ALSO BY GREGG HERKEN

The Winning Weapon:
The Atomic Bomb in the Cold War, 1945–1950

THIS IS A BORZOI BOOK
PUBLISHED IN NEW YORK
BY ALFRED A. KNOPF

COUNSELS
OF WAR

COUNSELS
OF WAR

Gregg Herken

ALFRED A. KNOPF   NEW YORK   1985

THIS IS A BORZOI BOOK PUBLISHED BY
ALFRED A. KNOPF, INC.

Grateful acknowledgment is made to Jerry Vogel Music Company, Inc., for permission to reprint an excerpt from "MacNamara's Band" by Shamus O'Connor and J. J. Stamford. Printed by permission of the copyright owner, Jerry Vogel Music Co., Inc., 501 Fifth Avenue, New York, NY 10017.

Library of Congress Cataloging in Publication Data
Herken, Gregg.
Counsels of war.
Bibliography: p.
Includes index.
1. United States—Military policy. 2. Nuclear weapons.
3. Military research—United States—History—20th century.
I. Title.
UA23.H45   1984   355'.0335'73   84-47876
ISBN 0-394-52735-6

Manufactured in the United States of America
First Edition

For Aven

The greatest trust between man and man is the trust of giving counsel. For in other confidences, men commit the parts of life; their lands, their goods, their children, their credit, some particular affair; but to such as they make their counsellors, they commit the whole: by how much the more they are obliged to all faith and integrity.

—SIR FRANCIS BACON,
"Of Counsel"

No lesson seems to be so deeply inculcated by the experience of life as that you should never trust in experts.

—LORD SALISBURY

CONTENTS

ACKNOWLEDGMENTS

More than sixty people—including three former secretaries of defense, four ambassadors, seventeen nuclear strategists, and twenty-two atomic scientists —consented to be interviewed for this book. Many were interviewed more than once. Almost all were generous with their time and patience. In one case a Reagan administration official granted an interview on his first day in office; in another a retired general changed his vacation plans so I could talk with him. While I did not necessarily agree with everything the experts had to say, I am both grateful and indebted to them for saying it. My hope is that all will feel they have been dealt with fairly. The responsibility for this book is, in any case, mine alone.

Other people to whom I have always been grateful—but am more so now —are the friends I stayed with during my research around the country, including Rick Laubscher and Judith Woodard in Berkeley, John Zielske in Los Angeles, and Sam and Barbara Dyer and Dana Trier in Washington, D.C. The Morse Fellowship, the Griswold Fund, and Yale's Center for International and Area Studies provided support during much of the time spent researching and writing. Arthur Singer of the Sloan Foundation brought to my attention its valuable videotape histories of Project Charles, the H-bomb decision, and the Cuban missile crisis. My thanks also to the people at the McHenry Library of the University of California, Santa Cruz, and to Irene and Peter Bashkiroff of Valira Farm in New Preston, Connecticut, for providing a place to write.

Finally, I would like to acknowledge the inspiration of two early and still preeminent thinkers about the unthinkable. British military historian Sir Basil Liddell-Hart was, for a brief time, my teacher at the University of California, Davis—where he was kind enough to ask an awed and anxious freshman his opinion of American strategy in the Second World War. Though I did not have occasion to meet Bernard Brodie—who died in 1978, and whose office in the Hall of Graduate Studies, by coincidence, I now occupy—his books and articles on nuclear strategy were in many ways the starting point for this effort. It was while Brodie was at Yale in 1946 that he wrote the three sentences that have been, ever since, the essential statement of the theory of deterrence: "Thus far the chief purpose of our military establishment has been to win wars. From now on its chief purpose must be to avert them. It can have almost no other useful purpose."

Brodie's concise formulation is no longer as generally accepted as it was in 1946. But one point of this book is that some thirty-eight years later he has yet to be proved wrong.

Gregg Herken
Yale University
May 1984

PROLOGUE

Operation Eggnog

It began—as everyone knew it would—in Europe: a virtual repeat of the "damn foolish thing in the Balkans" that Bismarck had prophesied would first plunge the world into war. As in 1914, the powder train leading to the Third World War was sparked by an assassination. The implication of the KGB in the murder of a popular eastern European leader seeking some measure of independence from Moscow for his homeland provoked world-wide anti-Soviet riots. The Russians, fearful of losing their satellite empire, responded with force—ultimately launching a massive invasion of western Europe. The Soviet onslaught, however, was stalled and eventually routed by NATO's use of tactical nuclear weapons.

The first atomic bomb to fall on the United States landed midway between the Capitol and the Jefferson Memorial, incinerating the government and incidentally snapping the top off the Washington Monument. A nuclear airburst directly above the intersection of Madison Avenue and 33rd Street instantly obliterated New York's garment district and set fires the length of Manhattan. Inadequate civil defense preparations and a stampede of mad-dened animals fleeing the burning stockyards contributed to bomb casualties in Chicago.

American retaliation was limited initially to industrial and military tar-gets in the Soviet Union. Among Russia's cities only Moscow was hit—and then "reluctantly," the provisional U.S. government later declared—several weeks into the war. But reciprocal nuclear raids against Soviet and Ameri-can cities characterized the next three bloody years of fighting, until a daring drop behind the Urals by ten thousand Allied commandos destroyed Russia's remaining stockpile of atomic bombs. Facing certain defeat, the communist leaders in the Kremlin were overthrown in a second Russian revolution. The new government, after first declaring a democracy in Russia, surrendered unconditionally to the United States.

. . .

So went "Operation Eggnog," a fictitious nuclear war fought on the pages
of *Collier's* magazine in October 1951. Today many of the details of the
Collier's scenario would be seen as plainly outdated—if not touchingly
naïve. The pipe bombs that Soviet agents plant in the lockers of Grand
Central Station—supposedly touching off a panic among New Yorkers in
1951—would probably be more irksome than terrifying to the present generation of commuters. Belonging to a different era, too, is the aftermath of
the magazine writers' hypothetical war. By 1960, barely five years after
the war's end, *Collier's* has "fashion-starved" Muscovites jamming a
newly constructed football stadium for the first showing of postwar
styles from the West. A theater troupe composed of former Red Army
officers is then performing *Bezdelniki i Zhenshchiny (Guys and Dolls)* at
the Bolshoi.[1]

But in some fundamental respects the 1951 vision of a nuclear war between
the United States and the Soviet Union more closely resembles the present-
day treatment of that subject than the specter of apocalypse that haunted
the Western imagination from the mid-1950s to the late 1970s. The *Collier's*
notion of a Soviet-American nuclear war shares common ground with several contemporary accounts of a possible Third World War, and with the
Defense Guidance of the Reagan administration for a "protracted" nuclear
conflict with Russia. Like these, the war of *Operation Eggnog* was thought
to be winnable—indeed, it was won.[2]

The contrast between the optimistic dénouement of *Operation Eggnog*
and the apocalyptic vision of only a generation ago indicates that thinking
about the unthinkable in this country has been transformed. The fact that
the 1951 account accords so closely with some of the official expectations
concerning a nuclear war some thirty years later suggests that this thinking
has traveled full circle.

Since 1945, American policy on nuclear weapons has been sometimes determined—and always influenced—by a small "nucleus" of civilian experts
whose profession it has been to consider objectively the fearful prospect of
nuclear war. Scientists, think-tank theorists, and cloistered academics have
traditionally formed this elite fraternity of experts—and it has been, for the
most part, a fraternity—who study a subject that did not even exist before
Hiroshima.

Curiously, military professionals have made few recognized contributions
to the body of theories concerning nuclear war—in part because the armed
services have understandably stressed operational planning over abstract
conceptualizing, but also because, until recently at least, such thinking
seemed to be actively discouraged in the nation's military academies. The
uniformed military, one civilian strategist claimed with some exaggeration,
"have been, with no significant exceptions, strictly consumers" when it

has come to "the basic ideas and philosophies about nuclear weapons and their use."[3]

Inevitably, the experts on the bomb have been likened to a "nuclear priesthood," whose members, suffering "a guild complex," have endlessly wandered the Pentagon's corridors like "Jesuits through the courts of Madrid and Vienna," their judgment clouded by "the heady wine of military strategy, methods of destruction and power politics." Initiates in what many perceive as a dark art, the experts speak their own arcane language and engage in esoteric controversies, seemingly comparable—in their debate over MIRV, for example—to the dispute in thirteenth-century theology over how many angels could dance on the head of a pin.[4]

But the notion of a nuclear priesthood, while evocative as a metaphor, is misleading if taken literally. In no sense have the scientists who design the weapons and the strategists who theorize about their use constituted a conspiracy. Their debates, even while scholarly in tone, have also never lacked for passion. Within their own ranks they have branded each other "nuclear scholastics," "nuclear accountants," and even "nuclear polemicists."

As George Orwell observed about the Spanish Civil War, the study of nuclear strategy suffers from a plethora of acronyms. Some critics have suggested, with reason, that obfuscation has become the ally and words like MAD (mutually assured destruction) and NUTs (nuclear-use theorists) the weapons in the expert's war to make the subject unintelligible to laymen. It has also seemed a subject strangely unsuited to academics—a fact that prompted one of the strategists' critics to remember Edmund Burke's comment on the nineteenth-century advocates of prison reform: "In the groves of *their* academy, at the end of every vista, you see nothing but the gallows."[5]

Apart from their expertise, however, the experts differ in no important way from anyone else in their concern about the bomb. Most have been drawn to study it less out of what Joseph Conrad termed "the fascination of the abomination" than in the spirit of Leon Trotsky's grim admonition that "while you may not be interested in war, war is interested in you." They, too, demonstrate the "controlled schizophrenia" that Arthur Koestler in *The Call Girls*—his novel about experts—claimed was the common ailment of the atomic age. Koestler's main character says, "On the one hand, we lead sheltered academic lives, pursuing our scientific quests *sub specie aeternitatis*—in the sign of eternity as it were." Like the majority of people in the two generations since Hiroshima, the experts "are caught," as was Koestler's hero, "between the Scylla of complacency" and "the Charybdis of panicky hysteria."[6]

Relying upon interviews with scientists, strategists, and the policymakers of eight presidential administrations, as well as upon declassified documents and published sources, this book is a history of the nuclear era, told from the perspective of the civilian experts on the bomb. It attempts to trace the course of thinking about the unthinkable from Hiroshima to the present time as a way of explaining not only where we are but how we got here. In the process it rejects the previously popular notion that the subject of nuclear weapons is so technical and complex that it is best left up to the experts—a view, incidentally, that few among the latter seem to share.

As esoteric as the contemporary debate over nuclear weapons and nuclear war has become, this book claims that it is not primarily or even importantly a debate over secret numbers, mysterious acronyms, or rival technical analyses. It is, instead, a competition between deeply held and often unstated beliefs—some of which only tangentially concern nuclear weapons. Behind it are rival perceptions not only of the Soviet Union but of the United States. It is a debate whose impact upon the history of the years since Hiroshima has been fundamental. Its course affects not only the understanding of our past, but the direction of our future.

PART ONE

MISSIONARIES

There is nothing in Man's industrial
machinery but his greed and sloth: his
heart is in his weapons.

—GEORGE BERNARD SHAW,
Man and Superman

1

—

Present at the Creation

For an entire generation the atomic bomb was cause of a revelation—a moment of epiphany. Most Americans first learned of the bomb from Hiroshima. For the scientists who had built the weapon, however, Hiroshima was the second coming. They had been present at the creation.

Evident at the beginning was a split in the scientists' ranks concerning their reaction to the bomb. "Some wept. A few cheered. Most stood silent," physicist Robert Oppenheimer remembered of the group that witnessed the first atomic bomb illuminate the New Mexican sky before dawn at Trinity —the name that "Oppie" himself had chosen for the site of the test at Alamogordo. Oppenheimer's own impression of the bomb would call to mind the passage from the Hindu scripture, the *Bhagavad Gita,* where Vishnu takes on his multi-armed form to impress the prince and says, "Now I have become death, the destroyer of worlds." That remark, and Oppenheimer's later comment that because of the bomb the physicists had "known sin," would become symbols of the scientists' remorse over creating the weapon. But on the morning of July 16, 1945, the dominant attitude among those at the Trinity site—Oppenheimer included—was a mixture of wonder and pride. The doubts would come later.

Isidor Rabi remembered Oppenheimer's "high-noon strut" immediately after the explosion. It was not until the light of the bomb had died away that Rabi began to develop goosebumps. George Kistiakowsky, the Russian émigré who designed the bomb's plutonium core, jumped for joy at the moment of the explosion and impulsively embraced Oppenheimer. "Kisty" would reflect in subsequent days that the very last thing seen by the last person on earth might be the incredible, searing light of the bomb. Frank Oppenheimer, Robert's brother, remembered wondering whether the deep-throated reverberations of the blast, whose echo continued to bounce off the surrounding mountains, would ever end.

Robert Wilson did not appreciate the significance of the moment until hours after the bomb had gone off, when he and a jeepload of other scientists drove up to the crater caused by the explosion. The group had gone out to ground zero at top speed to minimize their exposure to radiation—on the way passing their more cautious colleagues in a lead-lined tank, to whom they "made rude Italian gestures," Wilson said. They stopped when they got to what seemed the shore of a miniature sea of green glass—desert sand fused by the million-degree heat of the atomic explosion. "I was overwhelmed by that," Wilson recollected. The following month he and Frank Oppenheimer became founding members of the Association of Los Alamos Scientists—ALAS.

Ironically, it was not a scientist but a military man who was the most eloquent witness at Trinity: Brigadier General Thomas Farrell, deputy to the director of the Army's Manhattan Project, General Leslie Groves. The effect of the bomb "could well be called unprecedented, magnificent, beautiful, stupendous and terrifying," Farrell wrote in his report to Washington. "It was that beauty the great poets dream about but describe most poorly and inadequately." Farrell said that he, too, was inadequate "for the job of acquainting those not present with the physical, mental, and psychological effects.

"It had to be witnessed to be realized."[1]

Not everyone who saw it was as awed by the bomb as Farrell, however. Physicist Edward Teller was unmoved—until he lifted his heavy welder's goggles. The effect, he later wrote, was "like opening the heavy curtains of a darkened room to a flood of sunlight." Teller thought it significant that the desert winds almost immediately began to shape the bomb's mushroom cloud into a giant question mark. Standing several days later on the spot where the bomb had gone off, General Groves had been singularly unimpressed. "Is that all?" he reportedly asked. One of the scientists with him thought that Groves seemed to expect a hole going to the center of the earth.[2]

Nor did all of those at Trinity on that day share Oppenheimer's subsequent feeling of guilt for a role in building the bomb. One who didn't was Ernest Lawrence, the Berkeley physicist who designed the cyclotrons that produced the uranium for the Hiroshima bomb. After the war Lawrence pointedly amended Kistiakowsky's famous comment. He said that he thought the *first* person on earth had probably seen what the scientists witnessed.[3]

"We knew the world would not be the same," Oppenheimer said of that day. His remark might also have been applied to the world of the atomic scientists. Kenneth Bainbridge, the physicist put in charge of the Trinity test, had had perhaps the earliest and the best understanding of that fact. Turning to Oppenheimer in the fading glow of the atomic fireball, Bainbridge said simply: "Well, Oppie, now we're all sons-of-bitches."[4]

·   ·   ·

If Trinity can be said to have opened a crack in the scientists' ranks, Hiroshima widened it. After the explosion at Alamogordo those who had built the bomb were no longer unanimous in their opinion of what should be done with it. With the atomic bombing of Japan their views would move even farther apart.

Rabi had been saving two bottles of expensive Scotch to celebrate victory —one for the fall of Hitler, and one for Japan. When Germany surrendered, he and his colleagues had only a short toast and went back to work on the weapon they expected to end the war. At Japan's surrender the second bottle went unopened. Robert Wilson became physically ill upon hearing the news of the casualties at Hiroshima. Robert Oppenheimer, who resigned as director of the Los Alamos nuclear laboratory at war's end, told friends that the beautiful mesa where the bomb had been built should be given back to the Indians.

But other scientists praised the atomic bomb for saving lives by putting an end to the war, and stayed at Los Alamos to work on the next generation of nuclear weapons. The split at the lab was particularly striking to Luis Alvarez, a colleague of Lawrence's at Berkeley and one of the few Los Alamos scientists to be sent overseas after the Trinity test to prepare the atomic bombs that would be dropped on Japan. Alvarez had been in one of the B-29s that accompanied the *Enola Gay* on its bombing run over Hiroshima. His first reaction upon seeing the black, roiling cloud that rose from the city was that the bomb had missed its target entirely. "It looked like it had landed on a forest," Alvarez said. "I didn't see any sign of a city." He remembered thinking that Lawrence would be furious when he learned that they had wasted all of his uranium blowing up trees.

When Alvarez returned to Los Alamos from the war he was amazed at the change that had taken place in the mood of the scientists: "When I came back I felt like Rip Van Winkle. I felt I didn't know the people. Everybody was moaning and wringing their hands."

There was another group of men for whom the atomic bomb was a revelation that would change their lives—the academicians and theorists who became the nuclear strategists, the abstract thinkers about the unthinkable. For almost all of this number, Hiroshima was the first inkling of the new world of the atomic age. As had been the case with the scientists, the reaction of the strategists was initially one of awe and national pride, later giving way to questions and growing doubt.

Yale professor Bernard Brodie immediately recognized that the bomb would have a revolutionary effect upon strategy. He told his wife upon hearing of Hiroshima that the event meant all his previous work concerning the effect of technology upon warfare was obsolete. Within six weeks of the atomic bombings, however, Brodie was at work on a book that would set forth the theory of nuclear deterrence.

For William Borden, a young veteran and law student at Yale when Brodie was writing his book, the news of Hiroshima had "a galvanic effect." "I decided instantly that this was the most important thing in the world," Borden later said of the bomb, "and couldn't understand why everyone else was not equally impressed." The atomic bomb inspired Borden, in fact, to write a book on nuclear strategy that was very different from Brodie's. After Hiroshima, Borden would come to play a key role in the development of the new generation of weapons far more destructive than the atomic bomb, and in the process would accuse one of the first bomb's inventors—Robert Oppenheimer—of deliberately hindering the development of the nation's nuclear arsenal.

Albert Wohlstetter was struck not only by the fact of the atomic bomb but by the official descriptions of it. A government-employed mathematician vacationing with his wife at their Long Island summer home the day Hiroshima was bombed, Wohlstetter saw "a cosmic impiety" in Truman's comparison of the atomic bomb to the source from which the sun draws its power. In later years Wohlstetter would repeatedly bring to the attention of the military and the American government a fundamental truth about strategy that should have been learned at Pearl Harbor—how a defending force that is vulnerable to attack may provoke rather than deter aggression.

Paul Nitze—one of the first Americans to stand in the rubble of Hiroshima—marveled then at the extent of the destruction. But he was also impressed at the number of people who had nonetheless managed to survive. Nitze immediately began to question, he said, the "common, popular view" that the atomic bomb "was an absolute weapon and that this changed everything." An investment banker before the war, Nitze would become an eminent authority on nuclear weapons and an adviser to five presidents regarding their use.

Like the atomic scientists, the divided response of the nuclear strategists to the first atomic bomb foreshadowed, in some degree, their later differences. The split was apparent even before the light had entirely faded from the explosions that lit up the American desert, and later incinerated two Japanese cities.

For the experts, the sides had already been chosen. The lines were drawn.

2

Shadow of the Sword

By the end of the first week after Hiroshima the idea of nuclear war was not only thinkable to the strategists, it was already becoming familiar. Bernard Brodie had been a member of the Yale faculty only five days when the atomic bomb was dropped on Japan. Yet the thirty-five-year-old associate professor would later be deemed "first—both in time and in distinction" among America's nuclear strategists.[1]

When Brodie arrived at Yale he had already established a considerable reputation as a strategic thinker. A graduate student in international relations during the isolationist 1930s, Brodie and a classmate who also became a nuclear strategist, Klaus Knorr, had rebelled at the time against the curriculum's seemingly exclusive emphasis upon international law, economic theory, and the history of the League of Nations. The subject of strategy, Brodie later wrote, was "an intellectual no-man's land" between the airy courses at Chicago and the "military science" taught at the service academies. "We realized something had been left out," confirmed Knorr: "the concept of power."

Brodie confided to Knorr while they were students the fear that his doctoral dissertation concerning the impact of technology on nineteenth-century naval warfare would go not only unpublished, but unnoticed, given the antimilitary mood of the nation at the time. Instead, Brodie's dissertation, *Seapower in the Machine Age,* became a kind of academic best-seller when it was published shortly after the outbreak of the Second World War. A sequel, *A Layman's Guide to Naval Strategy,* sold more than fifty thousand copies and was adopted as a textbook at Annapolis after the author agreed to remove the offending word "layman's" from the title.[2]

During the war, Brodie worked in Washington as a propagandist until accepting the offer of a teaching job at Yale. He was finishing a long treatise concerning the battleship's imminent comeback in warfare when the bomb fell on Hiroshima.[3]

As a careful reader of the nineteenth-century military theorist Clausewitz,

Brodie was keenly alive to the role of irony in history. A consistent theme throughout his work concerned how military innovations were rarely appreciated by their own originators, but were often better employed by their inventors' enemies—as was the case with the ship's armor invented by the French in the 1800s and used with devastating effect against them by the British navy.[4]

Brodie also appreciated how the advent of the machine gun had made a cruel but little-appreciated joke of martial valor by 1914, and a vast graveyard of Europe four years later as a result. But as late as 1941—virtually on the eve of Pearl Harbor, in fact—Brodie argued that the human spirit had not yet suffered the fate of technological obsolescence in war at sea. "It is exceedingly rare that the advent of a military invention at once renders existing equipment obsolete," he had written in his first book. "The indomitable spirit at the helm and at the gun counts as much as ever."[5]

"When a change comes," Brodie later admitted, "it is best if it is unequivocal." He was one of the first to realize that the atomic bomb represented such a change. Little more than a month after the end of the war against Japan, Brodie had written a remarkably prescient essay on the significance of the new weapon to peace and war. At a time when most in the nation's military services were arguing that the bomb had changed warfare only by making necessary larger armies, navies, and air forces, Brodie claimed that Hiroshima "heralds a change not merely in the degree of destructiveness of modern war but in its basic character." "The atomic bomb is not just another and more destructive weapon to be added to an already long list. It is something which threatens to make the rest of the list relatively unimportant."[6]

Six weeks later, while rubble still lay in the streets of Hiroshima and Nagasaki, Brodie expanded upon this theme in a manuscript he edited of his own and his colleagues' thoughts on the bomb. His choice for the book's title, *The Absolute Weapon: Atomic Power and World Order,* reflected his feeling of how completely the bomb had changed the world.

In Milton's *Paradise Lost,* Brodie explained, Adam is told by the angel Raphael about an "absolute weapon" that the loyal angels used against Satan and his seraphim followers in Heaven's civil war after the Fall. Raphael recounts that while the devil at one point came close to winning that war by "an infernal device"—akin, Brodie noted, to artillery—the fortunes of the climactic battle turn when the good angels unveil a weapon so powerful that, according to Milton, it "tears the seated hills of Heaven from their roots" and hurls them at the foe. This absolute weapon, however, is copied in time by the fallen angels and used in turn against the heavenly host. With both sides making use of it, the destruction of Paradise itself seems inevitable when the timely intervention of the Deity on the side of the loyalists gives them the victory.

The traditional story seemed to Brodie an appropriately cautionary tale. Raphael's prediction in *Paradise Lost* that the absolute weapon would appear among men "in future days, if malice should abound" seemed to have come true with the Second World War. The creative genius behind the inventors of heaven's absolute weapon, Brodie observed, would have proved suicidal had it not been for divine intervention at the last trumpet. The inventors of the earthly version, he thought, could ill afford to rely upon such dramatic intercession for their own salvation.[7]

The truly revolutionary thing about the atomic bomb, Brodie argued in *The Absolute Weapon,* was not merely its unprecedented destructiveness but equally the fact that such devastation could occur with unique suddenness, and that there was no known defense against it. Contemptuous of what he termed the "preatomic thinking" of the military services and of other civilian theorists who denigrated the bomb's power, Brodie claimed that there was little likelihood of developing an effective counter to nuclear weapons, and even less chance of doing away with them altogether. It was instead necessary, he wrote, "to develop the habit of living with the atomic bomb."[8]

It was because humanity had never before encountered an absolute weapon that Brodie expressed the hope it might be possible to live with the bomb in peace. Paradoxically, the impetus to such hope, he felt, came precisely from the weapon's incredible destructiveness. It was this destructiveness, Brodie wrote, that made the bomb not only a potentially decisive instrument of attack but also "a powerful inhibitor to aggression"—and hence an unexpected asset to peace. "Even if no measures are conceivable which will quite remove the shadow of a sword of Damocles," he concluded, "it is possible that the threads by which that sword is suspended may be strengthened."[9] In short, the solution proposed in *The Absolute Weapon* to the problems created by the bomb was to replace the traditional military aim of defeating an enemy once war occurred with the goal of preventing his attack in the first place.

Brodie and his associates among what would henceforth be known as "the Yale group" certainly did not invent the concept of deterrence. The term itself—whose French root means "to frighten from"—appeared as early as 1820 in the *Oxford English Dictionary.* The principle of deterrence was already well established at least by the time of the Greek city-states, whose populations were held hostage in war for the acts of their leaders.[10] But it was Brodie, in the shadow of Hiroshima, who would be responsible for popularizing the concept of deterrence, and for emphasizing its unique applicability in the case of nuclear weapons. In one of the two essays that he wrote for *The Absolute Weapon,* he expressed in a few sentences what would become the basic statement of the theory of deterrence for the next two generations: "The writer . . . is not for the moment concerned about who will *win* the next war in which atomic bombs are used. Thus far the chief purpose of our military establishment has been to win wars. From now on its chief purpose must be to avert them. It can have almost no other useful purpose."[11]

While Brodie and his colleagues at the Institute of International Studies were working on *The Absolute Weapon* in the weeks just after the war, across the street from their offices at the Hall of Graduate Studies a twenty-five-year-old student at Yale's law school, William Liscum Borden, was writing a radically different book about the atomic bomb. In contrast to the restrained optimism of his elders, Borden's was a dark and gloomy vision of the future.

"Lic" Borden was a representative—almost stereotypical—example of the well-groomed and wealthy elite that thrived in the clublike camaraderie of the prewar Ivy League. He had been a prodigy at St. Albans prep school in Washington, D.C. He was editor of the *Yale Daily News* when he gradua-ted from the university at the top of the class of '42. Articulate, self-confident —some thought justifiably arrogant—Borden while an undergraduate had been an iconoclast, yet one who believed that responsibility came with wealth and power, and who held that only the privileged can make a true revolution.[12]

As was common with many students then at Yale, Borden had undergone a political conversion from isolationism to interventionism as the Second World War approached—a conversion completed with dramatic suddenness in his senior year on the day the Japanese bombed Pearl Harbor. Unlike the rest of his fellows, however, Borden documented his intellectual coming of age in a column he wrote for the *Yale Daily News* titled "Straws in the Wind."

Warning in the fall of 1940 against "quixotic, dewy-eyed idealism" that could lead to involvement in the European war, Borden had used his column to endorse the presidential candidacy of the Socialist Norman Thomas. The previous summer, Borden and Burton K. Wheeler had even shared the platform with Thomas at a Washington antiwar rally. Some six months later, however, Borden confessed to a youthful change of mind about the war —concluding that since it was impossible to change human nature, it was first necessary "to alter institutions so as to nullify the tragic flaws in man that necessitate war." By the fall of 1941, he had joined with many of his peers in lamenting the bleak "triviality" of undergraduate life. He was, he wrote, yearning after "something to fight for."[13]

Only five days before Pearl Harbor, Borden announced his completed conversion to interventionism in a column headlined "The Case for Immedi-ate War Against Japan." His call there for a "preventive war" against the Japanese was actually a tongue-in-cheek gimmick that he had used success-fully in a debate at Princeton the previous week. Ironically, it anticipated the actual rationale behind Japan's day of infamy—only applying it in reverse.

Borden was as surprised as the rest of his classmates the following Sunday by news of the Japanese attack. His column two days later in the *Yale Daily News* had rallied—with undergraduate hyperbole—to the vision of an American century following the war. "At the end," Borden predicted, "Americans will be in control, from the sun-drenched sands of Africa to the crowded hinterlands of Cathay."

Borden's idealistic zeal survived his college days, prompting him to enlist right after graduation and to volunteer for flight training in bombers rather than the more glamorous fighter school preferred by his classmates. It was in late 1944, while piloting his B-24 Liberator back from a nighttime mission of dropping supplies to the Resistance, that Borden had experienced an instant of revelation as a German V-2 rocket destined to strike London hurtled past him. "It resembled a meteor, streaming red sparks and whizzing past us as though the aircraft were motionless," Borden wrote. "I became convinced that it was only a matter of time until rockets would expose the United States to direct, transoceanic attack." The sight of the V-2 gave him the "emotional impetus," he claimed, to write a book about the coming transformation of warfare when he got home.[14]

Borden had already been discharged from the Army and begun writing the book at his family's cabin in upstate New York when he heard the news of Hiroshima. Like the experience of seeing the rocket, the word of the atomic bomb gave Borden's writing a new sense of urgency. The urgency that the author felt about the book's message was also expressed in its title: *There Will Be No Time: The Revolution in Strategy.*

Completed shortly after he returned to Yale to study law, Borden's book appeared in the summer of 1946, within weeks of *The Absolute Weapon.* Both the iconoclasm and the idealism that had characterized Borden as an undergraduate were evident in his book. He had only just learned of the existence of Brodie's book, Borden later said, when he was putting the finishing touches on his own. It was partly for reasons of youthful pride that he never took the initiative to meet Brodie and the other authors of *The Absolute Weapon.* But another reason for Borden's aloofness was his feeling, he admitted, that the professors were "intuitively wrong" about the bomb.

Thus, though Borden would subsequently acknowledge Brodie's book as a "stimulus" to his own ideas, he thought particularly wrong the assumption in *The Absolute Weapon* that the atomic bomb would remain scarce in the world's arsenals for some time to come. The premise that America's atomic monopoly would endure was part of what Borden contemptuously termed the "hocus-pocus, medicine-man mood" that then surrounded the subject of the bomb—a mood fostered, he thought, "by the venerable elders of the tribe."

A main premise behind Borden's book was that atomic bombs would soon also be available to America's enemies in large numbers, and that these bombs would in the future be carried to their targets by intercontinental-range rockets. While doing the research for his book Borden had been stunned by the ease with which scientists and military figures alike had seemed to discount the coming danger. Deploring such complacency as misplaced, Borden thought it in equal measure dangerous. His previous experience with the military mind—including his acquaintance with an uncle who was a high-ranking Army officer—had already convinced him that the atomic bomb was a matter far too important to be left up to the generals.

Ironically, the predictions Borden made in *There Will Be No Time* resembled in some respects the future forecast in *The Absolute Weapon.* Borden, like Brodie, thought that the great danger in a world of many nuclear-armed states would be that of a blindingly fast sneak attack: "a rocket Pearl Harbor." Unlike Brodie, however, Borden, as a former bomber pilot, did not believe that even the terrific destructiveness of nuclear weapons would create a lasting obstacle to their use. Instead, he thought that peace in such a world could only be a temporary and tenuous truce between wars that would inevitably be fought with nuclear weapons.[15]

Borden attacked as a "fallacy" what he termed "the mutual-deterrent thesis" on which Brodie and others had pinned their hopes for peace. There was, he argued, only one choice facing humanity in the atomic age: between world federalism—which would either put the bombs under international control or eliminate them altogether—and nuclear war. "The essential point is that an armed peace cannot persist indefinitely, that either war or voluntary federalism must resolve the truce," Borden wrote at the end of his book. There was to be, he predicted, no living with the bomb. "Unless a world government intercedes in time an attack on the United States will surely come."[16]

Having come to temper his idealism with pessimism after the war, Borden envisioned the atomic age as a grim, almost Hobbesian predicament of incessant conflict, where warring states would recognize few if any moral restraints. Atomic bombs might be used by an aggressor not only against an opponent's cities directly, Borden thought, but even to melt the polar icecap in order to flood his coastline, or to remove the sheltering ozone layer above the foe's homeland. An enemy would probably strike when the nation was most vulnerable, he predicted—during the indecisive interregnum of a lame-duck president, for example, or in the depths of winter, when the population's resistance to radiological or biological warfare would be lowest.[17]

But there was another, somewhat less apocalyptic and also perhaps more probable direction that a future nuclear war might take. Hiroshima, Borden wrote, had cast the strategic bombing campaigns of the Second World War in "a weird and sardonic light." America's next war would probably resemble the last solely in the way it was begun—with a calculated and unprovoked attack upon the nation's military forces. The difference in the atomic age was that the first blow might prove so decisive it would be the only one struck. "A full-scale atomic war will not be won on pulverizing cities and industry," Borden predicted, "but by destroying the enemy's military power of retaliation."[18]

The war would be a "one-dimensional aerial duel" fought "between highly decentralized military systems," where civilian casualties might be incidental and almost negligible. Any aggressor would probably refrain deliberately from striking at enemy cities—at least in the initial attack, Borden reasoned—not only for fear of retaliation in kind, but so as to focus his assault upon the foe's military forces. With the enemy thus disarmed, his cities and the people living in them would become hostages to the attacker's will. If a sufficiently early and decisive blow could be struck in what Borden called this "war-between-the-bases," not only might the prospective conflict be kept limited in terms of the damage it would cause, but it could be decisively won.[19]

In order to guard against the threat of a sneak attack on a scale far larger and more destructive than Pearl Harbor, Borden predicted that the United States would have to base its future nuclear-tipped intercontinental-range rockets in underground protective "hedgehogs" located well away from cities, and "on undersea platforms scattered throughout the world's oceans."[20]

But the fundamental changes he forecast in the realm of military strategy and international diplomacy were not the only transformations that would be necessary because of the advent of the bomb. The cost of preparedness in the atomic age would not be slight, Borden warned—nor even entirely economic.

One impetus behind his writing of the book, he later admitted, had been his concern with what he felt was "America's happy-ending complex," and the nation's Second World War–induced concept of a "Hollywood peace." Borden believed that both were delusions after Hiroshima. "Preparations for war," he wrote in the book, "will involve steps distasteful to the American public without the threat of war to justify them—and no preliminary threat is to be anticipated, because of the premium on surprise." Since Borden assumed that a dictatorial enemy would be intent upon striking the first blow, the United States would have to depart from tradition by taking steps to prepare for the next war that would "surpass—not merely equal—the dictator's preparations." Beyond maintaining military superiority over any enemy or likely combination of foes, Borden thought the need to "give precedence over all international problems to defense" necessitated as well "an American secret intelligence second to none."[21]

There would be other necessary changes seemingly inimical to the interests of a democracy. The likelihood that there would be little or no warning of the outbreak of war, and the chance that the "issue of victory or disaster could be decided within a few hours," required that the president be granted unprecedented powers in peacetime. Among these might be the authority to "order any war to be prosecuted to a successful conclusion, regardless of the cost." So long as a "vital minority" of civilian defense workers remained loyal to the government, Borden argued, the cause for which the war was being fought need not even have the broad support of the American people.[22]

The effect that the atomic bomb might have in transforming American life was one of the things that Brodie and his colleagues had considered in *The Absolute Weapon.* The prospect of having to fundamentally restructure democratic society to prepare for a nuclear war was one of the reasons, in fact, why Brodie had concluded that the emphasis should be upon preventing, rather than winning, such a war. Brodie thus considered—and rejected in his book—proposals made in the wake of Hiroshima that the nation make itself less vulnerable to attack by dispersing its population and industry, or by creating new "linear" or "cellular" cities whose size would be restricted by law.[23] The evident futility of defending against nuclear weapons—and the radical transformation of American life that the effort would require nonetheless—had reinforced Brodie's conviction that it was necessary, instead, to learn to live with the bomb.

Like the reaction of the atomic scientists—for whom the atomic bomb was either the symbol of creation or a presentiment of doomsday—the difference between Brodie and Borden defined the two very different ways that the nuclear strategists came to look at the atomic bomb immediately after Hiroshima.

With minor variations, the positions taken by the two men endured as the opposite poles of a debate that would rage for the next forty years among the experts on the bomb. It would be a debate not about two opposing strategies, but over the emphasis in strategy that should go toward preparations for fighting and winning—or preventing—nuclear war. It would also be a debate as remarkable and often angry as the men and events which sparked it.

For Brodie, a rationalist with no direct experience of war, hope for the future lay in a paradox: the nation had to prepare for a war it did not intend to fight. For Borden, an idealist who blamed idealism for the last war, there was to be no avoiding the reality of a future nuclear conflict. The fact that he dedicated *There Will Be No Time* to the memory of his college roommate, killed in the Pacific war, underscored the dire warning contained in that book. Borden's choice of a line from Matthew Arnold's "Hymn of Empedocles" as the book's epigraph keenly revealed the depth of his own disillusionment: "Because thou must not dream, thou need'st not despair!"

· · ·

The books by Brodie and Borden were read by a relatively small number of people—those Americans who, in the wake of the war just ended against Germany and Japan, were already concerned with the coming dangers of the atomic age. The impression that most citizens had of the atomic bombings was taken not from the work of the early nuclear strategists, but from a book by a young war correspondent born in China of missionary parents, and, coincidentally, a graduate of Yale.

John Hersey's account of the first atomic bomb dropped upon a city was published in August 1946 in *The New Yorker,* which devoted an entire issue to the story. The year before Hiroshima, Hersey had won a Pulitzer prize for *A Bell for Adano,* a novel about a small town in Italy during the war. Hersey was on a troopship in the Pacific when he heard the news of the atomic bombing. As soon as the ship docked he had begun making plans to see the stricken city.

When he visited Hiroshima, Hersey despaired of describing the devastation caused by the bomb. The ultimate inspiration for the *New Yorker* story was Thornton Wilder's novel *The Bridge of San Luis Rey,* which describes the daily lives of a handful of individuals, all of whom are killed when the bridge they are crossing collapses. Wilder's book concerned why those particular people had become victims of a random fate. Hersey's interest was in how some victims of the first atomic bombing had managed to survive it.

When later published as a book, *Hiroshima* alternately horrified and fascinated readers by its graphic portrayal of six people whose individual lives were nearly ended—and all abruptly changed—by the bomb. The story was read in installments over nationwide radio and became the subject of newspaper editorials and church sermons. The physical effects of the atomic bomb were described in vivid detail for the first time to many Americans, including this account of a Methodist missionary who returned to Hiroshima right after the bomb fell:

> He was the only person making his way into the city; he met hundreds and hundreds who were fleeing, and every one of them seemed to be hurt in some way. The eyebrows of some were burned off and skin hung from their faces and hands. Others, because of pain, held their arms up as if carrying something in both hands. Some were vomiting as they walked. Many were naked or in shreds of clothing. . . . Almost all had their heads bowed, looked straight ahead, were silent, and showed no expression whatever.[24]

At the same time Hersey's story appeared, a rival perspective on Hiroshima was being presented by the U.S. government's thoroughly researched and carefully prepared report on the atomic bombing, part of its multivolume *Strategic Bombing Survey* of the air war against Germany and Japan. While few people read the *Survey*'s slim volume on Hiroshima and Nagasaki—and it certainly had less popular impact than Hersey's book—in one sense the government's account would be more influential: it was the official view of the atomic bombings. Distilled from more than two hundred volumes of reports by a variety of experts who had personally studied the damage and interviewed over seven hundred survivors in the two cities, the *Survey* recounted the destruction of Hiroshima and Nagasaki in full, but dispassionate, detail.[25]

The man in charge of the report, Paul Nitze, later described how he was "seized right off the bat" by the task of assessing the damage caused by the atomic bomb. As one of the directors of the bombing survey, Nitze was among the first Americans to arrive at Hiroshima after the bombing. Nitze had been a government expert on foreign economic policy before the war, and he was intuitively skeptical of claims that the atomic bomb "changed everything." From his lifelong tendency "to put numbers and quantities on arguments," he undertook the task of precisely measuring the physical and other effects of the atomic bomb—"to put calipers on it, instead of describing it in emotive terms." "We tried to put quantitative numbers on something that was considered immeasurable," he said of the effort.

Nitze found the bomb's physical effects surprisingly easy to gauge. Unlike Hersey, he even discovered some cause for hope in the seemingly boundless wreckage and debris of the aftermath. The *Survey* would describe Nagasaki after the bomb as looking "like a graveyard with not a tombstone standing." But it also argued that casualties in the city might have been reduced by as much as 30 percent if the inhabitants had received some warning of the attack. Engineers among the *Survey*'s experts reported that reinforced-concrete buildings built to withstand earthquakes had best survived the atomic blast. Even a portion of Hiroshima's trolley line, they noted, was back in service two days after the attack—with 80 percent of the system restored to operation at the end of two weeks.[26]

In the case of Nagasaki, the report observed that the city's shipping industry had been "virtually unaffected" by the atomic bomb, which landed well inland of the port and on the other side of a range of hills. In both cities the experts found evidence that contradicted the popular impression of an all-consuming holocaust: people wearing substantial but light-colored clothing received burns less severe than those wearing dark or flimsy garments. The window glass that Hersey described as killing or maiming thousands of Japanese near the epicenter of the explosion had actually protected others, farther away, from the bomb's initial pulse of radiation—which the *Survey* found was ultimately the bomb's deadliest effect.[27]

The *Survey*'s unstated conclusion seemed to be that the destruction wrought by the atomic bomb, terrible as it might be, was still finite—and survivable. Nitze believed that he was able to measure the devastation exactly, in the process making the specter of the bomb comprehensible. Exclusive of radiation effects, the damage done to Hiroshima, he calculated, had been equivalent to that of conventional bombs carried by 150 B-29s. For Nagasaki his calculation was 210 bombers.

To Nitze the greatest surprises in the *Survey* came with the measurement of the atomic bomb's psychological effects. He discovered, for example, that civilian morale had not suffered an immediate collapse in the two cities after the bombs fell, despite the suddenness and the near-totality of the destruction. The *Survey* noted how Nagasaki's prefectural government the day after the bombing had called for "a rehabilitation of the stricken city and an aroused fighting spirit to exterminate the devilish Americans."[28]

What Nitze found to be one of the most common initial reactions of survivors to the bombings—"aimless, even hysterical activity"—eventually gave way to feelings of anger, hatred, and in some cases admiration for the bomb and its inventors. A few fanatical Japanese still clung to the hope of final victory. The supposedly absolute weapon, the *Survey* concluded, had ultimately not even been decisive in Japan's surrender.[29]

The *Survey* summary and recommendations, which Nitze drafted, explicitly posed a question that surely had been in the minds of readers of Hersey's book as well: "What if the target for the bomb had been an American city?"

Nitze's answer was hardly one to engender complacency, but it was not nearly so dire a comment on the atomic bomb as that made by Hersey's account. While reminding that "to avoid destruction, the surest way is to avoid war," Nitze nonetheless urged as precautionary measures that the United States decentralize its vital industrial and medical facilities, consider a nationwide shelter system, and arrange to evacuate its cities under the threat of war.[30]

Readers of Hersey's *Hiroshima* and of the *Strategic Bombing Survey* might have found it difficult to believe that both books described the same event. In an important sense, of course, they did not.

Hersey's account of the atomic bombing had been from the viewpoint of the victim. Nitze's was—purposefully—from the viewpoint of the victor. The difference in their perspective was, almost literally, the difference between the heavens and the earth: between the bomber and the bombed.

It was the difference that strategic bombing and the atomic bomb had made.

3

The Road from Guernica

The notion of striking at the enemy from the air was probably conceived at the same time as the idea of powered flight. The goal of compelling the enemy's surrender by inflicting pain upon his civilian population predated even that. The latter was the purpose of Britain's naval blockade of Germany in the First World War, and of the Germans' use of zeppelins in 1917 to bomb London—which induced the first case of mass hysteria brought about by the threat of death from above. But inaccuracy and other problems meant that the results of bombing in the First World War fell far short of the expectations held by air-power promoters. The after-action report of a German aerial raid upon a British airfield demonstrated the problem: "Theoretically, it was a beautiful shot, practically it hit a turnip."[1]

The modern concept of strategic bombing was the particular creation of military and civilian theorists writing between the world wars. Italian air-power enthusiast Giulio Douhet, whose book *Command of the Air* was published in 1921, first popularized the idea that a large industrialized nation could be defeated in war by strategic bombing alone. By the 1930s Douhet's disciples included Hugh Trenchard and Charles de Gaulle in Europe and Billy Mitchell in the United States.[2]

The rising influence of these and other promoters of victory through air power assured that a significant part of the coming conflict would be fought in the skies above some of the world's principal cities—despite the fact that the feasibility of Douhet's decisive "knockout blow" from the air had yet to be demonstrated. The only occasion where bombing alone proved decisive before the Second World War was the quelling by the Royal Air Force of a revolt among Iraqi tribal villagers in 1922. Nonetheless, the following year this was the grim vision of a future attack on Britain's capital:

> London for several days will be one vast raving Bedlam, the hospitals will be stormed, traffic will cease, the homeless will shriek for help, the city will be in pandemonium. What of the government

at Westminster? It will be swept away by an avalanche of terror. Then will the enemy dictate his terms, which will be grasped at like a straw by a drowning man. Thus may a war be won in forty-eight hours and the losses of the winning side may be actually nil![3]

Douhet wrote that the first and most vital target of an air force should be the enemy's own fleet of strategic bombers. But he and his disciples had also been quick to recognize the bomber's potential for creating terror among a country's civilian population. This prospect—and the fact that there had been no rival air armadas to be destroyed either in the Spanish Civil War or when Japan invaded China in the 1930s—accounted in part for the later shift of the primary target in air-power theory from the enemy's armed forces to his civilian population. The bombing of cities in Spain and China during that decade showed how attacks on civilians seemed to offer the best hope of inflicting "the greatest damage in the shortest possible time," according to Douhet's dictum.[4]

The point that the raids on Guernica and Shanghai, like the 1917 attack on London, had proved psychologically devastating to civilians—but were not militarily decisive—was seemingly either not grasped or deliberately ignored by air-power theorists. It was a point not widely appreciated, indeed, until after the Second World War. Before that conflict, the shift to civilians as the principal target of strategic bombing had come about almost inadvertently. During the war—and after—it would be deliberate.

The experience of strategic bombing after 1940 showed most clearly how the brunt of modern war was gradually moved from the soldier to the civilian. Prior to the outbreak of war, the Plans Division of the British Air Ministry had concluded that a bombing offensive against Germany's air force and aircraft industry offered the best chance of limiting damage to Britain itself in the event of hostilities. A subsequent study by Britain's Bomber Command, however, concluded that the losses likely to be incurred in attacking the Luftwaffe would eliminate most of the RAF's entire force of bombers in less than two months. The search for alternative targets for the air arm led, inescapably, to cities.[5]

Even on the eve of the Second World War, top military leaders in Britain publicly rejected the idea of targeting German civilians—for reasons that turned out to be as much pragmatic as ethical. Fearful of devastating reprisals in kind should the RAF attack German cities, the chief of Britain's Imperial General Staff argued that "it is entirely to our advantage to keep within the accepted codes for the conduct of war." This proscription upon bombing civilians was reflected as well in an August 1939 communiqué of British and French staff officers, who pledged "that we have no intention of attacking the civil population as such."[6]

The words "as such" proved portentous. As early as 1918, Hugh Trenchard, Britain's foremost air-power proponent, had denounced "the indiscriminate bombing of a city for the sole purpose of terrorizing the civilian
population" as "contrary to the dictates of humanity." But it was an entirely
different matter, Trenchard wrote, to bomb munitions workers who were
also civilians. "Moral effect is created by the bombing in such circumstances," he argued, and was "the inevitable result of a lawful operation of
war—the bombing of a military objective."[7]

Throughout the 1920s, Trenchard—whose nickname, "Boom," reflected
his enthusiasm for strategic bombing—espoused the psychological or
"moral effect" of bombing civilians, which he claimed was likely to be both
a less costly and a more effective strategy than attacking the enemy's forces
directly. Cities containing the enemy's wartime industries would become the
prime targets, on the theory that it was easier to overcome the enemy's will
to resist than to destroy his means of resistance. "The personnel," Trenchard
argued succinctly, "are not armed and cannot shoot back."[8]

Because of Trenchard's influence there already existed, one historian of
strategic bombing later wrote, a "half-articulated faith in terror bombing in
the higher ranks" of the Air Staff and of Bomber Command by the outbreak
of the Second World War. It was this faith—the basis for which had yet to
be either examined or challenged by 1939—that gave the impetus to the
decision of Britain's military leaders that the first wartime priority should
be the destruction of Germany's war machine: "the morale which sustains
it, the supplies which nourish it, and the hopes of victory which inspire it."[9]

By 1941 both Britain and Germany were guilty of bombing residential
areas located near war industries, owing to the inherent inaccuracy of bombing at that time.[10] Certainly for both belligerents the Douhetian "knockout
blow" against the other's forces had fallen short, Britain's in a costly but
ineffective raid in 1939 upon the German fleet, and Germany's in the foiled
attempt to destroy the RAF during the Battle of Britain a year later. By the
end of the second year of war, total casualties among bomber crews were
actually higher than among those they had bombed on the ground.[11]

A major shift in British targeting policy occurred in early 1942. It was
brought about not by a change in strategy but by the belated discovery of
the extent to which inaccuracy had undermined the effectiveness of the
bombing campaign thus far. The RAF's bombs, the Air Ministry found,
were consistently landing far from their targets. The fault was not with the
bomber crews so much as with the circumstances under which they conducted the bombing, and with their equipment. Bomber Command's decision to stage exclusively nighttime raids over Germany had cut down on
losses, but accuracy had suffered even more as a result.[12]

On Valentine's Day in February 1942 the Air Ministry informed Bomber
Command that henceforth "the primary object of your operations" was to

focus "on the morale of the enemy civil population and, in particular, of the industrial workers." The RAF was instructed to employ its bombers to that end "without restriction." Lest there remain any doubt that the real target of the new direction was to be the people in their homes, a clarification was forthcoming from the chief of the Air Staff. "I suppose it is clear that the aiming points are to be the built-up areas, not for instance, the dockyards or aircraft factories," he wrote. "This must be quite clear if it is not already understood."[13]

As the emphasis of strategic bombing shifted progressively from military to civilian targets, the Air Ministry for the first time employed the euphemism and circumlocution that would later become familar to a generation grown accustomed to modern warfare. The month after the Valentine's Day order, Lord Cherwell, Churchill's scientific adviser, announced that it would be Britain's intention to "dehouse" German workers. "Investigation seems to show that having one's house demolished is most damaging to morale," Cherwell claimed. "People seem to mind it more than having their friends or even relatives killed."[14]

By the middle of 1942 there seemed to be little alternative to bombing civilians, since raids were being conducted on a growing scale by a burgeoning Allied bomber force. As well, the promised technological advances of the so-called "wizards' war," which were supposed to make precision bombing possible, had by that time either had disappointing results or been countered by the Germans.[15]

Yet the fact that the strategic bomber as an instrument of war had come to resemble a bludgeon more than the rapier of Douhet's imagination was seemingly not acknowledged by Bomber Command, which, officially at least, maintained that it was conducting selective strikes against the enemy. (The inherently approximate nature of nighttime "blind bombing" became evident when an RAF raid upon Essen did such extensive damage to neighboring cities that the Germans were unable to determine which had been the intended target.) By the time of the thousand-bomber raids that summer, accuracy had all but ceased to be a concern in strategic bombing. The RAF was area-bombing "in fact, if not in intent," one chronicler of the air war concluded.[16]

The American experience of strategic bombing was initially a reaction against the British performance. A 1926 U.S. Air Service manual had dismissed terror bombing as unlikely to prove decisive in war, and American airmen were instructed in training that attacks on cities would be made only in reprisal to enemy raids. As inspired by Douhet, the principal target of the fledgling American air force remained the opponent's air force. Lectures given at the Army Air Corps Tactical School in the 1930s showed a subtle change when they emphasized the bombing of industrial targets as a way of undermining the enemy's morale. But Air Corps instructors nonetheless upheld the prohibition against killing civilians in declaring that "the real target is industry itself, not national morale."[17]

As was the case with the British, the shift in American targeting to include cities—and ultimately to focus on them—had its origins in pragmatism rather than military dogma. The costly daylight bombing of heavily defended German industrial targets that the British abandoned late in 1940 was subsequently given up by the Americans as well. An alternative strategy directed against vital "chokepoints" in the Germany war economy—particularly oil refineries and ball-bearing plants—also brought high losses and disappointing results.[18]

Like the British, the Americans too discovered that "precision" bombing, even in daylight, was often a misnomer. The Army Air Forces' continued belief in the efficacy of such bombing, one of its own historians wrote, was more "a matter of faith than of knowledge empirically arrived at." The German economy—thought to be already under severe strain in 1941 because of British bombing—proved to be both more resilient and more adaptable than had been imagined by air-power theorists. At the peak of intensity of Allied raids against aircraft industries, indeed, German fighter production actually tripled.[19]

Despite the frustration and disappointments encountered in their conduct of the air war, American commanders at first resisted British pressure to join the RAF in the area bombing of German cities to break morale. As had been the case with the British, the aversion of Army Air Forces leaders to terror bombing had its roots in practical as well as moral grounds. Wartime AAF doctrine specified that area bombing to affect morale was not to be undertaken until nearly the end of the war, when the enemy's society was on the verge of collapse. The problem, logically, was in knowing when that collapse was imminent. As the scale of the Allied bombing offensive increased in the summer of 1942 there came to be a kind of *post hoc* quality to the argument that morale bombing was justified because the German war machine was on its last legs. It became more difficult, accordingly, to distinguish between the RAF's nighttime "blind bombing" and the AAF's daytime "precision bombing" in terms of the results.[20]

In at least some instances, American commanders resorted to the same sort of rationalization that their British counterparts had used to justify the mounting toll of German noncombatants. The "way to stop the killing of civilians," suggested AAF commander H. H. "Hap" Arnold in 1943, "is to cause so much damage and destruction and death that civilians will demand that their government cease fighting." By February 1945, the head of the AAF in Europe, General Carl Spaatz, explained the bombing of Dresden —where tens of thousands of civilians were killed—as representing "not a change in priority but a shift in emphasis" on the part of U.S. bombing policy, since the American target had been the city's railroad marshaling yards. More than four years before, a member of Britain's Air Staff had similarly justified the killings of civilians as a "by-product" of bombing, where the "primary intent" had been "to hit a military target in the sense of a power station, a marshalling yard or an oil plant." Later, Bomber Command had declared that "this by-product should become an end-product."[21]

The blurring of targeting distinctions that began for the AAF in Europe culminated in its bombing campaign against Japan. The commander of the 20th Air Force in Japan, Curtis LeMay, was instructed by Arnold's staff to give first priority to attacks upon cities rather than industrial targets. Illustrative of the way that LeMay assessed the effectiveness of this bombing was his answer when Arnold asked when he thought the war would end. LeMay calculated that his bombers—which were attacking a Japanese city a day by the spring of 1945—would run out of targets that fall. LeMay thus reasoned, he later wrote, "that if there were no targets left in Japan, certainly there wouldn't be much war left." Indeed, nighttime incendiary raids on Japanese cities—such as those over Tokyo during March 1945—killed more people than either of the atomic blasts at Hiroshima and Nagasaki.[22]

The emphasis late in the war upon strategic bombing's supposed morale effect was shown as well by the choice of Hiroshima as a possible target for the atomic bomb. The relatively flat terrain of the city and the fact that it had not been previously bombed were both reasons why Hiroshima was picked to demonstrate the unique power of the bomb.[23]

The process of illusion—or, perhaps, of self-deception—that had accompanied the shift to civilian targeting at every step was evident also in the atomic bombings. When making the decision to use the weapon against Japan, President Truman wrote in his personal diary that he had instructed Secretary of War Stimson to make sure "that military objectives and soldiers and sailors are the target and not women and children." "The target," Truman wrote on July 25, 1945, "will be a purely military one and we will issue a warning statement asking the Japs to surrender and save lives."[24]

Many years after the atomic bombings, a British physicist who had worked for Bomber Command during the war concluded, with regard to strategic bombing, that the destruction of Hiroshima had been "an afterthought."[25]

It would be more accurate to say that the atomic bombings were a culmination. The road to Hiroshima had actually begun at Guernica.

The postwar debate that should have arisen over the effects of strategic bombing was preempted by the atomic raids on Hiroshima and Nagasaki. While the experience of bombing in the Second World War proved Douhet wrong on "almost every salient point he made," nonetheless "the utility of strategic bombing could no longer be questioned" because of the atomic bomb, Bernard Brodie wrote after the war.[26]

Brodie himself would later come to question that summary judgment. But the widely held view that the atomic bomb played a decisive role in Japan's surrender had the effect of salvaging Douhet's ideas and rescuing the victory-through-air-power school of thinking right after the war. Douhet and air-power doctrine thus emerged from the war triumphant—even after official reports by both the United States and Britain concluded that strategic bombing had been neither the only nor even the most important cause of victory.

Britain's own postwar strategic bombing survey—written by a committee of Bomber Command experts—was expressly critical of the area bombing conducted by the RAF. "The actual effort expended on bombing Germany in manpower and resources was greater than the value in manpower and resources of the damage caused," the *Overall Report* concluded. It also claimed that morale attacks aimed at inducing Germany's defeat had been effective only insofar as they had incidentally disrupted or destroyed German transport and communications.[27]

The recounting of the experience of strategic bombing evoked memories and arguments that many in Britain after the war felt were best forgotten. The *Overall Report* proved so unpopular with the postwar Labour government that the document was suppressed by the Air Ministry. Contrary to custom, no monument to Bomber Command was erected among the war memorials at Westminster—nor was a campaign medal struck at war's end for those who had taken part in the air offensive. "It is hard to look back across a generation on such a night's work as the destruction of Darmstadt with any pride," one historian of the bombing offensive reflected. "Morality had little part in it," another summarized of the campaign.[28]

America's *Strategic Bombing Survey,* while larger and more comprehensive than its British counterpart, expressed similar doubts about the utility of the bombing. The chokepoint strategy employed by the AAF was generally deemed a failure, though the *Survey* argued that bombing did contribute significantly to the collapse of the German economy once Hitler's Reich was finally beset by invading armies. Particularly effective during this last stage of the war, the *Survey* concluded, had been Allied bombing of German synthetic-fuel plants and electrical utilities, the destruction of which had hastened—but not caused—the final collapse.[29]

As with Britain's *Overall Report,* the most ambiguous and controversial of the American *Survey*'s findings concerned the effect that bombing had had upon civilian morale. The American account of the European war argued that bombing "appreciably affected the German will to resist," and "did little to stiffen resistance through the arousing of aggressive emotions of hate and anger." However, in a later passage, the American report conceded that sustained heavy bombing of cities "soon led to diminishing returns in morale effects," and that morale in heavily bombed German cities was no worse than in cities receiving only a fraction as many bombs. The survey also acknowledged that German arms production had increased steadily until mid-1944, despite the bombing and "in spite of declining morale." The decrease in production thereafter was attributed only in part to the effect that bombing had upon the will of German civilians.[30]

The conclusion of the *Survey* contradicted the basic assumptions held by the victory-through-air-power school and challenged the justification behind the dropping of the atomic bombs. The Japanese, the *Survey* claimed, would probably have surrendered before the planned American invasion of their home islands "even if the atomic bomb had not been used."[31] Contrary to the prediction of prewar air-power enthusiasts, it was ultimately the enemy's *means* of resistance—not his spirit—that strategic bombing had come closest to breaking.

4

Only One Carthage

The conclusions of the bombing survey notwithstanding, the absolute weapon came to dominate American strategy—absolutely—in the years just after Hiroshima. The Air Force's belief in the bomb was partly a faith born of desperation. More than any other service, it had anticipated an enduring U.S. atomic monopoly. As late as the summer of 1949, only a matter of weeks before the first Soviet atomic test, an Air Force appendix to the nation's only long-range plan for a war with Russia had confidently predicted that the monopoly would last for several more years—and that even a decade hence the United States could still enjoy a ten-to-one superiority over Russia in the number of atomic bombs.[1]

Complacency and optimism had vanished almost overnight with the news of the Soviet bomb—in its wake the prediction of a tenfold nuclear advantage over Russia a decade hence was reversed. But the popular antipathy to universal military training and Truman's pledge of a reduced peacetime defense budget had already committed the nation to the so-called strategy of the air-atomic offensive by the time the Russians matched America's technological coup. The centerpiece of Air Force thinking by 1950 was the atomic bomb—if only because of the lack of alternatives. Consequently, deterrence was not so much adopted there as accepted by default. The Air Force's war planning after 1949 thus acquired an almost schizophrenic quality in its premise that the air-atomic strategy would either prevent a war or win one.[2]

After the publication of *The Absolute Weapon,* Bernard Brodie had been hired by the government to conduct a survey of military attitudes toward the atomic bomb. Brodie was struck by the extent to which the old concept of a sudden, decisive attack from above had become enshrined in the new Air Force because of the bomb. Douhet's "knockout blow" and Trenchard's "thunderbolt" were suddenly joined by the postwar concept of the "atomic blitz."[3]

In the summer of 1950, Brodie presented the case for strategic bombing in an article that came to the attention of Air Force planners, who were then eagerly seeking a rebuttal to the discouraging conclusions of the wartime bombing survey. Offered a job with the Air Targets Division of Air Force Intelligence as a result, Brodie willingly abandoned Yale and also deserted his first sponsor, the Navy, the service most resistant in adapting to the bomb, in hopes that he might be able to play a direct role in shaping military strategy around the absolute weapon.[4]

It was while working for the Air Force, where he had access for the first time to nuclear secrets, that Brodie began to realize how his earlier work on the bomb had been—in a literal sense—academic. While still at Yale he had commented on the confusion and ambiguity of public statements made by military spokesmen concerning how a "significant" number of atomic bombs "might prove decisive" in war. Once in the government, Brodie discovered that Air Force leaders themselves had been kept in the dark by the Army's Manhattan Project until the spring of 1947 on exactly how many bombs were in the nation's nuclear arsenal. Hence they had been unable before that date to plan realistically for an atomic war with Russia.[5]

Brodie was as shocked as the Air Force had been to learn just how few bombs there were. All but one of the atomic bombs originally produced at Los Alamos had been exploded. If the Japanese had not surrendered in August 1945, the atomic "rain of ruin" with which the United States had threatened them some weeks earlier would have simply—and abruptly— stopped. Fully two years after Hiroshima the American nuclear arsenal consisted of exactly thirteen atomic bombs, only one of which could have been readied for use in less than two weeks. But a year earlier the Air Force's draft of a nuclear war plan had proposed dropping a total of fifty atomic bombs upon twenty cities in Russia.[6]

A crash program to increase the output of the nation's atomic laboratories as well as a series of technical advances in nuclear weaponry had increased the number of bombs in the arsenal to fifty by the end of 1948. Foremost among these technological breakthroughs was perfection of the "fractional crit" experimented with in the early days of Los Alamos, whereby a fraction of what had hitherto been considered a critical mass of plutonium could be used to create an atomic explosion. Further improvement in the design of the bombs made it possible to double their yield using the same amount of fissionable material. Henceforth, not only would the weapons themselves become more powerful but their numbers would begin to increase at an almost exponential rate.[7]

The growth of the arsenal after 1948 aside, the fact that the Air Force lacked the necessary number of specially modified B-29s to carry the bombs —and the weaponeers trained in how to assemble and arm them—continued to frustrate its efforts to plan for a single, mammoth atomic raid against

Russia in the event of war. It was not until after the outbreak of the Korean War that President Truman finally agreed to relax civilian control over the weapons sufficiently to allow the military to transfer atomic bombs to overseas bases within range of Russia.[8]

What Brodie in his role as a civilian consultant found at least as disturbing as the country's surprising lack of preparedness for nuclear war was the "preatomic thinking" that he felt still predominated in the services even five years after Hiroshima. Nowhere, he thought, was this trait more evident than in the Air Force's selection of targets, which he considered the "essence of air strategy." He was amazed, Brodie later confided, by the "sheer frivolousness and stupidity" with which the Air Targets Division had treated "the No. 1 strategic problem confronting the U.S. at the time": the question of where and when in wartime to drop the atomic bombs that were now being produced at an ever-increasing rate.[9]

Brodie complained that the Air Force had, in effect, drawn up a "bombing schedule" rather than a war plan, in which the rate at which the bombs were being delivered from Los Alamos and not military requirements had become the main determinant of strategy. As more bombs became available, the Air Targets Division had simply added more cities and industries in Russia to its list. By the time Brodie arrived, the number of places in Russia designated as targets had swollen from the original twenty to over one hundred, with a total of three hundred bombs assigned to their destruction.[10]

Air Force planners met only one afternoon a year to decide on the strategic principles underlying the target list, and Brodie saw this as indicative of their virtual disregard of the subject. While ostensibly based upon "the latest available air-force intelligence studies," Brodie claimed that the rationale behind the choice of targets in Russia was often taken—verbatim—from the text of the *Strategic Bombing Survey* on the bombing of Germany and Japan.[11]

There was, Brodie remarked, a more than passing similarity between the logic and language of the wartime *Survey* and that of the current war plan. In the same words that Bomber Command had used to justify the bombing of German cities, the Joint Chiefs of Staff subsequently argued that the destruction of Russian cities "would be a by-product of the campaign to cripple Soviet war-making capacity." There was also, Brodie complained, the same willful glossing of the obvious in the Air Force's war plan. Although "population *per se*" was specifically exempted as a target in that plan —as it had been during the Second World War—the atomic bomb's inherent destructiveness and the growing number of weapons to be dropped inevitably meant, he pointed out, that "urban areas in general" would be the real targets.[12]

The disarray that Brodie found in strategic targeting was in large part the result of a debate within the Air Force that had been carried over from the wartime bombing survey. That debate had its origins in rival claims concerning the effectiveness of the RAF's so-called "Rail Plan" versus the AAF's "Oil Plan." The controversy over whether the British bombing of railroad marshaling yards in cities such as Dresden had been more important than the American bombing of synthetic-fuels plants in causing the Nazi war machine to grind to a halt had ultimately become so heated that initial plans for a joint Anglo-American bombing survey were abandoned.[13]

In the postwar Air Force the debate had become personified in a three-way split between that service's chief of staff, Hoyt Vandenberg, its director of intelligence, Charles Cabell, and the head of its Strategic Air Command, Curtis LeMay. Each man cited the "lessons" of the bombing survey when arguing his case in the debate, which came to have all the appearances and passions of a religious controversy involving rival interpretations of scripture. Its effect was to delay approval by the joint chiefs of an official target list in the event of nuclear war.[14]

Vandenberg and Cabell both argued, in line with classic air-power doctrine, that the principal target in strategic bombing should be the enemy's vital "war-supporting industry." But Vandenberg considered Russia's oil-refining capacity a more critically vulnerable target than Cabell's choice, Soviet electrical utilities. LeMay—the only one of the three to have commanded a large bomber force during the war—dismissed the distinctions made by both Vandenberg and Cabell, arguing instead that the first-priority target in a future war should be what it was in the past: the lives and psychological well-being of the civilians who worked in the enemy's factories.

A failed nighttime mock raid upon Dayton, Ohio, by SAC in 1948 had disabused LeMay of the notion that precision bombing was possible even in the atomic age. Not a single one of the bombers in the hypothetical attack had found its target and completed its mission. The SAC commander subsequently cited the incident to bolster his case for bombing cities *in toto* rather than specific industries. "LeMay," Brodie later wrote, "preferred to find his industrial targets within cities rather than outside them, so that bombs which missed their primary targets would still knock over bricks rather than trees." (In the incessant arguments that he had with Vandenberg and Cabell on this point, LeMay liked to recount a story about how he had once led an attack against a particular aircraft-manufacturing plant in Tokyo, and in the process serendipitously discovered the benefit of bombing civilians. Because of bad weather, the bombers missed the factory buildings altogether and dropped their bombs accidentally upon the surrounding residential areas. But since most of those living in the houses had been workers at the plant, production there had stopped.)[15]

Brodie found that this debate at the highest level of the Air Force, combined with the far greater power of atomic bombs, resulted in some strange compromises in the planning for nuclear war. The original aiming point for the attack upon Moscow, for example, had been the spires of the Kremlin. When an electrical power station was subsequently discovered by Cabell's targeters only a mile south of the government's headquarters, however, ground zero was shifted to a point midway between it and the power plant. In many Russian cities on the target list some bombs were designated to be dropped on electrical utilities, some on oil refineries, and some on railroads—in what was essentially just an adaptation of the strategy that the bombing survey concluded had not been decisive in the Second World War.[16]

Another idea that Brodie found the Air Force had adopted from the bombing survey was what he termed its "collapse thesis": the belief that Russia would simply surrender under the onslaught of the atomic blitz. Brodie discovered that Vandenberg, Cabell, and LeMay all subscribed to this theory—despite the evidence of two Pentagon studies done in 1948 and 1949. Those studies had concluded that the Air Force would probably not be able to carry out the kind of attack on Russia it planned, and that, in any case, such an attack would probably not knock Russia out of the war. So ingrained was the idea that the Soviet Union would collapse as a result of the air-atomic offensive, Brodie noted, that in 1950, when he asked an Air Targets Division officer how the latter expected a Russian collapse to come about, the officer had "seemed to think it was a bizarre question." "The SAC mission was simply 'collapse,' " Brodie marveled.[17]

Brodie's knowledge of the war plan convinced him that the Air Force was intent upon using the absolute weapon to repeat not only the experience but even the mistakes of the Second World War. In a detailed study that he completed in the spring of 1951 for Vandenberg, Brodie pointed out how Britain's *Overall Report* had concluded that the bombing of Germany's electrical grid did not significantly affect war production until a point so late in the war that most of the factories using electricity had already been destroyed. Until that time, demand had decreased in step with supply. The same phenomenon applied to the destruction of Germany's oil refineries and synthetic-fuel plants.[18]

More important, Brodie argued, was the fact that the military-civilian distinction in targeting, which four years of strategic bombing with conventional weapons had gradually worn away, became all but meaningless with the advent of the atomic bomb. Virtually without regard to what was being aimed at, the real target in a Third World War, Brodie claimed, would be what it had been in the Second—people—since "cities would most certainly have been hit." No one in the Air Force—and least of all LeMay—had taken into account the moral implications of the war plan's emphasis upon the destruction of cities, though that emphasis blatantly contradicted a top-secret statement of war aims made by the Truman administration in 1948.[19]

Brodie suggested that the Air Targets Division adopt a radical new approach to the thinking and planning for nuclear war—one that would, in effect, reverse Douhet's axioms. He argued that cities and civilians should be spared in a war rather than made its first victims. His approach was specifically in reaction to LeMay, who, like wartime Bomber Command, regarded civilian casualties as a by-product or "bonus" in the bombing of industries. There was, Brodie told Vandenberg, "no justification for regarding whatever large scale slaughter results from our bombing as a 'bonus.' " More was to be gained "by holding cities hostage than in making corpses."[20]

Brodie's alternative was to launch "sample attacks" against carefully selected targets in Russia. The purpose of such attacks would be to demonstrate to the civilian population that the real target of American retaliation was the Soviet government—not the Russian people. One inspiration for the sample-attack idea had come from Brodie's previous experience with psychological warfare, where he was impressed with the effect that leaflets warning of a coming attack had had on Japanese morale. Rather than a single massive atomic blitz, the kind of air-atomic offensive Brodie envisioned the United States undertaking would strike at only a few Russian cities, warning their populations beforehand of the impending attack, and allowing time for evacuation. The point of those raids would not be to cause economic or psychological collapse, Brodie claimed, but to induce something that the communist leadership feared most: anarchy. The "distaste of the Russian people for the regime which covers them," he wrote, "might be the nation's single greatest asset in a war with the Soviet Union."[21]

The key to Brodie's idea was restraint—not only in the selection of targets to bomb in Russia, but in the pace at which the war would be conducted. Convinced that restraint had been completely lost sight of in the strategy of atomic blitz, Brodie even recommended to Vandenberg that the rate at which nuclear weapons were being added to the arsenal be deliberately slowed—a suggestion certain to be regarded as heresy in the Air Force, which had consistently urged that the government increase the production of atomic bombs.[22]

Brodie was probably not surprised, therefore, when the Air Force reacted with a marked lack of enthusiasm to his ideas. Vandenberg looked at his report, Brodie claimed, "rather hastily one afternoon" while its author waited in the corridor outside his office. Though Brodie thought that his report was one of the most insightful of his career, the Air Force, he later learned, either lost or destroyed it. Despite repeated entreaties, Brodie was never able to discuss his recommendations at length with either Vandenberg or Cabell. LeMay reportedly told him that his idea of restraint was "contrary to the principles of war."[23]

In fact, some thought of restraint had previously entered into every consideration of the bomb's use since the dawn of the atomic age. In the spring of 1945, Secretary of War Stimson had ordered General Groves to strike Kyoto from the list of Japanese cities that were possible targets for the atomic bomb. Stimson had feared that the destruction of a historic cultural shrine might so embitter the Japanese that they would turn toward the Russians after the war. The same had been true of Tokyo—though that city was later put back on the list as a target for the third atomic bomb. "Even if the Japs are savages, ruthless, merciless and fanatic, we as the leader of the world for the common welfare cannot drop this terrible bomb on the old capital or the new," Truman wrote in his private journal of the decision to spare Tokyo and Kyoto.[24]

Similarly, at the peak of the 1948 Berlin crisis, an aide to Dean Acheson had suggested to Secretary of State George Marshall that the United States drop an atomic bomb on Russia. "If we were to atomic bomb the Soviet Union," Marshall had asked the aide, "what targets would you choose?" The latter subsequently reconsidered his idea of bombing Leningrad, with its art treasures at the Hermitage.[25]

For somewhat different reasons, Air Force planners, too, apparently decided to spare Leningrad and Moscow at this time. The first draft of a plan for a nuclear war with Russia had included the two cities on the list of targets to be destroyed at the outbreak of the conflict. Some time later, however, both were removed from that list in a revision of the plan, which now specified that the two most important Russian cities would not be hit with atomic bombs before the second week of the war: a reflection perhaps of the tacit—if belated—realization of war planners that those Russians with the authority to surrender had to be spared. By the time that Brodie arrived at the Air Targets Division, the status of Moscow and Leningrad as "prompt targets" in a nuclear war had been restored.[26]

Instead of receiving a hearing for his ideas on an alternative to the atomic blitz, Brodie was informed by Vandenberg that his proposed air-strategy study—which the strategist intended to base upon the wartime bombing survey—had been canceled. It was undoubtedly clear to Brodie when he resigned as a civilian consultant to the Air Force late in the spring that the service was not interested in restraining strategic bombing but was, indeed, headed in exactly the opposite direction. A farewell lecture that he gave at this time on the "lessons" of strategic bombing from the Second World War was certainly not what the Air Force wanted to hear. "What should it teach us?" was the rhetorical question that Brodie posed about the bombing as the subject for the lecture. His answer was foreign to the very spirit of the postwar Air Force: "It should teach us humility."[27]

With no interest in returning to the quiet of academic life after serving as a consultant to the Pentagon, Brodie accepted an offer from the newly founded Rand Corporation, the pioneering "think tank" established, ironically, by the Air Force to foster new ideas in strategy.

Together with a few other academics, Brodie had begun producing papers for Rand shortly after its inception in 1949. He now intended to write the history of strategic air warfare that the Air Force had canceled shortly after his report to Vandenberg. Brodie might even have hoped that his new book would end the debate the bombing survey had begun. The study was to be patterned after his earlier book on naval power, and presumably would have taken the case for selectivity and restraint in targeting further than his brief report for Vandenberg.[28]

But another impetus for Brodie's new book was probably his realization that there already existed a need for some fundamental rethinking of the unthinkable. Many of the assumptions that he and others had made about the bomb in *The Absolute Weapon* were obsolete only five years after Hiroshima.

The irresistible advance of technology was one reason for that obsolescence. Brodie had assumed that the very great difficulty and cost of making atomic bombs, as well as the relative scarcity of uranium in the world, would make the absolute weapon a rare commodity in national arsenals for some time to come. He also thought that the seemingly inherent bulkiness of the first atomic bombs would make them virtually impossible to conceal and both difficult and expensive to carry to a target. "It couldn't fit in a suitcase," Brodie stated categorically about the bomb in his 1946 book.[29]

But the technological prowess that made it possible by the spring of 1948 to construct a nuclear weapon twice as powerful as the one that destroyed Nagasaki and only half its size undermined both of Brodie's assumptions at a single stroke. The absolute weapon was becoming not only more powerful and more efficient but also more available and hence, perhaps, more usable.

During his time in office, President Truman had approved four successive increases in the production of fissionable material for bombs. The dire situation of atomic scarcity that had existed at the beginning of his administration was sufficiently resolved near its end so that the number of bombs said by the joint chiefs to be required for war planning doubled between 1949 and 1951—and by the latter date even included some provision for "a postwar stockpile." The production rate of atomic bombs by the end of the Korean War in 1953 was triple the 1950 rate. Ironically, even as Brodie tried to introduce the notion of restraint into nuclear targeting, the major prior causes of such restraint—the limited number of bombs and their inefficiency —had begun to disappear.[30]

But the most spectacularly wrong of Brodie's predictions in 1946 concerned the duration of the nation's nuclear monopoly. The earliest of his estimates of how long it would take the Russians to get the bomb had matched that of the majority of atomic scientists: from three to five years. Curiously, as time passed without any evidence of a Soviet bomb, Brodie began to revise his original estimate upward in line with the Truman administration's expectation that the monopoly would endure for at least a decade, and probably longer. Brodie's newfound complacency was reflected in his 1947 comment that the difference between the Soviet atomic-bomb effort and the Manhattan Project was "the difference between a backward technology and an eagerly progressive one." Less than eighteen months later, however, the Russians too had the absolute weapon.[31]

It was while Brodie was at Rand that an event as portentous as the Soviet atomic test occurred. Even before the atomic bomb was a reality, scientists had recognized the theoretical possibility of a second generation of nuclear weapons—what was called the thermonuclear "superbomb," or simply the "Super." The Super promised to solve the problem of the scarcity of fissionable materials for all time, since it would be fueled by hydrogen, the most plentiful element in nature. Unlike the fission or atomic bomb, moreover, the destruction that could be caused by the Super's thermonuclear reaction was in principle without limit. A war fought with superbombs could be, perhaps literally, world-ending.[32]

The dramatic implications of the Super were soon evident to Brodie and other civilian analysts at Rand. One of those who knew firsthand of the work being done on the superbomb told Brodie that he had indeed chosen the right title in *The Absolute Weapon*—but that he had written the book about the wrong bomb.

The implications of the Super were further magnified for Brodie when he learned from another co-worker at Rand of the possibility that in just a few years ballistic missiles might be able to carry superbombs to targets halfway around the world in minutes. This revelation came within weeks of the first successful test of a prototype hydrogen bomb by the United States in the fall of 1952. World-girdling rockets had been dismissed as fantasy by some scientists and Air Force figures only a few years before.[33] But by 1953, they were already on the way to becoming reality.[34]

The advent of bombs a thousand times more powerful than those dropped upon Japan, and of missiles able to deliver them upon the homeland of a future foe virtually without warning, created "a drastically different situation" than that which had existed in the immediate aftermath of Hiroshima, Brodie wrote a year after the first test of the Super. He despaired "of the necessity of exploring the implications of the new type [of bomb,] when we have not yet succeeded in comprehending the implications of the old." In a 1953 lecture to the Air War College on nuclear strategy, it was with a mixture of wonderment and despair that Brodie noted how previous limitations upon the effectiveness of strategic bombing—such as accuracy—would in the future matter "astonishingly little" because of the advent of the Super and the ICBM. Technology, not strategy, had finally fulfilled Douhet's vision of a war fought—and decided—in an afternoon.[35]

The Super "sort of swamped Brodie," recollected Herman Kahn, his Rand colleague at the time. "He gave up on defending against hydrogen weapons." Bruno Augenstein, the physicist at the think tank who told Brodie about the unexpectedly rapid progress toward an ICBM, similarly thought that the Super "undid" the strategist: "It jolted him [Brodie] intellectually."

In later years, Brodie himself would acknowledge that it was the sudden appearance of the hydrogen bomb—more than any refinements in atomic bombs—which caused him to admit that his vision in *The Absolute Weapon* was obsolete. The nature of the change in Brodie's thinking was reflected in the revised subject and title of the book he had long planned on air strategy. *Strategy in the Missile Age* was a far more worried account than his first book on the bomb. In 1946, Brodie had written that even the atomic bomb was "not so absolute a weapon that we can disregard the limits of its destructive power." Before the breakthroughs on the ICBM and the H-bomb, he had consoled himself with Adam Smith's admonition to a young disciple "that there is a great deal of ruin in a nation."[36] Brodie now recognized that because of the new weapons, there would never again be enough.

One of the ideas that Brodie subsequently backed away from—but did not entirely abandon—was his early notion of nuclear deterrence in *The Absolute Weapon.* After the Super, Brodie no longer felt as comfortable with the almost total reliance he had put upon the threat of nuclear weapons to prevent nuclear war. Now those weapons seemed to pose an equal threat to the survival of the nations that possessed them.

At the same time, Brodie was stymied in his search while at Rand for an alternative to the reliance upon deterrence. The idea of a "sample attack" upon enemy cities which he had unsuccessfully promoted to the Air Force as an alternative to Armageddon also enjoyed a brief vogue at the think tank. But his and the other civilian analysts' enthusiasm for the idea paled quickly once the Russians had their own atomic bomb and could respond to sample attacks in kind. Increasingly pessimistic after 1950 about limiting the number of weapons in American or Soviet nuclear arsenals, Brodie thought it might be possible to introduce restraint of another sort—in the choice of targets to be struck in wartime, for example. In *The Absolute Weapon* he had anticipated that the continued scarcity of bombs would mean the targets of a future war would be those things most highly prized by the enemy, particularly his cities. But there might be a kind of mixed blessing, Brodie thought, behind the vast increase in the number of nuclear weapons that seemed a consequence of technology and the arms race.

At Rand, Brodie even briefly entertained the same idea of a nuclear "war-between-the-bases" that William Borden had written about years earlier. But the same rapid increase in the number and power of nuclear weapons that undermined Brodie's faith in deterrence ultimately caused him to doubt as well that a nuclear war fought with hydrogen bombs could be controlled. Quick calculations showed that even a selective attack upon the Soviet Union, in which only military targets were struck, would still kill as many as two million Russian civilians.[37] A "separated target system" whose aim was to limit damage in the event of war was not feasible, Brodie concluded. The kind of restraint he had wanted to bring to war planning with the atomic bomb seemed much more difficult—if not wholly impossible—once both sides had the Super by 1954.

In an exchange of letters that year between Brodie and Borden—the only correspondence ever between the two men—the differences in their outlook on nuclear war were shown to be stark and undiminished. But now it was Borden, not Brodie, who seemed to find some hope for the future. The author of There Will Be No Time wrote optimistically about how in a nuclear war where military targets were hit first "there might be only one Carthage, and if the loser surrendered before the consummating blow against cities was actually delivered, there would be no Carthage." Brodie's reply was curt and gloomy. He evidently found the prospect of "only" one Carthage both slight and unconsoling, since he thought the single restraint on nuclear weapons "which can be made to stick, if any can be made to stick," was simply whether or not they would be used in a conflict.[38]

The pessimism that subtly began to enter Brodie's thinking at Rand seemed itself a tacit admission on his part of how much the world had changed since Hiroshima.[39] The Air Force, at first "preatomic" in its attitudes, Brodie charged, responded with alacrity to the Super, and now had adapted perhaps too well to the grim and swollen calculus of the thermonuclear age.

The restraint that Brodie had thought always deficient in Air Force war planning with the atomic bomb was, he claimed, almost entirely missing once the Super entered the arsenal. Air Force requirements for more bombs, Brodie noted, seemed to increase at an ever-growing rate, in disregard of the greatly magnified power of the Super. In 1947 the joint chiefs had deemed four hundred atomic bombs "sufficient" to defeat the Soviet Union in a war. By 1950 that estimate had doubled. Two years later, the Air Force general to whom Brodie had vainly preached the doctrine of restraint, Hoyt Vandenberg, announced that the United States might have to destroy a total of six thousand targets in the Soviet Union in order "to prevail" over Russia in a war. By the following year the number of bombs in the inventory—nearly a thousand—was evidently increasing at a faster rate than targets could be added.[40]

The rapid growth of the stockpile and the advent of the Super did solve at least one persistent problem that had plagued Air Force targeters since

Brodie's brief stint as a civilian consultant on the war plan. The three-way debate between Cabell, Vandenberg, and LeMay over whether to target railroads, electrical utilities, or cities was finally made moot by the increasing number and power of the bombs available to SAC. Aiming points that previously had been located over individual factories were shifted in the Air Force's 1954 war plan "Reaper," where the center of the city itself became the designated ground zero. As an increasing number of Supers entered the arsenal it even became possible to plan the destruction of two or more cities with a single blow by dropping a superbomb between them. The Air Targets Division for which Brodie had worked was eventually terminated as a specific organization within the Air Force, its task having become almost superfluous.[41]

"Inflation occurred because of the hydrogen bomb," observed Herman Kahn—who continued as a civilian consultant to the Pentagon on war planning long after Brodie had abandoned the field. Kahn once pointed out to his Rand colleague how inflation had fundamentally changed war planning, overturning Brodie's earlier objection that a strategy intent upon destroying military targets alone was impossible, since at least two million Russians would be killed nonetheless. "By today's exaggerated standards, one or two million *is* a separated target system," Kahn told Brodie.

The language of Air Force war planners reflected this inflation as well. SAC's targeting of "urban-industrial areas" came to be characterized as "city-busting" in the jargon of the new thermonuclear age. LeMay's notion of "bonus damage" was supplemented by the concept of an "optimum mix" of industrial and military targets, whose destruction would maximize the bonus of civilians killed. If war broke out, LeMay intended to drop virtually the entire American nuclear arsenal upon Russia in a single raid. He allegedly told aides that his ultimate goal was a single bomb—one that would destroy the whole country.[42] The evidently complete abandonment of restraint by Air Force war planners inspired a kind of cynicism in Brodie's subsequent writings on nuclear strategy. Citing the "orgiastic" destruction that SAC seemed intent upon, Brodie accused the Air Force of creating not a war plan but a "war-spasm." He branded as senseless the competition among and between the military services to destroy targets in Russia not once but many times—characterizing the result with a new word: "overkill."[43]

The change in Brodie's own attitude toward the subject he had embraced so eagerly in 1945 was evident in a series of magazine articles he published in the mid-1950s based on his classified work at Rand. Questioning in a 1955 *Harper's* article whether it was really necessary "to shoot from the hip" —and thus destroy the enemy's society at the outset of war—Brodie professed to find a qualified source of hope in the fact that war between East and West had remained limited in the case of Korea. The same technology that had resulted in the horrific Super, Brodie noted in the article, also made possible a new generation of smaller and less destructive "tactical" nuclear weapons, which might conceivably be used instead of world-ending Supers in any future war between the great powers.[44]

But there was no illusion on Brodie's part that even such a limited nuclear war could remove the lurking danger of a world holocaust, or resolve the paradox of deterrence. The prospect of living with the Super, he thought, had changed the face of war—and with it the meaning of strategy.

"There is a stark simplicity about an unrestricted nuclear war that almost enables it to be summed up in one short sentence: Be quick on the draw and the trigger squeeze, and aim for the heart. One then has to add: but even if you shoot first, you will probably die too!" Brodie wrote in *Harper's*. "This brings us a long way from the subtleties of a Clausewitz, a Jomini, or a Mahan," he argued. "It brings us even a long way from Douhet, the prophetic theorist of strategic air power. It brings us, in short, to the end of strategy as we have known it."

Brodie's conclusion that strategy "had hit a dead end" because of the Super represented a culmination as well in his own career as a strategist. Since Hiroshima that career had been marked by a gradual but progressive erosion of his early faith that deterrence made it possible to live with nuclear weapons. It was the erosion of this faith that had led Brodie to endorse the development of tactical nuclear weapons as a "second line of insurance" between the conventional forces of the West and SAC's fearsome superbombs. A war fought with Supers, he warned, would cause the United States and Russia to suffer the fate of the legendary fighting Kilkenny cats—who consumed each other.[45]

Brodie privately admitted his doubts in a 1954 letter to a friend. He wrote that he had come to have a certain contempt for his fellow strategists, who seemed oblivious to the changes in strategy that nuclear weapons had brought about. He had barely begun his seminal book on air warfare, Brodie informed the friend, when "as I progressed it became clear that 'strategy' and 'unlimited war' are simply incompatible in a world of H-bombs."*

---

*Brodie's insight may have been truer than he knew. In 1983 a distinguished group of scientists concluded that the smoke and fires from burning cities after a nuclear attack might trigger a global "nuclear winter"—enshrouding the earth in darkness and eventually extinguishing all life. The nuclear winter effect might have been produced as early as 1953—according to these scientists' calculations—by the thousand or so atomic bombs that the Air Force was then planning to drop on Russia in the event of war. But nuclear winter would almost certainly have been the result had war occurred the following year—when the hydrogen bomb began to enter the arsenal in significant numbers. There was, indeed, a chilling and unintended irony in the name of the war plan approved by the joint chiefs in July 1954: "Reaper."[46]

5

Straws in the Wind

The "great dilemma" of the atomic age, Bernard Brodie had written in 1948, was that "the conviction *on all sides* that war is too horrible ever to be contemplated [could be] sustained only by making every possible effort to prepare for war and thus to engage in it if need be."[1] Ten years after Hiroshima that paradox was no closer to being resolved, though the world had seemingly developed the habit of living with nuclear weapons—as Brodie, but not Borden, believed it would. Ironically, the popularizer of nuclear deterrence had by that time begun to lose faith in his original proposition. The widely divergent lives of Brodie and Borden a decade after 1945 reflected the split in the world of the nuclear strategists.

After receiving his law degree in 1947, Borden decided against a career on Wall Street and took a job in Germany offered him by an overseas relief agency. The young attorney's trip to Europe was cut short when he received an invitation to lunch from Brian McMahon, a neighbor of Borden's parents and Connecticut's freshman senator. The meeting with McMahon came about as the result of a letter that Borden and two law school colleagues had sent to the legislator some weeks earlier.

The trio jokingly dubbed their letter "the Inflammatory Document," since it contained ideas that Borden had thought too radical to express in his book. Foremost among these was Borden's urging that the Truman administration issue a nuclear ultimatum to Russia while the United States still enjoyed an atomic monopoly. In what the youthful idealist considered a ringing phrase, the letter to McMahon recommended that the nation in effect throw down the gauntlet to the Soviets: "Let Stalin decide—atomic peace or atomic war."[2]

McMahon had made the atomic bomb a proprietary concern in the Senate and was the author of legislation for the domestic control of atomic energy. His reputation in Congress was reflected in his nickname there—"Mr. Atom." Borden's letter to McMahon proposed that the senator persuade Truman to use the nuclear arsenal as a threat, forcing the Kremlin into accepting the kind of world federalism outlined in *There Will Be No Time*.

McMahon did not endorse the idea of a nuclear ultimatum in his meeting with Borden, though he did acknowledge—winking conspiratorially and tapping his temple for emphasis, the latter remembers—that the idea had considerable merit. At the end of the luncheon McMahon offered Borden a job on his staff. Becoming the senator's legislative assistant, Borden was subsequently disappointed to find his employer's ambitions concerned less with the world of the atom than with the chairmanship of the Senate Foreign Relations Committee—and, ultimately, the White House. Borden soon realized that McMahon—a flamboyant Irish Democrat who dressed nattily even by Senate standards, and whose trademark was a diamond stickpin—worried more about his constituency than about the bomb.

But Borden's disappointment was salved by the fact that McMahon gave him the authority to draft virtually all of the senator's position papers and statements on the atomic bomb. The unexpected Democratic sweep in the 1948 election suddenly advanced the fortunes of both men, putting McMahon at the head of the Joint Congressional Committee on Atomic Energy, with Borden becoming its executive director at the age of twenty-eight. From their newfound positions of prominence, the two early the next year set out to uncover the truth behind a subject that had obsessed Borden since writing his book and that was, in fact, the premier secret in Washington: the exact number of bombs in America's nuclear arsenal.

The question raised by McMahon and Borden immediately ran into a stone wall from the Army and former Manhattan Project director Leslie Groves, who remained the chief custodian of the atomic secret. Groves' continuing and unyielding refusal to divulge the number of bombs in the stockpile eventually resulted in a tense standoff in the president's Oval Office between the senator and the general. Truman—perhaps as chagrined as Groves by the fact that the vaunted atomic arsenal still consisted more of shadow than of substance some years after Hiroshima—sided with Groves in the dispute.[3]

Borden's witnessing of an atomic test at the Nevada proving grounds shortly after the run-in with Groves reinforced his belief that a nuclear war need not mean the end of history, particularly if it was limited to strikes at military targets. Borden admitted to being surprisingly unimpressed by "the absolute weapon." "What's all the excitement over these little things?" had been his first reaction to the test. Though the "immediate and certain" war he predicted in 1946 had yet to occur, Borden thought the error of his forecast was in the timing—not in the prediction itself.

The complacency that Borden felt had always surrounded the subject of the bomb disappeared abruptly with the unexpectedly early news of the first Soviet atomic bomb, which evidently stunned both Groves and Truman into disbelief.[4] Since the surprise Russian bomb gave the size of the American atomic stockpile suddenly increased significance, McMahon and Borden renewed their request to know the numbers in the aftermath of the Soviet test. This time their efforts were rewarded with a special briefing by the Atomic Energy Commission, established as a result of McMahon's legislation. The briefing confirmed to Borden what he had always suspected was the real reason for the extraordinary secrecy around the subject of the nation's nuclear arsenal: the shockingly small number of bombs.

Alarmed by the fact that the arsenal consisted of only a fraction of the number of bombs generally believed, Borden was even more concerned to read a subsequent, top-secret AEC assessment of the Soviet bomb which concluded that the Russians might already have embarked upon development of the Super. Analysis of the radioactive debris carried into the upper atmosphere by the 1949 Soviet atomic test indicated that the Russian bomb was at least as advanced as the one the United States had dropped upon Nagasaki, and this finding sparked fears that it might also have contained a thermonuclear component.[5]

These disclosures persuaded Borden that the nation needed to embark upon what he later termed "a feverish quest for atomic abundance." Other recent initiates into the real atomic secret—including conservative Republican Senator Bourke Hickenlooper, who until the Russian test had been one of McMahon's principal foes in Congress—willingly endorsed the quest.[6] The "situation of nuclear plenty" that Borden said he, McMahon, and others now sought for the nation included not only the scientists, raw materials, and weaponeers to assure that America would continue to have superiority in atomic bombs, but also the means to develop the next generation of superbombs.

The first part of their quest was to be the greatly accelerated and expanded production of atomic weapons, which Truman almost immediately approved. But the real focus of Borden's effort was upon a crash effort to build the first Super. At Borden's suggestion, McMahon created a special subcommittee in his congressional committee to act as a lobbying force for the hydrogen bomb. Together with AEC commissioner Lewis Strauss, McMahon and Borden mapped out a strategy for promoting the weapon's development and recruited sympathetic scientists to testify on behalf of that cause.

Borden's actions in promoting the Super were reminiscent of both the ideas and the passion contained in his column at Yale, his book, and the "Inflammatory Document" that launched his crusade for atomic abundance. Opponents of the Super among the scientists and in Congress warned Truman that McMahon and Borden would attempt "to blitz" him into proceeding with the weapon without considering alternatives.[7]

The desperate idealism that had always motivated Borden was evident as well in the urgent tone of the two letters that he wrote to the president under McMahon's signature in November 1949. "The profundity of the atomic crisis which has overtaken us cannot, in my judgment, be exaggerated," the first letter read. "The specific decision that you must make regarding the Superbomb is one of the gravest ever to confront an American president." The sense of dire warning that had characterized *There Will Be No Time* was present as well in Borden's final appeal to Truman: "If we let the Russians get the Super first, catastrophe becomes all but certain—whereas, if we get it first, there exists a chance of saving ourselves."[8]

The fight over the Super was to become a centerpiece in the struggle between advocates of "nuclear plenty" like Borden and those who, like Brodie, urged restraint upon the government in the development of nuclear weapons and the planning for their use. The superbomb debate would eventually engage many of the scientists who had built the first nuclear weapon. Because of their involvement, those scientists would themselves become an issue in the debate over the Super.

Truman's decision in January 1950 to approve an urgent effort to develop the hydrogen bomb, and the subsequent approval he gave to another expansion of atomic bomb production, seemed to confirm the ascendancy of the group urging more, not less. Since the president's decisions were taken in the wake of fresh revelations concerning the activities of Soviet "atom-spies" and amid the shock created by the Russian bomb, however, they represented not so much an independent choice as a confirmation of the previous policy.[9] The real choice for the nation in the matter of nuclear weapons was yet to come.

Significantly, even the attainment of nuclear plenty and the decision to build the Super did not necessarily diminish the threat that Borden believed still confronted the nation. In his book he had predicted that an atomic attack upon the United States would be "preceded by extensive espionage and by propaganda stressing the aggressor's good intentions and desire for international cooperation." Borden had also warned that a democracy, because of its emphasis upon personal freedom, was far more likely than a dictatorship "to have spies circulated in its midst."[10]

To combat this threat Borden had urged in 1946 that the United States respond "by expanding the Federal Bureau of Investigation somewhat and by extreme care among those charged with research and weapons production."[11] The almost daily press reports about espionage since he had written those words convinced Borden that the country had ignored his warning.

Preparing to leave the government in early 1953, following the Republican election victory and the death by cancer of Brian McMahon, Borden's latent concern with espionage focused upon the career of one scientist in particular —Robert Oppenheimer, the "father" of the atomic bomb who had nonetheless become one of the most prominent opponents of the Super. It was not only Oppenheimer's opposition to the hydrogen bomb that aroused Borden's suspicions, but what the latter claimed was "the pattern of activities" in which the scientist had been involved before and after the Manhattan Project.

Oppenheimer's radical affiliations had first come to Borden's attention shortly after the young lawyer became McMahon's aide. A subsequent personal encounter with the eminent scientist had persuaded him, Borden said, that Oppenheimer was "a born leader and a natural manipulator—a con man." Borden's continuing involvement in the H-bomb controversy further convinced him that Oppenheimer was using his well-known influence with fellow scientists to obstruct development of the hydrogen bomb.

Ironically, another impetus behind the charges that Borden would eventually level against Oppenheimer had its origins in a breach of security for which Borden himself bore responsibility. Before departing the Joint Committee on Atomic Energy, he and a few other committee members had resolved to acquaint their successors with a brief history of the development of nuclear weapons. Behind the historical facade of the "A-Bomb Chronology" and the "H-Bomb Chronology" that Borden and the others wrote, however, was an inflammatory allegation. Borden charged that both weapons programs had been marked by delay, cutbacks, and malfeasance for which one individual above all others was responsible: Robert Oppenheimer.

Akin to Senator Hickenlooper's claim five years earlier that the AEC was guilty of "incredible mismanagement," Borden's chronologies were less an actual history based on fact than a lawyer's brief charging Oppenheimer with willful obstruction of the national quest for atomic abundance. Neither Borden nor anyone else on the committee overtly recommended a course of action to its new members. But what they left behind them, in the chronologies, was plainly intended to be a legacy of doubt.[12]

The final spur for Borden to act on his suspicions regarding Oppenheimer was an incident that occurred in the preparation of the "H-Bomb Chronology." On his way home by train after conferring with a scientist at Princeton about the Super, an aide to Borden accidentally left a top-secret draft of the "H-Bomb Chronology" in the restroom of his Pullman car. (The irony as well as the magnitude of the mistake was compounded when it turned out that the train had been carrying a delegation traveling to the capital to protest the impending execution of the Rosenbergs for the theft of the atomic secret.) Though the FBI searched frantically for the document—and the hapless aide's briefcase was minutely dissected on the committee's green-baize conference table—it was never found.

What FBI director J. Edgar Hoover pointedly came to call "the Borden incident" prompted the dispatch of an anonymous letter to the Senate—written by Hoover himself—protesting the lax security surrounding atomic secrets. The letter reportedly led to a personal reprimand of Borden by President Eisenhower. When he finally left the government that spring,

Borden was conscious of having inadvertently become an example of the kind of carelessness with nuclear secrets that he had warned about in his book.[13]

Six months after Borden returned to private life as an attorney for the atomic-power division of Westinghouse, it was gallingly apparent to him that the finger-pointing chronologies had had little impact. Oppenheimer's influence in the government and his public popularity seemed undiminished —a fact underscored by the scientist's report in the July 1953 issue of *Foreign Affairs* on the disarmament panel he had been appointed to by Truman the previous year.[14] Borden, finding his last, albeit veiled warning thus unheeded, was inspired to frame his suspicions about Oppenheimer in the form of a letter to Hoover.

While he was still working for the committee in Washington, Borden had compiled a list of some four hundred questions concerning Oppenheimer's activities and beliefs that formed his essential case against the scientist. It was not, Borden later averred, these four hundred questions "but a thousand things" about Oppenheimer that prompted him to write the five-page, single-spaced letter which he sent to Eisenhower as well as Hoover in November 1953.

The considered, carefully legal language of Borden's letter did not mask the extraordinary nature of his allegation. Though Borden had no evidence beyond what was already in Oppenheimer's FBI file—which he had reviewed before he left the committee—he concluded in the letter that "the worst is in fact the truth," and that "more probably than not" Oppenheimer was a Soviet agent.[15]

Like Bernard Brodie's surprisingly frank conclusion that nuclear strategy had hit a dead end with the Super, Borden's last inflammatory document marked a kind of culmination in his own crusade for the hydrogen bomb, and against those who opposed it. Borden had, unwittingly, already contributed to the paranoia about atomic secrets. He later conceded that Eisenhower's decision—against the advice of some superbomb proponents—to proceed with a formal investigation into Oppenheimer's loyalty may have had its origins in the president's concern with security, which itself had been inspired in part by Borden's own transgression in the case of the "H-bomb Chronology."

The Oppenheimer trial and its aftermath perhaps irretrievably embittered relations among atomic scientists. It would widen further the split in their ranks that had its origins at Alamogordo and Hiroshima, and that was advanced further by the Super debate.

The source of Borden's "feverish quest for atomic abundance" and for the Super could be found even earlier, in the urgent appeal of his book, or in the ideals honored in his college newspaper column. Borden's Yale roommate had sensed his friend's near-fanaticism when he wrote the dedication to a privately published volume of "Straws in the Wind." "He seemed," the classmate wrote of Borden, "to be always trying to free himself of the lies of the world in order to find something to believe in."[16]

In Borden's crusade for the Super—and against Oppenheimer—he had found it.

6

—

That String Untuned

When Paul Nitze returned to Washington from the war he found that "quite different things had achieved the center of the stage," he said. "The interest was no longer with how to organize our defense. The thinking that was central in some people's minds was, 'How do you return to normalcy most rapidly?' "

At the Pentagon, Nitze was shocked to discover how rapidly postwar demobilization had dismantled the nation's victorious armies, fleets, and air armada. He learned from Navy Secretary James Forrestal, for example, that because of this pell-mell return to civilian life the Navy, only a year after the war, was unable to put together a single carrier task force. Forrestal had wanted to send the task force into the Mediterranean to impress the Russians, who were balking at their wartime pledge to withdraw from Iran. But the ships lacked sufficient crew members even to leave port. As distressing to Forrestal as the dismantling of the country's defenses was the popular mood in the United States just after the war. "The country," he warned, "was going back to bed at an alarming rate."[1]

Shortly after he returned home, Nitze had approached New York's Robert Moses about implementing one of the recommendations made in the bombing survey. He wanted Moses to endorse the idea of incorporating bomb shelters in the construction of all big buildings going up in New York. Moses, however, told Nitze his idea "was mad—absolutely mad." "Nobody," he informed Nitze, "will pay any attention to that."

Nitze had been surprised by the reaction to his idea, but in time, he said, he came to realize that Moses was right. "The issue then," Nitze pointed out, "was not whether one group or another was right about what the impact of these weapons upon military affairs was, but the attitude was 'forget the whole darn thing and let's go back to normalcy.' "

The rapid disintegration of the nation's mammoth military machine, and the postwar mood of the citizenry, left Nitze personally persuaded that the temporary mainstay of America's defense would necessarily be its atomic arsenal. But he found that there was still no general agreement, even in the Pentagon, over the future of the bomb. There were instead, he noted, three contending schools of thought on the subject within the military and in the country at large.

The first conceded that the bomb had made modern war more terrible—"perhaps by two orders of magnitude in terms of destructiveness"—but nonetheless believed that there might still be a solution to the threat of the bomb, or even a counter to the fearsome weapon. "The second school, a very small minority," Nitze said, "took the view that these weapons were so horrible that they required an entire change in grand strategy." But the majority in both the services and the government, he believed, "and perhaps ninety-nine percent of the population," had simply ignored the changes brought about by the bomb.

Nitze subscribed to the views of the first school. He thought Brodie's theory of deterrence "went too far" in putting emphasis upon the destructiveness of nuclear weapons.

Nitze's view of the Soviet Union accorded well with the developing hard-line policy of the Truman administration toward Russia, which focused upon containing Soviet expansion around the globe. The author of the containment policy was George Kennan, the administration's ranking Russia expert, whose anonymous *Foreign Affairs* essay in the summer of 1947 titled "The Sources of Soviet Conduct" rallied Forrestal and other key government figures around the idea.[2]

Kennan had been perhaps purposefully vague about the means by which the United States would contain Russia, mentioning in his article such things as economic sanctions, "the preponderance of world public opinion," and even "moral example." But to Forrestal—and to Nitze—there was little question that the real barrier to Russian aggression would have to be the atomic bomb: not only was the threat of the bomb a unique advantage that the United States enjoyed over the Soviet Union in the early years of the Cold War, but the threat had the added virtue of being implicit—and hence independent of the popular will.[3]

The job that Nitze took in the State Department after the war dealt with international trade and finance. But his continuing—and growing—interest was with the military and political implications of nuclear weapons. In 1949 that interest became a vocation when Secretary of State Dean Acheson appointed him to the department's Policy Planning Staff, then headed by Kennan. While Nitze and Kennan became friends, the differences in their views of containment remained strong. Kennan argued that the threatened use of force lay outside the purview of diplomacy; yet he admitted that he deliberately thought very little about the atomic bomb. Kennan told Nitze that spring, in the midst of a war scare over Berlin, that he felt two divisions of Marines would be sufficient to accomplish the military ends of containment—a notion the latter thought "nonsensical."[4]

Nitze believed, to the contrary, that the military capabilities of a nation were inseparable from its intentions, and hence that much more than moral example and diplomacy would be required to frustrate Russian ambitions. The briefing that Nitze received from the Atomic Energy Commission shortly after the Soviet atomic test on the status of America's nuclear stockpile awakened him to the extent to which deterrence had heretofore relied upon bluff. Like Borden, Nitze had become convinced that rearming the country should be a first priority.

Nitze's concern with the nation's military weakness and its irresolute will caused him to ally himself later that year with those promoting development of the Super. Initially he had been persuaded by Oppenheimer, the Policy Planning Staff's scientific adviser, that the Super probably would not work and that the effort to build it might divert scarce resources from the accelerated production of atomic bombs. A subsequent briefing by superbomb proponent Edward Teller, however, had convinced Nitze of the weapon's feasibility. There was, moreover, no doubt in his mind concerning what the consequences would be if the Russians got the Super first: "They would have hegemony right away."

The debate over the Super opened a division in the ranks of the State Department as deep and wide as that among the atomic scientists. In a seventy-nine-page memorandum to President Truman, Kennan argued against a crash effort for the Super, claiming that present nuclear weapons already demonstrated "a certain top-heaviness as instruments of our national policy." Kennan had previously expressed his concern to Truman that the country was "traveling down the atomic road rather too fast." The Super, he implied, would only speed the juggernaut along. Near the end of his memorandum, Kennan quoted lines from Shakespeare's *Troilus and Cressida* which he thought particularly apt in the case of the Super: "Take but degree away—untune that string/ And hark what discord follows."[5]

While sympathetic to the arguments of Kennan and others against the hydrogen bomb, Acheson ultimately sided with proponents of the bomb's development. "I've listened to Oppie as carefully as I know how," he told his aide Gordon Arneson. "But I don't know what the hell he's talking about. How do you disarm an adversary by example?" After the brief meeting where Truman approved a crash program for the Super, Acheson had responded in a similar way when Kennan voiced foreboding that the decision would inevitably lead to an arms race, and eventually to war. If Truman had decided against the Super, Acheson told Kennan, the latter would be well advised to "put on a monk's robe and a tin can and announce that the end of the world is nigh."[6]

But Acheson's bravado only masked what were evidently deep-seated doubts. Arneson remembered how Acheson was unusually solemn after Truman's decision on the Super. There remained, the aide said, a hint of uneasiness in the secretary of state's reassurance on that occasion. "You know," Acheson told him, "we make these weapons so that we may never use them."[7]

Kennan's departure from the government following the H-bomb decision elevated Nitze to the top post at the Policy Planning Staff, guaranteeing him a prominent role in drafting the review of containment policy that Truman had ordered in the wake of the Soviet atomic bomb test. Intended in part to placate those who had unsuccessfully opposed the Super, this fundamental reassessment of the nation's response to Russia had its origins, in Nitze's own view, with Oppenheimer's comment to him during the superbomb debate that no one had yet considered how to conduct foreign policy in a world armed with H-bombs. He decided to undertake this review of foreign policy, Nitze said, with Oppenheimer's comment in mind.[8]

The product of Nitze's effort was embodied in National Security Council Memorandum Number 68, presented to Truman in the spring of 1950. In substance NSC-68 was less a review of past policies than a new recommendation that the nation rearm to fight the Cold War. The first ten pages of the fifty-page top-secret document presented Soviet-American rivalry in almost Manichæan terms. To critics on the committee drafting the review, Nitze defended his characterization of the Cold War in NSC-68 as a struggle between "free" and "slave" worlds. If "we had objectives only for the purpose of repelling invasion and not to create a better world," he argued, "the will to fight would be lessened."[9]

The frightful vision of a possible future that Nitze presented in NSC-68 could have been borrowed from William Borden's *There Will Be No Time.* Central to Nitze's thesis was the contention by Rand analyst Nathan Leites that the unswerving "operational code" of Soviet leaders inclined them toward preventive war. Previously, official expectations in Washington were that war would most likely come about as the result of Soviet "miscalculation." But Nitze warned in NSC-68 that four years hence—by 1954, "the year of maximum danger"—the Russians would for the first time have enough atomic bombs to "seriously damage this country." Under those circumstances, he thought, "the Kremlin might be tempted to strike swiftly and with stealth."[10]

The four alternative policies that NSC-68 proposed as a response to this threat seemed less an analysis than thinly veiled advocacy. The first proposal —a continuation of current policies—Nitze thus deemed not only likely to be suicidal, but no longer acceptable to the American public in the wake of recent setbacks. Equally doomed to failure and unacceptable to the people, NSC-68 claimed, was either a return to isolationism or the admittedly

alluring prospect of a preventive nuclear war against Russia. The final
alternative proposed in the document was what Nitze termed a "more rapid
building up of the political, economic, and military strength of the free
world."[11]

The military buildup recommended by NSC-68 was intended to be across
the board. Estimates of its cost were deliberately not included with the
document sent to Truman. But Nitze argued in NSC-68 that the administration would be able to triple its previous defense spending without sacrificing
the nation's standard of living. Privately, Nitze and the other authors of the
study calculated that the reconversion of the peacetime economy to fight the
Cold War might require a one-third cut in the construction of new houses,
the retooling of Detroit to produce tanks instead of cars, and even a possible
end to the production of television sets and home radios "in order to meet
military demands for electronics."[12]

Nitze, however, professed to see necessary sacrifices on the home front as
a kind of hidden blessing. "The whole success of the proposed program,"
he wrote in NSC-68, "hangs ultimately on recognition by this Government,
the American people, and all free peoples, that the cold war is in fact a real
war in which the survival of the free world is at stake."[13]

The nation's resolve to confront the communist challenge was a particular
concern of Nitze's in NSC-68—especially in light of the country's demobilization and the rebuff his shelter proposal had received. "The democratic way
is harder than the authoritarian way," that document argued,

> because, in seeking to protect and fulfil the individual, it demands
> of him understanding, judgment and positive participation in the
> increasingly complex and exacting problems of the modern world.
> A free society is vulnerable in that it is easy for people to lapse into
> excesses—the excesses of a permanently open mind wishfully wait-
> ing for evidence that evil design may become noble purpose, the
> excess of faith become prejudice, the excess of tolerance degenerat-
> ing into indulgence of conspiracy and the excess of resorting to
> suppression when more modern measures are not only more ap-
> propriate but more effective. . . .[14]

The many disadvantages that the United States suffered in its dealings
with the Soviet Union could only be offset, Nitze claimed, if the nation
maintained a continuing military advantage over the Russians. "In coping
with dictatorial governments acting in secrecy and with speed, we are also
vulnerable in that the democratic process necessarily operates in the open
and at a deliberate tempo," he wrote in NSC-68. "Weaknesses in our situation are readily apparent and subject to immediate exploitation. This Government therefore cannot afford in the face of the totalitarian challenge to
operate on a narrow margin of strength. A democracy can compensate for

its natural vulnerability only if it maintains clearly superior overall power in its most inclusive sense."[15]

The argument that Nitze gave in NSC-68 for maintaining strategic superiority over Russia was developed further in a *Foreign Affairs* article he wrote some six years later, when he was no longer in the government. Even the Cold War, Nitze reminded in that article, was "an atomic cold war," where nuclear weapons were akin to the pieces in a game of chess: "The atomic queens may never be brought into play; they may never actually take one of the opponent's pieces. But the position of the atomic queens may still have a decisive bearing on which side can safely advance a limited-war bishop or even a cold-war pawn."[16]

To Nitze, nuclear weapons were not only a necessary part of military strength, but could be a surrogate for national will. He believed the enemy's perception of American strength and will was as important as their reality in the great power game. In that game, the bomb was both a symbol of power and its instrument. The presence of the bomb might thus only cast a shadow over the relations of Russia and the United States—but it was a specter that subtly haunted the diplomacy of the cold war. It was for this reason that Nitze drew a distinction in his *Foreign Affairs* article between the government's "declaratory policy" on nuclear weapons—the "statements of policy which we make for political effect"—and its actual or "action policy."[17] Just such a distinction had been behind his rejection in NSC-68 of the suggestion that the United States declare it would never be the first nation to use nuclear weapons.

The idea of a no-first-use pledge had been proposed in the years just after Hiroshima by a number of those who hoped by that way to introduce restraint into the nation's nuclear strategy. George Kennan, in his long memorandum to Truman advising against development of the Super, had urged that the president make such a pledge to the world. The idea of a promise of no first use also occurred to Bernard Brodie. A few years after Kennan, Brodie wrote scornfully of the nation's evident desire "to remain free to *initiate* atomic strategic bombing regardless of Soviet acts or intentions during war." Brodie asked rhetorically, "And what is the potential price for such freedom?"[18]

Nitze believed the freedom to use nuclear weapons first was a necessary part of containing Russia. A no-first-use pledge, he wrote in NSC-68, "would be interpreted by the U.S.S.R. as an admission of great weakness and by our allies as a clear indication that we intended to abandon them." Any uncertainty that the United States might deliberately create about its intentions concerning the bomb was itself an ally, Nitze argued, in the protracted struggle with the Soviet Union. But there was as well another—and less abstract—reason for maintaining nuclear superiority over Russia, he admitted.

Nitze was as contemptuous as Brodie of the Air Force's nuclear war plans, though in Nitze's case it was because he believed the military had vastly overrated the destructiveness of the weapon. He ridiculed General Cabell's idea that it would be possible to destroy Russia's railroad system "with just a few atomic bombs." The Russians, Nitze noted, "had railroad marshaling yards all over the place," and the Second World War bombing survey had shown that the tracks at least could be repaired in as little as twenty-four hours.[19]

Though Nitze acknowledged that traditional concepts of victory no longer applied in the atomic age, he thought that the bomb did not so much rule out the possibility of winning as simply give it a new meaning. If containment failed and an all-out war between the United States and Russia ensued, he argued in his 1956 *Foreign Affairs* article, American nuclear superiority would still allow the nation to win the war—albeit in a pro-scribed meaning of the term. It was not "in the sense of being richer, happier or better off after such a war" that victory was possible, Nitze wrote, but in the sense of "a comparison of the postwar position of one of the adversaries with the postwar position of the other."[20]

The winnable nuclear war that Nitze envisioned was, in fact, the war between the bases that William Borden had written about more than a decade before. In Nitze's war, as in Borden's, both countries would deliberately spare the other's cities, striking only at military targets and leaving the urban areas and their populations as hostages to the outcome of the battle of the bases. "In this sense it is quite possible that in a general nuclear war one side or the other could 'win' decisively," Nitze claimed. "The side which has lost effective control of the intercontinental air spaces will face a truly agonizing decision," he concluded: "It may still have the capability of destroying a few of the enemy's cities. But the damage it could inflict would be indecisive and out of all proportion to the annihilation which its own cities could expect to receive in return." The "adversary's entire country" —"including cities, industries, means of communication and remaining military capabilities"—would then lie open to its enemy's will.[21]

His critics would argue that Nitze deliberately exaggerated the Russian threat in painting the dire scenarios of NSC-68 and his later *Foreign Affairs* article. The point of NSC-68, Dean Acheson subsequently admitted, was not so much to propose a specific course of action as to "bludgeon" the government into adopting a general position from which specific actions would follow. The case for rearmament in the Truman administration, Acheson noted, had to be made "clearer than the truth."[22]

Coming as it did upon the heels of Senator Arthur Vandenberg's celebrated advice to Truman and Acheson that they would "have to scare hell out of the American people" in order to gain the necessary support for containment—and its product, the Truman Doctrine—NSC-68 had the desired effect. Taking a day off to read the document, one of Truman's cabinet officers had been both fascinated and terrified by NSC-68.[23] Subsequent efforts by Nitze to sell NSC-68 to the Truman administration proved superfluous. The president gave his official approval to the "more rapid building up" of the nation's military strength within weeks of the communist invasion of South Korea, even though Truman had yet to receive a firm estimate of the buildup's cost.[24]

Korea, seemingly the first of the "proxy wars" that Nitze and NSC-68 had predicted, focused attention upon nuclear weapons as well as conventional forces in that buildup. By the time the war broke out, Nitze had become the government's ranking civilian expert on the bomb and the policies surrounding it. When Truman let slip at a press conference that he was considering the use of nuclear weapons in Korea, it was Nitze whom presidential press secretary Charles Murphy had frantically called upon to defuse the controversy. Nitze was as well Truman's own choice to personally reassure British Prime Minister Attlee that America would not use the bomb irresponsibly. Finally, Nitze was one of those in the administration to recommend against a desperate proposal made by Stuart Symington when the Chinese unexpectedly entered the Korean War later in 1950. Symington had urged that the administration abandon the policy of containment and the long-term buildup of NSC-68. Instead, he proposed that the nation employ its atomic bombs immediately against China, and threaten Russia with their use.[25]

The fact that Truman on at least two occasions did indeed give some thought to using the bomb in Korea showed the extent to which nuclear weapons had come to dominate American military strategy by the early 1950s, being considered in one case as even a substitute for diplomacy.[26] But the final ascendancy of the bomb in containment was less the result of any conscious design than the combination of technology's implacable advance, the enmity of the Cold War with Russia, the misunderstood lessons of the previous war, and the continuing lack of any real alternative.

Against this background it was Borden's feverish quest for atomic abundance that won out against Brodie's lone call for restraint in nuclear strategy. The increase in the number and power of nuclear weapons in the decade after Hiroshima—as well as the planning for their possible use—showed the virtual abandonment of restraint. Indeed, Paul Nitze's NSC-68 demonstrated how nuclear superiority had become an integral part of America's military and political strategy to contain Russia—though, ironically, U.S. war plans of the time left no doubt that a nuclear war, if it occurred, would be neither as limited nor as controlled as Borden and Nitze had envisioned.[27]

The strategists' failure to put limits upon nuclear weapons was not yet a cause of despair. Brodie's doubts about the direction of nuclear strategy and the arms race were shared by many of those experts who included the bomb's creators—the atomic scientists.

7

The Wizard Warriors

Isidor Rabi remembered most the bitterness and disappointment that followed Hiroshima. Of all the scientists, it was Rabi's longtime friend and colleague from Los Alamos, Robert Oppenheimer, who probably felt this disillusionment most intensely. As the recognized leader of the scientists, Oppenheimer was the one among them in the best position to speak out against their creation.

Since he had been director of the wartime laboratory, Oppenheimer clearly felt a special sense of responsibility for the bomb. When he resigned that post a few weeks after the end of the war, Oppenheimer predicted in his farewell speech that if atomic bombs were henceforth "to be added to the arsenals of a warring world, or to the arsenals of nations preparing for war, then the time will come when mankind will curse the name of Los Alamos and Hiroshima." His subsequent anguished comment to Truman that he felt he had blood on his hands prompted the president to dismiss him as "a cry-baby scientist," but Oppenheimer nonetheless remained the preeminent expert adviser to the government on nuclear weapons: one whose special knowledge and eloquence caused him to be much in demand at congressional hearings on the postwar fate of the bomb.[1]

Rabi would later recall the early hopes that he and Oppenheimer had had for controlling nuclear weapons. He remembered in particular Christmas Day in 1945, which the two men had spent at Rabi's high-rise apartment on New York's Riverside Drive, watching chunks of ice in the Hudson River below turn pink in the fading light of sunset. Oppenheimer had ruined the moment, Rabi said, by suddenly bringing up the subject of the atomic bomb.

At the time, Oppenheimer was head of the panel of experts that Dean Acheson and AEC chairman David Lilienthal had recently appointed to come up with a workable scheme for the international control of atomic energy. President Truman had already committed his administration to an attempt to realize international control through the United Nations. Oppenheimer was enthusiastic about a technological solution he had devised to head off the impending nuclear arms race—an international authority modeled after the UN which would have control over the world's high-grade uranium ore. He proposed to the panel that the authority could "denature" the ore to make it usable only in peaceful applications. But the fact that the ore could still be "renatured" for use in bombs—albeit at great expense—persuaded Rabi that Oppenheimer's solution was a desperate measure, more political than technical in character.[2]

The "Oppenheimer plan" was substantially modified in the months before being introduced to the UN in the summer of 1946. Responsible for the most drastic changes was Bernard Baruch, the seventy-six-year-old financier and philanthropist chosen by the administration to present the international control plan to the UN. The Baruch plan differed fundamentally in both letter and spirit from Oppenheimer's original inspiration, abandoning the scientist's ambitious concept of an international authority as well as the idea of denaturing. In the aftermath of Russia's outright rejection of the Baruch plan at the end of 1946, Oppenheimer's initially high hopes for control of the atom plummeted. "I am ready to go anywhere and do anything," he told Lilienthal in despair, "but I am bankrupt of further ideas."[3]

For Oppenheimer, a glimmer of hope had briefly surfaced again late in 1949 with the beginning of the debate over the Super. Like many scientists and some figures in the Truman administration, he saw a decision for the superbomb just after the Russians' atomic test as a potentially irreversible step in the direction of a nuclear arms race. On the other hand, a decision not to develop the Super could be a fateful step away from such a race. Oppenheimer viscerally recoiled from the prospect of an unlimited Soviet-American competition in nuclear arms. The atomic tests that were carried out in the Pacific and at the Nevada proving grounds after the war had left a few scientists "jaunty" and "full of jolly little reminiscences," noted one observer, but they made Oppenheimer and many other veterans of Trinity "awed and anxious."[4]

Along with five of the six other scientists who made up the Atomic Energy Commission's General Advisory Committee, Oppenheimer—the head of that committee—hoped to use its influence to ward off development of the Super. In a climactic meeting of October 1949 that was not attended by the one member, Glenn Seaborg, who conditionally supported the Super, the committee recommended without dissent to Truman that he not proceed with the weapon.

Perhaps because they realized that a judgment on the morality of nuclear strategy was beyond their charter, the committee members decided to combine the ethical argument against the Super—upon which their real opposition rested—with various technical arguments against developing the weapon. The result gave their report a strangely divided, almost schizophrenic quality. Thus, while they said that they thought a crash program would have a better than even chance of success within five years, they cautioned that whether or not the weapon worked, it would nonetheless take scarce raw materials and talent away from the speeded-up program to produce atomic bombs—and hence also divert the effort to develop a generation of nuclear weapons smaller and less destructive than present bombs. The Super, in fact, threatened to reverse the direction of that effort. Later, Oppenheimer would argue in private that an American crash program to develop the Super might even inadvertently help the Soviets, who could unlock the secret of the thermonuclear breakthrough by analyzing the fall-out produced by U.S. tests.[5]

But behind the argument made against the Super on technical grounds was a more fundamental moral objection in the scientists' report that the Super would carry "much further than the atomic bomb itself the policy of exterminating civilian populations." In order to make the ethical objection even clearer, two of the scientists on the committee, Rabi and Enrico Fermi, appended their own letter to the GAC report. The hydrogen bomb, Rabi and Fermi wrote, was by its very nature "a weapon of genocide," and "necessarily an evil thing considered in any light." The choice to forgo development of the terrible new weapon, they argued, was "a unique opportunity" for restraining "the totality of war and thus of limiting the fear and arousing the hopes of mankind."[6]

Rabi and Fermi proposed a choice for the president that was lacking in the committee's overall report. The scientists suggested that, rather than either approving a crash effort for the Super or abandoning the bomb entirely, Truman might consider proceeding with development of the weapon while simultaneously approaching the Russians about an agreement to ban testing of the Super. Since neither side would dare deploy a new type of weapon it had never tested—and because any test of a Super would surely be betrayed by fallout—such a ban seemed to Fermi and Rabi the next best alternative to forgoing the weapon altogether.

At the end of the October meeting, Oppenheimer reportedly offered to sign both the Rabi-Fermi letter and the general report, but finally decided to affix his name only to the report. The attitude of the scientists there, Rabi thought, was summed up by James Conant. Conant, who had advised Franklin Roosevelt to develop the atomic bomb in 1940, felt that the Super "would just louse up the world even more." Conant would later tell Lilienthal that the discussion over developing the Super also had some uncomfortable similarities with the brief debate over whether to proceed with the atomic bomb. It was, he said, like "seeing the same film, and a punk one, for the second time."[7]

The recommendation of the committee against a crash program for the Super became a rallying point for both sides in the debate over the weapon.

Luis Alvarez, the Los Alamos physicist who had witnessed the dropping of the atomic bomb on Hiroshima, vainly urged Oppenheimer on the eve of the decisive meeting to support the Super. Alvarez had made the same futile appeal to Lilienthal—and was shocked when the latter refused even to discuss the subject. Instead, the AEC chairman had turned his chair around and gazed morosely out the window.[8]

Along with Ernest Lawrence, once again his colleague at Berkeley, Alvarez had been recruited to the cause of fostering the Super by Edward Teller, the guiding spirit behind the hydrogen bomb's development. Shortly after the committee report, Teller, Lawrence, and Alvarez met with Brian McMahon and William Borden in Los Angeles to discuss ways of promoting the Super to Truman.

Teller had been deeply interested—some thought obsessed—with the prospects for the Super since the day he arrived at Los Alamos in the spring of 1943. The conflict between Oppenheimer and Teller started soon afterward. Oppenheimer had wanted Teller to do some of the calculations concerning the implosion method that would be used in the "Fat Man" bomb dropped upon Nagasaki. Teller, however, had become so distracted by the idea of the Super that Oppenheimer finally gave the work to an eager young British scientist, Klaus Fuchs. It would later come out that Fuchs had passed what he learned from the work to a Soviet contact at weekly meetings on a bridge outside Los Alamos.

According to some of his colleagues at the wartime lab, Teller seemed unimpressed by—even disdainful of—their efforts to build the atomic bomb. When one physicist left Los Alamos at the end of the war, Teller had refused to take his place as head of the Theoretical Division there. In turning down the post offered him, Teller allegedly told a colleague that he was already working on a more important project. "I'm making an alarm clock," Teller had said. "One that will wake up the world."

The tension between Oppenheimer and Teller continued after the war, and even increased. Teller later claimed that he had been among the scientists urging that there be a harmless demonstration of the atomic bomb before its use against a city. He charged that Oppenheimer, as head of the group of scientists advising Truman's Interim Committee on the use of the bomb, had used his influence to veto the suggestion, thereby ensuring that atomic bombs would be dropped on Hiroshima and Nagasaki.[9]

The feud between Oppenheimer and Teller prompted many of the scientists at Los Alamos to take sides in the dispute—a development that would further personalize the debate over the Super. Oppenheimer's champions alleged that it was the ambition to supplant him as the most influential scientist in Washington that ultimately lay behind Teller's advocacy of the Super. One thought that Teller's crusade was even the result of a conscious, cynical choice. "I have quit the appeasers and joined the fascists," Teller reportedly told him in explaining his decision to oppose the GAC report.

There was an ironic—even bizarre—quality to the rivalry between the guilt-ridden father of the atomic bomb and the aspiring father of the Super. One of those who knew both men remembered Teller boasting—in an obvious allusion to his rival's famous comment in the aftermath of the Trinity test—that he and not Oppenheimer was the real prince of darkness and destroyer of worlds. Teller supposedly told a colleague that he expected to be a prisoner of the Russians in a matter of months if the United States did not proceed with the hydrogen bomb.[10]

Truman's decision for a crash effort to develop the weapon seemed to settle the long-standing dispute of the rivals in Teller's favor. Despite the warnings to Truman of a "blitz" by the Super's supporters, no such intense lobbying had been necessary. Instead, the decision of January 31, 1950, had been overtaken by the events of the preceding months—including the surprise of the Soviet bomb the previous summer, and the arrest just days before of Russian spy Klaus Fuchs. The meeting in the Oval Office had gone on only seven minutes when the president announced that he had made up his mind on the hydrogen bomb. The brief ethical argument that Lilienthal had started to make against the Super was, the AEC chairman recalled, "like saying 'no' to a steamroller."[11]

Truman himself subsequently admitted that his mind had been made up the previous month when he had approved yet another increase in the production rate of atomic bombs. His answer to Oppenheimer's warning that the superbomb might sap the effort to build existing nuclear weapons was to proceed with *both* types of bombs. Some weeks before, Truman had summarily rejected a suggestion by scientists that the public be given a say in whether or not to develop the Super.

Such had been the atmosphere at the January meeting that there was not even discussion of the proposal that Truman approach the Russians about a ban on testing thermonuclear weapons, though the idea contained in the letter by Rabi and Fermi was briefly discussed in the State Department and was also mentioned in Kennan's long memorandum. In the wake of Klaus Fuchs' arrest, Acheson thought it best not to raise the issue of the ban at the meeting with Truman. A final determinant of the president's decision, Acheson's aide remembered, was the fact that the single question Truman had raised at the meeting concerning development of the Super—"Can the Russians do it?"—could have only one possible answer.[12]

The rift between Oppenheimer and Teller and within the ranks of the atomic scientists did not, however, end with Truman's decision for the Super. Nor did it stop a year later, when an inspiration from mathematician Stanley Ulam led Teller to design a wholly different version of the superbomb. The thermonuclear breakthrough represented by the Teller-Ulam "trick" removed the original objection of the Super's foes that the bomb was unworkable. But their more fundamental objection—that the weapon was inherently an instrument of genocide—remained.

Even after the new theoretical breakthrough, progress on the Super was slow, and Teller's allies attributed this in part to deliberate efforts by Oppenheimer to forestall its development. Alvarez accused his former colleague at Berkeley of persuading some of the atomic veterans at Los Alamos not to work on the new bomb. Teller, too, thought that there was a conscious effort to slow or even stop work on the Super. It was for that reason that he lobbied —successfully—for establishment of a second nuclear weapons laboratory, at Livermore in California.[13] Shortly after Truman announced creation of the second lab, AEC General Manager Kenneth Nichols, a leading proponent of the Super, asked Teller why he appeared so concerned about the progress being made on the bomb. Teller responded, according to Nichols, that he was not worrying about the situation of the bomb, but instead "worrying about the people who should be worrying about the situation."[14]

For many of those who sided with Teller, the superbomb decision seemed a long-awaited vindication. Alvarez felt that the Super was as much a consequence as a cause of the tension between Oppenheimer and Teller— in that the inspiration which led to the thermonuclear breakthrough might have been lacking had there been no sense of rivalry between the two men.

Alvarez remembered how Teller's victory had taken a tangible form in the fall of 1952, with the test of the first Super. On the last day of October— Halloween—he, Teller, and Lawrence had gathered at the seismograph on the Berkeley campus to see the results of the test of the "alarm clock" that Teller had been working on since 1943. As soon as the instrument's needle jumped, Teller measured the squiggle it made on the graph paper and performed a quick calculation on his slide rule. He announced that the explosion had been the equivalent of ten million tons of TNT—almost a thousand times the size of the bomb at Trinity.

On the way back up the hill to their offices at the university's Radiation Laboratory, Teller apologized that "Mike"—the successful Super's code name—had been so destructive. He told his colleagues that the reason lay in the fact that so many people in Washington had been threatening to cut off money for the H-bomb if the test didn't work. As a consequence, every time Mike's creators discovered some possible way to make the bomb more powerful they had included it in the design.

"Everything worked," Alvarez recalled.

For some of the scientists who had vainly opposed the Super, Truman's decision to ignore their advice was cause not only for bitterness and disillusionment, but for a reappraisal of their role as advisers. Physicist Cyril Smith, a Los Alamos veteran and a friend of Oppenheimer's, resigned from the AEC's General Advisory Committee after the superbomb decision.

Behind the reappraisal by Smith and others lay a fundamental rethinking of the scientist's duty to the government. Teller wrote in 1947 that the atomic scientists had "two clear-cut duties: to work on atomic energy under our present administration, and to work for a world government which alone can give us freedom and peace."[15] But another physicist—a foe of the Super —expressed a growing sentiment when he declared that "the duty of a scientist in peacetime was to prepare for the next war."

Oppenheimer himself did not dissent from this view, at least initially. "Very early in the game," Oppenheimer would later testify, he and the other scientists working for the Atomic Energy Commission had decided "without debate"—but "with some melancholy"—"that the principal job of the Commission was to provide atomic weapons and good atomic weapons and many atomic weapons."[16]

They had remained true to that task in succeeding years—until the Super, when the growing doubts of the scientists concerning their role crystallized in opposition to the weapon. The passage from Ecclesiastes that one of the scientists quoted with regard to the hydrogen bomb expressed a sentiment that certainly would have been foreign to them before the advent of atomic energy, and before Hiroshima: "For in much wisdom is much grief/ and he who increases knowledge, increases sorrow."[17]

For a number of the atomic scientists, doubts concerning their role as advisers and the unalloyed beneficence of technology had first surfaced in Project Lexington, a 1948 MIT study sponsored by the Air Force on the feasibility of building a nuclear-powered bomber. Lexington was the first example of an institution that would gain importance and notoriety in later years—the "summer study," a research project carried on under government contract at a major university during the months when its faculty was freed from teaching.

The participants in Lexington were able to supplement their academic salaries by advising the government. Initially, a majority of the scientists who took part in the study were imbued with the same enthusiasm and faith in their technological prowess that had characterized the work for the Manhattan Project. But, gradually and progressively, a sense of disillusionment with the purpose and direction of the project had set in. While Lexington would not be officially abandoned until the start of the Kennedy administration, its effect much earlier had been to undermine the seemingly blind faith of those scientists who believed that every problem might have a technological solution.*

---

*Project Lexington's failure was both prolonged and ignominious. Even though the technical problems associated with the nuclear-powered bomber were never resolved, a more pressing worry was what would happen if one of the planes crashed. "There was no way to prevent a disaster from

Despite the failure of Lexington, a far more ambitious summer study was inaugurated two years later. Also at MIT, it included many of the same scientists who had worked on the ill-fated nuclear-powered bomber. While ultimately more successful than Project Lexington, Project Charles—a study of continental air defense—raised the larger question of the utility of technical solutions even when they worked. From its inception, Charles showed the practical difficulties of trying to separate technology and strategy from politics.*

Well before Project Charles, the Air Force had decided to subordinate its effort to defend the nation against air attack to its preparations for an atomic blitz of Russia should war occur. The Army had henceforth taken over the role of defending against Russian bombers. But little emphasis or funding had gone into the project, because of the dominance of the Air Force's air-atomic strategy. So entrenched was the spirit of the offensive in the Air Force's nuclear strategy—and so controversial the subject of the nation's coming under atomic attack—that Truman's decision to approve the air defense study at a secret Oval Office meeting with its sponsors was accompanied by the president's stern admonition that he didn't "want a single goddamn one of those present talking to the press."[19]

With the critical support of Secretary of the Air Force Thomas Finletter, whose efforts had initiated the project, Charles survived repeated efforts by others in that service to redirect its efforts away from air defense, or to scuttle it altogether. "It was an uphill battle with the Air Force to get them to think at all about defense," commented one of the participants in Project Charles. "The Air Force didn't want it," said another flatly.[20]

Jerrold Zacharias, a leading figure in Charles, was one of twenty or more physicists at MIT recruited to work on the project. Another key scientist in the effort would be Jerome Wiesner. As workers at MIT's Radiation

---

becoming a catastrophe," one of the scientists observed on this point. The official report on the project concurred, noting bluntly that "the site of a crash will be uninhabitable."

Eisenhower's defense secretary Charles Wilson compared the bomber to a "shitepoke": "a great big bird that flies over the marshes"—"that doesn't have much body or speed to it or anything." The Kennedy administration official who would finally cancel the project—on which $1 billion had been spent by 1960—was amazed at how long Lexington had survived. It was, he said, upon discovering that Lexington was still in the budget, like "coming downstairs in the morning and finding a dead walrus in your living room."[18]

*Charles was only the first of a number of summer studies at MIT that became known as the Cape Cod series. Project East River was concerned with civil defense shelters; Project Troy with countermeasures to radio jamming; and Project Beacon Hill with aerial reconnaissance and intelligence-gathering. According to a participant in Project Charles, MIT's James Hubbard, the code names were chosen because "they conveyed absolutely nothing." Names associated with flowers or animals were rejected for the summer studies, Hubbard said, in keeping with Winston Churchill's observation that he would never want to tell a child his father had been killed in "Operation Bunny Hug." Hubbard himself had preferred *Atropos* as the name for the air defense study—in tribute to one of Greek mythology's three Fates, who snipped out man's destiny with fast-cutting shears.

Laboratory during the war, both Zacharias and Wiesner had been involved in the development as well of the atomic bomb.

Zacharias' introduction to the Manhattan Project had been as a member of the group trying to reduce the size of the first nuclear weapons so that they would fit into the bomb bay of a B-29. His experience with Project Lexington had taught him, he said, "one of the most important things about a study: you've got to allow people to argue the general issues; not just look at technological ones." Zacharias' interest in continental air defense had begun right after the Russians got the atomic bomb. It had received another spur with Project Hartwell—another summer study of 1950, on antisubmarine warfare. It was while serving as an adviser on Hartwell, in fact, that Zacharias began to question the direction that his work for the government was taking.

During the project Zacharias learned that the Pentagon in 1950 had plans to increase the size of America's atomic arsenal to exactly 452 bombs—a number, he discovered, that reflected not the Air Force's calculations of military necessity, but simply the limit of its annual budget.[21] The prospect of more than four hundred atomic bombs inspired Zacharias to envision a nuclear war of dimensions never before imagined. But the grimness of that vision was compounded by his knowledge of another secret.

Some two years earlier he had been told of the results from the tests of the more powerful and efficient atomic bombs that Los Alamos developed after the war. In the late 1940s the AEC had experimented with exploding the bombs close to the ground instead of in the air, like the bombs dropped on Japan. The unexpectedly large amounts of lethal radioactivity released in those tests had surprised even veteran atomic scientists, few of whom had hitherto appreciated the problem of fallout from nuclear weapons. Subsequent experiments had shown that atomic bombs with forty times the yield of the weapons used in the Second World War—and proportionally greater fallout—were theoretically possible. "Those of us who had been in the business knew that twenty kilotons was small potatoes," Zacharias recalled.[22]

His insight into the future of nuclear war prompted Zacharias to draw a diagram on the blackboard at one meeting of Hartwell's scientists. The figures in the diagram depicted the categories of damage that could be expected if progressively larger numbers of atomic bombs were dropped on the United States. The first category Zacharias put on the board was "a few bombs on target," followed by "a dozen bombs on target." He stopped when he got to the third and last category of "a hundred bombs on target." It was pointless to go further, Zacharias told his colleagues, because this was a number greater than what he imagined the nation could survive—even though it was less than one-quarter of the number of bombs that the United

States already planned to drop on Russia in a war. Zacharias simply described the third and final category as "the horrors."[23]

Like Zacharias, a variety of often conflicting motives characterized those who worked on Charles. One economist who would win a Nobel Prize for his later work allegedly joined Charles so he would be able to afford to resurface the driveway of his Boston home. A physicist who likened his work on the atomic bomb to original sin professed to think of his involvement in Project Charles as atonement.[24] The indeterminate nature of some problems —and their solutions—was evident when the air defense study was expanded to a full year. The extension prompted Zacharias to quip of Charles, "Summer studies and some are not."

The worsening news from Korea and the nuclear arms race already underway with Russia provided, for most, a patriotic motive for their labor. The lasting memory of one participant in Charles was the scene where he and his coworkers huddled silently around a radio, listening in a mood of foreboding and despair to Douglas MacArthur's farewell speech to Congress. Another Charles alumnus, a renowned mathematician, responded directly to the fears that arose from the project. Shortly after the Russian test of an atomic bomb, he had moved from Boston out to the suburbs. When the Soviets tested their first Super, however, he decided to move back into the city.[25]

The product of Charles was a massive, three-volume report entitled "Problems of Air Defense." It concluded that a defense of the United States against Russian bombers was feasible and should be undertaken promptly, combining a distant-early-warning radar network—the DEW Line—with a system of computers—the Semi-Autonomous Ground Environment, or SAGE—originally developed at MIT to control commercial air traffic.[26]

Critics of Charles in the government and elsewhere immediately questioned the $2 billion cost of the proposed air defense effort and pointed out that the system would take years to put into place. Skeptics charged that the MIT researchers had deliberately underestimated the difficulty of shooting down attacking bombers so as to make a stronger case for air defense. The ensuing controversy over the Charles report hardened positions on both sides in the scientists' debate over defense—particularly when a special facility, the Lincoln Laboratory, was created at MIT to work on the practical problems of shooting down bombers.

But the greatest and most persistent opposition came, predictably, from the Air Force. That service saw the "defense-dominated" emphasis of Project Charles as a threat to both its traditions and its future. "We can build it," Zacharias told a colleague of the air defense system outlined in the Charles report. "But I promise you we won't." Air defense, Zacharias claimed, was finally "sold to Truman over the dead body of the Air Force."[27]

The reaction to the Charles report demonstrated how technology, strategy, and politics had become all but inseparable in the atomic age. Two years after the start of Charles, one of the young physicists recruited by Zacharias to work on Project Lamplighter—a spin-off study of how to intercept enemy bombers over the oceans before they got to the United States—recalled the almost missionary zeal that by that date imbued the subject of air defense.

Richard Garwin had been only seventeen when the bomb was exploded at Trinity. By his own choice he never witnessed a nuclear explosion in the years after he went to Los Alamos, though he contributed to the early development there of the Super.[28] While working on Lamplighter, Garwin was struck not only by the intensity of his colleagues but by their dedication to proving that a defense-dominated strategy could work. "If these people don't come to the right conclusion," Garwin claimed Zacharias once told him, "then I'll dismiss them and begin another study." Air defense, Garwin thought, had begun to assume some of the aspects of a crusade among the scientists opposed to the military's emphasis upon the atomic blitz. "We all knew the conclusions we wanted to reach," admitted one of the scientists involved in the summer studies.[29]

In spite of the scientists' effort to promote a defense-dominated strategy as an alternative to the atomic blitz, the verdict of Charles—like that of the GAC report—was unable to blunt the offensive emphasis in American nuclear strategy. Thus, even though the Charles report was endorsed and approved by President Truman, it was soon evident to politically well-connected scientists like Oppenheimer that the air defense study would have little or no effect upon the Air Force.

Early in 1951, Thomas Finletter had picked Oppenheimer as one of those experts to take part in the study of strategic air warfare that Bernard Brodie was urging upon the Air Force. In February of that year, Oppenheimer and Brodie had talked about the proposed study in Washington. The following spring, however, Oppenheimer learned that Brodie had abruptly left his job with the Air Force, and that the planned review was canceled.

It was equally clear to Oppenheimer in succeeding months that his own influence with the military, if not in the government, had begun to wane. Even before the controversial GAC report, efforts had been made to exclude him from a role in analyzing the results of atomic tests. Those efforts were revived after the scientist made plain his opposition to development of the Super.[30]

The mounting sense of despair that many scientists felt about the direction of the nation's nuclear strategy was discussed among Oppenheimer, Rabi, and another Los Alamos veteran, Charles Lauritsen, in the fall of 1951, during a week-long informal seminar on the subject at Oppenheimer's Princeton, New Jersey, home. Their dominant concern, Rabi remembered, was with how the growing number of nuclear weapons in the world could be substantially diminished without endangering the security of the United States or its allies. Beyond air defense, the three scientists considered how a greatly increased buildup of conventional forces might allow NATO to defend Europe without resort to nuclear weapons. The previous summer, in fact, Oppenheimer and Lauritsen had been involved in a summer study of how small nuclear weapons might be able to defeat a vastly superior conventional force.

The impromptu discussions in Princeton had their origins in the scientists' recognition of the changing nature of the atomic age. In 1948, a widely read article by Oppenheimer had lamented how the atomic bomb seemed almost necessarily a weapon "of aggression, of surprise, and of terror," where "the elements of surprise and terror are as intrinsic to it as are the fissionable nuclei."[31] Ironically, the same technological advances which would rapidly increase the number of strategic nuclear weapons in American hands that year also made possible smaller, cheaper, and more discriminative atomic bombs for tactical use in a war.

The prospect of tactical nuclear weapons invalidated his earlier comment about the inherently aggressive nature of the bomb, Oppenheimer believed —and reawakened his hope that the technology which had brought such weapons into being might also be used to control or diminish the threat they now posed to humanity. Unlike the orphaned cause of air defense, moreover, the idea of tactical nuclear warfare as an alternative to the atomic blitz had found a ready sponsor in the Army. That service—after continually losing out to the Air Force and its air-atomic emphasis in budget battles—retaliated in the summer of 1951 by pursuing a Cal Tech study of tactical nuclear weapons and warfare. Dubbed Project Vista, the purpose of the study, according to the Army's slogan, was "to bring the battle back to the battlefield."

Many of those who had worked on the bomb at Los Alamos and later on Project Charles were likewise participants in Vista, whose principal members included Manhattan Project alumni Robert Bacher and Robert Christy, MIT's Wiesner and Zacharias, and other scientists from Cal Tech. Rabi and Oppenheimer were kept informed of Vista's progress by Lauritsen, who became a key figure in the project.

The chief interest of Vista was the nonnuclear defense of Europe. The conclusion of all those involved in the study, thought Wiesner, was unremarkable. It was simply that "the people who could best defend west Europe and Britain were the west Europeans and the British." Vista's hopes, another remembered, lay with "the local heroes—the naked boys who could throw Molotov cocktails."[32]

Many of the recommendations of the Vista report only reaffirmed suggestions made earlier and elsewhere—such as the observation that better intelligence was needed on the Soviet Union. The controversial part of the study concerned tactical nuclear weapons and the possibility of their use in a nuclear war. It was on this issue that the scientists of Vista were unable to agree.

While he had played no direct role in the study itself, Oppenheimer was asked by Vista's participants to aid in their dispute by agreeing to write the fifth and final chapter of the report on the military utility of tactical nuclear weapons. The choice of Oppenheimer as arbiter was partly at Lauritsen's urging, but the decision was as well a logical one, given both his famous affability and his prestige in the government. Behind the selection was almost certainly a realization on the part of the scientists that their report was bound to spark dissent. As in Project Charles, the Air Force had tried in vain to stop or at least redirect the work on Vista—a mission on which it was evidently joined by the Navy. Bacher recalled that every week the same Navy captain and Air Force colonel would visit the Pasadena hotel where the study took place, hoping to persuade its members to abandon their efforts.[33]

The crucial chapter of the Vista report that Oppenheimer wrote recommended that the resources of the nation's nuclear weapons laboratories, which had hitherto focused their efforts upon building bigger and bigger bombs, be divided three ways henceforth between strategic nuclear weapons, tactical nuclear weapons, and the thermonuclear Super. The final version of the report additionally urged that the Air Force's Strategic Air Command be supplemented by an enlarged and nuclear-armed Tactical Air Command, whose responsibilities would include the defense of Europe with atomic as well as conventional bombs. Oppenheimer himself made a personal case for reordering the nation's defense priorities when he accompanied a delegation of Vista scientists to Europe in December 1951. Reportedly, Oppenheimer's briefing on the promise of tactical nuclear weapons in the defense of Europe particularly impressed Dwight Eisenhower, who had recently been appointed supreme commander of Allied and American forces there.[34]

Oppenheimer would later testify that he never believed nuclear weapons, once they were used, could be limited to a tactical role in warfare. He subsequently claimed, as well, that he and the other authors of the Vista report had not intended their recommendations to supplant SAC, or to blunt the offensive emphasis of the nation's nuclear strategy.

However, the Air Force would in time charge—with some reason—that the smaller and less deadly nuclear weapons proposed in the Vista report were plainly meant to be something more than just an adjunct to the nation's swelling strategic arsenal. Indeed, in a draft version of the controversial fifth chapter, Oppenheimer seemed to argue that tactical nuclear weapons could even substitute for SAC and its Supers. As he had in the AEC committee report, Oppenheimer suggested that for ethical reasons the United States might wish to withhold its atomic blitz in the event of war. But the final version of the chapter had deleted that passage.[35]

Coming as it did upon the heels of Charles, Vista was thought by some to be part of a concerted attack on the victory-through-airpower thesis of strategic bombing that had come to dominate postwar American nuclear strategy. The Air Force succeeded in suppressing the Vista report within the Pentagon, even recalling those copies of the document and its supporting evidence that remained in the hands of its authors.[36]

Oppenheimer unwittingly lent credence to the Air Force's fears when he agreed to serve as head of a special Presidential Panel of Consultants on Disarmament that Truman and Acheson appointed in April 1952. The panel's report, not completed until the following year, contained many of the recommendations in Charles and Vista that were already anathema to the Air Force. The report of Oppenheimer's panel urged, therefore, that more effort be put into the nation's neglected air defense. It was likewise critical of what it characterized as a headlong effort to build as many bombs as soon as possible, without regard to alternatives or consequences. Oppenheimer and his colleagues concluded with a bleak vision of a future arms race, one where both the United States and the Soviet Union would have thousands of nuclear weapons, and in which declining hopes for peace would rest on the fragile and "strange stability" such a stalemate would create.[37]

The panel's report reintroduced a theme that had been included in the AEC committee's recommendation against the Super, but was ignored or forgotten there. The government, it urged, "should adopt a policy of candor toward the American people" in "presenting the meaning of the arms race." The "central fact" of which neither the public nor the government was "responsibly aware," the report claimed, concerned the almost explosive growth on both sides in the number and power of nuclear weapons during the seven years that had passed since the bombing of Hiroshima.[38]

Rabi later came to suspect that the disarmament panel was an attempt by the Truman administration to "co-opt" Oppenheimer and other disaffected scientists into once again working for the government. Oppenheimer himself, however, evidently saw the panel and its report as a kind of crossroads in his attempt to turn back the arms race. His hope that the Truman administration, too, might see it as such quickly vanished when Acheson summarily rejected the first act of candor urged by the panel—that their top-secret report be made public.

Instead, the report was forwarded without comment in early 1953 to the Eisenhower administration, which agreed with Acheson's judgment that there was nothing to be gained by releasing it to the public. Oppenheimer's frustration at what he took to be the deliberate suppression of the "Candor Report," as it became known in the government, prompted him to take the risky step of making the panel's conclusions public.

"There has been relatively little done to secure our defense against the atom," he wrote in the July 1953 issue of *Foreign Affairs.* The military, Oppenheimer claimed, had deliberately neglected "many technical developments that have not yet been applied in this field and that could well be helpful." Oppenheimer went on to attack in the article not only the nation's offensive nuclear strategy but the kind of thinking that had brought it into being, and the obsession with secrecy that continued to shield it from the public. He cited as an example of such thinking the comment made to him by one high-ranking military official that "it was not really our policy to attempt to protect this country, for that is so big a job that it would interfere with our retaliatory capabilities." Oppenheimer wrote, "Such follies can occur only when even the men who know the facts can find no one to talk to about them, when the facts are too secret for discussion, and thus for thought."[39]

Initially, Oppenheimer noted, he had agreed with what he said was the government's "rule of the atom": " 'Let us keep ahead. Let us be sure that we are ahead of the enemy.' " But subsequent events, including the advent of the Super, had convinced him that there was indeed no possibility of winning the nuclear arms race, since there would inevitably come a point when both the United States and Russia had enough bombs to destroy the other: "The very least we can conclude is that our twenty-thousandth bomb, useful as it may be in filling the vast munitions pipelines of a great war, will not in any deep strategic sense offset their two-thousandth."

Rabi thought Oppenheimer's *Foreign Affairs* article represented no new current of thinking, but only a decision by his friend to make those thoughts public. Thus Rabi felt that both he and Oppenheimer had long since come to the conclusion that there could be no technological solution to the problems raised by the bomb, and no winner in the nuclear arms race. (He began to understand how the Russians felt, Rabi said, when a Soviet scientist had complained to him that the attitude of Americans toward the Soviet Union was reminiscent of the Roman senator Cato's famous injunction concerning Carthage. "Your people are always saying 'Cartago delenda est,' " the Russian told Rabi.)

The attack on Oppenheimer had begun two months before his *Foreign Affairs* article appeared. In the May 1953 issue of *Fortune,* Charles Murphy, one of the magazine's editors, charged that the government's summer studies had been converted by a cabal of scientists led by Oppenheimer into a conspiracy aimed at undermining the nation's defenses. Murphy, a retired Air Force officer, claimed that the members of the cabal were known among themselves by their initials: ZORC, for Zacharias, Oppenheimer, Rabi, and Charles Lauritsen.[40]

Murphy wrote in his article "The Hidden Struggle for the H-Bomb" that

"Oppenheimer had transformed Vista into an exercise for rewriting U.S. strategy," one which "questioned the morality of a strategy of atomic retaliation." After the Vista report had been rejected in the Pentagon, Murphy claimed, Oppenheimer had personally taken part in an effort to get its recommendations accepted. The article branded Project Charles "an extension in the U.S. of the Vista idea," and hence part of a "fortress concept" and an "electronic Maginot Line" that would be fatal to American security. Quoting Air Force Secretary Finletter, Murphy concluded that "there was a serious question of the propriety of scientists trying to settle such grave national issues alone, inasmuch as they bear no responsibility for the successful execution of war plans."[41]

A far more serious charge against Oppenheimer was filed the following November with William Borden's letter to FBI director Hoover and President Eisenhower alleging that the scientist was probably a Soviet spy. The upshot of the letter would be the AEC-sponsored hearings into the matter of Oppenheimer's loyalty that began in April of 1954. Raised in the course of those hearings were many of the four hundred questions about Oppenheimer that Borden had collected over the previous eight years. But at the inquiry's heart was the fundamental—if unstated—question of Oppenheimer's true allegiance. Behind that question was the scientist's alleged "pattern of activities," and particularly his involvement in the controversial summer studies.

It was while on a visit to Cal Tech and Vista that Borden had observed what he felt was Oppenheimer's almost Svengali-like effect upon his colleagues. Another witness hostile to Vista, the Air Force's chief scientist, David Griggs, claimed to have seen the fateful ZORC written on a blackboard by Zacharias, and later mentioned in a telephone conversation. The elusive acronym, in fact, would occupy a disproportionate part of the three weeks and nearly eleven hundred pages of testimony in what became known as the Oppenheimer trial. The importance of ZORC was symbolic—as a test not of the opinions of the scientists around Oppenheimer, but of their veracity.[42]

Indeed, the questions put to Oppenheimer showed that what was really being challenged in the hearings was not the technical judgment of Oppenheimer and his allies among the scientists, but their character. It was, as Finletter had hinted, the propriety of those scientists that was open to question, because of their opposition to the strategy of atomic blitz and to the Super. The charge that "Dr. Oppenheimer opposed the nuclear-powered aircraft," "failed to enthuse" about the hydrogen bomb, and disparaged the "offensive emphasis" of American nuclear strategy were among the first and the last arguments made for denying his security clearance and hence ending his role as a government adviser.[43]

While many of the accusations made in the hearings concerned Oppenheimer's leftist associations as a student and professor at Berkeley before the war, a great deal also revolved around alleged improprieties related to his postwar involvement with the Super, Charles, Vista, and even the Baruch plan. Among these were his persistent claim that weapons-grade uranium could be effectively and permanently denatured, despite the scientific evidence to the contrary; his continued reservations about the Super even after the bomb had been shown to be feasible; the allegations that he had persuaded other scientists not to work on the superbomb project; a mistake in the final chapter of the Vista report that substantially overestimated the amount of damage that tactical nuclear weapons could do; claims he was alleged to have made at the time of Project Charles concerning the feasibility of shooting down as much as 90 percent of an attacking bomber force; and Oppenheimer's charge that Finletter and others in the Air Force had encouraged the idea of a preventive nuclear war against the Russians.[44]

But there was perhaps a special irony in one of the accusations leveled against Oppenheimer concerning his role in the "Candor Report": used as evidence against him was Oppenheimer's urging that the government divulge the number of bombs in the nation's nuclear arsenal—the same recommendation that McMahon and Borden had made to the Truman administration five years earlier. Rabi would be one of the few witnesses called in Oppenheimer's defense to argue that his loyalty was beyond question, and his service to the country tragically unappreciated. "What do you want—mermaids?" he finally challenged the interrogators in exasperation.

The decision of the AEC board to deny Oppenheimer access to future atomic secrets was a public humiliation for the scientist, though hardly a guilty verdict to the charge of treason. One unintended result of the trial was to bring about a long-delayed climax in the feud between Oppenheimer and Teller. Teller's testimony at the hearings on behalf of the government—as a witness for the prosecution, in effect—outraged those scientists for whom "Oppie" had always been the hero, and the inventor of the H-bomb his nemesis.

Teller's words were in fact carefully chosen. They represented less an actual accusation than some particularly damning praise for Oppenheimer's complex personality, and his extraordinary career of influence as a government adviser. "In a great number of cases," Teller said, "I have seen Dr. Oppenheimer act—I understand that Dr. Oppenheimer acted—in a way which for me was exceedingly hard to understand." Teller went on to declare that he "would like to see the vital interest of this country in hands which I understand better and therefore trust more." "If it is a question of wisdom and judgment, as demonstrated by actions since 1945," he told the panel in conclusion, "then I would say one would be wiser not to grant clearance."[45]

It would be later debated whether Teller's testimony played that important a role in the AEC panel's verdict, which relegated Oppenheimer to a life of virtual academic exile at Princeton's Institute of Advanced Studies. Oppenheimer's friends would also subsequently disagree as to whether Teller actually intended to do the damage that they believe he did. But it was the motivation behind the attack on Oppenheimer that most alienated the scientists from Teller. "Teller put the knife in Robert's back and twisted it," said one who had once been a friend and colleague of both men.[46]

There would be no doubt among Oppenheimer's allies that Teller did not expect the reaction he received for his testimony. Some weeks after his appearance at the AEC hearings, Teller and his wife, Mici, returned to Los Alamos to attend one of the periodic reunions of the atomic scientists. Outside Fuller Lodge, the wartime lab's social center, Teller encountered Rabi and Robert Christy. In his typically effusive manner of those days, Teller rushed up to Christy with his hand extended. Christy only stared at the hand before wordlessly turning on his heel and walking away. "I won't shake your hand either, Edward," Rabi told Teller. Teller was crushed by the snub. He and Mici left the reunion and Los Alamos shortly thereafter.

The lessons each side in the Oppenheimer-Teller feud drew from its outcome proved as different as the scientists themselves. But both sides acknowledged that the effects of the two men's rivalry outweighed the immediate issues involved, and transcended the fate of either. "In 1950 the question was raised," Teller subsequently said about the role of scientists working for the government. "And in 1954 it was settled."

Teller said it was only because he had become "a politician" that the superbomb was finally built. "The majority of my fellow scientists went out of their way to use their scientific influence to prevent our work on the hydrogen bomb." The suspicion and hostility aroused by the debate over the Super, Teller believed, "culminated and concluded at the time of the Oppenheimer hearings"—but its effects endured long after in the unwillingness of many American scientists to work for the government to develop new weapons.

"What happened over the Oppenheimer case not only polarized the scientific community, but brought about the situation that at least 90 percent of the scientists—and probably more—considered it immoral to cooperate in any way with the military," Teller reflected. Nearly thirty years after the AEC's verdict in the hearings, he claimed that the nation's "present military weakness goes back to those days."

William Borden later thought the effect of the verdict was "to remove physicists from the category of an anointed species." Because of his obvious bias in the case, Oppenheimer's accuser did not play as large a part in the hearings as he had wished. He had initially wanted to be prosecutor in a trial for treason, Borden said, so that he might confront Oppenheimer directly with his allegations; and he admitted that the AEC's conclusion that the scientist had been "less than candid" with investigators fell far short of a substantiation of his, Borden's, most serious charge. Nonetheless, in retrospect he thought it "the turning point in converting scientists back to human beings."

For the scientists themselves—at least for those who had sided with Oppenheimer—there was a different moral altogether in the verdict: one that concluded what seemed to have been a deliberately cautionary tale. Rabi protested that the mysterious ZORC and the meeting of three of its four supposed members at Oppenheimer's home in the fall of 1951—a meeting characterized in the hearings by Griggs as a conspiracy "to work for world peace or some such purpose"—represented no more tangible or serious a cabal than the earlier meetings of Teller, Alvarez, Lawrence, and Borden for the purpose of promoting the Super. The principal difference between the two opposing groups, in the view of Rabi and other scientists, was that Teller's side had triumphed.

Some of the scientists professed to find a shift in the attitude of the government toward them in the wake of the Oppenheimer trial. In at least a few cases, it was more than just the government's attitude that changed. During 1954, MIT's Jerome Wiesner—a veteran of both Charles and Vista—came under attack by Senator Joseph McCarthy for his earlier role in a related summer study, Project Troy. Troy's purpose had been to seek countermeasures to the Soviet jamming of the Voice of America, also under investigation by McCarthy's committee.

Wiesner would indirectly prove Teller's point about the legacy of Oppenheimer's bitter experience being a change in the scientists' attitude toward working for the government. There was still, said Wiesner, "a feeling of mission underlying the motivation of most scientists" after the Oppenheimer hearings. That feeling, he thought, had had its origins in the wartime Manhattan Project, and lingered in the postwar faith that technology could at least diminish—even if it could not quite remove—the threat created by nuclear weapons: "We believed that the United States was in mortal danger and we had to do what we could—technically—to protect it. We all believed it. Before we became suspicious."

The result of their suspicion, reflected another veteran of the summer studies and a colleague of Wiesner's at MIT, was "a nagging concern in the technical community about the Oppenheimer hearing"—"a gnawing concern about where this was going." In retrospect, he agreed with Wiesner that there had been a kind of "hysteria" behind the scientists' motivation that was not recognized at the time. "We were very naive."

That naiveté was reflected, the scientist thought, by the fact that he and his colleagues had never considered in their study of air defense the possibility that the United States, not the Soviet Union, might land the first blow in a nuclear war. All had universally assumed that, like the Manhattan Project, the summer studies were the result of a national emergency—the Cold War. They had never stopped to consider, he said, that this was an emergency which might never end.

But an even more fundamental oversight—he felt a generation after Charles—was the assumption that had subtly dominated the work of all the scientists during the summer studies, an assumption that was the legacy of their wartime work for the Manhattan Project and that they had not questioned since, though he believed it was plainly outmoded in the atomic age. Their only concern in those days, this scientist said, had been "with *when* —not *if*—there would be another war."

8

The Santa Monica Priory

Oppenheimer's conclusion that the problems created by nuclear weapons might be beyond the power of the experts—even that of the bomb's creators —to remedy was a belief not widely shared at the Rand Corporation, the Air Force–created think tank. The successor to Project Rand (the name was an acronym for "research and development") the corporation had its origins in a wartime contract signed between the Air Force and Douglas Aircraft to provide civilian advice on the development of new bombers. Generals "Hap" Arnold and Curtis LeMay were among the early boosters of the project, whose first assignment was to modify B-29 bombers so that they could carry the atomic bombs that would be dropped on Japan.[1]

While the Air Force would later pride itself on respecting the independence of its creation, the heads of that service often made plain that they felt no obligation to accept the advice of Rand's civilian experts. After reading a report on a plane designed at the think tank, for example, one Air Force veteran reportedly volunteered the observation, "I wouldn't strap *my* ass to that Rand bomber."[2]

The physicists and engineers at Douglas were joined soon after the war by a phalanx of social scientists and mathematicians, many of whom were recruited by Rand's John Williams at a 1947 conference of economists in New York City. The exact sort of work they would be doing at Rand was kept from the new recruits, but one of their number caught an inkling of his future role in the fact that the title of Rand's math department was the Department of Military Worth.[3]

Initial relations between the Air Force's generals, Douglas' engineers, and Rand's new academic theorists had not been smooth. In addition to a natural clash of temperaments—the engineers complained that the social scientists absent-mindedly put coffee cups on their blueprints—there came to be a growing resentment among Rand's veterans over the newcomers' rising influence. By the time that Rand finally separated from Douglas and became a private corporation in 1948, it had three hundred employees at its oceanside headquarters in Santa Monica, and its Social Science Division was expanding at a rapid rate.[4]

There was an early tension as well between the scientists at Rand and their counterparts at colleges and universities. The think tank's physicists tended to consider themselves pragmatists and problem-solvers, in contrast to what they regarded as the abstract thinkers who inhabited the universities. The result was a rivalry that was constant, and not always good-natured.

Outside scientists objected, for example, to a 1948 Rand study which concluded that continental air defense was technologically unfeasible because of the ease with which the defending radars could be blinded by an attacker. Even after the accidental discovery of radar's backscatter effect in Project Troy had largely removed this objection, the opposition of Rand's scientists to air defense had continued. A few at the think tank even hinted that the undiminished enthusiasm of their MIT counterparts concerning the Dew Line was due to the fact that the latter could find no other use for the Whirlwind computer developed by the university at government expense.

A more subtle—and probably more important—cause of the rivalry had its roots in the fact that Rand's scientists were often more politically conservative than those in academia, some of whom had refused to work on the Super. A majority of Rand's physicists had supported the development of the hydrogen bomb. Other early projects done at Rand, besides the air defense study, included an analysis of the Soviet economy and a report on the "operational code" of Russia's Politburo used by Paul Nitze in the writing of NSC-68.[5]

What virtually all at Rand would come to consider its "golden age" began shortly after the think tank gained independence, when its experts undertook the study of what one of their number later called the "deep elements of strategy." Theirs was a search, he said, for nothing less than "the strategic sense" of the atomic age. It was the allure of this search that had drawn Bernard Brodie to Rand after his brief stint in the Air Force's Air Targets Division. Brodie continued writing his book at the think tank on the lessons of strategic bombing even after his work was interrupted by the Super.

A friend and colleague of Brodie's at Rand felt that its sole client of those days, the Air Force, was alternately attracted and repelled by the work there, but nonetheless always fascinated by the "Rand style." The hallmark of that style was the thorough and dispassionate analysis of a problem, whose solution was presented in the course of a forty-five-minute oral briefing. Before any Rand briefing could be presented outside the think tank it first had to pass the notorious "murder board"—a review committee composed of the corporation's top leadership—and then be presented before an open audience of eager and often hostile critics.

Almost from its inception, the Rand style assumed two different forms. One was the classic, historical kind of analysis that Brodie's work epitomized. The other was the quantified approach of Rand's economists and other social scientists, whom Brodie dubbed—at first admiringly, later derisively—"the scientific strategists."[6]

The techniques of statistical analysis and econometrics that this latter group applied to the analysis of military problems were essentially an outgrowth of the pioneering methods of operations research developed during the Second World War. In that war, operations research had first been used to prescribe the most efficient search patterns for Allied destroyers hunting German submarines. Later, it was adapted for use in strategic bombing to bring about the terrible firestorms that consumed cities in Germany and Japan. As the war progressed, operations research had been gradually transformed from a kind of inspired art to a grisly science. In the process, it had transformed in turn the nature of warfare.

The difference in their methods of analysis aside, the experts at Rand in the early 1950s were united by a shared motivation and a common goal. "There was sort of a missionary attitude," one remembered. "It was like being on the frontier—the cutting edge." "All of these people were missionaries," another of the strategists confirmed. "But that's because they all ended up with a message that they thought was just terribly important to get across."

For a number of those analysts who came to Rand—and who later became the best and the brightest of the Kennedy administration—the first introduction to strategy had been at a British hamlet called Princes Risborough, near High Wickham, almost two years after Pearl Harbor. The small group of American advisers there—Charles Hitch, Henry Rowen, Carl Kaysen, and Walt Rostow among them—worked and lived in rickety temporary housing expropriated in the wartime emergency from England's Road Research Institute. All were part of what one later acknowledged was "a children's crusade." The oldest among them was thirty-three; most were still in the twenties. Hitch, a Rhodes scholar, was teaching economics at Oxford when the war broke out. The others had been graduate students at MIT or Harvard when they were recruited for the secret wartime work in England. But there was a common attitude of idealism and patriotism among them. "We were winning the war," Kaysen observed.

The work of the Americans at "Pine Tree"—the code name for the operation at Risborough—was, in his words, "to create a new form of poetry": combining the technical skills of photoanalysis with the developing science of econometrics to estimate the amount of damage that Allied bombers were doing to the German war effort. Kaysen had originally "gotten into railroading," he said, by picking targets among Japanese railheads and marshaling yards in Manchuria for the Research and Analysis branch of the American Office of Strategic Services. He had been assigned to do the same at Risborough with German targets. For both Kaysen and Hitch, as for most of the Americans there, the work at Pine Tree was a high point in their individual careers and lives. "This was a business which nobody knew how to do," Kaysen explained. "It was a very exciting war," Hitch affirmed.

In order to assess the effectiveness of the Allied bombing offensive, the Americans had compared aerial photographs of bomb damage to the roofs of German homes and factories—the only kind of damage visible from the air—with photographs of bombed cities in Britain of similar size where the effects upon population and industry were already known. Since clouds typically covered much of northern Europe between October and April, aerial photography of German cities was only possible an average of two days during each of those months. Consequently, the experts at Risborough had to use the techniques of operations analysis pioneered in England to estimate the number of bombs that were hitting their targets.[7]

Hitch recalled that what he and the others found out about bombing accuracy by this method "proved *very* unpopular with Bomber Command." Their discovery was that the cloud cover which so hindered the photographing of enemy targets hampered British and American bombardiers no less. Hitch estimated that at least 90 percent of Allied bombs fell as much as two miles from the intended target. While he and the other Americans acknowledged that the results were good at "dehousing" the German population, in the Air Ministry's term, they concluded that the bombing was having only a minor impact upon the enemy's vital war industries.

The Allied bombing surveys would later confirm the work of the Risborough experts. The surveys found that much of Germany's war machine was dispersed to the countryside by the bombing or driven underground. The effect of the bombing had been further reduced when important industries were given priority by German air defense workers and by military firemen, while workers' houses were bombed and burned to the ground with little interference. In spite of this incessant pounding, the analysts of Pine Tree were surprised to find, enemy civilian morale did not seem to suffer markedly from the bombing. In German cities, as in London during the Blitz, the onslaught created a mood of stoicism and even defiance.[8] As skeptical as they became at Risborough about the contribution of strategic bombing to victory, Hitch and Kaysen discovered after the war that their pessimistic figures had in fact overestimated bombing's effectiveness to a considerable extent.

The Americans at Pine Tree were dismayed when—despite the evidence of their research—the bombing of German cities not only continued but intensified. Their cynicism grew when it became evident that the shift in bombing strategy from a concentration upon industry to virtually indiscriminate attacks upon cities was more a result simply of the growth of the Allied bomber fleet than of any sudden new insight by military planners.

Kaysen began to suspect that Bomber Command's disregard of the work done at Risborough ultimately meant that the air offensive would be conducted independent of its results. His suspicions were confirmed when near the end of the war he was sent to AAF headquarters in Washington, where he was able to read the secret teletyped messages exchanged between various air force commanders. The latter were already preoccupied with the role of their service after the war, and with gaining independence from the Army. "The reason they were bombing all the time was to get a good record," Kaysen said. His final, futile attempt to shift the emphasis of strategic bombing away from civilians was the role he played in drafting an alternative plan for air support of the Normandy invasion. The plan would have used fighters to knock down enemy-held bridges as a substitute for the massive bombing of railroad yards located in or near cities.

At war's end, most of the Americans at Pine Tree had returned to civilian life. Kaysen went back to graduate school, Hitch to teaching economics at Oxford. Both learned of the atomic bomb from the newspapers. But their interest in military strategy, awakened at Risborough, remained. They were recruited to work at Rand, each said, in part because they found academic life too boring after their wartime experience.

The brunt of their criticism of strategic bombing while at Risborough had concerned its effectiveness in relation to its costs, as measured in terms of lives and materials. "Cost-effective," indeed, was a term that Hitch would coin while working at Pine Tree. The Americans had raised moral objections to strategic bombing only when the RAF proposed Operation Thunderclap in 1944—a single massive raid meant to exploit the terror potential of bombing by deliberately killing as many people as possible in one square mile at the center of Berlin.[9] In the face of opposition from British military leaders as well, Thunderclap had been canceled.

This one case aside, the ethical implications of strategic bombing were not a major concern of the experts at Pine Tree, Hitch and Kaysen both readily admitted. "We were young and pretty bloodthirsty," the latter remembered. "And we were winning the war."

The realization that the atomic bomb would make the consequences of strategic bombing that much worse for civilians became a common concern of the so-called "wizards of Risborough" after the war. Hitch and Kaysen recognized that the bomb's power made it necessarily an even less discriminate weapon than high-explosive and incendiary bombs, whose fearsome effects their work had already documented. The result was that noncombatants would bear the brunt of strategic bombing more than ever.

It had been "perfectly apparent" to him at Pine Tree, Hitch said, "that we were causing enormous damage to civilians—that we were causing enormous casualties." This fact, and the prospect that the bomb would magnify the effect of bombing on civilians, began, in his words, "to grow on him" after the war. Hitch and the other experts who had been at Risborough began looking, while at Rand, for an alternative to the deliberate and wholesale slaughter of civilians in modern warfare. Theirs was a search for a way to return war to the soldiers.

Bernard Brodie's interest in imposing some restraint upon American nuclear strategy matched that of Pine Tree's alumni at Rand. For all, the advent of the Super gave a sudden and unexpected impetus to their efforts. Beginning in the fall of 1952, an informal seminar composed of Brodie and some of Risborough's veterans—dubbed rather self-consciously the Strategic Objectives Committee—met regularly at lunchtime on Rand's patio, or inside on smoggy days in Santa Monica. The members of the committee were not long in deciding that a "counterforce" strategy—the "war between the bases" described by Borden—was the most promising alternative to the "city-busting" envisioned by the planners of the atomic blitz.

The earliest exposition at Rand of a nuclear strategy designed to avoid killing civilians in a war had been in a paper that same year by Victor Hunt, a member of Rand's Social Science Division and an occasional participant in the meetings of the Strategic Objectives Committee. Hunt's tragic death shortly thereafter removed an eloquent spokesman and advocate for counterforce strategy, but the idea of hitting military targets instead of cities in a nuclear war continued to be a topic of animated discussion at Rand's luncheon seminars.[10]

Another participant in the Strategic Objectives Committee who became particularly interested in counterforce strategy at this time was Andrew Marshall. Like most of the group's members, Marshall was an economist. One of the first studies he did at the think tank had concerned the economic effects of bombing in the Second World War.

Marshall and Herbert Goldhamer, a social psychologist at Rand, had worked together on another of the think tank's earliest projects—a study to determine if the percentage of draftees rejected for psychological reasons was increasing in the United States. The relatively high number of potential recruits deemed mentally unfit for military service during the Second World War had concerned top officials in the Pentagon, who feared that a postwar trend toward mental illness in civilian life could adversely affect mobilization for a future war. The study conducted by Marshall and Goldhamer, noted a Rand colleague of theirs, "was to determine whether or not the country was going crazy." (The two researchers concluded that it was not —or at least not at a rate which should concern the military. Using census figures for the state of Massachusetts going back as much as a hundred years, Marshall and Goldhamer reported in their study, "Psychosis and Civilization," that the incidence of mental illness in society had remained remarkably consistent over time.)

Marshall knew something else of significance that few others in the Strategic Objectives Committee—or at Rand—were aware of. His association with two important figures in Air Force Intelligence, Joseph Loftus and Spurgeon Keeny, as well as his own personal connections with the Central Intelligence Agency, made Marshall perhaps uniquely qualified among those at Rand to know exactly how practical a counterforce nuclear strategy actually was. After a summer spent at the European headquarters of Air Force Intelligence in Germany, Marshall, Loftus, and another member of the Rand seminar, James Digby, returned to Santa Monica personally convinced that counterforce was feasible, and that it would greatly limit the damage and casualties on both sides in a nuclear war. Not incidentally, Marshall and the others realized that such a strategy might even allow SAC virtually to disarm the Soviet Union in the event of war without striking directly at Russian cities.

It was while in Germany that Marshall discovered how the Air Force and the CIA had, in fact, "inherited" a great deal of information about Soviet military targets from the Second World War—including detailed photographs of Russian military bases from captured German and Japanese sources. The fact that such bases were generally fixed and permanent installations meant that Air Force targeters could even rely upon old prerevolutionary maps of Russia, or upon a more modern cartographic project undertaken by Soviet mapmakers in the 1930s. During the Second World War the results of that project had fallen into German, and then American, hands. Other kinds of technical intelligence—such as the performance characteristics of Soviet bombers, and information gained from the CIA's interception of Russian radiocommunications—proved helpful in making a counterforce strategy feasible.

Spurgeon Keeny—a physicist and a Russian expert, and another of Marshall's friends—was at this time civilian head of the Air Force's Special Weapons Section, the division with responsibility for the bomb. Keeny later confirmed of the Air Force's targeting of Russia that "very early in the day we had identified major parts of their atomic energy program—even down to the aim points." "We not only knew locations. We knew where to drop the bombs."

Back at Rand, Marshall and Loftus were surprised at the resistance they encountered from others—including their colleagues on the Strategic Objectives Committee—to their efforts to promote counterforce as an alternative to bombing cities. Brodie was one of those who had begun to despair of the possibility of limiting damage in a nuclear war because of the Super, and he remained skeptical of the idea that any such war could long be kept limited. Another occasional member of the committee, Albert Wohlstetter—who was uninitiated into the secrets known to Marshall and Loftus—doubted that the Air Force would know where to drop its bombs in a war between the bases.

Marshall and Loftus concluded ruefully that the principal obstacle to counterforce at Rand was the ignorance of their colleagues, whose lesser security clearances did not permit them to know the extent to which counterforce was possible, and in fact had already entered into Air Force targeting. The mistaken view "that you just didn't know the targets," Marshall said, remained "strongly embedded" at Rand. When he and Loftus hinted vaguely to their colleagues that knowing the location of Soviet military bases might not be the problem they imagined, the two had simply been rebuffed. "We felt under some restrictions due to security," Marshall explained of their reasons for not arguing a stronger case.

It was not only secrecy but what Marshall characterized as "the excessive narrowness of Rand assumptions" that he and Loftus had had to struggle with in their effort to return war to the soldiers. "People at Rand remained fixed in their thinking about strategic bombing, which was mostly the bombing of industry at this time," Marshall recollected. "Basically, in the late 1940s the concept was that if the Soviets attempted to invade Europe, one would try to damage their economy and thereby cripple them for subsequent mobilization. This was a notion of the Second World War fought over again —but with this early crippling blow."

Eventually, the resistance and doubt that he and Loftus encountered caused them to abandon what Marshall called "their few, small, tentative efforts" to win Rand over to counterforce thinking. "There was," Marshall said, "only so much ignorance that one man could prevent."

The ignorance—and isolation—of analysts at Rand was a source of quiet derision in the Air Force. In retrospect, Keeny thought that the experts at the think tank looked "pretty stupid." "Asking the people at Rand" about nuclear strategy, he thought, "was like asking people in the street."

But the Air Force's own thinking, Keeny conceded, was itself a barrier to counterforce strategy. Military bases in the Soviet Union had appeared on the Air Force's target list since SAC's inception. In 1949, after the Russians tested their first bomb, Soviet atomic energy facilities and stockpiles had in fact been given the highest priority in Air Force targeting.[11]

But hitting military bases had always been considered by SAC's leaders an adjunct—not an alternative—to bombing cities. So intent was the Air Force upon hitting so-called "urban-industrial targets" that the Joint Chiefs of Staff had not finally gotten around to approving a counterforce target list for the Air Force's nuclear war plan until 1953. Even afterward, SAC commanders like Curtis LeMay and Thomas Power made it repeatedly plain to Keeny and others that they considered any deliberate effort to save

Russian lives and limit the damage to the Soviet Union as nonsensical—if not treasonous.[12]

SAC's objection in principle to counterforce was accompanied by a host of pragmatic objections. Despite the interest of some in Air Force Intelligence, counterforce strategy entailed a discrimination and a finesse that seemed simply foreign to the temperament and strategic sense of SAC's commanders. "LeMay," Keeny lamented, "never did think beyond World War Two."

Indeed, LeMay objected vehemently to the idea of fragmenting or holding back the single, massive, and coordinated nuclear onslaught that was known in SAC as "the Sunday punch." He openly ridiculed the prospect of using his strategic bombers either to blunt a Soviet invasion of western Europe or to "dribble in" with attacks on individual Russian military targets, which would mean greater exposure of the bombers and their crews to Soviet air defenses. Keeny vividly remembered a briefing of the Air Force war plan when someone in the audience had questioned the ability of SAC's bombers to get past Russia's new surface-to-air missiles. LeMay, who was in the audience, had stridden to the podium and unceremoniously brushed the hapless briefing officer aside. "This was the kind of attitude that was causing SAC problems," LeMay snapped. When he became head of the 20th Air Force during the war against Japan, LeMay recounted, one of the first things he had done was to have enemy air defenses pointed out to him on a map. Stabbing with his finger for emphasis at the map of Russia next to the lectern, he told how he had identified the targets: "And there they were—there, there, and there. I'd just draw a line right down the middle of 'em," LeMay said. "You'd lose some planes but you'd knock 'em out as you went along."

Even after the Super had greatly reduced SAC's vulnerability to Russian defenses—which were not expected to survive an attack with hydrogen bombs—LeMay remained opposed to counterforce. Keeny finally concluded that LeMay's real objection to the strategy was philosophical, not practical. The restraint that counterforce envisioned was not only lacking in the SAC commander's vision of a nuclear war—LeMay's intent was quite the reverse.*

---

*In his memoirs, LeMay graphically depicted the destruction that could be wrought by just one of SAC's bombers: "It lugs the flame and misery of attacks on London . . . rubble of Coventry and the rubble of Plymouth . . . blow up or burn up fifty-three per cent of Hamburg's buildings, and sixty per cent of the port installations, and kill fifty thousand people into the bargain. Mutilate and lay waste the Polish cities and the Dutch cities, the Warsaws and the Rotterdams. Shatter and fry Essen and Dortmund and Gelsenkirchen, and every other town in the Ruhr. Shatter the city of Berlin. Do what the Japanese did to us at Pearl, and what we did to the Japanese at Osaka and Yokohama and Nagoya. And explode Japanese industry with a flash of magnesium, and make the canals boil around bloated bodies of the people. Do Tokyo over again."[13]

. . .

Those few who were privy to the operational side of SAC's philosophy were, like Brodie and Keeny, able to see that fact quite clearly. Another at Rand with that privilege was a former student of Brodie's at Yale, William Kaufmann, who had been recruited in 1949 by his former mentor. His first inkling of the implications of the atomic age, Kaufmann said, had come after reading a 1946 essay by E. B. White in *The New Yorker* that forecast the day when many nations might have nuclear weapons in orbit around the earth. The specter had profoundly impressed the young political scientist.

Shortly after arriving at Rand, Kaufmann had taken part in an Air Force–sponsored study of nuclear targeting that already included Hitch and Kaysen and would be briefly joined by Brodie. Kaufmann's assignment took him to the Air War College in Montgomery, Alabama, and brought him into close contact with the Air Force officers whose task it would be to drop the bomb in the event of war. He and they had "talked late into the night," Kaufmann remembered, on the subject of nuclear strategy and targeting.

Kaufmann learned at these sessions how "the targeting had gotten extraordinarily sloppy," because of the phenomenal growth of the atomic stockpile and the invention of the hydrogen bomb. Between 1953 and 1955 the stockpile had virtually doubled, bringing the total of bombs in the arsenal to nearly two thousand. But an even more dramatic change was represented by the addition of the Super to the inventory. The "bonus effect," or collateral damage to civilians, that would result from the enormous amounts of lethal radioactivity created by multimegaton hydrogen bombs exploded at ground level was expected to multiply earlier estimates of Russian casualties severalfold.[14]

By 1955, SAC planners envisioned destroying at least three-quarters of the population in each of 118 cities in Russia. Total casualties in the Soviet Union and eastern Europe from a nuclear war were expected to exceed seventy-seven million, of whom approximately sixty million would be fatalities.[15]

The destruction inherent to SAC's war plan was "so horrendous," Kaufmann recalled, "that it would have amounted to wrecking several countries." "The final impression," commented another stunned witness at a SAC briefing, "was that virtually all of Russia would be nothing but a smoking, radiating ruin at the end of two hours."[16]

The apocalyptic nature of Air Force war planning encouraged renewal efforts at Rand, and especially among the members of the Strategic Objectives Committee, to find an alternative to "city-busting." But Bernard Brodie remained unpersuaded that striking only at military targets was such an alternative. Attacking "the enemy's bases or his industrial economy with superbombs would be practically indistinguishable from hitting his cities, with obvious consequences for populations," Brodie wrote in the book on strategy he was then finishing at Rand. It would be "idle," he claimed, to discuss striking at the enemy's military forces instead of his population "*unless* planners were actually to take deliberate restrictive measures to refrain from injuring cities."[17]

Brodie's own disappointing encounter with the Air Targets Division had already shown him that the Air Force had no interest in such a restrictive approach. In 1953 he proposed again—this time to Eisenhower's AEC chairman, Lewis Strauss—that the United States refrain from hitting Soviet cities in the event of war so long as the Russians recognized the same prohibition regarding American cities. But Brodie found Strauss no more sympathetic to the idea than the Air Force had been.[18]

What would turn out to be Brodie's last, remaining hope for introducing restraint to the missile age lay in the prospect he raised in his book that the United States and Russia might, in a future conflict, restrict the use of nuclear weapons to small tactical bombs employed outside each other's borders. The possibility that a conventional war between the great powers could remained limited—something previously discounted by most strategists—had been demonstrated in Korea, Brodie pointed out in his book. Yet the most likely arena for a future limited nuclear war, he argued, was not Asia but Europe.[19]

Brodie's notion of a limited, tactical nuclear war as an alternative to a world-consuming holocaust found few supporters at Rand, even among his fellows on the Strategic Objectives Committee. One who did sympathize with the idea, however, was Rand physicist Samuel Cohen.

Cohen considered his presence at Rand to be partly the result of fate's intervention. A displaced and homesick graduate student from California attending MIT in 1943, Cohen had decided to skip his physics class one cold December day. Ironically, the decision caused him to be enlisted in the Army's Manhattan Project—whose recruiting officer had gone to the college's dormitories instead of its classrooms because he did not wish to draw attention to the top-secret project. Cohen became a minor-level scientist at the wartime lab's Theoretical Division, but he missed the climactic test of the bomb at Trinity when he slept through his alarm.[20]

Cohen's interest in the effects of radiation began when he joined the Physics Division at Rand in 1947, where he was assigned to work on shielding problems for the nuclear bomber of the ill-fated Project Lexington. The problems were never solved. But in the process of learning about them, Cohen said, he became "sort of hooked on radiation."

Cohen's fascination with radiological warfare was further piqued by a secret visit he made to South Korea at the height of the war. The purpose of the trip, made at the behest of Rand and the Air Force, had been to assess the practicality of using nuclear weapons in Korea. Cohen could find no reason to warrant use of atomic bombs in the war, but a jeep ride through the heavily bombed city of Seoul had impressed him with the destruction that merely conventional weapons could cause. "There was just about nothing left," he remembered. The experience had changed his thinking about the nature of warfare: "I was a total innocent. It made a mark on me."

It was while he was back at Rand, Cohen said, that he "really became obsessed with tactical nuclear weapons." Cohen admitted to being "a little appalled" by the results of a 1953 war game played at Rand. He discovered in the course of the game that the Air Force planned to drop hundreds of Hiroshima-size nuclear weapons upon western Europe in the event of a Soviet invasion. "They paid no attention to collateral damage," Cohen said of Air Force planners. "What they were mainly interested in back then was bombing targets in eastern Europe and as far into Russia as the airplanes would reach." In Cohen's view, the Air Force's Tactical Air Command had "set about to become a junior SAC—a forward-based SAC." Brodie was similarly surprised at this time to find that the Tactical Air Command in Europe had gone so far as to remove the bomb racks from its planes so that they could carry only nuclear weapons.[21]

The Air Force's resistance to the idea of small, discriminative nuclear weapons was explained, Cohen and Brodie thought, by that service's rivalry with the Army and Navy. Since the Army was the only service promoting the development of tactical nuclear weapons, the Air Force's reaction to the idea of using such weapons was bound to be one of hostility and suspicion.

The extent to which the Air Force had wedded itself to large and indiscriminative nuclear weapons was brought home to him, Cohen said, when he visited a friend at the Air Research and Development Center in the mid-1950s. Looking around at the projects being studied by the center, Cohen remarked to his friend that there did not seem to be much emphasis by the Air Force upon how to use nonnuclear weapons to stop a nonnuclear attack. The friend had offered to show Cohen the "total effort in my shop" devoted to conventional munitions: "See that sergeant over there? He's it."

"Everything," Cohen marveled, "was nuclear."

Brodie and Cohen were not the only ones at Rand to be appalled at the way the military was planning to use nuclear weapons in the event of war. Malcolm Hoag's first assignment when he joined Rand in 1952 from the economics department of the University of Illinois was to guess the most likely place in Europe where the Soviets might attack. (The degree to which the Russian threat had already come to dominate the work at Rand was impressed upon him, Hoag said, when he befriended Brodie. Hoag had expected the strategist to talk about Clausewitz's classic *On War*. Instead, Brodie urged the new recruit to read *The Operational Code of the Politburo* by Rand's Nathan Leites.)

Like Brodie, Cohen, and virtually everyone else at Rand, Hoag became one of the players in the so-called "scratch-pad wars" that the Math Department devised in the early 1950s. The most often played war game concerned an invasion of Europe by the Red player. The game ended either when Blue destroyed Red's homeland or when Red's forces broke through to the Channel. "At that time," Hoag recalled, "Blue beat hell out of Red."

However, on one occasion he and a teammate "invented a new Red threat," Hoag said. Instead of attacking the United States at the outset of the game—the tactic preferred by previous players—he and his partner concentrated almost all of Red's forces in a conventional invasion of Europe: "We dropped mines everywhere. We closed every port on both sides. And we won."

He and his colleague were accordingly outraged when the Rand referee threw out the results of the war game. "We had used the wrong parameters," Hoag said he and his incredulous teammate were told. He recalled with amusement how both had subsequently charged up to the director of the project. "What the hell is going on?" they demanded. "You're depriving us of victory."

But there was a serious as well as a surprising lesson that he and others at Rand drew from the simulated wars, Hoag said. Confronted with the prospect of a Red occupation of Europe, the Blue players "had dropped nuclear weapons all over the map." "The people who had refereed the exercise were horrified because there was nothing left of Germany," Hoag remembered. This had become the important object lesson of the game, he felt. "If there was anybody left at Rand who believed in 'massive retaliation' as a sensible policy for the United States," Hoag said, "well, after they played the game they didn't believe that anymore. . . . It showed the fallacy of treating Europe—a place concentrated with people—as just a place to drop bombs on. As we looked ahead, we saw it was going to get worse, not better. It really brought home to everybody what a nuclear war would look like."

More extensive war games conducted in Europe in the early and middle 1950s confirmed his point. In the course of one of those simulations, more than 350 Hiroshima-size bombs were exploded in just a two-day period. It was later estimated that German civilian casualties would have exceeded two million had the combatants been using real, rather than hypothetical, bombs. At the end of another such war game—where seventy somewhat larger atomic bombs were used in an area the size of Greece and Portugal —referees concluded that had the game been an actual war most life in those countries would have simply "ceased to exist."[22]

Projected casualty figures of this magnitude—and the European reaction to them—understandably diminished enthusiasm at Rand for the idea of limited nuclear war among all except, apparently, Cohen and Brodie. The latter continued to defend tactical nuclear weapons and the idea of a limited nuclear war in Europe as a "second line of insurance," and as an additional hedge to deterrence approaching the time of a nuclear stalemate between the United States and Russia.

"Amazed disbelief" was the reaction of his colleagues, Brodie said, to his idea of a limited nuclear war. It was, he wrote, "a completely accepted axiom that all modern war must be total war."[23]

Some of those at Rand who did not agree with Brodie's ideas could nonetheless sympathize with his reasons for presenting them—and were likewise surprised by the hostility they provoked. Herman Kahn, a frequent participant in the work of the Strategic Objectives Committee, professed to being "shocked" at the response to Brodie in what Kahn called Rand's "cocktail circuit." "Brodie—like everybody else in our circle—was very hostile to the use of tactical nuclear weapons," Kahn remembered. It was initially a "kind of intellectual integrity," he felt, that had prompted Brodie to study the subject and to adopt a devil's-advocate argument for their use in war. "But Rand reacted," Kahn said, "the same way that liberals react —that Brodie was encouraging it."

Cohen agreed that his friend's hapless identification with the cause of limited nuclear war was what caused Brodie ultimately to be "pushed out" of the closed intellectual circle at Rand. Cohen felt that Brodie's interest in tactical nuclear weapons had been a natural outgrowth of his belief in deterrence: "He kept on saying, 'Look, it's working. Why fool around with it? Why change the strategy of NATO? What need is there?'"

Like Marshall's attempt to promote the idea of striking only at military targets in a war, however, there proved to be little receptivity at Rand to Brodie's notion of restraining nuclear war in terms of the size of the weapons and the location of the battlefield. A decade after the founding of Rand, the intellectual differences over nuclear strategy that surfaced at meetings of the Strategic Objectives Committee had grown into intense rivalries and even personal animosity among the experts in Santa Monica. Brodie "was very unhappy—even bitter—about the treatment he was getting," Cohen remembered. He and Brodie felt increasingly isolated at Rand. "When are you going to stop working on all these foolish ideas?" one of Cohen's colleagues asked him.

9

A Bolt from the Blue

Beyond Andrew Marshall's counterforce strategy and the theories of Bernard Brodie and Samuel Cohen about limited war there were other ideas about nuclear weapons that originated and evolved at Rand during the mid-1950s. One of these was the dawning realization that the Strategic Air Command—the nation's premier instrument of retaliation and the chief deterrent to Soviet aggression—might itself become the target of an enemy attack.

Brodie had recognized as early as 1946 that a strategic force which became vulnerable might cease to be a deterrent and become, instead, a magnet for attack. He wrote in *The Absolute Weapon* that reducing the vulnerability of American military forces was "one way of reducing temptation to potential aggressors."[1] It was a lesson that the nation had supposedly—and painfully—learned at Pearl Harbor.

But in the years since the Second World War, SAC had seemingly been slow to acknowledge the problem of strategic vulnerability. Even after the Russians had ended the American nuclear monopoly and begun to develop long-range strategic bombers of their own, there seemed little awareness of or concern with the prospect that the United States might be suddenly disarmed by a Soviet sneak attack. What was true of the Air Force was initially true of Rand—which, ironically, had more interest in the Russians' potential vulnerability than that of SAC. Strategic vulnerability was the same coin as counterforce strategy, but its other side.

Beginning with a 1951 Rand study of where to base SAC bombers overseas, the vulnerability question grew from an interest to a near obsession for Albert Wohlstetter, a logician with a background in mathematics and philosophy. Since his student days, Wohlstetter had been intrigued by the writings of American philosopher Charles Sanders Peirce, particularly the latter's notion of "fallibilism"—the idea that the unexpected and the uncertain form the most important aspect of any inquiry.

Shortly after Pearl Harbor, Wohlstetter became a quality-control specialist for the government's War Production Board. When the war ended he had stayed with the government, becoming involved in the effort to find housing for the twenty-five thousand ex-GIs being demobilized each day. In both jobs he had demonstrated enormous energy and a prodigious capacity for work. Some of Wohlstetter's fondest memories were said to date from the early postwar days in the capital, when he would often stay at his office until three in the morning and return home only long enough to shower, change clothes, and have a snack. (One of his colleagues at Rand said that this regime continued until the day Wohlstetter fell asleep at the wheel and ran into the side of a bus.) Casting about for what he might do after the country had returned to peacetime, Wohlstetter had just received a fellowship to do research in probability and statistics for the Department of Agriculture when he was asked to come to Rand.

Initially, he had been unenthusiastic about the basing study proposed to him by Hitch, then head of Rand's Economics Department. Wohlstetter freely confessed that he knew very little about military matters *per se*—his friends at Rand said that it had been a revelation, for example, when Wohlstetter learned that the "B" in B-29 stood for "bomber." Only a week after he reluctantly agreed to do the basing study for Rand, however, Wohlstetter had become fascinated by the evidence he found of fallibilism in the nation's nuclear strategy.

The source of the error, he thought, concerned the assumptions that the Air Force made from its experience of strategic bombing in the Second World War—assumptions which had gone unchallenged since. Air Force planning for a possible nuclear war with Russia had been based on that experience, where Allied bombers at their bases had remained relatively secure from enemy attack through the duration of the war. Wohlstetter realized in his study of nuclear war planning that SAC's strategists had essentially ignored Pearl Harbor, which for Americans had been the earliest and most costly lesson of the previous war.

"Strategic doctrine was to overleap the enemy's military forces and go to the industrial heart that supported them," Wohlstetter said. The issue that dominated SAC's planning was the question "How do you—despite bad weather and enemy opposition—penetrate through local defenses and destroy enemy targets?" Wohlstetter marveled that "consideration *started* with the penetration problem." The question that he posed at the start of his study of the basing problem was more fundamental: "What if the bombers don't even get off the ground?"

The most important determinant in deciding where to base its bombers had been overlooked by SAC in Wohlstetter's view. That decision should hinge, he argued, on whether the bombers were intended to strike first or to retaliate against an attack on the nation. Since it was already axiomatic in American military doctrine that SAC was a retaliatory force which, by definition, would strike second, the Air Force's apparent disregard of the effect that a Soviet first strike would have upon its bombers seemed to Wohlstetter a logical lacuna of monumental proportions.

The simple question that Wohlstetter posed as the inspiration for his basing study began a year and a half of virtually uninterrupted work. Aided by other analysts who emulated his work habits, such as economists Henry Rowen and Fred Hoffman, Wohlstetter's basing study came to epitomize the work of the so-called "scientific strategists" at Rand. Although the Air Force denied them access to its top-secret war plans, Wohlstetter and his co-workers were nonetheless able to divine accurately that service's preparations for war by reading unclassified SAC manuals like the *Mobility Planner's Guide*—which instructed military personnel on what to take with them if suddenly sent overseas in a crisis.

Each of the questions that the group posed in its basing study was intended to peel away a level of complexity, like the multilayered skin of an onion or the acetate overlays that the Air Force put on its bombing maps. What are the best routes for bombing Russia if the bombers are unopposed? What are the best routes given opposition? Which of those routes are especially well defended?

Wohlstetter and his colleagues dubbed their approach to the problem "opposed-systems analysis" in order to distinguish it from the systems or operations analysis of their peers at Rand. The difference lay in the fact that the enemy could be expected to create a new problem for each solution they found. One of those in the group likened the difficulty of the task to designing a house to be built upon a shifting foundation, or to solving an equation when it is known that some of the figures are wrong.

Unlike systems analysis, Wohlstetter explained, opposed-systems analysis "had tension built into it." To him it was a point of pride that "*his* Russians didn't fly through the DEW Line," in what Rowen scornfully called the "U.S.-preferred Soviet strike" that seemed to be the basis of SAC planning. Those at Rand who were not involved in the basing study remembered how at odd hours Wohlstetter, Rowen, and Hoffman could be found on their knees in the basement of the main building, poring over maps spread out on the floor, pondering the least-expected and hence the best avenues of approach for Russian bombers planning a surprise raid upon SAC.

Whenever possible, the Wohlstetter group liked to ask their questions in person. At March Air Force base, near his home in Los Angeles, Wohlstetter inquired of the chief of maintenance how long it would take for the bombers at the base to take off armed and ready. The number of hours cited was several times the official SAC figure. Rowen found that even a near miss with a single atomic bomb would have torn the wings off the bombers parked wingtip-to-wingtip on the tarmac at a SAC base in Morocco. Despite its assumption of a quick, decisive war, Wohlstetter discovered that the Air

Force had stockpiled "acres of machine tools" overseas for restoring and rebuilding the bomber fleet in the *second* year of a nuclear conflict with Russia. The answer he and the others received to their questions, Wohlstetter said, "would probably have stunned most people."

The end result of their effort was a 426-page top-secret report on bomber basing that was later reduced to a summary a quarter that length, and then further condensed to a forty-five-minute briefing using a few dozen charts.[2] Wohlstetter presented the briefing for the first of what would eventually be ninety-two times in the winter of 1952 before the famous "murder board" of Rand's leadership. His introduction had been suitably—and purposefully —dramatic.

"In a strike using only a fraction of the capability we assign them in 1956, the Soviets would destroy 90 percent of our bombers and tankers based in the United States," Wohlstetter began. "If the remaining few planes went overseas, as they would according to our mobility plan, they would be flying from the frying pan into the fire."

Existing plans, Wohlstetter explained, deployed the bulk of SAC's bombers at overseas bases within close range of their targets in Russia. In the event of a crisis or the actual outbreak of war, these planes would be joined by longer-range bombers flown from SAC bases in the United States. Once assembled at these forward bases, the bombers would launch the nuclear "Sunday punch" that was the centerpiece of SAC's strategy. Yet little—if any—consideration had been given in that plan to the possibility that the Russians might preempt the impending atomic blitz by simultaneously striking SAC bases overseas and in America. The nation's real deterrent strength, Wohlstetter said, was not the total number of bombers in SAC's inventory —or even the total number of planes expected to penetrate Russian defenses —but the number that would survive the initial Soviet attack and be able to reach their targets, and that number was small indeed.

The briefing presented a grim account of what Wohlstetter argued was the nation's woefully inadequate preparation for a nuclear war. Air Force planners had estimated that the bulk of SAC's bombers could be airborne within an hour of the mobilization order. The Rand group claimed that it might take SAC most of a day to get a single bomber aloft. During that time, Wohlstetter warned, it would be possible for Russian bombers flying under American radar and along approaches that skirted air defenses to destroy SAC and disarm the United States.

In the briefing, as in their report, the group tried to anticipate all the questions and objections that doubters and SAC's defenders might raise. Accordingly, their calculations had taken into account such esoterica as the radar reflection characteristic of a certain type of Russian bomber and the rate of fire of defending American fighters. (Wohlstetter felt their effort at thoroughness was vindicated when the question about radar reflections came up in a later briefing. *"Nobody,"* his associates had assured him, "would ask *that.* ")

The implicit message contained in the briefing was unambiguous. "SAC was so vulnerable," Rowen said, "that you had to prop it up at each barrier so that it could be knocked down at the next." The initial response of Rand's management at the end of the briefing was silence. Wohlstetter later said he was unsurprised by the reaction. "I had just told them," he reflected, "that the most powerful force in the history of the world was really quite vulnerable, and at the outset of a war would be lying there in pieces."

In the lengthening silence, John Williams, the mathematician who had brought Wohlstetter to Rand, quietly relit the pipe that he had theatrically let fall from his mouth when the briefing began. Finally, someone in the room broke the spell with an observation that in time would seem prophetic: "The impact of this study will be the greatest that Rand has ever had. If, Albert, General LeMay stays in the room after your first two sentences."

The SAC commander was not in the audience during the briefings of the basing study that Wohlstetter, Rowen, and Hoffman soon began giving at the Pentagon and Air Force bases around the country. The initial reaction of SAC's deputy commander, General Thomas Power, to the Rand presentation was noncommittal.

Two events that occurred while the Rand team was making its rounds began to affect not only the conclusions of the basing study, but also the reception it would receive at SAC headquarters and in Washington. One was the Russians' test of a prototype hydrogen bomb in the summer of 1953. The other was the realization, which came from the work of Rand analyst Bruno Augenstein, that missiles capable of carrying hydrogen bombs to their targets half a world away in a matter of minutes might be closer to realization than previously thought.[3]

The combined threat represented by the specter of a hydrogen-bomb-tipped intercontinental-range missile had been one of the reasons why Brodie decided that the conclusions of *The Absolute Weapon* were obsolete. It affected Wohlstetter's thinking as well. He and his co-workers thus realized there would no longer be time for the United States to escape surprise by dispersing its deterrent force in advance of war. This fact would cause Wohlstetter and Hoffman to conclude, in a second basing study they completed in 1954, that SAC might have to shelter as well as disperse its future bombers and missiles to make them a less attractive target for a Soviet attack.[4] But even before making that recommendation officially, Wohlstetter altered his briefing to account for the sudden urgency that the Soviet Super and the impending advent of the ICBM gave to the question of SAC's strategic vulnerability. One of the young Rand analysts who accompanied him on the briefing tour, Alain Enthoven, reportedly began carrying with him a scale model of the shelter that Rand proposed for the bombers.

The recommendation of Wohlstetter's study that all of SAC's bombers be based in the United States instead of overseas unwittingly involved the Rand group in a prolonged internecine struggle within the Air Force between SAC and the Air Staff over the planning for a nuclear war. Upon the Air Staff's recommendation, the influential Air Force Council eventually accepted many of Rand's recommendations—including Wohlstetter's suggestion that SAC adopt a "fail-safe" system, whereby bombers would return to their bases after an alert unless they received a positive and coded signal to proceed to their targets in Russia.[5] (Wohlstetter said he borrowed both the term and the concept behind it from the memories of his childhood, when he had briefly considered becoming a railroad engineer and was fascinated with how train accidents were avoided.)

The case that Wohlstetter made for SAC's vulnerability was also furthered by some timely and ironic proof of fallibilism. A freak tornado that hit a Florida SAC base in September 1952 helped to make Rand's point about the unexpected fragility of the bomber force when it destroyed or damaged several planes sitting on the runway. An unscheduled exercise the following summer aimed at testing the Air Defense Command seemed, as well, to confirm Wohlstetter's claims about the feasibility of a surprise attack on the United States. Using the unorthodox approaches that he and the others had plotted out for a hypothetical Soviet attack, SAC's bombers were able to achieve complete surprise in the mock raid, penetrating to their targets virtually without opposition.[6]

Beginning in 1954, SAC would cease to rely upon overseas bases to launch the planned atomic blitz. As Rand had suggested, the Air Force's fleet of bombers would henceforth be based in the United States and refueled in flight on their way to targets in Russia.

Despite the generally favorable response Wohlstetter's briefing received in military circles and even from Air Force officers outside SAC, it was not until the spring of 1955—more than two years after the group's first presentation—that the long-awaited showdown with LeMay occurred. Reportedly, LeMay was said to have at first endorsed Rand's thesis on SAC's vulnerability—mistakenly believing that the basing study's recommendations would include increasing the total number of SAC's bombers to make up for those lost in a Soviet attack.

Hoping to defuse in advance the SAC commander's well-known objections to civilian strategists in general and those of Rand in particular, Wohlstetter and Hoffman had sat in the audience on the occasion that LeMay was briefed on the basing study. To give the briefing additional clout, Wohlstetter arranged to have it presented at the Pentagon by the head of the Air Staff. The latter had only gotten a few sentences out, however, before LeMay interrupted and the presentation, as Wohlstetter remembered, "began to crumble." He and Hoffman sat helplessly while LeMay argued that SAC's solution to the vulnerability problem was not shelters and dispersal—but new bombers that would fly higher, faster, and farther than the existing force.

The briefing "dissolved," Wohlstetter said, when the briefer referred to Rand's dispersal plan for SAC's bombers, which the Air Staff was then considering but LeMay had not yet seen. "*What* dispersal plan?" LeMay had bellowed from the audience. The remainder of the briefing, Hoffman recalled, was taken up by a heated exchange between LeMay and the Air Staff officer concerning the need for new bombers.

Several months after the fiasco at the Pentagon, Wohlstetter and the president of Rand, Frank Colbaum, briefed LeMay personally on the basing plan at SAC headquarters in Omaha. The presentation this time included no complex charts or graphs. Instead, Wohlstetter referred only to a single sheet of paper containing a few calculations. At the end of the impromptu presentation, Wohlstetter thought that LeMay had ultimately come to accept much of Rand's argument concerning SAC's vulnerability.

But one of the basing study's recommendations to which LeMay's opposition—then and later—proved unyielding was the matter of shelters for SAC's bombers. "Concrete has never been attractive to LeMay," Wohlstetter conceded reluctantly. One final, belated attempt by another member of the Rand team to raise the question prompted the response from LeMay that SAC, in fact, had always had a policy concerning shelters. "Really?" the young analyst responded eagerly. "What is it?" he asked.

"Piss on shelters," LeMay replied.

Contrary to Rand's assumptions, the problem of strategic vulnerability had not been entirely ignored in the Air Force. Nor was LeMay's seemingly cavalier dismissal of the threat to SAC's bombers necessarily a sign of reckless disregard. The sardonic reply that one SAC officer gave to Wohlstetter's warning about strategic vulnerability—"They wouldn't *dare* attack one of General LeMay's bombers"—was indeed not only indicative of a certain attitude in the Air Force, but a statement of expectations there. SAC's complacency about the threat of surprise attack was—in LeMay's view at least—both deliberate and well founded.

The topic of preventive war—meaning an unprovoked attack by the United States on the Soviet Union—had been discreetly discussed in some government and military circles since the advent of the atomic bomb. It was one of the four possible courses of action that Paul Nitze had proposed with NSC-68 in 1950. A few members of Congress urged that the Truman administration embark upon such a war in 1949, shortly after the Russians had shown that they too had the bomb. Secretary of State Dean Acheson—who had reprimanded the enthusiasts of preventive war on that occasion—privately acknowledged later that there was an undeniable attraction to the idea of disarming the Russians while the United States still had the chance.[7]

Similarly, though Truman would subsequently dismiss a member of his administration for suggesting the idea of a nuclear attack on the nation's enemies, the president's personal diary revealed that he considered the possibility in the course of the Korean War. Truman's successor would likewise acknowledge somewhat wistfully the advantage to striking first.[8] As William Borden's 1947 letter to McMahon was perhaps the first to show, the related notion of a nuclear ultimatum to Russia had an early as well as a long lineage.[9]

Preventive war was an occasional topic of discussion, too, among the nation's military leaders. Public comments favorable to the idea were expressed during the late 1940s or early 1950s by Chief of Naval Operations Admiral Robert Carney, director of the Air War College Orville Anderson, and Navy Secretary Francis Matthews.[10] The charge that Air Force Secretary Thomas Finletter once spoke out positively about "policing the world with H-bombs" would be made in the course of the Oppenheimer hearings.[11]

In his memoirs, Curtis LeMay confirmed that the alluring prospect of a sneak attack on the Russians was discussed among SAC's commanders at various times—though it was never actually proposed to the White House. "There was, definitely, a time when we could have destroyed all of Russia (I mean by that, all of Russia's capability to wage war) without losing a man to their defenses," LeMay wrote. "We at SAC were the first to perceive this potential. We had constructed it to a point, and had our weapons ready."[12]

Thomas Power, LeMay's successor as commander of SAC, was even more forthright on the subject in his own memoirs. Power thought it "evident that we may have to take military actions of various types which, with certain qualifications, might fall under the public's broad concept of 'preventive war.'"[13]

But in every case, the alternative of preventive war was finally rejected by civilian and military leaders alike as inimical to the nation's principles, and contrary to the popular will. While a Pearl Harbor–like attack on Russia "might be desirable," the Joint Chiefs of Staff acknowledged in the late 1940s, "it is not politically feasible under our system to do so or to state that we will do so."[14] NSC-68 branded the idea of preventive war "generally unacceptable to Americans," "repugnant," and "morally corrosive." In the fall of 1950, Truman had fired Navy Secretary Matthews after the latter urged that the United States become the first "aggressors for peace." The American people would never tolerate the use of the bomb for "aggressive purposes," Truman told an aide.[15]

Orville Anderson's comment about "wiping out Russia's five A-bomb nests" also eventually led to his ouster. "Starting an atomic war is totally unthinkable for rational men," Truman claimed in his farewell address to the nation as president.

Eisenhower, from the evidence, felt no differently. In 1954, when it became clear that the Russians too had the Super, a study group formed in the Pentagon by the joint chiefs told Eisenhower that he might wish to consider "deliberately precipitating war with the U.S.S.R. in the near future."[16] But Eisenhower on several occasions rejected the idea of preventive war while president, and even before. "We are not going to deliver the first blow," he had declared when still Army chief of staff.[17]

While preventive war *per se* was clearly ruled out of American strategic planning, the possibility of *preempting* an impending Soviet attack was not. Preemption—or an "anticipatory counterattack" in SAC jargon—was recognized in Air Force doctrine and in the nation's declared policy on nuclear weapons to be a morally justified and even militarily necessary response to the enemy's preparations for war. As early as 1945 the joint chiefs had argued that the United States should be prepared "to strike the first blow if necessary" whenever "it becomes evident that the forces of aggression are being arrayed against us."[18] At one point the chiefs were even considering—under the category of "provocations" that might justify such a step—the occasion when the Soviets developed the capacity for "eventual attack against the United States or defense against our attack."[19] Preemption found equal justification in the political strategy for dealing with Russia. Though it had rejected preventive war, NSC-68 acknowledged the need to be "on the alert in order to strike with our full weight as soon as we are attacked, and if possible, before the Soviet blow is actually delivered."[20]

The notion that the United States and not the Soviet Union would be the first nation to use nuclear weapons in the next war was not only the expectation of SAC planners; it was also the principal idea upon which most of their planning was based. Since the earliest American planning for a nuclear war, the guiding assumption had been that the conflict would probably begin as the result of a crisis or a confrontation that took place beyond the borders of the United States and Russia, most likely in Europe. Because at least the first stage of that conflict would thus be far removed from this country, American military planners believed that there would be ample time—the Army projected an entire year—to mobilize U.S. forces for the fight overseas.

Even after the Russians had nuclear weapons and the ability to attack the United States directly, the great majority of military planners still believed that there would be enough warning of an impending Soviet attack to launch SAC's bombers before the blow fell. Few if any in the Air Force at this time feared the hypothetical prospect of a "bolt from the blue"—an unprovoked Russian attack on the U.S. homeland preceded neither by crisis nor by warning.

The nether region that existed between preventive war and preemptive attack was also recognized by SAC's commanders. LeMay and SAC expected to receive an "unambiguous strategic warning" from U.S. intelligence of a Soviet attack—though exactly what constituted such warning was evidently not well defined either by LeMay or within SAC.[21] A similarly deliberate vagueness was inherent in Power's idea of the "assumption of the initiative," which he claimed SAC would undertake once Russia's belligerent intentions became clear. It "would be a grave mistake," Power wrote in his memoirs, "to give the Soviets the impression that we would never strike first."[22]

Privately, SAC's leaders were less circumspect in expressing their belief that the United States would be the first to use nuclear weapons. At a secret briefing on the Air Force war plan in early 1954, LeMay, according to one witness, claimed that the idea of striking second was "not in keeping with United States history." "I want to make it clear that I am not advocating a preventive war," LeMay explained at the briefing. But, he said, "I believe that if the U.S. is pushed in the corner far enough we would not hesitate to strike first." On another occasion, according to a member of Air Force Intelligence, LeMay told a gathering of SAC pilots that he "could not imagine a circumstance under which the United States would go second."[23]

Evidently a more direct concern for LeMay as well as subsequent SAC commanders was whether America's civilian leaders would grant them the authority to preempt a Soviet attack for which there was, in SAC's definition, unambiguous strategic warning. Despite their disclaimers on preventive war, neither Truman nor Eisenhower while in office ever specifically ruled out the possibility that the United States would preempt a Soviet attack and be the first to use nuclear weapons. Indeed, the Eisenhower administration's explicit threat to retaliate "massively" and "at a time and a place of our own choosing" against unspecified acts of Soviet aggression seemed entirely in accord with SAC's thinking on preemption. "Massive retaliation," one historian of the doctrine observed, implied "massive preemption."[24]

Yet LeMay and his subordinates in SAC did not seem burdened with doubts over whether they would get the necessary permission if the time came. "We know we will get the weapons when the bell rings," SAC's director of operations assured those assembled at the 1954 briefing. It was evident on this occasion that not only LeMay's thinking but the very persona of the general had come to dominate SAC war planning. The "exact manner in which SAC will fight the war is known only to General LeMay," the briefer told his audience.[25]

In fact, it is likely that few in the government or at Rand actually knew enough details of Air Force war planning to appreciate the extent to which American nuclear strategy by the mid-1950s was based upon the premise that the United States would land the first blow with the bomb. One of those at Rand who had an understanding of this fact from his acquaintance with the actual war plans would later characterize Wohlstetter's imaginative hypotheses concerning one-way, suicide attacks by Russian bombers as a case "of making up a threat against which to plan": one that reflected "neither the Soviet threat nor Soviet thinking."

Ironically, what Wohlstetter and his colleagues in the basing study warned the Air Force the Russians might be able to do to SAC came very close to what SAC and LeMay were actually planning to do to the Russians.

The vital difference was that LeMay and SAC intended to do it first.

Only a decade after its inception, Rand seemed to many of its pioneers already in decline. By the late 1950s, "Mother Rand" appeared suddenly dowagerlike in its lack of tolerance for Brodie's advocacy of tactical nuclear weapons or for Marshall's arguments on counterforce. Some of Rand's problems were the unintended consequence of its own success.

Part of that success had been in popularizing the subject of nuclear strategy. The notoriety Rand received had made public figures of several of the analysts there. One example was Herman Kahn, whose lectures on what a nuclear war might be like became a fixture at Rand as well as the Pentagon, and were eventually published in a best-selling book.

Kahn left Rand at the end of the 1950s—a victim, he said, of its lapse into conformity. A warning sign of Rand's ossification had appeared, Kahn claimed, a few years earlier, after he and other members of the Strategic Objectives Committee were enlisted in a mammoth Air Force–sponsored study of air power. Kahn and a colleague had proposed an annex to the study concerning the feasibility of civilian defense against atomic attack. Kahn expected the Air Force to oppose his idea, but he was surprised when opposition had also come from the president of Rand, Frank Colbaum. "It was widely assumed that the civil defense study was done because the Air Force wanted it," Kahn recalled. "Actually, it was done over the dead body of the Air Force and the dead body of the president of Rand."

Kahn's stubborn perseverance with the project led to a direct confrontation with Colbaum. Kahn accused the latter of bowing to Air Force pressure; Colbaum accused Kahn of misrepresenting the civil defense study, which threatened to absorb the original Air Force project. "Basically I said that the study would be dull and uninteresting," Kahn remembered of the dispute. "It got very interesting and Colbaum thought I promised to keep it dull."

In a few cases, ideas that originated at Rand not only entered the popular domain but became the focus of a public debate, as when the ill-chosen name of a 1958 study sparked a congressional investigation. The study had concerned whether it might be possible to have a limited nuclear war; its conclusions were later published as a book. But it was the book's title— *Strategic Surrender: The Politics of Victory and Defeat*—more than its contents or its conclusion, that created the uproar. Mistakenly thought to advocate that the United States lay down its arms in the event of a war with Russia, the book inspired a unanimous congressional resolution against future use of government funds to sponsor any study envisioning the nation's surrender.[26]

The gradual widening of concern with nuclear weapons beyond the scientists' laboratories and the briefing rooms at Rand also led to the rein-volvement of academics at top universities in the debate. In 1957, Harvard government professor Henry Kissinger published an influential book, *Nuclear Weapons and Foreign Policy*, which borrowed heavily from the work of Brodie and others on the subject of tactical nuclear weapons. Kissinger's argument that limited nuclear war was a possible alternative to Armageddon essentially repeated the case that Brodie had made—unsuccessfully—before his colleagues at Rand in earlier years. (So close was the book to Brodie's work, in fact, that the latter accused Kissinger in a letter of having "deliberate and petty motives" for not acknowledging its source.)[27]

The publication of *Nuclear Weapons and Foreign Policy* caused the dormant controversy over limited war to flare up again at Rand. In a lengthy review of Kissinger's book, William Kaufmann savaged its author for becoming almost "lyrical" about nuclear war, and for engaging "in a great deal of wishful thinking" about the subject. Kaufmann was equally critical of Kissinger's motives in providing an intellectual justification for the Eisenhower administration's nuclear strategy of massive retaliation. "Kissinger," Kaufmann observed dryly, "is nothing if not fashionable."[28]

A year later, the idea of controlled nuclear war was given a new and broader definition in a conference at Princeton, when Rand strategist Klaus Knorr suggested that the use of tactical atomic weapons in Europe was not the only example of how nuclear war might be fought for limited objectives and with limited effects. Knorr hypothesized that a nuclear war between the United States and Russia could conceivably be stopped after both sides had "exchanged" one or more cities. But the reception Rand's strategists and other academics at the conference gave Knorr's idea of a limited *strategic* nuclear war was, according to another participant, "lukewarm" at best.

The tensions that had always underlain Rand's relations with the Air Force began to come more into the open by the end of the 1950s as well. A notable change from the early days at Rand was the increasingly personal nature of what had started as intellectual differences. Certainly the most personal and bitter of those rivalries was that between Brodie and Wohlstetter.

Paradoxically, the two men shared similar interests and hobbies. Beyond their common link in the study of nuclear strategy, both were stereo buffs and connoisseurs of French cuisine. Each was married to a brilliant woman with a career and impressive accomplishments of her own. (Roberta Wohlstetter's book on Pearl Harbor presented the historical evidence behind her husband's theory of strategic vulnerability, though the couple regarded their work as separate and independent.[29] Fawn Brodie became interested—as did Bernard—in the psychological makeup of leaders. She wrote several biographies of famous figures, including a Pulitzer Prize–winning study of Thomas Jefferson.)

Relations between Brodie and Wohlstetter ultimately personified the tension that had always existed between the two forms taken by the Rand style. Privately, Wohlstetter disparaged Brodie's intuitive approach, characterizing it with thinly disguised scorn as "in the essay tradition." One of those who had worked with Wohlstetter on the basing study credited Brodie with writing the "primer on nuclear strategy." But he said that most at Rand "had, in effect, gone on to graduate school and left Brodie behind."

For his part, Brodie discounted the worth of Wohlstetter's painstakingly quantified analysis. There was, Brodie objected, a kind of false precision and an illusory aura of certainty to the results. After some initial enthusiasm for the scientific strategists, Brodie had come to radically reassess the value of their work. "Experience" had shown him, Brodie wrote to a friend, that "the great majority of them (though with conspicuous exceptions) show an astonishing lack of political sense."[30]

Lost sight of in the clash of their personalities was the fact that Brodie and Wohlstetter represented not only different examples of the Rand style, but equally a different understanding of Rand's "strategic sense." Brodie's intuitive approach took into account the likely intentions of the enemy; Wohlstetter's was a self-consciously limited focus upon the enemy's capabilities. Relations between the two men worsened further with the ascendancy of the scientific strategists at Rand by the end of the 1950s. The fame accruing to the successful basing study meant henceforth that Wohlstetter—not Brodie—was accorded the status of "high priest of deterrence" in journalistic accounts of the work at Rand.[31]

In the view of some of Brodie's friends, his personal differences with Wohlstetter were responsible for his curious shift on the subject of deterrence. From his early view that there should be a kind of "qualitative prohibition" against the use of any nuclear weapon, Brodie had come to embrace tactical nuclear weapons and the doctrine of limited nuclear war. What had started out as an intellectual exercise appeared to have turned into a sort of bizarre infatuation. Attacks on Brodie, moreover, just seemed to harden his position and to separate him further from the majority at Rand.

By the end of the 1950s Brodie's isolation was virtually complete—as was the triumph of the scientific strategists. Those who had been drawn to Rand as missionaries had become either heretics . . . or zealots.

Thomas Schelling, who knew both Brodie and Wohlstetter at Rand, later commented on the changes that their rivalry had brought about. "When I first met them, I found that Brodie, Kahn, and Wohlstetter were a fascinating group to eat lunch with and got along beautifully," Schelling recalled. "I could detect very little competition or rivalry among them. There was a very collegial feeling that they were all developing a tradition for how to think about nuclear weapons. They were complementary to each other and got along fine."

When Schelling returned to Rand in the early 1960s, after a five-year stint in the government, he was struck by the difference in both the people and the attitudes there. Wohlstetter, Schelling thought, had become "remarkably arrogant." Brodie, in contrast, was "a very unhappy person—very much out of it." "Brodie was just terribly, terribly hurt" by the rejection of his colleagues at Rand, Schelling remembered. "It finally got to where Brodie and Wohlstetter could hardly bear to be in the same room together."

10

Setting Back the Clock

The military policies of the Eisenhower administration the strategists at Rand had railed against were themselves undergoing change by the end of the think tank's golden years—though those changes were not necessarily the result of their efforts. During his first few weeks as president, Eisenhower had been presented with the report of Oppenheimer's Disarmament Panel. At nearly the same time, the new president was urged by Paul Nitze—in what the latter considered a kind of "valedictory"—to adopt a revised version of the containment doctrine inherited from Truman.

The Disarmament Panel's report proposed that Eisenhower be more candid with the American public on the subject of nuclear weapons and consider a fresh diplomatic initiative with the Russians to lessen the chances of nuclear war. Nitze's recommendation was that Eisenhower substantially increase defense spending, rebuild America's conventional forces, and institute a mammoth program of shelters meant to protect the population from atomic attack.

Eisenhower chose to reject the advice of Oppenheimer and Nitze alike. But several weeks later, in the course of what would become known as the Solarium study, the president was confronted by his own advisers with a similar set of fundamental choices for the administration's foreign and military policies.

The alternatives offered in the Solarium study were essentially those of NSC-68, though the option of a return to isolationism was excluded at the outset in the 1953 reassessment of containment. The prospect of preventive war that Nitze had mused about in 1950 had also undergone a subtle change three years later. Instead, Eisenhower was urged to consider telling the Russians that they faced the certain prospect of war in two years unless they agreed to negotiate their differences with the West.[1]

The course finally chosen by the president was the same containment policy that the United States had followed for most of the past decade—though Eisenhower's secretary of state, John Foster Dulles, privately informed both the original architect of that policy, George Kennan, and its later interpreter, Nitze, that both the nomenclature and the personnel of the previous administration would have to go to give at least the appearance of change. Kennan had returned to the government long enough to take part in the Solarium study, but he was pointedly not asked to remain. Nitze, already identified in the Republican administration as "an Acheson man," he said, later joined the critics of Eisenhower's foreign policy. The center-piece of that policy was still the containing of Soviet expansionism, but the rhetoric which now surrounded containment stressed—by way of contrast —"liberation" and the "rolling back" of the Iron Curtain.[2]

The major change of substance was Eisenhower's "New Look" military strategy, which accelerated the trend begun under Truman of using nuclear weapons as a lower-cost substitute for conventional forces. Despite the initial qualms that he expressed during the 1952 campaign about the strategy of massive retaliation—Eisenhower once said he would not run on a plat-form which made "retaliatory striking power," in Dulles' phrase, the key-stone of America's defense—as president he sanctioned the increasing reliance upon nuclear weapons as an answer to the Russian threat. The already great and growing role of nuclear weapons in the New Look was subsequently confirmed in Dulles' celebrated speech of January 1954 threat-ening to retaliate "massively" against Soviet aggression.[3]

Starting in 1953, even before the New Look was announced, the Army had begun deploying the first of the tactical nuclear weapons that were the end result of Vista. "Atomic weapons have virtually achieved conventional sta-tus with our armed forces," Eisenhower stated later that same year. The president's assertion, though startling and somewhat exaggerated, was sub-stantially valid. The New Look and the Army's so-called "Pentatomic" strategy envisioned the prompt use of tactical nuclear weapons if an enemy force larger than a brigade crossed the border into western Europe. The intent of American military strategy, Eisenhower confided to selected mem-bers of Congress in 1954, was "to blow hell out of them in a hurry if they start anything."[4]

But the spirit at least of Oppenheimer's "Candor Report" remained alive in the Eisenhower administration—as became evident in a speech the presi-dent made in the spring of 1953. The inspiration for the speech to the American Society of Newspaper Editors had been Defense Secretary Charles Wilson's suggestion that a personal appeal for disarmament by Eisenhower might disarm the administration's critics, if not the Russians. The speech that launched Operation Candor—later redubbed "Operation Wheaties," and eventually the "Atoms for Peace" program—would be the only real outcome of the 1952 Disarmament Panel's work.[5]

Ironically, after the president's speechwriters and advisers had produced nearly a dozen versions of "The Chances for Peace," the one eventually chosen by Eisenhower came from the pen of Paul Nitze. It included a graphic account of the material and human costs of the nuclear arms race. "Every gun that is made, every warship launched, every rocket fired signifies, in the final sense, a theft from those who hunger and are not fed, those who are cold and are not clothed," the president intoned. What followed was Nitze's careful calculation of how many schools, hospitals, and homes were sacrificed to build bombers, fighters, and destroyers.[6]

Operation Candor and the speech that launched it led to Eisenhower's controversial proposal in the United Nations some months later to share the technology of peaceful nuclear power with developing nations. At the end of the year, Eisenhower proposed increasing government spending on housing and social services while further decreasing the money for defense. But, contrary to Wilson's optimistic expectations, Eisenhower's prestige and the seemingly selfless motives behind the Atoms for Peace plan failed to defuse the foreign and domestic criticism aimed at the administration because of its nuclear emphasis. Skeptics of the program charged that the government's attempt to spread atomic power plants around the world was at best misdirected altruism—"Watts for Hottentots," some derided it—and at worst a new and dangerous step toward the proliferation of nuclear weapons.[7]

The reaction to "The Chances for Peace" within the administration inadvertently showed the tensions that already divided the government over the issue of the arms race and the Russians. Nitze later thought his authorship of the speech to have been "the last straw" in his stormy relations with Dulles, who finally fired him as head of the State Department's Policy Planning Staff some weeks later. The hostility that Dulles had shown to its proposal for Soviet-American cooperation prompted as well a falling-out between the president and his secretary of state. "If Mr. Dulles and all his sophisticated advisers really meant that they can *not* talk peace seriously, then I am in the wrong pew. For if it's *war* we should be talking about, I *know* the people to give me advice on that—and they're not in the State Department," Eisenhower said in reaction to Dulles' rumored criticism of the speech.[8]

But it was not Dulles alone who stood in the way of "The Chances for Peace." The earnest hopes for disarmament that Eisenhower expressed during his first term also did not receive much encouragement from events. A number of those scientists who helped to build the first bomb had initially professed enthusiasm for Eisenhower's effort to beat swords into plowshares —either out of a desire to see some good come from their discovery or, as some admitted, from a sense of atonement.[9]

But there had been, since the early optimism of the summer studies, a fading hope on the part of the atomic scientists that their efforts could stop or even significantly slow the arms race with Russia. Increasingly, technology itself had become a force in that race: what was at first thought to be a boon was soon recognized as a curse. The same technological break-through that made smaller and more discriminative nuclear weapons feasible, therefore, also made it possible to build larger and more destructive bombs more efficiently. The alternative with which Oppenheimer and the Vista report had tried to confront the Truman administration proved to be a false choice: it was possible to build *both* the Super *and* tactical nuclear weapons.

There seemed at times even a perverseness to technology's headlong progress. As with Vista and the Super, the same science that brought Project Charles into existence had in time caused it to be overtaken and rendered obsolete. The intercontinental-range ballistic missile foreseen at Rand in the early 1950s was a reality before the end of the decade, in part because of the efforts of experts who had also worked on Charles. Members of the Pentagon's Strategic Missiles Evaluation Committee—the so-called Teapot Committee—like Jerome Wiesner and Charles Lauritsen saw their earlier accomplishments in air defense utterly undone by their work on the ICBM. The bomber threat they and Project Charles had thought to guard against turned out to be the wrong one. Charles' multibillion-dollar Distant Early Warning picket line of radars, its battery of vacuum-tube computers, and its phalanx of supersonic interceptions became operational just in time to be overflown by the hypersonic missile, Wiesner noted wryly.[10]

As the history of Vista and Charles showed, there was a dynamism to military technology which seemed ultimately to favor the aggressor, frustrating and confounding the search for defensive countermeasures. A "technological imperative"—which decreed that every offensive weapon that could be built, would be—was the cause of his own bitter disillusionment with technology, one veteran of the summer studies said.

Even those scientists who opposed the development of new weapons on ethical grounds bowed to the unslowable pace of technological development. The theoretical breakthrough that had made the Super possible was so "technically sweet," Oppenheimer said during his loyalty hearings, that he had no longer been able to oppose development of the hated weapon. It was his profession's "intellectual arrogance"—as demonstrated by Oppenheimer's comment—that another scientist engaged in building nuclear weapons, Freeman Dyson, blamed for compounding the problem created by technology's advance. "Defensive weapons," Dyson wrote, "do not spring like the hydrogen bomb from the brains of brilliant professors of physics." *"Defense,"* Dyson concluded with emphasis, *"is not technically sweet."*[11]

The disillusionment and concern that some scientists felt about the direction of the arms race was portrayed by them in a graphic way. Since the founding of the Federation of Atomic Scientists in 1947, its monthly *Bulletin* had carried on its cover the figure of a "doomsday clock," its hands just minutes from midnight—the exact number of minutes varying with the editors' degree of pessimism concerning the prospect of nuclear war. In 1949, after the first Russian bomb, the hands of the clock were moved from their original position at seven minutes before twelve to just three minutes short of the final hour. In 1953, after the United States exploded a true hydrogen bomb and the Soviets had tested the thermonuclear principle behind the Super, the clock was advanced another minute, to the closest it had ever been to midnight. For the next seven years, until the end of the Eisenhower administration, it would remain at two minutes to twelve—belying their feeling, these scientists said, that time was in fact running out.

The near-certainty that the Russians would in time develop their own intercontinental ballistic missiles with hydrogen bomb warheads was the reason for Eisenhower's creation of a "Technical Capabilities Panel" in the spring of 1954. Admitting publicly for the first time that "the Soviets now have the capability of atomic attack on us, and such capability will increase with the passage of time," Eisenhower appointed MIT president James Killian to head the group of scientists and engineers whose task it would be to recommend measures for reducing the dangers of surprise attack.[12]

Killian was a logical choice to lead the panel. A 1948 article he wrote on air defense had been one of the inspirations behind Project Charles. Another figure who would become a guiding spirit of the panel was Assistant Secretary of the Air Force Trevor Gardner—a man whom Killian described as "technologically evangelical," and who was also a major force behind the Teapot Committee on the ICBM.[13]

Initially, the Killian panel covered much of the same ground as Wohlstetter's second basing study, which Rand had recently completed for the Air Force. But one of its members recalled how the panel soon "got enthused on the idea of defense." "Theirs was a great belief," he said, "in all the things technology could do."

Among the panel's many ideas for bolstering defense was its recommendation that the ICBM program be accelerated and that the nation develop an antimissile missile. Another development urged was that of a jet-powered high-altitude reconnaissance airplane, able to fly with impunity above Russian air defenses and to photograph in detail all that was below. Originally conceived in Project Beacon Hill, an offshoot of Charles, the U-2 spy plane would be able in theory to resolve speculation in the West about Russia's military capabilities, and hence assuage American fears that the Soviets might be planning a sneak attack.[14]

The possibility that the spy plane would also be ideally suited for pinpointing strategic targets in the Soviet Union was not played up in the Killian panel's final report—though it was certainly a thought that had already occurred to the Air Force.[15] Hitherto, up-to-date intelligence on Russia had usually been gathered from brief but deliberate penetrations of Soviet airspace by American planes flying along the borders. Those overflights had been both provocative and dangerous. Several of the supposedly "accidental" incursions had resulted in the planes' being shot down, with the loss of their crews. For all that, the results had been disappointing in terms of the information gained.[16]

An alternative suggested by Rand as early as 1946 and later tried by the Air Force—floating huge, instrument-laden balloons over Russia—had proved too expensive and unreliable. Some of the balloons were apparently shot down by the Russians; others were carried by erratic winds far from their intended targets. (One unexpected difficulty encountered with the project, code-named Moby Dick, was the problem of procuring enough plastic film to build the mammoth balloons—"when all the big money is in seat covers and carrot-wrap," recalled one of the participants.)[17]

Eisenhower approved development of the U-2, but the spy plane's existence would become one of the administration's premier secrets. Upon the president's order, the top-secret project was not even mentioned by the Killian panel in its report to the National Security Council in early 1955. Despite the early enthusiasm that its authors had for technical solutions to the problems of defense, there was a curious quality to the conclusions of their report. Beyond the recommendation that the nation "push all promising technological developments," the members of the Killian panel admitted that even with the utmost scientific prowess, both sides in the arms race were destined to eventually reach a situation of irreducible stalemate—where "attack by either side would result in mutual destruction."[18]

The panel attempted to qualify its pessimism with the observation that "we need not assume that this state is unchangeable or that one country or the other cannot move again into a position of relative advantage." Yet there was sufficient doubt underlying even this prospectus for the experts to put their final statement in italics: *We see no certainty, however, that the condition of stalemate can be changed through science and technology.*

Eisenhower ultimately accepted most of the recommendations of the Killian report. But its members' exhortation that their findings should inspire "a sense of urgency without despair" fell rather flat with the president, who plainly felt neither urgency nor despair in confronting the problems of defense. A month after he received the Killian report, Eisenhower made the widely quoted observation about nuclear weapons that in "the case of strictly military targets and for strictly military purposes," he could "see no reason why they shouldn't be used just exactly as you would use a bullet or anything else."[19]

The bravado of that offhand remark belied Eisenhower's personal feelings on the subject of nuclear war. The same month he compared nuclear weapons and bullets, the president declared that there was a time "when a lead is not significant in the defensive arrangements of a country." "If you get enough of a particular type of weapon," he reflected, "I doubt that it is particularly important to have a lot more of it."[20] It was only because of the weapon's "psychological importance," Eisenhower said later, that he had decided to approve the Killian report's recommendation on speeding up development of the ICBM. He still intended to hold the missile program to only a fraction of what the Air Force wanted, the president told aides in confidence.[21]

Privately, Eisenhower regarded the course of the arms race with mounting concern. That race had shown a steady, almost geometrical, increase in both the number and the power of the weapons that were both its object and its result. And yet, paradoxically, as the grim calculus of destruction grew ever more inflated, so too did the amount of devastation that experts imagined the nations could endure.

From the original twenty Russian cities on the Air Force's 1946 target list, the number of places in the Soviet Union on which atomic or hydrogen bombs would be dropped in a war had swollen only a decade later to nearly three thousand. What in 1948 had been deemed sufficient to bring about a Soviet "collapse" was, a few years later, only a small fraction of the destruction that would be visited upon Russia in order for the United States to "prevail" in a nuclear war. Curiously, the fact that multimegaton hydrogen bombs gradually replaced the kiloton-size atomic bombs of earlier war plans seemed to have virtually no effect upon the ever-increasing number of bombs in the inventory and targets on the list.[22]

A similar inflationary phenomenon occurred in calculations of how much destruction the United States and its society might survive. Here, too, the magnifying effect of the Super was evidently ignored. In 1948, Jerrold Zacharias had not thought it possible for the nation to survive more than a hundred atomic bombs dropped on it. Two years later, Paul Nitze in drafting NSC-68 had calculated the "year of maximum danger"—1954—from his estimate of when the Russians would be able to drop two hundred atomic bombs on the United States. In 1952, the report of Oppenheimer's Disarmament Panel—which had warned of the tendency of Americans to think of nuclear war as a "one-sided conflict"—concluded that the nation would probably be unable to endure the destruction caused by the six hundred to fifteen hundred atomic bombs that the Russians were expected to have in their arsenal after "a few years." In 1955, the Killian report confirmed that the Soviets probably not only had that number of bombs already in their stockpile, but that their arsenal now included hydrogen bombs, which in a few more years could be carried by rockets to targets in the United States.[23]

The effect of this awful, apocalyptic cadence upon Eisenhower was cumulative. A few months after he received the Killian report, the president spoke to the National Security Council of the "chaos and destruction" that a nuclear war would mean for the country. So widespread would be the devastation, Eisenhower said, that only the Army would be able to restore order in its aftermath, and the country's democratic institutions might never recover.[24]

It was presumably with these dire facts in mind that the president, soon after the Killian report, undertook the effort of opening what he termed "a tiny gate in the disarmament fence." Eisenhower's "Open Skies" proposal actually grew out of a recommendation from another presidential commission of experts. The Quantico Vulnerability Panel—so called because it met on the grounds of the Marine base in Virginia—was composed of administration figures and nonscientists given the task of identifying ways that the United States might exploit the Soviets' diverse vulnerabilities. A related concern of the group was with proposals that Eisenhower might make to Soviet leaders at the upcoming summit meeting in Geneva.

Headed by Nelson Rockefeller, the Quantico panel had been quick to conclude that foremost among the Soviets' vulnerable spots was their mania about preserving Russia as a closed society. It was equally obvious to the panel that the inaugural flight of the U-2 scheduled for the coming year was likely to compound the Soviets' paranoia.

Overruling opposition from the Air Force's representative on the panel, the majority of its members recommended that Eisenhower gain some diplomatic leverage from the U-2. Specifically, they urged that he propose in advance of the spy plane's maiden flight that the U.S. and Russia exchange blueprints of their respective military bases and allow reciprocal overflights without interference.

Virtually all on the panel expected the Russians to turn down the offer. Open Skies, they recognized, would offer a "decided intelligence advantage" to the United States—which was already, by comparison, an open book to Soviet intelligence. ("I see what you fellows are doing—you are trying to open up the Soviet Union," exclaimed the joint chiefs' chairman, Admiral Arthur Radford, when the proposal was explained to him.) A Russian rejection of the proposal, on the other hand, would disarm the "peace offensive" that the administration feared the Soviets might launch at the summit. Such a rejection, some thought, could well force the president to approve the dramatic increase in military spending that Walt Rostow and others on the panel were urging, but that Eisenhower had thus far resisted.[25]

To the great surprise of the panel's membership, Eisenhower proved to be "deadly serious" about Open Skies, according to Rostow.[26] The president even departed from his prepared remarks at the opening meeting of the July summit to make the proposal personally—a dramatic and uncharacteristic *coup de théâtre* for Eisenhower that was given an unexpected touch when a freak summer thunderstorm drowned out the president's closing words and suddenly plunged the conference room into darkness.

Despite Eisenhower's earnest intent, the Russians summarily dismissed the Open Skies proposal as "a bald espionage plot." Nikita Khrushchev's response later caused Eisenhower to conclude lamentingly that the Russians were "short-sighted" and determined *at all costs to keep the U.S.S.R. a closed society.*" But at the time the president, even though discouraged, had not yet entirely given up hope for an agreement in Geneva. According to Rostow's account, following the formal adjournment of the summit Eisenhower and his interpreter "rushed down the corridors of the Palais des Nations to the Soviet delegation offices for one more try." Fatefully, the Russians had already left.[27]

The Soviet rejection of Open Skies at the Geneva summit did not lead, as Rostow and others had hoped, to a decision by Eisenhower to increase defense spending. But it did reveal once again—and accentuate—the differences between the president and John Foster Dulles on the subject of the Russians and the nuclear arms race. Dulles at one point had tried to dissuade the Quantico panel from even making its recommendation to Eisenhower —believing, he told a friend, that the president was "so inclined to be humanly generous, to accept a superficial tactical smile as evidence of inner warmth, that he might in a personal moment with the Russians accept a promise or a proposition at face value and upset the apple cart."[28]

Behind Dulles' opposition to Open Skies was both a deep-seated fear and a guarded hope. His hope was that the United States—if willing, in his words, "to run the full mile" in the arms competition with Russia—might be able decisively to outdistance its opponent.[29] The notion that America, because of its superior economic and technological position, would be able to win the arms race with the Soviets had been present in NSC-68. It was evident as well in the thinking of some of the members of the Quantico panel. But Dulles was perhaps the most outspoken among those in the Eisenhower administration to advocate the position that victory could be gained either by getting so far ahead as to persuade the Russians to abandon the contest or by running the Soviet economy into the ground.

At one point Dulles' opposition to Open Skies had led him to consider resigning from the administration if the Russians accepted the proposal. He might "have to be the Devil at Geneva," the secretary of state told a confidant. But the fact that the Russians had preempted that role at the summit made Dulles' sacrifice unnecessary.

In the wake of the summit's failure and the subsequent collapse of what was briefly thought of as "the spirit of Geneva," Eisenhower reluctantly gave his approval for the first of the ultrasecret U-2 flights over Russia. The premier flight of the spy plane the following November effectively closed the question of Open Skies for some time to come.[30]

11

Staring into the Abyss

The attack on the New Look that began shortly into Eisenhower's first term intensified after his reelection. Critics charged that the administration's threat of massive retaliation against unspecified acts of Soviet aggression had ceased to be credible once the Russians, too, had hydrogen bombs in quantity. They complained as well that the war-hero president was reluctant to spend enough on the conventional forces that offered an alternative to the use of nuclear weapons. Eisenhower's opponents claimed either that he was running the wrong arms race or was unwilling to run one at all.

With the publication of his 1956 *Foreign Affairs* article on the contradiction between the government's "declaratory" policy and its "action" policy on defense, Paul Nitze officially became one such critic. He explicitly rejected the notion that Eisenhower had increasingly come to accept—namely, Nitze wrote, "that an 'atomic stalemate' has developed or is about to develop" between the United States and Russia. American military superiority could be maintained "indefinitely," Nitze argued, so long as the nation's alliances and its resolve remained strong.[1]

Albert Wohlstetter was another authority on nuclear weapons who had become progressively more concerned with the Eisenhower administration's evident complacency in the face of the Russian threat. Wohlstetter felt a growing frustration that the government and the military had at best only partially heeded his warnings concerning the nation's perilous vulnerability. Like Nitze, he felt that the threat contained in massive retaliation was already hollow, and that the administration's rigid adherence to the nuclear strategy of the New Look was a sign of its intellectual bankruptcy. The nuclear balance that seemed to be coming into existence between the United States and Russia, Wohlstetter argued, was not stable and enduring, as the administration seemed to believe, but tenuous and fragile. Retaliation to a Soviet attack would almost certainly not be massive, he felt he had proved. Indeed, it might not be forthcoming at all.

Wohlstetter was aware that there was some sympathy for his views within the administration—particularly from Air Force officers in the Pentagon, and among members of the Joint Chiefs of Staff. Twice those who had heard his presentation on strategic vulnerability had tried to arrange for Wohlstetter to brief the president himself. But each time the opportunity had been denied at a higher level.

Wohlstetter blamed those around Eisenhower for shielding him from the ominous truth. Assistant Secretary of Defense Donald Quarles—who coined the term "sufficiency" to describe the goal of the administration's military policy—had been one of the obstacles to his briefing of the president. Quarles evidently thought the conclusions of the Rand basing studies unduly pessimistic and alarmist. The reason he gave for denying Wohlstetter's request to brief the president supposedly concerned the state of Eisenhower's health: he, Quarles, allegedly feared that the president—who had recently suffered a heart attack—might find Wohlstetter's revelations about the vulnerability of SAC too shocking to be borne.[2] It was, Wohlstetter later said, "a really bad moment" to realize that he could not tell the president of the United States about the impending danger of nuclear war.

The threat of nuclear war had hardly passed from Eisenhower's concerns. In the spring of 1957 he approved the formation of yet another commission of experts to study the problem of defense. Eisenhower's decision to create a new blue-ribbon panel came about in part because of the constant urgings of critics both inside and outside the administration that he increase defense spending to counter the Soviet threat. But the step had not necessarily meant any change from the growing pessimism with which Eisenhower had come to regard the prospects of surviving a nuclear war. That attitude had been reaffirmed following a 1955 briefing that the president received at the Pentagon. The presentation concluded that there would be "no significant difference in the losses we would take" if the Soviets attacked only military targets in the United States, Eisenhower told aides. "It would literally be a business of digging ourselves out of the ashes, starting again," he noted disconsolately.[3]

The following year Eisenhower asked the members of the National Security Council to contemplate the consequences when "we reach a point where we will have passed the limits of what human beings can endure."[4] The response of the council had been to propose a $40-billion system of shelters and other measures to protect the civilian population from nuclear attack. Similar studies sponsored or undertaken by the Rockefeller Foundation, Herman Kahn at Rand, and the MIT summer study code-named "East River" had earlier made the case for shelters.[5]

The 1957 "Security Resources Panel" appointed by Eisenhower was headed by California attorney and Rand board chairman Rowen Gaither. The president had intended the panel to consider only the narrowly defined subject of civil defense and shelters. But the nature of its members' concerns virtually guaranteed that they would extend their charter to include a wholesale reassessment of the administration's military policy. Prominent among those chosen by Gaither and his steering committee, therefore, were many critics of that policy.

Among the nearly one hundred experts assembled by the Gaither committee were the early veterans of Los Alamos and alumni of summer studies like Charles and Vista—including Isidor Rabi, Jerome Wiesner, James Killian, Herbert York, and Spurgeon Keeny. The New Look's critics among the strategists were equally well represented on the panel in the persons of Nitze, Wohlstetter, and Andrew Marshall. When Gaither took a leave of absence from the committee for reasons of health, his place was taken by a Boston defense contractor who was chairman of the NSC's Security Resources Board, Robert Sprague. Significantly, Nitze was Sprague's choice to write the committee's final report to the president.[6]

As the panel expanded in size, so did the scope of its study. Wiesner remembered how the Gaither committee "grew like a cancer" once its members decided to broaden the subject of their inquiry. Their inspiration, he recalled, was the question Eisenhower posed when he first assembled the group at the White House. "If you make the assumption that there is going to be a nuclear war," the president had asked the experts, "what should I do?"

From Eisenhower's broad injunction there had been an "almost infinite regression," Wiesner said, in the questions the committee decided to focus its attention upon. The initial consideration of building shelters spread to measures that might be taken to protect the nation's missiles and bombers as well as its citizens. A related concern became what kind of weapons— offensive or defensive—the military budget should buy. But, Keeny noted, there was at least one common theme that united the group's search for solutions. "The emphasis," he said, "was on solving it technologically."

Perhaps because Nitze would have the largest role in drafting the Gaither committee's final report, both its language and its argument paralleled that of his earlier tocsin of alarm, NSC-68. The Gaither report even included a subtle recasting—and rescheduling—of Nitze's idea of the year of maximum danger. Warning of "an increasing threat which may become critical in 1959 or early 1960," the Gaither report identified that threat as the unexpectedly early development by the Russians of the ICBM—a weapon category in which the Soviets already "probably surpassed us," the experts concluded gloomily. The looming specter of a surprise Soviet missile attack prompted the Gaither committee to urge extensive and immediate steps to protect the nation's retaliatory forces and its citizens—steps that might cost as much as $50 billion over the following few years.[7]

There was a stark contrast between the conclusion of the Gaither report

—titled "Deterrence and Survival in the Nuclear Age"—and the findings of
Killian's panel just two years before. Gone entirely from the Gaither panel's
recommendation was Killian's call "for a sense of steady confidence without
complacency, a sense of urgency without despair." The country, the Gaither
report hinted, was now tottering on the brink. "If we fail to act at once,"
it advised, "the risk, in our opinion, will be unacceptable." "It was like
looking into the abyss and seeing Hell at the bottom," former defense
secretary Robert Lovett said of reading the report.[8]

Significantly, the committee's dire prognosis accepted implicitly Wohlstetter's warnings about the critical vulnerability of SAC. The briefing that
the Rand strategist had never been allowed to give the president was presented instead to the attentive experts on the committee, who made its
warning of strategic vulnerability a central premise of their report. Wohlstetter remembered how both Nitze and Sprague had been "visibly affected" by
the briefing. Neither, he thought, had hitherto been fully aware of the
dimensions of the danger facing the country.

Sprague, in fact, had already witnessed what seemed to be tangible evidence of Wohlstetter's thesis when a SAC mock alert at which he was an
observer turned into a debacle. General LeMay's effort to reassure Sprague
that the slip-up was not as worrisome as it seemed—since SAC was planning
to land the first blow in any case—unwittingly added to Sprague's unease.[9]
But Wohlstetter thought the turning point of Sprague's conversion on the
question of vulnerability—and the dénouement of the Gaither study—had
occurred when Sprague called those who knew the most about the subject
into his office at the Pentagon to resolve the controversy.

Present there, besides Sprague and Wohlstetter, were LeMay and the
director of a twenty-six-volume study on continental air defense recently
completed by the Army. The Army report had concluded that SAC and the
nation were actually at little risk of being caught on the ground by a Soviet
sneak attack. "How is it possible to say what you say?" Sprague asked
Wohlstetter after the Army's representative had presented his report. Wohlstetter replied that the difference between his view and the Army's concerned the amount of time it would take for SAC's bombers to become
airborne—an interval he claimed was much longer than the Army's estimate.

This answer prompted Sprague to ask another question of the men around
him: "If war broke out today, how long would it take for SAC's bombers
to get off?"

"Forty-five minutes" was the Army officer's unhesitating reply.

LeMay, who until this moment had observed the debate in silence,
removed the ever-present cigar stub from his mouth only long enough to say
the two words that Wohlstetter thought finally settled the argument:

"Nine hours."

. . .

The climactic showdown over the vulnerability question that preceded Sprague's conversion and the Gaither committee's final report acquired even greater significance because of the Soviets' launching of the world's first artificial satellite, *Sputnik,* only the month before. Like the outbreak of the Korean War in the wake of NSC-68, the advent of *Sputnik* in October of 1957—combined with the successful Soviet test of an ICBM the previous summer—gave an accidental, if especially timely, impetus to the conclusions of the Gaither report.[10]

Yet neither *Sputnik* nor the Soviet missile came as a complete surprise to most of those on the Gaither panel. The Russian government had some time before announced its intention of launching a satellite, and the Gaither committee was quietly informed of the missile test shortly before it occurred by one of their own members—Richard Bissell, the man in charge of CIA's U-2 program. As head of the CIA's clandestine services directorate, Bissell said he had warned agency director Allen Dulles early in the Eisenhower administration that "one of these days the Russians are going to put something in orbit." Bissell told Dulles that the satellite would probably have little military significance, but that it "would have tremendous psychological impact" on the West.

The reaction of the Gaither panel's experts to Russia's technological achievements was, accordingly, one less of shock than of frustration. Rand's representatives had reason to be particularly nonplussed. A 324-page Rand study of 1946 had not only anticipated earth-orbiting manmade satellites but even predicted that the first nation to launch one would score a significant psychological coup with world public opinion. (Rand's rivals among the scientists from MIT on the Gaither panel had no cause for self-congratulation either. A study that some of their number had done for the Air Force on what the world might look like twenty years hence—completed the week of *Sputnik*'s launching—had all but ignored the possibility of space exploration.[11])

In *Sputnik*'s aftermath it was plainly the hope and probably also the expectation of administration critics on the Gaither panel that the alarmist tone of their report would awaken in Eisenhower a new urgency in responding to the Soviet threat. Most expected the same affirmative, almost unquestioning response that Truman had given to NSC-68 seven years before, in what now seemed remarkably similar circumstances. The response to the present danger then had doubled the nation's defense budget in little more than a year.

The reincarnation of that threat in 1957 was said by Gaither's experts to justify another redoubling, and contained the almost certain prospect of other increases to come. Consequently, the Gaither report urged that Eisenhower not only embark upon construction of a vast civilian shelter program but that he likewise approve virtually every military proposal ever to have been the subject of a summer study or a Rand contract. Privately, at least a few of the panel's members felt even that did not go far enough. So pessimistic were they about holding the lead in the arms race that they quietly asked Eisenhower to reconsider the possibility of a preventive war against Russia while the United States was still ahead.[12]

Given the public's image of *Sputnik* as the latest manifestation of the Russian threat, the response of Eisenhower and Dulles to the formal presentation of the Gaither report at a White House meeting of early November 1957 was surprisingly negative. Nitze characterized the reaction of the president and his secretary of state there as, simply, "not helpful." Throughout the long briefing, Eisenhower sat silently, a notepad balanced on his knee. Dulles—apparently having second thoughts about running "the full mile" —aggressively questioned the usefulness of the committee's recommendations and, just as avidly, their cost.[13]

Wiesner, who was also present in the Oval Office that afternoon, particularly remembered a comment by Eisenhower at the end of the briefing, after he had thanked the members of the Gaither committee for their efforts over the previous six months. Recalling that his instructions to them had been to recommend the course of action he should take if there was going to be a nuclear war, Eisenhower said that he now realized he had asked the wrong question. "You can't have this kind of war," the president declared matter-of-factly. "There just aren't enough bulldozers to scrape the bodies off the streets."

Eisenhower's comment was, Wiesner reflected, "a real sea change" for the president. It was also the inspiration, he said, for a fundamental shift in his own thinking, and that of several others on the Gaither committee. The recommendations of the Gaither report had actually been unanimous, made without any sign of dissent. But in its aftermath the report was questioned, Wiesner said, by many of its authors. While suppressed by them at the time, those doubts remained unstilled.

In the course of the Gaither study, Wiesner had gone even further than Wohlstetter in urging that SAC bases be ringed by antiaircraft and antimissile missiles as a hedge against surprise attack. Wohlstetter concluded that such countermeasures were impractical. As his study of the problems of vulnerability and surprise attack progressed, however, Wiesner was impressed in a way he had not been during Project Charles with the difficulties of trying to defend against atomic attack. It was, he said, not so much the material cost of the Gaither experts' advice on how to prepare for a nuclear war that caused him to question its utility, but rather what seemed to be the inherent futility of defense. It was the latter, Wiesner claimed, that he and a few other colleagues on the panel "never got over": "I couldn't comprehend the usefulness of the difference between forty or fifty million and eighty or ninety million dead." Behind the premises contained in their report, Wiesner thought, was a hidden fallacy. "It became clear that if you were certain that war was going to occur you'd take a lot of costly steps. But even then you couldn't do much."

It was the human as well as the social costs of preparing for a nuclear war that finally changed Wiesner's mind. A turning point in his attitudes occurred in the course of one briefing on civil defense, when Rand analyst Herman Kahn had suggested that the residents of Manhattan might emerge from thousand-foot-deep shelters after a nuclear war and resume something like their normal lives. "We became increasingly convinced," Wiesner said, "that the distortion of society would be such no one would tolerate it."

Spurgeon Keeny had by this time reached a similar conclusion. Keeny, too, was struck by the seemingly insurmountable problems faced by defense, and by the impact the committee's recommendations would have had upon American society. "The more I learned of it the less enthusiastic I became about defense," Keeny said. "There was no longer any question but that you would lose the whole society, even though you could save lives." Keeny thought "the complex of technological solutions" that he, Wiesner, and others came up with in the course of the Gaither report had only created greater problems of another dimension.

In retrospect, he believed that the Gaither report represented "the high water mark of the belief that a technological solution could be found." "The whole experience," he said, "left a lot of people with a very bad feeling: Is this really the way to solve the problem? Do you want an underground society—a garrison state?"

As a result of the Gaither committee's work, scientists who had previously worked on developing offensive weapons began to have a new appreciation of the difficulties of defense in the nuclear age. Herbert York, for one, later acknowledged his involvement with the Gaither panel as the inspiration for a major shift in his thinking. Before, as a member of the Teapot Committee on the ICBM, York had counted himself among those urging new and better weapons, and increased spending on defense. After the president's rejection of the panel's findings, however, he started to question his earlier assumptions.

"In the period after the Gaither report," York remembered, "people began to calm down—calmer voices took over." He claimed that as a consequence he "learned nuclear moderation from Dwight Eisenhower."

Another step in this conversion was York's discussions with banker John McCloy, an Eisenhower adviser and a top member of the Gaither panel. Shortly after the committee's report to the president, McCloy had asked York what the alternatives to a defense buildup might be. (McCloy, who over the course of his career would be an adviser to five presidents, professed never to have been overawed by experts or their expertise. He had once learned the secret, he told friends, of making impressions and giving advice. Upon meeting General George Patton during the Second World War, McCloy had asked the celebrated military hero if he had ever read the leather-bound volumes of Clausewitz and Jomini that were conspicuously displayed in his command tent. "Hell, no," Patton had answered. "But it impresses the hell out of the war correspondents.")

His meeting with McCloy, York admitted, was the first occasion when he thought about the alternatives to more weapons "in general terms, as opposed to just putting out fires." He had only realized then "that you're not forgoing a solution by putting limits on what you do," York said. "Because there is no solution—at least no technical solution."

The underlying mood of skepticism and doubt among some members of the Gaither panel was subtly revealed in the report's conclusion that even if all of its recommendations were accepted, "there will be a continuing race between the offense and the defense." "Neither side can afford to lag or fail to match the other's efforts," the report warned. "There will be no end to the technical moves and counter-moves." Given the almost despairing tenor of their vision of the future, it is not surprising that the Gaither report's authors chose to emphasize a present opportunity as an alternative to an accelerated arms race: *"This could be the best time to negotiate from strength, since the U.S. military position vis-à-vis Russia might never be as strong again."*[14]

The fissures of dissent among the experts who wrote the Gaither report would not be evident to the public for some time. But to the experts themselves, the report would seem in retrospect the beginnings of a fundamental change in the attitude of scientists toward the arms race. It was the start, Wiesner said, of his own belief "that there is not only a technological interaction in the arms race, but a political interaction—in which we are the driving force." "People went two ways," Keeny observed of the response to the report. "Either 'the report is right'—or to seeking a political solution."

The most important reader of the Gaither report—Eisenhower—was plainly inclined toward the latter course. Less than a month after the briefing in the Oval Office, the president appointed eighteen of the scientists who had worked on the report—including Killian, Keeny, York, and Wiesner—to a permanent Science Advisory Committee.[15] York thought that Eisenhower had decided upon the committee—and its mission—even earlier. At the end of the Gaither briefing, York said, the president had made a request of him and some of the other scientists. "Why don't you fellows help me with this nuclear test ban?" Eisenhower asked. "Everybody in the Pentagon is against it."

The experts' doubts were responsible for a curious fillip in the Gaither report that seemed out of keeping with its otherwise fervent call to arms. Indeed, it seemed a tacit admission of the arms race's futility. Almost lost in the forty-page report—and perhaps intended only as a needed counterpoint of optimism there—was a reference to "the great importance of a continuing attempt to arrive at a dependable agreement on the limitations of armaments and the strengthening of other measures for the preservation of peace."[16]

Eisenhower had indicated his earnest and continuing interest in that effort by his 1953 speech to the UN, the Open Skies initiative, and his plea that the scientists join him in support of a nuclear testing ban. The idea of such a ban had been proposed to the UN only months after Eisenhower's "Chances for Peace" speech. Popular interest in the ban was aroused later in 1954, when the unexpectedly powerful test of an American hydrogen bomb in the Pacific exposed members of the Japanese fishing boat *Fortunate Dragon* to an errant, fatal cloud of radioactivity. The harmful properties of fallout—little understood even by scientists before the late 1940s—finally became known in the public debate that followed the *Fortunate Dragon* incident. By 1956 the long-term effects of radiation from nuclear testing had become an important issue in that year's presidential campaign, as well as a subject of growing personal interest to Eisenhower.[17] With the formation of the President's Science Advisory Committee, those scientists the president had asked to join him in the campaign for a test ban came to be in the front ranks of that effort.

Natural allies of the scientists were the growing number of academic theorists recently drawn to the study of nuclear strategy. Dubbed "the Charles River Gang" because of their connection with Harvard or MIT, many members of this intellectual alliance—such as Thomas Schelling, Henry Kissinger, and Morton Halperin—were attracted to the topic of nuclear weapons and war, despite the nearly universal feelings of *Angst* it engendered, by the frank allure of a career open to talent.

The study of nuclear strategy had, in their view, reached an intellectual plateau by the middle to late 1950s. Early pioneers among the nuclear strategists like Bernard Brodie had by that time either fled the field in controversy or taken a mandatory vow of silence in choosing to work for Rand and the government. "I discovered it was a wide-open field with room for amateurs like me," Schelling said of his reason for turning from economics to strategy. Schelling's year-long leave of absence from Harvard in 1958 to go to Rand was illustrative of the often symbiotic relationship that had meanwhile developed between the world of academia and the think tank.

Like the majority of atomic scientists, the worldly philosophers of Cambridge regarded disarmament as a noble but wholly unattainable goal. Theirs "was an effort," one said, "to take a long-overdue step toward recognizing the role of military force in the modern world." As a consequence, he accepted the need—and also the worth—"of collaborating with the countries that are potential enemies."

Since this approach not only welcomed but actually sought a stalemate in the nuclear arms race, it understandably proved anathema to those who wished to gain a unilateral advantage in that race, as well as to those whose goal remained nuclear disarmament. But for its proponents—especially those academicians and scientists who had silently recoiled at the implications of the Gaither report—this new realism seemed a fresh and hopeful middle road. It was one that offered an alternative to both blind hope and paralyzing despair; one whose novelty was expressed by its name, which seemed to contain a certain internal tension, if not an outright contradiction —"arms control."

The intellectual roots of the arms control movement would later be traced by some of the atomic scientists among its champions to the initial, tentative efforts of one of their colleagues, Leo Szilard. Szilard had persuaded Albert Einstein in 1939 to sign the letter to President Roosevelt that eventually led to creation of the Manhattan Project. After the war, Szilard personally promoted the cause of the bomb's international control from the lobby of a Washington hotel, culminating with his creation of the Council for a Livable World.

The first privately arranged meeting of Western and Soviet scientists at Pugwash, Nova Scotia, in 1955 had been another such landmark. But the broadening of arms control into an ecumenical cause was most evident in a 1958 Harvard summer seminar on the subject attended by scientists and a broad spectrum of other academics. The publication the following year of the seminar's proceedings in a special edition of *Daedalus*, the journal of the American Academy of Arts and Sciences, sparked a general interest in arms control and represented to some its intellectual coming of age.[18]

What united the academic advocates of arms control with the disgruntled skeptics on the Gaither panel—and divided this group from the panel's enthusiasts—was not a professional or even an entirely political allegiance but a difference of perceptions. The essential distinction between the two groups concerned the degree of belief or doubt that a decisive and lasting advantage in the arms race—perhaps even a victory—was possible. This difference divided those among the Gaither panel who were willing to continue running that race from those who now dedicated themselves to slowing it and making it less dangerous. The self-named "arms controllers" professed disbelief that a meaningful unilateral advantage in nuclear weapons over Russia was possible—or desirable.

To defenders as well as detractors of the Gaither panel, Eisenhower's response to its report was vitally important as a symbol. A concern with demonstrating the national will had been behind the report's recommendation for a multibillion-dollar shelter program. Such a program, it argued, would "symbolize to the nation the urgency of the threat" and "demonstrate to the world our appraisal of the situation and our willingness to cope with it in strength." Similarly, an appendix to the Gaither report had emphasized that steps taken to defend American citizens against attack "would symbolize our *will to survive,* and our understanding of our responsibilities in a nuclear age."[19]

Eisenhower's wholesale rejection of the report at the briefing in the Oval Office had thus been a refutation as well of its stress upon mobilizing public opinion and demonstrating national will—as all who had been present there were doubtless aware. The president's decision to spurn—and later suppress —the top-secret report prompted some among its authors to consider other ways of pressuring Eisenhower into acting upon its recommendations. Reconstituting the Committee on the Present Danger—which had helped persuade Truman to approve the defense buildup urged by NSC-68—was one expedient discussed, but ultimately rejected as likely to appear too partisan.[20]

Instead, in the weeks following Eisenhower's rebuff, details of the report were deliberately leaked to sympathetic journalists and to the administration's foes in Congress. The initially slow dribble of leaks that began in November of 1957 had swollen to a torrent by year's end, culminating in a highly publicized press conference on Capitol Hill sponsored by Eisenhower's congressional critics. The disclosures there were plainly intended to draw public attention to the scarifying conclusions of the Gaither report and to force the president's hand. Particularly highlighted was the report's conclusion that the Russians had "probably already surpassed" the United States in the development of intercontinental ballistic missiles, and would soon have a commanding lead in that area.[21]

The controversial claim gave rise to an evocative expression that had never been used in the actual Gaither report, but that would nonetheless come to haunt Eisenhower for the remainder of his time in office, ultimately capturing the public debate over defense: the "missile gap."

12

The Equal and Opposite Danger

Even before the public controversy over the Gaither report, Eisenhower was aware of substantial opposition to his efforts at arms control. As his comment to York indicated, the president saw the Pentagon as one source of that opposition. But another was within his own administration.

In 1957, during talks at Geneva, the Russians had accepted in principle a restricted version of the Open Skies proposal that Eisenhower had made two years earlier. Under the terms of the revised accord, the Soviets would have been allowed to overfly western Europe and the eastern seaboard of the United States, in exchange for which American overflights of the westernmost part of Russia were to be permitted. At the time the United States was already overflying a large part of the Soviet Union with the U-2.[1]

The reaction of John Foster Dulles to the apparent revival of Open Skies had been to withdraw the earlier American offer and to recall the overeager U.S. representative at Geneva, Harold Stassen. By his action Dulles seemed intent upon rebuffing even symbolic signs of cooperation with the Russians —so-called confidence-building measures.

Subsequent efforts to induce some thaw in the diplomatic cold war with Russia had fared little better. Following years of deadlock between American and Soviet negotiators at Geneva on the subject of a nuclear test ban, however, a Conference of Experts—on the American side composed mostly of representatives from the newly established President's Science Advisory Committee—suddenly seemed to make unexpected progress toward that goal in the summer of 1958. Atomic scientists from both the United States and Russia agreed that a necessary measure for policing a test ban—a means to detect clandestine nuclear explosions—was theoretically feasible, and would require only a few foreign inspectors on each country's soil.[2]

Another encouraging sign at Geneva was the fact that the Russians had departed from their usually obdurate behavior by offering to suspend nuclear testing—albeit after they had completed their latest round of tests. As with the Open Skies proposal, the agreement between the scientists was so unexpected that it took place in a political vacuum. The highest-ranking State Department official at the talks had been a twenty-eight-year-old foreign service officer.[3]

A diplomatic convocation at Geneva in the autumn to follow up on the success of the summer differed entirely in form, substance, and, ultimately, results from the Conference of Experts. "It was a very strange meeting," said Keeny, who had been there as well as at the original gathering in his capacity as one of Eisenhower's science advisers. The swollen assemblage of professional diplomats that composed the Committee of Principals contrasted sharply with the small enclave of scientists meeting the previous summer. The negotiators of East and West maneuvered constantly throughout the fall months and into the winter over how many inspection stations would be allowed in each country to detect forbidden nuclear tests, how many inspectors could be present at each station, and how many suspected violations of the ban constituted proof of cheating.[4]

More summary was the failure of the Soviet-American talks that were held concurrent with the test ban negotiations on reducing the mutual fear of surprise attack.[5] Herbert Scoville, another of the president's science advisers in Geneva, thought that Eisenhower's effort to gain support for arms control by inviting a political spectrum of representatives to the surprise-attack conference had actually foredoomed the result. The United States, Scoville remembered, had fielded "a delegation beyond belief"—but one nonetheless where he felt "Air Force types" had predominated.

Gerard Smith, the president's personal representative at the talks, confirmed that the conference had been "a circus." Like Scoville, Smith thought that the interest of both sides in a propaganda advantage in the talks had undermined the hope of easing tensions. "When all of these commanders arrived in their big Stratofortresses at Geneva air field," Smith recalled, "the Soviets probably thought this was a demonstration of air power."

The man chosen to head the 105-member American delegation to the conference, Albert Wohlstetter, agreed that the unwieldy size of the venture was itself an invitation to disaster, and a cause for parody. "Have you found your opposite number yet among the Albanians?" a colleague jokingly asked him on the conference's opening day. To Wohlstetter, the bloated dimensions of the conference mirrored the unrealistic hopes of its promoters. When the talks collapsed the following January with agreement only on the conference's title, it was with amusement as well as some bitterness that he noted the length of the final communique—it averaged 2.8 words for each of the ten nations represented. But notwithstanding the disappointment that attended its demise, Wohlstetter did see the conference as containing a kind of lesson: it showed the scientists behind the effort, he said, to be "starry-eyed" and "very naïve people who suffered from exaggerated hopes."

Shortly after returning home from Geneva, Wohlstetter published a widely read *Foreign Affairs* article entitled "The Delicate Balance of Terror."[6] Though he subsequently denied that the article's purpose had been to draw attention to his warnings about SAC's potential vulnerability, its effect was to spur the public debate on defense that had begun after the launching of *Sputnik* and the leaking of the Gaither report. The article thus explicitly challenged the contention—first made in the 1952 report of Oppenheimer's Disarmament Panel—that a "strange stability" would inevitably result when both the United States and Russia had large stockpiles of nuclear weapons.

Wohlstetter's concern was that deterrence—far from being inherently stable and even "automatic," as in the public's view—was actually quite fragile, and required "an urgent and continuing effort." His worry was not with a hypothetical missile gap, he took pains to point out, but with what he felt was an impending "deterrence gap" between the United States and Russia. Such a gap, he warned, would expose America's unprotected missiles and bombers to a disarming attack from the Soviet Union. The great danger, Wohlstetter argued, was that the nation would return to its "deep pre-sputnik sleep" as a result of the popular enthusiasm for arms control. Behind the current American mood of complacency, therefore, was an unspoken assumption that "Soviet leaders will be rather bumbling, or better, cooperative."[7]

Varying perceptions of the Russian threat were subtly at the heart of the differences between Wohlstetter and the group of atomic scientists he disparaged as "technologists." The twin dangers of surprise attack and accidental nuclear war were, Wohlstetter admitted, "inseparable." If wars could only begin by accident it would not be necessary to have a system that warned of attack. On the other hand, if surprise attack was the only danger it would merely be necessary to have the warning of an imminent attack automatically trigger the retaliatory blow. "The solution," Wohlstetter argued, "was somewhere in the middle."

At Geneva, Wohlstetter claimed, the scientists had virtually ignored the danger of surprise attack in their single-minded obsession with lessening the danger of accidental war by mutual agreements with the Russians: "It was," he objected, "as if they thought that it was the *United States* that would launch a surprise attack."

The scientists credited their own efforts for the public interest in and early successes of arms control. They attributed Eisenhower's 1958 decision to accept the Soviets' offer of a moratorium on nuclear testing to a combination, therefore, of popular pressure and their own discreet lobbying. "If it hadn't been for the President's Science Advisory Committee, arms control wouldn't have gotten anywhere," said Scoville. "The initiative came from the scientific community—especially PSAC," Keeny said of the test ban.

Like Keeny and Scoville, Herbert York considered Wohlstetter's fear of surprise attack exaggerated, and misplaced. "The notion that you have to protect your strategic forces from surprise attack was strongly in the air beginning about 1950 among the technical people," York claimed: "Because of Pearl Harbor you didn't have to discuss the notion of surprise attack. It was in your bones that the Russians are perfidious, that surprise attack is the way wars start, and that appeasement doesn't work."

Another self-professed arms controller, Thomas Schelling, believed it was not the actual threat of a sneak attack, but the mutual *fear* of such an attack that constituted the real danger. A member of the American delegation at the surprise-attack conference, Schelling characterized this unappreciated threat as "the reciprocal fear of surprise attack." Mutual fear was the result, he claimed, of a runaway cycle of "he thinks we think" in the relations of the United States and Russia. The logical progression of that cycle, Schelling argued, put this fear in motion: "he thinks we think he'll attack; so he thinks we shall; so he will; so we must."[8] Nuclear war was less likely to occur as the result of a premeditated bolt from the blue, Schelling felt, than by a desperate decision—fueled by this logic—to strike first in a time of crisis.

The collapse of the surprise-attack conference and the inconclusive wrangling of the test ban negotiations that continued into the winter of 1959 shattered the optimism felt by the arms controllers only the previous summer. At that time the editors of the *Bulletin of Atomic Scientists* had celebrated the involvement of technical experts in the talks at Geneva as "a new approach to the stalemated problems of the arms race," and even "a radical innovation."[9] Since then, that approach had disappointed by its results, and the scientists had increasingly come to blame "politicians" for the failure of arms control. It was perhaps more out of hope for the future of the new decade than in recognition of any tangible progress toward lessening the danger of nuclear war that the *Bulletin*'s editors decided, in 1960, to move the hands of their doomsday clock back five additional minutes from the final hour.

The fate of the Gaither report evidently confirmed Eisenhower's decision to move toward arms control. By every account, the president was furious with those he suspected of leaking the top-secret document. Even after the furor over the report had begun to die down, Eisenhower remained adamantly against the wholesale arms buildup the Gaither panel urged. When told by the joint chiefs in December 1959 that military requirements made it impossible even to consider a cutoff of the production of fissionable materials for bombs—an idea first broached in the Atoms for Peace program—Eisenhower remarked with exasperation that he was "completely unconvinced as to the validity of these so-called requirements."[10]

Earlier in the year, the president had voiced the same skepticism when asked to approve construction of a new nuclear reactor that would produce weapons-grade plutonium. "They are trying to get themselves into an incredible position of having enough to destroy every conceivable target all over the world, plus a three-fold reserve," he complained of the military and its war plans.[11] Eisenhower was increasingly aware that the New Look's early reliance upon nuclear weapons lay behind the services' ever-mounting requirements and budget requests, and the Topsy-like growth of war planning.

Partly in an effort to bring these requests under control, Defense Secretary Thomas Gates instituted in 1960 the idea of a "Single Integrated Operational Plan" to replace the independent and often competing war plans of the military services.[12] The point of the SIOP had been to avoid the wasteful and often gruesome duplication of nuclear war planning, where some targets were assigned a number of bombs sufficient to guarantee their destruction many times over. As with a similar attempt made at the end of the Truman administration, Gates' effort failed by his own admission, and the number of cases of "overkill" had continued to grow. Eisenhower would note with some amazement that the number of bombs the United States planned to drop on Russia in the event of war had increased nearly three-hundredfold between his service as Army chief of staff and the end of his presidency.[13]

Even the principal architect of the nation's massive retaliation strategy, John Foster Dulles, began to regret its excessive reliance upon nuclear weapons and to search for an alternative. Gerard Smith thought that the secretary of state's awakening to the inherent limitations of brinkmanship was both sudden and dramatic. It was, Smith remembered, on November 7, 1958—exactly a year after the briefing on the Gaither report—that Dulles ordered the joint chiefs, the secretary of defense, and the individual service secretaries to assemble at the Pentagon. The secretary of state informed the gathering, according to Smith, that the threat of massive retaliation, though it had worked in the past, was now "a wasting asset." "We would have to move to a new doctrine and to new weapons," Dulles told his audience. "And it was up to the military side of the house to get cracking."

Dulles' remarkable admission came shortly after doctors had diagnosed the cancer that would kill him less than two years later. His successor as secretary of state, Christian Herter, reached a similar conclusion about the country's overreliance upon nuclear weapons after only a brief time in office.[14] But Eisenhower himself—perhaps the first to admit the need for a change—evidently felt constrained from making it by the inherited legacy of the New Look. At the president's request, a year-long study of limited war begun by the members of PSAC in the fall of 1959 was carried out under the assumption that American commanders would not use nuclear weapons of any kind. But Eisenhower ultimately chose to disregard the findings of the study—concluding that "we were unfortunately so committed to nuclear weapons" that the premise they would not be used in a war was "unrealistic."[15]

That Eisenhower still did not question another unremarked assumption of American nuclear planning was quietly evident when he agreed with members of the Gaither committee, after their White House briefing, that "we must not allow the enemy to strike the first blow." As late as January 1960 the president was briefed by Air Force General Nathan Twining, then chairman of the Joint Chiefs of Staff, concerning "certain questions relating to pre-emptive attack under conditions of conclusive advanced warning." Yet, increasingly, Eisenhower's personal concern was more with how to avoid nuclear war—not how to fight one. At the meeting with Twining, for example, he had reiterated his view that "the biggest thing today is to provide a deterrent to war."[16]

During succeeding months, Eisenhower moved in the opposite direction to that pointed out by his critics and in the Gaither report. In March 1960, at a cabinet meeting, he declared that "We have got to try to make some progress somewhere in the disarmament area," specifically citing the need for a test ban. Eisenhower disagreed with the anti-ban advice of CIA deputy director John McCone at that meeting, and indicated instead his willingness to take some risks in order to get a permanent end to the testing of nuclear weapons.[17]

Like many citizens, the president occasionally despaired of the future direction of the arms race—as was plain in a telephone conversation with John Foster Dulles the following month. "How are we ever going to be able to scale our programs down?" Eisenhower had asked rhetorically of the dying Dulles. In "the long run," he concluded, "there is nothing but war —if we give up all hope of a peaceful solution."[18]

At the time he made the comment to Dulles, Eisenhower's own hopes for the test ban and for a solution to the other problems created by the arms race lay in the summit meeting scheduled with Soviet premier Khrushchev the following month in Paris. The planned Paris summit—itself the result of a meeting at Camp David with Khrushchev in the summer of 1959—was meant to be the forum for discussions between the two leaders not only over the test ban, but on such perennial problems in East-West relations as the status of Berlin. State Department papers prepared for the summit indicated that Eisenhower planned to reintroduce the Open Skies proposal there, as well as to discuss unspecified plans for the mutual "reduction of secrecy and suspicions."[19]

The very fact that the president intended to meet with Khrushchev to discuss the test ban had already aroused controversy among the administration's critics, and even within Eisenhower's own circle of advisers. One of those in the first camp, Senator Stuart Symington, charged in Congress as early as the summer of 1958 that the administration "heavily underrated Soviet missile development." Citing secret CIA estimates, Symington claimed that the Russians were likely to have a force of up to five hundred ICBMs two years hence, when the United States would have a mere two dozen.[20]

Eisenhower had initially felt that twenty to forty ICBMs would be a sufficient addition to the nation's deterrent force. The day after the launching of *Sputnik,* however, he had doubled that number to eighty. Mounting domestic pressure to increase U.S. missile production in subsequent months prompted the president to raise this figure to two hundred and, later, four hundred missiles. But Eisenhower consistently rejected pleas that he consider further increases—even in the face of Secretary Gates' blunt warning that he and other administration figures "were being subjected to severe attack and were receiving little support or defense" for their stand against more missiles. Angered when he learned that the Air Force and SAC were still appealing his decision on the missiles at the end of his administration, the president had finally exploded in exasperation: "Why don't we go completely crazy and plan on a force of 10,000?"[21]

In private, Eisenhower admitted he was temperamentally disinclined to believe claims of significant military or technological "gaps." As evidence of how such hypothetical threats had been overblown in the past he could cite the case of the celebrated "bomber gap"—where the Russians, after introducing the prototypes of two new bombers at a May Day fly-by, had produced only a fraction of the planes that doomsayers warned would soon fill the sky.[22]

But, in fact, Eisenhower also knew much more than his critics—and even many supposed experts—about the Russians' missile program.

After an inaugural flight over eastern Europe in early 1956 to test the spy plane's cameras, the U-2 had completed five missions over Russia by the end of 1957. The first overflight of the Soviet Union had taken the plane directly over Moscow and Leningrad—an audacious move that stunned even Dulles. Another had flown along the Baltic coast, and one had penetrated deep into the airspace of southern Russia. A Soviet diplomatic protest concerning the overflights brought a temporary grounding of the U-2, but the plane had taken to the air again by the time the Gaither committee began its deliberations.[23]

In spite of the fact that a member of the committee, Richard Bissell, was head of the U-2 project, others on the committee were not made aware of the sensitive intelligence gathered by the plane's cameras and electronic sensors. Indeed, they were not even informed of the spy plane's existence— which was evidently kept a secret from all but those who ran the program, the president, the Dulles brothers, and Vice-President Nixon.

The U-2's early missions uncovered few surprises about Soviet military strength.[24] Though the Russians' ability to track the plane proved "better than we had hoped," according to Bissell, they were unable to shoot it down. A significant find came early in 1957, when one overflight accidentally discovered a Soviet missile test center at Tyuratam in central Russia. Analysis by the CIA's photointerpreters disclosed that the few liquid-fueled rockets seen on test stands at the site were not operational ICBMs, but probably represented the kernel of a missile force then under development.

On the basis of the U-2's pictures and other information the CIA possessed relating to Russia's industrial potential, the agency's National Intelligence Estimates Board predicted that the Soviets might have a dozen operational ICBMs by 1960—a number that would allow them to hit each of the twelve bomber bases in the United States before SAC could launch its planes. The "very terrifying prospect" that he and others at the CIA envisioned, Bissell said, was "that the Russians would have a fair number of a weapon when we didn't have any." While Bissell admitted that the information behind this estimate was "still very incomplete" by 1957, it was his and the CIA's assumption "that the Russians would move just as fast as they could" to build the ICBMs they had tested which underlay the desperate prognosis of a missile gap.

Few in the Eisenhower administration were initially inclined to challenge the CIA assessment. Members of the President's Science Advisory Committee, including Herbert York and Jerome Wiesner, had been among the first to warn of an impending missile threat. As the U-2 overflights failed to confirm the existence of a gap, however, doubts grew. Wiesner began to question the CIA's premise after he asked an agency analyst how many missiles the Russians were capable of building in the next few years. "Ten thousand" had been the reply. In retrospect, Wiesner realized that he and others in the administration had been asking the wrong question of the CIA's experts. The important unknown was how many missiles the Russians were *likely* to build.

The difficulty skeptics had was in trying to prove a negative hypothesis. "There was no evidence that there was no missile gap," York noted. "It was the reverse of that." It was the failure to find evidence of a missile gap that gradually made a skeptic of York and others in the Eisenhower administration.

Like York, most experts were guarded in expressing doubts about the missile gap. The head of Eisenhower's science advisers, George Kistiakowsky—the physicist who had jumped for joy at Trinity—discreetly marveled to colleagues at how "leisurely and relaxed" the Soviet missile program seemed to be.[25] The slow pace of Russian ICBM development contradicted not only the CIA's expectations but Khrushchev's boast that his nation was turning out rockets "like sausages." Others took the failure to find a gap as itself a foreboding sign. One Pentagon analyst who studied the U-2 photographs found the absence of Russian rockets "interesting and disturbing." If the Soviets were not building ICBMs, he wondered, then what *were* they building?

The possibility raised by the Air Force that the Russians might have skillfully hidden their missiles from the prying eyes of the U-2 created pressure for more overflights. But as early as 1959, Eisenhower himself had evidently joined the ranks of skeptics about the gap. He mused to members of PSAC that the Russians might be having the same problems with their missiles that the United States was then encountering with its own. The president's skepticism blossomed into openly expressed doubt shortly thereafter, when Eisenhower assured Killian "that the Soviets were not as strong as many claimed."[26]

By early 1960 he and others among the science advisers were "internally convinced," York said, that there simply was no missile gap. But there remained "a genuine ambiguity" in the administration about the gap, he remembered, as a result of the fact that the U-2 had never been able to photograph all of Russia, owing to persistent cloud cover and the limitations of its range. Only gradually had the doubters come to outnumber the believers.

In January 1960, the CIA finally acknowledged that its initial assumption of a Russian crash effort to build ICBMs had been in error. The Soviets, the CIA reported, evidently decided not to mass-produce the type of missile tested in 1957. Instead, they had moved on to the development of a second-generation ICBM. By that fall the Pentagon's analysts concurred with the CIA's revised estimate. In the spring of 1960, Eisenhower could even point to the Soviet missile program as evidence of America's technological superiority. "The one thing they have done is to use for space exploration engines which they originally built for missiles because they did not have good, small warheads," he observed at a cabinet breakfast. "We found out, however, how to make small warheads and therefore did not need to build the big engine," Eisenhower said.[27]

By that summer, moreover, pictures from the CIA's new Discoverer satellite had begun to supplant the still inconclusive evidence gathered by the U-2. Unlike the spy plane, the high-resolution cameras in orbit were able to photograph all of Russia in the space of a single day. The photographs gained by the CIA's satellite program, Project Corona, strengthened the case against the missile gap. Like the U-2 project, however, very few outside a select number in the administration and the CIA knew of the existence of Corona.[28] (The satellites were not a secret from the Russians, of course. The first successful launching of a Discoverer in August 1960 followed thirteen consecutive failures caused, Bissell said, "by every kind of malfunction." One of the satellites unexpectedly fell to earth near Spitzbergen, Norway. "We had a cow over that," Bissell remembered. The satellite was never found, and the CIA concluded that it might have been picked up by the Russians.)

As a former military man, Eisenhower may have been particularly reluctant to divulge state secrets. Whatever the reason, the president persistently refused to disclose why he lacked concern over the missile gap and why he was unwilling to increase defense spending dramatically—despite repeated importunings from others in his administration. When the government came under public attack in Congress during February 1960 for "complacency, introduction of politics into Defense affairs, and with having downgraded our intelligence"—the result of its lowering of the estimate for Soviet missiles in line with the CIA's revised report of the preceding month—Eisenhower simply made light of the charges at a meeting with administration defense officials. On that occasion he protested that "some other people are talking too much." According to the minutes of the meeting, Eisenhower "stated with vehemence that he has been opposed to giving such detailed figures to Congressional groups—particularly those whose only interest seems to be to misuse them and misrepresent their meaning." (He evidently even included in this category the head of the CIA, Allen Dulles. Eisenhower confessed to being "very troubled" by "the indication that Mr. Dulles may be giving too many figures to Congress.")[29]

Repeated protests came from the Pentagon—especially the Air Force—that there remained undiscovered phalanxes of Soviet missiles. For those who continued to claim that the Soviets had hundreds or even thousands of ICBMs hidden across the trackless Russian steppes or underneath the arctic tundra, the missile gap was not myth but an article of faith.

One of Eisenhower's science advisers professed to having been "appalled" when, during a visit by government officials to SAC headquarters in Omaha, General Thomas Power trooped the entire delegation into a vault to show the most recent pictures taken by Discoverer. Power had pointed out to his audience where in the pictures he thought Russian missiles might be hidden. The amazing thing about the incident, recalled the scientist, was not only the breach of security involved—no one there besides him and Power was supposed to know of the satellite's existence—but the fact that the sites identified by the SAC commander as clandestine launching pads for Soviet ICBMs included grain silos, haystacks, and even vacant fields.

It was perhaps with the hope of silencing such claims—and finally exploding the missile gap as a myth—that Eisenhower in the spring of 1960 approved a final U-2 mission just before the Paris summit. The area to be photographed in the mission included a part of Russia where there was rumored to be a new bomber or ICBM base. The suspected location had always either been shrouded by clouds or out of the U-2's range during previous overflights. The "important information" that the spy plane sought, Secretary of State Herter later observed delphically, "was likely to be unavailable at a later date."[30] What was fated to be the last mission of the U-2 over the Soviet Union began when one of the spy planes took off from Turkey in cloudless weather, headed for the Russian city of Sverdlovsk.

As Eisenhower himself surely realized, there were a multitude of ironies surrounding the collapse of the Paris summit. He had looked forward to the meeting as "the culminating act" of his presidency. But the shooting down of the spy plane on May 1, only a matter of days before the planned meeting with Khrushchev, became the ostensible reason for the Russians' cancellation of the summit. Eisenhower had recognized in the wake of the Soviet rejection of Open Skies how the uncertainty that the Russians were able to create in the West about their military capabilities was their most jealously guarded advantage. The fact that the U-2 had been able to pierce the veil of secrecy—and to reassure Eisenhower that the United States had not fallen behind the Russians—made the scheduling of the summit possible.

Significantly, Eisenhower's concern with the U-2 program had grown to the point where, in December 1958, he "questioned continuation of the overflight reconnaissance program" in a meeting with his intelligence advisers. According to the minutes of that meeting, the president's worry was not only that one of the planes might be shot down, but that the program itself —whose military application was now certainly clear to the Russians— interfered with his effort to improve Soviet-American relations. The question which he was facing, Eisenhower told the group, "is whether the intelligence which we receive from this source is worth the exacerbation of international tension which results." It was the president's view that "we have located adequate targets." But Eisenhower's feeling that "there should be a reevaluation of the U-2 program as such" was not endorsed by representatives of the CIA and Air Force—who insisted that "the intelligence is highly worthwhile."[31]

By confronting Khrushchev with the possibility that his bluff might be called on the missiles at Paris, the U-2 may subtly have led to the summit's undoing. A State Department assessment of Khrushchev's reasons for scuttling the meeting concluded, therefore, that the Soviet leader had probably already decided not to go to Paris—and only used the U-2 incident as a convenient pretext.[32]

Even after the U-2's existence became public knowledge, Eisenhower continued to reject appeals from within his own administration to expose the missile gap as chimerical. The president pointedly ignored Herter's urging that he "let the Soviets know we know" by releasing the information gained in the overflights. Eisenhower likewise rebuffed presidential candidate Nixon's desperate plea that he announce "there is no intelligence gap just as there is no deterrent gap."[33]

In retrospect, Jerome Wiesner thought that Eisenhower at the end of his term simply preferred a less direct way to let the world know the truth about the missile gap. Having served since 1958 as a science adviser to Eisenhower, Wiesner was "astounded," he said, when the president approved a request from candidate John Kennedy that the scientist join the Democrat's 1960 campaign. In his dual capacity as adviser to both the Republican president and the Democratic presidential candidate, Wiesner was admonished by Eisenhower not to divulge any classified information about Soviet or American military capabilities. But Wiesner thought that the president's real intentions were clear.

Despite the fading of his hopes for a final meeting with the Soviet leader, Eisenhower had long since cast his lot with those advisers who were urging an attempt at controlling the arms race and easing the tensions of the Cold War. Scientists like York, Wiesner, and Keeny saw the turning point as the president's summons to them in the wake of the Gaither report to help in the effort for a nuclear test ban. This explained the seeming paradox contained in Eisenhower's warning in his farewell address about the "unwarranted influence" of a "military-industrial complex" upon national policy. But virtually unnoticed in that same speech was Eisenhower's expression of concern with "the equal and opposite danger that public policy could itself become the captive of a scientific-technological elite." Keeny thought that this comment referred specifically to those who had leaked the Gaither report.

The culminating irony of Eisenhower's presidency was the fact that he himself had done more than anyone else to raise the role of experts and expertise to prominence in the government, with his creation of the President's Science Advisory Committee and of special panels like those headed by Killian and Gaither. By the end of his two terms, Eisenhower had seemingly come to regret his reliance upon experts—but the process by which the latter had risen to influence already seemed irreversible.

In Wiesner, York, Keeny, and others, the scientists' role recognized by Eisenhower would grow in importance during the administration of John Kennedy—whose victory in the 1960 campaign was due in substantial part to concern with the missile gap and to Kennedy's charges of the Republicans' alleged malfeasance in providing for the nation's defense. Prominent as well in Kennedy's campaign and later in his administration would be those theorists who at Rand had been among the earliest and most persistent critics of the nation's nuclear strategy.

During the fifteen years since the dawn of the atomic age this nucleus of experts had for the most part merely witnessed the making of strategy and policy on the bomb. They had remained on the sidelines of the great national debate over defense.

Henceforth, they would be at its center.

PART TWO

CRUSADERS

We are abstract, and therefore cruel.
—DOSTOEVSKY,
The Brothers Karamazov

13

Accidental Judgments,
Casual Slaughters

The first few weeks of the New Frontier were—appropriately enough—a time of discovery.

One of the earliest and most startling revelations came to Kennedy's secretary of defense, Robert McNamara. McNamara had been at the Pentagon only four days when a B-52 bomber carrying two twenty-four-megaton hydrogen bombs disintegrated in flight over North Carolina. Five of the eight-member crew parachuted to safety, and the parachute on one of the bombs floated it also gently to earth. The other bomb, however, fell unimpeded from the wrecked plane and broke apart upon impact, pieces of it penetrating more than fifty feet into the soggy farmland.

An investigation showed that five of six safety devices designed to prevent the bomb from exploding accidentally had failed at the moment of impact. "Only a single switch prevented the bomb from detonating and spreading fire and destruction over a wide area," one physicist testified at a subsequent hearing.[1]

McNamara learned during the investigation that the crash of the bomber had been only one of scores of such accidents involving nuclear weapons since the start of the atomic age. Two of those prior mishaps had involved the inadvertent launching of short-range American missiles carrying nuclear warheads. The North Carolina incident, by far the most serious nuclear accident to date, prompted McNamara to order new fail-safe interlocks installed on the weapons in the nuclear arsenal. The close call, he admitted, had also profoundly impressed him with the danger of accidental nuclear war.

Only a short time after the B-52 crash, there occurred what McNamara later characterized as "a massive false alarm" at the North American Air Defense Command of a Soviet missile attack on the United States. The false alarm underscored to McNamara the fact that not even new safety switches on the bombs would remove the threat of an accidental nuclear war. What he termed "that great danger" was one of the factors which caused him to decide there was no circumstance under which he as defense secretary would recommend a retaliatory nuclear strike on the evidence of warning alone.

Because of these incidents, in fact, the conviction grew with McNamara that the president should withhold the final authorization for a retaliatory blow even after the first bomb or bombs had fallen on the United States— until he had had a chance to inspect the damage and to communicate personally with Russian leaders.

The North Carolina accident and the false alarm at NORAD headquarters brought home to the novice defense secretary a danger whose dimension he had hitherto not appreciated—the threat of a nuclear war caused by inadvertence. Less than a month after going to the Pentagon, McNamara gained a vivid understanding of what a deliberate decision for war would mean when he was briefed on the Single Integrated Operational Plan (SIOP) that the Kennedy administration had inherited from Eisenhower.

Herbert York was one of those who accompanied the defense secretary to Omaha, where SAC commander Thomas Power himself gave the briefing. A former targeting consultant for the Air Force, York was already well aware of what the war plan contained. But he remembered being impressed anew with a sense of drama as the group descended to SAC's war room, where the presentation was to take place.

On one side of the high-ceilinged chamber, covering the entire wall, was a map of eastern Europe, Russia, and China. As the briefing began, Power explained by way of acetate overlays how the SIOP would be carried out in the event of war with Russia. The first overlay indicated the location of Russian military bases and atomic stockpiles that would be struck by the first wave of SAC bombers. The second overlay showed as little dots the Russian cities that were targets for the attack's second wave. York recalled that McNamara seemed surprised both by the number and the extent of the dots covering the map. But it wasn't until the third overlay came down that he appeared to stiffen in his seat. The last transparency showed the fallout pattern that was expected to result from the nuclear blitz. While the dark splotches did not quite cover the map of Russia, York noted, they nonetheless represented "one hell of a lot of fallout."

In response to questions posed to Power, McNamara learned that carrying out the SIOP would cause the deaths of perhaps 350 million Russians, Chinese, and eastern Europeans in a matter of hours. The war would result in the destruction of up to 90 percent of the cities and towns in the Soviet Union—some 2,500 targets in all, or virtually every locality "above the size of Tomsk," York pointed out. McNamara discovered during the briefing that SAC had targeted cities in China and eastern Europe as well as

Russia—Albania, for example, would be virtually obliterated because it was the site of a large air defense radar—and that vast amounts of lethal radiation resulting from the attack would inevitably drift into neutral and perhaps even friendly countries.[2]

Seeing McNamara's startled reaction, Power—who had initially refused the defense secretary's request for the briefing—tried unsuccessfully to downplay the devastation shown on the map. To McNamara—who seemed transfixed by the fatal shroud of fallout which enveloped Helsinki—the SAC commander gave a reassurance which York thought particularly "bizarre." "I want you to understand, Mr. Secretary," Power said, "that the two hundred rads you see is what some damned fool would get who went out his front door and stared up into the sky for two days." The comment only widened the gulf between Power and McNamara. York remembered McNamara's "stunned" expression at the end of the briefing. It was, he reflected, the first time that the defense secretary had "looked the subject of nuclear war down the throat."

McNamara—plainly more alarmed than reassured by Power's briefing and by the events of his first days in office—resolved shortly thereafter to speak with Kennedy personally about what the president intended to do if the dread contingency envisioned by strategic planners ever arose. At a meeting of the two men in the Oval Office, McNamara outlined to Kennedy what he thought the president's reaction should be if he ever received a call from SAC headquarters informing him that the country was under Russian attack.

McNamara claimed to have recommended that instead of immediately releasing control of the weapons to the military Kennedy should, in that event, instruct the SAC commander to join him at Andrews Air Force Base outside Washington. From there, McNamara said, the two men could board a plane to fly over the place where the first Russian bomb had reportedly landed, after which—if Kennedy was certain it was not an accident—he should return to the capital and attempt to contact the Soviet premier to find out if the attack was deliberate and, if so, whether it would be sustained. Though General Curtis LeMay or others would probably balk at this plan, McNamara said, he urged Kennedy to remain firm in refusing to authorize the carrying out of the SIOP against the Russians until the president knew "the size of their attack and the intention of their attack."

McNamara subsequently admitted that Kennedy's reaction to his remarkable proposal was noncommittal. But he was neither surprised nor disappointed by this response. Even if the president had accepted what McNamara described as a policy of "no-second-strike-until," it would have been impossible to announce such a drastic change in nuclear strategy to the public or the Russians.[3] Yet McNamara thought that Kennedy at the time had "fully agreed" with what he had had to say about the danger of an accidental nuclear war. For McNamara it was a preeminent concern—and remained so throughout his seven years as defense secretary.

Even before McNamara talked to him on the subject of nuclear war, Kennedy had been given reason to rethink some of his early positions in the campaign concerning the question of defense. Foremost among these had been his claims concerning the celebrated missile gap. In the course of his bid for the presidency, Kennedy and his supporters had deliberately and effectively transformed the question of the gap into a national referendum on the adequacy of America's response to the Soviet threat. Despite Jerome Wiesner's avowed efforts to persuade Kennedy's aides and speechwriters like Paul Nitze not to overemphasize the gap, it had become one of the central issues in the campaign. With Kennedy's election, the widespread public belief in the missile gap had received a kind of official endorsement. (Wiesner at the time justified his unwillingness to correct Kennedy's claims as the result of a concern that he not disclose the secrets of Project Corona. Years later, however, Wiesner acknowledged that his sympathy for Kennedy's candidacy may have caused him to be a bit *too* discreet.)

Conclusive evidence that there was no gap—or, rather, that the gap entirely favored America—was forthcoming within days of Kennedy's election. Analysis of photographs taken by the Discoverer satellite launched that November confirmed Russia's vaunted missile superiority as purely illusory. But the passing of the missile gap as a military concern did not remove it as a political worry for the president. Called into the Oval Office to present the incontrovertible evidence against the gap, Wiesner was somewhat surprised at Kennedy's reaction. The president had greeted the news with a single expletive—delivered, Wiesner said, more in anger than relief.

There had been a mixed reaction at Rand as well to the truth about the missile gap. The existence of the overhead reconnaisance program came as a revelation to most of those at the think tank, to which the newly installed administration had already turned in recruiting defense experts critical of the policies of the Eisenhower administration. One of that select number, Daniel Ellsberg, eagerly accepted an invitation to join the Kennedy administration but delayed his departure for Washington in order to complete a project underway at Rand. It was shortly after he had arrived in the capital that Ellsberg learned from another Rand alumnus in the Pentagon the secret that few back at Santa Monica knew.

Ironically, the persistence of faith in the missile gap among Rand's analysts was an indirect result of their attack upon the New Look. Stung by leaks and criticisms in the wake of the Gaither report, the Eisenhower administration in 1959 had decided to withhold from Rand and other think tanks under government contract the top-secret National Intelligence Estimates prepared by the CIA.[4] The last such estimate seen by those at Rand had reflected the generally held assumption of the time that the Russians were mass-producing the type of ICBM tested successfully two years before. Subsequent CIA reports based upon evidence gained from the U-2 and the Discoverer satellite drastically revised those figures downward, but Rand's experts had never seen the corrected estimates. (Some veteran skeptics at Rand, accustomed to the Air Force's inflated estimates of the Soviet threat, discounted the figure of Russian missiles by as much as half. What they could not know was that the resulting number still exaggerated Russian military capabilities by a factor of ten.) "Rand's beliefs were preserved in amber from the height of the missile gap," Ellsberg claimed.

When a former colleague from Rand violated security regulations to show him the photographs taken by the Discoverer, Ellsberg was "stunned," he said, by what the pictures showed. The Russians not only lacked the two hundred or more ICBMs that the Gaither report had predicted they might have by 1961; they actually had fewer than what the CIA defined as an "initial operating capacity" of ten missiles. The analysts at Langley, Ellsberg said, had in fact found only four intercontinental-range missiles in Russia, all of them exposed aboveground at a single launching complex at Plesetsk, and each requiring hours to be readied for firing: "That meant that they could have been destroyed by one sortie of one bomber armed only with high explosives."

Intent upon acquainting those at Rand of the surprising truth behind the missile gap—but at the same time reluctant to violate his secrecy pledge by letting them know the source of his knowledge—Ellsberg arranged a mock briefing in the same room where Wohlstetter had first presented his findings on SAC's vulnerability. The fifty or so analysts who attended, Ellsberg remembered, included many of those who had also been present on that occasion; the atmosphere was marked, he thought, by the same eager air of anticipation.

Ellsberg began the briefing by noting that while he normally did not use charts, in this case he had followed the example of Herman Kahn and prepared some. He had in fact prepared three large placards for the presentation—each stenciled "Top Secret" in bold red letters—which he began to unveil in order before the group. The first one, according to Ellsberg, read, "Yes, Virginia, there is a missile gap." There was, he said, no response from the audience to this news other than a few nods and reaffirming murmurs. The second read, "It is currently running at ten to one." There were again, he noted, only grunts of confirmation. Ellsberg paused for dramatic effect before revealing the third and final chart. It read: "In our favor."

There was, Ellsberg recalled, an almost universal reaction from the audience to this last bit of information. He thought it could be summarized in one word: "Bullshit." Since he had already agreed not to divulge the source of his information, however, Ellsberg was unable to persuade the uninitiated

at Rand of his claim. The idea that the government had consistently overestimated the number of Russian missiles was still regarded there as "eccentric," he said.

Ellsberg vividly recalled the frustration he felt at the strictures secrecy had
put upon him; how they had first kept him and still prevented others from
knowing the truth. It was a frustration Ellsberg would encounter again in
subsequent years—and decide to overcome.

More than just Rand's misestimate of the missile gap troubled those who
left the think tank to become the Kennedy administration's celebrated "whiz
kids." "You realize, don't you, that Rand can never be the same again,"
Charles Hitch told Alain Enthoven shortly after the two alumni of Pine Tree
left to go to Washington.

Becoming head of McNamara's new System Analysis division, Enthoven
found his new concerns were far removed from what they had been in Santa
Monica. The "Rand style" suddenly seemed to him anachronistic in the
world of the New Frontier. Soon after he arrived in Washington, Enthoven
had written a letter to Bernard Brodie disparaging one of Rand's most
hallowed traditions—the forty-five-minute briefing. "Quite frankly," he informed Brodie, "I am sick of Rand's emphasis on communicating everything in this fatuous way." He cited as an example of such frivolousness the
occasion when Herman Kahn had given a briefing on nuclear war and the
first comment from the audience was the observation that Kahn's pants were
unzipped. "The rest of the discussion was given to criticism of the appearance of the briefing charts," Enthoven noted scornfully.[5]

Another Kennedy recruit, Morton Halperin, had gone to Rand directly
from Yale, but remained there only a year before joining McNamara's staff
at the Pentagon. Halperin became immediately aware of the tension between
the insiders and the outsiders of Rand. He thought that tension had been
almost palpable during a government-sponsored conference on limited war
held at Princeton in the fall of 1961. Halperin remembered the delegation
from Rand had been "startled" by his confirmation that the missile gap was
illusory—a fact already so well established in the Pentagon by then, Ellsberg
said, that it was increasingly difficult for the initiates "to hide their degree
of boredom" with their former colleagues. Halperin saw the split at the
Princeton conference as one of personality, ideology, and even age. It had
marked in his mind, he said, Rand's "last hurrah."

The missile gap became a particular symbol of the rift between those who
joined Kennedy's administration and those who stayed behind at Rand. The
shootdown of the U-2 had provided the first inkling that some of those at
Rand, like Andrew Marshall, had reason to claim a counterforce strategy
was feasible, since the United States knew where the targets were in Russia.
But the myth of the missile gap lived on at Rand—even when the issue had

long since been resolved in Washington's official circles. "It was as if my briefing had not occurred," Ellsberg said.

He believed that one reason for the stubborn refusal of Rand's analysts to admit that there was no gap stemmed from the fact that they "had been totally hoaxed and entirely misled by their sponsor—the Air Force." The persistence of false assumptions there proved, Ellsberg felt, that "Rand's theorizing had no relation to reality." Wohlstetter's basing study, for example, had entirely missed the point that it was Russia's vulnerability to attack —not its own—that properly concerned the Air Force, because of the emphasis upon preemption there. Ellsberg eventually came to realize, he said, that some of the attitudes and beliefs he and others had accepted without question at Rand not only differed from reality, but were pure fantasy.

Ellsberg's own journey of discovery had begun even before he joined the Kennedy administration. Like many of the strategic *Wunderkinder* who would later be recruited from Rand, the thirty-year-old theorist arrived in Washington with a reputation already established for hardheaded—or cold-blooded—thinking about nuclear war. When Ellsberg returned to his alma mater, Harvard, some years after graduation to give a Rand-sponsored lecture entitled "The Art of Coercion," one of his former professors thought that in the talk Ellsberg had elevated torture to a principle of statecraft. Another lecture by Ellsberg, "The Political Uses of Madness," made an equally inventive—and chilling—point by arguing the advantages of irrationality in diplomacy, especially when threatening the use of nuclear weapons.[6]

Ellsberg himself thought this kind of studied objectivity was what had recommended him for the study of nuclear warfare that Rand began in 1959. That same year he became a consultant to the Eisenhower administration on nuclear war planning. For a period of several weeks, locked within a steel cage in a heavily guarded area, Ellsberg had pored over the Pacific fleet's portion of the Joint Strategic Capabilities Plan, the document that would direct American forces in the event of a war with Russia. Later, upon joining the Kennedy administration, Ellsberg would be allowed access to the successor to that plan—the SIOP.

Upon first beholding the SIOP, Ellsberg said, he was "appalled" by what he saw. No less remarkable than the indiscriminate nature of the destruction planned for was its seeming wantonness, he thought. Disbelieving the casualty estimates contained in the plan, Ellsberg had asked for a confirmation from the joint chiefs. Their reply confirmed not only the numbers but also what Ellsberg felt was the extraordinary callousness of the military to the prospect of a monumental loss of civilian life. "That *was* a shocker," Ellsberg recalled. His "attitude toward the joint chiefs," Ellsberg said, "was very much affected by that answer—by what they had come to." The SIOP "represented the pathology of military bureaucratic thinking to a degree that was almost unimaginable," he said. "I thought they were the most dangerous, depraved, essentially monstrous people. They really had constructed a doomsday machine." (Ellsberg was not alone in his outrage. Another young civilian who was briefed on the war plan at this time told colleagues that he thought its authors should be simply lined up on the White House lawn and shot.)

An example of what Ellsberg considered "the half-baked, simple-minded, and even crazy quality" of the war plan was the military's collective obsession with bombing Moscow. Adding up the number of weapons aimed at the Russian capital, Ellsberg found that the city would be the target for a total of 170 atomic and hydrogen bombs—its inhabitants the victims, in effect, of service pride: "Everybody who could put a weapon on Moscow did so. If you could somehow jury-rig a vehicle so that your unit could have a weapon on Moscow, you did it."

Initially inclined toward "a continuous contempt" of military planners for their excesses, Ellsberg later began to realize that there was a kind of hidden logic in the war plans that he and others at Rand—isolated until then from the top secrets—had but dimly perceived. Central to that planning were certain assumptions about a nuclear war that its planners might steadfastly deny in public, but privately recognized to be true. This included the knowledge that the United States actually had overwhelming nuclear superiority over the Soviet Union, and the likelihood that this country—not Russia— would be the first to use nuclear weapons in a war. Only those assumptions explained, Ellsberg said, why the war plans "looked just absolutely—just incomprehensibly—irrational in view of what we thought was the strategic situation."

Before seeing the SIOP, he had believed official statements that American war planning envisioned a retaliatory second strike upon Russia in response to a Soviet nuclear attack. At Rand and later in McNamara's Pentagon, Ellsberg said, he found that the actual plans assumed the United States would use nuclear weapons first, in a coordinated and massive attack that deliberately held few bombs in reserve.

An incident that occurred shortly after he joined the Kennedy administration confirmed his dawning suspicion, Ellsberg said, that war planning had been conducted all along on the assumption that the United States was militarily superior to Russia, and that this country would strike first with nuclear weapons. At that time, he noted, the Air Force still stubbornly clung to its claim of Russian missile superiority—though the administration was privately persuaded of the unreality of the gap. In June of 1961, therefore, the head of the Air Force's war planning division had declared that Soviet ICBMs numbered between 120 and 160. That same month the officer responsible for SAC's estimate of Russian strength had speculated that the Soviets might have as many as a thousand intercontinental-range missiles.

The following August, Ellsberg visited SAC's underground headquarters as a member of the Pentagon team reviewing war plans in the wake of McNamara's briefing by General Power. Aware that the previous week—at the height of the crisis over Berlin—the Air Force had discreetly advised Kennedy that civilian losses in the United States would probably not exceed ten million if the nation struck first, Ellsberg asked the SAC briefing officer how many of the thousand missiles he credited the Russians with had actually been located and targeted. "Approximately two hundred" had been the reply, according to Ellsberg. When he noted to the SAC spokesman that the existence—by the Air Force's own reckoning—of eight hundred untargeted Soviet missiles would seem to undermine its recommendation that Kennedy stand fast on Berlin, the briefing officer responded with a query—in what Ellsberg said he took to be "sincere mock horror"—whether it was being suggested that SAC had doctored its estimates to inflate the Russian threat. That was not his intent, Ellsberg demurred. But he also pointed out, he said, how the Air Force was defeating its own purpose by emphasizing only the highest number in its estimate of Soviet missiles. The interest of SAC might be better served, Ellsberg suggested, "by portraying the whole range of uncertainty—including the lower end."

Privately, Ellsberg felt he understood the rationale behind the Air Force's persistence in claiming there was a missile gap. Such an exaggerated estimate justified that service's argument for a much larger missile force of its own. But its estimate of ten million American dead, Ellsberg felt, meant that the Air Force and SAC *knew* its own figures on Soviet missiles were greatly overstated. (He believed they had arrived at the figure by adding the population of the five boroughs of New York to that of the one or two cities on the West Coast that might be struck by missiles on Russian submarines that survived SAC's disarming strike.) "The prediction that SAC was making in 1961 which sounded as insane as predictions could be—and which also contradicted their estimates of what the Soviets had—were actually quite realistic," Ellsberg said. "In retrospect, that ten million estimate reflected to me that the joint chiefs all knew—including SAC—that what they [the Russians] had was four missiles."

When the CIA's drastically lower estimate of Soviet missile strength began circulating in Washington a month after his visit to Omaha, Ellsberg thought it significant that neither SAC nor the Air Force bothered to contest it. Indeed, later that fall each independently admitted that its figures on the missile gap had been in error. "The missile gap hoax was both absurd and costly to the Air Force," Ellsberg pointed out. He thought it was the Air Force's belated recognition of this fact—not the increasing burden of evidence—that finally brought about the sudden demise of the gap that fall: "If you're trying to sell a first-strike capability you couldn't talk about eight hundred missiles you couldn't find."

· · ·

If, as Enthoven wrote, McNamara's Pentagon "operated under the theory that information was power," then the theorists who stayed behind at Rand were plainly considered powerless by those who went to Washington. Within days of arriving in Washington, the "whiz kids" began the fundamental review of American defense policy that McNamara had decided upon shortly after assuming office. Like the efforts that preceded it—including NSC-68, the Solarium study, and the Gaither report—the reassessment ordered by McNamara was not long in developing a life, and a legacy, of its own. Unlike them, however, it would not be shaped—or warped—by the assumption of Russian strategic superiority.

McNamara's discovery of the dangers of accidental nuclear war had convinced him, he later said, that the redefinition of American strategy would have to take place "within a very short time." While president of Ford he had had little prior interest in or knowledge of nuclear strategy. Before he came to the Pentagon, McNamara had read only one book and one article on the subject—Henry Kissinger's *Nuclear Weapons and Foreign Policy* and Wohlstetter's "Delicate Balance of Terror" essay—though he had studied the problems of strategic bombing in the Second World War. Yet the experience of even a short time in office had dramatically awakened him to the responsibilities and dangers that attended the bomb.*

Neither doubt nor unfamiliarity afflicted those whom McNamara selected from among Rand's representatives to carry out the new Pentagon study. Particularly prominent among the group of so-called "defense intellectuals" were the veterans of Risborough at Rand: Hitch, Enthoven, and Rowen. Two other experts from Pine Tree, Carl Kaysen and Walt Rostow, had already gone to work at the White House, and were temporarily recruited to work on the Pentagon review of nuclear strategy. Despite repeated entreaties from his former co-workers, Albert Wohlstetter remained at Rand. Malcolm Hoag—the unexpected winner of the think tank's war game in the 1950s—joined the team at the Pentagon, working until the early hours of the morning on the strategic review.

The man chosen by McNamara to direct the effort, Paul Nitze, was likewise lacking neither in experience nor in opinions on nuclear strategy. A few at Rand, particularly Bernard Brodie, waited in vain for a summons from the White House. When one was not forthcoming, Brodie surmised—

---

*McNamara was not the first to become so aware. Truman's decision to drop the atomic bombs on Japan later brought to the president's mind Horatio's speech in the last scene of *Hamlet:*

> "Of accidental judgments, casual slaughters,
> Of deaths put on by cunning and forced cause,
> And, in this upshot, purposes mistook
> Fall'n on the inventors' heads . . . "[7]

correctly—that his views on tactical nuclear warfare were out of favor on the New Frontier.

Enthoven thought the intent of the ninety-six questions that McNamara posed to the group as the inspiration for their study "was to shake everybody up." Almost all engaged in the effort remembered how its effect was to re-create, if only briefly, the intense excitement of working at Rand in the early days. Enthoven compared it to "an intellectual crap game." He, Hitch, and Rowen would often assemble in Hitch's office at the end of a day and reflect upon how they had been able to put into practice the theories they had talked about at the think tank.

Even if they were not directly involved in it, McNamara's rethinking of nuclear strategy struck a sympathetic chord among many fresh recruits to the New Frontier. Kaysen openly ridiculed the Basic National Security Plan, the BNSP, inherited from the Eisenhower administration as the "bean soup"—a reflection upon the nonspecificity of its contents as well as the impenetrability of its style. Kennedy's national security adviser, McGeorge Bundy, had a similar contempt for the war plan originating with SAC and the Air Force. "The first line was usually one that extolled us 'to prevail,' " he remembered. Bundy said he considered "prevail" in this context to be consciously "a word of art," intended to justify a continuing and open-ended expansion of the arsenal. Early in the administration, Bundy, McNamara, and Kennedy had decided that they would strike the offending verb from their revision of the war plan. "We didn't want that kind of language to be thrown back at us by the joint chiefs," Bundy said.

Bundy concluded that the unrestrained destruction called for in the SIOP was the antithesis of strategy. "We're planning to shoot everything off at once," he explained to Kennedy.[8]

14

The Germans in McNamara's Band

If it was not evident within the first few days they were in Washington, it became clear in succeeding weeks to the group calling itself "McNamara's Band" that there were limits beyond those of the imagination upon the changes they could bring to the New Frontier.* A day or so after Jerome Wiesner briefed him on the truth behind the missile gap, Kennedy had called Charles Hitch, who was at home recovering from the pneumonia he had caught on the wintry morning of the inaugural. "I'm going to have to make a statement about the missile gap," the president told him. But no such statement was forthcoming from Kennedy then—or ever.

Instead, an almost offhand remark by McNamara at a press conference the following month, in which he declared that the Russians had no advantage in missiles, touched off an immediate public furor over the gap. Kennedy partisans, remembering the claims made by the candidate during the campaign, accused McNamara—a Republican—of sabotaging the Democratic administration. The subdued and somewhat cryptic announcement by an undersecretary of defense several months later that American retaliation would inflict more damage than a Soviet attack upon the United States

*From a turn-of-the-century music hall song:

"Oh, the drums go bang, the cymbals clang,
The horns they blaze away,
McCartney pumps the old bassoon
While I the pipes do play.
And Hennessey, Tennessey tootles the flute
And the music is somethin' grand
Oh, I am the only German in MacNamara's Band."
by Shamus O'Connor and J. J. Stamford

—even if the Russians struck first—implicitly belied the notion of a gap, but received little public notice.[1]

The possibility that the administration was unable—or even unwilling—to correct the impression of national military weakness contained in Kennedy's campaign rhetoric came as a surprise to some of those who had been at Rand and were now in the government. Yet the fact that America was already "second to none" militarily, in Kennedy's electioneering phrase, had not seemed to affect the momentum for rearmament—where the persisting illusion of weakness suddenly seemed to count for more than the reality of strength. The public continued to suffer from "gaposis," Kaysen noted.

The first test of Rand's influence upon McNamara was to come in the reassessment of nuclear strategy, where the civilian experts at the Pentagon almost immediately ran into a conflict with their counterparts in the military.

As they had since the dawn of the atomic age, the three services had rival views of how and where a future nuclear war would be fought. Among these, the Army's notion of a protracted campaign in Europe, where both large and small nuclear weapons might be used, had been quickly dismissed by McNamara for the same reasons it was once burlesqued by a Navy spokesman: as being "based on the shipment of unavailable goods, supplied and loaned by people who have been killed, from ports that have been destroyed, on ships that would be better advised to steer for Tierra del Fuego." It had also long been axiomatic with Air Force commanders, according to one, that the war "would be over for months and months" before the Army finally arrived at the gates of the Kremlin.[2]

A joint Army-Navy war plan intended to supplant the Air Force strategy of atomic blitz—called, with unintended irony, "the Alternative Undertaking"—had been drawn up at the height of the controversy over massive retaliation during the Eisenhower years. But it was abandoned in 1960 when the creation of the SIOP reaffirmed the supremacy of SAC.[3]

By the time Kennedy and McNamara assumed office, the central premise of the Army-Navy alternative to SAC—that deterrence could be guaranteed by a much smaller number of weapons, provided they remained relatively invulnerable to attack—had become the principal argument behind the fleet of missile-firing submarines that Eisenhower tentatively approved by the end of his term. McNamara received a detailed briefing on what the Navy termed a strategy of "finite" or "minimum" deterrence only a day before the bomber accident in North Carolina. The Navy briefing had followed a twenty-minute CIA presentation which confirmed that the long-presumed phalanx of Soviet ICBMs was actually a hollow specter. This concatenation of events evidently left McNamara persuaded that the projected fleet of submarines—whose two hundred missiles would be able to destroy virtually every city of any size in Russia—offered a less vulnerable, less dangerous, and more reliable alternative to SAC's bombers and missiles.[4]

In contrast to the Navy's notion of minimum deterrence, which focused the nuclear threat upon cities, virtually all of Rand's civilian advisers around McNamara had been longtime advocates of a counterforce strategy. In the case of those who were veterans of Pine Tree, advocacy of counterforce had begun even earlier. The idea of returning war to the soldiers—abandoned by Andrew Marshall in frustration—had been taken up again at Rand in a 1956 study initiated by James Digby. Since Digby's principal interest was with avoiding civilian casualties, this approach had been dubbed "neo-counterforce" at Rand—to distinguish it from the Air Force version of counterforce, which viewed the killing of civilians as more a "bonus" than a liability.

The Air Force itself experimented briefly with the idea of a neo-counter-force, or "no-cities," doctrine at this time. By the late 1950s a new group of relatively youthful converts to counterforce had risen within the ranks of the Air Staff, whose head, General Thomas White, initially received their ideas with favor. A so-called New Approaches Group had even been created by Curtis LeMay to study the merits of the idea. LeMay's interest was explained by the fact that he, like others in SAC, was avidly looking for a rebuttal to the Navy's argument for missile-firing submarines, which threatened to break the Air Force's monopoly on strategic forces. The Air Force found it in the charge that the Navy's carrier-based planes lacked the range and its submarine-fired missiles the accuracy to carrying out a counterforce strategy.

The sudden vogue in ideas that had been anathema in the Air Force only a few years earlier was thus the result less of a new open-mindedness than of more parochial concerns. LeMay overcame his early resistance to missiles and counterforce once it became evident that the explosive growth of the U.S. nuclear arsenal compared to the number of military targets in Russia meant that SAC could afford to apportion its bombs more freely—aiming them at secondary airfields or even at individual missiles in the Soviet Union. The prompt destruction of the relatively few missiles in Russia would remove their threat not only to American cities, but to SAC.[5]

Ultimately, the restraint urged by the young Turks within the Air Staff was deemed "weak and unpatriotic"—and their proposal to reduce the size of SAC's bomber force "eccentric"—by officers like LeMay and Thomas Power, who replaced White as Air Force chief of staff in 1960. By the following year the report of the "New Approaches Group" had been sidetracked within the Air Force, its staff disbanded, and its authors reassigned.[6]

But the idea of purposeful restraint in a nuclear war remained alive at Rand, chiefly in the work of analysts like Digby and William Kaufmann, Brodie's former student who had broken with his mentor over the issue of tactical nuclear war. By the spring of 1960—within a week of leaving his teaching job at Yale to return to Rand—Kaufmann was engaged "full blast," he said, in developing the no-cities idea. He discovered that in his absence more than a dozen analysts had also begun thinking about counterforce, testing their theories in computer-run games that were an updating of the early "scratchpad wars" fought on yellow-lined legal pads. In the new and more sophisticated version of these games, players lost points when they killed or injured noncombatants in attacks on military targets.[7] Counterforce, Kaufmann thought, had finally achieved the status of "a developed theology" at the think tank.

The suddenly emergent possibility that the administration might adopt a nuclear strategy focused almost exclusively on killing civilians prompted Rand's advocates of counterforce at the Pentagon—Hitch, Enthoven, and Rowen among them—to arrange for Kaufmann to brief McNamara personally on the no-cities doctrine. After rehearsing the presentation before Digby at Rand, Kaufmann traveled to Washington and gave the briefing in McNamara's office, seated across from the defense secretary, Enthoven, and a stand-in for Hitch, still bedridden with pneumonia. Reading from notes scribbled in his tiny, Dickensian scrawl on a dozen index cards, Kaufmann in the course of two hours set forth the case against minimum deterrence and for a counterforce nuclear strategy.

Later, Kaufmann thought that one of his most persuasive arguments with McNamara had been the examples in which the threat from a small, seaborne force might not be enough to deter Soviet aggression. He specifically mentioned the possibility of a serious confrontation with the Russians over Berlin or Cuba. In such cases, Kaufmann claimed, the president would face the unenviable alternative of either destroying Russian cities—inevitably inviting reprisals in kind—or surrendering. Using an expression that Kennedy himself had coined during the campaign, the choice, Kaufmann said, would be between "holocaust or humiliation."

The ability to respond to a Soviet attack without hitting Russian cities would extend deterrence, Kaufmann argued, in those situations where all-out retaliation was not warranted. While the actual prospect of nuclear war might be disappearingly small, disarming the Russians at the outset of such a war could drastically reduce American casualties. "If a war ever got started you wanted to stop it as soon as you knew how," Kaufmann pointed out. "Why blow everything up when all you wanted to do was stop it?"

Kaufmann's intercession with McNamara had the desired result. "Within a week he had reversed himself," Kaufmann said of the defense secretary's brief flirtation with minimum deterrence. "I talked him out of it." McNamara himself later admitted to having been "very impressed" with Kaufmann's presentation. In the weeks that followed the winter of 1961, McNamara moved away from minimum deterrence, asking the coterie of analysts from Rand to recommend specific changes in the strategic planning passed down from Eisenhower.

"Rand," as Bundy would observe, "was on the payroll."

Despite the fact that secret CIA estimates in 1961 forecast a coming American superiority over Russia of two or even four to one in the number of intercontinental missiles—the actual ratio would prove greater—the administration decided to proceed with plans for the missile force ordered when most Americans believed that the United States needed to catch up to Russia. One reason for their decision, Enthoven reflected, was the fact that Kennedy and McNamara faced "just one hell of a battle" over any move that would have reduced the missile force—particularly since McNamara had already eliminated or cut back eight other major weapons programs during his first weeks in office.

By the time the new administration was underway, the number of missiles in the Air Force's budget request had soared to twenty-four hundred from the eleven hundred tentatively approved by Eisenhower but left unbudgeted at the end of his term. While Enthoven was convinced that both Kennedy and McNamara personally favored a smaller number of missiles—the figure of six hundred was frequently mentioned—the recommendation forwarded from McNamara to the White House was only one hundred missiles less than Eisenhower's final figure.[8]

Since he had paid very little attention to the politicking of the military while at Rand, Enthoven admitted, his first experience with the defense budget proved an education. In order to get money for several new surface ships, for example, the Navy had included in its 1961 budget request only two of the more than two dozen Polaris submarines it actually expected to receive. When Enthoven inquired about this curious accounting procedure, the admirals replied that they considered Polaris a national rather than a Navy program, and hence they expected the money for it to come from outside that service's budget.

"I used to think that the whole damned Navy was a national program," Enthoven retorted heatedly. "What you fellows are telling us is that if we're willing to put up the money for your aircraft carriers and cruisers and all, then you're willing to run a few Polaris subs for us."

"To hell with that way of thinking," Enthoven told the admirals.

Herbert York—who stayed on in the administration during the transition from Eisenhower—agreed with Enthoven on the primacy of politics in the missile decision. York thought that the only real freedom Kennedy and McNamara had in making the decision on the missiles was in the type of weapons to buy—not their number. To York, present during the earliest stages of the debate, the reason why the new administration stuck to the high figure was that the number represented a kind of "independent variable"—

one independent of the number of missiles the country's security actually required. Thus it was not the number of missiles that the Russians had or even the number of targets in the Soviet Union that dictated the thousand-missile force, York claimed, but the seemingly immutable logic of strategic precedents going back to a time before Hiroshima.

It was "because a thousand was a round number," he said, that both Kennedy and Eisenhower had arrived at the figure, despite their supposedly opposite views on defense. Before the advent of the ICBM, America's post-war deterrent force had consisted of about two thousand bombers, the approximate size as well of the air armada sent against Germany and Japan in the Second World War. While the nature of both the weapons and the enemy had changed radically since then, the figure of one thousand seemed to York to retain a "mysterious"—almost totemic—"significance" in the military's calculations of its own requirements.[9]

York was at the February 1961 meeting of Kennedy and his aides when the missile decision had been first discussed with the new president. On that occasion he had been prepared to argue the case, York said, for a halving of the projected force—to five hundred—in light of what was then known about previous overestimates of the Soviet missile threat. Instead, York found that the reductions McNamara announced in the number of SAC's bombers would be exactly made up for by the number of missiles the administration now planned to build. York felt that military tradition, not function, had been the determining factor in the administration's missile decision.

Notwithstanding the fact that most of Rand's experts felt they now had a precise answer to the inquiry at the center of McNamara's ninety-six questions—"How much is enough?"—they discovered that there was nonetheless a pressing political necessity for more. A month into the New Frontier, McNamara had called both Hitch and Enthoven to his office and asked them to note on separate slips of paper what decision *they* would make on the number of missiles. When Enthoven balked at this request, protesting that he was not qualified to advise on how money which had been allocated should be spent, McNamara had persisted. "I'm paying you to tell me how many of these things I should have," he reminded them. The advice that both he and Hitch gave McNamara, Enthoven remembered, was "build a thousand as fast as you can and then wait and see."

Back in his office shortly after the meeting, Enthoven received another call from the defense secretary, who asked him to devise a comparison relating the number of missiles to the damage they could inflict upon Russia. McNamara told Enthoven of his personal view—inspired, perhaps, by the minimum-deterrent argument—that the ability to destroy between 20 and 50 percent of Russian society would be sufficient to deter any Soviet attack upon the United States. His own quick calculations, McNamara said, showed that no more than four hundred hydrogen bombs of one megaton each were necessary to accomplish that gruesome task.

The curve that Enthoven drew ascended rapidly from its starting point until it reached the figure of several hundred missiles. Between that number and a thousand missiles, however, the curve was essentially flat. Additional missiles between the figure of a thousand and twenty-four hundred—SAC's request—represented only a small increase in the amount of destruction. "They would only make the rubble bounce," said Enthoven.

Curiously, a characteristic of Russia's cultural anthropology contributed to the flatness of the curve at the higher numbers. The concentration of nearly half of the country's population in relatively few major cities, and the proximity of those cities to military bases, meant that it would prove difficult to kill less than a quarter of the Russian civilian population even if attacks were aimed only at military targets—and equally difficult to kill a much larger percentage unless many more bombs were used. What Enthoven would come to call "the flat-of-the-curve argument" became the basis for McNamara's recommendation to Kennedy that the nation build as many as a thousand ICBMs—but no more.

There were at least a few in the administration—including one of Enthoven's former associates from Rand—who charged that the curve he plotted for McNamara represented more of a *post hoc* political rationale than a mathematical verity. ("When you know a decision is right, you just have to make it," Enthoven had allegedly told a colleague about McNamara's earlier decision to cancel a new bomber on the grounds that it would not be cost-effective.) Carl Kaysen, Bundy's aide at the White House, thought that Enthoven might even have put the reference points on the graph paper *after* the curve was drawn. Kaysen's suspicions were aroused by the fact that the number of missiles needed to assure the destruction of between a quarter and a half of Russia's population and industry just happened to coincide with the number the administration had decided to acquire.

Compared to Enthoven's experience with the budget, Kaysen's exposure to the practical politics of Washington was both earlier and more sustained. While working on his first assignment for Kennedy, a study of the civil defense program, he had been surprised to find that virtually no government officials—the president included—cared to hear about plans to evacuate them from the capital in the event of war. Reportedly, Kennedy was stunned when Kaysen innocently suggested that he sleep in the White House bomb shelter and send his wife out of Washington during the Cuban missile crisis.

Kaysen also differed from the other veterans of Pine Tree in that he remained unpersuaded of the advantages to a counterforce strategy. While at Rand he had become a convert to the minimum-deterrence ideas that McNamara originally toyed with but was talked out of by Kaufmann. After the February 1961 meeting with Kennedy, Kaysen, along with science advisers Wiesner and Keeny, had become convinced that the country needed no more than four hundred ICBMs to deter Russia. Anticipating the political pressures likely to be upon the president, however, the trio had agreed for tactical reasons to raise the figure to six hundred.

Kaysen said he once pointed out to Enthoven how the flat-of-the-curve argument could be used against the thousand-missile rationale as easily as against SAC's figure of twenty-four hundred missiles. "Look, Alain, you've shown that the curve is flat in the upward direction," Kaysen objected. "But it's also flat in the downward direction," until it reached the figure of four hundred missiles. "You could diddle the curve," Keeny confirmed of Enthoven's calculation. But even though Enthoven eventually conceded their point, Kaysen and Keeny said, he remained adamant on the thousand-missile force. The administration's unyielding insistence on the number of missiles convinced Kaysen that McNamara and Kennedy might be seeking to get the higher number in order to achieve some diplomatic leverage on the Russians. In response, he wrote a memorandum to the president in the early fall. Its message, Kaysen said, "was that you can't get more than deterrence from nuclear weapons."

The final decision on the missiles was made in a meeting the day after Thanksgiving at the presidential compound near Hyannisport. The occasion was "the first big session on the subject without the generals," Wiesner remembered. Disagreements there were without recrimination, though at least one protest contained the hint of a warning. Theodore Sorensen, a presidential confidant, cautioned Kennedy that the missile buildup would inevitably spur the arms race. Another adviser, a defender of the thousand-missile force, countered Sorensen by reminding Kennedy of the very narrow margin by which he had been elected in a campaign that emphasized defense issues. Others in the group agreed that political pressure—especially from the military services and Congress—figured prominently in Kennedy's decision for a thousand ICBMs. The administration would be "politically murdered," McNamara predicted, if the president approved a smaller number. It was, he reportedly told Kennedy, "the best that we can live with."

Kaysen was not surprised that politics had ultimately been determining in the decision. He was reminded by the Hyannisport meeting of a White House luncheon once held for the leader of Guinea, where Kennedy had made fun of his own close election victory. The ceremony had started off badly—the host was unable to converse with his guest, who spoke only French. Kennedy had finally abandoned both toasts that the State Department and Kaysen suggested he make, to propose one of his own: "To the kind of president I would like to be—eighty percent of the vote."

. . .

Although Kaysen, Wiesner, and Keeny were disappointed by the missile decision, Rand had already had a profound effect upon the administration's defense policies. In the interregnum between Kennedy's election and the inauguration, Hitch, Enthoven, and Rowen began to put into practice the theories they discussed at Rand when the assumption of U.S. strategic inferiority held sway. Their ideas included speeding up the various missile programs, placing more of the missiles underground or in submarines to make them less vulnerable to a Soviet attack, and phasing out SAC's increasingly imperiled bombers.

Another theory implemented at this time was an outgrowth of Wohlstetter's basing studies, which had suggested putting SAC's unprotected ICBMs in underground concrete silos. The inspiration for hardening the missile sites came from Wohlstetter's experience with prefabricated housing during the war. Air Force officers had originally rejected the idea as impractical—until Wohlstetter and a mining-engineer friend from those days were able to convince them of its feasibility.*

The changes in American nuclear strategy proposed by the "whiz kids" in the summer of 1961 were already being carried out by the fall. Chief among these was a complete revision of the SIOP and abandonment of the inherited Basic National Security Plan—Kaysen's despised "bean soup." The two options that the original SIOP had given the president for responding to a Soviet attack were increased to five in the new version, in accordance with the administration's publicly declared policy of flexible response and "graduated" deterrence.[10] So eager, in fact, was McNamara to begin the shift away from the old war plan that he cabled SAC commander Power in the early autumn with instructions to incorporate the new options in the target list immediately, rather than wait for the changes to be announced in the official defense posture statement the following June.

Between the briefing that Kaufmann gave McNamara in February on the no-cities concept and the missile decision the following November there had been another occasion where the advice of Rand's experts—had it been taken—would have had the profoundest effect imaginable upon the nation's nuclear weapons policy.

The embarrassing setback Kennedy suffered at the Bay of Pigs in the spring of 1961 centered attention briefly upon Cuba, which had likewise been an issue in the election campaign. (Two of the planners of the invasion fiasco

---

*Wohlstetter's aides liked to point out that Nikita Khrushchev had a similarly difficult time convincing the Soviet military of the worth of underground silos. In his memoirs, the Russian leader wrote that the notion of putting missiles in silos had occurred to him as a result of his mining background and his role in building Moscow's subway. Khrushchev was finally able to persuade Russian generals of the idea, he said, when he pointed out that the Americans were doing it.

during the Eisenhower administration had been Richard Bissell, head of the CIA's U-2 program, and Charles Cabell, the former chief of Air Force Intelligence when Bernard Brodie was at the Pentagon. Both men were forced to leave the agency in the wake of the disaster.) To Kennedy, the Bay of Pigs had seemed a self-inflicted wound for the administration—one that he might even learn something from.[11]

He was not so philosophical over Berlin, which was the centerpiece of his confrontation with Khrushchev at the Vienna summit in June. It was Berlin that Kaufmann had used as an example of why minimum deterrence would not work; why the president needed options other than the extremes of suicide or surrender. For Kennedy, the rancorous encounter with the Soviet leader over the encircled city was an occasion for bitterness and even near-despair. Significantly, the clear margin of nuclear superiority that the United States then enjoyed had plainly not deterred Khrushchev from issuing an ultimatum on Berlin. (Ellsberg recalled how the joint chiefs had been furious when Kennedy suggested in a speech at Vienna that the United States and Russia were essentially equal in missile strength—when in fact the United States was far ahead.)

"He's imprisoned by Berlin," one cabinet member said after a meeting with the president that summer. "These were strange, moody days," confirmed presidential aide Arthur Schlesinger. "Cuba and Laos had been side issues," Schlesinger observed. "But Berlin threatened a war which might destroy civilization." Kennedy, he wrote, "thought about little else that summer."[12]

Kennedy's premonition upon taking office that there would be trouble with the Russians over Berlin—an impression certainly reinforced at Vienna —came true within weeks of the ill-starred summit, when Khrushchev threatened to abandon the postwar Allied agreement on the city by signing a separate peace treaty with East Germany. The Russian ultimatum prompted the most serious crisis over Berlin since the Soviet blockade of the city in 1948. In the midst of the renewed crisis Kennedy instructed Paul Nitze to form a task force within the administration to consult with America's allies and to advise him on a proper response to the Russian provocation.

Virtually all in Nitze's Berlin Task Force—which included Rand's acolytes as well as crisis veterans like Dean Acheson—immediately came to the conclusion that there was little the United States could do to defend the threatened city with conventional forces. "No matter what we tried in these hypothetical cases the Soviets stomped on us," recalled Kaufmann.

The fact that Truman's advisers reached the same conclusion thirteen years earlier, during the first Berlin crisis, caused the dispatch of the first "atomic-capable" bombers to overseas bases within striking distance of the Soviet Union. In 1961—as in 1948—civilian officials were chagrined to find that existing war plans still directed that nuclear weapons be used almost immediately in the event an Allied military probe in the direction of Berlin was halted by Russian troops. Administration figures thus learned that the flexible response they and Rand's experts were planning for American strategy had not yet been incorporated into the SIOP. In early July, Bundy advised the president of the task force's unanimous opinion "that the current strategic war plan is dangerously rigid," and that it "may leave you with very little choice as to how you face the moment of thermonuclear truth." The war plan was so constructed, Bundy told Kennedy, "as to make any more flexible course very difficult."[13]

Two different U.S. military responses—each of which involved the use of nuclear weapons—were studied by Kennedy's advisers after the crisis escalated in mid-August with the building of the Berlin wall. In a "crisis simulation" exercise—patterned after Rand's war games, and played at Camp David by members of the task force the following month—Thomas Schelling, the referee of the game, proposed a novel way of demonstrating American resolve over Berlin: a nuclear "warning shot" exploded dramatically—but harmlessly—over an isolated place in Russia like the island of Novaya Zemlya.

A pioneering game theorist at Rand as well as an avid devotee of mystery novels, Schelling the year before had published an influential and highly imaginative book on how people and nations engaged in tacit bargaining. The book, *The Strategy of Conflict,* contained advice on how to resolve crises of various sorts—from cab drivers trying to negotiate their way through New York traffic to dynamite-truck drivers at an impasse on a narrow mountain road, as well as for nuclear-armed nations engaged in the sort of confrontation that had now developed over Berlin.[14] The idea of signaling the Russians with a warning or "demonstration" detonation of a nuclear weapon followed logically from Schelling's book.

But it was not an idea received with favor by members of Nitze's task force. "If you're going to use them you should be very serious about them, and not blow one up over a test base," Kaufmann objected. Bundy raised the practical protest that the initial trajectory of a nuclear-tipped missile aimed at an obscure place in Russia would be the same as that of a missile aimed at the Kremlin—pointing out that Soviet leaders would be understandably disinclined to believe American assurances as to the real target. Later, Bundy said he thought it would have been "irresponsible for the administration not to have considered the possibility of using nuclear weapons in the crisis—but even more irresponsible to have actually used them."

Among the most vehemently opposed to Schelling's proposal was Nitze himself. The head of the task force feared that the use of nuclear weapons to demonstrate resolve could backfire—in that the Russians, too, might begin firing warning shots. "If we used three they might use six," Nitze reasoned. At some stage in the test of wills, moreover, one side might decide to use its weapons for something beyond a mere demonstration. "When that happens," Nitze said, "then you know that you're in for keeps and you've lost a hell of a lot." He accordingly dismissed the idea of the nuclear warning shot as "a mug's game."

With the apparent exception of a senior NATO commander, the reaction of America's allies to a nuclear demonstration was equally negative. When Lord Mountbatten, the head of Britain's Defence Staff, visited McNamara's office that August, the latter had asked his opinion of what action the United States should take in the crisis. At the time the Russians had begun to interfere with planes flying the air corridors to Berlin—indicating they would not permit a repetition of the airlift that had saved the city in the 1948 crisis.

Since Mountbatten in his discussion with McNamara failed to raise the possibility of using nuclear weapons, the defense secretary had finally broached the issue himself. "My God," Mountbatten replied, "anybody who thinks of that is mad!" McNamara reportedly told the Englishman that he, too, had concluded the use of nuclear weapons in the crisis would be "irresponsible."

The other use of nuclear weapons studied by a few of Rand's experts in the task force was far more ambitious: a disarming first strike against Russia in the event that war seemed about to erupt over the crisis. Kaysen, one of the authors of the first-strike plan, later thought that it had its origins in a question posed by another member of Nitze's group concerning the feasibility of such an attack. But the impetus for the idea, Kaysen admitted, had come even earlier: in the wake of the disastrous Vienna summit. Working quietly that June with Henry Rowen, Nitze's deputy at the Pentagon, the two men together drafted what Kaysen characterized as "a first-strike plan to show that we could have a successful, clean first strike." One of those in the administration who learned of the plan called it a "clever first strike," in that it was designed to catch Soviet forces unalerted and at their bases.

Kaysen and Rowen consulted other analysts from Rand in the preparation of their plan. One remembered the debate that had been raging when he arrived at Santa Monica in 1957 as to the possibility of using a missile to destroy a missile on the ground. He was struck by the fact that four years later his theoretical calculations were being used by Pentagon civilian analysts in a practical plan to destroy Soviet missiles while inflicting a minimum number of casualties. Another Rand alumnus thought that the seeds of the first-strike plan drawn up by Kaysen and Rowen had been in Kaufmann's no-cities briefing of McNamara. The satellite photographs that finally exploded the myth of the missile gap had thus also pinpointed the location of Russia's 190 strategic bombers and handful of ICBMs. "We could really dust them up" was the inescapable point, he thought, of Kaufmann's briefing.

The hypothetical nuclear attack on Russia would have used "everything" in the American strategic arsenal, Kaysen later noted of the plan, which was outlined on just a few sheets of paper. He and Rowen decided to keep it a secret from military planners not only because of its obvious sensitivity, but because the two feared that a few in the Pentagon might embrace the idea with an embarrassing degree of enthusiasm.

The proposal was discreetly considered by some within the administration's inner circle during the tense few weeks of the Berlin crisis. Enthoven remembered being present in McNamara's office during discussions "about just what such a strike would look like and how you would go about it." But he thought those discussions "not extraordinary," insofar as the United States had always reserved to itself the right to use nuclear weapons in the face of Soviet aggression. "It was just one of the things that was looked at along with everything else," Enthoven noted.

Kaufmann himself later downplayed the significance of the first-strike proposal: "There were those who explained the possibilities and who said, in effect, 'Look, you should understand what is open to you.' One knew certain things and could see certain options open."

But even those who scorned the idea that the United States should land the first blow in a nuclear war were "fascinated," Kaufmann admitted, by the plan. Uncertainty, he said, proved to be perhaps the single greatest argument against a first strike: "It's amazing how people who had no mathematical background discovered distribution. Very quickly they'd come to understand that if you're honest then there may be a 90 percent chance of success, but there was also a 10 percent chance it will all go haywire." The result, Kaufmann noted, was that "they'd lose interest in fifteen minutes."[15]

While Kaysen and Rowen came to consider their own plan more an intellectual exercise than a practical solution to the Berlin crisis, the fact that they would even consider a preventive war against Russia was a source of outrage to others in the administration. The response from within the government to the first-strike plan was more negative than the reaction to Schelling's warning-shot idea. "Go away, you're crazy" was in effect what Sorensen told Kaysen when the latter informed him of the plan. A Kennedy speechwriter who had written a secret history of the missile gap controversy at the president's request, Adam Yarmolinsky, also reacted to the proposal "with shock," he said. The subsequent resignation of one of Bundy's aides would allegedly be in protest to the first-strike plan.[16]

McNamara, as well, rejected the idea out of hand. He had precluded the use of nuclear weapons as a response to the crisis in his conversation with Mountbatten the previous month, and there was no sign of any inclination on his part to reconsider that decision. But there was a lesson of sorts to be drawn from the crisis, the defense secretary evidently concluded. More than a year later, in November 1962, McNamara warned Kennedy that what the Air Force truly sought by its budget requests was "a full first-strike capability"—one whereby, as in the plan devised by Kaysen and Rowen, "we would be able to attack and reduce Soviet retaliatory power to the point at which it could not cause severe damage to U.S. population and industry."[17] McNamara would strongly urge Kennedy to spurn Air Force wishes and forgo the option of first-strike capability.

Kennedy plainly concurred in McNamara's recommendation. The United States had—almost by inadvertence—acquired the means to devastate Russia while suffering disproportionately smaller casualties in return. Kennedy's missile decision, made on political rather than military grounds, dramatically increased the American ability to strike first. But there was never any indication that the president considered nuclear war an alternative to diplomacy in the confrontation with Russia.

Significantly, Kennedy had received his first briefing from the joint chiefs on what such a war might look like shortly after he returned from the Vienna summit. The hypothetical casualty figures he heard on that occasion —150 million dead on both sides in the first eighteen hours—would later be cited publicly by him as proof that neither side could win a nuclear war. Although the Air Force had privately assured him that American losses would probably only be a small fraction of that number, particularly if the United States struck first, Kennedy obviously found this fact small consolation. "Only fools," he told a reporter from the *New York Post,* could believe in the possibility of victory in a nuclear war.[18]

While Berlin did not cease to be a focus of East-West tensions, at least the danger of war over the city gradually faded as the deadline for Khrushchev's ultimatum passed. But only a year after the Berlin crisis, in a confrontation with a different enemy, the prospect of preventive war would be raised again in the Kennedy administration—this time by the president himself. When intelligence reports in the summer of 1962 indicated that China was preparing its first test of a nuclear weapon, Kennedy had asked Averell Harriman, his special envoy to Moscow, to elicit Khrushchev's views concerning "means of limiting or preventing Chinese nuclear development." Harriman's instructions revealed that Kennedy was interested specifically in the Russian leader's "willingness either to take Soviet action or to accept U.S. action aimed in this direction."[19]

While no action would be taken by either nation to preempt development of the Chinese bomb, the idea of a disarming strike on China survived into the Johnson administration, and may have remained alive with Soviet leaders after Khrushchev.[20] The possibility of preventive war against Russia was also apparently raised on at least one other occasion during Kennedy's presidency.[21] But he continued to reject the desperate allure of using nuclear weapons. Although the crisis over the Russian missiles in Cuba still lay ahead, what Bundy aptly characterized as the president's "moment of thermonuclear truth" had—unbeknownst to the public—already passed.

15

Eyeball to Eyeball

It was not until the summer of 1962 that Robert McNamara decided to inform the public and America's European allies of the changes that he and Rand's experts had brought to the nation's nuclear strategy. By that date, most of those changes—including the complete revision of the SIOP—had already taken place. Not all of those around McNamara thought the disclosure a good idea. William Kaufmann opposed making public the new emphasis upon counterforce and "damage limitation" in a nuclear war for fear of the unpredictable emotions it might arouse. Daniel Ellsberg did not object to an official announcement of the new strategy *per se,* but he thought it a mistake to represent the change "as a marvelous thing for the new administration to run on." Almost certainly, McNamara did not expect the reaction his announcement would receive.

One apparent reason behind McNamara's adoption of the no-cities doctrine was the hope that he might thereby head off France's development of its own nuclear *force de frappe*—the independent deterrent which threatened to make the coordination of Allied nuclear retaliation to a Soviet attack increasingly difficult, and heightened the risk of an accidental nuclear war. The Russians themselves were another intended audience for the announcement of the change in strategy, since they too would have to adopt the no-cities idea if there was to be any hope of keeping damage limited in a nuclear war.

Yet the reaction of the allies—particularly the French—to the novel idea of a controlled nuclear war was reportedly "incredulous" when McNamara presented it that May to a secret meeting of NATO ministers at Athens.[1] White House aide Adam Yarmolinsky, a consultant on that speech, thought that McNamara used it less as a means to inform the allies "than as a club to beat the French." The Europeans, McNamara learned, continued as they had during the Eisenhower years to look to the deliberately open-ended threat of American nuclear retaliation to deter the Russians. It was clear by the French reaction, moreover, that they intended to proceed with their own nuclear deterrent in any case.

NATO's less than enthusiastic response to the new strategy caused McNamara to be more cautious when introducing it to the American public. Accordingly, he asked a number of those in the administration to write their own versions of the pending speech. One of those consulted—Ellsberg— thought that McNamara's original speech to NATO, which Kaufmann had drafted, and a revised rendition by Yarmolinsky were both too "insouciant" about the prospect of nuclear war. Ellsberg felt that one reason for the negative Allied reaction to McNamara's message had been the latter's optimistic—even smug—assurance about "the cold-blooded and horrendous calculations of how the United States would do better in a nuclear war." This was a consolation "which the American public wasn't remotely prepared to celebrate," he said. Ellsberg feared that the popular domestic reaction to McNamara's speech might be "very negative" as well.

A month after the NATO meeting in Athens, the defense secretary told a commencement audience of the University of Michigan at Ann Arbor that the United States now had a nuclear strategy which aimed first at "the destruction of the enemy's military forces," and thereby gave the foe "the strongest imaginable incentive to refrain from striking our own cities."[2] To McNamara's disappointment, Ellsberg's prediction concerning public reaction to the no-cities idea was borne out. McNamara's gambit seemed ironic, since popular approval for the change had not been necessary—the changes in the SIOP having gone into effect the previous fall. "Ann Arbor," Kaufmann later observed, "was simply a reflection of what had already been instituted." Moreover, the shift to counterforce itself marked no sudden departure in American war planning, since that had always aimed at military targets.

But the effect of McNamara's speech, and of a widely cited comment that Kennedy had made some three months before, was to focus attention upon some of the implications behind such planning—implications which had hitherto been missed or deliberately ignored by most Americans. "Khrushchev must *not* be certain," Kennedy had said, "that, where its vital interests are threatened, the United States will never strike first."[3] The Ann Arbor speech by McNamara and the president's remark for the first time raised the prospect in public that the United States, not the Soviet Union, would be the more likely nation to use nuclear weapons first in a conflict. "If you're going to shoot at missiles," observed one critic bluntly, "you're talking about first strike."[4]

The simple fact that the optimum way to limit damage in the event of nuclear war would be to land the first blow was surely as obvious to McNamara and his civilian experts as it had been to SAC's commanders more than a decade before. Indeed, the certain knowledge by 1962 of America's strategic superiority over Russia made a disarming U.S. first strike an even more attractive proposition than it had been then, as McNamara was doubtless aware. Significantly, the second SIOP retained the original's option of a preemptive first strike "in response to unequivocal strategic warning."[5] The fact that the Kennedy administration had already secretly considered—and rejected—the option of a first strike during the Berlin crisis clearly had not removed the subject from discussion entirely.

It was the unexpected costs of preparing to fight a limited nuclear war as much as the greater danger that such a war could break out because of miscalculation or accident that caused McNamara to back away from the no-cities doctrine. What Ellsberg took to be the sudden and surprising switch of the Air Force on counterforce strategy in 1961 after long resisting the idea was explained a year later, he thought, when that service requested a whole new variety of weapons to implement McNamara's war-fighting strategy. (Typical of the unforeseen consequences of no-cities was SAC's request for a new strategic bomber, the B-70, following Kennedy's missile decision the previous November. McNamara had confided to Herbert York that he had "shot down" the new bomber by approving another Air Force request for a short-range missile, the Skybolt, to be launched from existing bombers. By the following July, however, both the Skybolt and the B-70 were resurgent in budget requests by the Air Force—which justified the weapons as necessary to destroy Soviet military targets missed or overlooked in the initial counterforce blow.)[6]

In retrospect, McNamara would dismiss the no-cities idea as "relatively unimportant," and his Ann Arbor speech as having had only "a very limited role to play." By the early fall of 1962, in fact, he was already beginning to move away from the new strategy he had accepted from his civilian advisers the year before. The reason given was not only the unexpected military demands that counterforce had given rise to, but the resistance that strategy had encountered abroad and at home. As his November 1962 memo to Kennedy indicated, probably not the least important of the reasons for McNamara's disenchantment with counterforce was the dangerous implication the strategy had for an American first strike. That concern and the subsequent course of events would eventually transform McNamara's step back from nuclear war-fighting into a headlong retreat.

For all the concern over Berlin, it was Cuba that ultimately caused the Kennedy administration the greatest anxiety about nuclear war. The irrefutable photographic evidence of early October 1962 that the Russians had surreptitiously begun to install offensive missiles on the island sparked the thirteen-day-long confrontation—during which Kennedy at one point estimated an even chance of nuclear war. Almost certainly the president's concern was not that the Russians had decided upon a deliberate course of aggression, but that a miscalculation on their part might lead to war.

There seemed some reason for Kennedy to worry. He had come away from the Vienna fiasco the previous year with the impression that Khrushchev seriously underestimated him because of his youth and inexperience. The fact that the Soviet leader would gamble by putting the missiles in Cuba seemed a confirmation of that presumed earlier misjudgment.[7]

It was the fear the Russians might make the same miscalculation as had European leaders in 1914 that haunted Kennedy during his presidency, Theodore Sorensen noted.[8] The possibility that nuclear war would begin by an accident or an error in judgment in fact preoccupied not only Kennedy and McNamara by 1962, but many of those around them. "I became convinced and Bundy became convinced—and this is a conviction we discussed at great length—that no rational politician was ever going to decide to start a nuclear war," said Kaysen of this time. (Later, Kaysen would be reminded by the crisis of an incident in 1961, when Kennedy had ordered an Air Force fighter squadron to Saudi Arabia in response to the Egyptian bombing of Yemen. He remembered in particular "the anxious care with which Kennedy would ask me to remind him what the rules of engagement were." Kennedy, Kaysen said, "was just terribly conscious of the responsibility." Some months later the president again reluctantly followed the counsel of his advisers by ordering the American commander in Berlin to detain a Russian officer whose troops had caused a minor provocation at the Allied war memorial in the city. "Okay, Carl, send the cable," Kennedy told Kaysen in giving the order. "But remember—if he doesn't stop, it's your war.")

Unlike Berlin, the use of nuclear weapons was evidently never considered in the case of Cuba. Those on the Executive Committee of the National Security Council that Kennedy convened to advise him on the crisis discussed only the expedient of using conventional forces. A few of the members of the "Ex Comm" had also served on Nitze's Berlin Task Force the previous year, and that experience may have affected their attitude toward dealing with the Cuban crisis. One suggestion which initially predominated at Ex Comm meetings, therefore, was for a precision air attack on the missile bases themselves, followed almost immediately by invasion. As he had in the case of Berlin, Bundy thought the military's appellation of "surgical" to describe the air attack curiously appropriate—though in a way that its advocates had not intended. "Surgery," Bundy observed, "is generally bloody, messy—and not final."

McNamara remembered the climactic Ex Comm meeting on the first Sunday of the crisis, after the group had eaten breakfast in the upstairs living room of the White House. On that occasion Kennedy had gone around the room, asking the sixteen men present whether they supported the air strike and invasion plan or an alternative—a naval blockade or "quarantine" of

Cuba. The vote was nine to seven for the air strike and invasion, but Kennedy had nonetheless decided on the blockade. Both McNamara and the president's brother, Robert, evidently played a major role in that decision, the latter having objected earlier that the president would not become "the Tojo of the sixties" by ordering a surprise attack on Cuba. The comparison may have been especially jarring to those who were aware of the discussions during the Berlin crisis, where Kennedy had passed up the opportunity for a far more ambitious Pearl Harbor–style attack on Russia.

Khrushchev's capitulation in agreeing to remove the missiles from Cuba defused the crisis and made academic what steps beyond a blockade the administration might have been willing to take. Nearly a generation later, the principal members of the Ex Comm would conclude that the chief lesson learned from the experience concerned how little America's unquestioned nuclear superiority had counted in the showdown with Russia. McNamara had come under fire in 1962 for pointing out that the Soviet missiles in Cuba did not materially affect the strategic balance. At the time of the crisis, in fact, the Soviet Union had possessed fewer than fifty intercontinental-range missiles and fewer than two hundred strategic bombers—compared to the nearly three hundred American ICBMs and fifteen hundred bombers of the Strategic Air Command.[9] "We did not count missiles on either side," professed Secretary of State Dean Rusk of the Ex Comm's deliberations. "It was not a slide-rule calculation," confirmed McNamara of the decision to confront the Russians. "Nuclear played a zero role in Cuba." Indeed, some time later both McNamara and Bundy speculated that America's nuclear superiority may have been a *cause* of the crisis—in that the Russians might have undertaken the desperate gamble with the hope of quickly redressing a strategic imbalance which seemed to them unendurably dangerous.[10]

What seemed the imminence of war over Cuba may also have subtly affected the administration's thinking about nuclear weapons at the time. "If one of these goddamned things was launched against New York, Washington, or Miami," McNamara told Kennedy at one point in the crisis, "it would destroy so many people that you, Mr. President, would never want to accept that risk." McNamara later mused, "If that was the case with one, think what a limited nuclear war would look like."

The crash of the B-52 and the frightening presentation by Power during his first days in office had awakened McNamara to the particular horror of a full-scale nuclear war, whether begun by accident or by deliberate act. His reflections upon the crisis in Cuba convinced him that the hope of fighting a limited nuclear war was both futile and dangerous. An incident that occurred shortly after the missile crisis tended to confirm that conviction—and incidentally underscored the fact that not everyone shared McNamara's view of the lessons to be learned from Cuba.

Khrushchev's message accepting Kennedy's ultimatum to remove the missiles had arrived in Washington on Sunday, less than forty-eight hours before a decision on the air strikes would have to be made. According to Robert Kennedy, there was at least one high-ranking military figure who advised that the president disregard the Soviets' capitulation and proceed with the air strikes on Tuesday anyway.[11]

Some evidently wished to exploit U.S. nuclear superiority beyond the borders of Cuba. Four months after the United States and Russia had gone to the brink over the island, one of McNamara's civilian analysts had happened to be at a meeting in the Pentagon where Curtis LeMay, then head of the Air Staff, was recounting what he felt were the conclusions to be drawn from the crisis. "The Soviets are rational people," LeMay had told the gathering. The fact that the United States had both tactical superiority around Cuba and overwhelming nuclear superiority over the Russians meant that there had been no real risk during the crisis, LeMay said. "The problem had been the flap at the White House," he recounted. "The thing to do next time," LeMay concluded, was "to head these people off."[12]

What concerned McNamara in the wake of the Cuban missile crisis was not only the fact that LeMay and perhaps others believed the United States could win a nuclear war by striking first, but the possibility that the Russians might think this view was becoming dominant in the administration. "My God, if the Soviets thought that was our objective, how would you expect them to react?" he remarked some years later.[13]

A month after the showdown with the Russians, McNamara wrote to Kennedy expressing his concern with the direction of counterforce strategy. "It has become clear to me that the Air Force proposals are based on the objective of achieving a first-strike capability," he noted of the latest budget requests. "What is at issue here is whether our forces should be augmented beyond what I am recommending in an attempt to achieve a capability to start a thermonuclear war in which the resulting damage to ourselves and our Allies could be considered acceptable on some reasonable definition of the term." As he had the previous year, McNamara advised Kennedy that they should both make clear their rejection of the Air Force's thinking.[14] Kennedy, as McNamara was aware, had already made it plain to one prominent proponent of a first-strike capability, General Power, that the administration would not sanction a limitless military buildup. At a meeting in the Oval Office between the president and Power, the latter had referred to a time in the future when the nation would have a force of ten thousand ICBMs. Kennedy had interrupted Power in midsentence. "What was that you said, General?" he asked. When Power began again, Kennedy had again interrupted, saying, "General, we'll never have ten thousand ICBMs in place."

McNamara nonetheless felt he had to go further to make the administration's intentions clear and to rein in the Air Force. In January 1963, he instructed Kaufmann to inform high-ranking Air Force officers they were no longer to use no-cities and the damage-limitation doctrine as a basis for future strategic planning.[15]

McNamara made a concurrent effort to reassure the American people that he did not believe in a winnable nuclear war. Only a month after the missile crisis, he proclaimed publicly for the first time that the Soviets would be able to devastate the United States in a nuclear war—regardless of whatever action this nation might take. A top-secret Pentagon study McNamara received in 1964 confirmed that the hope of limiting damage to the United States in a nuclear war was fast slipping away. Russia's own growing fleet of missile-firing submarines and its emulation of the American invention of encapsulating ICBMs in hardened silos made a U.S. nuclear strategy of counterforce and damage limitation increasingly difficult—if not altogether futile, the report concluded. By this time McNamara was convinced that the mutual destruction of both countries would be the result if Russia and the United States ever entered into war.

But—as had been the case with no-first-use—the political costs of conceding that the nuclear arms race had reached a stalemate ultimately deterred McNamara from making an official announcement of his views. McNamara had been reminded of those costs the day columnist Stewart Alsop came to his office with a secret CIA report confirming that the Russians were sheltering their missiles in concrete silos. Alsop had wanted to warn the defense secretary of what he saw as a new and dangerous development. While McNamara refused to comment on the report, he assured Alsop that if it were true his own reaction could only be relief. Making Russian missiles less vulnerable to attack would stabilize the arms race, he pointed out, since it would cause the Soviets to have less fear that the United States would strike first. (It was with the idea of similarly reducing the chance of accidental war that McNamara, shortly after he assumed office, approved the discreet leaking to the Russians of the know-how behind the permissive-action link [PAL] devices this nation used to prevent unauthorized or accidental launching of its missiles—hoping that the Russians would, in this case, copy the American secrets.) After the interview, Alsop had printed in his nationally syndicated column that McNamara approved of the Russians' gaining in strength. "All hell broke loose," McNamara remembered of the reaction. "In that kind of environment it would have been very difficult to get public acceptance" for his changing ideas on nuclear strategy, he reflected.

McNamara's change of mind was certainly noticed by those around him. Shortly after the Cuban missile crisis, Henry Rowen recalled, the emphasis of the memos that McNamara wrote Kennedy on the subject of nuclear strategy "shifted abruptly" from the no-cities idea and counterforce—back to the emphasis upon deterring, rather than fighting or controlling a nuclear war.[16] Instead of counterforce, these Draft Presidential Memoranda as well as McNamara's own public statements stressed a new concept that he had coined: "assured destruction." Significantly, the term "damage limitation" was explicitly ordered stricken from the memorandum that Enthoven and Rowen drafted for Kennedy's signature in the fall of 1962.

Enthoven, too, thought that McNamara's about-face had been prompted by his belated recognition of the implications behind counterforce: "One of the reasons why McNamara backed off the no-cities doctrine is that it was being erroneously interpreted as a theory whereby thermonuclear war could be made tolerable, and therefore fought and won. Gradually he turned against it because it seemed to be getting bent out of shape."

McNamara's conversion on nuclear strategy in turn affected the attitudes of those who had come to Washington from Rand, including some of the earliest advocates of no-cities and counterforce. By the end of the Kennedy administration, Daniel Ellsberg had begun to ridicule the assumption that he said previously formed "the absolute core of the strategists' mutual identity": "We all agreed that we must be willing to blow up the western hemisphere if Russian troops crossed the borders of Germany."

The long-pressing burden of the strategists' earliest assumptions, however, proved difficult to shake. Particularly hard for some to envision was an acceptable alternative to the historic reliance upon nuclear weapons. After taking part in a Rand simulation of a Soviet-American nuclear war, Malcolm Hoag had had the same kind of epiphany he experienced in the 1955 war game for Europe. "My God, the casualties are unacceptable," Hoag said. "We were spending four times as much on strategic offense as defense. What if we did it the other way around?"

Hoag's revelation led him to prepare a briefing for his colleagues at Rand on an alternative nuclear strategy, where the emphasis would be upon defense rather than retaliation. "I made the calculations, drew nice curves, and had a breakthrough," he recalled. But at the end of his presentation, Hoag realized he had overlooked the obvious, and ended up by throwing his charts and graphs away.

"I concluded that beauty is not truth. If you knew that you were going to have a war, then my method was best. But deterrence, of course, focuses upon not fighting."

Others thought that McNamara had gone too far too fast in his retreat from counterforce. Albert Wohlstetter felt that a widely quoted observation by Dean Rusk about the Cuban crisis had missed the point. Rusk had said that when the United States and Russia were "eyeball to eyeball" over Cuba, it was the Russians who "blinked." "The Russians blinked," Wohlstetter agreed, "but the United States had a nervous breakdown." Some in the Air Force, one historian of the administration has written, regarded as "the ultimate heresy" McNamara's comment after the crisis that a strategic stalemate might be a positive good.[17]

There was widely perceived to be a personal element behind McNamara's move away from the ideas he had embraced—with confidence, if not enthusiasm—just a short time before. One of his successors remarked that "as McNamara got more deeply into these matters, he found them viscerally repugnant." The grim but dispassionate analyses of nuclear war done in the joint chiefs' Strategic Evaluation Committee at the Pentagon and by his own civilian advisers, McNamara himself later admitted, "made it appear less and less tenable to consider a nuclear war": "We acquired a capacity to make these studies very quickly. We could almost sit at a desk and do these studies ourselves. It got to the point where I could damn well do it in my head."

The Kennedy administration's sudden and tragic end did not halt McNamara's move away from the new strategy. Nor did it remove the causes for that shift in his thinking. Shortly after the inauguration of the new president, McNamara went to Lyndon Johnson with the same advice he had given Kennedy some three years earlier on the contingencies to be followed in the event of nuclear war. As had been the case with Kennedy, McNamara believed that with Johnson, too, he had in effect "a private pledge of no-first-use" of nuclear weapons, and a commitment that the president would not authorize an act of nuclear retaliation until he was personally certain that the nation was under deliberate attack by the Soviets.

McNamara recognized that his decision to put less reliance upon nuclear weapons put a correspondingly greater emphasis upon nonnuclear forces in the strategy of flexible response. That there was a need to redress the serious imbalance between nuclear and conventional forces in the American arsenal had been one of the conclusions reached in the review of military policy McNamara ordered shortly after arriving at the Pentagon. Correcting that imbalance had been an issue during Kennedy's presidential campaign, and was an even earlier concern of Kennedy's military adviser, Maxwell Taylor. Taylor had been Army chief of staff during the Eisenhower years and was author of a 1959 book, *The Uncertain Trumpet*, that provided both the term and the rationale for flexible response.[18]

The same coterie of experts who carried out the reassessment of American nuclear strategy at the start of the Kennedy administration—Nitze, Enthoven, and Rowen—had likewise taken part in the review of conventional strategy. As with the ideas about nuclear strategy, many of the new theories of conventional war had had their origins at Rand. Chief among these was the notion of the "firebreak"—the theory that a massive Soviet invasion of western Europe could be slowed by NATO's conventional forces, and then halted by the threat to use nuclear weapons. The possibility that NATO might be able to stop the Red Army without using nuclear weapons had been "a very far out, minority view" at Rand as recently as the late 1950s, said Enthoven, "because of the widespread assumption of the overwhelming mass of Soviet forces." But war games of the sort that Enthoven, Rowen, and Hoag had played at Rand, as well as more realistic exercises in Europe, convinced most strategists that an all-out conventional war was at least preferable to a Soviet-American nuclear *Götterdämmerung*.

Since the beginning of the Kennedy administration, even those strategists previously most often identified with the theory of limited nuclear war in Europe—like Henry Kissinger—had come to affect a kind of public transubstantiation of their earlier view. The few holdouts who stubbornly continued to make a case for tactical nuclear warfare—particularly Bernard Brodie and Samuel Cohen—faced increasing isolation and derision. The low point for Brodie was probably the 1963 conference of strategists that he attended in England, during a year's leave from Rand. At this gathering he attacked the conventional-force firebreak idea and defended his advocacy of tactical nuclear weapons. Brodie's arguments, however, simply "got the back of the hand" from others present, including former secretary of state Dean Acheson, according to one participant. Even his friends thought Brodie's ideas on fighting a limited nuclear war in Europe "bizarre," if not "ludicrous." Brodie, for his part, ridiculed Rand's firebreak theory as having its origins in the frequent grassfires in the hills near Santa Monica.[19]

William Kaufmann was author of another book about limited nuclear war. But he, like Kissinger, had since abandoned the idea. By the 1960s Kaufmann thought that even small tactical nuclear weapons "were just too powerful to have any tactical use." He became persuaded of that view during a 1962 demonstration of a new Army weapon—a recoilless rifle capable of firing a nuclear warhead. Derided by critics as "a nuclear hand grenade," the Davy Crockett could be fitted atop a jeep and fired by a crew of only three men. The Army unintentionally compounded the weapon's public-relations problem with its slogan "A Davy Crockett in every pocket." At the test firing, Kaufmann had upset his host, General Charles Bonesteel, by laughing.

Kaufmann thought the Army's strategy for fighting a nuclear war in Europe similarly "ludicrous in a sinister kind of way"—in that it simply substituted nuclear weapons for conventional ones. War games played at Rand and in the field had shown that casualties among civilians as well as soldiers "just mounted astronomically" as soon as even the smallest nuclear weapons were used. The employment of such weapons by NATO, Kaufmann became convinced, would be strategically suicidal. When allied players resorted to nuclear weapons in those games, he said, "NATO just loses faster."

But the idea of using conventional forces to stop a Soviet invasion of Europe was unpopular both at home and among America's allies. The greatest difficulty, Enthoven thought, lay not in stopping Russian troops but in overcoming the fixed idea among the military that it "wasn't feasible" to halt the Red Army without resorting to nuclear weapons.

As had been the case with the missile gap, Enthoven believed that NATO's pessimism was an example of the military's becoming needlessly enslaved by the tyranny of false numbers.[20] Years of overstating the Russian threat, he noted, had had the effect of "bending U.S. strategy out of shape" by putting an almost exclusive emphasis upon nuclear weapons. Like the Air Force in the missile gap, Army and NATO commanders belatedly came to realize that they were hurting their own cause by proclaiming the Red Army's invincibility. Enthoven found the British Defence Staff so gloomy about the prospect of holding the Russians back that it had issued its Army of the Rhine only three days' worth of ammunition. "You can be damned sure that the war won't last more than three days in that case," he scolded the British.[21]

The political pressures and military prerogatives that had stood in the way of changes in the nation's nuclear strategy proved an obstacle as well in the shift to a greater conventional emphasis. When rejecting Hoag's proposal that McNamara devote a substantially greater part of the military budget to conventional forces, Enthoven had supposedly claimed that Hoag's idea "won the cost-effectiveness argument by thirty percent"—but it would embarrass the defense secretary by creating a furor in Congress and among the allies. Hitch thought an earlier clash with LeMay over a new rifle for SAC had been a kind of parable of the problems faced by those in McNamara's band. The Pentagon's Comptroller and his co-workers in Systems Analysis thought the case for the M-16 "overwhelming," Hitch said. He remembered, however, being called into LeMay's office one day over the issue. "I agree with everything you say about the M-16 rifle," LeMay told him. "But it's none of your goddamn business. It's the business of the chief of staff of the Army."[22]

Resistance to the idea of substituting troops for nuclear weapons confronted the Kennedy administration at virtually every level. In the summer of 1961—after Kennedy's decision to call up the reserves during the Berlin crisis had dramatized to him the extent to which the nation was dependent upon the bomb—he ordered a greater emphasis to be made upon rebuilding conventional forces. But the prospect of increasing the defense budget and of reinstituting conscription proved as politically unattractive to America's NATO allies as it was at home.

During the rethinking of military policy at the start of the administration, a formal pledge that the United States would not be the first to use nuclear weapons had become a topic of considerable discussion and even some consensus among McNamara's civilian advisers. A public no-first-use pledge to supplement the informal promise that McNamara felt he had from the president was among the recommendations that Morton Halperin and Malcolm Hoag circulated within the government at the time. As with the no-cities doctrine, however, the no-first-use idea had provoked hostility as well as incredulity when McNamara brought it up with the Europeans in his secret speech at Athens in 1962.

Despite the assurances that it would be possible for NATO to match or even exceed the Warsaw Pact forces confronting it in Europe, the social, economic, and political costs of such a step had finally been seen as prohibitive. "Our European allies had different perceptions and we didn't want to get them all shook up," Enthoven explained of the reason for drawing back on flexible response. Ultimately, Enthoven, Nitze, and Rowen were obliged to postpone the effort to bolster NATO. But their commitment to the goal remained. "We never abandoned the idea that we should have a conventional capability of about the same size and strength as the Soviets," Enthoven said.

For all, a final and graphic illustration of the problems the administration would encounter with the allies over nuclear weapons was the fate of the multilateral force—which at one point had been thought of as a sort of middle ground between a no-first-use pledge and the threat of massive retaliation. The idea of a separate stockpile of nuclear weapons under joint European and American control had actually originated with the Eisenhower administration.[23] Since then, the aim of the MLF had been to preclude German development of an atomic bomb and to prevent France's defection from NATO. Either event, it was feared, might result if the Europeans began to doubt that the United States would risk a nuclear war on their behalf. The concept of the MLF had been revived in the Kennedy administration when discussion of the no-first-use pledge and McNamara's announcement of the no-cities doctrine had reportedly awakened such doubts.

The MLF had also been adopted by self-professed "Europeanists" in the State Department as a way to promote the dream of a unified Europe. "The multilateral concept," even a supporter acknowledged, "was essentially theological." "It was pure form—symbolism without substance," a detractor charged. Shortly after the MLF was brought up again by the Kennedy administration, it had become a topic of criticism—and ridicule—at home. The initial notion of missile-firing submarines with mixed American and European crews had had to be abandoned when Admiral Hyman Rickover —for whom the nuclear Navy was a kind of private satrapy—privately informed Kennedy that he would not allow Frenchmen on his vessels.

Like the no-cities idea and the no-first-use pledge, the MLF was never officially renounced by the Kennedy administration, but quietly allowed to fade into oblivion. Its original justification had ended with France's split from NATO, and the fading of the specter of a German bomb. After the Cuban missile crisis, moreover, the last and perhaps the most important reason for the MLF ceased to exist: henceforth few could doubt Kennedy's willingness to risk a nuclear confrontation with Russia.

In lieu of the multilateral force, McNamara substituted a secret Nuclear Planning Group consisting only of NATO's defense ministers and himself. The purpose of the group was to decide under what circumstances nuclear weapons would be used in the event of war in Europe. McNamara assured that the meetings of the group would remain deliberate by seating its ten members at a round table whose size could accommodate only that number, and by forbidding anyone there from reading a prepared statement or position.

McNamara's Nuclear Planning Group notwithstanding, the failure of the MLF and the frustrations encountered with the strategy of flexible response underscored the difficulty that the Kennedy administration faced in attempting to move away from a generation-long dependence upon nuclear weapons. So subtle and protracted was the demise of the MLF that even Bundy would be unaware of its passing. In the summer of 1963, Bundy said, he had gone to Kennedy to express his personal view that "the MLF had had it." Bundy's revelation evidently came as no surprise to Kennedy. "Where have *you* been?" the president had asked sardonically.

For all the differences of style and substance that Kennedy, McNamara, and their advisers tried to draw between themselves and their predecessors, the final attitude of the New Frontier toward nuclear weapons bore a remarkable resemblance to that of Eisenhower at the end of his second term.

In November 1963, just before Kennedy's death, McNamara had for the first time in public held out the tentative prospect that future defense spending would level off—and might actually "decline a little."[24] The previous summer, the extent to which Kennedy himself had begun to move away from his early thinking about the arms race was evident in the speech he gave at American University on the dangers of nuclear war. That topic was almost certainly a central concern as well of the secret correspondence that Kennedy had continued with Khrushchev after the missile crisis. The conciliatory rhetoric of Kennedy's American University speech contrasted sharply—and deliberately—with the call to arms of his inaugural.[25] Kennedy's proposal in the speech that the United States and Russia launch a renewed effort for a ban on nuclear testing seemed an equally dramatic departure from the administration's early and unparalleled missile buildup. By the early fall of 1963, the test ban had become an almost consuming interest for both Kennedy and McNamara.

The political and bureaucratic pressures that acted to bring the administration's military buildup into being, however, also acted to sustain it. The speech in Dallas that Kennedy had intended to give the day he was assassinated was one extolling the administration's record in achieving the nation's as-of-then-unchallenged strategic superiority. Another purpose of the speech, the president's aides said, was to have laid the basis for future efforts at arms reductions with the Russians.

It was all the more ironic, therefore, that the tangible legacy of the Kennedy administration would be the thousand-ICBM force and the concept of nuclear war-fighting that McNamara introduced into U.S. war planning. It had proved far easier to undertake those changes than to undo them. Kaufmann noted that the defense secretary continually postponed a second revision of the SIOP—in which he intended to officially replace the concept of damage limitation with assured destruction. Bundy thought it significant that he and McNamara had been in the Oval Office, discussing ways to counter the Navy's latest request for more missile-firing submarines, when the word came from Dallas of Kennedy's death.

Despite all of the experts' efforts, the vital question that McNamara had posed at the beginning of the New Frontier—"How much is enough?"—remained unanswered at its end.

16

False Dawn

Scientists who became advocates of arms control at the end of the Eisenhower administration were chagrined to find the most stalwart opponents to a nuclear test ban in the Kennedy administration among their own kind. Since the diplomatic fiascos at Geneva and Paris, the issues separating the scientists on the test ban had become perhaps less technical than polemical. One illustration of the resulting rancor—and occasional misunderstanding—was the dispute between test ban opponent Edward Teller and Teller's chief nemesis in the debate over the ban, chemist Linus Pauling.

Pauling accused Teller of trying to defuse public concern over fallout with claims that radioactivity was actually beneficial to living organisms, and necessary to the process of evolution. Teller had at one point even proposed renaming the standard measure of radiation exposure—the rad—a "sunshine unit." (The inspiration for the change in nomenclature may have been more innocent than Pauling supposed. The idea thus evidently came from a ghoulishly misnamed government study, Project Sunshine, which analyzed the bones of stillborn infants to verify the claim of test ban proponents that fission products from aboveground nuclear explosions accumulated in the bone marrow of children.)[1]

So emotionally charged had the issue of radioactive fallout and its effects become by the late 1950s that both sides in the test ban debate made claims and statements which were at least a source of confusion, if not an actual misrepresentation of the facts. The scientists' "numbers game" became a classic example of how disagreements among experts created bafflement for laymen. Pauling, for example, portrayed the harmful effects of radiation in terms of the number of children whose deaths were statistically probable as a result of exposure to fallout from nuclear tests. Teller, using the same data, compared the effects of fallout to the average number of days that an individual's life might be shortened by exposure to hospital X-rays, cigarette smoke, or the sun's rays. It was in extending this argument to include the presumed role of cosmic rays in evolution that Teller made the controversial claim of how the long-term effects of radiation might even be beneficial to humans.[2]

Another expert who became caught up in the test ban debate, Herman Kahn, found it was possible to make enemies on both sides. Kahn professed amazement at the reaction to his article on the effects of fallout, published while he was still at Rand. The article had claimed that continued atmospheric testing in the Pacific by the United States would eventually cause ten thousand cases of bone cancer worldwide—creating a one-in-three-million chance that any particular individual would be so afflicted. The response to Kahn's article was almost uniformly irate, but for different reasons. "Half of the mail said, 'You bastard—why are you scaring the hell out of people by saying ten thousand when the important figure is one in three million,' " Kahn recalled. "But the other half said, 'Why are you saying one in three million when the important point is ten thousand?' "

A physicist drawn into the test ban controversy, Freeman Dyson, thought that its high and low points coincided with a spring 1960 article he wrote for *Foreign Affairs* opposing the ban. Dyson claimed in his essay that the renunciation of nuclear testing by the United States would eventually find the nation "in the position of the Polish army in 1939, fighting tanks with horses." Some years later, after he had become a test ban supporter, Dyson rejected both the tone and the substance of his earlier argument—even as he defended its motive. His anti-ban essay, Dyson wrote, was "an act of personal loyalty to Edward Teller and to his colleagues with whom I worked at Livermore." But it was also, he conceded, "a desperate attempt to salvage an untenable position with spurious emotional claptrap." Dyson said he accepted the case for the test ban one evening in 1962, when he had plotted the number of nuclear explosions occurring since 1945. His chart showed a doubling of nuclear tests every three years.[3]

Behind the continuing public dispute over the effects of fallout, other issues —equally controversial, but kept hidden from the public because of their security classification—were the subject of arguments between pro- and anti-ban scientists. One such claim, originating with two Rand physicists opposed to a ban, concerned the possibility that the Russians might be able to test nuclear weapons secretly and in violation of an agreement, by exploding them in huge underground salt caverns. The physicists' theory was that the size and geology of the caverns would mask—or "decouple"—the telltale shock waves created by a nuclear explosion and relied upon by monitors to betray clandestine tests.[4]

The "big-hole" theory, as it was called, had initially been ridiculed by scientists who studied the detection problem at the 1958 Geneva conference. Subsequent underground experiments by the United States, however, had pointed to the conclusion that masking a nuclear test was at least theoretically feasible. It was not until an actual nuclear test in a Mississippi salt cavern had demonstrated the practical difficulties to decoupling that the big-hole theory was reluctantly abandoned by its sponsors. "The big-hole managed to derail the test ban for some time," ruefully acknowledged one proponent of the ban.

The prospect that the Russians might be able to evade detection by testing nuclear weapons deep in outer space or on the far side of the sun or moon was next raised by Teller, who attributed a hidden and sinister motive to the Soviets' participation in the space race. But here as well, pro-ban scientists discounted the danger of such cheating as exaggerated or fanciful—and certainly of a cost out of proportion to any possible gain. "If you assume *that* level of conspiracy, then you sacrifice any hope of arms control," observed physicist Wolfgang Panofsky. "One has to temper these technical-possibility arguments with some kind of value judgment. The irony is that you almost hoped the adversary would waste his resources on such methods."[5]

Panofsky served with Teller in the 1950s on a government panel investigating the feasibility of nuclear testing in outer space. The panel had concluded that such testing, while possible, would be enormously more expensive and less technically valuable than tests conducted on or under the earth's surface. It was a device Panofsky invented that had measured the shock waves from the first nuclear test at Trinity site. Some years later, at Oppenheimer's request, he wrote the top-secret "Screwdriver Report" on how to foil enemy efforts at smuggling nuclear weapons or radioactive materials into the United States. (The detectors Panofsky designed for airports and ship terminals were discreetly in use throughout the 1950s. But, according to their inventor, they detected only one supposed nuclear terrorist—a hapless woman attempting to smuggle a hundred radium-dial watches in her corset.) Panofsky's experience as a technical representative at Geneva in 1958 had convinced him that a ban on nuclear testing was both necessary and attainable. Even after the technical objections to such a step had been met, however, Panofsky conceded that there remained "strongly divided opinion" among scientists concerning the ban.

The sudden resumption of atmospheric nuclear testing by Russia in 1961—following a three-year moratorium proposed by the Soviets and agreed to by Eisenhower—predictably drove the two sides in the scientists' test ban debate even further apart. Stunned proponents of the ban sought to rally their position by noting that Khrushchev had at least announced his intention to end the moratorium beforehand, rather than secretly resuming nuclear testing in the hope of avoiding detection. But test ban opponents like Teller pointedly observed in rebuttal that the timing of Khrushchev's announcement hardly reflected well on the ability of the West to detect Soviet intentions: "I do know that the CIA assured us that if the Soviets were planning to have a test series we would know at least a month in advance. We did find out about it ahead of time—namely, forty-eight hours ahead of time, when Khrushchev announced it."

Hopes for an eventual ban remained alive, despite the resumption of unrestricted testing in the atmosphere by both the United States and the Soviet Union during 1962. Indeed, the resumption of nuclear tests unexpectedly gave a new impetus to the test ban movement in the United States— and possibly in Russia. The effect of the gigantic sixty-two-megaton hydrogen bomb with which the Russians inaugurated their resumption of nuclear testing thus unintentionally underscored the urgency of a ban. The greater-than-expected power of the explosion evidently frightened Khrushchev as well as the mammoth bomb's own creators—some of whom apparently shared the Soviet leader's opinion that they were tampering with the unknown.[6]

But there were conflicting lessons drawn from the moratorium's end. For some, the similarly unanticipated results of a parallel series of American nuclear tests made a case for continued testing to develop new weapons; for others, those tests bolstered the case for a ban. Opponents of the ban argued that a new round of tests might lead the way to a new generation of nuclear weapons, useful in developing a defense against missiles or as a means to blind enemy defenses in the event of nuclear war. They pointed out how a high-altitude test of a U.S. hydrogen bomb in the Pacific during 1962 had effects beyond what its designers had imagined—knocking out lights and setting off burglar alarms in Honolulu, some eight hundred miles away.[7]

"It was scary," said one scientist about the unexpected results of another high-altitude test, which temporarily caused an artificial band of radioactivity around the earth. "We thought we had created a new Van Allen belt."

The promise of revolutionary new weapons eventually became the most serious argument against a ban on testing. During the Eisenhower administration, Teller and others had claimed that a test ban would preclude the United States from developing a new generation of nuclear weapons which could prove decisive in a limited war in Europe and might reduce American casualties in the event of an all-out war with Russia. Eisenhower admitted that he found this the most compelling case against a test ban; it was also the reason why he had initially rejected a moratorium on nuclear testing.[8] Preeminent among the new generation of nuclear weapons that opponents of the ban claimed could be developed by continued testing were those that would be theoretically "clean," or relatively free of the long-lived fission products that composed radioactive fallout.

Since his visit to the bombed-out city of Seoul during the Korean War, Samuel Cohen had appreciated the potential for an atomic weapon that would kill by a dazzling pulse of short-lived ionizing radiation—reminiscent of the death ray of science fiction—rather than by the effects of heat, blast, and debilitating fallout. But it was not until a decade later that Cohen, while on a visit to the weapons laboratory at Livermore, had come across a practical way to make the destructiveness of nuclear weapons more discriminative.[9]

The inspiration for the enhanced-radiation weapon, or "neutron bomb," had originated with a Livermore project to develop a fallout-free nonfission trigger for small hydrogen bombs that could be used tactically in warfare. Both Rand and the military, Cohen claimed, had been "largely unsympathetic" to the proposal made in his 1958 Rand report for a nuclear weapon that killed primarily with radiation. "Since the Air Force was not enamored of tactical nuclear weapons there was no emphasis put on it," he said.

His efforts to interest the Eisenhower administration in the neutron bomb also met with failure. Despite repeated entreaties and the personal intervention of the president's brother, Cohen was never able to present a briefing on the neutron bomb to Eisenhower—and was eventually proscribed by the Air Force from giving the briefing to anyone in the Pentagon, he claimed.[10] (Cohen recalled that on one occasion he at least came close to briefing Eisenhower. When he arrived at the White House, however, the president was practicing putting in the Rose Garden and had left strict instructions not to be disturbed.)

The real breakthrough on the neutron bomb, Cohen admitted, came about as the result of "Washington politics." Called before a closed Senate hearing in 1959 by test ban opponents, the self-professed "father of the neutron bomb" found allies among those in the military who resented the Air Force's dominance in the military budget, as well as among those who hoped to resume atmospheric testing. "The Navy fell in love with it," Cohen remembered. Locked in its annual struggle with the Air Force over the defense budget, and in search of a justification for its politically imperiled fleet of aircraft carriers, the Navy had seized upon the neutron bomb as one nuclear weapon that could be uniquely its own preserve. Subsequently promoting the weapon "in a wild swing of briefings" throughout official Washington, Cohen said, he nonetheless did not consider himself a lobbyist for the neutron bomb: "Everybody else was lobbying. I was a captive salesman. I had been picked by a group."

Part of the group that adopted him, Cohen pointed out, "genuinely shared" his belief in discriminative nuclear weapons—"but another part of the group was trying to put an end to the nuclear test moratorium." Years later, Cohen conceded that he had been "extremely naive" in thinking the almost overnight popularity of the neutron bomb reflected support for his idea of more "humane" nuclear weapons. He realized that promoters of the bomb's development by renewed testing sought it primarily as a political weapon against the moratorium and a permanent test ban. Because of the larger political issues behind the neutron bomb, some of those scientists who had most vehemently opposed Project Vista and tactical nuclear weapons only the decade before now became the most fervent supporters of the neutron bomb.

A chance encounter between the father of the hydrogen bomb and the father of the neutron bomb in a hallway at Rand in the early 1960s confirmed Cohen's opinion that cynical ulterior motives lay at the heart of his pet project's sudden popularity. When Cohen ran into Teller the moratorium had already ended, nuclear testing had resumed, and the Livermore lab that Teller directed had recently been given the task of developing enhanced-radiation weapons. "Sam, I can't thank you enough for what you've done," Cohen claimed Teller told him. "But then Teller," Cohen said, "got that typical leer on his face and added: 'Tell me, Sam. What *have* you done?'"

As Cohen groped for a reply to the barbed jibe, Teller simply turned and walked away. "Until that time, in my own egotistical way," Cohen reflected, "I thought I was just being loved and appreciated."

Cohen's triumph was also short-lived. The enthusiasm for the neutron bomb "just suddenly died," he recalled, amid the resurgent public concern with fallout in the wake of the moratorium's end.

In addition to opposition from scientists like Teller, resistance to a test ban came from within the Kennedy administration itself, and from Congress. Shortly after becoming president, Kennedy had ordered a comprehensive reassessment of arms control negotiations to accompany the review of military strategy. One of the scientists who had participated in the arms control review thought the discussion there of a Soviet-American ban on the testing of new intercontinental ballistic missiles—a proposal first considered during the Eisenhower years—now "disappointing" and even "unreal." He believed, therefore, that the opposition to a permanent test ban had become institutionalized within the government while the moratorium had been in effect.

In fact, Kennedy was reportedly furious to learn that some of the most effective opposition to the test ban came from his own CIA director, John McCone. McCone had volunteered the help of the agency's technical experts to other opponents of the ban in Congress. The CIA's analysts subsequently aided Senator John Stennis' Armed Services Committee in making its case, based upon circumstantial evidence, that the Russians were secretly violating the test moratorium. While the moratorium was still in effect, Kennedy accused the Atomic Energy Commission of violating his direct orders by making its own clandestine preparations to resume nuclear testing in Nevada.[11]

Opponents of the test ban in Congress also found an eager ally in the military. At one point Air Force Intelligence allegedly had as many as thirty people assigned to the single task of proving that the Russians were cheating on the moratorium. "Every time a plane flew from one point to another in the Soviet Union," noted physicist Herbert Scoville, "the Air Force claimed it must have dropped a bomb en route."

Scoville, then head of the CIA's science and technology directorate, said that he and his staff investigated Air Force claims of Russian cheating in three separate studies and found no substantiation for the charge. Herbert York similarly concluded that the question of Soviet cheating had become an article of faith for some, regardless of the evidence. In a confrontation with McCone during the fall of 1960, York repeated his conviction that the Russians were not violating the moratorium. "That's practically treason," McCone had snapped.

Even after the moratorium's sudden and disappointing demise, test ban proponents took heart in the fact that the Kennedy administration still had an Arms Control and Disarmament Agency as part of the State Department. The new organization—originally dubbed the "Peace Agency"—had grown out of an inspiration of the 1960 presidential campaign, as the beginning of what one of its creators hoped would be "a countervailing force" to the Pentagon. Since its inception, however, ACDA, too, had become embroiled in partisan politics and stymied by worsening relations with the Russians. While the word "disarmament" remained in the agency's title, there was no longer any question that its principal effort would be directed toward the more limited and seemingly more realistic goal of arms control. One reason for the politicalization of ACDA, Kennedy administration officials acknowledged, was the fact that an early and particular focus of the new agency would be the negotiations for a test ban.[12]

While many experts were persuaded of the merits of a ban on nuclear testing well before the fall of 1962, the Cuban missile crisis lent a new touch of urgency to the talks that had been going on in Geneva since 1958. George Kistiakowsky, Eisenhower's chief science adviser, who had meanwhile returned to Harvard to teach physics, dismissed his class at the height of the crisis—gripped by the despairing fear, he told his students, "that war is at hand." Another Los Alamos veteran who had been a technical adviser at Geneva, Cornell physicist Hans Bethe, thought the missile crisis was both a reprieve and a providential warning. So, too, did physicist Leo Szilard— who flew to Switzerland during the crisis in the expectation, he told a friend, of being "the first refugee of the Third World War." (After he returned to the United States, Szilard remarked to his friend that the destruction of a backyard fallout shelter belonging to an anti-ban scientist in a California grass fire during the missile crisis proved not only "that God exists, but that He has a sense of humor.")[13]

Kennedy's decision in the spring of 1963 to "lean into" the stalled test ban negotiations seemed as well to have a connection to the near-brush with nuclear war. In talks with the Russians that were revived as a result of the president's initiative in his American University speech, Kennedy publicly rededicated himself to the goal of a permanent ban on all nuclear testing.

For the president and his chief negotiator in Geneva, Averell Harriman, that goal seemed tantalizingly close—and increasingly urgent—by the summer of 1963. The specter of a Chinese atomic bomb had thus begun to haunt the test ban talks after the Cuban crisis.[14] At the same time, the exposure of the myth of the missile gap and the weathering of the missile crisis had removed what was almost certainly a reason for Khrushchev's long-term and adamant opposition to on-site inspection: the fear that the U.S. government might call his bluff concerning the real number of missiles and attempt to exploit America's strategic advantage.

The number of on-site inspections had always been the outstanding issue of disagreement in the test ban talks. A steady improvement in detection techniques and—perhaps more important—a series of political compromises by U.S. and Soviet negotiators after the Cuban crisis had progressively reduced the number of inspections that U.S. experts said they required from a supposedly irreducible minimum of twenty to just five. The Russians, however, were willing to allow only three. Over the two disputed inspections the talks had remained deadlocked for several months.

While the impasse over the number of inspections persisted, early hopes for a complete or comprehensive ban on nuclear testing had faded correspondingly. Because of the deadlock, Kennedy and Harriman began to despair of achieving their original aim of a comprehensive test ban. The military services and the two nuclear weapons laboratories had meanwhile become a nexus of domestic opposition to such a ban. But the most important resistance remained in Congress, remembered Carl Kaysen, who served as liaison between the administration and congressional committees holding hearings on the test ban. (Responsible for instructing pro-ban scientists on how to testify before John Stennis' conservative Senate committee in late 1962, Kaysen recalled being advised by deputy defense secretary John McNaughton to "horse-shed" the witnesses. In the Illinois farm country where McNaughton grew up, it was a tradition for a circuit court judge to coach a friendly witness on his testimony in a horse shed near the courthouse before a trial. City-bred, Kaysen simply thought that McNaughton had misspoken; but he enthusiastically volunteered to do all that the task required. "We did a much better job on Stennis that time," he said.)

Despite the fact that Khrushchev had twice before rejected the idea of a partial ban on nuclear testing, Soviet opposition to such an interim measure —which would allow testing underground and required no on-site inspection—began to waver in the late spring and early summer of 1963. Beset on all sides, the idea of a comprehensive test ban "just stopped dead" that summer, Kaysen recollected. "It just sort of fell apart," Spurgeon Keeny said of the proposal, for which he had also been a spokesman in the administration. Final evidence that the Russians too had decided to pull away from a total ban came with a classic example of Soviet indirection. When a U.S. geophysicist arrived in Moscow that summer to continue discussions with a Russian counterpart regarding on-site inspection, the American was simply told by Soviet officials that their scientist could not be found.

With the collapse of the comprehensive test ban proposal, the idea of a partial or limited ban as a compromise measure quickly gained ground in the United States. Indeed, in the aftermath of the total ban's demise, Keeny considered that "the limited test ban became a political necessity." The final breakthrough on the stalemated talks in Geneva had come about on political, rather than technical, grounds. Kennedy's renewed call for a test ban in his American University speech was the turning point in the negotiations, according to the president's aides—as well as by Khrushchev's own subsequent account. When Freeman Dyson, by then an adviser to the Arms Control and Disarmament Agency, returned to ACDA later that summer following a year spent at Princeton, he found that "the atmosphere had completely changed" regarding the chances for a test ban.[15]

The signing that August—only hours short of the eighteenth anniversary of the atomic bombing of Hiroshima—of a treaty banning nuclear weapons tests in the atmosphere, in outer space, and underwater became the crowning achievement of Kennedy's brief time in office. "No other accomplishment in the White House gave Kennedy greater satisfaction," wrote Theodore Sorensen.[16] Initially, Kennedy's enthusiasm was unquestionably shared by those experts who had lobbied for the test ban. Jubilant over the treaty with Russia, the editors of the *Bulletin of Atomic Scientists* moved the hands of their doomsday clock to the farthest it had ever been from the final hour—twelve minutes away from midnight.

But it would become evident to the scientists in succeeding months that their celebration had been premature. Even some of the test ban's foremost supporters later conceded that theirs had been a hollow victory at best—a meaningless triumph that obscured the defeat of what may have been a last, best hope. "When you stop to think of what the advantages were to us of stopping all testing in the early 1960s when we were still ahead of the Soviets it's really appalling to realize what a missed opportunity we had," Harriman concluded of the comprehensive test ban some twenty years later. Glenn Seaborg, a member of Oppenheimer's General Advisory Committee in 1950 and chairman of the AEC under Kennedy, came to share Harriman's view. He and other scientists claimed that the Soviets benefited more than the United States from subsequent nuclear tests.[17]

Because the partial test ban did not eliminate or even necessarily reduce nuclear testing but merely forced it underground, it was destined to have little or no effect upon the development of new and more deadly nuclear weapons, including those whose promise Teller and others had used as an argument against a ban. Ironically, the neutron bomb's feasibility had been demonstrated by underground tests conducted during the negotiations on the test ban. In the late spring of 1963—just before the breakthrough in those talks occurred—the prototype of future enhanced-radiation weapons was perfected in a series of subterranean explosions.[18] "The limited test ban was more an environmental measure than arms control," Keeny reluctantly concluded. "It made the world safe for testing."

While the partial test ban did not lessen the pressure for more and better nuclear weapons, it did illustrate a curious reversal of roles in the scientists' generation-long debate on defense. A sign of the trouble ahead for arms control had been present in Senate ratification hearings on the test ban treaty that began in the fall of 1963—but the warning was ignored then amid the celebratory mood of the treaty's supporters. In a closed session of those public hearings, Edward Teller had seized upon what his critics considered the last and latest of his weapons against the ban. It was an arsenal that had started with the big-hole theory and included the neutron bomb.

Teller argued in a secret annex to the ratification hearings that continued high-altitude nuclear testing was necessary if the nation hoped to perfect a means of destroying Russian missiles in flight. Atmospheric tests carried out by the United States just before the ban had, in fact, tentatively borne out the contention—made by him and the two Rand physicists who were authors of the big-hole theory—that X-rays released by a nuclear explosion in outer space could incapacitate the warhead of a missile in midflight. Teller's troubling but almost totally isolated testimony against the test ban and for development of a defense against missiles had had no effect upon the outcome of the Senate hearings, which ended in an overwhelming endorsement of the test ban treaty. Indeed, so impressed was Kennedy with the outpouring of public support for the treaty, he told science adviser Jerome Wiesner that if he had known the depth of popular support for an end to nuclear testing he would have continued to press for a comprehensive test ban.

Teller's futile plea for an antiballistic missile—an ABM—in the closed Senate hearing seemed, in retrospect, the hand-sized cloud that portended the gathering storm. In spite of the test ban's popularity in the administration and among the public, the apparent triumph of arms control that the treaty represented was both highly qualified and short-lived. The glow of optimism which suffused the ranks of those who proudly called themselves arms controllers at the end of the Kennedy administration would seem, in hindsight, to be the light of a false dawn.

17

Mad Momentum

The obvious advantage that the intercontinental-range missile would give the attacker had been a principal impetus to development of the ICBM. Only a year after Oppenheimer was stripped of his security clearance—in part for supposedly overstating the effectiveness of a defense against bombers—the Eisenhower administration had approved a program to develop a defense against missiles. The problem of countering the missile threat had been acknowledged then to be even greater than that faced by Project Charles, because of the remarkable speed with which missiles could reach their targets, and because of the devastation that would result if only a single missile slipped past the defenders. For a number of years after the search for an ABM had begun, a defense against ballistic missiles—while recognized as theoretically feasible—was thought to face technical obstacles that could prove insurmountable.[1]

By 1958 the Army had been assigned the ABM project as a result of the Air Force's demonstrated lack of enthusiasm for continental air defense. The following year, Eisenhower vetoed an Army plan to deploy a prototype defense against missiles on the advice of scientists, who argued that the proposed system could be easily countered by the Russians.[2] Among the physicists advising against the ABM had been Richard Garwin, an early recruit to one of the progeny of Project Charles—Project Lamplighter.

Garwin pointed out that the technical flaws of the Army's ABM included the difficulty of detecting enemy missiles soon enough to destroy them, and the problem of distinguishing between the actual missiles and accompanying decoys. He blamed the Army's misplaced faith in its antimissile missile in part upon a lack of imagination shown by the Air Force, which had been assigned the task of overcoming the missile defense in various tests. In each of those trials the Air Force, Garwin said, had made all of its decoys the same. He and other scientists noted that a real attacker would almost certainly be more ingenious, using a variety of decoys to deceive the defense. They had demonstrated their point by inventing their own decoys, some of which were as simple as foil-covered balloons. "That dampened the ardor of the Army's people," Garwin recalled.

His early experience with Lamplighter, he claimed, had taught him how defense projects could take on a life of their own—a lesson that seemed relevant as well in the case of the ABM. When confronted with irrefutable evidence that a particular design for their ABM would not work, the Army sponsors of the weapon would invariably return with a somewhat modified design. After once again advising the Army to take its latest version of the ABM back to the drawing board, Garwin and others among the president's science advisers had been given an especially gloomy briefing by the same service about the rapid progress supposedly being made by the Russians toward developing their ABM. The briefing prompted the experts to suggest wryly that the Army simply copy the Soviet system. Some weeks later Garwin and the others had had to demonstrate that even the Soviet-style ABM proposed by the Army could be thwarted by a determined and technologically sophisticated opponent.

The still unresolved technical deficiencies of a missile defense lay behind President Kennedy's decision to reject yet another ABM design in 1962.[3] As with Eisenhower, Kennedy's science advisers had unanimously recommended against the Army's latest antimissile missile. But in Kennedy's case it may have been the opinion of McNamara that played the decisive role. McNamara's opposition to the ABM was based upon considerations, therefore, that were practical as well as technical. He acknowledged that some of the problems of intercepting missiles in flight had been overcome since the Eisenhower years, though the difficulty of distinguishing between real and apparent missiles remained. But for McNamara it was the fact that the ABM failed the test of cost-effectiveness—it was likely to cost the United States more to build than it would cost the Russians to counter—which lay behind his recommendation that the president not commit the nation to a missile defense.

Except for the administration's initial review of nuclear strategy, Alain Enthoven said, the ABM debate was the only other occasion when McNamara became "deeply involved with strategic issues." A 1963 meeting between the two men illustrated for Enthoven how McNamara's attitude toward the ABM had changed along with his thinking on nuclear strategy. Skeptical that any defense against missiles would ever be practical, McNamara had instructed Enthoven to prepare a case for and a case against the ABM. The head of the Pentagon's System Analysis Division had likened the problem then to that of the flat-of-the-curve argument he had made for Kennedy's missile decision. Accordingly, Enthoven presented McNamara with two separate sets of charts and figures—representing two widely different estimates of the ABM's prospective cost.[4]

"What is the assumption that makes for the difference?" McNamara had quizzed him after the study was finished. When Enthoven explained that the variance was caused by the CIA's high and low estimates of future Russian missile strength, McNamara asked him to prepare another set of tables exploring various Soviet responses to an American ABM. "Instead of just constraining the Russians to be like our intelligence estimates say they're going to be—with implicitly no response to our ABM—tell me what it would look like if we bought the ABM and they don't respond, or if they respond in varying amounts," he instructed Enthoven.

"We found that the Soviet response was the most critical variable," Enthoven recalled of his subsequent study. "If we spent forty billion dollars on an ABM they might be able to spend ten billion and completely offset it."

Enthusiasts of a missile defense charged that the same political considerations hidden in the flat-of-the-curve argument against more ICBMs were subtly present as well in McNamara's cost-effectiveness case against the ABM. In reality, Kennedy's decision to continue funding research on a defense against missiles was probably motivated less by the faith that an effective ABM would be the result than by the hope that this partial measure would at least deflect criticism of the administration by the military and Congress.[5] Within a year of the president's decision not to deploy the ABM, nonetheless, the claim that the Russians were well ahead of the United States in perfecting a defense against missiles came to dominate the ABM debate, overshadowing the technical arguments for and against the weapons, and once again pitting expert against expert.

A warning of how bitterly contested the ABM issue would become was the long and passionate controversy it provoked at Herman Kahn's think tank. Kahn had left Rand in 1960 to found the Hudson Institute in the Washington Irving country of upstate New York. The fact that the physicist's resignation had been prompted in part by Rand's objections to his evident fixation upon fallout shelters may have explained the beginning emphasis at Hudson upon defense against atomic attack. Kahn's advocacy of civil defense came to encompass not only so-called passive measures like shelters, but more active steps to limit damage in a nuclear war—such as the ABM. Even some of Kahn's earliest supporters thought that his interest in civil defense at Rand had become a kind of obsession by the time he founded Hudson. After one visit there, Thomas Schelling told Kahn that a more appropriate title for his think tank would be "The Institute for Active Defense."

Reacting to what he claimed was Rand's stultifying, "hothouse" intellectual environment, Kahn deliberately chose to surround himself at Hudson with an ecumenical group of intellectuals who held contrasting—and often conflicting—views. Because at Rand there had been much emphasis on rank, Kahn, in another departure from hallowed Rand tradition, allowed each member of Hudson to choose his or her own title. The unifying trait of the group assembled, Kahn argued, was its sense of mission. "Eight out of ten of us were idealists," he said. "We were going to save the world."

Kahn himself remained unquestionably the major figure at Hudson in terms of both intellect and force of personality. It was impossible to be there, according to Schelling, "without being under exceedingly strong unconscious pressure to accommodate with the dominant view." He noted that some of those who had initially disagreed with Kahn when they first came to Hudson changed their views completely, and in a few cases became zealous converts to a belief they had earlier regarded as heresy: "It's a bit like the notion that a reformed communist is more like a communist than anyone else."

Among the first recruits to the staff at Hudson were pacifist A. J. Muste, head of the Quaker Fellowship of Reconciliation, and mathematicians Jeremy Stone and Donald Brennan. Described by various friends as "determined," "strong-minded," and "a man of tremendous pride," Brennan had been one of the organizers in 1961 of the pioneering *Daedalus* conference on arms control, later editing a collection of essays inspired by that meeting. Brennan immodestly labeled this volume "the bible of arms control."[6] Brennan also liked to boast that he had received his Ph.D. from MIT in record time for the shortest doctoral dissertation ever approved there—a single mathematical formula on a single sheet of paper.

"Don liked to feel he was a key architect of whatever position he participated in," remembered Schelling. Friends thought it significant in this regard that Brennan chose to give himself the rank of president of Hudson.

It was his own constellation of personality traits as well as the dominant influence of Herman Kahn that Brennan's former colleagues felt was behind the radical transformation he underwent at Hudson. Jeremy Stone—the son of radical journalist I. F. Stone—looked upon Brennan initially "as a source of deliverance" at the conservative institution, he said. Stone later thought that Brennan's stunning about-face on arms control was the culmination of a personal transformation, which began over the issue of the ABM.

In 1962, following the success of the *Daedalus* conference, Brennan had organized a convocation of American and Soviet experts on defense into something called the Joint Study Group. An inspiration for the idea had been the Pugwash conferences of Russian and American scientists. But, unlike Pugwash, the Joint Study Group included nuclear strategists as well. A paper that Stone wrote making a case against the ABM was to have been read at the group's first assembly, scheduled for Moscow in 1963.

Even before that inaugural meeting, however, the Americans in the Joint Study Group decided that Brennan's mercurial personality was likely to prove a major obstacle to its progress. "Don would very carefully ponder over something to say, and in the end say the wrong thing," explained Stone.

"Everybody agreed that the Joint Study Group was a good idea—but the attitude concerning its head was 'anybody but Brennan.' "

His peers' choice of another figure to lead the group understandably rankled Brennan, who felt he had been betrayed by the very people he had agreed with earlier on the subject of arms control. "Apparently, Brennan didn't recognize that he had this effect on everybody," Stone said. "Brennan felt rejected by the doves. His attitude was: 'if only they'd have been nicer.' "

An incident during the Moscow meeting evidently pushed Brennan further toward a break with his colleagues and a recantation of his former beliefs. Before the trip to Russia, Brennan's chief concern, Stone thought, had been whether the United States and the Soviet Union would be able to agree to forsake a defense against missiles. During a meeting with Russian scientists, however, one of their number had identified a picture on the wall as that of the newest model Soviet ABM. Henceforth, Stone claimed, "Brennan argued that the Soviets couldn't be dissuaded" from the ABM: "No longer for Brennan was it that you can't negotiate the ABM away, but that now you shouldn't. He concluded that the Soviets were going ahead with ABM—regardless."

Once Brennan was back at Hudson, friends thought that his crusade for an American ABM to match what he now argued was a headlong Soviet effort in missile defense became a sort of mania. Stone felt that Brennan even tried to outdo Herman Kahn in his enthusiasm for the ABM. Former collaborators on the *Daedalus* volume were dismayed by what they considered Brennan's defection from the cause of arms control. "Brennan became infected by the idea of defense," Stone said. "The trip to Moscow turned him around. Not in the sense that the Russians converted him, but just that he had a different view. He began to believe that it was possible for the defense to overwhelm the offense." Brennan's advocacy of the ABM eventually caused a rift between him and those who had been his friends and colleagues.

Stone left Hudson in early 1964, by which time, in his view, Brennan's stand for the ABM had alienated most of his associates. "People drifted away from him because they couldn't stand dealing with him," Stone said. His own departure from the institute, he admitted, was prompted in part by the pro-ABM stance at Hudson—and undertaken with such alacrity that both he and Kahn later characterized it as more a "flight" than a resignation.

By that time, also, the increasing divisiveness of the ABM issue had given the debate its own politically charged lexicon. The terms "hawk" and "dove" had first come into vogue at the time of the Cuban missile crisis; their use was already becoming common in the growing controversy over Vietnam. Stone thought their appearance at Hudson in the context of the ABM controversy reflected the developing tendentiousness of the debate over a missile defense—and the polarization that followed in its wake. The "flight of the doves" from Hudson, he said, was what finally "pulled the props out from under Brennan": "Brennan lost his bearings. Once the anchor was up, he slowly drifted to the right. It was not only the isolation of Hudson, but the whole attitude there. He was living and working in a place without doves."

Following a particularly vicious and personal exchange between the two men in the *Bulletin of Atomic Scientists,* Stone concluded that Brennan "had gone over the edge on the subject" of the ABM. There was, he reflected, "a mocking irony" to the fact that Brennan's chief antagonists in the debate over missile defense were now the very members of the Joint Study Group he himself had founded: "It was almost as if Brennan believed that if it wasn't for this group there would be an effective ABM." Like Wilson after Versailles, Brennan had convinced himself, Stone said, "that only a small group of willful men was keeping the country from the ABM."

Donald Brennan represented perhaps the extreme case of those who reversed their views in the defense debate as the Soviet Union drew abreast of the United States in the nuclear arms race. Edward Teller had undergone a similar, if more gradual, change of heart on the issue of tactical nuclear weapons by the time of the test ban controversy. Originally opposed to the effort to develop smaller and more discriminative bombs, Teller and his allies had come to embrace the new weapons as a way to break the stalemate in the strategic arms competition with Russia.

But the earliest champions of a defense-dominated nuclear strategy had also changed their minds on the subject since the early 1950s. Most of those scientists who joined with Oppenheimer then in supporting the development of nuclear weapons that were less destructive or better suited for defense had come to oppose such weapons when they led to theories of limited nuclear war and to the ABM. In the decade between the 1950s and the 1960s, each side in the debate on nuclear strategy had traded places with the opposition. The question that now concerned the scientists was not whether the United States could regain a decisive lead in the arms race, but whether the nation *should* upset the tenuous balance that currently existed.

Two prominent scientists who had undergone a change of heart on that question were Herbert York and James Wiesner. For both men the seeds of doubt sown at the time of the Killian and Gaither studies had matured over subsequent years into a complete conversion of views. As one of those who helped to develop the ICBM, York had become convinced that the defender was forever doomed to run one lap behind the attacker in the arms race. The apparent promise that technology held out for a final, decisive advantage in that race was, York thought, a deceptive and false allure—one he termed "the fallacy of the last move." Wiesner's own career had brought him by a different path to the identical conclusion. His early involvement with Project Charles and his role as science adviser to presidents Kennedy and Johnson thus persuaded him that the United States, not the Soviet Union, had consistently been "the driving force" in the arms race.

In the summer of 1964 the two men decided to make their private conversions a matter of public record. With an essay published that October in *Scientific American,* York and Wiesner identified the essential conundrum of the nuclear arms race as that "of steadily increasing military power and steadily decreasing national security."[7] Since the controversial conclusion of their article was purposefully intended to be a rallying cry for arms control, they put it in italics: *"It is our considered professional judgment that this dilemma has no technical solution."*

In retrospect, York felt the article and its declaration to be "a personal turning point." It was as well, he thought, a kind of landmark for the scientist-advocates of arms control. Jeremy Stone told both York and Wiesner that while they had not been the first scientists to reach their conclusion, they were at least the first to put it in italics.

Significantly, the controversy the article created when it was widely quoted in newspapers and magazines centered less upon York and Wiesner's argument for a comprehensive test ban than upon their case against the ABM. Both the authors and their critics acknowledged, therefore, that the article's real importance was as a symbol of the scientists' loss of faith in the ability of science to win the arms race. "If the great powers continue to look for solutions in the area of science and technology only," York and Wiesner had written, "the result will be to worsen the situation. . . . The clearly predictable course of the arms race is a steady open spiral downward into oblivion."

The article was "outrageous," "an incitement," and an example of "dirty pool," charged Paul Nitze—who as secretary of the navy in the Johnson administration had wanted to print an immediate rebuttal to the essay, but was dissuaded from doing so by McNamara. Nitze thought the article's implicit message—"the more effort put into defense, the worse the result" —marked the first resort to polemics in the ABM debate. He professed to find ominous parallels, indeed, between Oppenheimer's position that the Super was both impractical and immoral and the argument by York and Wiesner that the ABM couldn't—and shouldn't—be built.

Nitze thought the technical evidence cited by the two scientists to support their claim equally as misleading—or disingenuous—as Oppenheimer's controversial claims for tactical nuclear weapons in Project Vista. He and other critics of the article pointed to two factual errors it contained. A chart showing the effects of various nuclear weapons had been reversed in printing, though the correct relationship was presented in the text. Equally,

York's claim in the article that the cost of a missile increased proportionally with its size was contradicted by the experience of the American missile program.

While few charged that the misrepresentations were deliberate—York later attributed them to errors made by the magazine's editors while he was on vacation in Mexico—the real controversy was never on technical grounds in any case. When one of the article's detractors demanded that York print a retraction of the questionable chart, he said that the physicist flatly refused, with the argument that the ABM's advocates already "had too much power and had to be fought in any way possible."

Like Nitze, Herman Kahn understood York and Wiesner to be making a deliberate assault upon the principle of active defense. "They start out: 'It is quite clear that there is no defense system that is guaranteed to work. Therefore, let's try arms control.'" Kahn protested, "My position was that it's quite clear arms control is not guaranteed to work—therefore, let's try defense." In Kahn's view, York and Wiesner had violated "a moral, legal, and fiduciary responsibility" to remain nonpartisan by reason of their status as science advisers to two administrations. "They had no right to lend their name to that article unless they were going to be judicious." The article appeared less than a month before voters went to the polls in the 1964 presidential contest between Johnson and Barry Goldwater, and to Kahn this was confirming evidence of unforgivable bias on the authors' part. The impression of bias was heightened, York conceded, when a political documentary sponsored by the Democratic party was televised nationwide the weekend before the election. The film at one point presented the distinctive roar and mushroom cloud of a nuclear explosion, over which York was heard to say: "Sorry, Senator Goldwater, we just can't risk it." (The comment had been made in the course of Senate testimony on an unrelated issue, but York was both flattered and embarrassed, he said, to receive a telegram from the newly elected Lyndon Johnson the following week with the message "Thank you very much.")

Johnson's election proved a victory for those who opposed the ABM—if only because it ensured that Robert McNamara would continue as defense secretary. Just as he had quietly backed away from counterforce and damage limitation in nuclear strategy in the wake of the missile crisis, McNamara discreetly but decisively retreated even further from the ABM after the election. The move away from a missile defense was part of McNamara's general aversion to the idea that it was necessary—or even desirable—to try to defend against enemy attack if the result of that effort was only to lead to the development of new and more destructive offensive weapons. For the same reason, the fallout shelter program announced with some fanfare at the outset of the Kennedy administration had been all but abandoned, upon McNamara's advice, only a few years later.

Like his turnabout on the no-cities doctrine, McNamara's decision against the ABM was the result of his own independent judgment, and ignored the advice of some of his civilian experts. Enthoven felt that it was because the ABM failed the cost-effectiveness test that McNamara "gained the insight that we ought to try to put negotiated limits on this." But McNamara himself professed to becoming convinced around the time of the test ban treaty "that we should accept more of the risks arising from arms limitation."

Able by 1964 to point to that treaty as well as to the hot-line agreement as evidence of successful negotiations with the Russians, McNamara shortly after the election began urging Johnson to follow up the diplomatic initiative begun by Kennedy. In private meetings with the president, McNamara stressed the point that he had earlier raised with Kennedy: that an unrestricted continuation of the arms race would result not only in the development of more threatening weapons in the nuclear arsenals of the United States and Russia, but eventually in the addition of new and possibly less disciplined competitors. McNamara's point was dramatically underscored some months later by China's test of its first atomic bomb.

Beyond China's pending entry into the nuclear arms race, there was, McNamara told Johnson, another compelling reason to pursue talks with the Russians. At the time, he pointed out, the United States enjoyed unquestioned nuclear superiority over the Soviet Union. But that advantage was almost certainly a wasting asset. Privately, McNamara admitted to Johnson that the missile buildup of the Kennedy administration had been "in excess of what we really need to assure deterrence." That fact, together with "statements from some of our people that we should have a first-strike capability," had probably "stimulated the Soviets to build far more than they otherwise would have built," McNamara said.[8]

McNamara's arguments ultimately persuaded Johnson. Originally one of those in Congress to warn of an impending missile gap, Johnson as president would concede that the estimates on which he had based his warning "were way off." "We were building things we didn't need to build," he later admitted. "We were harboring fears we didn't need to harbor."[9]

Personally inclined to favor a missile defense when he came to office, Johnson nonetheless acted upon the advice of McNamara in deciding once again to defer deployment of an ABM in 1965. Yet Johnson also appreciated —more than McNamara—the political pressures then building for the ABM. By 1964, American intelligence had confirmed that the Russians were constructing an ambitious but technologically primitive defense against missiles around Moscow. When McNamara steadfastly refused to yield to

congressional pressure for an American antimissile missile, denying approval for the weapon, Congress in defiance had appropriated the money for
the ABM nonetheless. As in his earlier confrontation with Congress over the
B-70 bomber, McNamara publicly vowed that he would not spend the
money for the ABM. But Congress was only one source of pressure for
missile defense. "At one point almost everyone in the building was for
ABM," McNamara said of sentiment at the Pentagon.[10]

Eventually, Johnson agreed to a compromise proposed by McNamara
that promised to satisfy both the latter's principles and the president's own
instinct that there was a political necessity for some kind of ABM. In a
climactic meeting at his Texas ranch during early December 1966, Johnson
approved McNamara's idea for an approach to the Russians on controlling
the arms race. The president's surprise endorsement was in exchange for a
promise from McNamara that he would spend the money on the ABM if
those talks proved fruitless.[11]

Although McNamara recognized the danger that a limited ABM system
might only generate pressures for a more comprehensive defense against
missiles, the showdown at the ranch represented nonetheless a substantial
personal coup. His triumph on the ABM was all the more remarkable given
the fact that all five of the joint chiefs had also been at the meeting with
Johnson, and each had opposed the compromise. (McNamara claimed that
at the time of the test ban debate he had locked the joint chiefs and himself
together in a room—telling them no one could leave until they all at least
understood each other's position.) Jubilant over the arrangement when he
returned to the Pentagon, McNamara was unable to persuade two other
administration officials, the U.S. ambassador to Russia and the deputy
secretary of state, that Johnson had actually agreed to the plan. The two had
finally telephoned the president personally to confirm McNamara's account.

In order to ensure that Johnson would not change his mind on the ABM,
McNamara the following month assembled all the past and present members of the President's Science Advisory Committee in the Oval Office. The
unanimous opinion of the experts concurred with the view of representatives
from the three principal contractors for the proposed ABM that an effective
defense of American cities against an all-out Soviet attack was unfeasible for
the foreseeable future.

Despite the fact that McNamara had Johnson's approval that winter to
begin the arms talks with the Russians, the first meeting of Soviet and
American leaders did not take place until the following summer, when
Johnson met Soviet president Alexei Kosygin—at a point midway between
the White House and the Russian mission to the United Nations—in Glassboro, New Jersey. Seated just to the right of the president and directly across
from Kosygin, McNamara was disappointed that the two leaders "weren't
getting anywhere" in their discussion of putting limits upon the ABM.

Equally frustrated, Johnson had finally asked McNamara to tell Kosygin why the United States was opposed to defending against missiles.

"Mr. President," McNamara told Kosygin, "it's very simple. You go ahead with the ABM and our response is not going to be an ABM. Our response is going to be an increase in offensive forces." McNamara confessed to Kosygin that such a buildup would be neither wise nor in the interest of either country, but he stressed his original point that the United States would be able to counter any defensive move that the Russians might make. "There's not a damn thing you can do to stop it," McNamara told the Russian. "Nothing that you do will we *allow* to stop it."

Kosygin, McNamara remembered, was made "absolutely furious" by this threat. Pounding the table for emphasis, he accused McNamara and the United States of pursuing a reckless and immoral nuclear strategy. "We are defending Mother Russia—that's moral," Kosygin allegedly declared. "You are increasing your offensive forces—that's immoral." Kosygin even blamed his persistent insomnia upon the failure of Americans to distinguish between offensive and defensive missiles.

One of the most surprising things to McNamara about his heated exchange with Kosygin at Glassboro was "the tremendous philosophical gap" he felt it revealed between Soviet and American thinking on nuclear strategy. For McNamara, the talks at the summit had been discouraging, since the pace of technological development meant that the effort to control the ABM was now in a race with plans for its deployment. In the time between Johnson's decision of late 1966 and the Glassboro meeting, moreover, domestic pressures for a missile defense had continued to grow. McNamara subsequently concluded that the summit had been an ill-prepared arena to begin talks on a subject as complex as arms control. "We were just trying to get it started," he said of Glassboro.

The public turning point for McNamara on arms control came with a speech that fall in San Francisco. Like his remarks to the graduating class at Ann Arbor some years before, McNamara's speech to the American Society of Newspaper Editors did not propose a major change; it simply announced one that had already taken place. In this case, the speech was a personal and frank admission of the shift that McNamara's own thinking had undergone in his nearly seven years as defense secretary. Significantly, he made no mention there of the possibility of fighting a nuclear war or of limiting the damage such a war might cause. Indeed, McNamara's perfunctory defense of U.S. policies seemed to accept implicitly a fundamental criticism of his actions at the Pentagon. The central theme of the speech— written right after Glassboro—thus echoed the scientists' point about the futility of seeking a technological solution to the arms race.

"There is a kind of mad momentum intrinsic to the development of all nuclear weaponry," McNamara claimed. "If a system works—and works

well—there is a strong pressure from all directions to procure and deploy
the weapon out of all proportion to the prudent level required." Dominating
what McNamara termed "the intrinsic dynamics of the arms race" was "an
action-reaction phenomenon" that fueled the race. It was this phenomenon,
McNamara stressed, which had inspired an American military buildup that
was "both greater than we had originally planned and more than we require."[12]

Near the end of his speech—and contrary to its whole thesis—McNamara
surprised many in the audience by announcing the decision to deploy a
"thin" ABM shield around the United States to defend against missiles
launched from China. The anti-ABM scientists whose thinking the speech
had so plainly mirrored up to that point were among those stunned by the
announcement.

At their meeting with McNamara and Johnson the previous January, a
majority of science advisers had specifically opposed the idea of a limited
ABM system to counter the yet-to-appear missile threat from China. Richard Garwin thought McNamara's talk to the newspaper editors "one of
the most eloquent speeches against the ABM"—until its closing lines.
"The speech was 90 percent 'why we don't have an ABM and don't need
one,' " said Garwin, "and 10 percent, 'nevertheless, it is prudent and
necessary . . .' " He and other anti-ABM scientists believed that the real
motivation behind McNamara's ABM announcement had been the need to
protect the Johnson administration from partisan charges that it was lax on
the issue of defense. It was not an "anti-Chinese ABM" that McNamara
intended to deploy, Garwin reflected, but "an anti-Republican one."

McNamara admitted at the time of his speech that the decision to go
ahead with the thin ABM system—dubbed Sentinel—was a "truly marginal" choice.[13] As he and Johnson discovered soon afterward, however,
what McNamara had termed a "modest" missile defense proved inadequate
to protect the government from attack by both sides in the ABM debate.
Anti-ABM scientists pointed out that McNamara's threat at San Francisco
"to run faster" than the Soviets unless the latter demonstrated restraint in
the arms race contradicted the logic of the speech. ABM proponents, while
welcoming Sentinel as a long-overdue step, objected that it was still inadequate, and—more important—that it was aimed at the wrong opponent.
Herman Kahn charged, for example, that McNamara had deliberately reduced the effectiveness of Sentinel against a Russian attack by orienting
some of its radars so that they would be unable to detect missiles coming
from the Soviet Union, a way of tacitly assuring the Russians that the ABM
was not directed against them.

As at Ann Arbor in 1962, another intended audience for McNamara's San
Francisco speech was doubtless the Russians. His encounter with Kosygin
at Glassboro had impressed upon him, therefore, the degree to which the

arms race had become a source of confusion as well as competition in American relations with Russia. It was for the Russians' benefit that his speech had emphasized the distinction between retaliation and striking first —stressing the point that, despite U.S. nuclear superiority, the aim of American nuclear strategy remained deterrence. While he later defended the Kennedy administration's missile decision as justified at the time, McNamara conceded that it had been "necessitated by a lack of accurate information." In the end, he admitted that it "could not possibly have left unaffected the Soviet Union's future nuclear plans."[14]

McNamara was certainly aware as well that, since Glassboro, Soviet leaders had been agonizingly slow in responding to his initiative on limiting nuclear arms. For some time prior to that effort, American reconnaissance satellites had monitored a steady Soviet missile buildup—of the magnitude predicted at the time of the missile gap, but which had hitherto failed to materialize. McNamara observed this buildup without alarm, evidently believing—in line with his theory of the action-reaction phenomenon—that the Russians intended to match but not to exceed the American missile force in size.

McNamara's inclination and that of most of his advisers was to reject the opinion of those who held a less sanguine view of the Soviet missile buildup. Among the latter were Bruno Augenstein and Andrew Marshall at the Pentagon. In 1963, when the first evidence of the Russian buildup had been confirmed, Marshall and Augenstein independently predicted that the Soviets would either accept the position of strategic inferiority to which they had been relegated or else attempt to achieve superiority in the number of missiles. But neither analyst had shared McNamara's view that the Russians would probably settle for being merely the strategic equal of the United States. McNamara thought the best the Russians were likely to achieve would be an "expensive" kind of nuclear inferiority to the United States. "We never contemplated in those days the possibility that we would find ourselves seriously outnumbered by the Russians in strategic forces," Enthoven admitted.

The fact that the Soviet missile buildup continued apace even after the American buildup had stopped was certainly part of the justification for Sentinel. But McNamara had also made it clear to Kosygin at Glassboro that unless the Soviets showed restraint in the future on the ABM, the response of the United States would not be an equivalent defense against missiles—but deployment of a new kind of offensive weapon which, in turn, could start another dangerous cycle in the arms race. McNamara repeated that message in his San Francisco speech. The United States had "already initiated offensive-weapons programs costing several billions in order to offset the small present Soviet ABM deployment," he announced.

In what turned out to be a fatefully ironic decision—one that McNamara himself would later lament—his effort to slow the arms race by countering the ABM with a new weapon had instead only increased its mad momentum. McNamara's attempt to stop or at least redirect that race gave it, indeed, a new impetus, and one that would soon seem all but irresistible.

The technological imperative that led to a defense against missiles led—inevitably—to a means of overcoming that defense. From the outset, the easiest and least expensive means of ensuring that a missile would be able to penetrate to its target had been to equip it with decoys—"penetration aids," in the argot of the weaponeer—designed to deceive the defender. The realization that the attacker "could put a warhead in as easily as a balloon," observed Richard Garwin, ineluctably followed among the scientists. The possibility of putting several warheads on a single missile proceeded in turn.

The advent of the hydra-headed weapon that would be acronymed MIRV —for multiple independently targetable reentry vehicles—seemed an unavoidable next step to the scientists developing countermeasures to the ABM.[15] "Early on, it was realized that the best way to defeat ABM was MIRV," noted Cal Tech's Marvin Goldberger, who, like Garwin, was one of the scientists to work on both projects.

The idea behind MIRV had been under study since at least 1958. The weapon was further refined at Rand in the early 1960s, when some of its supporters had unsuccessfully used MIRV as an argument against the nuclear test ban.[16] In 1964 McNamara had approved its development, and the following year MIRV had been mentioned for the first time publicly in a *Life* magazine article.[17]

In retrospect, some professed to see in MIRV a triumph of technical inadvertence. Few of the experts in McNamara's Pentagon or even among the weapon's creators professed an appreciation at the time of the threat that MIRV would eventually pose to the stability of the balance of terror. "I didn't see—and I don't think anyone else saw—the implications of MIRV for the strategic balance," Enthoven said. "It was seen as a normal product improvement. It gave us a good argument for why we didn't have to buy more forces."

MIRV "was developed as a technological capability," remembered Harold Brown, McNamara's technical adviser in the Pentagon. It was only later, Brown thought, that "people started looking around, saying 'What good is this?' " Ultimately, Brown felt there were three possible answers to that question. First was MIRV's "ability to put warheads at a precise place." Second was its attraction as a means "to cover a growing Soviet target list." Finally was the fact that "it was less expensive to do it this way."

"The sole justification for it was that the Soviets were going ahead with an ABM system," McNamara subsequently remarked of his own reason for approving MIRV. While he had always recognized the danger that the weapon might develop into something more than a countermeasure to missile defense, McNamara said, his decision had been taken in "the hope that the Russians would come to their senses and stop deploying ABM—in which case we would not have deployed MIRV."

Some later argued that a limitation on multiple-warhead missiles could have been discussed as early as the Glassboro summit. Instead, the talks there had been dominated by the issue of ABM, which then seemed the greater threat. "We thought we could get by without deployment," McNamara noted ruefully of MIRV years later.

In fact, though MIRV's threat to deterrence would be fully understood only after the weapon had been tested and deployed, the virtually unanimous support its early development received had had behind it a variety of reasons and rationales. MIRV's popularity was accounted for in part because it was —as much as a weapon can be—all things to all people. Along with McNamara and Enthoven, scientists like York and Wiesner approved going ahead with MIRV as a way to undermine the Army's argument for ABM and the Air Force's perennial call for still more missiles.[18]

At the same time, MIRV had received early and critical support from the Air Force as a weapon ideally suited to a counterforce strategy and to the idea of damage limitation in a nuclear war—concepts that McNamara, but clearly not all in the Pentagon, had abandoned. McNamara ultimately used MIRV's suitability for counterforce as an argument against the case for more missiles. The fact that each American missile, with MIRV, would theoretically be able to destroy two or more Soviet missiles in their silos had thus been one of the unpublicized reasons that McNamara gave to the military for approving the MIRV project in the first place, and for accelerating its development in 1965.[19]

Ironically, the flat-of-the-curve graph and the cost-effectiveness arguments that McNamara and his civilian experts used successfully against other military budget requests backfired in the case of MIRV. Multiple-warhead missiles easily passed the defense secretary's own test of cost-effectiveness in terms of the expense and effort it would take the enemy to counter MIRV. (In at least one case, excess was the unexpected result of an attempt at restraint. In the mid-1960s McNamara had approved a plan to put from ten to fourteen small nuclear warheads on the Poseidon submarine-launched missile then under development. He rejected the alternative of three larger warheads proposed by the Navy in the belief that the more numerous but smaller warheads would appear less threatening to Russia's land-based missile force. However, by the early 1980s—when the Trident II, a third-generation sea-based missile, was being developed—unanticipated improvement in accuracy meant that each of the ten to fourteen warheads on every submarine-launched missile would be theoretically capable of destroying a Soviet missile in its silo.)

"MIRV was just too good," concluded one account of how and why the weapon came to be: "It contributed to the solution of too many political problems of the Administration and the civilian authorities in the Pentagon."[20] Indeed, so unquestioned was the multifaceted utility of MIRV that a scientist involved in the project since its inception could not remember any single occasion where a conscious decision had been made to proceed with the weapon—or when an objection had been raised.

The concept of the strategic "triad" was another example of how a deceptively simple step in the arms race could have far-reaching and unintended results. Some of the scientists who supported McNamara in his early decisions on MIRV thought, in hindsight, that both he and they had fallen into a similar kind of trap with the triad.

McNamara allegedly first used the term in 1964 in an attempt to end the services' perpetual feuding over the military budget. The strength of deterrence, he had explained then, rested in effect upon a tripod. The three legs of the tripod were represented by the Air Force's bombers, its land-based missiles, and the Navy's missile-firing submarines. Like the no-cities doctrine and McNamara's ideas on counterforce, however, the concept of the nuclear triad had subsequently taken on a life of its own. Thereafter both the Navy and the Air Force imbued the idea with something approaching the sanctity of holy writ—using it to justify requests for further generations of bombers as well as new land- and sea-based missilery.

MIRV had been intended by McNamara as an argument against those requests, since the effect of the weapon would be to multiply severalfold the destructiveness of the missiles that the services already had. But MIRV, as the triad, illustrated the practical difficulty of undoing the changes that McNamara had brought to American nuclear strategy—starting with the official shift to the doctrine of damage limitation and counterforce. "The Chiefs kept coming at him with damage-limiting proposals involving new offensive weapons," recalled one of McNamara's aides.[21]

The central paradox in American strategy between deterring and fighting a nuclear war—the paradox that McNamara inherited upon becoming defense secretary—was not resolved during his tenure. Instead, McNamara's own thinking on the subject had gone full circle by the time he left the Pentagon. At the end of his remarkable intellectual journey—a journey shared and occasionally inspired by the crusading experts who joined the Kennedy administration—McNamara had finally arrived back at the conclusion he reached after confronting the specter of nuclear war for the first time. Despite the early importance that he and the experts once assigned to controlling and limiting nuclear war, the obvious emphasis of American strategy by the end of the Johnson administration in 1968 was back where it had been in Truman's time—upon deterrence.

As weapons like the ABM and MIRV showed, technology and domestic politics as much as nuclear strategy and military doctrine were motive forces in the arms race—a point that McNamara himself had seemed to concede in his landmark San Francisco speech. In spite of McNamara's well-deserved reputation for managerial skill, his years as defense secretary were characterized by decisions and events whose results were uncontrolled and unexpected—and where, indeed, the outcome often seemed all but unavoidable.

His choice of MIRV—a decision he hoped would kill the ABM—had breathed new life into it instead. His attempt to slow the arms race by deploying only a limited defense against missiles had not been able to prevent the greatest acceleration of that race in history by the end of his term. Yet the controversy over missile defense nonetheless endured. As events developed, it outlasted even McNamara.

By February 1968, some six months after his muted *cri de coeur* in San Francisco, McNamara was gone from the Pentagon. A month later, Lyndon Johnson—who had finally forced the ABM upon McNamara—declared that he would not seek reelection as president. Fatefully, the abrupt departure from office of the two men was not because of any decisions concerning nuclear weapons, the issue that had preoccupied McNamara since his first few days in office and remained his greatest concern at the end. Rather, the direct cause of their leaving was a conflict that neither Johnson nor McNamara—nor any of the civilian experts who advised them—had shown much interest in or alarm about. But it had gradually come to obsess—and engulf—them all.

The crowning irony of McNamara's years in office was the fact that the kind of war he and the experts had been preparing for—and perhaps even expecting—never came. The experts' ideas and theories on warfare were tested not in Berlin or Cuba, but in southeast Asia—in Vietnam.

18

A Long Twilight Struggle

What seemed to be the alternative prospects of accidental war or surprise attack had preoccupied most of those who thought about nuclear war since the dawn of the atomic age. Which dread contingency was the greater danger had, indeed, become a major part of the defense debate—as the protracted feud between the strategists and the scientists showed. By the mid-1960s the possibility that a nuclear war might begin and develop like a conventional war, becoming a protracted conflict, seemed by contrast an isolated and lonely obsession of analysts like Bernard Brodie at Rand. The almost exclusive concern elsewhere was with how a nuclear war might begin —not with how it might be fought or brought to an end. Behind this narrow view was the all-but-unchallenged assumption of the time that such a war would be both brief and world-ending.

For a small group of nuclear strategists, however, the lack of consideration given to what might happen after the outbreak of a nuclear war represented a peculiar gap in the thinking of their colleagues. To Herman Kahn, this oversight had seemed a strategic lacuna of grand proportions at Rand —one he self-consciously set out to avoid at Hudson. Part of the fixation of Rand's analysts with the causes of war, Kahn believed, was explained by the dramatic but historically exceptional case of Pearl Harbor. Kahn felt that the complex and tangled roots of the First World War had also discouraged strategists from studying how war might develop gradually, inexorably— but also more plausibly—from something like a minor diplomatic crisis.

"We used World War One as an example of a scenario that would never pass anybody's examination," Kahn said of a study begun at Hudson on the origins of war. The results had underscored the unpredictability of events as well as of human behavior. "There were at least eight instances that would never pass anybody's examination," Kahn remembered, "including, for example, the Kaiser signing a blank check and then going on vacation." The implausibility of the historical record before Pearl Harbor—and the shock that event would have upon the American psyche—had made it difficult, he believed, to imagine a war that did *not* begin with a sneak attack. (When Kahn asked two new recruits at Hudson to consider how a nuclear war between the United States and Russia might be terminated, the duo had returned after thirty minutes complaining that they could find no convincing way to get such a war started. Kahn suggested a Soviet invasion of West Germany as "the least implausible" *casus belli.*)

Another reason for the strategists' blind spot concerning the conduct of a nuclear war, Kahn claimed, was the unwillingness they shared with the general populace to look the specter directly in the eye—in his phrase, "to think about the unthinkable": "The reason why the level of understanding was so low is that nobody was willing to take the subject seriously."

The unreality of the strategists' world was dramatically made clear to Kahn by the results of an informal poll that he, Thomas Schelling, and another colleague from Rand had taken of their colleagues there in 1960. Asking the analysts' opinions of the most likely way a nuclear war might begin, Kahn was surprised to find "that 90 percent of the effort at Rand had gone into looking at 'out-of-the-blue' attacks, rather than at wars which began as a reply to provocation or to a conventional invasion." Yet the same strategists, he marveled, believed that such an unprovoked surprise attack was the *least* likely cause of war. "By their own judgment they were looking at the wrong problem."

Nor did Rand's counterparts in the military do much better in his 1960 poll, Kahn said: "Pentagon studies at this time assumed a Soviet attack upon the United States and American reprisals within one to ten hours." Those studies had also assumed as a variant for planning that the U.S. retaliatory blow against Russia would land either at four, at six, or at eight p.m.—and that the Russians in the meantime would take no action to evacuate their cities. "I didn't understand the reasoning that ten to twenty hours after the war started—and one to ten hours after bombs had been dropped on the United States—the Russians were still going about their business as usual." "If they just walked out of town it changes casualties by a factor of ten," he complained to Pentagon planners. "What do your calculations have to do with anything?" Kahn challenged them.

Back at Hudson, Kahn and his colleagues decided there were at least eight ways that a nuclear war might start—and that it was necessary to anticipate and plan for each one of them. Though Kahn himself said he viewed the question of using nuclear weapons as "akin to a religious issue"—"At some psychological level I find nuclear war unthinkable," he admitted—his concern was with how a nuclear war might be fought and won, and not only with how it could begin.

Consequently, a series of lectures that Kahn prepared on fighting and surviving a nuclear war had been much in demand at the Pentagon and at Rand. In 1959, not long before he left Rand to set up the Hudson Institute,

Kahn spent several months at Princeton's Institute for Advanced Study assembling his lecture notes into the book that he intended to be an atomic-age updating of Clausewitz's classic *On War.* "Herman had his amanuenses follow him around the country while he gave his famous three-day talks," Thomas Schelling remembered. "They taped it, gave him a thousand-page transcript, and he took a year off to write the book." Of the unwieldy result, *On Thermonuclear War,* Schelling said: "He almost got it into shape."[1]

Since the nearly seven-hundred-page book was taken directly—even ver-batim—from Kahn's lectures, it was often difficult for readers to separate the form from the content of what became known simply as *OTW.* To Schelling, Kahn's book and his lectures alike reflected the distinctive per-sona of their author. "His message was that the subject of nuclear war is too important to be left to slogans," he said of Kahn. But Schelling and Kahn's other associates and friends came to question whether there wasn't a mes-sianic urge hidden behind his marathon writing and speaking. Observed Schelling: "You couldn't tell whether it was like Bob Hope—he loved an audience—or because he had a mission to save the world."

Arguably, the flaws of Kahn's book on nuclear war were also those of its author. Its repetitiousness gave it "a bolero-like style," complained one critic. Even Kahn's admirers thought *On Thermonuclear War* an example of what some at Rand called "Hermanism"—after Kahn's penchant for hyperbole. Brodie, for example, objected to Kahn's coining of the term "wargasm" to describe an all-out nuclear conflict. "So grim a subject does not exclude an appropriate kind of humor used very sparingly," Brodie scolded, "but levity is never legitimate."[2] Another former Rand colleague compared Kahn's attitude toward critics who pointed out contradictions in his book to that of Walt Whitman: "He was vast. He contained multitudes." (Kahn himself acknowledged that supporters and detractors alike often found common ground in criticizing his work. Concerning a revision of *On Thermonuclear War* he was working on at the time of his death in 1983, he said: "People who don't like it will say, 'unsound, but creative.' People who do like it will say, 'creative, but unsound.' ")

Certainly Kahn's own impishness about such a grave subject as nuclear war invited misunderstanding. One such case concerned the book's discus-sion of the "doomsday machine"—a fanciful device meant to ensure peace by blowing up the world as the penalty for aggression.[3] He had actually borrowed the idea from physicist Leo Szilard in order to burlesque the concept of deterrence. Critics, however, mistook Kahn's subtle satire for advocacy. Another section of the book that uniformly outraged reviewers contained Kahn's helpful hint that fallout shelters should contain individual dosimeters—so the shelters' occupants would be able to distinguish real victims of radiation sickness from hypochondriacs and malingerers.[4]

The most outspoken among Kahn's many critics was mathematician

James Newman, who in March 1961 wrote a review of *On Thermonuclear War* for *Scientific American*. Newman confessed he had at first thought the book "a hoax in bad taste," and its authorship mythic. Upon learning that both were authentic, Newman dismissed the epic as "thermonuclear pornography," suggesting that Kahn's first name might more properly be "Genghis."[5]

The editor of *Scientific American* refused to print the rebuttal that Kahn wrote to Newman's scathing review—or even to allow the strategist into his office. But the snub only inspired Kahn to write a sequel to the first book, for which he borrowed the title of his unprinted rebuttal—*Thinking About the Unthinkable*. Kahn also announced that he allowed his children to burn a page of Newman's *The World of Mathematics* over the sink each evening after dinner.

Kahn was certainly not the only strategist to popularize the subject of nuclear strategy. Thomas Schelling had left Rand around the same time as Kahn in order to return to Harvard and finish writing *The Strategy of Conflict*. The popularity of his book, while less than that of Kahn's opus, would bring Schelling's name as well before the public. (He had once before narrowly missed notoriety. Shortly after returning from the failed Geneva surprise attack conference in 1958, Schelling had written an innovative essay for *Foreign Affairs* on the problems of strategic surprise and vulnerability. The editors rejected the article because they had already agreed to publish Albert Wohlstetter's essay on the same theme, "The Delicate Balance of Terror." Schelling subsequently included the article as a chapter in his book titled "The Reciprocal Fear of Surprise Attack.")[6]

The Strategy of Conflict stressed many of the same points about the inherent fragility of deterrence and the importance of demonstrating resolve in a crisis that were features as well of Kahn's lectures and books—though it was Schelling, not Kahn, who came the closest to putting his theories into practice. The nuclear demonstration or warning shot that Schelling actually proposed to detonate over the Soviet Union during the 1961 Berlin crisis had first appeared as an idea in his book, published the year before.[7]

The oblique literary style of both Kahn and Schelling, and their peculiarly metaphorical use of language, also inevitably left them exposed to a great deal of hostile criticism. No less startling for being true, therefore, was Schelling's reflection in a later book, regarding Hiroshima, that against "defenseless people there is not much that nuclear weapons can do that cannot be done with an ice pick." He continued, "And it would not have strained our Gross National Product to do it with ice picks."[8]

Not surprisingly, their critics often confused the eccentric style of the strategists' writings with their substance, ridiculing both. Kahn's comparison of the adolescent game of "chicken" with the behavior of nations at the brink of war was meant to be merely descriptive—not an endorsement of the practice. (Though Kahn did suggest that in order to win the game—in which two cars race toward a cliff until one driver becomes the first to jump out or veer away—a contestant should deliberately appear either drunk or crazy by staggering around the car before getting into it, and then throwing the steering wheel out of the window.)[9]

Kahn and Schelling, like most strategists, defended their apparent insensitivity to the consequences of nuclear war as a necessary kind of objectivity. Each responded to the charge of callousness with a disdain that bordered, in Kahn's case, on outright contempt. Kahn defended the strategist's objectivity, not unflatteringly, with the detachment necessary to the occupation of surgeon. Once criticized for cold-bloodedness, he reportedly confronted his critic with the rhetorical question: "Would you prefer a nice warm mistake?" When one outraged legislator similarly asked a rhetorical question of Kahn in a congressional hearing on prospective American casualties in a nuclear war—"Ten million or one hundred million dead," the congressman had declaimed, "what is the difference?"—Kahn had coolly replied, "Ninety million, Senator." Kahn once admitted in another context: "I don't understand people who aren't detached."[10]

In Kahn's case, the language and style of his books on nuclear strategy were surely more radical than the ideas they contained. Subsequent critics pointed out that the most obvious flaws in his argument concerned matters not of morality, but of interpretation and fact. Upon first reading a draft of *On Thermonuclear War,* Daniel Ellsberg, Kahn's colleague at Rand, had thought the book "reckless and mad." Ellsberg was particularly disturbed by Kahn's argument that the United States needed the ability to strike the first blow in a nuclear war—even if it had no intention of doing so—in order to make American nuclear threats against Russia more credible. In characteristic fashion, Kahn had drawn a distinction in the book between a "credible first-strike capability"—in which the United States would have some ability to disarm Russia in a first strike, and hence could expect a threat to do so to be taken seriously—and a "splendid first-strike capability"— whereby the United States would be virtually certain not only of being able to carry out a successful first strike, but of making its threat to do so stick.[11]

"The irony is that when Kahn was talking about the strategy we might want for the future, he was describing what we already had," Ellsberg reflected years later. Kahn's book, Ellsberg said, "had been based upon the assumption that we all shared at Rand": the assumption of Russia's military superiority. Like most of the other analysts there, Kahn had accepted the mythical missile gap on faith. "But the 'splendid' capability is what we already had," Ellsberg claimed.

.   .   .

More telling than the strategists' error concerning the assumptions that guided American nuclear strategy was the failure of Kahn, Schelling, and others to foresee the importance of a phenomenon that would eventually come to dominate the subject of strategy: the process of escalation, by which crises become wars, and small wars become larger ones. Significantly, the topic of escalation was given only a few paragraphs in *On Thermonuclear War,* and then merely as it related to how accidents could lead to a wider war. Escalation was not mentioned at all in Schelling's *Strategy of Conflict.* [12]

In the writings of virtually all nuclear strategists, the treatment given the subject of escalation was both belated and incomplete. *Thinking About the Unthinkable*—published the year of the Cuban missile crisis—contained a sixteen-rung "escalation ladder" which started at the lowest level of diplomatic disagreement and ended in all-out thermonuclear war. But Kahn's later critics pointed out that only three of the steps on the ladder did not involve the use of force, and no consideration at all was given to the thought of reversing the process—of "de-escalating" the conflict.[13]

As had been the case with the concept of limited war in Korea, the theory of escalation actually followed by some time its practice in the expanding war in Vietnam. The gradual escalation of the insurgency there into the "long twilight struggle" that Kennedy had unwittingly prophesied in his inaugural address required a rethinking of strategy by the strategists, the majority of whom had hitherto barely considered the subject of guerrilla war.

Most strategists' initial response to Vietnam, indeed, was to adapt their theories about nuclear war to the very different kind of conflict taking place in the jungles of southeast Asia. In a 1965 book titled *Arms and Influence,* Schelling praised as an exemplary case of "signaling" President Johnson's 1964 decision to launch reprisal raids against North Vietnam following the incident in the Gulf of Tonkin. "A good way to describe the American response is that it was *unambiguous,*" Schelling wrote. "It was articulate. It contained a pattern. If someone asks what the United States did when its destroyers were attacked in the Gulf of Tonkin, there is no disagreement about the answer."[14] Further comparing the U.S. raids to the action of a farmer who ties the chicken that his dog has killed around the dog's neck, Schelling developed his point about informing the enemy simultaneously of America's intentions and resolve: "To the dog we cannot explain; we cannot tie a dead chicken around a dog's neck and *tell* him it is because he bit the postman. We can *tell* the North Vietnamese, though, that we are destroying their PT boats because they attacked our ships. . . ."[15]

In a book published the same year as *Arms and Influence,* Herman Kahn showed that he, too, intended to deal with the previously neglected subject of escalation—which had by now resulted in the first massive U.S. troop commitments to that country—in his typically thorough way. Accordingly, the rungs of Kahn's new escalation ladder climbed forty-one steps from "ostensible crisis" to "spasm or insensate war." While the brunt of *On Escalation,* like Kahn's earlier books, concerned nuclear war rather than jungle insurgencies, the plain implication was that strategists might learn lessons from the guerrilla war in Vietnam. (Not all agreed. Kahn's escalation ladder was later published, without comment, in a science-fiction anthology.) Like Schelling, Kahn's book described the U.S. response in the case of the Gulf of Tonkin as an "exemplary" way to communicate threats to the enemy.[16]

The books of Kahn and Schelling showed that, from an early date, Vietnam cast a wide net for the nuclear strategists. But they were not the first nor the only ones to become so ensnarled. Even Brodie—one of the first strategists to dissent from the war—publicly defended the bombing of North Vietnam in 1965 as both warranted and effective. Brodie and Schelling, though not Kahn, would in future years come to oppose both the bombing and the war.[17]

Despite the subsequent turnaround of some strategists on Vietnam, many persisted in the belief that the theories they had devised concerning nuclear war could be applied with success there—or vice versa. The notion of "compellence" that Schelling promoted in his first book he linked with American bombing of North Vietnam in the second. The strategy of "controlled escalation" and the related "attrition-pressure-ouch" theory that Kahn used to explain the conduct of the war in Vietnam might have equal relevance, some strategists hinted, to the course of a nuclear war with Russia. An underlying assumption shared by both Kahn and Schelling— and, in fact, questioned by few strategists—was that the United States could either use or at least threaten enough force to compel the enemy to surrender.[18]

The real combat in Asia made plain a truth that simulations and scenarios never could reveal: that the strategists' theorizing on war and its nature contained fundamental flaws. In differing ways and not at the same time, Vietnam would prove all of the strategists wrong—and some of them more wrong than others.

What was true of the strategists regarding Vietnam applied as well to the atomic scientists as a group. Only belatedly did the guerrilla war in Asia become a focus of interest and concern to those who had built the bomb. When it did, even those scientists who had long since abandoned the hope that technology could win the nuclear arms race apparently believed that it might make a difference in Vietnam. Their lingering faith was particularly evident in the origins of what became known as the "McNamara line."

In the spring of 1966, Robert McNamara had asked the scientists of the elite Jason group for advice in harnessing America's technological prowess to the war effort in Vietnam. Jason member Marvin Goldberger observed of McNamara's request that its effect was to revive "the original Charles River gang—Zacharias, Kistiakowsky, Kaysen, Rabi—the whole mafia." Goldberger thought the spirit that had originally prompted this group to take part in Project Charles inspired as well their approach to the new assignment: "They became carried away with their own World War Two triumphs, and the idea that we might in fact be able to do something that would decrease the temperature of the war and actually help bring it to an end." Goldberger admitted that at the time he, too, had shared this spirit. Only years later did he and the other scientists who answered McNamara's call realize, Goldberger said, that they had been "very naive—extraordinarily naive."

To another member of the Jasons, George Rathjens, the assignment was confirming proof that McNamara had rejected his advice of some four years before. A brief visit to Vietnam in 1962 had convinced him, Rathjens said, that there would be no technological solution to the war. Events since then had not changed that view, though Rathjens believed he was still in the minority among the Jasons in 1966.

The Jasons' study of Vietnam arrived at some conclusions that were critical of U.S. conduct of the war. Their report to McNamara in the fall of 1967 suggested, for example, that the body count being used to gauge the progress toward victory in Vietnam was probably greatly inflated. Another finding seriously questioned the military efficacy of America's bombing of North Vietnam.[19] But a majority of their colleagues, both Goldberger and Rathjens felt, were "enthusiastic" about a third and final part of the study. The last section of the Jasons' report concerned the prospects for an "electronic battlefield"—a sophisticated array of sensors and weapons meant to confront the insurgents with a technological no-man's-land in the demilitarized zone between North and South Vietnam.

Goldberger later said that his own doubts about the direction of the war had surfaced the year before, but he had chosen then not to discuss them with his colleagues. He and Rathjens had each endorsed the idea of the electronic battlefield. But their endorsement had been made, both men claimed, without passion, and amid growing doubts that the scheme would work. Both thought the optimism of the scientists concerning the effectiveness of what they dubbed "the Barrier" or the "McNamara line" sprang— as had the early optimism of Project Charles—from a hidden desire to avoid the most likely alternative. In the early 1950s, that had meant the continued offensive emphasis in American nuclear strategy. In the mid-1960s, it meant the continuing escalation of the Vietnam War.

The faith that their solution represented an alternative to the bombing of

North Vietnam was part of what Goldberger meant by the Jasons' extraordinary naiveté. "It was part of our arrogance at that time to believe that if the system worked perfectly, the military would support us and abandon the air war," Goldberger said. "I learned then a fundamental aspect of the military mentality: Any incremental advantage is worthwhile."

Goldberger came to view his and the Jasons' support for the electronic battlefield idea as a parable of the scientists' role in the war—as well as an occasion for personal remorse: "I regard this as a fundamental mistake that I made, and that all of the rest of the 'gang' made. It was the only thing that we could see to direct the war against combatants. But what we should have done when Mr. McNamara came to us with this proposal was to spit in his eye."

19

The Lost Crusade

Like the nuclear strategists, the novelists and filmmakers who imagined Armageddon between the early 1950s and mid-1960s almost always assumed that nuclear war would be the result of either a sudden accident or a calculated act of madness.[1] The war that was the subject of a book or movie sometimes started with a deliberately planned sneak attack. The whimpering end portrayed in the best-known book of this genre, *On the Beach,* had its origins in a 1914-style catalytic war begun by the Albanians and the Chinese. Yet the prospect that a nuclear war between the United States and the Soviet Union might gradually evolve from a conventional conflict fought elsewhere was all but ignored in American fiction—even though many civilian strategists as well as SAC's planners came to believe that a nuclear war would be most likely to start with a limited war in Europe.*

The popularity of books and films on nuclear war had the effect of focusing public attention not only upon the subject itself, but upon those whose profession it was to think about the unthinkable. Generally, however, the emphasis there was upon the danger of technological malfunctions, or madmen. Occasionally, life came close to mocking art.

One of the earliest and best-known fictional accounts of an accidental war, *Red Alert,* was written in 1958 by an RAF bomber pilot, Peter George.[3] In the novel, a deranged SAC base commander orders his bombers to attack the Soviet Union. Most of the planes are shot down, with the willing connivance of a panicked and chagrined American government. But one errant bomber gets through to Moscow with its bombs, requiring the U.S. president

---

*Understandably, this theme was not ignored in Europe. A BBC documentary-style film of a hypothetical nuclear war, *The War Game,* began with the Russians overrunning NATO. The film was so gruesomely realistic that British censors banned it from television for a number of years. The response of a survivor in Frank Herbert's novel *Alas, Babylon* to the question of who won the war expressed an attitude typical of how most American novelists treated the subject: "We won it. We really clobbered 'em . . . Not that it matters."[2]

to sacrifice New York in exchange for the Russian capital. In the novel, the nascent nuclear war ends there.

George had been inspired to write the book by an unremarkable incident that occurred one rainy afternoon at the SAC base in England where he was stationed. In the barrackslike ready room at the base, he and other bored pilots had begun a game of stacking empty coffee cups on a table. Nearby, jet bombers struggled into the air on a practice alert, rattling the crockery on the table with the roar of their engines. Unattended and unnoticed by the airmen until it was too late, a single coffee cup suddenly danced off the table in the vibration of a passing jet and shattered on the floor. Someone then remarked casually: "You know, that's how World War Three is going to start."

Shortly after George's novel was published in England, a review of the book came to the attention of American filmmaker Stanley Kubrick, then researching a nonfiction film on the danger of accidental nuclear war. After reading the book, Kubrick decided to hire *Red Alert*'s author to write the script for the proposed documentary. The filmmaker at the same time discreetly enlisted a number of academic strategists as advisers on the film. One of those was Thomas Schelling, who had written the review read by Kubrick, and who later professed to find in *Red Alert* "the only good analytical work in those days about how wars got started." Together, the three men, said Schelling, "spent a long afternoon trying to figure out how to get the war" of the proposed film started.

Kubrick's collaboration with Schelling was followed by meetings with other nuclear theorists, including William Kaufmann, Albert Wohlstetter, and Herman Kahn. The producer apparently even offered to name the forthcoming film after Wohlstetter's seminal essay "The Delicate Balance of Terror." But Wohlstetter declined the offer with thanks. (He was concerned, he said later, that Kubrick was both "too bloody an artist" and "too enthusiastic about the bomb"—and hence that the film might portray too graphically what could happen if deterrence failed.)

Wohlstetter was subsequently thankful for his instinctive caution—since at some point in his research Kubrick evidently decided that his film would be more effective as *grande farce* than *cinéma vérité*. [4] Wohlstetter, Schelling, Kaufmann, and Kahn were surprised and somewhat embarrassed to discover in *Doctor Strangelove* that they had unwittingly abetted a satire of their own profession—especially since the movie's outcome differed fundamentally from that of the book on which it was based. As the film ends, so does the world.

Doctor Strangelove was originally intended to be as much a spoof of the military mind as of the civilian thinkers about the unthinkable. But the almost cultlike popularity of the film as black comedy derived from its chief character and namesake: Strangelove, a strategist from the "Bland Corporation," pointedly overcomes his physical and psychological paralysis in Kubrick's film only as all life on earth is annihilated.[5] By inference, the real villain of the film is not Strangelove alone, but the cohort of civilian experts —and their Russian counterparts—responsible for creating the insane system that first sends the fatal bomber on its way, and then makes the consequences of that mad act world-ending. Kubrick chose to emphasize this point by deleting from the movie a scene he had originally intended to be its finale—a pie fight involving the Russian ambassador, the president, and others present in the Pentagon war room. As the subtitle Kubrick chose for his film makes clear, its most damning indictment is reserved for those who have "learned to stop worrying and to love the bomb."

Doctor Strangelove and a related book and film of the same time about accidental nuclear war, *Fail-Safe,* prompted some to remark upon the uncomfortable degree of verisimilitude between real-life experts like Kahn and Schelling and the fictional figure of Kubrick's film.[6] What inspired the most vehement criticism of the experts, however, was not the portrayal of their role in a fanciful apocalypse but their implication in the real war in Vietnam. The steady escalation of that war beginning in the mid-1960s created a corresponding increase in the number and volume of antiwar critics. Much of the latter's criticism was aimed at the civilian strategists and scientists who were thought to be among the earliest supporters of the war—if not its actual architects. The early attack upon the experts—like the criticism of the war itself—concerned less the efficacy than the morality of their advisory role in Vietnam.

Deadly Logic, a 1966 book highly critical of the strategists both as a group and individually, charged that the experts' abstract theorizing was not so much thinking about the unthinkable as "quantifying the unquantifiable," and even "applying the inapplicable." Author Philip Green claimed that the moral culpability of the academic strategists—among whom he listed Kahn, Schelling, Wohlstetter, and Kissinger specifically—was even greater than that of elected officials, on the grounds that "the responsibilities of those who develop ideas are greater than the responsibilities of those who apply them."[7]

Two years earlier, a similar kind of intellectual broadside had been aimed at the strategists by mathematician Anatol Rapoport in a book titled *Strategy and Conscience.* As with Green's book, the focus of Rapoport's concern was the civilian nuclear strategists. But Vietnam inevitably provided the backdrop to the book. Discussing the prospect for a rapprochement between the groups he dubbed the "disarmers" and the "armers" in a chapter called "Is a Dialogue Possible?," Rapoport summarily answered his own rhetorical question in the negative.[8]

Neither Rapoport's nor Green's indictment of the strategists could be as damning, however, as that contained in a 1967 publication, *The Report from*

Iron Mountain. As recounted in a front-page story in the *New York Times,* the report supposedly presented the results of a top-secret government inquiry into "the feasibility and desirability of peace."[9]

Readers of the *Times* article and of the leaked report could readily understand why the government had wanted to keep the study from the public. Composed of a number of distinguished but unidentified experts in various fields, the "Iron Mountain Study Group" had concluded that a durable peace was not only unlikely in the world, but actually undesirable. International harmony, the experts claimed, could never hope to replace the traditional and historic benefits associated with what they termed "the war system"—among them being economic prosperity, political stability, and technological progress.

Most readers of *The Report from Iron Mountain* were predictably outraged by the study and its conclusions. "Whoever wrote this book is an idiot," proclaimed Henry Kissinger in a review written for the *Harvard Crimson.* However, at least a few reviews of the book—including those appearing in the journal *Transaction* and in the *New York Herald Tribune* —expressed gratitude and relief that the report and its authors had finally dared to say what everyone secretly knew to be true. Earnest efforts by various experts—including Herman Kahn—to deny participation in the study group or authorship of the report were publicly discounted.

Not only scandal but mystery surrounded *The Report from Iron Mountain.* Leonard Lewin, the writer to whom the report had supposedly been leaked, resisted repeated importunings to reveal the identity of "X," the member of the study group who Lewin claimed had given him the document. Lewin's reticence was understandable—since he himself was the mysterious "X" and sole author of the controversial report. He later confessed that the inspiration for the hoax came from a satirical magazine to which he was a contributor. He had been emboldened to the effort from the spectacular success of similar satires, such as Jonathan Swift's notorious *A Modest Proposal.* Like Swift's classic essay, his book was intended, Lewin said, "to be a provocation—to provoke outrage." But even he had not expected it to be accepted as authentic so readily. "The book is what it is," he simply told doubters while the hoax lasted.

"The astonishing thing to me," Lewin reflected, "was that those who thought it might be a hoax were people without any background in the subject. The people who took it seriously were professionals." "Is this one of ours?" Johnson's national security adviser, Walt Rostow, allegedly asked of the report at a cabinet meeting.

The obvious target of the book had been what Lewin called "the value-free analysis of the Iron Mountain mentality." His purpose had been to ridicule those self-consciously engaged in thinking about the unthinkable. But he was among the most surprised at how the reaction to the book showed the extent to which the Iron Mountain mentality had become pervasive—even unquestioned—in the land. Like a nuclear-age equivalent of Swift's *Modest Proposal, The Report from Iron Mountain* proved that moral outrage had atrophied to the point where the outrageous had become commonplace.

In what seemed to some antiwar critics an almost classical kind of retribution, Vietnam gradually but inexorably came to dominate the careers of those strategists who had at first ignored the conflict in Asia, and then turned to it as a proving ground for their theories concerning war. As the military stalemate in Vietnam continued despite the increasing American commitment, the effort there began to seem less and less an exemplar of "compellence" and "of making the punishment fit the crime" than an indictment of those theories and their authors. Some of the latter, however, persisted in the belief that America would prevail in Vietnam, attributing the protracted failure there to a choice of tactics, not strategy.

Bernard Brodie cited Polonius' advice to Laertes when discussing Vietnam in a 1966 book, *Escalation and the Nuclear Option:* "Beware/Of entrance to a quarrel/but, being in,/Bear't that th' opposed may beware of thee." One of the first to argue from Vietnam that wars involving major powers could be kept limited, Brodie conceded in his book that the use of nuclear weapons by the United States in Vietnam, while perhaps militarily advantageous, was politically unwise.[10]

The possibility of using nuclear weapons in Vietnam was a contingency peculiarly unremarked by most advisers on Vietnam—though it did not go entirely unconsidered. In private discussions as well as at high-level meetings among experts, the prospect was discussed—if only to be dismissed. Freeman Dyson, then a consultant to the Arms Control and Disarmament Agency, recalled a government meeting in 1966 when an official of the Johnson administration had offhandedly proposed using nuclear weapons in the war "now and then, just to keep the other side guessing."[11]

But the idea of employing nuclear weapons in Vietnam remained for the most part a matter of speculation and rumor. One of Dyson's colleagues among the Jasons, Richard Garwin, repeatedly traveled to Vietnam on visits concerned with construction of the "McNamara line"—visits that were widely but wrongly connected, Garwin said, with consideration of nuclear weapons. Even self-proclaimed "hawks" on the war, like Edward Teller, opposed using nuclear weapons in Vietnam on pragmatic grounds. "Only a few idiots—and they were really idiots—suggested the use of nuclear weapons in Vietnam," Teller said. In retrospect, he claimed that he could "hardly think of a decision that would have been more irrational." The reason: "Because you do *not* use nuclear weapons against guerrillas." To have done so, Teller concluded, "would have been in our worst possible interest."

Teller's opinion was evidently shared by at least one secret, government-funded study. That fact notwithstanding, critics of the war feared that the "nuclear option" remained very much alive among the contingencies studied for the war. The use of tactical nuclear weapons as a final resort in the defense of the beleaguered Marine garrison at Khe Sanh, for example, was reportedly discussed by President Johnson and the joint chiefs in 1968.[12] The popular outcry following an unverified rumor that the president and military commanders in Vietnam had formed a special study group to select targets for nuclear strikes in North Vietnam provoked immediate denials from those involved, and may finally have put an end even to consideration of nuclear weapons in the war.

As Brodie and others were aware, it was not only the lack of any clear military utility to such a course, but also the political fallout that would inevitably accompany the use of nuclear weapons in Vietnam that made the option unworkable—if not unthinkable. For at least a few among the war's early supporters, the very fact that the government would even entertain such a course was cause for alarm.

Daniel Ellsberg admitted his attitude toward the government had never quite recovered since the shock of learning the grisly details of American nuclear war planning at the outset of the Kennedy administration. Ellsberg had nonetheless been an early and outspoken promoter of the counterinsurgency theories that remained in vogue at Rand and in the government. Friends said they had begun to notice an apparent change of heart concerning the war on Ellsberg's part shortly after his return from a 1967 tour of Vietnam for the Pentagon and Rand. Engaged in a study of Vietcong motivation for Rand, Ellsberg had been particularly impressed with the evidence of the enemy's dedication and morale. A marine reservist, Ellsberg had come back from the front with both his optimism about the war and his health undermined. "They don't call it a 'jaundiced view' for nothing," observed Thomas Schelling about this period of growing disillusionment in his Rand colleague's life.

Before going to Vietnam, Ellsberg had participated in a Harvard debate on the war with faculty member Samuel Huntington, an originator and steadfast proponent of counterinsurgency doctrine. On that occasion Ellsberg had argued for a military victory in the war, whereas Huntington had counseled that success in Vietnam depended upon winning over the hearts and minds of the people. "Their analyses were almost identical," Schelling recalled. "Except that they came out on opposite sides."

While in Vietnam—according to another of his former colleagues at Harvard—Ellsberg wrote to Huntington conceding that the latter had been right in the debate. By the time Ellsberg returned to the United States, the earlier positions of the two debaters were exactly reversed. But Ellsberg had by then also begun to doubt that a political solution in Vietnam would be possible unless it was preceded by widespread political and economic change—a transformation he despaired of after witnessing firsthand the corruption of the Saigon government.

Never a man of measure even in the estimation of his friends, Ellsberg underwent "a psychological as well as an intellectual conversion" on the war because of his experiences, former colleague Stanley Hoffmann believed. An important step in that conversion, Ellsberg himself claimed, had been his subsequent involvement as director of a Rand study of the military options available to the United States in Vietnam. When one member of that study group tentatively broached the subject of using nuclear weapons in Vietnam, Ellsberg said that he had purposely cut short the discussion by announcing that he "refused to be associated with a piece of paper that even mentioned the possibility of the use of nuclear weapons": "I wanted that to be literally unthinkable."

Those experts who tried to distance themselves from the war found Vietnam pursuing them with dogged persistence. Pentagon comptroller Charles Hitch left the Johnson administration in 1965, before the first massive U.S. troop commitment to Vietnam, to become president of the University of California. At Berkeley, however, Hitch found himself in the middle of a maelstrom of student protests against the war and his alleged implication in it. Well before his return to academia, ironically, the pioneer of cost-effectiveness had privately concluded that there was a danger to misapplying its methods. When an eager young acolyte once spoke of elevating systems analysis to a principle of government, Hitch quickly deflated the idea with the observation that systems analysis had yet to solve the problem of rush-hour traffic in Cambridge.

One of Hitch's aides who remained at the Pentagon, Alain Enthoven, discovered to his chagrin that the war's critics seldom recognized a distinction between those analysts who helped to head off the ABM and those who had played a part in escalating the fighting in southeast Asia. An early and rare attempt to apply systems analysis to Vietnam, Enthoven remembered, had been a study of the military utility of the air war. The study concluded not only that the bombing failed to be cost-effective, but that the quantity of explosives recovered by the enemy from dud American bombs probably exceeded that destroyed by the bombing. Enthoven later defended the work that he and his band of systems analysts did as an implicit argument against further escalation of the war—an argument, he claimed, that McNamara himself eventually found compelling.[13]

For McNamara particularly, the Vietnam war had developed from a minor irritant to something approaching a consuming obsession by 1967. During that time he had gradually lost faith in the ability to win what he —even before the protesters—had come to regard as "McNamara's war."

His subsequent career offered unwitting proof, in fact, of how the war's spoiling effect extended beyond Vietnam.

The experts' own developing doubts about the value of their expertise surfaced, Enthoven thought, in a revealing incident near the end of his and McNamara's tenure. Since the early 1960s the two men had devised and updated yearly a Strategic Force Comparison Table that showed the relative number of Soviet and American bombers and missiles. Prior to his January 1968 testimony before Congress on the military budget, his last appearance there as defense secretary, McNamara had called Enthoven into his office and instructed him—"in a resigned voice," the latter recalled—"to get out 'the table.' " McNamara asked Enthoven how the number of submarine-launched ballistic missiles for each side had been arrived at on the chart.

"Here's what we do," Enthoven had explained. "We subtract the number of subs that are not ready for sea on our side, then take the remaining number and multiply it by sixteen for the number of missiles. For the Russians it's just the same. You take the number of submarines, you subtract the number that are not ready for sea . . ." Enthoven's explanation abruptly stopped. "Oh my God, don't tell me!" he exclaimed. "We didn't subtract the number for the Russians!"

There was a lesson to be learned, Enthoven reflected, in the oversight he and McNamara had committed—one that might be as fairly applied to Vietnam as to the balance of nuclear forces, and that gave reason for humility when dealing with both: "You assume that there is an information system that will tell you what you want to know. But that just isn't so. There are huge amounts of misinformation and wrong information."

For most of those who wrote on strategy, as for the nation generally, the Tet offensive in the spring of 1968 marked a turning point in attitudes toward the Vietnam war. After Tet, many of the experts who had since become the war's critics joined the growing number of citizens—for the first time a majority—who opposed continuing the effort in Vietnam. Besieged—sometimes literally—on university campuses around the country, academic strategists like MIT's William Kaufmann and Harvard's Thomas Schelling became acutely aware of the fact that Vietnam offered no middle ground. Kaufmann thought the protests in Cambridge responsible for a "kind of hiatus" in the study of anything related to the military or to strategy. "If you taught anything having to do with foreign affairs you got rocks through your windows," said Schelling.

As the "McNamara line" had become a source of division among the Jasons, so the war itself became a cause of increasing controversy among the strategists. A letter that Schelling drafted to send to Washington protesting the escalated bombing of North Vietnam split the original members of the "Charles River gang"—and drew a quick rebuff from one of its former members: Henry Kissinger. But the doubts about the war that first troubled and later consumed colleagues like Ellsberg were little evident in the work of other strategists, like Kahn, who remained firm in their support of the war.

For antiwar critics, the evidence that the strategists had been wrong on Vietnam was reason to doubt the wisdom of the experts on other matters. The year before Tet, Kahn and an associate at Hudson had decided to temporarily abandon the field of nuclear strategy to write a lengthy and number-filled prognosis for the next thirty-three years, titled *The Year 2000*.[14] Prompted in part by a childhood fascination with science fiction, Kahn's excursion into "futurology"—a term he claimed to have coined—was dominated by the same ebullient outspokenness and irrepressible optimism that had characterized his earlier books on strategy and nuclear war.

But in the view of Kahn's detractors—both then and later—the new genre suffered the same defects as the old. They pointed out how Kahn's prediction that by century's end American cities would have burgeoned in size to form urban "megalopolises"—with San Francisco and San Diego becoming a single heavily populated and industrial strip on the California coast dubbed "Sansan," dwarfed only by "Chipit" and "Boswash"—ignored basic and essential elements of demographics, economics, and even human nature. Critics also noted that Kahn's long-term "surprise-free predictions" forecasting a concurrent worldwide increase in both population and material wealth contrasted sharply with the contemporary evidence of global famine, poverty, and war—the most current example of which was, of course, Vietnam. Several reviewers of *The Year 2000* accordingly thought Kahn's effort at prescience likely to be not merely wrong but spectacularly wrong.[15]

The predictions that Kahn made concerning Vietnam caused his powers as a prospective Nostradamus to be further called into question, and doubts to be expressed as well about his reputation as one of the "prophets of nuclear realities," as a reviewer of *On Thermonuclear War* had written. A study of the Vietnam War that Kahn and others at Hudson completed in 1967 mirrored the most glowing of the Johnson administration's own forecasts in predicting an American victory in Vietnam within two to five years. The Hudson study, commissioned by the government and forwarded to the Military Assistance Command in Vietnam, was most critical of the Army's search-and-destroy tactics, suggesting instead that the military pursue the more traditional objective of seizing and holding territory. The emphasis of the study throughout, said one of its authors, was upon "a planned victory campaign."[16]

Kahn and his fellow analysts at Hudson were among the few whose optimism was not dimmed by Tet. Within months of the North Vietnamese and Vietcong offensive, Kahn had contributed to a book that gave a resoundingly affirmative answer to the rhetorical question raised by its title: *Can We Win in Vietnam?* Kahn's essays in the volume were perhaps the most determinedly sanguine about the prospects in Vietnam. America's failure in the war to date stemmed from its lack of a coherent "theory of victory," he asserted.[17]

The effect of Vietnam was to point out that the principal differences among the strategists concerned neither strategy nor tactics in the war, but the unstated assumptions behind America's involvement. Lacking the complex quantification of his books on nuclear strategy or the untestable esoterica of his predictions regarding the future, Kahn's writings on Vietnam showed that—like the Iron Mountain mentality of Lewin's satire—his thinking on the war was not value-free but subtly value-laden. In the highly charged emotional atmosphere of the Vietnam debate after Tet, the experts' self-professed detachment seemed but a poorly concealed kind of advocacy.

On occasion, even the pretense of objectivity was abandoned. Kahn argued in the book on Vietnam and in a subsequent *Foreign Affairs* article that the United States had a responsibility to stay in the war because of the "moral claim" the South Vietnamese had upon their American ally. Charging that an American "sellout" in Vietnam would reveal U.S. policy there to be, by successive degrees, "stupid," "incompetent," and "immoral"—he later added "criminal"—Kahn defended a continued involvement in the war as both just and necessary.[18]

Kahn's ethical argument on Vietnam was mirrored by other strategists who remained resolute on the war, such as Hudson colleague Morton Kaplan.[19] Upon reflection, Kaplan and another Hudson alumnus with diametrically opposed views on the war—Jeremy Stone—agreed that Vietnam finally revealed a fundamental truth about the strategists and their profession. The war, Stone thought, had exposed the myth that think tanks like Hudson were only modern-day Delphis for Kahn and like-minded seekers of truth. Hudson, he said, professed to be "a nuclear-war ivory tower," but the illusion of objectivity had finally been shattered by the guerrilla war in Vietnam. Stone felt that the war had likewise exposed the true nature of Hudson's founder and best-known figure. "His heart," he said of Kahn, "is that of a hawk."

The extent to which the Vietnam war had removed the middle ground on a variety of issues not directly connected with it was evident as well in the course of an experts' seminar on the future of American foreign policy, held in Chicago during the tumultuous summer of 1968. Unable to arrive at any substantive agreement on the subject, the participants—who included Ellsberg, Kissinger, and Wohlstetter—decided to publish their deliberations as a book bearing the revealingly tentative title *No More Vietnams?*[20] Unwittingly, the seminars—which took place only weeks before the confrontation between antiwar protesters and police in the streets outside—became a microcosm of the experts' debate on the war.

In those sessions the experts who were now sharply critical of the war saw U.S. involvement as neither an accident nor an isolated mistake, but as the symptom of more fundamental errors. "The Vietnam war had brought on a crisis not only of policy but of the theory behind the policy," said Stanford political scientist Theodore Draper. Among the theories needing reexamination, he claimed, was the whole doctrine of limited war. Citing Schelling's earlier praise for the Gulf of Tonkin reprisal raids, Draper argued that something "must be wrong if one of the outstanding theorists of 'limited war' could not see, at least a year and possibly two years later, where the Gulf of Tonkin action would or could lead us."[21]

Ellsberg thought it was not the theory of limited war *per se* that had been at fault in Vietnam, but the "attitudes and expectations associated with the American way of war"—specifically, Americans' "widespread belief" in "the efficacy and acceptability of aerial bombing . . . aimed at the will of the opponent via his industrial and population resources." Ellsberg saw the emphasis upon body counts in Vietnam as a related and gruesome extension of this aptitude for measuring war aims in terms of the number of enemy killed.[22]

Critics of the war at the seminar recounted how the bombing, the "McNamara line," and the government's confessed "orchestration" of military escalation were all examples of what one strategist called his profession's "fascination with technique." By the seminar's end what was originally intended to be an examination of American strategy and policy had become instead a judgment—and sometimes a self-indictment—of the experts themselves. "The policy has failed, and so has the theory," Draper concluded. "We need a new policy; and before we get it, we may have to work out a new theory."[23]

The relevance of Vietnam to their theories about nuclear war was a point rarely raised by the experts after Tet. Yet, as it had in the Chicago seminar, the guerrilla war in southeast Asia filled almost everyone's vision of the future. "Whatever became of nuclear war?" Wohlstetter had inquired almost imploringly at one point in the group's deliberations.

In a way that perhaps not even the experts themselves were quite aware of, Vietnam had already affected the thinking about the unthinkable. The crusade begun so enthusiastically and on so many fronts back in 1961 had gradually been abandoned in the course of the war. There seemed a particular irony in the fact that the analyst who had been the first to make an academic case for the strategy of torture and coercion, Daniel Ellsberg, came to identify most closely with the tortured and coerced victims of the war near its end. "He was a believer in 1965, an apostate in 1967, and a believer in something else by 1969," wrote a biographer of Ellsberg. "Vietnam," Ellsberg himself observed, "destroyed the center."[24]

The final step in Ellsberg's transformation, which had begun with his disquiet over war planning and the missile gap, was his decision in 1970 to leak the so-called Pentagon Papers—a multivolume, top-secret study of decision-making in Vietnam, ordered by McNamara near the end of his tenure in the hope that it could explain how the nation had become ensnarled in the war. The case of the Pentagon Papers was an extreme but not a unique example of how Vietnam had incited heresy. "The career of Daniel Ellsberg casts a glaring light on the divergent paths of his ex-colleagues," noted one of the growing number of critics of the war and the experts.[25]

Another of Vietnam's unintended victims would be the strategy of flexible response. The "ability to intervene anywhere created the need to intervene everywhere," observed Brodie about the military policy of the Kennedy administration. The theory of limited war was challenged in the wake of Vietnam even by some who were among its originators. Robert Osgood remarked how "Vietnam showed the things we took for granted couldn't be taken for granted." "What was perhaps a surprise and a shock to some strategists," he reflected, "was the limited utility to the use of force." The experience of Vietnam also caused Osgood to question, he wrote, "the whole interwar experience about opposing aggression" that "had become attached to limited war doctrine and had become axiomatic—so axiomatic that people never thought about it." Because of the war, "it became obvious that there were limits to which one would pursue such an abstract point, even when it applied primarily to American prestige."[26]

" 'Expertise' has been consulted but mere assertion has been delivered," charged one of the strategists' detractors concerning Vietnam. "One realizes," noted another critic pointedly, "with what misplaced abstractions the calculations of counterforce war and 'limited nuclear war' have been conceived."[27]

For a few experts, their loss of stature in the public's eyes because of the war led to a kind of self-imposed exile from the profession they had made a career. Lost in Vietnam in these cases was not only the crusade but the crusaders.[28] The impact of Vietnam was as heavy upon such strategists personally as upon the theories of war they had propounded. Shaken along with the popular faith in the experts' wisdom was the confidence the experts themselves had possessed in the soundness of their own basic attitudes regarding such things as national will and the rationality necessary to deterrence. The implicit assumptions that virtually all had made regarding the ability and the willingness of the United States to continually up the ante in Vietnam—to achieve "escalation dominance" in the strategists' phrase—was later admitted by some to have been missing a vital human element. "When we recall how we discussed methods for demonstrating 'our superior resolve' without ever questioning whether we would indeed have or deserve to have superiority in that commodity," Brodie wrote after Vietnam, "we realize how puerile was our whole approach to our art."[29]

It was perhaps because of this new sense of uncertainty that the "hiatus" which Kaufmann said the Vietnam war had created in the study of strategy extended as well at this time to the implementation of changes in the planning for nuclear war. Since 1967, Kaufmann and others among McNamara's aides had been urging him to revise the SIOP to bring it into line with the move away from counterforce begun by the defense secretary years earlier. But McNamara had continually postponed the revision—remaining fixated instead upon Vietnam.

Curiously, while Vietnam was often subtly at the center of the experts' debate, the war as such never became its focus. By 1969 the hopes of victory in Vietnam that almost all the experts once shared had given way to a pressing concern with avoiding the worst consequences of defeat. In the process, assumptions that had gone unchallenged for more than a generation came under attack. The self-promoted aura of objectivity that the experts maintained until Vietnam had finally broken down not only because of the war, but because of the end of unquestioned American nuclear superiority. Less than a year after Tet, the subject of Vietnam was recognized by all to have become an intellectual no-man's-land—and the question of missile defense to be once again the high ground.

PART THREE

APOSTATES

And if thou gaze long into an abyss,
the abyss will also gaze back into thee.

—NIETZSCHE

20

The Balance of Error

In February 1967, Robert McNamara received a long letter from Albert Wohlstetter concerning the ABM. Wohlstetter's letter, which Alain Enthoven had urged him to write, argued the desirability of eventually expanding the anti-Chinese missile defense McNamara then had under consideration to include protection for America's land-based missiles against Soviet attack. Wohlstetter agreed with McNamara that an ABM defense for the missiles was premature, but he envisioned a not too distant future when such protection might be the only guarantee against a disarming Soviet first strike.

It was Wohlstetter and Fred Hoffman who had first anticipated the vulnerability of land-based missiles in the basing study they completed for Rand in 1954. That study had also been the first to propose putting American missiles in underground silos as a temporary solution to the vulnerability problem. But the two men conceded in the study that even "this defense would have a finite life, and would probably not serve beyond the end of the decade of the sixties." Wohlstetter and Hoffman concluded, in fact, that the problem of the missiles' vulnerability simply might not have a permanent solution.[1]

In the course of the intervening years, Wohlstetter's native optimism had returned. By the time of his letter to McNamara he had become convinced that an active defense of the ICBMs would preserve the deterrent value of the land-based part of the strategic triad for years to come. Not the least important among Wohlstetter's other arguments for the ABM was his claim that it would reassure America's allies that the nation was not moving toward the "familiar but untenable strategic doctrine of minimum deterrence." Wohlstetter reminded McNamara several times in the letter that he "would like very much to have a chance to talk with you soberly and at some length" about the ABM.[2]

Since he was leaving the Pentagon, McNamara declined Wohlstetter's suggestion of a meeting. Some close to the developing ABM debate thought it characteristic of McNamara that he would choose to cite the part of Wohlstetter's letter that applauded the anti-Chinese system, while ignoring the case for a defense against Soviet missiles. One ABM proponent even charged that Wohlstetter had been "fooled" by McNamara into writing the letter.[3]

In reality, a principal motivation for Wohlstetter's letter had been the fact that he was becoming—as he later said—"progressively unhappy" with McNamara and the Johnson administration's defense policies. Wohlstetter thought misleading and even disingenuous, for example, McNamara's public statements concerning what constituted "tolerable" or "acceptable" damage in a nuclear war—particularly the latter's calculation of the degree of destruction that would be sufficient to deter the Russians. Since McNamara's first exposition of assured destruction, that figure had varied from one-half to one-third of the Soviet Union's population and industry. There was a kind of false precision behind such calculations, Wohlstetter charged: "This was McNamara at his worst. He liked to have a nice hard number."

Wohlstetter protested that the seemingly precise formulation behind the policy of assured destruction was merely a convenient argument against spending more on defense, and hence that the policy itself was "a numbers game—a polemic." He thought the Johnson administration's idea of simply comparing the number of Soviet and American missiles—regardless of their size or yields—similarly "a bad argument used by McNamara to counter a bad argument put forward by the joint chiefs." The refined techniques of quantitative analysis that he had helped to introduce to McNamara's Pentagon were, in Wohlstetter's view, being abused and subverted in the case of the ABM. "The problem with the use of numbers," Wohlstetter reflected, "was that you've bequeathed them to people of bad faith and to people of good faith as well."

Wohlstetter's letter to McNamara opened up a new and wider front in the experts' debate on a missile defense at a time when most of those engaged in the controversy—including Johnson and McNamara themselves—assumed that the issue had been settled. McNamara had predicted in 1967 when announcing the modest anti-Chinese ABM "that pressures will develop to expand it into a heavy Soviet-oriented ABM system." But not even he had imagined that those pressures would be so insistent, or that they would develop so quickly. Since then, lobbying for an expanded missile defense had become increasingly intense, despite McNamara's disclosure in his final report as defense secretary that the threat from China was developing more slowly than had been expected.

But it was not until a year after Wohlstetter's letter that the anti-ABM scientists joined the escalating battle over a missile defense, with the March

1968 publication of a *Scientific American* article by Richard Garwin and Hans Bethe. The two physicists attacked there the feasibility of the ABM in general and questioned the particular utility of the Sentinel program announced by Johnson and McNamara. Like the widely noted article by York and Wiesner on the arms race that had appeared four years earlier in the same magazine, the essay by Garwin and Bethe immediately assumed a symbolic importance because of the reputations of its authors.[4]

Garwin had decided to write the article to express publicly for the first time his opposition to the ABM. Previously, his growing doubts about a missile defense had been voiced only to his peers in private discussions and at classified conferences. Bethe, on the other hand, was a recognized veteran of earlier defense debates—including that over the Super, which he had refused to work on. Since then he had become a vocal and consistent opponent of missile defense in all its incarnations. Together, the two men represented a certain consensus of scientific opinion as well as a joining of forces in the ABM controversy. While different in age and experience, therefore, they were nonetheless alike in the reasons for their opposition to the new weapon.

The idea for the *Scientific American* article was suggested to Garwin and Bethe by the magazine's editor at a meeting of the American Association for the Advancement of Science the previous December in New York. The article's ostensible purpose was to set forth the technical case against missile defense apart from the political and strategic considerations that embroiled the issue. In their essay, Garwin and Bethe argued that an effective defense of American cities against the missiles of a sophisticated and determined opponent was then impossible and would be likely to remain so, since every missile that evaded the defender could destroy an entire city. Thus disposing of the case for a blanket or "area" defense of cities, Garwin and Bethe claimed that an alternative "site" or "terminal" defense of protected ICBMs—while eliminating some of the problems associated with city defense—could certainly be overwhelmed by a skillful and resolute opponent.

Ever impressed with the resiliency of the arguments put forward by the ABM's proponents, Garwin and Bethe were nonetheless surprised at the vehement reaction their article provoked. Reportedly, shortly after the article appeared, Army Secretary Stanley Resor—a prominent ABM advocate —circulated a memorandum in the Pentagon urging that government scientists denounce and discredit it. Garwin found that his stand against the ABM drew fire from both sides in the debate. The physicist saw his own role in the controversy as that of lending technological expertise and moral support to the ABM's foes—"as a flag-carrier rather than a soldier," he said. But he was criticized nonetheless by other anti-ABM scientists—who branded him a reluctant warrior because of his belated involvement in the public controversy—as well as by ABM supporters among the scientists, one of whom called him a traitor.[5]

The stir created by the article opened his eyes, Garwin said, to the fact that there would be little neutral ground in the upcoming public debate of the experts over the ABM. But there was one point in his subsequent rebuttal to critics which perhaps both sides in the dispute could accept. It embodied an elemental truth about the experts' debate that was often over-looked—or deliberately ignored by them. The two sides in the ABM controversy, Garwin wrote, "differ primarily not on technical facts but in technical judgments and political opinions."[6]

There were other aspects of the ABM controversy in the spring and summer of 1968 that suggested it might be unique among the many debates over defense. Foremost among these was the involvement for the first time of an informed public. While the ABM had not been a significant issue in the 1968 campaign—Vietnam dominated that contest, as it had in 1964 and would again in 1972—the decision of the newly installed Nixon administration the following March to proceed with an expanded program to protect U.S. ICBMs against Soviet attack had the effect of mobilizing popular sentiment against the ABM.[7]

Even before the administration's decision, anti-ABM sentiment had begun to find expression in citizens' meetings and at congressional hearings, where scientists like Bethe, Garwin, Herbert York, and Jerome Wiesner spoke out against the weapon. The scientists as a group were accorded an almost religious deference by their listeners. "You're here because you're against the ABM," Bethe joked with an assembly of students and faculty at MIT. "I'm here to tell you why you are."[8]

By the summer of 1968, protest rallies and Vietnam-style "teach-ins" against the ABM in Chicago, Seattle, and Boston—all identified as prospective sites for the system—had given the opposition to missile defense a kind of populist image. This public debate contrasted sharply with the closely held controversies that had developed around previous weapons like the Super. Indeed, the plainly emotional question facing the public of having nuclear weapons in close proximity—the so-called "bombs in the backyard" issue—dominated popular consideration of the ABM from an early date. (The Army's initial fear, ironically, had been that protests would occur in those cities *not* designated as ABM sites. Switching the location of sites only created new opponents. A congressman from Washington State who had initially supported the ABM, for example, was persuaded to join the opposition after the Army said it would shift Seattle's site to the island in Puget Sound where he had a home.)

The procession of congressional hearings on missile defense that began in 1968 and continued into the following year eventually defined two fundamental challenges to the ABM from the experts. Critics doubted, first, that there was an imminent threat to America's land-based missiles to be defended against. Second, they questioned whether the particular ABM program proposed by the government would work well enough to counter such a threat if and when it did emerge.[9]

Indicative of the profound shift in the attitude of scientists toward defense since the days of Project Charles, many of those who had earlier been in the forefront of the effort to defend against bombers now became leaders in the opposition to a defense against missiles. Defense itself was "a delusion" in an era of hydrogen bombs and intercontinental missiles, wrote Herbert York. On the other side, some of those whose previous support of the Super had identified them with the offensive emphasis of American nuclear strategy—Edward Teller and Paul Nitze, most notably—were, a generation later, in the position of endorsing a defensive nuclear strategy by promoting the ABM.[10]

Not everything was changed in the controversy over missile defense, however. The new ABM debate, like the old, was characterized by charges and countercharges in which each side impugned the other's motives. Proponents claimed that anti-ABM scientists had rejected the latest version of the weapon—dubbed Safeguard by the Nixon administration—even after conceding that its task of defending missiles was more realistic than Sentinel's task of defending cities. This proved, ABM supporters said, that the opposition to missile defense was on grounds more ideological than technical. Believing that Safeguard had removed the scientists' main objection to the ABM, Nixon's national security advisor, Henry Kissinger, reportedly complained of being personally betrayed when their opposition to missile defense continued.[11]

In Wohlstetter's view, an alternative to the ABM proposed by Garwin—launching the nation's ICBMs upon verified warning of a Soviet attack—demonstrated that the scientists and their allies opposed the ABM "philosophically, and at any price." He accused anti-ABM scientists of using underhanded tactics in their opposition to Safeguard. In particular, Wohlstetter charged that after the Nixon administration announced the emphasis of Safeguard would be upon defending missiles and not cities, Bethe's favorable comments regarding a site missile defense were deleted from the transcript of his Senate testimony by the ABM's foes in Congress.

Safeguard's opponents, for their part, claimed that the new ABM differed from Sentinel only in its name and its cost. Missile defense itself seemed to them a symbol of the self-sustaining dynamics of the arms race. The "ABM appeared to have all the characteristics of a solution in search of a problem," Herbert York wrote. Jeremy Stone similarly thought the ABM "a weapon in search of a mission."[12]

But the experts' debate on the ABM by the spring of 1969 remained where it had always been—upon the alleged technical merits or demerits of the weapon itself. What amounted to the closing arguments for and against a missile defense were made by Albert Wohlstetter and Wolfgang Panofsky during Senate hearings at this time, in a confrontation subsequently known to both sides as "the battle of the charts."

Panofsky's credentials as a physicist and arms control advocate were well established in advance of his testimony. Besides having played a major role in the ill-starred 1958 Geneva conference on surprise attack, Panofsky some years later had written a widely read *Foreign Affairs* article which argued that the United States and Russia would indefinitely remain the nuclear captive of the other. What Panofsky termed the "mutual hostage relationship" of the two superpowers was immutably fixed, he claimed, simply because of the incredible destructive power of the weapons each side possessed. It would remain the dominant factor in their affairs, he argued, unless both countries disarmed. In Panofsky's view the effort to change that relationship was not only futile but dangerous. Its effect could not alter the actual strategic balance, therefore, but it might undermine faith in that balance.[13]

The kernel of Panofsky's Senate testimony concerned not the balance of terror *per se,* but his specific contention that Safeguard was inadequate to the task of defending the nation's missiles. Both Panofsky and Wohlstetter had come to the Senate hearings as reluctant—and, indeed, almost inadvertent—witnesses.

One evening when the congressional hearings on Safeguard had just gotten underway, Panofsky had a chance encounter at the San Francisco airport with David Packard, a deputy defense secretary in the Nixon administration. Panofsky told Packard on that occasion that he agreed with the administration's goal of defending American missiles, but that Safeguard "used the wrong hardware for the right mission." When Packard later testified at the ABM hearings conducted by Senator William Fulbright that Safeguard had the support of prominent scientists, he cited his brief conversation with Panofsky as evidence, prompting Fulbright to immediately call Panofsky as a witness.[14]

Like Panofsky, Wohlstetter had remained purposely aloof from the ABM debate in Congress, following it only in the newspapers, he claimed. Wohlstetter's detachment ended, however, when ABM opponents in the hearings challenged his assertion that the nation's ICBMs would soon be vulnerable to a Russian surprise attack. Because his own calculations were being called into question—and because he and Fred Hoffman had been the first not only to identify the problem of strategic vulnerability but to suggest a solution —Wohlstetter said he felt an obligation to enter the fray.

It was soon evident that the Nixon administration and its allies in the ABM hearings had made a major mistake in believing that the support of scientists like Garwin and Panofsky for the *principle* of defending missiles against missiles would translate into support for Safeguard. This belief ignored the fact that there were, as Garwin had acknowledged, more fundamental technical and political issues underlying the ABM debate. Panofsky effectively disarmed ABM proponents during the course of his testimony by agreeing with the administration that a defense of ICBMs would be strategically prudent. But—he quickly pointed out—"on narrow technical grounds" alone the particular ABM proposed by the government would be unable to safeguard the thousand-odd Minuteman missiles that were the mainstay of the nation's land-based deterrent force.[15]

In closed sessions, Panofsky demonstrated by means of prepared charts that the Safeguard program suffered from what he termed "a glaring defect." It was the same fatal flaw that had always bedeviled the defense in its perpetual contest with an attacker: the defender could always be overwhelmed by guile and superior numbers. Since the number of intercepting missiles to be stationed at each Safeguard site remained secret, the essential defect that Panofsky pointed out did not enter into the public debate on the ABM. It became, however, the focus of the experts' secret debate.

Panofsky thought that Wohlstetter's counterarguments at these closed sessions—while painstakingly prepared and "very elaborate"—failed to convince Fulbright and the other nonexperts at the hearings, and served instead only "to confuse" the senators. At the same time, Wohlstetter's point that Safeguard would at least be adequate to guarantee the survival of a minimum deterrent force of American missiles left open the question that he himself had raised earlier: just how large would such a force have to be?

Several observers at the closed hearings agreed that Panofsky's testimony generally carried the day in the battle of the charts, convincing most there that an effective defense for the bulk of America's missiles remained unfeasible. But they also thought that it was the contrasting attitudes of the witnesses—as much as the substance of their arguments—that had made the decisive difference in the debate. Panofsky himself felt the climactic moment in the hearings had come when Donald Brennan, testifying in favor of Safeguard, contended that it was "most unlikely" nonexperts could arrive at a sound judgment on the ABM. When Brennan further suggested that the concepts behind a missile defense might be too complex for him to explain to laymen, Fulbright, a smile stuck on his face, responded acidly: "You go right ahead and try, Doctor."

A few weeks after the battle of the charts, Wohlstetter and MIT physicist George Rathjens argued the other major claim of ABM opponents—that the threat Safeguard was meant to defend against was neither imminent nor certain. The key issue in their dispute involved rival calculations of Russian and American military capabilities. Differing estimates of Soviet capabilities and intentions, in fact, subtly underlay the disagreement of the strategist and the scientist—just as they figured prominently in both the public and the closed sessions of the ABM hearings by the summer of 1969.

Wohlstetter's case for the ABM hinged upon his calculation that America's entire force of Minuteman and Titan missiles could become vulnerable to a Soviet first strike by 1974 or 1975, the earliest date by which Safeguard would go into operation. Rathjens countered with the argument that the nation's land-based missiles would remain safe from a disarming attack at least until the end of the decade, and that in any case the other two legs of the strategic triad—the missile-firing submarines and the bombers on alert—would remain invulnerable to a first strike for the foreseeable future.

There could no longer be any disputing that the Russians had undertaken a rapid and massive missile buildup in the previous few years. At issue was how long that buildup was likely to continue, and whether it represented only a reaction to the American missile buildup begun under Kennedy, or something far more portentous and sinister.[16]

Wohlstetter professed to find Rathjens' figures on missile vulnerability and accuracy "incredibly careless." He claimed that when he tried to talk to Panofsky and Rathjens about reconciling the disputed numbers his efforts were rebuffed. Concluding that there was more than just a casual element of neglect in the calculations of the scientists opposing the ABM, Wohlstetter said: "The fact of their sheer carelessness betrayed a kind of attitude toward these matters."

By the time they ended later that summer, the ABM hearings had raised either directly or indirectly all of the fundamental points in contention between the experts concerning Russian motives and the stability of deterrence—and resolved none of them. The Senate's decision in early August to fund the Safeguard program by the narrowest of margins—a single vote—had seemed once again to end the debate on missile defense, while in fact it left the controversy surrounding the issue intact.[17]

Each side in the experts' debate ultimately agreed that the question was decided by Congress and the public apart from the merits of the case. Garwin shared the view of the anti-ABM Arms Control Association, which concluded that the outcry provoked by the plan to locate ABM sites close to populated areas—the "bombs-in-the-backyard" argument—had probably doomed the project from the outset. Wohlstetter concurred that the specter of nuclear weapons in the neighborhood and the public's related fear of nuclear accidents had been "the most effective but probably the weakest argument against the ABM."

Just before the Senate vote the issues in the ABM debate had been made more complicated by yet another shift in the Nixon administration's rationale for missile defense. But the effect of this last-minute change in the government's strategy had only been to undermine the case for Safeguard.

ABM opponents pointed out how the administration's new claim that Safe-guard was needed as a "bargaining chip" in the upcoming negotiations on limiting strategic arms tacitly conceded the point that the weapon could no longer be justified on its own terms. The closeness of the Senate vote demon-strated, finally, the extent to which serious doubts about the ABM lingered.

Though inconclusive, the ABM controversy had an effect upon the partic-ipants. Like the debate over the Super, the ABM hearings also had repercus-sions lasting long after the issue itself had been decided. "Most of those involved in the ABM debate felt that it had significant effects on the scientific community," Rathjens wrote.[18] James Killian believed that the Nixon ad-ministration's refusal to appoint an independent group of scientists to study the problem of missile defense departed from the long-standing tradition which Killian's own Technical Capabilities Panel and the Gaither commit-tee had upheld.[19]

As Nixon's chief science adviser, Richard Garwin thought that the presi-dent's decision to bypass the scientists on the ABM had unwittingly helped to undo Safeguard. The study of missile defense that Nixon commissioned the National Security Council to do had thus ignored, Garwin claimed, the many technical problems which the committee was aware of: "All of this would have been prevented if they had just talked to the committee." Gar-win concluded that Nixon's snub of the scientists was one of the things which had rallied that group into a potent lobby against a missile defense. The anti-ABM lobby—many of whose members had supported without question the government's position in an earlier era—represented in his view a new and different tradition of independent experts speaking the truth to power. (Garwin's later testimony against another favorite administration project, the supersonic transport, was evidently the final straw for Nixon, however. He rid himself of the troublesome scientist and abolished PSAC shortly after his reelection in 1972.)

The wider gap that the ABM debate opened up between the scientists and the government was matched by the increased suspicion and distrust with which the public, because of the controversy, came to regard all experts—and even the claim of expertise itself. The gathering cloud of doubt that originated with the popular disillusionment over Vietnam had grown much larger by the summer of 1969 because of the missile defense controversy. To critics of the Nixon administration, the ABM seemed almost a parable of the protracted war in Asia. The fact that the government had repeatedly changed both the mission and the rationale of the ABM—from a defender of U.S. cities against Chinese attack to a defender of U.S. missiles from a Soviet first strike, and from a needed bulwark of deterrence to a mere bargaining chip—weakened not only the case for missile defense, but like-wise the public's faith in those who had made that case. "The credibility of the professional is on the line," warned Senator Henry Jackson—a longtime proponent of a missile defense—at the close of the ABM hearings.[20]

The dawning realization by both sides of the truth behind Jackson's remark accounted in part for the bitterness of feeling that remained in the ABM debate, even after the Senate vote had supposedly resolved the issue. As Garwin found, those most directly involved in the controversy necessarily bore the brunt of the passions it aroused. Exactly how contentious the issue of missile defense would become was made clear to Wohlstetter at a private meeting between witnesses for the ABM and skeptical journalists. The meeting had been arranged by columnist Joseph Kraft during the hearings, in the hope of bettering relations between the government and the press.

During that session, Wohlstetter was unable to dispel the journalists' conviction that the government had deliberately altered CIA estimates on the accuracy of Soviet missiles and the vulnerability of Minuteman in order to make a better case for Safeguard. "The *ad hominem* attacks were just terrible," Wohlstetter complained of the episode. "The press was in no mood to believe anything the government said." He remembered in particular how the Vietnam war formed a backdrop to the discussion on the ABM. "The government has lied so much, why should we believe them now?" NBC's John Chancellor had challenged. "It was very, very frustrating," Wohlstetter recalled of the meeting. "Vietnam made the thing an adversary relationship. Passions were determining: Vietnam passions."

Instances where the government had, indeed, deliberately misrepresented intelligence reports or willfully withheld damaging information about Safeguard undoubtedly did undermine the case of the ABM, as even its supporters admitted. But probably as harmful to the experts was the pall the debate itself cast upon their reputations for candor and accuracy. By the time the ABM hearings had drawn to a close, the popular attitude toward administration spokesmen on the subject was said to range from polite skepticism to open contempt.[21]

To Wohlstetter, the ABM case had raised some fundamental questions about the role of experts as government witnesses and advisers. At one point in the hearings, Senator Stuart Symington, a prominent ABM foe, had expressed nonetheless a sentiment with which Wohlstetter was in complete agreement. "How can an intelligent nonexpert check among conflicting expert testimony?" Symington asked despairingly. Wohlstetter thought that the real issue behind Symington's question was a variation of the point usually raised about the role of the military in a democracy: "How do you get civilian control of the scientists?"

The dispute that began between Wohlstetter and Rathjens in the Senate hearing room during the summer of 1969 continued into the fall with an exchange of letters in the *New York Times*. Their personal debate concerned such highly technical details as the blast resistance of Minuteman silos and the terminal guidance accuracy of the Soviet SS-9 ICBM—points that probably would have seemed minor to most laymen. Rathjens calculated that 20 percent of the Minuteman force would survive a Soviet attack five years thence if no defense against missiles existed. Wohlstetter's estimate was that only 5 percent would survive. Yet in the fifteen percentage points that separated Wohlstetter from Rathjens were two wholly different and conflicting perceptions of the future direction of the arms race.[22]

Mindful of C. P. Snow's comment about another famous feud between two experts, Henry Tizard and Lord Cherwell—that it could have been resolved in a day if the evidence had been submitted to the Royal Academy of Science—Wohlstetter asked the Operations Research Society of America, of which he was a member, to arbitrate his dispute with Rathjens.

Like the ABM debate itself, the ORSA review had a symbolic importance beyond that of the issues involved in the dispute. Rathjens characterized it as "a debate about the debate"—"one of the bitterest in the community since the Oppenheimer controversy." In fact, the ORSA incident evoked the same heated passions and charges of bias that had characterized the conflict of Teller and Oppenheimer twenty years before.[23]

The *démarche* with Wohlstetter seemed, in retrospect, "a funny debate" to Rathjens, since the principal question at issue was not the viability of the ABM but the theoretical vulnerability of Minuteman. The fact that Rathjens was not a member of ORSA—and that the panel it appointed to investigate Wohlstetter's charges included a researcher Rathjens had once fired, as well as another he had refused to hire—seemed proof to the scientist of the organization's bias in the case. The fact that both Wolfgang Panofsky and Jerome Wiesner had also been mentioned in Wohlstetter's indictment persuaded Rathjens that the real purpose of the review was not to check his figures but to discredit the scientists' movement against the ABM.

The private controversy over the ORSA investigation became public when the panel published its report in the summer of 1971, nearly two years after beginning its inquiry. The report essentially affirmed the charges in Wohlstetter's letter. Rathjens and other scientists, it claimed, had consistently overestimated the resistance of American missile silos to the effects of a nuclear blast while at the same time underestimating both the yield and the accuracy of Soviet warheads.

Reaction to the ORSA report divided, predictably, along lines that were already rigid at the time of the Super decision—ones that arguably had been formed in the first light from Alamogordo. Rathjens condemned the report as "biased," "technically incompetent," and overall "the most outrageous thing I've ever seen." Garwin decried it as "sophisticated operations research techniques applied to shaky assumptions." A special issue of the Federation of American Scientists' *Newsletter*—published in response to the

report and featuring contributions from many of those mentioned in it—
concluded that the study suffered from "important errors, and a host of
other indications of bias and inappropriate procedures."[24]

Edward Teller, on the other hand, thought the ORSA report "remarkable
for its competence and objectivity." A spokesman for the Nixon administration similarly praised the society and its panel for providing "a magnificent
service" and an "incremental act of leadership and good sense." The report
ultimately even provoked a temporary reopening of the Senate ABM debate,
in miniature, when partisans on both sides read statements about the investigation into the *Congressional Record* following a favorable account of
ORSA in ABM advocate Joseph Alsop's syndicated column.[25]

But the most significant thing about the ORSA incident was the two very
different lessons that those involved drew from it. To Wohlstetter, the
scientists' reaction to the report was indicative of "the general hysteria about
the ABM that existed at the time": "There was a rallying together of the
clan—of practically all of the scientists I had criticized." Revived by Wohlstetter's critics was the earlier charge leveled against him—one he always
steadfastly denied—that his appearances at anti-ABM and antiwar rallies to
defend the Nixon administration's position had been financed by the government at public expense.

One positive result of the ORSA investigation, Wohlstetter thought, was
to expose the anti-ABM scientists as a special-interest group and to challenge what he regarded as their "specious authority." But the question that
Wohlstetter felt had often been at the heart of the ABM debate remained
unresolved and even unaddressed in the ORSA report—"Is democracy
compatible with the use of experts?"

To the scientists who felt they were its target, the report represented the
first time since the Oppenheimer case when public doubts were expressed
regarding not their knowledge or wisdom but their intentions and motives.
In a retrospective written some years after the controversy, Rathjens
reached a bitter conclusion in summing up the report's significance. "So
much for the objectivity of science," he wrote.[26]

In ORSA's investigation, as throughout the ABM debate, the focus upon
technological minutiae had foreclosed any discussion by the experts of the
fundamental issues separating the two sides. Barely raised and never fully
discussed in the contest over numbers and analytical technique, for example,
was the critical question of how much more likely the theoretical vulnerability of America's land-based missiles made a Soviet surprise attack. The
question about the compatibility of experts and democracy that Wohlstetter
had thought implicit in the missile defense controversy remained, as well,
unresolved at its end.

Ironically, the future of the ABM no longer hinged upon the opinions and arguments of the experts in any case. The ABM debate itself had been rendered academic shortly after the Senate vote on Safeguard. Less than a week after Wohlstetter sent the letter to ORSA that sparked his confrontation with the scientists, the long-awaited Soviet-American negotiations on the limitation of strategic arms—the SALT talks—began in Helsinki.

21

A Race Toward
Reasonableness

Eugene Rostow—later one of SALT's foremost critics—remembered how the negotiations began with great drama and optimism, and almost immediately encountered a portentous snag. Though the Russians had agreed in the early summer of 1968 to the talks proposed by Johnson and McNamara, as the summer's end approached no substantive steps had been taken by either side toward the negotiations. Finally, one evening in mid-August, Secretary of State Dean Rusk hurried from a meeting with Soviet ambassador Anatoly Dobrynin on board the presidential yacht to give Johnson the news that the Russians wanted to begin the negotiations with him personally the following month in Leningrad.

The next evening it was Dobrynin's turn to rush to the White House to inform Johnson that the communist government of Czechoslovakia had "requested" the intervention of Soviet and Warsaw Pact troops to restore order in that country. Just before midnight, Rusk informed Dobrynin that because of the Czech invasion Johnson would not be traveling to Russia on the arranged date after all. When Dobrynin objected that it was already too late to cancel the visit—which the Soviet government was planning to announce in *Pravda* the following morning—Rusk waved the Russian's protest aside and said he would inform the Kremlin of the cancellation directly, with a "flash" or top-priority telegram. The message, Rostow remembered, had been conveyed in four blunt words: "The visit is off."

A week later the Democratic National Convention convened in Chicago. Neither the delegates who subsequently nominated Johnson's picked successor, Hubert Humphrey, nor the demonstrators in the streets outside protesting the administration's Vietnam policy were aware of the circumstances that had preempted what Johnson evidently hoped would be the final, unifying act of his presidency: an act that might, in time, even have removed the stain of the war from his legacy. A lifelong Democrat, Rostow thought it tragically ironic that the event watched by the whole world at Chicago was the disintegration—not the culmination—of Johnson's aspirations as peacemaker.

Despite the false start prompted by the invasion of Czechoslovakia, discreet efforts to begin negotiations on reducing strategic arms continued in succeeding months. Obstacles to that effort included not only Soviet repression of the Czechs' brief "Prague spring" but the lame-duck status of the Johnson administration, and President-elect Nixon's understandable reluctance to be bound by his predecessor's commitments on arms control. Yet Russian interest in SALT was evident in the fact that the Soviets themselves finally took the initiative in breaking the deadlock, with a move that showed uncharacteristic energy and even daring on their part.

It seemed especially appropriate that the person approached in the Soviet initiative was SALT's original architect, Robert McNamara. In his 1967 speech at San Francisco, McNamara had looked to the arms talks as a way of inaugurating "a new race toward reasonableness." Since leaving the Pentagon to become president of the World Bank, however, he assumed that he would play no direct role in the enterprise.

But on Veterans Day in 1968, while McNamara was a tourist in Red Square—having stopped off in Moscow on a trip to Afghanistan for the bank —he was approached by a foreign service officer from the American embassy with a message from the Russians. The aide told McNamara that Premier Kosygin and a deputation of other important Russians wished to speak with him about the stalled arms control talks. McNamara demurred, protesting that since he had joined the World Bank he could no longer speak for his government. The young diplomat had persisted. "What should I tell them?" he asked anxiously. "Tell them you couldn't find me," McNamara suggested affably. The aide looked incredulous—suddenly realizing that the former defense secretary simply didn't *understand.* Gesturing past McNamara's shoulder, he blurted out: "Who the hell do you think those people behind you are?"

The very fact that SALT would take place at all was evidence to arms control enthusiasts of a dramatic change in the arms race and the Cold War. The "SALT process"—as it would become known—was characterized from the outset by the same kind of highly technical and abstruse considerations that had stalled the arms control talks of the late 1950s and early 1960s. But there was a difference: the technological arcana of the experts' arguments —and the experts themselves—were no longer necessarily dominant in the case of SALT.

Spurgeon Keeny attended the opening round of SALT in Helsinki, just as he had its ill-fated predecessors—the conference on surprise attack and the Conference of Experts in Geneva—more than a decade before. Head of the science and technology directorate of the Arms Control and Disarmament Agency in the Nixon administration—in which capacity he had put two *purgatorios* by Hieronymus Bosch on his office wall as a reminder of what the world might be like without SALT—Keeny thought the beginning of the change in the Cold War had been signaled by the successful test ban negotiations. But he attributed the major difference in arms control that he felt SALT represented to a change within the ranks of the experts.

The original initiative for arms control, Keeny felt, had come from the scientists: "Most of the people in the government didn't understand any of this. Even the military was uncomprehending." Since that time, however, there had come to be, he said, "more and more people who know—or think they know—more about arms control, or at least are comfortable with it." These people were "no longer overwhelmed by the technology—by the avalanche of bombs, computers, and missiles."

The change that SALT represented was commented on as well by Gerard Smith, chosen by Nixon and Kissinger in 1969 to head the American negotiating team in Helsinki. Smith later observed of the origins of SALT that it was accompanied "by a tremendous influx of academics, lawyers, and bureaucrats in what in previous days would have been a straight military problem." Smith was himself a prominent Washington attorney rather than an elected official or career diplomat, and his appointment to head the U.S. SALT delegation seemed itself to symbolize a break with the past.

Both Smith and Keeny believed that the way in which statesmen replaced the scientists and the strategists in SALT portended progress in the negotiations. A similar change in emphasis, therefore, had heralded the breakthrough that resulted in the 1963 test ban treaty. As had been the case then, each man now felt that the importance given SALT by the superpowers was less the result of any true resolution of outstanding Soviet-American differences than of a changing attitude on the part of both governments toward the arms race.

That change, they agreed, was most evident on the American side. While Richard Nixon in his 1968 campaign had publicly endorsed the goal of regaining American nuclear superiority, the fact that Nixon replaced the term "superiority" with "sufficiency" within a week of his inauguration heartened SALT supporters. Nixon's pointed reference early in his presidency to Eisenhower's celebrated warning about the baneful influence of a scientific-technological elite was likewise contradicted by his administration's steady retreat on a missile defense—a retreat which seemed tacitly to concede the point of ABM opponents that the system was at least politically, if not technically, unfeasible. Nixon's final justification of the ABM as a bargaining chip in the upcoming negotiations with the Russians showed the extent, indeed, to which promoters of the weapon had ultimately seemed to side with its critics.[1]

But the champions of SALT in the United States claimed that a comparable change of mind on arms control seemed evident as well in the Soviet Union. As on the American side, the issue of a missile defense was at the heart of that change. "SALT-sellers" pointed out that one of the earliest delays in launching the talks had been Premier Kosygin's stubborn attachment at Glassboro to the ABM as a purely defensive—and even "humane" —weapon. By the time the SALT negotiations began two years later, however, the Soviet position on the ABM had clearly shifted. After some initial wrangling over whether the ABM fit into the category of a strategic weapon, the Russians had finally conceded the point to the United States and announced their willingness to consider not only limitations upon present ABMs but even an outright ban on their future development.[2]

Underlying the new optimism about arms control was not, its advocates emphasized, any newfound mutual perception of trust, but rather a newly shared perception of mutual interest on the part of the United States and the Soviet Union. This view was in accord with the belief of anti-ABM scientists that defending against missiles unsettled the certainty that both sides would be destroyed in a nuclear war, and hence that such a defense threatened the stability of the stalemated arms race. The very fact that the SALT process continued in earnest during the Vietnam war seemed to signify the quiet victory of the arms controllers—and to signal as well the tentative triumph of their attitude that there could be no winner in the arms race.

It was, in the scientists' view, this perception of mutual interest—one now shared by the American people, who gave arms control a political constituency—that moved the SALT negotiations in 1969 and 1970 through the innumerable technological complexities which had confused and confounded earlier efforts at controlling the arms race. The discernible difference in SALT was that the talks this time were no longer concerned just with the possibility of agreement, but with the mechanics of how such an agreement could be carried out. An early writer on the negotiations, John Newhouse, agreed that the really significant change was not just in the approach of SALT but in the attitude there. There was "much more to SALT," Newhouse wrote, "than meets the eye of many a systems analyst." "One of our objectives in getting the SALT talks started," McNamara recounted, "was to narrow the tremendous philosophical gap between the U.S. and the Soviet theories of nuclear strategy." He said of SALT: "Whatever else it's done, it sure as hell has done that."[3]

The possibility of a complete ban on ABM had been one of the early options considered by the American team at the talks, and was the solution person-

ally favored by Gerard Smith. Having rejected a proposed U.S. ban on
missile defense early in the talks, Smith's Soviet counterpart subsequently
expressed an interest in discussing the issue. After a lengthy hiatus—during
which the idea of an ABM ban was neither promoted nor specifically excluded by Washington—the Nixon administration late in the summer of
1969 proposed an entirely new negotiating position, adding it to the other
four options that Smith and the State Department had worked out at length.
This fifth proposal—Option E—apparently came directly from the White
House, though its earliest origins had included an eighty-five-page memorandum written by Albert Wohlstetter and others for Kissinger's consideration. Option E for the first time in the talks tied a ban on ABM to reductions
in the number of offensive weapons permitted to each side under the terms
of SALT.[4]

Protesting that the proposed reductions were in effect "nonnegotiable"—
since they clearly favored American strategic forces at the expense of Soviet
forces—Smith opposed the administration's decision to make Soviet acceptance of Option E a prior condition for consideration of an ABM ban. Little
more than a week after the proposal had been introduced and been summarily rejected by the Russians, Nixon personally instructed Smith to strike
the proposed ban on missile defense from the American position.[5]

In his own later account of the negotiations, Smith wrote that he was
unable "to see the logic" behind the reasons Nixon gave for abandoning the
effort to abolish the ABM. Smith speculated that "the President's central
motivation was to avoid what he thought would be a real fight with Congress
over a ban on ABMs." But the result of Nixon's action, he thought, was to
make the failure to consider proscribing missile defense an American responsibility. "As it was," Smith wrote, "we started a process from which we
backed away when the U.S.S.R. showed interest."[6]

Like Smith, others among those who initially entertained high hopes for
SALT felt the proposed ABM ban became a victim of the persistent quest
for advantage in the nuclear arms race—a quest which ensured that the arms
competition would continue within the terms of a SALT agreement. There
had been a brief time when those seeking to control—or even to end—that
race had thought themselves within sight of victory. But, as with the ABM,
consideration of a ban on MIRV was similarly averted in the SALT negotiations. The inability to stop MIRV—a technological Pandora's box—would
appear to this group in coming months as an even more significant failure
than what they considered the missed opportunity to ban forevermore the
ABM.[7]

Nonetheless, the signing at Moscow in May 1972 of two SALT treaties
—one limiting ABM deployment, the other limiting the number of offensive
weapons permitted to either side—seemed an occasion of barely restrained
joy for those who had come to identify themselves collectively and some-

times self-consciously as "the arms control community." To most arms controllers the two treaties were the culmination of an effort symbolically begun by Oppenheimer more than a generation before. The treaties seemed to represent, therefore, a substantial—if not yet final—acceptance of the idea that there could be no victor in a nuclear arms race.

The SALT treaties seemed as well a personal tribute to the efforts of Robert McNamara and to the strategic vision that prevailed at the time he left the Pentagon. In the peculiar logic of deterrence, the SALT agreements seemed to offer stability in the arms race through stalemate. The treaties thus seemed to ally political consensus with the forces of nature in creating a technological endgame which gave the final and decisive advantage to offense, and yet assured that neither side would survive—much less triumph by—an ultimate act of aggression.

At the treaties' signing there seemed little recognition among SALT's promoters that theirs was a very qualified and tentative success. Having moved their doomsday clock to within seven minutes of midnight following China's explosion of a hydrogen bomb in 1968, the editors of the *Bulletin of Atomic Scientists* put the hands back five minutes upon SALT's signing —to a position they had not occupied since the ratification of the 1963 test ban treaty. As had been the case then, many in the revitalized arms control community—including Keeny and Smith—believed that SALT might only have launched the momentum toward arms control, and that the race toward reasonableness could still lead to an outright ban on ABM and MIRV.

"A consensus did emerge on ABM," Keeny concluded of SALT's significance. "The fact of the treaty reflected a recognition that ABM wouldn't solve the problem." He believed the treaty also represented "a technological disillusionment" on the part of ABM advocates. Jeremy Stone similarly thought the Senate's subsequent approval of the SALT treaties indicated that "Wohlstetter and the other hawks ultimately accepted" the Nixon administration's closing argument for Safeguard as a bargaining chip—and accepted as well the implicit conclusion that the weapon's real utility lay in contributing to its own demise.

But exactly how shallow the supposed consensus on SALT actually was became increasingly evident in coming months. As with the partial test ban, the early enthusiasm that accompanied SALT's ratification began to dissipate in a remarkably short time. Like the initial apparent successes of arms control, the inaugural SALT agreements would seem upon reflection a remarkably grand battle for a surprisingly meager victory. Having won the equivalent of a skirmish on the battlements with the ABM, the arms controllers were oblivious to the breach already opened in the defense of SALT by its critics. They were consequently unprepared for the ensuing full-scale assault upon arms control and the premises underlying it.

· · ·

As early as 1969—in the midst of the ABM debate and shortly after SALT had gotten underway—the Hudson Institute's Donald Brennan publicly ridiculed the premises behind American nuclear strategy. Adding the word "mutual" to McNamara's "assured destruction" formulation for the purpose, Brennan had burlesqued the concept as particularly appropriate to its acronym—MAD. It was mad, Brennan argued, that the government "evidently preferred dead Russians to live Americans," and that the nation should seem content to live forever under a nuclear sword of Damocles rather than seek to defend itself against Soviet attack.[8]

Two years later—and some months before the American negotiating team went to Moscow to work out the last details of the SALT treaties—Brennan resumed his attack on MAD and SALT in the *New York Times.* "While technology and politics may conspire for a time to leave us temporarily in such a posture," Brennan wrote of the mutual-hostage relationship, "we should not welcome it—we should rather be looking for ways out of it." Announcing himself opposed to mutually assured destruction on pragmatic as well as political grounds, Brennan claimed that his principal objection to the strategy was ethical: "We should not deliberately create a system in which millions of innocent civilians would, by intention, be exterminated in a failure of the system."[9]

"Brennan created the MAD acronym and used it like a club," Jeremy Stone said of his former colleague at Hudson. Stone felt that Brennan's was "a PR man's role in the debate," with the latter simply using the morality argument as "a blind." (Brennan's invention nonetheless established a trend. Stone himself later coined Percentage Arms Reductions—PARs—as a substitute for SALT. Eugene Rostow subsequently proposed that SALT be replaced by START, standing for "strategic arms reduction talks.") But Brennan—who described himself as a "former MADvocate" and "the most forceful and persistent critic of mutual assured destruction ideas in the West"—was actually only one of those to challenge the assumptions behind American nuclear strategy at this time.[10]

Those Rand analysts who had been among the first to decry how modern war made civilians its victims denounced assured destruction for extending that process to its apotheosis. Henry Rowen later condemned the nuclear strategy that evolved while he was at the Pentagon as "a policy of genocide," and "a policy based on bluff." Fred Iklé—who, like Rowen, had pioneered in calculating the damage done by strategic bombing in the Second World War—charged that "our method for preventing nuclear war rests on a form of warfare universally condemned since the Dark Ages—the mass killing of hostages." Following Brennan's lead, Iklé complained that the strategy of mutually assured destruction made civilization a hostage to accident and miscalculation. MAD, he and other critics argued, was based on "the sort of reasoning that says 'Killing people is good, killing weapons is bad.' "[11]

The attack on MAD intensified with the signing of the SALT treaties. Testifying against Senate ratification of the treaties in 1972, Brennan claimed that arms control had in effect gotten its priorities reversed. The treaties did "the wrong thing well" in constraining the defense against enemy attack, Brennan said, and "the right thing badly" by not putting more severe limits upon offensive weapons.[12]

The subsequent defense of MAD was for the most part perfunctory and conducted without enthusiasm—a fact which showed the growing ambivalence of even its supporters for a doctrine that admittedly envisioned the possibility of mutual destruction. But the prompt ratification of the SALT treaties in the summer of 1972 indicated that the moral argument against mutually assured destruction was more confusing than compelling to a Congress and a public now plainly enthusiastic about arms control. Instead, the most serious challenge to American nuclear strategy and arms control would not be on the broad and emotional issue of ethics raised by Brennan, but on the more narrowly conceived grounds of probability.

Well before the signing of the SALT treaties, some who were witness to the negotiations privately conceded that SALT had a prospective Achilles' heel. SALT's political vulnerability lay in the fact that the treaties had ultimately been unable to deal with the strategic vulnerability of land-based missiles. In a 1972 book on the negotiations, John Newhouse mused about how a concern with Minuteman's theoretical vulnerability to Soviet attack—a subject that had been, he wrote, "a mostly arcane internal argument" in the American delegation since the start of the talks—"could blossom into a full-blown and contentious political issue" amid "renewed cries of a missile gap and heavy pressure from Congress to deploy new or improved weapons with all possible speed."[13]

The consequent "convulsion in the public mood," Newhouse predicted, might in turn prompt "a closely reasoned statement by some prominent member of the defense community," proclaiming "a sharp decline in America's political and strategic power." Newhouse posited how such a statement could lead to front-page articles in the *New York Times,* congressional investigations into defense spending, and—finally—the undoing of SALT. Newhouse's warning proved prescient. What neither he nor anyone predicted in 1972, however, was that among those responsible for SALT's unpopularity a decade hence would be one of its earlier sponsors.

In his memoirs, Gerard Smith recalled how the unresolved problem of Minuteman vulnerability had been a particular and persistent concern of Paul Nitze's. Smith remembered how "Nitze seemed under the most strain" among all on the American team regarding the disparity in the size of U.S. and Soviet missiles. The cause of that disparity—as Eisenhower noted in the

1950s—was the fact that Russian scientists had not been as successful as their American counterparts in miniaturizing the nuclear warheads carried on ICBMs. This inequality in size had increased as the Russians continued to build ever larger missiles capable of carrying heavier and more destructive payloads, while the size of the individual warheads on American missiles shrank as a consequence of technical improvements and MIRVing.[14]

Efforts on the American side to rectify this imbalance through the SALT negotiations had been summarily rebuffed by the Russians. Nitze, according to Smith, "worried about the long-run effect of this process on worldwide perceptions about the Soviet-American strategic balance," as well as about the "increasing vulnerability of American Minuteman ICBM siloes to attack by these large Soviet missiles." Nitze seemed, nonetheless, to have overcome his doubts and fears by the time the first SALT agreements were concluded. He publicly supported the treaties in his 1972 testimony before the Senate. But, privately, he expressed the feeling that future talks should focus upon limiting missile "throw-weight"—the size and/or number of the warheads that the missile could carry.[15]

Nitze's continued doubts concerning SALT caused some on the American delegation to profess skepticism concerning the genuineness and depth of his public commitment to arms control. Consistently throughout his career and as recently as a decade prior to SALT, these skeptics pointed out, Nitze had argued that military superiority over the Russians was vital to American interests. Smith, for example, "sensed" that Nitze's support for the ABM treaty stemmed more from his belief that a defense against missiles would not work than from any deep or abiding worry over the weapon's destabilizing effects.

Others went further in claiming that Nitze's support for arms control was merely tactical, and his endorsement of SALT dependent upon the condition that the preexisting American advantage in the number of strategic bombers and missile warheads be maintained. Such critics charged that Nitze's apparent interest in arms control—like his secret 1963 proposal that the United States and Russia freeze the number of missiles and bombers in their arsenals, when the U.S. was far ahead—actually masked an effort to keep the Soviets from catching up to the United States. While initiatives of that sort would certainly have favored the American side, for that reason they stood little chance of receiving serious consideration from the Soviets.[16]

The subject of this criticism denied that there was "another Nitze" on the matter of arms control. Nitze defended his freeze recommendation as seriously motivated, and explained an even more ambitious proposal by him three years earlier—in which he suggested that both the United States and Russia abandon their land-based ICBMs, and eventually turn their nuclear arsenals over to the United Nations—as "pursuant to the definition of an economist: a man who lightly passes over the minor inconsistency the better to press on to the grand fallacy."

By Nitze's own account he was first persuaded of SALT's "fatal flaw" as a result of studies done by an engineering designer at the Boeing Corporation's think tank in Seattle. As early as 1968, the author of those studies, Thomas (T. K.) Jones, had begun to be concerned with the coming problem of Minuteman vulnerability. The calculations Jones made then convinced him that improvements in Soviet missile accuracy and the advent of a Russian MIRV would put America's land-based missiles at risk much earlier than previously estimated.[17]

In 1970, under a contract to Boeing from the government's nuclear laboratory at Oak Ridge, Jones conducted a related study of the Soviet Union's civil defense program. His study reached another controversial conclusion: that the Russian shelter system would prove far more effective in reducing civilian casualties from a nuclear war than previous Western analysts had imagined.[18]

Jones' calculations were of far more than mere academic interest. If, as his figures indicated, Russian fatalities would be only a fraction of the quarter of the Soviet Union's population that McNamara had decreed as the minimum necessary to deter the Kremlin, then the validity of assured destruction strategy was subtly being called into question on its own terms. Similarly, if Jones' figures on the nearly imminent vulnerability of Minuteman were correct, that development—coupled with the Russians' previously underestimated ability to withstand nuclear attack—made the long-haunting threat of a Soviet surprise attack appear suddenly tangible.

"It was becoming quite clear that the strategies on the books were not useful in the world that was shaping up," Jones observed of his findings. "From 1950 to the 1960s the strategy of assured retaliation had made sense, since a Soviet attack would have exhausted their arsenal." But the Russians' missile buildup that had continued into the 1970s—and America's failure to respond in kind—had since made that strategy dangerously obsolete, he felt. His studies at Boeing had converted him, Jones said, from a supporter to an opponent of the nation's nuclear strategy and its arms control policy.

Nitze attested that the studies conducted by Jones—whom he termed "a brilliant analyst"—had had a similar effect upon him. In 1971, at Nitze's instigation, Jones joined the assembly of technical experts supporting the American negotiating team at SALT. Together, the two men said they tirelessly—but futilely—tried to incorporate into the final deliberations of SALT some formula acceptable to the Soviets that would redress the inequality in missile throw-weight, and thereby remove or at least diminish the coming threat to Minuteman. The frustration of their efforts increased

the resolve of Nitze and Jones to raise the issue at a later stage of SALT—
or, if need be, in another forum altogether. But by this time they had in any
case privately arrived at their own conclusions about where the Russians
were headed. The continuing Soviet military buildup, Jones said, "far out-
stripped any reasonable interpretation of MAD."

22

A Different Mental Approach

There was a kind of sublime irony to the curious, almost symbiotic relationship between nuclear weapons, Richard Garwin reflected. Garwin personally regretted that at the time of the ABM debate he and other experts opposed to Sentinel and Safeguard had not spent more time opposing instead the development of MIRV—which proved to be by far the greater threat to the stability of deterrence. But it was not until the summer of 1968 and the first successful test of MIRV by the United States, Garwin said, that he and others finally recognized how destabilizing MIRV would be.

Too late did they realize that, in the pantheon of nuclear weapons, MIRV was not only hydra-headed but Janus-faced. The solution it promised to the problem of the ABM created a new and more dangerous threat to the land-based missiles of both sides. Belated as well was the recognition that the greater throw-weight of Soviet missiles—and hence the fact that they would eventually be able to carry more warheads than American missiles—made the technological innovation of MIRV a greater threat to the United States than to Russia once the Soviets, too, had the new weapon.[1]

It was the destabilizing effect of MIRV on the arms race and the implicit threat it posed to SALT that the Jason scientists decided to emphasize in a 1969 report to Henry Kissinger. Their unanimous recommendation had been against the continued development and the eventual deployment of MIRV.[2]

The two MIT physicists who chaired the study group that produced the report, George Rathjens and Jack Ruina, had each hoped at the time that by putting an end to MIRV the ABM, too, could still be averted. Both believed that only by stopping accurate multiple-warhead missiles would a new and particularly hazardous round of the arms race be avoided. Like the opposition to ABM, the importance of halting MIRV had suddenly become an article of faith among the Jason scientists. For that reason, Rathjens thought Kissinger's summary rejection of the report's straightforward recommendation against MIRV especially foreboding: "Henry was angry because he wanted an options paper. Instead he got only one option. Not 'A,' 'B,' and 'C,' but only Option A—don't proceed with MIRV—and we told him nothing else was worth talking about."

Yet the confounding of MAD and the undoing of SALT were the result of more than just a lack of foresight, the arms controllers felt. Rathjens thought "disingenuous" the Nixon administration's refusal even to consider serious discussion of a MIRV ban in the SALT talks. Those negotiations seemed to him in retrospect not only the best but perhaps the last time that MIRV could be stopped, since the flight testing of the weapon by either side might have been monitored by satellites. Once those tests were completed, however, not even the electronic eavesdropping relied upon in SALT could give assurances that MIRV had not been deployed.

Despite the technological progress that had made verification of arms control agreements possible, the motive forces behind the arms race remained undiminished. To Rathjens, the decision by Nixon and Kissinger to proceed with MIRV reflected the persistence despite SALT of a technological imperative in that race—as did the administration's rejection of an ABM ban a year later. SALT had plainly not extinguished or even lessened the allure of a unilateral advantage in weaponry. As with the advent of both the atomic and the hydrogen bomb, some in Washington believed it would be many years before the Russians could duplicate America's technological achievement in developing MIRV.[3]

The administration's decisions on ABM and MIRV also ignored the Russians' own pledge—made in the immediate aftermath of the 1962 missile crisis—that they would never again allow an American strategic advantage to go unchallenged.[4] In 1970, while Rathjens was attending a Pugwash conference of Russian and American scientists in Wisconsin, Georgei Arbatov, a prominent Soviet expert on the West, had made a point of reminding him of that pledge. Both men were pessimistic about the prospect of avoiding MIRV. The obvious solution, they each felt, would be an agreement whereby the United States consented not to deploy MIRV in exchange for a Soviet concession not to flight-test its version of the weapon. Rathjens argued that the Russians would find out about any clandestine American deployment of MIRV because of the openness of U.S. society, while Soviet compliance with the agreement could be verified by satellite surveillance. Rathjens and Arbatov had ultimately agreed that the arrangement seemed equitable. But the history of the arms race caused them to doubt that another round of competition between the United States and Russia could be avoided.

Garwin, another member of the Jasons' study group on MIRV, reluctantly shared Rathjens' gloomy outlook on the arms race. Beginning with its inception and throughout its development, Garwin conceded, MIRV had seemed too promising a weapon to be avoided. Like Rathjens, he felt that the administration's decision to proceed with MIRV in spite of SALT contradicted its avowed goal of limiting strategic arms.

While still Nixon's science adviser, Garwin remembered cautioning Kissinger that the latter "would have difficulty getting straight answers to his questions" about nuclear weapons. After Kissinger's rejection of the Jasons' advice, Garwin began to suspect, he said, that it was not straight answers the national security adviser was seeking. His suspicions had been confirmed, Garwin felt, when Kissinger protested to him "that we had used up the intellectual capital of the 1950s arms control theorists." Garwin countered: "You *have* the ideas. There aren't any more ideas that anybody has been able to think of. You know what you're supposed to do and you're not doing it."

Years later—when the Soviets as well had installed MIRV on their missiles—Garwin would similarly dismiss Kissinger's seemingly contrite admission that the inability to stop MIRV had been perhaps the single greatest failing of the Nixon administration. Kissinger said he wished that he "had thought through the implications of a MIRVed world more thoughtfully in 1969 and in 1970."[5] It was, Garwin claimed, an even more telling comment on the dilemma of the arms race that Kissinger and Nixon *had* thought through those implications—and decided to press on with MIRV in any case.

The scientists' concerns had begun to be shared by some of the American diplomats at Geneva once it was clear that MIRV would work. In the spring of 1969, Gerard Smith urged the Nixon administration to formally propose a ban on MIRV's development and deployment in SALT. The idea of a moratorium on MIRV testing had first been suggested by U.S. scientists during the Johnson administration. But it was left out of the starting American position in SALT partly as a consequence of the long delays that stalled the talks.[6]

Fatefully, by the time the negotiations began the United States had already successfully tested the new weapon. Despite—or perhaps because of—that fact, public and congressional pressure for a ban on MIRV had increased: pressure that was related as well to the popular outcry against the ABM. The Nixon administration, while professing interest in the ban, had consistently opposed introducing it into the negotiations—even to the extent of a handwritten letter to Smith from Nixon warning that discussion of a MIRV ban with the Soviets by any member of the U.S. SALT delegation would result "in reprimand followed by dismissal."[7]

The possibility of a moratorium on the further testing of MIRV and a ban on the weapon's deployment had been ruled out for good by the spring of

1971, when the administration announced that an agreement on MIRV would require on-site inspection—a precondition that scientists argued was unnecessary and that was known to be historically unpalatable to the Soviets, who at the time had yet to test their first MIRV. Smith later concluded of Nixon's decision that the president "must have known that such a condition had little or no chance of being accepted."[8]

Many, if not most, on the American SALT delegation subsequently professed doubt that a MIRV ban would have been acceptable to the Soviets in any case. But Smith stressed in his own account that—as in the attempt to prohibit the ABM—the final discouraging word had come not from Russia, but from the United States. "Those of us who favored a ban finally got the point," he wrote. "Our side did not want a MIRV ban."[9]

Paul Nitze quit the American SALT delegation in the summer of 1974. His reason for leaving, he said, was the inability of SALT to deal with the inequality in missile throw-weight between the United States and Russia, and hence its failure to remove the Soviet threat to Minuteman. Early in 1974 the Soviets as well had begun to deploy MIRVed missiles, persuading Nitze that the problem of Minuteman vulnerability—which he had hitherto claimed to be only on the horizon—was now in fact imminent.[10]

Two years before his resignation, Nitze had proposed a radical solution to the vulnerability problem to his Soviet counterpart at the talks, Alexander Shchukin. Nitze told Shchukin that "if we really wanted to solve this problem of stability it would be easy." All that was necessary would be to scrap the existing ICBMs on both sides and replace them with much smaller missiles, which would not have sufficient throw-weight to carry multiple warheads, he said. Stability would be returned to the strategic equation, Nitze explained, because whichever side initiated an attack would wind up with fewer missiles than the defender. Moreover, verification of the agreement posed no real problem, because the number of small missiles on both sides would be so large that any cheating on a scale to be militarily significant would almost certainly be discovered.

Shchukin had agreed with him, Nitze said, "that the arrangement would be completely stable." But one problem, both men thought, was that the Soviet military would never agree to it. The other major obstacle to the plan that Nitze anticipated was inherent in the SALT process itself, as a result of the stress there upon limiting the number of weapons. Since it was cheaper to build a few large missiles than many smaller ones, he noted, "all the economics of the thing go for big MIRVed missiles." Paradoxically, the SALT process itself seemed to drive the arms race: "SALT put a premium on—made it necessary—to go to big MIRVed missiles," Nitze said.

At congressional hearings shortly after his widely publicized resignation, Nitze had branded the SALT talks the central fallacy in what he now termed the "myth of *détente.*" In a subsequent series of articles in *Foreign Affairs* and *Foreign Policy,* he recounted the reasons for his final conversion to the opposition of SALT. Central to Nitze's thesis was the claim made consistently throughout his career that strategic superiority counted for a great deal indeed, in peace as much as in war. Even if nuclear weapons were not used, Nitze argued, the nation possessing a superior number of them had a potentially decisive edge in diplomacy. In the event of war, meaningful superiority could still determine the victor—even in the nuclear age.[11]

Nitze's articles were intended in part to give a greater degree of verisimilitude to a controversial 1969 Pentagon study of a hypothetical Soviet attack on the United States. His avowed concern was that Russian leaders might be tempted to strike selectively at the nation's military targets, using only a fraction of their MIRVed arsenal, deliberately sparing American cities in the expectation that the president would ultimately rather accept limited civilian losses and an unfavorable peace settlement than risk utter destruction. It was not only possible but "highly plausible," he wrote, that Russian leaders would choose to strike first if faced with the kind of "crisis instability" that had once before led to war, in 1914.[12]

As Nitze himself admitted, his scarifying scenario of a thermonuclear Pearl Harbor was only an updating and a refinement of the counterforce nuclear war that he had predicted as early as 1956 might result if the United States lost its strategic edge to Russia. Like his 1950 warning of a coming "year of maximum danger" and his 1957 prediction concerning an impending missile gap, Nitze's 1976 endorsement of the notion of an impending "window of vulnerability" identified a new and previously unappreciated threat from Russia.

Nitze also acknowledged that the evidence for his argument concerning the new Russian threat came from the work of T. K. Jones. Jones quit the American SALT team some three months after Nitze, similarly frustrated by the intractability of the Russians, and unsettled by what he complained was the "fast pace" of the negotiations. Since returning to Boeing, Jones claimed to have found further evidence of an unremitting Soviet strategic buildup. A study he completed for the company in 1975 on improvements in Russian missile accuracy featured a dramatically more pessimistic conclusion than had the report done just four years before. Jones argued in the second study that if the current trend of Russian technical progress continued, the Soviets by the end of the decade might be able to destroy all important military targets in the United States and yet kill no more than six to twelve million Americans in the process—making the more than two hundred million survivors hostage, in effect, to the Kremlin's will.[13]

Almost as disturbing was the evidence of another new study by Jones on the Russian shelter program. It concluded that the Soviets were taking civil defense even more seriously than stated in his previous report, which itself had been far more pessimistic than official government estimates of the time. (A 1969 CIA study of Russian civil defense concluded, by comparison, that their shelter system was essentially an underground Potemkin village, intended more to impress American defense planners in peacetime than to protect Soviet civilians in the event of nuclear war.)[14]

Disputing the official view, Jones professed to find a rapid intensification of the Russians' civil defense program in recent years—one modeled, ironically, on plans that the United States had drawn up in the 1950s and since discarded. According to Jones, this new program aimed at protecting not only the bulk of the Soviet Union's urban population but also Russia's industrial base against the effects of nuclear war. The Russians' efforts to "damage-proof" their cities and industry had been remarkably successful, he claimed. So well had the Russians applied the lessons learned in their own experiments and from the published results of American nuclear tests, Jones argued, that by 1972 they were able to protect a machine factory—using only sandbags—to the point where it would sustain merely minor damage from a 1.5-megaton nuclear airburst less than half a mile away. While the United States had subsequently abandoned hope of even surviving a nuclear war, the Russians—Jones concluded—were preparing to win one.

The direful scenarios drawn by Nitze and Jones had made a public issue by 1976 of their previously private objections to the nation's nuclear strategy and its policy on arms control. Their argument that the Soviet Union had abandoned the implied consensus behind arms control by striving for the capability to carry out a disarming first strike raised the disturbing prospect that there was yet another unacknowledged strategic disparity between America and Russia—a "doctrine gap," in which the Soviets were moving inexorably toward a strategy of nuclear war-winning while the United States alone remained grimly attached to its strategy of mutually assured nuclear destruction. Such destruction, Nitze and Jones argued, seemed to be less and less assured on the Soviet side—and was now almost certainly not a mutual concern of both countries.[15]

The charge made by Nitze and Jones that the Russians were indeed seeking strategic superiority implied that the Soviets were not only playing by different rules than the United States in the SALT negotiations, but that they were engaged in a different game altogether. Their critique suggested that the real facts of SALT were now actually the reverse of what arms controllers in this country had always assumed. It was not the United States that was dictating arms control to the Soviet Union, Nitze and Jones claimed, but the Russians who were determining by their actions what America's future nuclear strategy would have to be. If the Russians were unwilling to give up the idea of fighting—and winning—a nuclear war the United States would have no choice but to follow suit. "After two to three years of testing we didn't find any Achilles heel in Soviet strategy," Jones said of his latest studies for Boeing. The change, he and Nitze concluded, would have to come from the American side.

The revision of nuclear war planning that McNamara had twice postponed and finally abandoned before leaving office was finally undertaken at the start of the Nixon administration. Within a matter of days of assuming office, the president and his national security adviser had followed the example of the previous two administrations by ordering a wholesale review of the nation's nuclear strategy and military policies. Nixon, Kissinger, and the new secretary of defense, Melvin Laird, were already on record as critical of the assured-destruction ideas inherited from McNamara. At the outset of his State of the Union address to Congress in 1970, Nixon had prepared the ground for the shift away from MAD by posing what was plainly intended to be a rhetorical question: "Should a president, in the event of a nuclear attack, be left with the single option of ordering the mass destruction of enemy civilians, in the face of the certainty that it would be followed by the mass slaughter of Americans?"

The review Nixon and Kissinger asked for was completed within six months of their request. But the actual changes in American strategy that it recommended did not come about until 1973, shortly after Nixon's reelection. They were preceded by a series of firings and reorganizations in the government in preparation for the second term. The promise made by one administration official "to get" those who had earlier opposed Nixon's policies was fulfilled with Richard Garwin's dismissal, the dissolution of the President's Science Advisory Committee to which Garwin belonged, and a purge of ACDA that replaced both Smith and Keeny.

Just as significant was the corresponding rise to prominence—or, in some cases, the reemergence in the government—of those strategists who had been among the first advocates of counterforce. Reflecting the return of Rand's influence during Nixon's second term was the role played by James Schlesinger, who directed the think tank's strategic studies program until 1969, and who later had a succession of posts in the scandal-ridden administration—including AEC chairman and head of the CIA. Appointed secretary of defense in 1973, Schlesinger returned to high positions at the Pentagon those whom one observer would describe as "the cohort of Rand alumni."[16]

Brought back to the Pentagon along with Rand's analysts was a vogue in the theories of counterforce and nuclear war-fighting, reintroduced by Schlesinger. A book that he wrote in 1958 while at the National War College had expressed concern with the "suicidal implications" of American nuclear strategy. Trained as an economist, Schlesinger was a latecomer to the coterie of counterforce theorists when he arrived at Rand in 1961, but later became a thorough convert to the thinking there. By 1967, for example, he included among the goals of arms control "to keep war at a low level and directed toward military rather than urban targets." The following year, Schlesinger wrote a treatise at Rand on controlled nuclear war reminiscent of the theories regarding "signaling" and intrawar bargaining that Thomas Schelling had popularized there many years before.[17]

Though he came to hold a number of jobs in the government, Schlesinger measured the beginning of his influence upon Nixon's thinking from his assumption of the directorship of the CIA in the spring of 1973. A slide presentation that he did then for Nixon and Kissinger had particularly impressed the president, Schlesinger thought, with the implications that a Russian MIRV and the much greater throw-weight of Soviet missiles would have for the strategic balance—despite SALT.

While previous briefings for Nixon had generally featured only pictures of new Soviet missiles, Schlesinger's presentation had been the first to portray dramatically the growing disparity in the nuclear strength of the two nations by using blue and red bar graphs representing the megatonnage each side's missiles could deliver. Another thing that "stunned" his audience on that occasion, Schlesinger remembered, "was the burst in Soviet research and development that took place immediately after the signing of the SALT agreement."

With the Nixon presidency embroiled in the Watergate scandal the following year, Schlesinger played a direct role in bringing about what he thought were necessary and overdue changes in American war planning. At a press conference in January 1974, he announced a "new nuclear strategy" for the United States—one that represented, Schlesinger claimed, "probably the greatest change in U.S. nuclear missile strategy in a decade." Arguing that the destruction of enemy cities "should not be the only option and possibly not the primary option" of the United States in the event of war, Schlesinger described as the essence of his new strategy a series of "limited nuclear options" that ranged from the destruction of individual missile silos, industries, or cities in the Soviet Union to the wholesale counterforce war-between-the-bases that William Borden had forecast almost thirty years before.[18]

In announcing the strategic doctrine that would henceforth bear his name, Schlesinger depicted the changes there as far-reaching. The "Schlesinger doctrine," however, was neither entirely new nor even entirely original with Schlesinger. It was, instead, the culmination of a two-year study done by a Pentagon panel of counterforce enthusiasts whose interest in the notion of a controlled nuclear war had continued even after McNamara had publicly abandoned any hope of being able to fight such a war. This group, as much as, if not more than, Schlesinger, was responsible for the return to counterforce thinking in the Nixon administration.[19]

．　．　．

As director of the Pentagon's research and engineering office, John Foster, the head of the panel conducting the review, occupied the same post previously held by Herbert York and Harold Brown. The executive secretary of the Foster panel, Air Force General Jasper Welch, had initially advised Foster against the review when apprised of it in December 1971. Welch feared that "there would be the greatest difficulty in getting cooperation" for such an ambitious reexamination of the rationale behind the targeting of nuclear weapons. It was Nixon's national security adviser who had finally cleared the way for the study, Welch said: "The big thing that Kissinger pushed was to make the thing practical. Because he knew that if you acted like you had things that weren't practical, then no leader would pay any attention to it."

One major departure from past practice urged by the Foster panel was adding what Welch termed "a great deal more flexibility" to the use of nuclear weapons in the war plan. He admitted that another big change was to remove deterrence from the category of an abstract theory and to assign it a human—indeed, a Russian—face: "We did have a notion that we ought to deter all three power centers in the Soviet Union: the Party, the Army—and I mean the Army specifically—and the technocrats, the guys who build factories." The practical difficulty with targeting Russia's leadership, Welch admitted, was in knowing "who's in charge at any one time." The Foster panel's solution, he said, "was to make sure that all three of those groups—if they were going to look at the war plan—would individually and personally and organizationally and culturally know that their part of the world was not going to survive."

The major purpose of the panel's review of U.S. nuclear strategy, according to Welch, was "to take into account the change in the international political situation since McNamara created the SIOP." Not only the nature of war but even the nature of the enemy had changed in the interim—a fact dramatically underscored by Nixon's recent visit to China. Yet more than a decade had passed—and the number of nuclear weapons in the American arsenal had grown almost exponentially—without any substantial changes to the three options that McNamara added to the war plan.

By way of contrast, the revised SIOP proposed by the Foster panel added an almost infinite range—"an entire spectrum," Welch said—of possible ways to respond to acts of Soviet aggression: "It explicitly targeted the Red Army and conventional forces more generally. It clearly recognized the difference between the Soviet Union and eastern Europe." The revised war plan also "dealt more explicitly with the issue of noncombatants"—in the process achieving what McNamara had originally set out to do with the no-cities doctrine: "It took residential areas off the target list explicitly—and provided even for residential area avoidance under certain circumstances, where one would reduce the effectiveness of the strike in order to avoid residential areas."

The report by the Foster panel eventually became the Schlesinger doctrine —in what was officially known as National Security Decision Memorandum Number 242, or NSDM-242. It incorporated into U.S. war planning what had earlier been some of the favorite—and most controversial—ideas at Rand. While nuclear demonstrations or "warning shots" were "explicitly, severely, and categorically thought to be sheer nonsense by everybody involved" in the study, Welch said, the idea of using nuclear weapons to signal intentions in the *course* of a war was more seriously considered: "There was a lot of discussion about signaling. But most of the academic chitter-chatter about it did not seem to be supported by those who knew something about it." (One of the Foster panel's discoveries, in fact, was that there existed no word or phrase in Soviet military jargon which corresponded to "collateral damage." "It was an interesting question," Welch mused. "How do you send a telegram when you don't speak the same language?" The answer turned out to be surprisingly obvious: "What you target signaled things pretty straightforwardly.")

The sweeping nature of the changes they proposed gave pause even to the authors of NSDM-242. Some six months of testing their hypotheses in war games and case studies—as well as in personal meetings with Schlesinger and Kissinger—followed completion of the panel's work. "After we got it all straight and everybody agreed to it, we sat around and made ourselves wonder whether we still liked what we were doing," Welch said. "So we set it aside for a few weeks and then came back and asked, 'Does anybody have any second thoughts?' " No one did. "Nothing changed after those meetings," Welch remembered. "I think everybody was pretty happy."

The revolution in military planning to which Schlesinger alluded at his 1974 press conference had thus, in substance, already taken place prior to his announcement. It perhaps owed more to technological innovation than to any profound revision of strategic thinking. In retrospect, the Schlesinger doctrine seemed an almost inevitable result of the phenomenal increase in the number of nuclear weapons that had occurred since McNamara's time.

Because of MIRV, the number of nuclear warheads in the nation's strategic arsenal had increased fivefold from when McNamara was defense secretary. The Soviet ABM system that the submarine-launched Poseidon missile was designed to overwhelm had been forestalled by SALT. But the MIRVed Poseidon had been added to the U.S. nuclear arsenal nevertheless. At first unable to find enough Soviet targets to keep up with the burgeoning rate of increase in the number of warheads, military planners adapted to the unanticipated abundance of bombs by adding whole new categories of targets to the revised SIOP. By 1974 the number of targets identified in the Soviet Union and marked for possible destruction in the event of war had risen to twenty-five thousand—several times the number of warheads in the arsenal before MIRV. The advent of accurate multiple-warhead missiles hence made the changes in strategic doctrine announced by Schlesinger not only possible but even necessary.[20]

What Schlesinger himself contributed to the new strategy was a sense of confident assurance and a novel rationale. Prior to 1974, members of the Pentagon's Joint Strategic Target Planning Staff, according to its director during the Nixon years, had set targeting policy "based on public statements by administration officials."[21] This attempt by military planners to divine the intent of civilian leaders through their public utterances had ended abruptly with Schlesinger, who replaced the vague and shifting criteria behind assured destruction with a new and presumedly less subjective measure—which included the ability to destroy at least 70 percent of the industries that the Soviet Union would need to recover from a nuclear war.

The primitive scratchpad war games of Rand's earliest counterforce theorists were replaced in Schlesinger's Pentagon by complex, computer-generated models of the Russian economy, studied with the intent of discovering its weakest and most vulnerable spots. The headquarters that would command and control Soviet forces in a nuclear war, the members of the Politburo itself, and the political leadership of Russia down to the oblast level were each in turn added to the lengthening target list.[22]

Perhaps the most significant change signaled by the new strategy was the "different mental attitude" that Schlesinger himself said NSDM-242 represented.[23] From the beginning of his tenure as defense secretary he had been intent, Schlesinger admitted, upon avoiding what he considered "McNamara's mistakes." He did not, for example, share his predecessor's "visceral repugnance" toward nuclear weapons. Indeed, Schlesinger thought it McNamara's particular "cast of mind"—as well as the Air Force's ill-advised campaign for counterforce—that had caused what he felt was McNamara's "premature" decision to back away from the no-cities idea and to embrace assured destruction.

"MAD just struck me as the wrong declaratory policy," Schlesinger said. Besides representing "a very sharp break in policy," he believed, it "lacked convincingness" and was "logically inconsistent," and "there were moral defects." Schlesinger's personal conviction that "what you declare in advance is designed to affect the psychology of the other side"—and, particularly, his private feeling that the United States shouldn't tell the Russians what it was *not* going to do—lay behind the emphasis he placed upon putting "selectivity" back into the war plan: "I was more interested in selectivity than in counterforce *per se.* Going after selected silos might be a way of delivering a message."

The changes he announced in the nation's declaratory policy on the use of nuclear weapons were not—in Schlesinger's mind at least—fundamental changes in actual policy. Instead, their purpose was to deliberately make uncertain what the American response to a specific Soviet provocation might be. Schlesinger privately discounted the danger raised by Nitze and others that the Soviets might deliberately begin a nuclear war in a crisis, if they perceived the United States as vulnerable. In secret testimony to Congress shortly after his public announcement of the new strategy, he summarily dismissed a disarming first strike as "impossible." Technical considerations alone meant that "neither side can acquire a high confidence first strike capability," he said. "I want the President of the United States to know that for all the future years, and I want the Soviet leadership to know that for all the future years," Schlesinger reiterated.[24]

Schlesinger discreetly admitted that the key to the nuclear doctrine which bore his name was a matter of changing psychological perceptions. He felt that one of McNamara's mistakes had been to assure the Russians that the United States would use its nuclear weapons only in retaliation. "Occasionally the Russians should read in the press that a counterforce attack may not fall on silos that are empty," he said. "Why give the Soviets that assurance?" (His view was apparently shared by members of the Foster panel. "You certainly didn't want to leave a war plan lying around where the Soviets would *know* that they weren't targeted," Welch explained.)

It was with the intent of removing such assurances from the calculations of Soviet planners, as well as to create a perception of renewed American strength, that Schlesinger decided to approve development of a new land-based missile shortly after he became defense secretary. This latest ICBM would be a marked departure from its predecessors because of its greatly increased throw-weight, its consequent ability to carry more warheads, and its improved accuracy—which would theoretically allow each American missile to destroy several Soviet missiles in their silos. The different approach behind the new missile was reflected even in its name—"missile experimental," or MX.

Though the MX had been proposed by a Pentagon study as early as 1967, it was not until 1971 that the Air Force, seeking to answer in kind the Soviet military buildup, had begun to lobby actively for the weapon. Counterforce advocates who rose to prominence in the Pentagon in Nixon's second term added their strong voices in its favor. As in the rationale behind his new strategic doctrine, Schlesinger justified the missile for reasons that were more concerned with psychology and diplomacy than strategy—as a way of altering Soviet perceptions of the United States, and of persuading the Russians to accept limits on missile throw-weight in SALT. Schlesinger's interest in the MX was as "a bargaining chip for arms control," he later averred. "I hoped we wouldn't have to deploy it."[25]

Critics of Schlesinger claimed that the change in degree he introduced to American war planning was so profound as to amount to a change in kind. Schlesinger's actions, they charged, created ambiguity and confusion about U.S. intentions not only among the Soviets but in the minds of Americans as well. Such critics accused Schlesinger of finally removing nuclear weapons from the category of symbolic totems, and of making nuclear war not only more plausible but to that extent more likely.

Robert McNamara considered Schlesinger's addition of a whole new range of so-called "limited nuclear options" a dramatic departure from the flexibility that McNamara himself had tried to introduce to war planning a generation before. The announcement of the Schlesinger doctrine, McNamara claimed, was the first indication he had had since his retirement as defense secretary that there still existed a school of thought in the Pentagon which considered fighting and winning a nuclear war something worth planning for.

Richard Garwin thought that Schlesinger's war-fighting doctrine and the new SIOP showed the final ascendancy in the Nixon administration of the "counterforce cabal" that had been active in the Pentagon since McNamara's days. It was no longer as a presidential science adviser but as an adversarial witness that Garwin testified in 1972 against two new counterforce weapons, the B-1 strategic bomber and the Trident II submarine-launched missile, whose development the Nixon administration had tentatively approved.[26]

Garwin objected that the B-1 and the Trident II, like the MX, "just didn't make sense" as bargaining chips in arms control. He felt, further, that the government's case for the new weapons was based on principles not only strategically unsound, but politically unwise: "In 1972 Kissinger came up with Trident and the B-1 to placate the hawks for SALT I. I think he was doing things that he felt were just a waste of money. It wouldn't hurt strategic stability to build more subs and bombers, and the spending of the money would be enough to take care of the arguments of the people who were unhappy with SALT."

Garwin said he protested at the time that Kissinger's approach "wasn't going to help—that critics will still argue we have inadequate throw-weight and will continue to argue that." But he had been ignored by the administration. While his opposition to the new weapons was unavailing, Garwin claimed to have found some rueful satisfaction in the fact that his prediction was borne out when the military demanded still more and newer weapons like the MX—demands that increased in the Nixon administration even after the Trident and the B-1 were approved.

· · ·

In the wake of the budgetary battles over the MX, the B-1, and the Trident II, there were signs that the first administration to take credit for moving American nuclear strategy away from MAD was beginning to regret the change. Initially, there seemed little doubt that Kissinger agreed at least in principle with the changes introduced by the Schlesinger doctrine. As early as his landmark 1957 book on nuclear weapons and foreign policy, Kissinger had thus identified as the most basic problem of strategy in the nuclear age that of "how to establish a relationship between a policy of deterrence and a strategy for fighting a war in case deterrence fails."[27] A secret White House memorandum that Kissinger had had a part in drafting during 1972 also seemed to accept a central premise of the new strategy when it defined "strategic sufficiency" as the forces necessary "to ensure that the United States would emerge from a nuclear war in discernibly better shape than the Soviet Union."[28]

But continued attacks upon the administration's SALT policy and the military's unrelenting budget requests seemed to awaken in Kissinger private doubts about the wisdom of the war-fighting approach to nuclear strategy. Those doubts surfaced during the 1974 Arab oil embargo, when Kissinger discovered that the most limited nuclear option envisioned by the Pentagon as a response to a Soviet invasion of Iran would involve the use of at least two hundred nuclear weapons. Protesting that two hundred bombs was too great a number to be considered merely a signal to the Soviets, Kissinger nonetheless felt that the next suggestion forwarded by the joint chiefs—using only two bombs—would convey an opposite but equally mistaken message about American resolve.[29]

Later that same year, Kissinger's reservations concerning the political and psychological utility of nuclear weapons became public, in a plaintive outburst directed at critics who claimed that SALT would guarantee the Russians a strategic edge. "What in the name of God is strategic superiority?" Kissinger had snapped. "What is the significance of it, politically, militarily, operationally, at these levels of numbers? What do you do with it?"[30]

By the end of the Nixon presidency, Kissinger was still looking for a definite answer to his question. Upon assuming the role of national security adviser in 1969 and being briefed for the first time on the SIOP, Kissinger had telephoned McNamara to protest that the war plan the latter had passed along to the Nixon administration seemed to be totally inappropriate to the purposes for which it was designed—namely, to deter a Soviet nuclear attack upon the United States. Such an attack would almost surely follow the war plan's projected use of nuclear weapons to stop a Russian conventional assault on Europe, Kissinger pointed out.

How could he have been secretary of defense for seven years, Kissinger asked McNamara, and left behind such a flawed plan?

McNamara, according to one account, readily conceded to Kissinger that the war plan was "inappropriate." But there were, he said, two "extenuating circumstances" which mitigated the sins of omission and commission in his nuclear strategy. First was the fact that it was possible, within the SIOP's five major options, to carry out selectively only a portion of the plan—"so that it wasn't as bad as it seemed," McNamara reassured. But second, and more important, McNamara said, was "the fact that it seemed extremely unlikely one would utilize the plan in the way in which the people who prepared it thought it might be utilized—that is, as a response to a conventional invasion."

"If you never used the SIOP—or any one of the SIOPs—to initiate the use of nuclear weapons, then they weren't as inappropriate as they might have seemed," McNamara told Kissinger. "But if you were responding to a conventional force or movement it was totally inappropriate," he admitted, "because it would just bring suicide upon yourself." McNamara evidently did not go so far as to tell Kissinger, however, what he had advised Kennedy and Johnson in their time—that under no circumstances should the United States be the first to use nuclear weapons.

Several years after this conversation, upon relinquishing the post of national security adviser, Kissinger privately conceded to McNamara that he, too, had finally been unable to make U.S. nuclear strategy any more "appropriate," in spite of all his efforts and despite NSDM-242.

The seven years that McNamara spent at that effort, Kissinger told him, had been followed by eight more where he had labored—in vain—after the same goal.

Gerald Ford's accession to the presidency in the summer of 1974 apparently created another skeptic regarding the changes in the Schlesinger doctrine. The story—perhaps apocryphal—went around Washington that when Ford was first briefed by Schlesinger on the SIOP's new limited nuclear options he had listened in stunned silence until the end, and then asked: "Okay, so what are my options?" Certainly the prolonged national agony over Vietnam that Ford inherited from Nixon and Kissinger did not encourage much optimism that the course of a modern war could be predicted—much less controlled. It was, in part, their differences over Vietnam that prompted Ford to dismiss Schlesinger in 1975. Schlesinger felt that he personally had been made to suffer the traditional fate of the bearer of bad tidings when he told Ford about Vietnam, "Mr. President, this is all over. *It is all over.*" Ford, Schlesinger explained, "is not the kind of fellow who doesn't believe that a turnaround can't bring you a victory in the fourth quarter."

But an even more fundamental cause of his dismissal than Vietnam, Schlesinger admitted, was his conflict with Ford over the military budget. He felt "ludicrous," Schlesinger told the president, about promoting *détente* and proposed cuts in the military budget after arguing for two years that the United States was falling behind the Soviet Union.

Even Schlesinger seemed to have some concern with the direction his new approach to strategy was taking by the time he left the Pentagon. The limitation that he hoped to put upon MIRVed throw-weight in SALT had never been introduced into the negotiations—largely, he said, because Nixon and Kissinger "desperately wanted an agreement" to offset the domestic effects of Watergate, and hence were "not prepared for anything long-term that would prevent counterforce capabilities developing on both sides." The result was that military pressure for ever more "selectivity" in targeting— and consequently for more weapons—had inexorably continued to grow.

Behind Schlesinger's discontent was his realization that, like McNamara's introduction of war-fighting to strategic doctrine, the return to counterforce in the Nixon administration unintentionally provided a justification for open-ended increases in defense spending. "Regretfully," Schlesinger reflected, "arms control never really got control of the process."

Ultimately, Schlesinger would protest that his own public emphasis upon "strategic asymmetries" in the size of Soviet and American missiles as well as his "intellectual calculations" concerning the vulnerability of Minuteman had been subverted by the critics of SALT. "I became increasingly worried when people began to talk about these *hypothetical* calculations as if there was a high probability that the Soviets were actually going to *do* it," he said. "It's one thing to use a hypothesis to test your forces. It is another to use it as a prediction. Things can get out of hand."

Despite their emerging doubts, the changes that Nixon, Kissinger, and Schlesinger brought to American nuclear strategy had by 1976 become a part of the SIOP—just as the changes introduced by McNamara to the war plan remained there after his subsequent change of mind. For Schlesinger's critics, the sole consolation was to find a kind of ironic vindication in the way his new strategic doctrine had backfired.[31]

Garwin, for example, thought the fact that the Schlesinger doctrine had escaped the control of its inventor a predictable and even inevitable consequence of the return to counterforce. As a civilian consultant on the Pentagon's nuclear-targeting staff, Garwin had gone to Schlesinger's office late in 1973 to confront him with what seemed a contradiction in the new targeting directive then under study. Instead of Schlesinger, Garwin had met with one of the uniformed authors of that study—a member of the group he had come to think of as the "counterforce cabal." When the Pentagon aide justified the shift in strategy in terms of what he called "the real need for a second-strike counterforce capability to destroy Soviet strategic forces," Garwin had dismissed that line of reasoning as "not serious." Thus a strike that was merely retaliatory, he pointed out, would necessarily find the Russians' bombers flown and their missile silos empty. "You're just trying to make it sound more acceptable by saying you want a second-strike counterforce capability," Garwin objected. "What you really want—but are not willing to say—is a first-strike counterforce capability."

It was this desire to regain the ability to strike first that Garwin felt was really behind the group's insistent and effective lobbying for the MX and the new submarine-launched missile, the Trident II, which would have sufficient accuracy to make it capable as well of destroying Soviet missiles in their silos. With a war-fighting strategy on the books and such counterforce weapons in place, the threat to Russia became, in effect, automatic, Garwin pointed out. There would be neither time nor occasion for Congress or the American public to sanction that threat—nor room, perhaps, for any human volition at all.

This hidden rationale, Garwin felt, also explained why the new generation of counterforce enthusiasts opposed his recommendation to modernize existing weapons rather than build new ones, and why they resisted his suggestion for eliminating Minuteman vulnerability by a policy of launching U.S. missiles upon warning of an attack: "They're selling the American spirit. They think the American spirit is sick, and its sickness is evidenced by an unwillingness to spend money on defense. They did not want to redress Soviet superiority because they wanted to claim it in order to arouse the nation . . . They *liked* to have Minuteman vulnerability and Soviet superiority. They would be lost without it."

Exactly how far counterforce advocates had gone during the Nixon and Ford administrations toward achieving their goal was evident to Garwin when he spoke with a colleague—a nuclear targeter in the Pentagon—in 1975, some months after Schlesinger had left the Defense Department. On this occasion Garwin engaged the young officer in a discussion of his own view of nuclear weapons—to wit, Garwin said, "that they were only for deterrence, and that all this idea of flexible response and a protracted closely managed war was nonsense." The targeter "looked at me as if I was some kind of fossil," Garwin remembered. "All the talk in the Pentagon was of these other aspects. People had long since gone away from the use of nuclear weapons as a deterrent."

23

The New Orthodoxy

Since Robert McNamara first cited a "greater-than-expected threat" from Russia as a justification in 1965 for proceeding with MIRV, the expression had become common in the rarefied and secret debate that raged within the government over the nature and dimension of the danger represented by the Soviet Union. McNamara at the time had privately expressed surprise at the rapidity and size of the Soviet missile buildup—but some doubt that it would ever match that undertaken by the United States during the Kennedy administration. Skeptics about "the threat," as it became known, including Spurgeon Keeny, had as early as the following year attacked the assumptions behind it as unnecessarily alarmist and rooted in "extremely crude analysis." By the late 1960s the issue was already one of the most contentious of the Cold War, since at stake was the true perception not only of the Soviets' military capabilities, but—by inference—of their intentions.[1]

The subsequent case for the greater-than-expected threat had been founded upon progressive improvements duly noted by American intelligence in a particularly large Soviet rocket, the SS-9, which the Russians first began to deploy in 1967. The following year—within a week of the successful inaugural test of an American MIRV—the Russians flight-tested a modification of the new missile with multiple warheads. These latter, however, were not independently targetable. Shortly after the Russian test, the Pentagon challenged the CIA's assessment that the SS-9 was not an effective counterforce weapon, claiming that it was in essence—if not in point of technical fact—a MIRV, and as such a threat to Minuteman. According to a controversial 1969 report by the Defense Intelligence Agency and to calculations by Albert Wohlstetter, the Soviets by the mid-1970s might be able to destroy as much as 95 percent of America's land-based ICBMs with "high confidence."[2]

Ironically, several years earlier the CIA's own analysts had concurred with Wohlstetter's initial prediction that U.S. land-based missiles would be vulnerable to a Soviet attack by the end of the 1960s. But by the close of that decade the experts at CIA had revised their estimate, concluding that Minuteman would not be at risk for perhaps another ten years. The public controversy over the ABM that was then at its peak—and the concern of Nitze and others about missile throw-weights and SALT then emerging—gave a sudden and ominous significance to the preferred azimuth of the SS-9, the "footprint" of its warheads, and the other technological esoterica that Henry Kissinger once characterized as the "talmudic distinctions" of arms control.[3]

The 1969 Pentagon report was cited in support not only of the dread scenarios of Soviet surprise attack later drawn by Nitze and Jones, but as the basis for Defense Secretary Melvin Laird's seemingly confident assertion during the ABM hearings that the Russians "were going for a first strike capability." Laird claimed: "There's no doubt about that."[4]

The opponents of ABM and the defenders of SALT hotly disputed Laird's assertion nonetheless, likewise challenging the Pentagon report, which they charged had tampered with intelligence data in order to make a case for missile defense and against a MIRV ban. Subsequently, even administration partisans acknowledged that the case for the greater-than-expected threat had perhaps been oversold in 1969.[5]

Morton Kaplan, the Hudson Institute analyst who participated in the Pentagon study, wondered at the time why the Air Force hadn't shown more alarm at its conclusions. They indicated, therefore, that the vast majority of America's missiles and bombers would be wiped out—even if the country received warning of an imminent Soviet attack.

The mystery was not cleared up to Kaplan's satisfaction until some years after the study was completed. "It turned out that the military lied to us on the capabilities of some of the weapons when we did the study," Kaplan said. He later learned, Kaplan claimed, that lower-level officials in the Defense Department had been instructed by their superiors to misrepresent the capabilities of American and Soviet weapons to the outside analysts taking part in the study.

A National Intelligence Estimate prepared by the CIA some months after the DIA study succeeded not in putting an end to the controversy but in provoking it anew. The CIA estimate thus concluded that the Russians neither had nor were they seeking the capability to disarm the United States. As in the ABM debate, charges of outright deception erupted again when the crucial paragraph disputing that the Russians sought a first-strike capability was removed from the CIA report at Defense Secretary Laird's insistence.[6]

The Nixon administration's decision to accept a partial limit on ABM but to deploy MIRV resulted in a temporary lull in the experts' debate over the greater-than-expected threat. The controversy resumed with characteristic fervor, however, when the second round of SALT negotiations began at

Geneva in the fall of 1972. At the heart of the renewed debate was a new charge by SALT's critics. Recent intelligence, they claimed, revealed a Soviet threat that was not only greater than expected, but greater even than what had been heretofore imagined. The summer after the SALT II talks began, the Russians had in fact tested what was indisputably a MIRV, with accuracy sufficient to make it a theoretical threat to Minuteman. The technical characteristics of the new missiles in the Soviet test series also seemed to confirm that their intended targets were, indeed, America's own land-based missiles.[7]

"One thing that was evident before the cheers had died down for SALT I," Albert Wohlstetter said, "was that the Soviet Union had a whole generation of new missiles that hadn't been anticipated—and with better accuracy." Wohlstetter believed that the battery of Russian missile tests in the summer of 1973 vindicated his prediction, made at the time of SALT I's signing, that the Soviets would exploit the loopholes in the treaty limiting offensive missiles to gain a strategic edge over the United States. "The things that were supposed to protect Minuteman were outmoded already," he concluded. "SALT was dead before the ink was dry on the treaty."

Well before the summer's surprises, Wohlstetter had been privately critical of what he considered the subjective judgment and almost Olympian detachment of the Central Intelligence Agency concerning the Soviet threat. Despite the role the CIA had played in exploding the myth of the missile gap, Wohlstetter claimed that the agency's analysts generally underestimated the danger that Russia posed to the United States.

In a 1967 study, Wohlstetter had calculated that, contrary to CIA estimates, the country was falling far behind the Russians in the amount of money spent on defense. He found that U.S. spending on strategic weapons when measured in constant dollars had declined as a result of the effects of inflation and the war in Vietnam. According to his figures, the nation's defense spending as a function of its gross national product had actually peaked in fiscal 1952. Wohlstetter's charts and graphs argued a statistical case which contradicted the appearance that more money than ever was being spent on the military, and certainly ran counter to the antiwar mood of that time. The overheated economy and the protracted Asian war, he warned, were sapping America's real strength in a way that national leaders seemed unconcerned by—and protesters in the streets blissfully unaware of.

In 1973, shortly after the revelations about Soviet missiles, Wohlstetter undertook a far more ambitious test of his thesis: a review of the CIA's estimate of the Russian threat over the past twenty-five years. When it was completed, Wohlstetter's survey charged that the agency had consistently underrated the Soviet menace for most of a generation. Claiming that there was a pervasive "myth of overestimation" surrounding CIA estimates—one that was exploded, for example, by the agency's continual underestimate of the number of intermediate-range missiles the Russians would eventually choose to build—he likewise disputed McNamara's view that an action-reaction phenomenon was at work in the nuclear arms race. Such theories, Wohlstetter wrote, were "massively in error." Since the early 1960s, he argued, only the Soviet Union had run such a race—while the United States had chosen either to walk at a slow pace or to stand still.[8]

Unlike Brennan's caricature of MAD or the abstruse critique of Minuteman vulnerability by Nitze and Jones, the point of Wohlstetter's quantified study was to show in irrefutable mathematical terms that the nation's perception of its principal enemy had been based all along on too rosy a view.[9]

By the mid-1970s there was yet to be, as John Newhouse had predicted, any single "convulsion in the public mood" that spelled the doom of arms control. But there was already, another observer of SALT wrote in 1975, a popular mood of "ambiguity and confusion" surrounding the subject.

Journalistic accounts in the fall of 1973 that hinted a second SALT agreement might be signed within the year had plainly proved too optimistic. Yet the growing disillusionment with SALT was gradual and undramatic. In 1973 as well, a funding request from the Pentagon for a more accurate guidance system to be fitted on the latest version of the Minuteman missile had been denied by Congress because of its counterforce implications. Significantly, the same program was reintroduced and approved by Congress the following year—as were other, successive improvements to the war-fighting capability of the nation's strategic arsenal.[10]

Not surprisingly, the official view of arms control seemed to mirror the popular mood. The initially spirited claims made on behalf of SALT by arms controllers had given way to what seemed at best a desultory defense, and increasingly a kind of desperate rearguard action. An interim SALT agreement worked out between Soviet and American leaders at Vladivostok in 1974 —though widely hailed at the time as a substantial achievement—seemed in succeeding months to confirm the failure of arms control to deal with the persistent problem of MIRV. The accord thus "restricted" each side to a MIRVed missile force so large that neither the United States nor Russia would be likely to reach the limit in several years of unrestrained building.[11]

It was perhaps appearance as much as reality that accounted for the subtle shift in mood. While President Ford had publicly justified his firing of Defense Secretary Schlesinger on the grounds that the latter opposed *détente*, within the year Ford himself ordered the controversial term struck from his administration's political lexicon. Critics of SALT charged that the steady Soviet missile buildup violated the spirit, if not the letter, of that accord. In fact, the burgeoning of each side's nuclear arsenal continued apace throughout this time as a consequence of MIRV, despite SALT—and even, SALT's supporters acknowledged, as "the price" of arms control. SALT, Wohlstetter observed, seemed to have become "a problem posing as a solution."

It was not, however, the sudden materialization of any new Soviet threat that led to SALT's final undoing, but the gradual reemergence of an old and familiar danger—seen in a new light.

Although it had grown steadily since 1972, the conservative opposition to SALT had always lacked a popular forum outside Congress. The Committee to Maintain a Prudent Defense Policy, to which Wohlstetter and Nitze belonged, lobbied for a missile defense in the late 1960s, but the signing of the ABM treaty had caused the organization to atrophy since then. The Coalition for a Democratic Majority, formed by a similarly minded collection of anti-McGovern Democrats after the 1972 election, suffered a like fate. "It never got anywhere," remembered Eugene Rostow, one of its founders.

Like his brother Walt, Eugene remained stubbornly hawkish on Vietnam long after most other members of his party had come to oppose the war. In a 1975 meeting at Rostow's house shortly before Thanksgiving, he and Nitze concluded that one of the reasons the opposition to *détente* had been ineffective during the Nixon and early Ford years was its unabashedly partisan nature. Incensed over the recent firing of Schlesinger, Rostow and Nitze resolved to create a new lobbying force that would carefully avoid its predecessors' mistakes. "We started over," Rostow said, "but with the same people and the same ideas." Their joint effort, he predicted to Nitze, would "be the most important thing you and I have ever done."

At lunchtime meetings in New York and Washington earlier in the year, Rostow and Charls Walker, a deputy treasury secretary in the Nixon administration, had already drawn up a prospective membership list for the new conservative lobby. Nitze agreed to serve as co-chairman with Rostow for the nascent organization. The name chosen in a March 1976 meeting of its members at the Metropolitan Club—the Committee on the Present Danger—was intended to be both traditional and auspicious. It was at the same place some twenty-six years earlier that the first Committee on the Present Danger had taken its name from Justice Oliver Wendell Holmes' injunction that no person had a right to yell "Fire!" in a crowded room unless there was a clear and present danger.[12]

The original committee, to which Nitze had also belonged, was founded at the nadir of American fortunes in the Korean War. Its guiding purpose had been to pressure the Truman administration into taking a more hard-line position with the Soviets and to increase spending on defense. Three years later, the implementation of Nitze's NSC-68, the course of the Cold War, and its own insistent efforts to awaken public opinion to the Russian threat had achieved the committee's initial goal beyond even its members' expectations, and it had disbanded.[13]

A generation after the original committee's dissolution, its namesake declared itself similarly committed to building "a fresh consensus" on the issue of defense. "Time, weariness, and the tragic experience of Vietnam" had undermined "the bipartisan consensus which sustained our foreign policy between 1940 and the mid-60's," Rostow wrote in the revived committee's first broadside: "The threats we face are more subtle and indirect than was once the case," with the result that "the awareness of danger has diminished in the United States." But the principal aim of the reconstituted committee remained the same as that of the original. As Rostow made plain, the specific target of its efforts would be the policy of *détente* with Russia, and that policy's foremost symbol and achievement—SALT.[14]

The feeling of Rostow and Nitze that their separate warnings about impending Soviet strategic superiority had been given little heed by the government and the public was behind the founding of the new Committee on the Present Danger. To its critics the committee represented "an elite aviary of hawks." Rostow defended it as "an educating—not a lobbying— organization." The committee's success in drawing attention to its message by early 1976 was, in any case, an indication of the end of the unquestioned consensus behind SALT and arms control.[15]

Even before the creation of the second Committee on the Present Danger, the official perception of the Soviet threat had begun to be transformed by the conservative critique of American defense policy. Appointed to the post of CIA director during the disintegration of the Nixon administration, William Colby yielded shortly thereafter to a growing number of the agency's critics in agreeing to a basic review of the CIA's prior estimates of Russian spending on defense. According to the newly revised estimate by the embattled analysts at Langley, the Soviets were now deemed to be spending twice as much yearly on their military establishment as previously thought.[16]

As subsequently acknowledged even by the CIA's critics, the light shed by this apparent statistical revelation was neither strong nor clear concerning Russian capabilities *or* intentions.[17] Andrew Marshall—the Rand alumnus whom Schlesinger appointed head of the Pentagon's Office of Net Assessments—conceded, therefore, that one possible interpretation of the agency's revised conclusion was that the Russian war machine performed at only half the efficiency previously thought. But a far more sinister inference could equally be made about Soviet intentions from the review, Marshall noted: the enemy was now seen as willing to make twice the sacrifice in his national economy to match—or surpass—the United States in military strength.

In a comparison of that strength, Marshall related the position of the United States relative to the Soviet Union to that of a big company historically twice the size of its closest competitor but now being overtaken by its rival. Besides the ultimate outcome of the race, what most concerned Marshall, he said, was how the contest appeared to spectators on the sidelines: "Our technical edge is gone and the competition is seen as significantly ahead." Accordingly, his fear was that "others who used to follow our lead will no longer do so."

But Marshall also saw cause for cautious optimism in the changing perception of Russia represented by the CIA's revised analysis. The attitude that the United States had fallen dangerously behind the Russians used to be "a minority view," he said. The fact that the CIA's analysts had accepted it meant that it was on the way to becoming a consensus.

The change in the CIA's estimate of Russian military spending was only the beginning of the revised perception of the Soviet threat. Ever since the publication of Wohlstetter's thesis concerning the myth of the arms race there had been a steadily building clamor—some of it raised by Wohlstetter himself—for an outside review of the danger from Russia on the model of ORSA's investigation of the ABM controversy. Détente's critics at the time of the Ford administration had renewed the call for such a review to counter what they alleged to be the "systemic error" and the "arms control bias" of the CIA's experts.

Another source of pressure for a comparative analysis was the President's Foreign Intelligence Advisory Board, a collection of senior government advisers established during the Kennedy administration to oversee the CIA and judge its performance.[18] By 1976 the membership of the board included Edward Teller and John Foster, head of the Pentagon panel that had drawn up NSDM-242. The outcry over Ford's firing of both Colby and Schlesinger the previous year—and the subsequent announcement by the two men that they had joined the Committee on the Present Danger—showed the extent to which disagreement over the Soviet threat was becoming an issue outside as well as inside the government.

As with the review of Russian defense spending, Colby initially resisted the prospect of engaging the CIA in what he derisively termed a "paper-and-pencil war" with its critics. His evident hope was that any substantially new view of the Soviet menace would originate within the agency itself. (One of the proponents of an outside review claimed that Colby, a devout Catholic, ultimately yielded to the logic that—as in the canonization of saints—there was a need for a devil's advocate against the CIA's estimates.) But Colby's successor as head of the CIA, George Bush, had already joined the growing ranks of the agency's critics, and readily agreed to the renewed demand for a paper-and-pencil war that followed Colby's dismissal in December 1975.

Since Bush shared the critics' view, it was hardly surprising that he chose from among the CIA's most vocal detractors for the "B-team" to review the Soviet threat. The "A-team," by inference, was the CIA itself. Several on the B-team had been founding members as well of the Committee on the Present Danger. Besides Nitze, other well-known conservatives on the nine-man team included its director, Richard Pipes, an *émigré* professor of Russian history at Harvard; and William Van Cleave, a defense expert who, like Nitze, was an early dropout from the SALT II negotiations.[19]

All on the B-team were veterans of the long-term intellectual rivalry over the American perception of Russia. Each, too, subscribed in some measure to what Andrew Marshall called "the minority view." Rand's Thomas Wolfe and the CIA's Robert Ellsworth had each promoted the "no-cities" doctrine during the Kennedy administration, and later applauded the return to counterforce under Nixon. Formerly head of the Defense Intelligence Agency, Lieutenant General Daniel Graham consistently branded CIA calculations of Russian strength as underestimates. Air Force General Jasper Welch had served on the Foster panel. The B-team's main technical consultants, who included Wohlstetter and T. K. Jones, mirrored the dominant view there. Another consultant, Air Force Major General George Keegan, was an early proponent first of the bomber gap and later of the missile gap, and remained true to his faith in the gap thesis long after most others had accepted it as chimerical.[20]

Predictably, the conclusions reached by the B-team about the nature and dimensions of the Soviet threat directly contradicted what had been the common wisdom of the CIA on the subject for many years. Specifically challenged by the B-team was the agency's long-standing contention that the United States had a technological lead in such things as missile accuracy, and the CIA's claim that Soviet preparations for civil defense would prove essentially futile in the event of all-out nuclear war.[21]

In cases where both sides in the competition conceded that uncertainty prevailed, the B-team consistently gave the benefit of the doubt to the Russians. In one instance where the CIA's analysts acknowledged that the accuracy of Soviet missiles could not be known with assurance, members of the B-team took this as evidence that Soviet missiles were probably more accurate than their American counterparts.

On nontechnical questions concerning such things as Soviet concepts of nuclear strategy and arms control, the B-team freely admitted to having "a more somber" view than that of the CIA. "It was more than somber—it was grim," one of the agency's experts later testified. "It flatly states the judgment that the Soviet Union is seeking superiority over United States forces."[22]

But the widest difference between the CIA and the B-team came in their analyses of Soviet intentions and motives. Neither side had access to any privileged information or new evidence regarding Russia. "It was almost a glass half-empty or a glass half-full kind of question," George Carver, one of the B-team's sponsors, acknowledged: "Were the Soviets only reacting or were they looking for an edge?" The answer, Carver said, "went back to the dynamics of the Soviet system." Yet the role that unstated premises played in their starkly different analyses of the Soviet threat remained virtually unacknowledged by both sets of participants in the controversy. "There was disagreement beyond the facts," noted one CIA analyst simply.[23]

As in the ORSA episode or the battle of the charts in the ABM debate, no decisive winner emerged from the paper-and-pencil war fought over the Soviet threat in 1975 and 1976. Victory—as much as the issue itself—depended upon the eye of the beholder. But one result of the B-team exercise, like that of the ABM debate, was to point out again the gap that existed between the experts. Moreover, the paper-and-pencil war did have a tangible effect upon subsequent CIA estimates concerned with Soviet intentions.

Henceforth the analysts at Langley tended to be more circumspect on the sensitive question of what the Russians actually intended. "Intellectually, that argument was not resolved," one observer said of the question of Russian intentions. "Politically, it was. Team B won."[24]

It was not in any single convulsion of the popular mood but as the result of a series of steady, wearing attacks and disappointments that the public attitude toward both the Russians and arms control had been transformed. There was in the wake of that transformation, observed Senator Daniel Moynihan, a supporter of the first SALT treaties, a "new reality" to arms control by the mid-1970s. This reality was rooted in the fact, Moynihan wrote, that the previous minority view of the Soviet threat—the view that the Russians intended "to surpass the United States in strategic arms and are in the process of doing so"—had since the start of SALT passed "from heresy to respectability, if not orthodoxy."[25]

24

The Window of Opportunity

The administration of Jimmy Carter would be one of the first victims of the new orthodoxy concerning the Russians, arms control, and nuclear war. As a presidential candidate, Carter had spoken often and evocatively about his lifelong "dream" of ridding the world of nuclear weapons. During the 1976 campaign he pledged as president to cut the military budget by as much as $7 billion.[1]

The scope of the changes in defense that Carter was considering when he came to office stunned some of those in Washington. During a preinaugural briefing on American war plans, the president-elect reportedly startled the joint chiefs by proposing that the nation's nuclear arsenal be reduced to a force of only two hundred missiles. Essentially the same minimum-deterrence idea that Robert McNamara had toyed with during his first few days in office, Carter's remarkable notion was immediately challenged by the chiefs and a phalanx of his own advisers. Like McNamara, Carter would never seriously propose the idea again.[2]

Yet—publicly at least—Carter gave no outside sign that he had abandoned his lifelong dream. His inaugural address accordingly promised to "move this year toward our ultimate goal—the elimination of all nuclear weapons from this earth."[3]

Carter's actions as a candidate indicated that the hope he expressed during the campaign for bettering relations with the Russians was genuine. It would, as well, remain alive in his administration. Insiders in the Carter camp thought significant in this respect a meeting that the candidate had with a number of aspiring appointees in the summer of 1976 at his Plains, Georgia, home. Among those present were Carter's future choice as secretary of state, Cyrus Vance; his secretary of defense-to-be, Harold Brown; and the man he would pick to head the Arms Control and Disarmament Agency, Paul Warnke. Paul Nitze—an early if seemingly incongruous supporter of Carter's candidacy who was rumored to be seeking the post of defense secretary—also attended the gathering.

Several of those at the pre-election meeting thought the presence there of Nitze and Warnke a curious juxtaposition. At one time the two men, both Democrats, were allies in a common cause. Since Vietnam, however, they had come to hold such diametrically opposed ideas on arms control and defense that there was wry talk in Washington of a "Paul-axis" concerning SALT.

The rivalry of Nitze and Warnke went back at least as far as their joint service as members of President Johnson's Senior Advisory Group on Vietnam—the so-called "wise old men," whose disheartening advice in the wake of the spring 1968 Tet offensive had finally persuaded Johnson to abandon both the presidency and the war. Their differences on Vietnam had been fundamental. Warnke joined the majority in urging Johnson to extricate himself and the nation from Vietnam, arguing that a communist victory there was "not going to have the least impact" on the future of American foreign relations.[4] Nitze, while critical of Johnson's policy in Vietnam, saw the contest as a test of national will—one whose importance went well beyond the immediate outcome of the war.

After Tet, Nitze had recommended that Johnson immediately send another thirty thousand combat troops to Vietnam—a step which, since it required calling up the Army Reserves, would have needed congressional approval. Johnson, already facing unprecedented opposition to the war, had balked at the move and sided with the majority urging him to seek negotiations. While sympathetic to the president's decision to back down, Nitze thought it a wrong and fateful choice for the nation as well as Johnson.

Since Vietnam, Nitze and Warnke had also been at opposite ends in the debate over arms control. In a 1975 *Foreign Affairs* article, Warnke compared the behavior of the United States and Russia in the arms race to that of "two apes on a treadmill," dismissing the significance—and even the possibility—of either side's gaining meaningful strategic superiority. Warnke had subsequently become one of the Democratic party's most prominent advocates of the SALT talks and of improving relations with the Russians.[5]

Those at the August 1976 meeting with Carter accordingly saw the presence of Nitze and Warnke as portending a symbolic as well as an actual turning point for the future government. One who attended the meeting professed "shock," therefore, when Nitze used the occasion to present a highly detailed exposition—complete with the graphs and charts that he and Jones had already made famous—of a hypothetical Soviet surprise attack on the United States. The presentation was intended to demonstrate vividly the vulnerability of Minuteman.

"It didn't go over very well," Warnke recollected of Nitze's unbidden and impromptu briefing. Nitze himself later acknowledged that his timing, at least, had been unfortunate. "He didn't want to listen," Nitze said of Carter. "He just got mad at me."

Actually, some of Nitze's ideas at the Plains meeting were probably in accord with Carter's own thinking. One example was Nitze's recommendation that the threat from MIRV be removed by development of a new generation of small, single-warhead missiles—the "Midgetman" that Nitze had suggested to the Russians four years earlier. Another was Nitze's interim proposal that both sides cut back to a force of no more than a thousand ICBMs apiece.

But Nitze's advisory that Carter would first have to increase defense spending, cut social programs, and deploy new weapons like the MX—since the Russians would not otherwise agree to negotiate seriously on things like Midgetman—failed to strike a sympathetic chord with the future president. While Carter did not disagree with what Nitze said was the "wholly solid premise that the avoidance of nuclear war is much more important than increasing welfare payments," both the style and the substance of Nitze's approach plainly misjudged the temper and the temperament of the future president.

The pre-election encounter of Carter and Nitze—which one witness baldly characterized as "a disaster"—unwittingly accentuated the differences between the two men and their respective points of view. "I didn't think he made any sense," Nitze said of Carter's plans to decrease defense spending. But that was clearly a minority view at the meeting. Others in the room after Nitze left derided his Midgetman proposal as "Paul's pinheads."

The humiliation Nitze suffered at Carter's hands in the August meeting seemed, in retrospect, a foreshadowing of the trouble the administration would encounter from conservative critics. Unheeded by Carter at the time of his election was a pointed warning and a veiled threat from the Committee on the Present Danger. A "strong and angry tide of concern about the safety of the nation is running throughout the country," wrote Eugene Rostow. Rostow professed himself "dismayed" at Carter's announced plans to cut the defense budget. A meeting between the president-elect and representatives from the committee in January 1977 "went badly," according to Rostow. Shortly thereafter, Carter was reportedly enraged at the committee when the top-secret B-team report was leaked to the press. In a move reminiscent of Nixon's decision to dismiss his science advisers and disband PSAC, Carter abolished the President's Foreign Intelligence Advisory Board, the guiding spirit behind the B-team report.[6]

The administration's subsequent problems were probably compounded by the fact that Carter showed little desire to compromise with his conservative critics—as his cabinet appointments soon showed. The year before Carter appointed him secretary of defense, Harold Brown had ridiculed the premise

that the Russians would ever gamble their entire society upon "a cosmic roll
of the dice" by attacking the United States. Though an early hawk on
Vietnam, Cyrus Vance had subsequently gone further than many self-professed doves in urging upon the Johnson administration a rapid withdrawal
from the war. Conservatives claimed that the gauntlet was thrown down—
and willingly accepted—when Carter nominated another outspoken liberal,
Theodore Sorensen, to be the next director of the CIA.[7]

Carter's choice of Washington attorney Warnke to head ACDA and the
SALT negotiations proved almost equally controversial. At the forefront of
the opposition to Warnke's confirmation by the Senate was Paul Nitze. In
addition to suggesting at those hearings that Warnke's judgment was un-
clear and inconsistent, Nitze attacked the nominee's views on the Russians
and the arms race as "asinine," "screwball," "arbitrary," and "fictitious."[8]

Though Warnke was finally confirmed as ACDA director, the closeness
of the deciding 58-40 vote and the bitterness of the confirmation fight in the
Senate left an anger on both sides that endured. Spurgeon Keeny, whom
Warnke would appoint his deputy at ACDA, thought the campaign against
his boss "despicable" and "without parallel in American history." Warnke
himself later made light of his confirmation "landslide." But he, too, was
doubtless aware that the controversy undermined his position as chief SALT
negotiator from the outset. "Like the position of the guy ridden out of town
on a rail—if it wasn't for the honor, I'd just as soon have not had the
experience," he quipped.

The battle over Warnke's nomination in the Senate became a harbinger
of the trouble that SALT as well as the administration was about to encounter from critics. At least a few veteran observers of the defense debate
thought it ominous for Carter's future that neither side seemed interested
in finding common ground. The story—illustrative, though almost certainly
apocryphal—circulated around Washington in the wake of Warnke's confirmation about a chance encounter at the Cosmos Club between the nominee and his nemesis shortly after the hearings. Wedged together into the
club's tiny elevator, neither man had spoken during the slow passage between floors. Only after Warnke stepped out on the club's second floor and
the elevator doors had closed was Nitze supposedly heard to mutter a single
word: "Traitor."

The Carter administration's discouraging experience with its domestic critics was followed soon afterward by the disappointment of its hopes for better
relations with the Russians and rapid progress on SALT. In the spring of
1977 a bold proposal that the president had approved—calling for "deep
cuts" in both Soviet and American nuclear arsenals and a ban on any new
ICBMs—was rejected outright by the Russians. Carter's hope, evidently,
had been that the Soviets would come back with a counterproposal. When

they didn't, there was intense disagreement within the administration over what the summary Russian rebuff meant.[9]

Warnke was one of the few who professed neither surprise nor disheartenment at the Russian rejection: "To the Russians it meant that the U.S. was going back on a deal. At Vladivostok we had agreed not to call for specific reductions in their heavy missiles. In effect, they were saying 'a deal's a deal.' " But even Warnke agreed with Carter's critics that the episode made the administration look naïve in dealing with the Russians—and hopelessly optimistic on SALT.

Such critics were also quick to point out how Carter's intimation that SALT II would stop the Soviet missile buildup was contradicted by experience—as well as by the very terms of the agreement that Gerard Smith and Warnke were endeavoring to work out with the Soviets. A series of Russian missile tests in the summer of 1978 revealed a new generation of even larger Soviet ICBMs, with unanticipated improvements in accuracy. The fact that the Russians had made these advances within the letter of the initial SALT treaties seemed to confirm the critics' point.[10]

By the summer of 1977 the campaign against the Carter administration's policies on arms control and Russia was well underway. While a second arms limitation treaty had yet to be negotiated with the Russians, it, too, was already under attack.

Among the most extreme examples of this anti-SALT critique was a July 1977 *Commentary* magazine article by Richard Pipes, a member of the Committee on the Present Danger and former director of the B-team. Pipes' article, "Why the Soviet Union Thinks It Could Fight and Win a Nuclear War," made plain that the challenge to SALT was equally a challenge to those who held to the assumptions and beliefs that underlay a generation of arms control efforts. It was an attack, indeed, upon most of the ideas and individuals behind American nuclear strategy and doctrine since Hiroshima.[11]

Pipes blamed "a coalition of groups" for silencing the opinion of the Strategic Bombing Survey that the atomic bomb represented no revolution in warfare. Each of those groups "for its own reasons," he wrote, depicted the bomb instead "as the 'absolute weapon' that had, in large measure, rendered traditional military establishments redundant and traditional strategic thinking obsolete." Pipes charged that Russian nuclear strategists had always held to the traditional view that the aim of strategy was to ensure victory. Americans, on the other hand, had eagerly but mistakenly embraced notions of deterrence and mutually assured destruction under the baneful influence of this coalition.

Pipes traced the source of this fundamental error back to the very beginning of the atomic age. "It represented," he wrote, "an act of faith on the part of an intellectual community which held strong pacifist convictions and felt deep guilt at having participated in the creation of a weapon of such destructive power." The result, Pipes claimed, was that the nation's nuclear strategy had entirely misjudged what the Soviets considered "unacceptable damage," and hence that America's supposedly formidable force of bombers and missiles actually posed an all-but-insubstantial threat to Russia. Pipes' conclusion—that all of the Soviet Union's cities "could be destroyed without trace or survivors, and provided that its essential cadres had been saved, it would emerge less hurt in terms of casualties than it was in 1945"—was a logical extension of the view expressed by T. K. Jones some years earlier.

An equally grim scenario of a prospective Soviet-American nuclear war was portrayed by Nitze, Jones himself, and other members of the Committee on the Present Danger and B-team alumni at a private two-day conference on "strategic alternatives" in the summer of 1978. Sponsored by the conservative National Strategy Information Center, the conference at Belmont House outside Baltimore, Maryland, was aimed explicitly at finding ways of influencing the Carter administration—though the talk there sometimes seemed more in the spirit of know-thine-enemy: "What kind of things would turn Carter around?" mused a member of the so-called Strategic Alternatives Group during one of their sessions. "What drives this almost religious zeal about ridding the world of nuclear weapons?"[12]

Both Nitze and Jones had earlier and at other forums hypothesized a nuclear war begun by a Soviet first strike. They claimed such an attack might destroy virtually all of the nation's land-based missiles in their silos, killing as many as a hundred million Americans at the loss of some ten million Russians. But the group at Belmont House provided a rare exposition of the fears behind this dire scenario, and its creators' proposed remedies.

There would be, Nitze explained, three phases in the "one-sided war" that he regarded as a possible consequence of the neglect of America's defense —including the "terminal phase in which the winner brings such pressure that he forces the other side to surrender." Nitze postulated that the Russians, having first evacuated their cities, would use no more than 50 percent of their ICBM force in the initial attack, destroying virtually all of America's land-based missiles and strategic bombers and as many missile-firing submarines as had not taken to sea. The remaining half of Russia's land-based missiles and all of the enemy's bombers and submarine-launched missiles could then be used to threaten American cities and force the United States to surrender.[13]

Civilian losses in the United States, Nitze calculated, would initially total ten to twelve million—but might reach as high as 180 million if the president did not yield to the Russian ultimatum. The final outcome, in any case, was not in doubt. The United States, he concluded, "was bound to lose the war."[14]

Other members of the symposium elaborated on Nitze's gruesome finale. The Russians were credited by Jones with the ability, concurrently with their attack on the United States, to overrun western Europe in a matter of days. In the second phase of the war the Soviets, it was thought, might re-deploy their tactical bombers to Cuba in order to put them within easier striking range of American cities. One participant speculated that the Russians might even sail their missile-firing submarines through the undefended St. Lawrence Seaway and into Hudson Bay with impunity.

In contrast to the utter devastation hypothesized for the United States in this war, T. K. Jones' calculation of Russian losses from the uncoordinated attacks that would be launched by America's now-crippled retaliatory force was as low as one or two million. He estimated that the Soviets' postwar industrial recovery could be complete in only two years if they made use of captured factories and slave labor in occupied western Europe. "In short," Jones concluded, "the situation right now with our present posture is that if we are threatened, we ought to give them what they ask for; if we are attacked, we ought not to shoot back."[15]

There was little disagreement within the Strategic Alternatives Group over where the blame for the current predicament lay. Most of the proposed solutions to what the participants considered America's perilous position of strategic inferiority—a crash ABM program and development of new and more powerful offensive missiles, for example—were either prohibited by current SALT agreements or likely to be outlawed by SALT II.

"The only way I can see to move the Executive Branch to seriously entertain the kinds of proposals we have been discussing here is if SALT fails and is not ratified," predicted Richard Perle, a young new-conservative and Senator Henry Jackson's legislative assistant. "Until it is disposed of, I think SALT will become a principal impediment to taking the kind of action we are talking about," Perle said at the group's concluding session: "It would be a stupendous political development if SALT were defeated." Former B-team member William Van Cleave agreed with Perle that SALT's defeat would be "the strongest possible call to action."[16]

But the Belmont House conference had not been entirely dominated by a chorus of negativism and despair. In addition to the "window of vulnerability" that most believed to imperil Minuteman, there was, the participants thought, a window of opportunity for the West—the prospect, T. K. Jones explained, of "less dangerous uplands" once the nation had passed through what he termed the " 'time valley' of maximum peril." Another analyst spoke in this connection of the "potential vulnerabilities which the Soviets have." The Russians, he suggested, "would be more concerned if we made a conscious effort to exploit these vulnerabilities."

Some of those at the Belmont conference had much earlier held out the prospect that the arms race itself could be used to exploit weaknesses in what was universally recognized to be the Soviets' greatest vulnerability: their economy. The idea of forcing the Russians into bankruptcy by a contest in military spending had been proposed by Nitze as far back as NSC-68. It was urged as well by the Quantico Vulnerability Panel at the time of Eisenhower's Open Skies proposal—and had been brought up again in Eugene Rostow's 1979 broadside against SALT. "The American people will spend and do whatever is required to assure the safety of the nation," Rostow wrote, "if their leaders tell them the truth, as President Truman did, and explain the central importance of nuclear weapons to our security and to the foreign policies we employ to protect it."[17]

The conference participants readily acknowledged how their ideas and recommendations represented a break—a discontinuity—from what had been the accepted wisdom on Soviet-American relations and on nuclear weapons for more than a generation. Uncertainty about Soviet intentions had been a fact of those relations throughout the years. Uncertainty about American intentions in a military contest with Russia was also a necessary element of deterrence as recognized in the limited nuclear options of the Schlesinger doctrine. But the members of the Strategic Alternatives Group argued, in effect, that uncertainty should be raised to its apotheosis in the 1980s. It was the key to what one at the final session termed the "quick fixes" and "technological breakthroughs" that might suddenly and unexpectedly allow the United States to leap forward in the arms race:

"One does things in a different way when one is strategically inferior," he said. "It is sort of like trying to deal with Ohio State with a bunch of puny 150-pound guards. You have got to be fast, you have got to be agile, and most all, you have got to be tricky. . . . This goes against the grain of what we have been doing for the last twenty years. It is going to go against the grain of what has been our approach to arms control proposals."[18]

The case against SALT did not go entirely unchallenged during the Carter administration. A 1978 review by the Arms Control and Disarmament Agency disputed the calculations behind T. K. Jones' estimate that the Russians could survive a nuclear war relatively unscathed. The ACDA report concluded that the United States and the Soviet Union were "roughly equally vulnerable" to nuclear attack—though the urban density of Russia and the tendency in Soviet society for people to live near their workplaces actually meant that Russian losses would be proportionally more than American losses in a war which led to attacks on cities. A similar ACDA study a year later noted that Jones' estimate of ten million Russian casualties following American retaliation was based on a highly suspect premise— namely, that the bulk of the Soviet Union's population would be evenly distributed across the barren Russian steppes and throughout the Arctic and Siberia at the time the war began.[19]

Defenders of arms control and deterrence pointed out how Nitze's scenario of a successful Soviet surprise attack assumed that most of America's submarines would be in port when the blow struck, and that all of the Russians' missiles would arrive at their targets simultaneously. These experts noted that the first assumption was contrary to the Navy's standard practice—and the second a violation of the laws of physics.[20]

In addition to those who challenged the figures on which the conclusions of Nitze and Jones were based, there were others who questioned the basic assumptions behind the conservative critique. Writing in the *Washington Post,* one authority dismissed Pipes' claim that the Russians believed they could fight and win a nuclear war as "rank hysteria in scholarly garb," and "worst-case alarmism."[21]

Since the Pipes article had directly attacked the group of which Richard Garwin was a foremost member—the atomic scientists—Garwin was moved to challenge its author to a debate. Pipes declined to debate Garwin, but agreed to meet with him in private shortly after the article came out. (Pipes also rejected, Garwin said, a subsequent offer from *Commentary*'s editor to publish a pair of articles by the two men presenting their arguments side by side.)

In retrospect, Garwin thought his encounter with Pipes a parable of the frustrations faced by those who tried to argue the pro-SALT side in the face of a changed political consensus. "Although he had been the leader of Team B and had access to all the information we had on the Soviet Union, he didn't have the least understanding of U.S. forces," Garwin said of Pipes. "He was just wrong." But the technical arguments were perhaps the least part of their private debate. "Pipes maintained that his conclusion was still valid, independent of the line of argument," Garwin remembered. "Pipes said that the evidence for his argument came from his deep knowledge of the Russian soul."[22]

It was not only the frustration of being unable to find common ground with SALT's critics, Garwin said, but his inability to realize an audience willing to listen to arguments *against* the opposition to SALT—either among the public or at congressional hearings—that he thought the most disturbing thing about the new attitude toward arms control. "It just died without arousing any interest," Garwin observed of the case for SALT.

25

From MAD to Worse

By the fall of 1978 the Committee on the Present Danger had joined with another neo-conservative organization, the American Security Council, to form the Coalition for Peace through Strength—a lobbying interest whose $2 million public relations campaign was explicitly designed to defeat the SALT II treaty before it came to a vote in the Senate. In books and pamphlets and on the occasion of testifying before congressional committees, Carter administration critics like Nitze, Rostow, and former B-team member Daniel Graham attacked SALT as—in Graham's words—"the acme of MADness." Arguments Nitze had first made in NSC-68 were raised again in the conservative opposition to SALT—as in the coalition's claim that strategic parity with Russia "is a condition that places the United States at a significant disadvantage."[1]

Even before the formal campaign to defeat the new treaty was underway, the opposition to SALT had achieved results. Former champions of arms control like Henry Kissinger remained publicly circumspect about SALT II. Political insiders in the Carter administration were said to have greeted with quiet relief the resignation of Paul Warnke as director of ACDA in 1977.[2]

Plainly, not all of the administration's problems with SALT were due to outside pressure. The president's clumsy handling of a Soviet training brigade suddenly "discovered" in Cuba—it was afterward acknowledged that Russian troops had been on the island since the 1962 missile crisis—gave support to critics' claims that the government was both inconsistent and incompetent when it came to handling the Russians. The administration's poor image had begun to be a source of increasing concern to Defense Secretary Harold Brown and, particularly, to Zbigniew Brzezinski, Carter's national security adviser. Approaching the final negotiations on the SALT II treaty in the spring and summer of 1979, Brzezinski resolved to dispel the appearance of weakness with a dramatic gesture: an announcement that the administration had decided to proceed with development of the MX missile.[3] Nowhere, in retrospect, would the change brought about in the Carter administration by its critics be more evident than in the president's decision on the MX and his subsequent revision of American nuclear strategy.

Since its origins in the Schlesinger doctrine as a counterbalance to Russia's massive ICBMs, the MX had seemed to follow the course of other technological measures and countermeasures in the arms race. Like MIRV, the solution represented by the MX defined a whole new problem. Initially promoted as a way to add stability to the balance of terror by ending the vulnerability of America's ICBMs, the MX, in fact, created a new instability by theoretically putting Soviet missiles at risk.

From the outset, counterforce enthusiasts in the Pentagon had recognized the war-fighting role that the MX could play in U.S. strategy by destroying Russian missiles in their silos. Thus its ten or more MIRVed warheads would each be an improvement in reliability, accuracy, and yield over the three warheads on the Minuteman missiles the MX was meant to supplement. Its technological proficiency made the MX not only the first American weapon capable of carrying out a disarming strike against Russian missile fields, opponents of the missile noted, but the first perhaps ideally suited to that task. The purpose of the MX—one of its supporters acknowledged— "was to be able to do to [the Russians] what they could do to us."[4]

Arms control proponents seeking a solution to the problem of Minuteman vulnerability had supported the missile for another quality entirely—its mobility. The end result was that the MX, like MIRV, had received critical support from both "hawks" and "doves" early in its development. Opposition to the missile's development was slow in coming; when it came, it was perhaps already too late.[5]

Like MIRV as well, the MX seemed a triumph of unforeseen technological consequences. As Wohlstetter had predicted a generation earlier, the challenge of protecting land-based missiles from enemy attack was beginning to seem insuperable by the beginning of the 1970s. Various schemes for moving the missile around on airplanes, trucks, trains, and even canal boats had been explored in the intervening years by the Air Force—whose principal concern, however, was always more with the MX's counterforce capability than with its invulnerability.[6]

By mid-1977 the "MX mafia," as the missile's proponents became known, had settled upon a basing scheme that combined protection of the MXs themselves with a plan to deceive any would-be attacker: a mammoth system of underground concrete shelters, only a fraction of which would actually contain a missile. During the following year this elaborate protection-and-deception scheme—variously termed the Alternate Launch Point System, ALPS, or the Multiple Aim Point System, MAPS, but soon known simply as "the shell game"—received the vital sanction of SALT critics like Paul Nitze.[7]

Carter's decision to cancel the B-1 bomber had prompted Nitze to predict, in what may have been a kind of self-fulfilling prophecy, that the MX would be the next major issue in the continuing defense debate. By 1978 the issue of the MX had moved to the forefront of the attack upon Carter's defense policies, though the president himself seemed one of the last in his administration willing to yield to pressures for the missile. Carter reportedly dismissed the MX and the shell game as "the craziest thing I've ever heard."

At the Belmont conference, however, Nitze had confirmed that there were others within Carter's inner circle who quietly supported the missile. Another participant at the conference spoke, in this connection, of a possible "trade-off between SALT on the one hand, and a set of strategic initiatives on the other."[8] "The problem seemed to be the president," Nitze said. "People do not dare to say certain things to the president. They seem to be intimidated."[9]

By the end of the year even skeptics—Carter included—who doubted that a Soviet sneak attack on Minuteman was a prospect in the real world were forced to admit, nonetheless, that Minuteman vulnerability and the MX had become a major political problem for the administration. The new series of Russian missile tests that summer had cast the problem in particularly stark relief. Nitze himself attributed Carter's decision to support the MX to the influence of the administration's critics. But more neutral observers did not disagree. It was the hope of Carter and his advisers, one observer wrote, that an official endorsement of the MX and the shell game "might induce Paul Nitze to support SALT II."[10]

As late as the winter of 1978, Carter was reportedly still toying with the prospect of scrapping all of the country's land-based missiles—a possibility that his cabinet officers and closest advisers had either long since abandoned or never entertained in the first place. Defense Secretary Brown argued with the president that the strategic triad should remain inviolate, if only to show the Russians that they could not make American nuclear strategy by pushing our deterrent out to sea. Brzezinski was inclined to go further than Brown, claiming that "geopolitical" as well as strategic considerations lay behind his support for the MX.[11]

Brzezinski favored the development of a counterforce weapon like the MX, he wrote, "in order to avoid the possibility that at some point in the future the Soviets would have more strategic military options than we did." Specifically, he feared "that if such a situation were to arise, the United States could be forced into significant political concessions in the course of a protracted crisis with the Soviets." Brzezinski was also frank enough to admit that the MX was a political necessity if the administration hoped to get Senate approval of the SALT II treaty.[12]

The climactic decision on the MX came in a meeting of Carter and the National Security Council in early June of 1979. Complaining at first that

Brzezinski was "jamming a decision down his throat," the president nonetheless "rather glumly" gave tentative approval to the missile when no one at the meeting raised objections. Carter's endorsement was just for the missile itself and not for the basing scheme, since still outstanding were the Soviets' objections, raised in the SALT negotiations, that the shell game would make verification of a treaty virtually impossible. The entry that day in Carter's personal journal noted only that he felt "disappointment" over the way the MX issue was resolved. "It was a nauseating prospect to confront, with the gross waste of money going into nuclear weapons of all kinds," the president wrote.[13]

Brzezinski took credit for "ramming through" another consequential decision on the MX in an NSC meeting two days later. Since the inception of the missile-experimental project, two sizes for the MX had been under consideration. The smaller model would have fit the Navy's submarines as well as the Air Force's existing Minuteman silos. An alternative version was both larger and even more destructive, but harder to move around or to conceal. Because of the larger model's liabilities, some of the MX's earliest and most fervent supporters in the Pentagon favored the smaller model—as, for example, did Defense Secretary Brown.[14]

But Brzezinski was ultimately instrumental in selecting the larger missile. What he characterized as "strategic and geopolitical factors" were, once again, determining in the choice. In his memoirs, Brzezinski cited among the reasons for the larger MX Carter's upcoming meeting later that month with Brezhnev and the criticism the administration was already under at home.[15]

"The bigger, the uglier, the nastier the weapon—the better" was how Paul Warnke explained the rationale behind the larger missile. The message being sent to the Russians by Brzezinski, Warnke thought, was in effect: "Shape up, Buster. We've got the ability to do you in. We're probably not going to do it—but it's an act of grace on our part."[16]

"Zbigniew Brzezinski gets the prize for settling the missile size," confirmed Jasper Welch, who had also been an advocate of the larger MX. "Brzezinski reasoned that it would not do politically for the U.S. to build a missile smaller than that allowed by the SALT II treaty," Welch said. "Carter's image would suffer."[17] One who had been present at the decisive NSC meeting agreed with Welch's assessment. "I think in the end the larger diameter made sense from a political point of view," noted Defense Secretary Harold Brown.

The Carter administration's decision that it would not only build the MX missile but build the largest and most destructive one possible showed the issues in the controversy to be largely symbolic, Richard Garwin thought. Garwin's protracted but futile opposition to the MX convinced him that the unstated arguments behind the missile were always more important than the official rationale offered on its behalf. Garwin had opposed the MX since its inception, believing its purpose to be a way of confronting the Russians once again with the threat of a disarming first strike. "If you want a first-strike weapon, why don't you say you want a first-strike weapon?" he chided MX supporters.

The price of the MX, Garwin warned at congressional hearings, might be the end of SALT and an arms race renewed with unprecedented intensity. He predicted that pressures would build if the weapon were deployed to abandon the shell game by filling the dummy shelters as well with real missiles, in a violation of SALT's limits upon offensive weapons. The next step would be the abrogation of SALT's ABM treaty in order to provide an active defense for the MX. Ultimately, even the 1963 ban on atmospheric testing would have to be abandoned in order to test the effectiveness of that defense.

Finding the momentum for the missile nonetheless irresistible, Garwin and another Jason physicist, Sidney Drell, proposed what they argued would be a cheaper, less vulnerable, and more easily verifiable means of basing the MX than the Air Force's shell game. Their alternative was actually a resurrected and modernized version of an idea for protecting ICBMs from attack that had first surfaced in a secret Pentagon study more than a decade before. Acronymed SUM—for "smallsub undersea mobile"—the scheme involved putting one or two of the MXs on each of what would be a fleet of miniature diesel-powered submarines stationed in waters off the nation's coastline.[18]

The resistance that Garwin and Drell encountered to the SUM idea persuaded them that the MX's vulnerability to Russian attack was not primarily—or perhaps even importantly—a concern of its supporters in the military. "Almost everybody in the Pentagon was against SUM," Garwin remembered. Diehards in the Air Force insisted on the larger version of the missile in part, he thought, because it could not be carried on submarines. But the Navy, too, preferred its much larger and more expensive nuclear-powered submarines to SUM. "Diesel subs just weren't sexy," Drell observed.

The two came to believe that, as in the abstract controversy over Minuteman vulnerability, at the heart of the case for the MX was an unremarked obsession concerning national resolve. Garwin thought this evident in the arguments that an Air Force briefing officer gave for the shell game and against SUM: "First, it will show the Soviet Union we are not about to concede the land-based leg of the triad. Secondly, it will allow us to threaten the Soviet Union's land-based force." This officer concluded—according to Garwin's account: "The result of these two virtues is that the MX will bring the Soviet Union to the bargaining table."

But Garwin felt the argument for MX as a bargaining chip in arms control to be both false and deceptive. The real reason for having the MX based upon land, he alleged, was to require the Russians in a war to take the final step of attacking American soil—and, conversely, to show the Soviets that the United States was willing to sustain significant casualties in defense of its interests.[19]

The idea of using the MX to demonstrate national will, Garwin claimed, also caused proponents of the missile deliberately to overstate the cost and vulnerability of the submarine-borne system while at the same time under-rating SUM's accuracy. When he and Drell pointed out to MX advocates in the Pentagon that SUM met each of the eleven requirements set for basing their missile, a twelfth and previously unstated criterion was, Garwin charged, promptly added: "Now they said, 'Well, sorry, but we didn't tell you that being land-based is also a requirement.' " At another hearing on the MX, Garwin and Drell were privately apprised by an Air Force representative "that they didn't understand the problem—which was not to provide the best basing mode for the MX, but the best *land-based* basing mode."

There was as well a final, unstated premise behind the case for the MX on land, Garwin and Drell thought. This was the argument that the United States had to put the big missile on its own territory if it hoped to persuade its European allies to accept shorter-range strategic missiles on theirs.[20] However, Garwin dismissed this rationale too as another example of the perverted reasoning and "loop thinking" that he said had always applied in the case of the MX: "We have to put the MX on land so that we can force our allies to put things on land that neither we nor they should ever have decided to put on land in the first place."

The triumph of the illogic behind the MX, he and Drell felt, had been Brzezinski's decision for the larger version of the missile—which they suspected was a way of finally torpedoing the SUM idea. The choice of the bigger and more threatening missile had been an expression of Brzezinski's concern with demonstrating not only the national will, therefore, but also the political will of the Carter administration. Unable to find an audience for the SUM alternative in the Pentagon, Garwin and Drell nonetheless believed they had extracted a promise from Brzezinski that they would be able to brief Carter personally on their basing scheme. But the briefing never took place. "Brzezinski said he didn't want it coming out that the Carter administration was once again uncertain on the MX," Garwin explained. "Brzezinski's argument was that he would rather deploy a vulnerable system than nothing at all—since what is required in the present political circumstance is to show that the United States can do *something.* "

It was not SUM but SALT that finally doomed the shell game. In the fall of 1979, Carter announced that he had decided to deploy two hundred MX missiles along a "race track" in Nevada and Utah—where individual missiles would be constantly kept in motion, dashing to the closest shelter upon warning of a Soviet attack.[21] Carter's decision was plainly intended to put an end to the long saga of the MX and the question of its basing. But the controversy over the missile endured nevertheless.

The same month that he made the decision to proceed with the MX, Carter signed the SALT II treaty with Brezhnev. In a subsequent speech to the Senate, the president reaffirmed that the MX was indeed "not a bargaining chip" but a permanent addition to the nation's nuclear arsenal. "The President's MX decision was a token of his firm determination not to let SALT inhibit the further modernization of our strategic deterrent," Brzezinski wrote with unintended irony.[22] More directly, Brown thought the MX decision in part "motivated by the need to show the hawks in the Senate that SALT was not a sign of administration weakness."

To foes of the MX, Carter's decision for the missile seemed a portentous turning point. The MX was "a monument to the failure of arms control," in Sidney Drell's judgment. It heralded the closing of what Drell termed the "window of simplicity" that had made arms control possible in the 1960s and 1970s. It would be, he reflected, increasingly difficult to verify any future agreement with the Russians because of new weapons like the mobile MX and the even more mobile and concealable cruise missile. Carter's decision was symptomatic of "a general retreat from belief in arms control," Drell felt.[23]

Senator Daniel Moynihan, a member of the Senate Select Committee on Intelligence that held hearings on the verifiability of SALT II, similarly thought the MX decision an example of the conundrum that arms control had become: "The SALT process has its premise in the doctrine of deterrence. The MX missile is incompatible with the doctrine of deterrence," he wrote. "The final irony of the SALT process," Moynihan reflected, was that it not only had "failed to prevent the Soviets from developing a first-strike capability; it now leads the United States to do so. . . . The process had produced the one outcome it was designed to forestall."[24]

There seemed a broad concurrence even among SALT's early supporters with Moynihan's bleak assessment. "Arms control has essentially failed" was the summary verdict of Leslie Gelb, a State Department official in the Carter administration, and one of SALT's former champions.[25] Paul Warnke blamed the MX, among other things, for sabotaging the proposal he had once made for a Soviet-American ban on all new ICBMs. "The MX," Warnke said, "was the illegitimate child of first-strike pressures plus politics." But also behind the MX decision, he felt, had been a miscalculation. "Carter thought also that the option should be left open—but that it would never be used." Warnke attributed the final outcome to political pressures upon the president: "Carter did not feel politically strong enough to implement what he genuinely believed in. Politically it was necessary to have the option of the MX."

Despite all the undeniably intense pressures upon Carter to choose the MX, the president's liberal critics had to concede that there was as well a kind of ineluctable logic behind the decision for the new weapon. It was the same logic that had been behind the development of MIRV, the Super, and even the first atomic bomb. It reminded Sidney Drell of a passage from Alexander Pope's *Essay on Man:*

> Vice is a monster of so frightful mien,
> As to be hated, needs but to be seen;
> Yet seen too oft, familiar with her face
> We first endure, then pity, then embrace.[26]

· · ·

The logic behind the MX decision would also lead Carter to complete what Brzezinski termed "a program for strategic renewal" within six months of approving development of the new missile. Following tradition, Carter had ordered a comprehensive review of nuclear strategy and war planning a few days after his inauguration. Initial indications were that the president intended the review to be the beginning of some fundamental changes, in accord with his announced goal of eventually ridding the world of nuclear weapons. Even after the shocked reaction of the joint chiefs to his ideas on minimum deterrence, therefore, Carter had quietly instructed Harold Brown to proceed with a study of the feasibility of significant reductions in the nation's strategic arsenal.[27]

When Presidential Review Memorandum number 10 was completed in the summer of 1977 it seemed to reflect the assumptions behind Carter's own thinking on the arms race and nuclear war. PRM-10 estimated that in an all-out war the United States would suffer at least 140 million fatalities and Russia 113 million, with three-quarters of the cities and industries in both countries destroyed. "Neither side could conceivably be described as a winner," one analyst said the study concluded. Significantly, PRM-10 had also essentially dismissed conservative claims of the nation's strategic vulnerability in declaring that neither side would benefit by striking first in such a war —since "whichever side initiates a limited nuclear attack against the ICBM forces of the other side will find itself significantly worse off," and vulnerable to retaliation from the surviving missiles and bombers of the other side.[28]

But there had been wide disagreement within the administration over the specific conclusions to be drawn from the review. "There were in fact three PRM-10 crowds—at least three," remembered Jasper Welch. "Early on, there was a question of where in the spectrum between pure deterrence and war-fighting the doctrine should be placed," Harold Brown confirmed. "There were some people who argued that war-winning is possible," Brown noted. "There were other people who said that only minimal deterrence is possible."

Brzezinski in particular challenged the memorandum's central contention that the United States already had sufficient strength to deter the Russians. His concern, he wrote, was not only with "the capabilities of the opponent whom we wished to deter but also his psychological-political predispositions as well as war doctrine." Barely two months after Carter asked Brown to study how dramatic reductions could be made in the nuclear arsenal, Brzezinski's own request to Brown showed that his thinking had taken a different turn entirely. Brzezinski asked Brown, therefore, for "a brief statement of the procedures for conducting war beyond the initial stage," as well as "a statement of the basic objectives to be achieved through limited nuclear options."[29]

A meeting of Carter, Brzezinski, Vance, and Brown in the summer of 1977 to resolve their differences over nuclear strategy produced no agreement beyond the decision that changes in the war plan should be further studied and a new targeting doctrine prepared for their consideration. Neither the president nor his secretaries of state and defense evidently endorsed Brzezinski's argument, the latter wrote, that "our old doctrine was politically and psychologically credible only as long as America was in fact superior"—and hence that there was an urgent need to adjust defense planning to what Brzezinski termed the "new reality."[30]

A further sign of the gap that separated Carter and his cabinet from Brzezinski on the subject appeared in the course of the briefing on the war plan that the group received the same day. Whereas Carter and Vance had reportedly recoiled with the horror typical of initiates into the SIOP—the subject was already long familiar to Brown—Brzezinski questioned the briefing officer in detail on how the United States proposed to fight, and win, the prospective nuclear war.[31]

The stirrings of change in American nuclear policy were evident the following year. By Brzezinski's own account, the "take-off phase" for those changes began in mid-1978, following his visit to the headquarters of the North American Defense Command. That visit had reinforced his belief that American strategic doctrine was "based largely on the experience of the sixties," he wrote, and that as such it was "less and less relevant to the late seventies and is likely to be altogether irrelevant in the eighties." Another sign of the impending shift in nuclear strategy, Brzezinski acknowledged, was the fact that he had by this time given the task of completing the agreed-to revision of the war plan to "a team of collaborators with considerable expertise and capacity for doctrinal innovation."[32]

One of those Brzezinski picked to carry out this revision was Jasper Welch, the Air Force general and former B-team adviser who was also a long-time advocate of the MX.[33]

Welch later drew a sharp distinction between the study of nuclear strategy Carter had originally ordered and Presidential Directive number 59, its eventual result: "PRM-10 was done by one group of Carterites. PD-59 was done by an entirely different crowd." (He noted as well that one staff officer who had taken part in the initial review was so savaged by the bureaucratic infighting over PRM-10 as to be nearly driven to suicide. "It was terrible, . . . terrible," Welch recalled.)

One of the first discoveries in the strategic review conducted by Brzezinski's NSC team was that some of the original goals established during the last revision of U.S. nuclear strategy—the Schlesinger doctrine—had still not been met. "There was in effect a call 'to get on with it,' " Welch remembered.

But the major flaw of previous doctrine, these analysts decided, was its lack of clarity. "It wasn't explicit about the fact that in order to deter the Russians you've got to tell them you're going to ruin their military forces," Welch said. At the time this vagueness had been deliberate: "Most of NSDM-242 did not require you to have any particular view on what a Russian was like. The whole point of it was not to lock future leaders into this particular leadership's view of the Russians, because we hoped to learn more about them over time." But the B-Team report, Welch noted, had finally settled the question of the Russians.

Welch felt the group's proposed revision of the war plan was "really a step in the same general direction" as NSDM-242. "It kept the stay-away-from-cities operations, it kept the China stuff, and it kept the eastern Europe sort of thing." But the result was to add a whole new dimension of sophistication and selectivity to the SIOP. The idea of separating ethnic minorities in the Soviet Union from Russians *per se* on the target list—in order to encourage the disintegration of Soviet power in the aftermath of war—had occurred to the drafters of NSDM-242. But the attempt had not "been profitable" back then, Welch said: "It was hard enough to get the eastern Europeans straightened out."

Improvements in missile accuracy and in military command and control —as well as the inexorable growth of the arsenal due to MIRV over the intervening years—made such selectivity feasible by the time of PD-59, he pointed out. Indeed, Carter's national security adviser had explicitly raised the prospect of ethnic distinctions in targeting during the briefing on the SIOP. "Brzezinski was very proud of saying, 'I want now even to distinguish between the Russians and the non-Russians,' " Welch remembered.

The "biggest hurdle" faced by their revision of the war plan, he thought, "was to make it perfectly clear that nuclear weapons have a very rightful place in a global conflict, not just in a spasm tit-for-tat." Envisioned by the planners were circumstances in which the United States might use nuclear weapons in support of conventional forces—or even to fight alongside former enemies: "Fighting may be taking place halfway between Kiev and Moscow, for all I know. Maybe it's taking place along the Siberia border—which is a fairly likely place for it—with Americans, Chinese, and Russians. But for the planning and for the construction of the thing, it doesn't matter."

As important to the origins of PD-59 as the technological changes since 1974 and the organizational changes that Brzezinski had introduced was the change in the attitude of Carter and other key administration figures toward the proposed "strategic renewal."

Harold Brown perhaps typified this change of view. While an early proponent of MIRV in McNamara's Pentagon, Brown's support for the weapon had seemed to come from an engineer's acceptance of its inevitability rather than from any true enthusiasm. Indeed, his legendary resistance to other technological innovations in weaponry reportedly earned him the Pentagon nickname "Dr. No." In 1975, while on a trip to Russia, Brown had distanced himself from the Schlesinger doctrine by rejecting the concept of nuclear war-fighting, declaring instead his belief that "only deterrence is feasible." Brown had also predicted that counterforce would have little future in nuclear planning by either side. "Facts do in the end prevail, whatever doctrine may assert," he observed on that occasion.[34]

Two years later, as Carter's defense secretary, Brown had seemed intent upon fulfilling his own prophecy when he became a willing supporter—some claimed an originator—of the administration's "deep cuts" proposal in SALT. As late as February 1978, Brown publicly derided the significance of the "window of vulnerability" claims that critics were raising against the administration and arms control. "Even if we did nothing about it," he wrote, "it would not be synonymous with the vulnerability of the United States, or even of the strategic deterrent."[35]

But by 1979—following the Russians' latest missile tests, and amid continuing attacks on the administration by its domestic critics—Brown's opposition to Brzezinski's notions of the new reality in nuclear strategy had begun to waver. "Harold Brown has now become much more interested in greater flexibility and is clearly moving away from a rigid deterrence posture," Brzezinski wrote in his private journal that spring. ("Cy Vance remains concerned and skeptical," he added.)

As if to confirm his change of mind, Brown admitted to the Council of Foreign Relations in April 1979 that "the growing vulnerability of our land-based missile forces could, if not corrected, contribute to a perception of U.S. strategic inferiority that would have severely adverse political—and could have potentially destabilizing military—consequences."[36]

While Brown would anger Brzezinski by not coming out strongly for the MX in their meeting with Carter two months later, he had by then already accepted the argument for the missile—even if a certain ambivalence on his part remained. Brown thus justified his support for the smaller version of the MX as a possible way of achieving progress toward a classic arms control goal: pushing the Russians' strategic deterrent "out to sea" by threatening their vulnerable land-based missiles.[37]

Paralleling Brown's change of mind on nuclear strategy was Carter's apparent change of heart about nuclear weapons. When making his decision on the MX, Carter had reacted to Brzezinski's arguments for the missile, the latter wrote, "by saying that much of the perception of Soviet superiority had been created by 'this group.' " While Carter's remark suggested that he was still personally disinclined to believe the Russians strategically superior, his action conceded the point made long before by his national security adviser "that perceptions can affect the gravity of the problem and that the perception was being created that the Soviet Union was stronger than the United States."[38]

Carter's shift to Brzezinski's point of view was gradual and grudging. But as early as the fall of 1978 he had signed a presidential directive originating in Brzezinski's office which declared that the nation's ability to survive a nuclear war was as important to deterrence as its ability to retaliate against Russian attack. A year later—on the occasion of introducing the SALT II treaty to the Senate—Carter seemed to finally abandon his lifelong dream of abolishing nuclear weapons, and likewise the goal of ending all nuclear testing that he had set at the beginning of his administration. He now professed to find, the president said, "a kind of strange stability" made possible by the possession of such weapons by both sides.

Two months after his speech before the Senate, Carter approved another presidential directive, PD-58, that set an altogether different kind of goal—in Brzezinski's words, "for the first time the United States deliberately sought for itself the capability to manage a protracted nuclear conflict."[39]

The final turning point in Carter's attitude toward nuclear strategy came at the end of 1979 with the Soviet invasion of Afghanistan. It was also that event which provided the catalyst for Brzezinski's order that the strategic directive under study since August 1977 be rapidly completed. In the spring and early summer of 1980—as the administration and the country were increasingly preoccupied by the hostage crisis in Iran—two other presidential directives signed by Carter telegraphed the nature of the impending change in strategy. Both set planning guidelines, therefore, for the reconstruction of America after a nuclear war.[40]

In mid-May of 1980, Brzezinski officially submitted PD-59 to Carter for approval. It contained the most sweeping changes yet in U.S. nuclear strategy, according to Brzezinski: "Till PD-59 was issued American war planning postulated a brief, spasmic, and apocalyptic conflict." The new directive, Brzezinski claimed, "marked an important new step in the evolution of American strategic thought." Carter signed the document that July following surprisingly little discussion of its implications, and after Brzezinski had overcome the objections of both Brown and Vance that a formal directive on the new strategy was unnecessary.[41]

One cause of the long delay in approving PD-59 was opposition within the administration to the change in strategy. Brzezinski's reason for seeking a formal presidential directive was also subtly linked with the fate of new war-fighting weapons like the MX. Previously, the drafters of NSDM-242 had deliberately avoided controversy, Welch noted, by advising only "on what you can do with the weapons you have." By contrast, he said, PD-59 "made the notion of acquiring weapons to better carry out the policy legitimate."

Brown's public announcement of the shift in nuclear strategy in August 1980 downplayed the significance of the change, characterizing it only as "a refinement" of the war-fighting ideas introduced by McNamara and Schlesinger.[42] The fact that the Carter administration chose to make the new strategy public suggested that, as had been the case with the changes introduced by McNamara and Schlesinger, one intended audience for PD-59 was the Russians. The new directive did indeed share some intellectual roots with the Schlesinger doctrine—which itself had gone much further than McNamara had been willing to go in arguing that a controlled nuclear war was possible. But the principal difference between the old strategy and the new was PD-59's assumption that it was not only possible to fight such a war—it was also possible to win it, perhaps decisively.

The theory of victory that was said to be contained in PD-59 revolved around distinguishing the political leadership of Russia as a target from the country's military command and control apparatus. "We were very clear even in '72 that there were two things—one was control over the forces, and the second was the national leadership," Welch said of NSDM-242. The changes that PD-59 introduced to the war plan made it possible to carry that distinction much further—even to the point of being able to "decapitate" the military leadership necessary for the conduct of the war, while at the same time preserving the political leadership needed to surrender. "The decision on what to go after would be decided by the sort of war," Welch confirmed. "Sometimes it would be the political leadership; sometimes the military leadership. Sometimes both; sometimes neither."

Behind PD-59's theory of victory was reportedly also the belief that the highly centralized nature of the communist system made it particularly vulnerable to the chaos and disruption that would inevitably follow a nuclear attack, and hence that this weakness itself might actually compel a Soviet surrender. PD-59 represented yet another break with the past in that it provided an explicit justification for counterforce weapons like the MX.

Welch admitted that PD-59 "didn't break much new ground" in terms of actual war planning. But he thought it a substantial departure in declaratory policy from the nuclear doctrine passed down from Nixon, Kissinger, and Schlesinger: "If you compare it to what was in the presidential document, then it was a whole lot different. There's very little of 242 in substance in the language."

Brown's bland contention that PD-59 represented only an "evolutionary" change in American nuclear strategy convinced few, even in the Carter administration.[43] The skeptics included as well two of his predecessors in the post of defense secretary—McNamara and Schlesinger.

Schlesinger felt that PD-59 represented a "sea change" from the doctrine he had introduced in 1974: "My emphasis had been upon selectivity." That selectivity, Schlesinger complained, had been "drowned out" by the sheer number of weapons added since then to the nation's nuclear arsenal. Equally significant, he thought, was the shift in emphasis with PD-59 "from selectivity and signaling to that of victory"—a shift that had accounted for the increase in the number of potential targets in Russia from 25,000 to 40,000 in only five years. Schlesinger concluded that PD-59 "took logic too far" by spinning out theoretical concepts "in a way that was still barely plausible on paper, but in my guess is not plausible in the real world."

Privately, Brown seemed to share some of Schlesinger's reservations about the new war-fighting doctrine. "I am not at all persuaded that what started as a demonstration, or even a tightly controlled use of strategic forces for larger purposes, could be kept from escalating to a full-scale thermonuclear exchange," he wrote in a personal statement appended to the public exposition of PD-59.[44] At William Kaufmann's suggestion, Brown also excised the controversial term "counterforce" from the directive and replaced it with the term "countervailing." "A countervailing strategy is a strategy that denies the other side any possibility that it could win—but it doesn't say that our side would win," Brown explained.

After he left the Pentagon, Brown conceded that the issue of nuclear war-fighting "had not been handled very well" in the Carter administration: "There were people in the government who believed in protracted nuclear war and even in prevailing in a nuclear war. The outcome was a rather uncomfortable compromise between those people and the people who believed mostly in deterrence."

In retrospect, he thought the origins of countervailing strategy lay in the only consensus that had been reached by the various drafters of PRM-10—on Russia: "What people were finally able to coalesce around is that deterrence requires you to deter the other side—not yourself. Therefore, you have to make some sort of judgment about what that takes. As soon as you say that, you're into very muddy ground—because the question is, 'What does it take to deter the Soviets?' Some people say, 'Well, for the Soviets, they have to know that if they start a war you'll win it.'"

"We started down that path and got into that morass," Brown said. "And PD-59 was the result."

Neither Brown's change in nomenclature nor the administration's repeated assurances that PD-59 was only an "evolutionary" change hid the appearance of a stark transformation in the assumptions behind American nuclear strategy. "It went against everything they believed in," Herman Kahn marveled of PD-59. A critic of the Carter administration on the other side, Paul Warnke, summed up the significance of the change when he claimed that with PD-59 Carter had gone "from MAD to worse."

It was a change, Warnke felt, that was destined to prove unavailing for Carter—either with the Russians or with voters at home. The president's approval of the MX and of PD-59 had been determined not by what either could do to the Russians in the event of nuclear war, Warnke was convinced, but by what both would theoretically achieve for the United States in peacetime diplomacy, by demonstrating American resolve. Another, not incidental purpose behind the decisions, Warnke believed, was to send a signal to the voters concerning Carter's own resolve.

In fact, PD-59 had been leaked to the press—prompting Brown's announcement of the new strategy—only two weeks before the opening of the 1980 Democratic National Convention. "The political side of the house recognized that Carter was perceived as being weak, so they wanted to give him muscles," Warnke said. "Had he been a shoo-in in 1980, there would have been no PD-59."

Warnke felt that at the heart of the administration's choice of a new nuclear strategy had been the same grand political—and strategic—fallacy that brought the nation the MX: "What they didn't realize was that all they were going to do was to reinforce the impression of weakness. It was just such a dramatic change from what they had been saying."

26

The Nuclear Gnostics

The changes introduced to nuclear strategy by Jimmy Carter had become fixed by the end of his presidency—regardless of the misgivings and reservations of those who inspired or approved them. Like McNamara's no-cities idea and the limited nuclear options of the Schlesinger doctrine, the war-fighting theories of PD-59 became part of the nation's war planning when they were incorporated into the latest version of the SIOP—which was itself almost immediately revised by the incoming administration of Ronald Reagan.

Andrew Marshall, the Pentagon official who would preside over the revision of the war plan in the new administration, professed to find "a kind of continuity and an evolution" to those changes that went back to the earliest thinking on nuclear weapons. The greatest break with the past, Marshall thought, was in the scale of the change—the fact that the number of weapons in the world had grown from a mere handful of atomic bombs in the years just after Hiroshima to arsenals containing tens of thousands of hydrogen bombs by the time Damocles approached middle age.

But accompanying the phenomenal increase both in the number and the destructiveness of nuclear weapons during the thirty-odd years since the first bomb was dropped had been a fundamental change of another kind: a growing sense of doubt. Paradoxically, this doubt seemed a legacy of the time when no nuclear weapon was dropped on an enemy and arms control agreements were signed between the two most likely antagonists. Arms control itself, ironically, had become a cause as well as a symbol of that doubt.

Despite SALT—or even because of it—the editors of the *Bulletin of Atomic Scientists* in the twelve years since the signing of the treaties in 1972 gradually moved the hands of their doomsday clock forward, from twelve minutes to only three minutes short of the zero hour by the start of 1984.

Doubt has, in turn, led to apostasy for many of the second generation since Hiroshima. In the fall of 1982, four prominent representatives of the first generation of the bomb—McGeorge Bundy, George Kennan, Robert McNamara, and Gerard Smith—wrote a widely publicized essay in *Foreign Affairs* urging that the American government pledge never to initiate the use of nuclear weapons, but only use them in retaliation against an enemy's atomic attack.

Each of the four, they pointed out, had "served in Administrations which revised their early thoughts on nuclear weapons policy." But the common impetus for their decision to break with the past by urging a course of action once considered heretical was the changed nature of the nuclear threat in the present day. "Questions that were answered largely by silence in the 1950s and 1960s," they wrote, "cannot be so handled in the 1980s." They concluded that it "no longer makes sense—if it ever did—to hold these weapons for any other purpose than the prevention of their use."[1]

The idea for the article came from Kennan, who as early as 1949 had urged that the Truman administration make such a no-first-use pledge. Since heading the SALT negotiations under the Nixon administration, Gerard Smith had come to fear that his accomplishments then were in danger of being undone. In 1969 Bundy had promoted the cause of arms control in a *Foreign Affairs* article titled "To Cap the Volcano." After the no-first-use article appeared, he proposed another major change in American military doctrine: adoption of a stated policy of "lesser retaliation," whereby the United States would respond to the enemy's first use of a nuclear weapon with a bomb smaller in yield. Bundy's proposal was, in effect, a reversal on the "signaling" idea popular at Rand a generation before.[2]

But it was McNamara, the progenitor of war-fighting in the Kennedy administration, whose thinking had undergone the greatest change over the intervening years.

Contrary to the protest of SALT's critics that arms control had gone too far, McNamara believed that "with hindsight, we didn't go far enough." "The whole thing could have been stabilized at a lower level, at a less risky level." McNamara mused that if the United States had, for example, given the Russians "some different signals, maybe we could have held their buildup down."

The foremost lesson McNamara drew from his own long and often bitter experience with nuclear strategy concerned the necessary limitations upon knowledge. He believed it "*absolutely* essential" that the leaders with control over nuclear weapons understand their responsibility from the outset. Indeed, McNamara had a practical suggestion along those lines. He felt it should be a constitutional requirement that the president, the secretary of defense, and all the key people of a new administration pass a one-hundred-hour course on nuclear weaponry—"the strategy, tactics, and potential scenarios involving their use"—before being allowed to assume office.

The beginning of wisdom for those leaders, McNamara thought, would be the acceptance of the two "overriding principles" he said he himself had adopted by the end of his seven years of practical experience with the subject: first, the recognition that "each side must maintain a stable deterrence—a nuclear arsenal powerful enough to discourage anyone else from using nuclear weapons"; second, the realization that "nuclear weapons have no military purpose whatsoever other than to deter one's opponent from their use."[3]

In the fall of 1983, McNamara's apostasy prompted him to recommend some eighteen other specific proposals for the future of arms control. His proposals were inspired, he said, by his feeling that past efforts by governments to limit nuclear weapons—as well as the current popular emphasis upon freezing the number of nuclear weapons in Soviet and American arsenals—had each "failed to address the basic issue": "The issue is not numbers; the issue is nuclear war. And nuclear war is not solely a function of numbers." McNamara's proposals emphasized returning stability to the balance of terror, instead of just a reduction in numbers.

In addition to a no-first-use pledge, this would mean the movement of nuclear weapons away from forward areas in Europe—where they would be overrun in a Soviet invasion unless used at an early stage of that conflict. Other of his proposals were aimed at reducing the number of strategic and tactical nuclear weapons in the West while making those that remained less vulnerable to attack, and at a corresponding increase in conventional forces. (By 1984, hostile reaction to the original no-first-use proposal—especially from the west Europeans—caused McNamara to modify his original idea. He urged that the West immediately announce a policy of "no-early-first-use," and begin a conventional buildup that would allow NATO five years hence to adopt a policy of no-first-use under any circumstances.)

Perhaps the most radical of McNamara's ideas was his suggestion for resolving the paradox that had always existed between the nation's declared policy of deterrence and its actual policy of nuclear war-fighting. In McNamara's revision, only deterrence would remain. Under his plan U.S. policy would announce in advance what it would do—and, more important, not do—with nuclear weapons.

McNamara admitted there "could be some slight reduction in the deterrent as a result of resolving" the long-standing contradiction between declaration and intent. But he thought that this slight erosion would be compensated for by the additional security provided by a conventional buildup. Moreover, any marginal decrease in deterrence, he felt, "would be more than offset by a tremendous reduction in the risk of nuclear war" as a result of accident or miscalculation—by far the greatest risk in his view. The alternative, McNamara claimed, was for the West to continue to put its hopes for peace on the increasingly fragile expectation that deterrence will never fail.

Despite the programmatic nature of the changes that McNamara proposed in American nuclear strategy, their effect would be nothing less than
revolutionary. The two overriding principles whose acceptance McNamara
said was a necessary precondition to his eighteen points represented, therefore, a direct contradiction of what had become one of the most fundamental
tenets of U.S. policy toward nuclear weapons: that it was necessary to
profess belief in the possibility of fighting and winning a nuclear war in order
for deterrence to work.

"Basically, American nuclear policy has been a stated policy of war-
fighting with nuclear weapons—from the beginning," McNamara argued.
In spite of his own efforts to move that policy away from war-fighting after
abandoning the no-cities doctrine—efforts, McNamara admitted, which had
not been entirely successful—the subsequent shift toward a counterforce and
then a countervailing strategy had continued, and even accelerated, that
trend. Yet the result, he thought, had been simply a more dangerous kind
of failure—culminating with PD-59 and its successor in the Reagan administration. "I have *never* had a human being explain to me how you can fight
a nuclear war," McNamara said. "It makes no sense to me."

Apostasy was a common result among those who, like McNamara, reflected on their own efforts to think about—and occasionally plan for—the
unthinkable. In a 1983 conversation, Henry Kissinger commiserated with
McNamara over the failure of their efforts to make sense of the SIOP. The
two men agreed that nuclear war-planning—despite all the energy and talent
that had gone into it—remained, in McNamara's words, "a morass."

Two of McNamara's best-known successors in the post of defense secretary agreed with him that war-planning had gotten out of hand by the 1980s,
but disagreed with him about the solution. "Of late I don't know what it
means," observed James Schlesinger of nuclear war-fighting strategy at the
end of 1983. The first defense secretary to take credit for bringing limited
nuclear options to the SIOP, Schlesinger thought the subsequent evolution
of war-fighting ideas suffered from "Whitehead's fallacy of misplaced con-
creteness": "In the first place, all of this is speculation and hypotheses. Who
the hell has ever tested these things? You wouldn't sell a toaster to the
American public without exposing it to continued tests, and yet here we talk
loosely about what nuclear weapons can do or not do on the basis of no data
at all."

Whatever nuclear war's uncertainties, Schlesinger nonetheless thought
that "the maintenance of credibility is important." The recent crisis in
American nuclear strategy, he felt, was a result of "blabbing about a war-
fighting strategy in order to maintain credibility"—when "credibility is
maintained much more by your demeanor than your words. . . . The name
of the game is to strike a balance between maintaining credibility with your

opponent and not at the same time sounding so damned shrill that you put your allies off."

While he understood the reasons behind his predecessor's change of mind, Schlesinger did not share McNamara's view that the United States should openly abandon its nuclear strategy of war-fighting. McNamara's "deep moral convictions have interfered with his clarity of thought," Schlesinger felt: "In an alliance which explicitly depends on the initiation by the United States of the use of nuclear weapons you cannot depend upon only mutually assured destruction or pure deterrence. That argument now is just as wrong as it was then."

Harold Brown agreed with Schlesinger. Brown, too, thought there was "an intermediate place" between deterrence and war-fighting, though he acknowledged that "it's hard to stop there." "My idea," Brown professed, "always has been that you've got to have these options, and to have as a declaratory policy that you've got these options—that is a way of enhancing deterrence." He continued to believe that "a nuclear war—particularly one involving strategic forces—is likely to escalate into an all-out exchange," Brown said. "On the other hand, I believe that you ought to have some capability to respond to a less than all-out attack with a less than all-out exchange."

It was this rationale, he claimed, that lay behind the change to a counter-vailing nuclear strategy during the Carter administration: "PD-59 is very clear on this. It says that you need the option [to destroy the Soviet leader-ship] but you certainly wouldn't want to use it, except if you had gone to an all-out strategic nuclear war on both sides." Unlike the war-fighting nuclear strategies of the past, the aim of countervailing nuclear strategy was "not 'to prevail,' " Brown said, "but to terminate hostilities at as low a level and at as favorable terms as possible."

Concerning the evolution of nuclear strategy, he felt that "what has varied is the degree of belief that nuclear war can be contained—and that nuclear attack might be usable as an instrument of policy": "It was clearly present in the early McNamara and then absent afterward. I think it returned with Schlesinger." Brown took credit "for pulling back some on the thought that the U.S. might initiate the use of strategic weapons in a previously nonnu-clear situation." However, he said, "I did not pull back to pure deterrence. And I think the Reagan administration has moved on to prevailing in a nuclear war—something I always had second thoughts about."

Apostasy was evident as well on the other side of the nuclear debate by the early 1980s—a result, in part, of the undeniable end of American strategic superiority. Only a year before his death in 1983, Herman Kahn advocated a position of no-first-use similar to the one urged by Bundy, Kennan,

McNamara, and Smith. The effect of Kahn's pledge, however, would have been to put greater—not less—emphasis upon nuclear weapons. Kahn said he was willing, therefore, to accept the disintegration of NATO as the cost of a declaratory policy of no-first-use by the United States. But he thought such a pledge should be balanced by a promise made with equal resolve and publicity that the nation *would* use nuclear weapons if it or its allies were attacked in kind.

Kahn's former Rand colleague Samuel Cohen likewise had changed his mind about nuclear weapons since the days of the think tank's golden age. The self-professed father of the neutron bomb, Cohen admitted to disowning his progeny as a result of the altered strategic equation. Together with Laurence Beilenson—friend and adviser to Ronald Reagan—Cohen announced in a January 1982 essay in the *New York Times Magazine* that he now advocated a new nuclear strategy for the United States, as a result of what he proclaimed to be the old strategy's failure. The creators of the old strategy "had decided unto themselves that the rest of the world would join in their beliefs to preclude the use of nuclear weapons—starting with the Soviets," Cohen charged. "They spun an ideology that flew in the face of common sense."[4]

Cohen said the group he contemptuously called the "firebreakers"— because of their belief in a "firebreak" between the use of conventional and of nuclear weapons—had subsequently found unexpected virtues in a weapon like the neutron bomb when the strategy of mutually assured destruction came under attack. "In contrast to their previous views, they found these things admirable indeed." But Cohen himself had long since concluded that neither the threat of assured destruction nor the rebuilding of conventional forces—nor even the deployment of the neutron bomb—was likely to prove a deterrent to Soviet aggression once American nuclear superiority had ended.

The Soviet Union's relentless military buildup, Cohen said, had caused him to lose his earlier faith that a nuclear war could remain limited. As a result, the new strategy Cohen and Beilenson advocated put more—not less —reliance upon the threat of nuclear weapons in American foreign policy. Like Kahn, Cohen envisioned the day when the United States, because of the relative weakening of its nuclear deterrent, would no longer be able to contain Russia and to protect its allies. When that time came, he thought, the country would face a critical choice: to abandon NATO altogether—or encourage allies like Germany to develop their own nuclear arsenals.

The "Fortress America" nuclear strategy that he and Beilenson championed, Cohen explained, put a premium upon "pushing technology" in the development of new offensive and defensive nuclear weapons. Its eventual adoption was as much a matter of practical necessity as choice, he thought, since the American people would ultimately reject the possibility of a limited nuclear war with Russia as readily as they had already rejected the prospect of a world-ending holocaust in the name of defending Europe. Though Cohen personally believed counterforce to be the best of all possible nuclear strategies, he acknowledged that it was "politically impossible": "What are the American people going to do—watch the war on TV?" he once challenged a counterforce advocate. "The country would just be enveloped by a great panic and the people would demand that we stop the war."

In its almost total emphasis upon nuclear weapons and regaining strategic dominance, the "new" nuclear strategy that Cohen and Beilenson outlined was frankly imitative of what they understood current Soviet doctrine to be. The original inspiration for their idea, Cohen said, had been a dual axiom from the ancient Chinese strategist Sun Tzu: "The best way to defeat an enemy is to defeat his strategy. The best way to defeat his strategy is to adopt it." But Cohen acknowledged that "the essential point" of their article was borrowed from a modern American adaptation of Sun Tzu's wisdom: "If you can't beat 'em—join 'em."

Clearly, the doubts that first gave rise to apostasy have subsequently inspired a prodigious rethinking of the unthinkable on the part of the experts. Out of this has come a kind of gnosticism about nuclear weapons—and a new approach by a second generation of strategic theorists. Like the original gnostics of the Christian faith—the dissident priesthood that radically reinterpreted the apostolic gospels shortly after the death of Christ—the nuclear gnostics consider themselves not so much heretics as possessors of a superior insight.*

An exemplar of the so-called "second wave" of strategists is Colin Gray, a Canadian-born theorist who worked throughout the 1970s as a member of Herman Kahn's Hudson Institute. As coauthor in 1980 of a controversial *Foreign Policy* article whose thesis was contained in its title—"Victory Is Possible"—Gray was one of the first of the new generation of analysts to argue for adoption of an explicit "theory of victory" in nuclear war.[6]

"Such a theory," Gray and his colleague wrote in that article, "would have to envisage the demise of the Soviet state. . . . The United States should plan to defeat the Soviet Union and to do so at a cost that would not prohibit U.S. recovery. . . . Washington should identify war aims that in the last resort would contemplate the destruction of Soviet political authority and the emergence of a postwar world compatible with Western values."

At the heart of the second wave's criticism of its intellectual forebears was

---

*Author Elaine Pagels wrote of these unconventional disciples: "Such gnostics acknowledged that pursuing *gnosis* engages each person in a solitary, difficult process, as one struggles against internal resistance." *Gnosis*—from the Greek for "knowledge" or "insight"—"is not primarily rational knowledge."[5]

Gray's charge that the first wave suffered from "an Armaggedon syndrome." The result, he wrote, is that the prior analyses of nuclear war appeared "to stop when the buttons are pushed." In contrast, Gray professed what he termed the more realistic view that "the United States may have no practical alternative to waging a nuclear war." Gray, indeed, has argued that nuclear weapons can be the instruments of victory over Russia in time of war or peace: "There is no way that the Soviet Union could win, or even draw, a high technology arms race with the United States."[7]

Should war prove nonetheless unavoidable, Gray hypothesized that the highly centralized nature of the communist state might make it uniquely vulnerable to the effects of nuclear war: "The Soviet Union might cease to function if its security agency, the KGB, were severely crippled," he wrote. "If the Moscow bureaucracy could be eliminated, damaged, or isolated, the U.S.S.R. might disintegrate into anarchy," he and his collaborator mused in their Foreign Policy article. Gray went further than most of his second-wave colleagues in suggesting that the United States might even choose to initiate the use of nuclear weapons in circumstances other than retaliation for a Soviet attack.[8]

As radical as the rhetoric of the second wave sounded, behind it were the arguments of more than a generation of critics of American nuclear strategy and arms control policy. Gray's scenario of a Soviet-American nuclear war, and his estimate of the likely number of Americans it would kill, mirrored, for example, the analyses of T. K. Jones and Richard Pipes. Gray's theory of victory acknowledged, as did Nitze's NSC-68, an intellectual debt to Rand analyst Nathan Leites' Operational Code of the Politburo, which inspired Gray's thoughts concerning the Soviet leadership's peculiar vulnerabilities. Elsewhere, Gray attributed his call for "the long overdue review of deterrence" to the inspiration of Donald Brennan.[9]

Not surprisingly, the nuclear gnostics among current strategists have held to basically conservative tenets concerning Russia, the importance of national will, and the political utility of nuclear weapons. "The Soviet military threat," Gray wrote, "tends to be seriously underrated." "The United States must give credible evidence of political will," he once argued regarding the lessons of the Vietnam war—which has a special significance in his analysis. The chief cause of America's failure in Vietnam, Gray charged, lay in the fact that the nation "was not willing to stay the course." But he placed at least equal blame for the defeat there upon the previous generation of American strategists. His predecessors, Gray claimed, had usually been "either wrong or cowardly" in their analysis of the Vietnam war.

The second wave's challenge was not only to the old guard's theories of nuclear strategy but to the values and assumptions of those theorists themselves. Deterrence, Gray wrote in one broadside, "is being brought to us by the same people that gave us Vietnam and a decade and a half of arms control experience, culminating in SALT." It was because of such past failures that Gray called for a "fundamental overhaul" of American strategic thinking—one that would take it away from its founding emphasis upon deterrence, and toward a wider consideration of nuclear war-fighting.[10]

It is not by their arguments but in their outspokenness that Gray and the other members of the second wave have differed most from earlier conservative critics of American nuclear strategy and arms control. They have thus dismissed outright what has passed for the common wisdom on nuclear weapons for nearly forty years. Decrying at the end of the 1970s "what RAND hath wrought," Gray contended that contemporary strategic studies suffered "from the pervasiveness of an attitude of undue respect for the recent past." His analysis specifically rejected what had been axiomatic in American declaratory policy and among American nuclear strategists since Bernard Brodie's famous dictum on deterrence—that military establishments in the atomic age had "almost no other useful purpose" than the prevention of war.[11] Such an attitude, Gray charged, consistently and willfully ignored the political utility of nuclear weapons. The other useful purpose for such weapons beyond preventing war, he argued, was to accomplish the aims of American foreign policy. The first requirement of "extended deterrence" or "deterrence-plus" was accordingly the regaining of American strategic superiority.

On the subject of the arms race as well, where the second wave differed most from previous critics of American nuclear policy and strategy was in the forthrightness of their views. Gray, for example, has been frank in proclaiming his belief that "the cause of international security is well served if the Soviet Union is placed at an enduring disadvantage in the arms competition."[12]

Gray's writings show how the argument of the second wave is less a revision of strategic thinking than its turning full circle. Ironically, his theory of victory gave an indication not only of where American nuclear strategy had been, but of the direction in which it was headed. Thus, in his prediction that "the USSR might disintegrate into anarchy" as the result of a nuclear war, Gray expressed a hope that was in fact the evident expectation of the war plan recently adopted by the Carter administration. The ability of the United States to disarm the Soviet Union by striking first—a capability that McNamara later professed to have been embarrassed by and worried about, and one that Schlesinger thought important only for appearances' sake—was openly sought by Gray as a definite asset. The goal of regaining this kind of strategic superiority was behind his and the second wave's advocacy of a revitalized civil defense program, of the ABM, and of new offensive weapons capable of destroying Soviet missiles in their silos. This goal was the basis for Gray's advocacy of abandoning arms control as inimical to American interests, and likewise the reason why

he supported the land-basing of the MX as a needed expression of national
will. The real significance of Gray and the second wave, indeed, would be
as a symbol of how—in the nuclear gnosticism of the 1980s—the theory of
victory in nuclear war had come to vie with deterrence for the status of
dogma.[13]

It was a sign of the nuclear gnostics' rising influence—as well as of the aging
of the strategists' old guard—that the gauntlet thrown down by the second
wave was not picked up by those who were the target of its critique. The
gradual confounding of nuclear strategy and of arms control over the last
generation occurred not because the champions of MAD and SALT had
been vanquished, but because they had—for the most part—chosen to flee
the field.

Bernard Brodie, in a rebuttal to Gray, repudiated the argument that
nuclear deterrence became outmoded with the end of American strategic
superiority. But Brodie essentially agreed with Gray's criticism of the "nuts-
and-bolts Rand types," and with his point about the failure of the strategists
in the case of Vietnam.[14]

Another prominent representative of the first wave of civilian strategists,
William Kaufmann, thought, with Brodie, that the nation should put a
declining rather than an increasing emphasis upon nuclear weapons. Kaufmann in the early 1980s considered that not much fundamental had changed
in the twenty years since he advised McNamara on nuclear weapons, despite
the new technologies and the changing vogue in strategies and strategists:
"The state of the art is not much different now. It's a stalemate. But,
unfortunately, neither side seems willing to recognize that it's a stalemate."

The originator of the no-cities doctrine dismissed as "silly" and as "airy,
fairy talk" the theories of Gray and other second-wave theorists on fighting
a controlled and limited nuclear war. Behind those theories, Kaufmann
thought, was a hidden and repressed longing for the lost "nuclear Acadia"
of American strategic superiority—a world that had always existed more in
the minds of the nation's theorists than of its leaders: "I've yet to see a
president who wasn't absolutely scared out of his mind by these things."

Kaufmann equally dismissed the second wave's argument concerning the
political utility of nuclear weapons, blaming the unintended consequences
of SALT for what he felt was the bomb's undeserved prominence: "The
irony is that the effort to gain some control over the weapons has overdrama-
tized their importance. Politically, they are of less significance than the
Grand Fleets of World War One. But they provide a backdrop. They put
limits—they cast a shadow." The present error, Kaufmann said, was to
make nuclear weapons "a centerpiece—rather than something that you have
to have in the closet."

Thomas Schelling—in 1960 called "the father of arms control"—was another pioneering strategist who blamed the good intentions behind SALT for creating the arms control dilemma of the 1980s. "The SALT process," he claimed, had "gotten perverted to where it was 180 degrees from its original intent." Like others among the missionaries, crusaders, and—finally —apostates of Rand, Schelling declared himself "not much impressed by any of the new wave people," and doubtful that their contribution was worthwhile, or even original: "By now you have people who were too young to be reading what was written twenty years ago, so they're laboriously working out the stuff that people worked out twenty years ago."

Since the end of the Vietnam war, Schelling admitted, his own interest had shifted from nuclear strategy to domestic issues like energy policy. His most recent writings on nuclear strategy concerned what he thought was the most likely kind of nuclear peril—a threat by terrorists to explode an atomic bomb in a major city. The "compellence" strategy that Schelling had initially applied to Vietnam now found application only in teaching people how to quit smoking. His reasons for leaving the field of strategy were, Schelling said, diverse. But foremost among them was the change that resulted from Vietnam: "I lost the access, I lost the audience, and I lost the motivation."[15]

Like the nuclear strategists, the atomic scientists as a group seemed as badly split in the early 1980s as they were at the time of the ABM debate or the Super decision, and over the same basic issues. There was, Wolfgang Panofsky and Spurgeon Keeny acknowledged, nothing new in the argument of their 1981/82 *Foreign Affairs* essay that there could be no technological solution to the arms race, despite the counterforce weaponry and doctrines developed by what they called the "nuclear-use theorists" over the past thirty years. "The NUTs approach to nuclear war-fighting will not eliminate the essential MAD character of nuclear war," they reiterated in their article. Their point was the same one Keeny and Panofsky had emphasized fifteen years earlier, in the wake of the Gaither report: "The thesis that we live in an inherently MAD world rests ultimately on the technical conclusion that effective protection of the population against large-scale nuclear attack is not possible."[16]

Keeny and Richard Garwin thought there had been, as well, an almost palpable sense of *déjà vu* among the scientists attending a conference on the prevention of nuclear war that summer. There seemed even a kind of symbolic presentiment about the conference's location—at Erice, in Sicily, near the legendary site where Odysseus had eluded the Cyclops. During the Second World War the surrounding region of Trapani had been heavily bombed in a campaign planned, in part, by one of the British scientists at the conference. The Englishman noted with wry irony how five thousand

tons of explosives had done terrible damage to the area during the war—
but that the group now assembled was talking about a war in which five
thousand million tons of explosives might be used.[17]

At Erice, Edward Teller had presented his now familiar case for the more
rapid development or deployment of weapons like the neutron bomb, the
B-1 bomber, and the MX. But Teller also lobbied for what he called a
promising "third generation" of nuclear weapons; these would include nu-
clear-pumped, space-based lasers and particle-beam weapons more accurate,
more discriminating, and hence more suitable to defensive use than their
predecessors. While "in the early days of the atomic bomb the most obvious
application was destruction," Teller told the conferees, "today the more
difficult but at the same time more relevant part of the development is the
development of defense—defense against atomic weapons, defense against
every kind of weapon, defense by atomic weapons, defense by every other
kind of conceivable weapons and invention." Readily acknowledging that
his proposal was not "novel," Teller nonetheless expressed "the hope that
this might be the last of these changes."[18]

Another familiar theme repeated by Teller at Erice was the importance
of civil defense—which he thought the Russians, at least, had come to
realize. "With preemptive evacuation they could hold casualties to within
5 percent of their population," he had claimed the previous year. "They
could wipe us out, really wipe us out—end us as a nation—using only a
fraction of their arms and still have enough to force every other country on
earth with the possible exception of China to deliver to them everything they
asked for—food, machinery, and slave labor."

Because of the situation of Soviet strength that existed in the 1980s, Teller
said, he no longer advocated the nationwide system of fallout shelters he had
promoted in the 1960s. Instead, he thought the superiority of America's
transportation system gave the United States a natural advantage over
Russia—if the United States adopted the Soviets' attitude toward civil defense. Teller claimed that preparation for the evacuation of American cities
in a time of crisis "could be done in such a cheap and such an inconspicuous
way" that the Soviets "wouldn't even try to attack."

As he had for the past decade or more, Garwin challenged Teller's contention that Soviet achievements in civil defense and in rocketry had made
traditional concepts of deterrence dangerously obsolete. Garwin explicitly
rejected the premise behind the latest changes in American nuclear strategy
—branding as "bizarre," for example, the "notion that the leaders of the
Soviet Union will be more deterred by knowing that there is a nuclear
warhead with their name on it." He likewise opposed spending money on
building new weapons when the modernization of existing ones would, he
argued, serve the purpose of deterrence.

But, beyond his critique of Teller, Garwin offered his own panoply of technological "fixes" for the problems of the arms race.[19] As well as the SUM idea of small submarines he and Drell had proposed earlier, these included some highly imaginative solutions to the hypothetical vulnerability of Minuteman based upon the "fratricide" effect Garwin and others had learned about at Los Alamos in the early 1950s—such as surrounding missile silos with steel rods to predetonate Soviet warheads the instant before they landed on their target, or even deliberately exploding U.S. nuclear weapons on American soil so that the resulting debris might destroy incoming Soviet warheads.

More controversial still was Garwin's revision of his earlier idea of solving the vulnerability problem by planning to launch land-based missiles upon warning of an attack—an idea that once prompted Wohlstetter to brand Garwin "a high-IQ madman." The physicist now proposed that the United States declare it would launch its missiles upon assessment that a Soviet attack was already underway—an assessment that Garwin felt could be made with virtual certainty by computer-connected sensors, before the nation's missiles and bombers were destroyed.[20]

Neither the original idea nor this revision, however, received much favorable notice from his colleagues. Launch on assessment, Garwin complained, was "a very good idea that was almost universally rejected—rejected by the people who wanted to spend money on new weapons, and rejected by most arms controllers—who say that anything is better than turning our fate over to computers."

An unintended result of the Erice conference was to show how—despite the stark contrast between the 1940s and the 1980s—the substance of the scientists' disagreement had remained essentially unchanged from the days of the first atomic bomb. Even the participants at the conference on the prevention of nuclear war likened the proceedings to a dialogue of the deaf.

"Teller just believes in technology," Garwin said of the meeting. "He fears and hates the Russians, just like so many central Europeans. They confuse the symptoms with the disease."

Teller himself thought the meeting at Erice showed how the "hawks" and the "doves" had switched sides since the early nuclear debate: "The doves were for MAD and for the building of more weapons, particularly by the Russians—or at least were not opposed to that—and they talked about how that was the way to avoid war. The hawks talked about really terrible things —like civil defense and ABM, stopping missiles and saving lives."

"A hawk is someone who wants to save lives," he said bitterly. "A dove is someone who wants to destroy as many lives as possible. Furthermore, this is logical. Because a dove is someone who believes that nuclear war is so terrible that it must be punished by the destruction of the human race —and if that should not happen all by its own, then we should do everything in our power to make it a reality."

What was most striking about the exchange at Erice was how little, not how much, things had changed among the atomic scientists in the years since Hiroshima. He was "deeply disappointed," Teller informed Garwin privately, by the latter's opposition to the development of new weaponry following his earlier work on such projects as the Super. Reportedly, Teller told colleagues that the outbreak of World War Three, should it occur, would be partly Garwin's fault. The disaffection of Garwin and other scientists, Teller said, was a cause of his own sleepless nights at the conference. He had thought about going home, Teller told a friend, but he had decided to stay to prevent Garwin from doing any more damage.

The passage of time—and even the inclusion of the Russians in a second Erice conference a year later—did nothing to lessen the distance between the American scientists. Garwin, in fact, described the discord at Erice in the summer of 1982 as "mind-boggling": "There was much greater dissent on the American side than there was between the Americans and the Soviets."

But there had been at the first conference one important departure from the past that was certainly obvious to all. Garwin saw it in the fact that among the traditional greetings and best wishes which foreign governments sent to their scientists at the conference, the telegram from the White House had been addressed not to the U.S. delegation as a whole, but to Edward Teller personally. Keeny saw it in the dramatic "prophecy" with which Teller had shocked the scientists at the end of the conference, in the course of a speech that had chronicled the long distrust of East and West since Neville Chamberlain's sacrifice of Czechoslovakia at Munich.

At the end of his speech, Teller said that "looking at past developments, looking at the lack of determination and unity in the West, looking at the continuing success of the Soviet Union (not in making its people more content but in extending its power), I predict that the Soviet Union will win."

In the stunned silence that followed this remark, however, Teller had immediately qualified his prediction with the observation that the West might yet be saved—"by a miracle." One such miracle had already occurred, he said, with the election the previous year of Ronald Reagan.

27

The Least Miserable
Option

It may be that the most notable result of the 1980 election was the Reagan administration's success in transforming—at least for a while—what a few years earlier had been regarded as heresy into something approaching common wisdom in the government. The change that the nuclear gnostics of the Reagan administration brought to American strategy and policy on the bomb was evident in the government's revised planning for nuclear war, its reform of arms control, and its announced intention of developing and deploying a new generation of nuclear weapons.

As in Carter's presidency, the depth and extent of the new administration's break with the past was at once indicated by the president's appointments. Laurence Beilenson and B-team chairman Richard Pipes both served as advisers during his campaign, and reportedly continued to influence Reagan after his election. Eugene Rostow, Paul Nitze, and Nitze's fellow Belmont House conferee Richard Perle all assumed leading, if competing, roles in formulating and carrying out the administration's approach to arms control. Colin Gray joined the General Advisory Committee on Arms Control and Disarmament. Nitze's technical expert, T. K. Jones, was appointed to a high-level post at the Pentagon. Rand veterans Andrew Marshall and Fred Iklé as well as counterforce advocate Jasper Welch were picked to carry out the traditional review of nuclear strategy that the president ordered during his first few weeks in office. In a symbolic step, Reagan reconstituted the President's Foreign Intelligence Advisory Board that Carter had abolished, placing at its head Edward Teller.

However ideologically disparate they might be on other issues, all of Reagan's appointees and advisers seemed united in their criticism of the military and political *status quo* inherited by the administration. All seemed to share, too, a common belief in the political utility of nuclear weapons.

Rostow had for some years publicly blamed America's failure in Vietnam upon the loss of American strategic superiority over Russia. Pipes branded "pernicious" Kissinger's suggestion in 1974 that the concept of strategic superiority had become meaningless. Perle felt that the frustration of Israeli military aims in the 1973 war with Egypt—contrasting with Israel's decisive victory in the 1967 war—was in part the result of Soviet nuclear blackmail made possible by the Russians' expanding strategic arsenal. The neo-conservative editor of *Commentary,* Norman Podhoretz—said to be another informal adviser to the Reagan administration—went the furthest in attributing political significance to the loss of American strategic superiority. Podhoretz reportedly claimed that the hostage crisis in Iran was a result of President Carter's decisions to cancel the B-1 bomber and not to deploy the neutron bomb.[1]

To the rank of experts whose collective voice had been dominant in the nation's defense policies for more than a generation, the rise to prominence within the government of the B-team alumni and the members of the Committee on the Present Danger marked a stunning and portentous change. "This crowd is different from every other," observed one arms control veteran. "There is no one among them who has any sympathy for the SALT process."[2] Herbert York was another who deplored the fact that those he termed "the crazier analysts" had risen to positions of influence and authority.[3]

Spurgeon Keeny and Richard Garwin claimed the change in personnel was symptomatic of an equally fundamental shift in official attitudes toward the Russians, nuclear weapons, and nuclear war.

"Many of the people who were instrumental in proposing candidate Reagan," Garwin said, "had a clear idea that we must build a capability to disarm the Soviet Union—to disarm them and destroy them—because the Soviets are unreliable, not understandable, they don't believe in God, they don't believe in capitalism, and therefore they can't have anything for us but malevolence." It was this motivation that Garwin blamed for the administration's buildup of nuclear weaponry—a buildup unprecedented in the United States since the Kennedy years: "They believe we can't lose by pursuing this route because either we will be able to use it, or we will be able to use it politically to coerce them, or—if the Soviets manage to get this capability—they will destroy themselves economically."

Keeny agreed with Garwin that the Reagan administration was a "watershed" in American nuclear strategy: "What's different now is that a lot of people who are in charge look at counterforce not as a broader deterrent but as part of the acceptability of war. A lot of them think that nuclear warfighting is not only possible, but very probable. . . . There is a big difference between just declaring this policy and actually believing it."

Keeny's chief concern was that the Reagan administration might in effect have "a secret agenda" that would mean the end of arms control. He feared the government's unstated intention was to abandon the existing SALT agreements by building a new generation of weapons, like the ABM, currently proscribed by arms control treaties. The development of such new weapons, Keeny argued, would in turn create pressures for resuming atmospheric nuclear testing and thus abrogating the twenty-year-old partial test ban treaty. The effect of the subsequent unrestrained buildup of nuclear weapons by both the United States and Russia would be to undermine efforts to stop the spread of nuclear weapons to other nations, whose leaders— pointing to the precedent of the "crazy Americans," Keeny said—would finally abandon the 1968 nonproliferation treaty and build their own bombs: "Then all the accomplishments of the last twenty-five years will be undone."[4]

Like the second wave of nuclear strategists, the Reagan appointees proved distinct from their predecessors not only in their attitudes but in their outspokenness—particularly in the case of the government's revised planning for nuclear war.

By the spring of 1982 the reassessment of American nuclear strategy called for by the administration had produced a comprehensive five-year "Defense Guidance" for the government. This document—dubbed Reagan-13—differed in some significant ways from its precursor, PD-59. While the avowed purpose of the latter had been to deny victory to the Russians in a nuclear war, the Reagan administration's Defense Guidance reportedly detailed for the first time how such a war could be decisively won by the United States. Reagan-13 pursued this point in contending that victory might not necessarily result from a brief exchange, but could be the final outcome of a "protracted" nuclear conflict lasting weeks, months, or— conceivably—even years. The Defense Guidance also raised the future prospect of fighting a protracted nuclear war in outer space.[5]

In some respects Reagan-13 was representative less of a major innovation in war planning than of a return to an even earlier way of thinking. Like the second wave, its chief novelty was its explicitness. But genuinely new was the evidence that at least some of its authors accepted without question the declarations they made concerning a winnable nuclear war—instead of merely professing that belief for the sake of making the idea of war-fighting more credible. Significantly, the unspecified goal of "prevailing" over the Soviet Union in the event of a nuclear war—stricken from American war plans since the Kennedy years—was explicitly reinstated as the U.S. aim in Reagan-13.

The break that SIOP-6 and Reagan-13 made with the past was perhaps most evident in the matter of targeting. The decision not only of when but of where to drop the bombs of a nuclear war had always been as much a political as a military question—as it was in 1945 when Kyoto and Tokyo were taken off the target list for the first atomic bomb, and later when Moscow and Leningrad were deleted as "prompt" targets in early war plans.

Starting in the 1960s, at least the illusion of restraint had been introduced to targeting, as the most destructive bombs were withdrawn from the American nuclear arsenal and the accuracy of missiles was increased. But the advent of MIRV had counteracted that trend by dramatically increasing the number of warheads on those missiles. As the number of designated targets in Russia rose correspondingly, some war planners began to express private doubts that the devastation resulting even from a supposedly controlled and limited nuclear war would be recognizably less than that of the "spasm" war planned for in the 1960s. SIOP-6—which allegedly targeted the entire political and military leadership of the Soviet Union, reportedly identifying some sixty "military" targets in Moscow alone—gave further cause for those doubts.[6]

Despite the magnitude of the changes in war planning over the years, Reagan administration officials like Andrew Marshall professed to find an essential continuity in the SIOP. In 1947, while defending the decision to bomb Hiroshima, Henry Stimson, Truman's former secretary of war, had characterized the atomic bombing of Japan as America's "least abhorrent choice." Overseeing the changes made thirty-five years later in the latest version of the U.S. plan for a nuclear war, Marshall claimed his effort was similarly that "of looking for the least miserable option."

Marshall specifically defended the premise of a controlled nuclear war. Reagan-13 and SIOP-6 had borrowed that premise from the nuclear strategy of the Carter administration, and then taken it further by detailing how the Soviet military and political leadership might be blinded, deafened, and ultimately beheaded by nuclear weapons. "People say that limited strikes are not very attractive," Marshall pointed out. "The question is, what the hell *is* attractive at that point?"

Marshall acknowledged that the Reagan administration's revision of war planning reflected a change from what American strategic doctrine had been in the recent past. To him, the most important change was that the United States had essentially decided to adopt the Soviets' approach to nuclear strategy. He believed that the Russians had "never, ever, even remotely" accepted the premise behind assured destruction. Marshall thought the assumption that they had—upon which he felt past American nuclear strategy and arms control policy was based—to be "in the first place arrogant, and [to] assume in some ways that we understand this better than they do." He said of the Russians, "They have had here, as in a number of other areas, probably a sounder and more intelligent doctrine than we have."

The United States, Marshall felt, had been consistently at a disadvantage as a result of the "asymmetry" in Soviet and American attitudes toward nuclear war. He conjectured that the Russians had "always had an underlying assumption that there really might be a nuclear war, and hence that you really have to prepare for how you would conduct yourself in that."

Similarly, he said, the Reagan administration had instituted changes in strategy based upon its view of the Russians and of nuclear war: "It's not a matter of trying to deter *anybody*—especially somebody like ourselves—but somebody like *them.* It's a question of saying, How do they keep score? What do they think is important? What are the objectives that they have—would have—if it came to the brink of using these weapons?"

Marshall conceded that behind the answers to those questions were, indeed, "perceptions in a way." "But you've got to distinguish between assessments and real calculations. You're trying to deter somebody like *that*—who doesn't think that a nuclear war is automatically the end of the world; who thinks that there is a hereafter, and that it will matter where their armies stand, whether they control Eurasia in the outcome. Are they an embattled country with hordes of Chinese streaming over the border and the east Europeans in revolt? The outcome *matters.* "

Marshall also thought the different ways that East and West depicted nuclear war was an indication of how the social psychology of Americans and western Europeans differed from that of the Russians. "In the fifties we were more or less serious about this sort of thing," he said of the Western attitude. But all that had changed, he felt, in the intervening years: "If you look at American and European movies that deal with this problem at all, they all deal with the crisis—the tension leading up to the use of nuclear weapons or the start of the war—and the war in the movie ends with the screen filled with mushroom clouds and so on. Now the Russians, of course, don't make movies about this. They're a society where they don't even publish plane crash accidents. They're not a society that evokes this kind of thing except at a level in a factory where people go through drills or in schools. But they're not making movies. If there were such a movie—my script for their movie—it's people digging out of the rubble and facing up to the challenge of the survival of the state six months after the big exchange."

Marshall imagined that any future nuclear war between the United States and the Soviet Union might initially follow the pattern of the strategic bombing conducted by Germany and Britain during the early part of the Second World War—where both sides had started out by deliberately aiming at military targets, avoiding attacks on cities, until eventually populations were bombed along with industries. "They really edged their way into this. Not because of the lack of capabilities, but because they didn't really want to start it."

It was for just such a protracted—and unpredictable—war that Marshall felt the Reagan administration's Defense Guidance provided: "Your opponent might have a substantial number of nuclear weapons that he might be planning to hit you with, periodically at six-month intervals. Unless you have some way of protecting yourself or deterring further use, you'll be defenseless."

In one way Marshall's views on fighting a nuclear war complemented those of his Pentagon colleague T. K. Jones on defending against a Soviet attack. Like Marshall's advice that the United States should emulate the Russians' strategic doctrine, Jones' recommendation to the Reagan administration was that the nation adopt a "Soviet-style civil defense program," combining evacuation with fallout shelters.[7]

Conceding that such an extensive program was "not suitable" for the United States at the time, Jones nonetheless thought that Soviet practices could be adapted to American culture. Rather than the ten hours of pick-and-shovel work by ten people that would build an adequate shelter according to Russian manuals, Jones suggested that American suburbanites could take six hollow-core doors, wrap them with plastic sheeting, and use them to cover a hastily dug trench in the backyard—an expedient, Jones added, which would incidentally also solve the ethical dilemma raised during the 1960s about admitting neighbors to the family's backyard shelter.

Jones believed with Marshall that there was a vital difference between Soviet and American attitudes toward nuclear war, and a corresponding asymmetry between the nuclear strategies of the two countries: "U.S. strategy is like poker while the Soviets' is like chess. If we bluff and lose, we lose the game. If the Soviets bluff and lose, they only lose one piece."

Unlike the United States, the Soviets, he said, "have prepared for social control" in the event of nuclear war. The Russians, Jones claimed, "reject the notion that all will die, whereas the West has convinced itself that it should surrender if threatened": "This is something that started with *On the Beach* and slowly evolved into this. Elements of the scientific community abetted it in the belief that if they could convince the Russians then the situation would be stalemated." A prerequisite for any substantive change in civil defense programs, he thought, was a change in the popular attitude of Americans toward the subject.

Significantly, Jones' own admitted optimism on the subject of humanity's surviving a nuclear war found its inspiration in an incident that occurred while he was on a skiing vacation in the Colorado Rockies, when a powerline had blown down onto a road and blocked traffic in the midst of a blizzard. Jones, a passenger in one of the stuck cars, sensed an incipient panic building among those trapped in the stalled vehicles during the rising storm—until one of the skiers had gotten out of his car and attempted to move the wire, inspiring others to join him in the effort. To Jones the episode had demonstrated the difference that team effort—and the initiative of a single individual—could make in a moment of crisis.

Acknowledging that a Soviet attack upon American Minuteman silos would certainly cause "inconvenience in St. Louis," Jones argued that it would nonetheless still be possible for the average Missourian to survive within a mile of a one-megaton nuclear blast by taking cover in a rudimentary shelter dug with a shovel in less than ten hours. It would be necessary to stay in the shelter for from five to seven days, he claimed, leaving it only a few moments each day—"for sanitary reasons and to get water"—before evacuating the area for one less contaminated by fallout. "A little bit of Yankee ingenuity," Jones said, would make it possible for citizens to gauge the danger of radiation exposure for themselves—by constructing a simple dosimeter "from plastic and tin cans from the kitchen."

Jones' interest in preparing to survive a Soviet attack was not limited to passive methods of defense. As a deputy undersecretary in the Pentagon's research and engineering directorate, his concern was likewise with reviving the inquiry into the feasibility of an active defense against missiles. There had been two important changes since the original ABM debate which made the issue worth raising again, he felt. "Technology was primitive back then," he said, "but it is now improved." Yet equally important to the more sanguine prospects for an ABM was the change in American assumptions concerning the Russians and arms control—a change that Reagan's election itself signified, in Jones' view: "The assumption back then was that the Soviets would agree with the United States on arms control. But the controllers didn't reckon with the expansion of the Soviet arsenal that allows them to hold forces in reserve to threaten us."

Jones' related concern was with updating the nuclear war-planning that the administration had inherited to reflect these changes in technology, attitudes, and assumptions. Previously, the plans had been "geared to a single action of button-pushing and that's it," he noted. "But we have to be able to hold these weapons and still control them." His specific interest was in modernizing the U.S. command and control of nuclear weapons so that once war was begun the United States could direct its escalation and its termination, and afterward maintain what Jones termed its "postwar power and influence."

In order to assure the Soviets that this nation would be able not only to survive a nuclear war but to prosecute it to victory, Jones proposed to supplement the existing National Emergency Airborne Command Post—the so-called "knee-cap" plane—with a number of specially designed underground command posts. His plan was to inform the Russians that the destruction of those bunkers would actually make it easier—not harder—for the United States to launch its missiles, thereby giving the Soviets the greatest possible incentive not to attack American command-and-control targets.

Jones acknowledged that the resulting system—dubbed "fail-deadly" by some—would be a logical reversal of the fail-safe policy that the United States had adopted in the 1960s to assure there would be no accidental or unauthorized use of nuclear weapons. But he felt the exigencies of the new situation warranted a complete change of view on the subject. He could even envision the circumstance in a Soviet-American nuclear war, Jones said, "where, at the extreme, a disgruntled citizen could twist two wires together and launch a missile."

The Reagan administration's nonconforming view of nuclear war was matched by its iconoclastic approach to arms control. Former Carter administration figures charged that Reagan's choice of men to represent the United States in the SALT talks and in negotiations with the Soviets on limiting the deployment of missiles in Europe revealed a far greater interest in rearmament than arms control. The appointment of Eugene Rostow to head the Arms Control and Disarmament Agency, of Paul Nitze to represent the United States in the so-called Euromissile talks, and of Edward Rowny—whose highly publicized defection from the SALT II negotiations in 1978 recalled the circumstances of Nitze's own resignation four years earlier—to initiate the parallel Strategic Arms Reduction Talks with the Russians occasioned wry comment from critics about "foxes guarding the henhouse." Adding to this impression was the acknowledged influence of the Pentagon's Fred Iklé and Richard Perle in formulating the administration's arms control policy.

One outspoken critic of that policy, Paul Warnke, branded his successors in ACDA "the extended deterrence group." "They have the idea of our nuclear force as being the rock on which the renaissance of the West was built in 1945, so they're for extended deterrence," he said. But Warnke thought the Reagan administration's interest in exploiting the supposed political utility of nuclear weapons beyond deterrence essentially antithetical to the whole purpose of arms control—in that extended deterrence involved regaining nuclear superiority and making first-strike threats. Behind it, moreover, was an attitude that almost certainly doomed serious efforts at negotiation. "When you have Ed Rowny reporting to Dick Perle there's no chance of getting anywhere," Warnke protested.

Warnke's former deputy at ACDA, Spurgeon Keeny, concurred. "If they wrote their own treaty they wouldn't support it," Keeny said of Reagan's arms control appointees. Indeed, Keeny thought them likely to oppose any agreement with the Russians out of principle—for fear that it might create a popular mood of false security, and hence imperil their planned defense buildup.

Early in his tenure as ACDA's director, Eugene Rostow admitted that the administration's new approach toward arms control was not to build upon the past but to depart from it. As a symbol of that departure, Rostow himself coined the START acronym that was to distinguish the upcoming series of negotiations with the Russians from the twelve-year-old SALT process.

Rostow thought that the administration's different outlook toward the Russians and arms control was evident early in Reagan's term—in the deliberations, for example, of a high-level committee on strategy chaired by CIA director William Casey. There was, Rostow recalled, a "general consensus" in the Casey committee "that the Russians had a lot of hostages to fortune." The committee felt, Rostow said, that the Russians had previously benefited in their diplomatic dealings with the West by taking the initiative and playing what he termed "the cow-in-the-parlor game": "They would bring a cow into the parlor and then offer to negotiate to take it out." The view of the Casey committee was that the Russians would not begin to negotiate seriously with the West until their own vital interests around the world came under similar diplomatic and even military pressure—in what one member of the administration would liken to "a full-court press."[8]

While sympathetic to the administration's goals, conservative veterans like Rostow and Paul Nitze sometimes found occasion to object to the methods urged upon the government in its approach to the Russians and arms control—especially by some of its younger and more ideologically inclined members. As early as 1950, in the drafting of NSC-68, Paul Nitze had argued the case for demonstrating a public willingness to negotiate with the Russians just for its political effects at home, irrespective of the prospects for an agreement. But thirty years later both he and Rostow evidently believed that the result of a generation and a half of arms racing, during which both sides had had setbacks and advances, had been to increase the chances that the Soviets would agree to limitations or even reductions in the number of nuclear weapons.

Rostow thus thought that Russia's protracted economic failure and recent signs of disintegration in the Soviet empire showed the leaders of the Kremlin to be "terribly strained": "They ought to want a period of stabilization in their relations with the West." But despite his own professed belief that "there's no way of *not* having arms control," there had been, Rostow acknowledged, from the outset a contrary strain of thinking in the Reagan administration. He felt himself "caught between the group that wanted an agreement with the Russians at any price and the group that wanted no agreement at all," Rostow said.

Among the latter Rostow included members of the "Madison group"— young ideologues who, when they had met weekly at Washington's Madison Hotel over lunch to discuss ways of blocking SALT II during the Carter administration, had been his allies. As an influence upon the Reagan ad-

ministration, however, the Madison group had become an obstacle to progress in Rostow's view. Its neo-conservative membership represented, he felt,
an altogether different tradition from the old-line conservativism with which
he and Nitze were identified—which traced its roots back to an internation-
alism that predated Pearl Harbor. Rostow thought the Madison group, by
contrast, "neo-isolationist," and "distrustful of all foreigners—including our
allies as well as the Russians."[9]

An example of what he considered the Madison group's baleful effect
upon arms control was the role played by Richard Perle—whom Rostow
considered its intellectual leader—in introducing the so-called "zero option"
to the Euromissile talks. Made public by the administration in the fall of
1981—less than two weeks before the talks on limiting short-range nuclear
missiles were to begin in Geneva—the zero option proposed that the Russians dismantle the entire force of SS-20 missiles they then had trained on
western Europe in exchange for a promise from the United States not to
deploy a planned force of cruise and Pershing II missiles still under development. While both accepted it as an opening gambit in the Geneva talks,
neither Nitze nor Rostow ever considered the zero option a serious negotiating proposal.

"It didn't take much astuteness to see that it was absolutely unacceptable
to the Russians," Rostow said. The fact that Perle, when presenting the zero
option to the administration, had urged there be no "fallback" position for
the United States in the Euromissile talks confirmed Rostow's opinion that
there were those in the government who opposed any agreement with the
Russians over the missiles in Europe. ("The interesting thing about that
proposal is that it originated with people who did not believe in arms
control," observed a former defense secretary about the zero option. "The
fact that it was not negotiable was not a disadvantage in their view.") But
the chief complaint that Rostow and Nitze had to the proposal was its
seemingly willful disregard of allied public opinion, already in outcry against
the cavalier statements of other Reagan officials concerning the Russians
and nuclear war.

What Rostow came to consider the showdown between the nuclear gnostics of the Reagan administration and the conservative veterans of arms
control came about nearly eighteen months after the start of the Euromissile
negotiations in Geneva. It resulted from an entirely new proposal originating with Nitze in the midsummer of 1982, and approved by Rostow as head
of ACDA.

Under the terms of Nitze's plan, the Russians would have had to destroy
more than 150 of the SS-20 missiles aimed at western Europe. In exchange,
the United States would agree to forgo deployment of the Pershing II
ballistic missile, whose ability to strike targets deep inside Russia with
unprecedented speed and accuracy reportedly made it the subject of the

Soviets' greatest concern at Geneva. The projected American force in Europe would instead be made up exclusively of three hundred cruise missiles—pilotless drones able to avoid detection and interception by flying near the ground and also capable of great accuracy. Since the subsonic cruise missile would take much longer than a ballistic missile to reach its target, however, and had insufficient range to penetrate deep within Russia, it did not pose as much of a first-strike threat as the Pershing II.[10]

His proposal was, Nitze reflected, "about as good a compromise as you could work out"—with the two hundred ten MIRVed warheads on the Russians' ballistic missiles roughly balancing the three hundred single warheads of the slower U.S. cruise missiles. Presented personally by him to his Soviet counterpart, Yuli Kvitsinsky, in the course of a mid-July stroll through a Swiss forest—where the two men had gone to avoid electronic eavesdropping—Nitze's simple page-and-a-half proposal had elicited an initially positive response. The governments of Germany and France, when briefed on the proposal by Rostow before he returned home, were reportedly also enthusiastic.

The reactions of the two governments most directly involved were, however, perceptibly cooler. Though the idea allegedly aroused the interest of Soviet foreign minister Gromyko, there was no sign from Moscow for two and a half months regarding the acceptability of the American proposal.[11]

When Nitze's so-called "walk-in-the-woods" formula was discussed at the first of two NSC meetings in Washington that summer, there had been no strong opposition to it—although the president, Rostow remembered, "was not happy about the proposal from the way that he looked." Both Rostow and Nitze at this first meeting had thought an occasion for optimism the fact that the joint chiefs raised no firm objection to the plan. While the sacrifice of the Pershing II meant that the United States would be unable to hit command-and-control targets in Russia with speed and precision, Nitze pointed out how the planned deployment of a modernized version of the Pershing I would still allow NATO to strike at second- and third-echelon military targets in the event the Soviets invaded the continent.

Moreover, Nitze noted at this meeting, the original justification for the Pershing II had by then disappeared. "The reason for the Pershing II was a political one," he later explained, "because the Germans had wanted it." The missile's role as a guarantor that Russian cities would be struck if European cities were destroyed seemed no longer necessary—ironically, the populations of the NATO countries had meanwhile expressed increasing concern that the Reagan administration's nuclear threats might be altogether *too* credible.

But an NSC meeting called on September 1 put an end to hopes that the Reagan administration might endorse Nitze's walk-in-the-woods proposal. It became clear at this gathering that, though the nation's military leaders were willing to consider abandoning the Pershing II, some in the country's highest political circles were not.[12]

Rostow remembered how Defense Secretary Caspar Weinberger argued at the meeting from a brief written by Perle—who had been on vacation during the first session—that "it wasn't yet time to abandon the zero option." Perle had earlier confided to associates his fear that Nitze had "set his sights on getting an agreement for its own sake." But it was ultimately the defense secretary's opposition to the proposal that was evidently complete and unyielding. "Weinberger turned against it even more violently than Perle," one participant recalled. "It was perfectly evident that Weinberger couldn't believe that Kvitsinsky had so deviated from instructions as to have gone along with the joint paper. He believed that it must have been a Soviet-instructed maneuver."

Another critic of the plan at this meeting was the president's national security adviser, William Clark, whom Rostow remembered as being "quite upset at the proposal." (There were obviously high feelings on both sides. After the meeting, Nitze allegedly told a colleague that Weinberger was "a goddamn fool" for not seeing the plan's advantages.) Reagan nonetheless sided with Perle, Clark, and Weinberger in disavowing Nitze's proposal.

In retrospect, neither Nitze nor Rostow felt that the Reagan administration's rejection of the walk-in-the-woods compromise represented a fatally missed opportunity—a promising road not taken in arms control. Though the Russians did not officially reject the plan until after the United States had already made public its own rebuff, Nitze believed the Kremlin's leaders had by that time already made "a policy decision that they were not going to permit any U.S. deployments, but were going to insist on substantial Soviet deployments." Subsequent to the walk in the woods the Russian position at the talks had hardened—a development Nitze attributed to the influence of what he called the "Z-forces" in the Kremlin: Zimyanin and Zagalin, members of the powerful secretariat of the Central Committee of the Communist party. After rejecting the walk-in-the-woods compromise, Kvitsinsky had no longer even distinguished between the Pershing and cruise missiles, "but simply insisted that 'a missile is a missile,' " Nitze said. "The decision at that time was no missile of either kind."

Yet, unlike Nitze, Rostow felt that the fate of the walk-in-the-woods proposal had had at least a symbolic importance. Dismissed by Reagan some six months later as ACDA's director, Rostow thought the summary rejection of Nitze's compromise signified the ascendancy in the administration of the Madison group's point of view. It marked the triumph, he said, of "a zealot's temperament"—one whose destiny, in time, was to be divided even against itself. The nuclear gnostics of the Reagan administration were, Rostow reflected, "a group of ideologues"—"humorless" and "paranoid." The depth of his own differences with them had been revealed, he thought, at the second of the meetings on the walk-in-the-woods proposal. The discussion there had not revolved around the merits of the proposal at all, he recalled, but over a more fundamental disagreement—one that went to the heart of the difference between the old and the new conservatives in the administration: "It was over how to deal with the Russians."

In the fall of 1983 there was a bizarre counterpoint to the walk-in-the-woods proposal.[13] Nitze speculated that what he termed Kvitsinsky's "outrageous behavior" in publicly attributing a Russian plan to American initiative—one whereby the Soviet Union would be allowed to keep some 120 SS-20s and the United States would forgo deployment of all cruise and Pershing II missiles—had had its origins in "one last attempt" by the Russian diplomat "to see what he could get." The quick and decisive rejection of Kvitsinsky's so-called "walk-in-the-park" gambit by all on the American side led the Russians to threaten to abandon the negotiations altogether as the time of the missiles' deployment approached.

Despite last-minute proposals by both sides—none of which, however, removed what had been the other's principal objections since the start of the talks—the Russians walked out of the Euromissile negotiations in November 1983, only weeks before the first cruise and Pershing II missiles were deployed and made operational in Europe. Within weeks, too, the Soviets abandoned the concurrent START negotiations as well as the talks that had been going on for more than a decade aimed at reducing Russian and American conventional forces in Europe.

Much earlier, the Reagan administration itself had decided to back out of the long-stalled negotiations over a comprehensive ban on nuclear testing —an avowed goal of every president since Kennedy—and to postpone discussion of a Soviet proposal for a ban on antisatellite weapons. In early 1984, members of the Reagan administration accused the Soviets of violating the 1972 ABM treaty by constructing a missile defense radar in Siberia. The Russians, for their part, warned that the administration's planned deployment of the MX and its proposed development of a space-based defense against missiles would constitute a violation of the SALT I treaties.

Following the collapse of arms control talks, Nitze accused the Russians of behaving "like an unspeakably dishonest horse trader" in negotiations with the United States: "If I were a businessman, I would never deal with them again."

But, reflecting upon his personal experience of nearly two generations of dealing with the Russians and nuclear weapons, Nitze thought that Soviet aims had remained "basically unchanging"—though there had been "some switches in strategy" and "great tactical flexibility" on the Russians' part, he said, as well as "a great deal of change in the environment" since the onset of the Cold War thirty-five years before: "All this demonstrates is that these things take a long time, and that thirty-five years is too short a time."

It was, Nitze thought, the United States that had undergone the greatest and most profound changes in the course of the Cold War. Were he to rewrite NSC-68 for the 1980s, Nitze said, he would change the form but not the content of that document: "The style was appropriate to the period." But one change, he noted, would be in the language used in NSC-68 "about the freedom of the individual being the touchstone" of Western values: "It was certainly true of that time, of the immediate postwar period. But today you talk about the freedom of the individual and nobody knows what you're talking about. The consensus that existed back then has broken down." His revision of NSC-68, Nitze declared, would "put even more emphasis on the importance of American will and resolve"—which was, he said, "still a problem, and will be forever. In a democracy you can never have unified opinion."

Nitze conceded that the 1957 Gaither report had overstated the ICBM threat from Russia. But he thought it came to the correct conclusions nonetheless—"even if the intelligence reports on which they were based turned out not to be right." A third major review of American nuclear strategy and policy that Nitze participated in during the Nixon and Ford administrations has not yet been made public. But its findings—like those of NSC-68 and the Gaither report—were sharply critical of the strategic *status quo,* and called for a greater effort on defense. The report was passed along to Carter at the start of his term, but, Nitze noted, "It never got anywhere."

In the wake of the suspension of virtually all arms control negotiations with the Russians by the end of 1983, Nitze professed neither optimism nor pessimism for the future. His attitude, he claimed, was reflected in the title of a recent book, *With Open Eyes,* by Marguerite Yourcenar, a member of the French Académie.

"I look at the world with open eyes," he said.

Beyond war planning and arms control, a final indication of how the Reagan administration felt the Russians should be dealt with was its decision on the MX. That missile figured, in fact, at the center of the strategic modernization that Defense Secretary Weinberger had initially predicted would cost $1.5 trillion over the next five years—subsequently revised to more than $2 trillion. Since President Carter had elected to build the MX and to deploy it along a "race track" in the American southwest, opposition to the missile had intensified. By 1984 the popular outcry against deployment of the MX rivaled that over the ABM more than a decade before.

The chief objection of MX opponents related not to the rarefied implications of nuclear strategy, but to a more pragmatic concern over the vast tracts of land and quantities of water that the missile would require. The MX race track—its supporters and critics were, curiously, each fond of pointing out—would be the most ambitious construction project undertaken since the Pyramids.

Intense public relations efforts by the Air Force to sell the missile and its basing plan to the public had been unable to overcome popular opposition to the missile in the American west. (The Pentagon's briefing on the various MX basing modes in one western town meeting evoked the comment from a particularly grizzled rancher that the only mode he was acquainted with was the "com-mode"—and that was where the missile belonged. Satirists in the *New York Times* and *Washington Post* suggested solving the basing problem by attaching the MX to migrating whales, or mused that it might be easier and cheaper to keep the missiles themselves stationary while the likely targets of a Soviet attack—the Pentagon and major cities, for example —were moved around the country instead.)

More than thirty basing schemes were finally studied for the MX by a committee of defense experts and scientists that the Reagan administration appointed in mid-1981 under the direction of Charles Townes, a University of California physicist. In addition to the original proposals for carrying the missile on trains, trucks, or boats or aboard specially designed airplanes, the Townes committee considered some new and highly imaginative ideas that were intended to anticipate any possible Soviet countermove.[14]

A common feature of these schemes was their theoretical suitability, in line with Reagan-13, for fighting a protracted nuclear war. Indeed, some plans even anticipated the world after the war. One novel plan envisioned hollowing out an entire mountain of rock and moving the missiles and their crews around on a circular track inside. In the event of war, giant hydraulic rams would be used to move the thousands of tons of debris created by a Soviet attack away from predug silos in the mountain's sides, allowing the missiles to be fired hours, days—or possibly months—later. The prospect that the Russians might try to defeat this scheme by using earth-penetrating nuclear warheads was anticipated in a scheme to dump additional tons of crushed rock on top of the silos built for the MX. Remotely controlled guns would shoot holes in any balloons or parachutes that the Soviets might use in an attempt to circumvent the rock shield by guiding the warheads gently and precisely to their targets.

In one additional touch worthy of Dr. Strangelove himself, it was proposed that a select group of volunteers—men and women with a carefully chosen range of skills and talents—live on the continuously moving, subterranean train, and that the underground community be equipped with nuclear reactors and hydroponic gardens to sustain life in what was termed "the post-attack environment." Planning for this hypothetical future society was complete in minute—and sometimes bizarre—detail. Thus a Pentagon contract for this study allegedly specified that signals along the train's right-of-way be visible as well as audible, since a great number of the

community's survivors would presumably have been deafened by the nuclear explosions occurring outside.[15]

There seemed, observed Richard Garwin, an "infinite regress" to the
measures proposed to make the MX invulnerable to Soviet attack. Even
after the Pentagon's rejection of the SUM system he and Sidney Drell had
devised for the MX, Garwin remained a consultant in the search for a
workable scheme to base the missile. The fact that, in spite of growing
opposition, the Air Force and the Reagan administration remained stubbornly attached to the MX showed, Garwin said, that counterforce and not
invulnerability remained the real rationale behind the missile. The Townes
committee's recommendation that the MX be based on land and in existing
silos seemed to confirm Garwin's point. It fulfilled, therefore, his earlier
prediction that the new missile would eventually wind up in the old shelters.
When he had first made that prediction, Garwin said, he was assured by a
Pentagon spokesman for the MX "that the last thing the United States
wanted was a silo-killing capability in a vulnerable basing posture."

The conclusion of the Townes report seemed to vindicate not only Garwin's prediction but equally Albert Wohlstetter's warning almost thirty
years earlier that the problem of strategic vulnerability might ultimately
prove unsolvable. Thus there was, the report asserted, "no practical basing
mode for missiles deployed on the land's surface."[16]

The debate on the MX was reopened by the Reagan administration's
announcement in the fall of 1982—citing the Townes committee's findings
—that it had decided upon a "closely spaced basing" scheme for the missile.
(In an effort to improve the image of the MX, administration officials also
gave it a name. Peacemaker, the first choice, was narrowly rejected for
sounding too much like "pacemaker." But critics pointed out that the
name finally chosen—Peacekeeper—had, even worse, a connotation of six-
shooters and the Wild West frontier.)[17]

The closely spaced basing idea counted upon the "fratricide" effect of
nuclear warheads to protect the MX. That phenomenon made a series of
nearly simultaneous nuclear explosions in close proximity theoretically impossible. Almost immediately, congressional opponents of the idea ridiculed
its "Rube Goldberg quality." But other, well-informed critics of the MX
suggested that the so-called "Densepack" idea left a shoe undropped: an as
yet undisclosed intention by the Reagan administration to abrogate the 1972
ABM treaty by giving the MX an antimissile defense, which was known to
be once again a subject of great interest in the Pentagon. Thus, the fact that
the closely spaced scheme created a narrow "threat tube" through which
Soviet ICBMs would have had to enter made it the plan perhaps best suited
to an active defense of the MX by an ABM.[18]

"An ABM *was* in the wings," confirmed one who helped formulate the

Densepack proposal: "In order to do that the United States would have had to renounce the ABM treaty of '72, and that was a very big step—even for the gentlemen who were in office. They hadn't really faced that. They had not thought through either the political or the strategic consequences."

Before the administration's intentions concerning the MX and the ABM were made clear, however, Densepack became the latest basing scheme to be overcome by domestic opposition. Skeptics in Congress, unwilling to authorize money for the proposal, persisted in questioning its cost and feasibility.[19] Even conservatives who had been among the first to express concern over the problem of strategic vulnerability—Albert Wohlstetter, James Schlesinger, and Paul Nitze among them—no longer disputed Paul Warnke's assessment that the MX basing problem had become "a monstrosity."

By the end of 1982 the Reagan administration's inability to sell the MX to Congress prompted the appointment of another prestigious panel of experts to study the problem and suggest a solution. Headed by Air Force General Brent Scowcroft—a long-time proponent of the missile—and relying upon two former secretaries of state and four secretaries of defense for advice, the second blue-ribbon panel on the MX reported back to the administration the following spring.[20]

Agreeing with the Townes committee that there was, in effect, no technological solution to the problem of strategic vulnerability, the members of the Scowcroft commission endorsed their predecessors' recommendation by proposing that the projected force of one hundred MX missiles be deployed in existing Minuteman silos—at least as "an interim measure." Balancing that recommendation, however, was the commission's urging that the present generation of vulnerable land-based missiles be replaced over the next decade by the smaller Midgetman missile that Nitze had proposed to the Russians and Carter. Less likely to be knocked out by a Soviet attack because it would be more numerous than present missiles, Midgetman, the Scowcroft report also pointed out, would pose much less of a threat to the Russians' land-based missile arsenal—and hence give both sides less of an incentive to strike first in a time of crisis.[21]

The Scowcroft commission's endorsement of the MX came as no surprise. "There was very little argument against the MX" within the group, one of its members recalled: "You started with a commission that was sympathetic to authorizing MX production. The question was to find the basing mode and the set of arguments that would pass muster on Capitol Hill." Despite the fact that "there were one or two people" on the commission who "were quite enthusiastic about this very small missile," he said their dominant concern had not been with Midgetman but with the MX. "For most of the members of the commission the small missile was a way of buying in political support on the basis that the total package would go through and that the MX would survive. Very few shared the belief on the Hill that somehow or other the small missile was a panacea."

Of the two reasons put forward in their meetings for proceeding with the MX—reducing the vulnerability of U.S. missiles, and threatening Soviet missiles in their silos—the second had clearly taken precedence in the deliberations of the Scowcroft commission: "We argued for more throw-weight. We argued for more counterforce capabilities as a way of buttressing extended deterrence. . . . The mistake that the administration made with all its grandiose talk about the 'window of vulnerability' and so forth was to put all the attention on silo vulnerability." But, this commissioner said, "That was *not* the main reason for deploying the MX. You would deploy it irrespective of eliminating the problem of the 'window of vulnerability'— as the administration proceeded to do."

The decisive argument in favor of going ahead with the MX—despite its acknowledged vulnerability—was in his view the unambiguous threat it posed to the Russians: "One of the things we hoped to convey to the Soviets is our capacity to go after their theoretically vulnerable land-based missile force. It is that which the acquisition of the MX missile provides to the United States. What one is indeed conveying to the Soviet Union is that here is a deployment that is fundamentally oriented toward reacting to an all-out Warsaw Pact invasion of western Europe." Acknowledging the overriding importance of perceptions in the MX decision, the members of the Scowcroft commission had concluded, he thought, that the larger warheads of the MX and its greater throw-weight would "convey more seriousness about counterforce" than existing U.S. missiles.[22]

There had been other recommendations that the commission had intended to make in its report. But its members decided to delete them from the final version for political reasons. A proposal for "super-hardening" the Minuteman silos meant to hold the MX was left out, this commissioner said, because of the group's fear of the possible reaction in the wake of the Dense-pack fiasco. "We could imagine people saying, 'Here is another set of dreamers and nuts.' " The other deletion concerned a passage in the report that "conveyed more hostility about the Soviet system than was wise," he felt. "It tried too much to enlist people in the crusade against the Red Menace. It suggested that opposition to U.S. defense policies was disloyalty."

The ultimate intent of the commission's recommendation for the MX was not to provoke the Russians but "to shore up deterrence," this member said in defense of the Scowcroft report: "There was no view in the commission that deploying in Minuteman silos was provocative. It is the Soviets who have created this overwhelming threat against western Europe. It is they who have created the circumstances that have made such a deployment necessary. We have told them for many years—some thirty-four years, in fact, explicitly—that in the event of a Soviet assault on western Europe we will respond. This gives us the means to respond. I do not regard that as provocative. I regard that as a prudent acquisition of the hardware necessary to live up to these threats."

The authors of the Scowcroft report acknowledged that as significant as its actual recommendations was what the report had to say—explicitly and implicitly—about nuclear weapons, arms control, and the Russians. Contained in the report, therefore, was the stark contention that the emphasis of the past twenty-five years upon reducing the number of nuclear weapons had been misdirected—that it was even responsible for the proliferation of nuclear warheads which once again threatened the stability of the balance of terror. In reaffirming the MX's original role and the prospective role of Midgetman as bargaining chips in future Soviet-American negotiations, the commissioners accepted as a basic premise that the arms race was a necessary and inseparable part of arms control. Already possessed of a seemingly irresistible momentum, that race was quietly conceded in their report to have an unassailable logic of its own as well.

Equally striking was the report's conclusion regarding what had been the guiding premise behind nuclear strategy since Hiroshima: "Deterrence is not an abstract notion amenable to simple quantification. Still less is it a mirror image of what would deter ourselves. Deterrence is the set of beliefs in the minds of the Soviet leaders, given their own values and attitudes, about our capabilities and our will." Failure to go ahead with the MX would "not communicate to the Soviets that we have the will essential to effective deterrence," the report warned. "Quite the opposite."[23]

Though represented as "a major new departure" in strategic thought, the Scowcroft commission's conclusion was, more accurately, the culmination of that thinking after almost forty years. By their last point about the nature of deterrence, the experts finally made explicit what had hitherto been only implied by previous blue-ribbon panels on the bomb—that nuclear weapons have made us a prisoner of shadows: the shadows that have grown in our understanding of the Russians; and the shadows that linger in the understanding of ourselves.

EPILOGUE

Present at the Re-creation

In the spring of 1983, the scientists who built the first atomic bomb returned to Los Alamos for a commemoration of their achievement forty years earlier. Since then the work of the weapons laboratory had diversified to include research into solar and fusion energy, microbiology, and space exploration. But two-thirds of the nation's nuclear weapons were still designed at Los Alamos. The reunion was also to be the occasion for a scientific conference where the atomic veterans were invited to give papers on their current work unrelated to defense. Isidor Rabi, eighty-six years old, warned the organizers that the theme of his paper would depart from the others dealing with time projection, particle accelerators, and lunar colonization. His paper's title, Rabi told them, was "We Meant Well."

The scene at the welcoming cocktail party held in Fuller Lodge on the first night of the anniversary was indistinguishable from the reunion of a college class where virtually everyone has made good. As at any such event, there was talk of children and grandchildren and recent operations, and of those who would not be there.

George Kistiakowsky—"Kisty," the physicist who jumped for joy at Alamogordo—had died the previous summer of cancer. During the last year of his life Kistiakowsky predicted that "there's only two ways this thing can end: Either there will be a nuclear war or there will be arms control with deep reductions on each side." Manhattan Project director Leslie Groves—who once called the scientists "the greatest bunch of prima donnas ever assembled in one place"—was dead nearly twenty years. But the name most often mentioned was that of Robert Oppenheimer. A typical picture of the physicist—drink and cigarette in hand—taken at Fuller Lodge more than forty years before hung on one wall of the Lincoln-log-style bunkhouse. It had been outside the same building, at another reunion shortly after the Oppenheimer hearings, that Rabi walked away from Edward Teller's proffered handshake. The two men had rarely spoken to each other since.

Rabi's talk the following day in the Los Alamos auditorium was delivered standing beside the lectern and without notes. He recollected of his and his colleagues' wartime work on the atomic bomb that it seemed, in retrospect, "almost immoral to have had such a good time working on such a thing. . . . But we had something to dedicate ourselves to." Rabi lamented that this sense of idealism had since vanished: "There is no way for scientists to escape responsibility for turning their creation over to people who have no respect or appreciation for it. People at that time understood this thing— its nature—much better than people understand it now. There was greatness then, folly now. . . .

"The way that things developed, the 'bomb' became a thing in itself," Rabi said. "The question became not how to protect ourselves, but how to destroy another culture—how to destroy human beings." The final result of the scientists' efforts, he thought, was that "nations are now lined up like people before the ovens of Auschwitz, while we are trying to make the ovens more efficient. . . .

"We meant well," Rabi concluded in a soft voice, "and we sort of abdicated. . . . We gave it away. We gave the power away to people who didn't understand it and now it's gotten out of our hands. We have to recover that."

As Rabi finished speaking, the audience stood and applauded. It was, one of the new generation of atomic scientists observed, only the third time he had heard of a standing ovation at the weapons laboratory. The first had been when Robert Oppenheimer returned to Los Alamos in 1946 to give a talk. The second was when Edward Teller had spoken there recently.

Teller's talk on the last day of the conference concerned the feasibility of a lunar laboratory. Many at the reunion thought the choice of topic portentous, though the paper itself remained strictly scientific and noncontroversial. It was only the month before that President Reagan in a nationwide speech had endorsed Teller's idea of a "third generation" of nuclear weapons —one that might make Oppenheimer's thirty-year-old idea of a defense-dominated strategy a reality. The president had spoken then of how lasers and particle-beam weapons based in space and capable of intercepting enemy missiles in midflight presented a "vision of the future which offers hope."[1]

But the prospect of a third generation of nuclear weaponry had generally failed to excite the imagination of Teller's former colleagues at Los Alamos. Indeed, some were reminded by it of James Conant's celebrated comment about the superbomb debate—that it "was like seeing the same film, and a punk one, for the second time."[2] Thus the president's so-called Star Wars proposal seemed to them but another rerun of that film. A White House dinner hosted by Teller on the eve of Reagan's speech had even been boycotted by some of the eminent Nobel Prize winners invited, and Richard Garwin once again challenged Teller on his ambitious ideas for space-based weapons in a debate held during the reunion. Garwin's colleague Sidney Drell felt that "going to space may be a throwback to the H-bomb. . . . People who feel we should go ahead with weapons in space are driven by the same passions." Drell thought that, like the decision on the Super, the administration's Star Wars proposal heralded a potential "watershed" in the scientists' generations-long debate on defense.

Teller himself agreed that the past played a major role in the current opposition to the idea. In an essay of reminiscences for the fortieth reunion, he wrote: "Oppenheimer's loss of security clearance partly introduced and partly solidified a deep division among the ranks of American scientists. Many scientists have never forgiven the damage that was done to a great scientist's reputation. While the origin of the feeling of distrust may have vanished from memory, the residual effect in the scientific community remains."[3]

It was this residual effect that Teller blamed for the resistance to his latest proposal to surge ahead of the Russians in the arms race—with an effort which he and his supporters argued might actually end that race for all time. Some at the reunion took Teller's very presence there to be an attempt at overcoming that resistance. Asked whether the passage of forty years and his attendance at the anniversary meant that there had been a reconciliation among the scientists, Teller had demurred. "I am reconciled," he said. "You will have to ask that question of others."

But the speeches given at the formal dinner on the last night of the reunion vividly demonstrated the extent to which the split between the scientists remained. In his talk, former Los Alamos director Harold Agnew—a passenger on one of the planes that had accompanied the *Enola Gay* on its mission over Hiroshima—justified the past and present work of the weapons laboratory as a regretful necessity. Concerning Hiroshima, Agnew told a story about a pair of NATO officers, both World War II veterans, whom he had recently met in Europe. One of the two, an Englishman, had asked the other, a German, how he came by his wooden leg. "In the Battle of Britain," the German answered. Agnew said that the Englishman's reply reflected how he, Agnew, had always felt about the decision to drop the atomic bombs on Japan. "Good," the Englishman had said. "You bloody well deserved it."

Victor Weisskopf, head of the wartime lab's Radiation Hydrodynamics group, decried the subsequent contribution of Los Alamos to "the craziest arms race in history—one that future generations will regard as a virulent case of a collective mental disease." Weisskopf's speech was a *cri de coeur.* "My friends," he said at its end, "all this is the outcome of our work. Can we be silent about it in our reunion?"

After the speeches a petition was passed around the room for the guests to sign. It emphasized, as had past petitions, the scientists' "special sense of responsibility" in calling for a halt in the production of nuclear weapons by the United States and Russia. The petition occasioned a brief and impromptu debate. A physicist at one table objected heatedly that he would sign such a petition only when Soviet physicists produced a similar document. One of the sponsors answered that, as representatives of a free people, American scientists had an obligation to take the initiative. The reluctant physicist remained unpersuaded. It was a debate that could have taken place forty years before—and did.

Isidor Rabi and Edward Teller rode on the same plane back to New York the following afternoon. Just before the plane landed in Chicago, where he would catch a connecting flight to Washington, Teller left his seat to talk to Rabi. Their conversation—one of very few between the two men in nearly thirty years—was brief but cordial. Teller asked Rabi to read his essay of reminiscences about Oppenheimer. Rabi suggested that Teller's proposed lunar laboratory might be useful as a base to detect and destroy asteroids that might otherwise hit the earth.

Did the breaking of their long silence—Rabi was later asked—change anything between the two men, or between the rival groups of scientists they had come to represent? "Nothing has changed," Rabi answered. It was not only Teller's testimony in the Oppenheimer case that was the cause of the rift, but his continuing support for new weapons with which Rabi disagreed. It was for the same reason, Rabi said, that he had broken with the arms controllers: "I've stopped going to their meetings. It's obscene to get people accustomed to megadeaths." Of the scientists, he said, "We have to talk to the country. I've given up on Congress."

"The problem of this generation," Rabi reflected, "is that they lost human sympathy. They lost an understanding of their own selves—of their own meaning. There has been an atrophy of the imagination, a decline of the moral sense." He particularly blamed the scientists for the change. "Science," he said, "is being destroyed in this race to destruction."

Rabi felt that the assemblage at Los Alamos during the war had been motivated by a different attitude than that now prevailing among the scientists. He thus objected to the comparison of the anniversary with a class reunion. "I've yet to see a class that had that spirit," Rabi said. "Or that was involved with such dreadful things."

Did he think that there was ever likely to be another gathering like that of the scientists at the wartime lab—with the same dedication, enthusiasm, and idealism?

Rabi's answer was unhesitating: "I certainly hope not. We had no doubts about what we were doing."

In contrast to the atomic scientists, there was no single event like the explosion at Alamogordo to mark a reunion for the nuclear strategists. But among their number, too, was a sense that a generation was ending—and that the original values were no longer revered.

"The arguments for using space (or indeed anything else) to fight, survive and win wars," one recent advocate of the Star Wars proposal remarked, "simply do not make any sense to people who throughout their careers—whether out of expedience or conviction—seemingly have traded on the premise that war can no longer be won or survived, or in any event should not be approached as a winnable, survivable proposition." Claiming that what he called "the ideological opiates of the past fifteen years" had "irrevocably closed the minds of a generation of policymakers, bureaucrats and top military officers," this analyst concluded: "There is, however, faint hope: people are available who are either older or younger."[4]

The older strategists—the first wave—have declined in both numbers and influence. The dean of this group, Bernard Brodie, died of cancer in 1978. By the end of his life Brodie had become disillusioned with the subject that he helped to inaugurate as a career. His interests had turned progressively away from nuclear strategy to a topic he evidently considered more important and tangible—the human and psychological motivations behind war.[5]

Brodie's final writings left no doubt that some of his ideas had changed fundamentally since the early days at Yale and during Rand's golden age. In notes prepared for testimony which he had planned to give before the Senate Foreign Relations Committee—testimony that was precluded by his final illness—Brodie wrote that he saw "no reason to regard Soviet policy as inherently more venturesome than an American policy that since World War II brought us into outright war in Korea and Vietnam, and to intervention in other areas of the world." Instead, he thought the United States could now afford to "virtually eliminate off-hand" its longstanding obsession with a surprise nuclear attack from Russia.[6]

On at least one topic Brodie's views remained virtually unchanged since his missionary days at Rand, however. More than twenty years after he wrote that strategy had "hit a dead end" because of the hydrogen bomb, Brodie seemed alternately bemused and irritated by the resurgence of what he termed "old-new ideas" on fighting and winning a nuclear war. In the draft of an article he was working on at the time of his death, Brodie observed that "regardless of which targets are given first priority, any thermonuclear war would inevitably mean the vast destruction of cities and populations on both sides." "Whatever else may be said about this idea," Brodie wrote of victory in a nuclear war, "one would have to go back almost to the fate of Carthage to find an historical precedent."[7]

The man who corresponded with Brodie in 1954 about the prospect of "only one Carthage" in a nuclear war—William Borden—had long since abandoned the study of strategy. In 1984 Borden was a successful attorney in Washington and, by his own admission, rarely thought about the subject anymore. The author of *There Will Be No Time* acknowledged that the timing of the prediction he made in 1946 of nuclear war "certain and inevitable" had been proved wrong—but not yet the prediction itself.

Another pioneering figure in nuclear strategy, Donald Brennan, died only two years after Brodie. Brennan's death at his own hand, said an associate, was, "like so many other things in his life, a rational choice." Brennan's despondency over the recent death of his wife had evidently been compounded by money problems, and by the feeling that his own most creative work lay in the past. Colleagues noted that his attitude toward nuclear strategy near the end had seemed increasingly distracted, even frivolous. One remembered how Brennan had wanted to include upon the roster of participants at an upcoming conference of strategists the young boatman he had met while on a rafting trip down the Colorado River.

Brennan's suicide was "the weirdest thing in the world," said his friend and co-founder of the Hudson Institute, Herman Kahn. Kahn noted in 1981 that the ideas on civil defense, the ABM, and nuclear war-fighting that he and Brennan had promoted at Hudson were only just coming into vogue with the administration of Ronald Reagan—for whose election campaign Brennan had served as an adviser. Kahn's own sudden and unexpected death in the summer of 1983 would come while he was in the process of finishing a nine-volume revision of his masterwork, *On Thermonuclear War.* "Some people will be aghast; others will just be appalled," he predicted of the reaction to the book.

Remarkably, the detachment that had always been characteristic of Brennan evidently continued up to the day of his death. In the month or so between the decision to end his life and the act itself, Brennan took unsuspecting friends out to dinner at an expensive French restaurant near the institute and charged the bill—knowing he would never have to pay it. "He had three weeks of an incredible high," Kahn recalled.

The legacy left by the coiner of MAD was, like Brennan himself, enigmatic. Two years after his death the personal papers he bequeathed to a colleague at Hudson were still in the black Cadillac that Brennan left behind in the institute's parking lot on the day he went home and shot himself. The car seemed to have been untouched in all that time. It was covered with a thick layer of dust and all four tires had gone flat.

On one subject, however, the memory of Brennan and of his work was clear and undiminished in the minds of those who knew him. Several recalled Brennan's last appearance before a Senate hearing on the future of arms control. On that occasion he specifically advised against the kind of negotiations he had been the champion of exactly twenty years before. Concluding his testimony, Brennan had shocked the hearing room into

silence by declaring in a loud voice—pounding the table for emphasis—
"You can't trust the Russians!"

The reunion of the atomic scientists as well as the deaths of Brodie, Brennan,
and Kahn underscored the passing of the first generation of experts and
advisers on the bomb. The world they have left behind is one fundamentally
changed because of their thinking. But, ironically, it is a world they did not
intend—and one that few if any of them had even dimly imagined.

As 1984 draws to a close, it is a world of six nuclear powers, more than
fifty thousand nuclear weapons, and a perilous peace. It is increasingly a
world, French historian Raymond Aron wrote shortly before his death in
1983, of "virile weapons and impotent men"—one where human prejudices
and assumptions have seemingly abetted technology in progressively removing destiny from our own hands.[8] The paradoxical consequence of making
nuclear bombs an expression of human will has thus been the creation of
weapons so advanced and sophisticated that human decisions may soon no
longer be required for their use. In our time the assumptions behind nuclear
deterrence have not been proved invalid, but they no longer go unchallenged. The world created by the experts is—for all these reasons—filled
with an unprecedented degree of doubt about the future.

Yet this doubt may, if nothing else, have finally and irretrievably shattered
the already riven world of the experts. "There is an underlying realization
already that there's something wrong with a lot that's being said," one of
the new generation of nuclear strategists recently observed. "There is a
fundamental readjustment in our thinking absolutely required, and it will
happen one way or another."

When concluding thirty years ago that nuclear strategy had "hit a dead
end," Bernard Brodie wrote that "what we now must initiate is the comprehensive pursuit of the new ideas and procedures necessary to carry us
through the next two or three dangerous decades." Those decades have
passed, and the time approaching seems immeasurably more dangerous than
that which Brodie envisioned. Neither the "launch-on-warning" strategy
proposed by those seeking both a solution to strategic vulnerability and an
alternative to producing new nuclear weapons nor the proposed building of
a Star Wars defense seems to offer a promising way out of the present
danger.[9]

One encouraging sign in the forty-year-long debate on U.S. nuclear strategy, however, has been the recent involvement of a new and a very different
group of nuclear gnostics—those whom Robert McNamara has termed that
debate's "potential victims": the vast number of American citizens who are
not experts on the bomb.

As early as 1948, when the first U.S. policy on the use of nuclear weapons was approved by the Truman administration, participation of the public in the strategic debate was explicitly discouraged by the government. Until recently, few had protested their exclusion. But two generations of the nuclear era have evidently changed this attitude on the part of the public, if not the government. "There is a realization," observed Paul Warnke, "that the experts don't have all of the answers—and possibly not any of the answers."

What strategist Robert Osgood once characterized as "the deference of the uninitiated, overawed by the secrets and rituals of the strategic priesthood," may be ending.[10] Indeed, the disillusioned scientists and strategists who in many cases now provide the organizing spirit behind the popular movement to reduce the threat of nuclear war have willingly played a subordinate role there.

The issues that should be addressed in any new nuclear debate are those which the experts themselves have seldom raised, and never really answered. Does the United States truly need the capability to launch a disarming first strike against the Soviet Union? Under what circumstances—and for what reasons—would the United States be the first to use nuclear weapons? Can and should this country continue to base decisions regarding nuclear weapons upon their supposed attribute as an expression of national will? And—finally—is there any real utility to the possession of such great numbers of these weapons beyond that of preventing their use?

A truly new nuclear debate—one that recognizes the old one has hit a dead end—might begin by acknowledging what Bernard Brodie described in his last book as the "absurdly simple idea" that nonetheless represented "the single most important idea in all strategy."[11] It is the idea contained in the question that the premier strategist of a different era, Clausewitz, said must always be posed before building any weapon or embarking upon any war: *De quoi s'agit-il?*—literally, "What is it all about? What is it for?"

It is a question at the heart of the concerns of the past forty years, and likewise at the center of the equally long argument among the experts. It would be a question unique to a new debate, in that seldom has it been asked about nuclear weapons and nuclear war.

Never has it received an adequate answer.

NOTES

Since this book is intended for a general audience, the chapter notes contain elaborations and suggestions for further reading as well as the sources for particular items of information. In those instances where a primary source such as a letter also appears in a secondary or published source, the latter has been cited. References have been avoided when the source of a direct quotation is indicated in the text. If the subject of an interview has requested anonymity for a remark the reference simply indicates "interview." Primary and secondary sources are cited in the Notes. The Bibliography contains a list of those interviewed as well as the published and unpublished sources for the book.

Abbreviations Used in the Notes

DOE	United States Department of Energy
GPO	Government Printing Office, Washington, D.C.
IISS	International Institute for Strategic Studies, London
MSS	Manuscript (Personal Papers)
USAEC	United States Atomic Energy Commission
USSBS	United States Strategic Bombing Survey

PROLOGUE

1. "Preview of the War We Do Not Want," *Collier's,* October 27, 1951.

2. See, for example, Sir John Hackett, *The Third World War: A Future History* (Macmillan, 1978); and Hackett, *The Third World War: The Untold Story* (Macmillan, 1983).

3. Bernard Brodie, "The Development of Nuclear Strategy," *International Security,* Spring, 1978.

4. Journalist Jonathan Schell has written of the civilian nuclear strategists: "Ordinarily, political men prefer to consult practice rather than theory, and are inclined to seek out men of broad experience to advise them, but on this one matter—the most important matter of all—they have been obliged to depend on the theorists themselves." Schell, *The Time of Illusion* (Knopf, 1975), p. 313. Other accounts of the strategists include Arthur Herzog, *The War-Peace Establishment* (Harper & Row, 1965); George Lowe, *The Age of Deterrence* (Little, Brown, 1964); Robert Levine, *The Arms Debate* (Harvard University Press, 1963); Colin Gray, "Strategic Studies: A Critical Assessment" (Hudson Institute, 1980); James E. King, "The New Strategy" (unpublished ms., Institute for Defense Analyses, 1972); Lawrence Freedman, *The Evolution of Nuclear Strategy* (Macmillan, 1982); and Fred Kaplan, *The Wizards of Armageddon* (Simon and Schuster, 1983). The contribution of European theorists is discussed in Michael Howard, *Studies in War and Peace* (Viking Press, 1971); and Raymond Aron, *The Great Debate: Theories of Nuclear Strategy* (Doubleday, 1965). The angel-pin/warhead-missile analog is noted in Strobe Talbott, *Endgame: The Inside Story of SALT II* (Harper & Row, 1979).

5. Burke is quoted in Michael Walzer, *Just and Unjust Wars: A Moral Argument with Historical Illustrations* (Basic Books, 1977), p. 269.

6. Arthur Koestler, *The Call Girls* (Hutchinson, London, 1972), p. 68.

CHAPTER ONE

1. Oppenheimer's reminiscences of Alamogordo are from a 1964 NBC television documentary, "The Decision to Drop the Atomic Bomb." A transcript of the interview of Oppenheimer used in the program is in the Robert Oppenheimer MSS, Library of Congress, Washington, D.C. Farrell's report is reprinted in Martin Sherwin, *A World Destroyed: The Atomic Bomb and the Grand Alliance* (Knopf, 1975), pp. 310–12.

2. Teller's recollection is in Edward Teller and Allen Brown, *The Legacy of Hiroshima* (Doubleday, 1962), pp. 17–18. The comment by Groves is quoted in Victor Weisskopf, "On Avoiding Nuclear Holocaust," *Technology Review,* October 1980, p. 29.

3. Interview.

4. Oppenheimer and Bainbridge made their remarks in the 1964 NBC television documentary "The Decision to Drop the Atomic Bomb."

CHAPTER TWO

1. Thomas Schelling, "Bernard Brodie (1910–1978)," *International Security,* Winter 1978, pp. 2–3.

2. Bernard Brodie, *Seapower in the Machine Age* (Princeton University Press, 1941); Brodie, *A Layman's Guide to Naval Strategy* (Princeton University Press, 1942).

3. Interview. On Brodie's wartime career, see Kaplan, *The Wizards of Armageddon,* pp. 16–22. The author is indebted to Professor Barry Steiner of California State University, Long Beach, for further details on Brodie's life in his soon-to-be-published book "Bernard Brodie and the American Study of Nuclear Strategy."

4. Concerning Brodie's own views on the study of strategy, see Bernard Brodie, *Strategy in the Missile Age* (Princeton University Press, 1959), pp. 7–11.

5. Brodie, *Seapower in the Machine Age,* p. 448.

6. Bernard Brodie, "The Atomic Bomb and American Security," unpublished mss., November 1, 1945, Yale Institute of International Studies.

7. Bernard Brodie, ed., *The Absolute Weapon: Atomic Power and World Order* (Harcourt, Brace, 1946). Brodie explained the "absolute weapon" imagery in *Strategy in the Missile Age,* pp. 3–5.

8. Some Navy officers asserted shortly after Hiroshima that their service had already developed a counterweapon to the atomic bomb—a claim that Brodie quickly shot down. *New York Times,* October 12, 1945. Equally fanciful was the charge made by air-power advocate Alexander de Seversky that atomic bombs were only marginally more destructive than conventional bombs; or the subsequent claim of a Navy commander that an atomic bomb exploded at one end of a runway would leave people at the other end unhurt. Concerning these and other early misestimates of the power of the bomb, see, for example, "Atom Bomb Hysteria," *Reader's Digest,* February 1946, pp. 82–97. Somewhat more reasonable were proposals of the time to relocate American industry or evacuate U.S. cities at the threat of war—but these ideas, too, Brodie dismissed as unfeasible. *The Absolute Weapon,* pp. 101–3.

9. Brodie, *The Absolute Weapon,* p. 73.

10. The other members of the Yale group were Frederick Dunn, Arnold Wolfers, Percy Corbett, and William T. R. Fox. On the origins of the concept of deterrence, see, for example, George Quester, *Deterrence Before Hiroshima: The Airpower Background of Modern Strategy* (Wiley and Sons, 1966); Alexander George and Richard Smoke, *Deterrence in American Foreign Policy: Theory and Practice* (Columbia University Press, 1974); and Herzog, *The War-Peace Establishment,* v–ix.

11. Brodie, *The Absolute Weapon,* p. 76.

12. Borden's background is also recounted in Philip Stern, *The Oppenheimer Case: Security on Trial* (Harper & Row, 1969), pp. 21–3.

13. William Borden, "Straws in the Wind," Special Collections, Sterling Memorial Library, Yale University.

14. William Borden, *There Will Be No Time: The Revolution in Strategy* (Macmillan, 1946), p. ix.

15. *There Will Be No Time,* pp. 29, 63, 175.

16. *There Will Be No Time,* p. 41.

17. *There Will Be No Time,* pp. 83–7, 175. Borden's vision of a "war-between-the-bases" anticipated that of George Orwell's *1984,* where the continual but inconclusive wars that engaged the novel's totalitarian regimes were fought far out at sea.

18. *There Will Be No Time,* pp. 87, 175. "Should the great-power foreign ministers assemble around a table in the year 1960," Borden predicted, "perhaps the vital unspoken question to be asked of each will be this: 'How many atomic bombs could your country activate on about thirty minutes' notice?' "

19. By contrast, Borden advocated "writing off the home front" in such a war: "Thousands of enemy paratroopers might be at large in industrial New England, without impeding the American war effort. . . . Occupation of the national capital itself would have but slight military value." *There Will Be No Time,* pp. 80–9.

20. *There Will Be No Time,* p. 113.

21. *There Will Be No Time,* pp. 175, 213.

22. *There Will Be No Time,* pp. 214–17.

23. Brodie, ed., *The Absolute Weapon,* p. 102.

24. John Hersey, *Hiroshima* (Knopf, 1946), pp. 39–40. Concerning the impact of Hersey's book, see John Latt and W. M. Wheeler, "Reaction to John Hersey's *Hiroshima,*" *Journal of Social Psychology,* August 1948, pp. 135–40.

25. U.S. Strategic Bombing Survey [USSBS], *The Effects of Atomic Bombs on Hiroshima and Nagasaki* (GPO, 1946).

26. *The Effects of Atomic Bombs,* pp. 18–22.

27. *The Effects of Atomic Bombs,* p. 20.

28. *The Effects of Atomic Bombs,* pp. 20–22.

29. The *Survey* concludes: "It cannot be said, however, that the atomic bomb convinced the leaders who effected the peace of the necessity of surrender." *The Effects of Atomic Bombs,* p. 22.

30. *The Effects of Atomic Bombs,* pp. 36–43.

CHAPTER THREE

1. The German report is quoted in David MacIsaacs, *Strategic Bombing in World War II: The Story of the United States Strategic Bombing Survey* (Garland, 1976), p. 21. Concerning the theoretical and historical roots of strategic bombing, see, for example, Anthony Verrier, *The Bomber Offensive* (Batsford, London, 1968); MacIsaacs, *Strategic Bombing in World War II;* and Quester, *Deterrence Before Hiroshima.*

2. On Douhet's influence, see Brodie, *Strategy in the Missile Age,* pp. 71–106. *Command of the Air* was not translated into English until 1942, but knowledge of Douhet's theories was widespread in the Army Air Force well before that date. See "American Military Ethics in World War II: An Exchange," *Journal of American History,* June 1981, pp. 85–92.

3. The quote is from British military historian J. F. C. Fuller and is cited in Quester, *Deterrence Before Hiroshima,* pp. 56–7. H. G. Wells wrote a vivid account of the feared air war in his futuristic novel *The Shape of Things to Come* (Macmillan, 1933).

4. Brodie, *Strategy in the Missile Age,* pp. 107–44.

5. The revision of Bomber Command's strategy is noted in Sir Charles Webster and Noble Frankland, *The Strategic Air Offensive Against Germany, 1939–1945,* v. 1, *Preparations* (HMSO, London, 1961), pp. 86–95. Concerning the shift to bombing cities and civilians, see also Frederick M. Sallagar, *The Road to Total War* (Van Nostrand Reinhold, 1969); and Max Hastings, *Bomber Command* (Dial Press, 1979).

6. Quester, *Deterrence Before Hiroshima,* p. 64. In 1932 former Prime Minister Stanley Baldwin created an uproar in a House of Commons debate when he stated a view that, though perhaps widely held, had never before been made so explicit: "The only defence is an offence, which means that

you have to kill more women and children more quickly than the enemy if you want to save yourselves." Baldwin is quoted in Hastings, *Bomber Command*.

7. Webster and Frankland, *Preparations*, pp. 95–6. Regarding how the supposed psychological effects of bombing became a major interest of strategic thinkers, see Harold Wilensky, *Organizational Intelligence: Knowledge and Policy in Government and Industry* (Basic Books, 1967), esp. p. 12.

8. Quester, *Deterrence Before Hiroshima*, p. 53; Hastings, *Bomber Command*, p. 49. Trenchard calculated bombing's "moral effect" upon civilians as twenty times the material damage caused— a figure he evidently arrived at after studying the experience of Londoners under bombardment by German Zeppelins in World War One. Curiously, proponents of "moral" or morale effect assumed that under equal strain enemy morale would collapse first—an example of ethnocentrism akin to the assumption of European general staffs before 1914 that the machine gun would only be a threat to troops of the other side. John Ellis, *The Social History of the Machine Gun* (Pantheon, 1975), pp. 149–66.

9. Webster and Frankland, *Preparations*, pp. 95–6.

10. Quester, *Deterrence Before Hiroshima*, pp. 117–20.

11. Sallagar, *The Road to Total War*, pp. 179–87.

12. Even in so-called "precision bombing" during daylight the three-hundred-yard radius in which it had been assumed most bombs were landing was found to be closer in fact to a thousand yards. A secretariat of the British War Cabinet established to investigate the accuracy problem discovered that of the bombers reporting successful attacks upon an industrial target, only one-third had actually dropped their bombs within five miles of the aim point. In raids conducted on moonless nights this figure fell to one-fifteenth of the bombing force. Webster and Frankland, *Preparations*, pp. 168–70; Sallagar, *The Road to Total War*, p. 92. Freeman Dyson, a physicist for Bomber Command, has noted how a superior there was able to make the accuracy seem better than it was. Faced with the prospect of submitting to higher authority a bomb plot whose three-mile radius showed only a few craters within the circle, he ordered the radius of the plot increased to five miles. Freeman Dyson, *Disturbing the Universe* (Harper & Row, 1979), p. 26.

13. Webster and Franklin, *Preparations*, pp. 474–5, 492. The Air Ministry's order is also quoted in Peter Pringle and James Spigelman, *The Nuclear Barons* (Holt, Rinehart and Winston, 1981), pp. 72–5.

14. The story of the "dehousing paper" is recounted in Hastings, *Bomber Command*, p. 127. A copy of Cherwell's report was henceforth paper-clipped to the mission orders of Bomber Command as an explanation of the government's policy. But, in fact, the investigation by British scientists on which Cherwell's "dehousing paper" was based—the "Hull and Birmingham Study"—came to very nearly the opposite conclusion.

15. Webster and Frankland, *Preparations*, pp. 313–20.

16. Sallagar, *The Road to Total War*, p. 92.

17. The change in the American doctrine of strategic bombing is noted in MacIssacs, *Strategic Bombing in World War II*, pp. 8–17; and Quester, *Deterrence Before Hiroshima*, pp. 73, 128.

18. Webster and Frankland, *Preparations*, p. 355.

19. *Preparations*, p. 355; Wilensky, *Organizational Intelligence*, p. 32.

20. Sallagar, *The Road to Total War*, p. 123; Webster and Frankland, *Preparations*, p. 299.

21. Arnold is cited in Ronald Schaffer, "American Military Ethics in World War II: The Bombing of German Civilians," *Journal of American History*, September 1980, p. 333; Spaatz in the subsequent issue of that journal, under "An Exchange." The way in which the "by-product" became the "end-product" for both the AAF and the RAF is noted in Sallagar, *The Road to Total War*, p. 123.

22. The shift in U.S. bombing policy from Germany to Japan is noted in Quester, *Deterrence Before Hiroshima*, p. 167; Sallagar, *The Road to Total War*, p. 128; and Henry Rowen, "The Evolution of Strategic Nuclear Doctrine," in Lawrence Martin, ed., *Strategic Thought in the Nuclear Age* (Heinemann, London, 1979), p. 136. LeMay is quoted in a Rand essay on the change in strategy from Europe to Asia. See Kevin Lewis, "Strategic Bombing and the Thermonuclear Breakthrough: An Example of Disconnected Defense Planning," Rand Corporation, April 1981, pp. 28, 59.

23. Gregg Herken, *The Winning Weapon: The Atomic Bomb in the Cold War* (Knopf, 1980), p. 3.

24. Robert Ferrell, ed., *Off the Record: The Private Journals of Harry S. Truman* (Norton, 1980), p. 53.

25. Dyson, *Disturbing the Universe*, p. 43. Robert Oppenheimer made essentially the same point in 1951 about the atomic bomb: "It is the decisive, even if not perhaps the final, step in a development that may have started at Guernica, and that was characterized by the blitz against London, by the British raids on Hamburg, by our fire raids on Tokyo, and by Hiroshima." "On the Military Value of the Atom," *Bulletin of the Atomic Scientists,* February 1951, p. 44.

26. Brodie, *Strategy in the Missile Age,* p. 101.

27. The *Overall Report* by Britain's Bomb Survey Unit is discussed in Hastings, *Bomber Command,* p. 346–8; Verrier, *The Bomber Offensive,* p. 29; and Webster and Frankland, *Preparations,* pp. 474–93.

28. Webster and Frankland, v. 2, *Execution,* pp. 22–5; Hastings, *Bomber Command,* pp. 350–1; Sallagar, *The Road to Total War,* p. 128. Shortly after the war, Winston Churchill vetoed the proposed monument at Westminster to Bomber Command's leaders. The bombing offensive remained a sensitive subject in both Britain and America forty years after its end. Hastings points out that Britain's official history of the air war contained forty-nine sets of statistics on the damage to German industrial production and hundreds of pages on the losses of British bombers and their crews, but no figures on the number of Germans estimated to have been killed or "dehoused" by the bombing. American passions on the subject of strategic bombing seem equally undimmed. See, for example, "American Military Ethics . . . An Exchange," *Journal of American History,* June 1981, pp. 88–91.

In his memoirs, Freeman Dyson wrote evocatively of a changing rationale that perhaps was fairly typical of the time:

At the beginning of the war I believed fiercely in the brotherhood of man, called myself a follower of Gandhi, and was morally opposed to all violence. . . . After a year of war I retreated and said, Unfortunately nonviolent resistance against Hitler is impractical, but I am still morally opposed to bombing. A few years later I said, Unfortunately it seems that bombing is necessary in order to win the war, and so I am willing to go to work for Bomber Command, but I am still morally opposed to bombing cities indiscriminately. After I arrived at Bomber Command I said, Unfortunately it turns out that we are after all bombing cities indiscriminately, but this is morally justified as it is helping to win the war. A year later I said, Unfortunately it seems that our bombing is not really helping to win the war, but at least I am morally justified in working to save the lives of the bomber crews. In the last spring of the war I could no longer find any excuses. [*Disturbing the Universe,* p. 31]

29. USSBS, *Over-all Report, European War* (GPO, 1945), pp. 64, 71, 95–6; Webster and Frankland, *Preparations,* p. 492.

30. USSBS, *Over-all Report, European War,* pp. 64–5.

31. The Survey concludes: "Certainly prior to 31 December 1945, and in all probability prior to 1 November 1945, the Japanese would have surrendered, even if the atomic bomb had not been used, and even if no invasion had been planned or contemplated." USSBS, *Japan's Struggle to End the War* (GPO, 1946), p. 13.

CHAPTER FOUR

1. Anthony C. Brown, ed., *Dropshot: The American Plan for World War III with Russia in 1957* (Dial Press, 1978). On the Air Force's postwar expectations and planning, see also Herken, *The Winning Weapon,* pp. 195–217; Jay Kelley and Desmond Ball, "Strategic Nuclear Targeting," unpublished paper, IISS, August 1981, pp. 10–17; and David Rosenberg, "American Atomic Strategy and the Hydrogen Bomb Decision," *Journal of American History,* May 1979, pp. 68–71.

2. One who participated in the planning for nuclear war wrote that "the task was seen as an extension of strategic bombing in World War II—greatly compressed in time, magnified in effect,

and reduced in cost" because of the atomic bomb. Henry Rowen, "The Evolution of Strategic Nuclear Doctrine," in Martin, ed., *Strategic Thought in the Nuclear Age*, p. 136.

3. Brodie wrote in a subsequent book on nuclear strategy that the Second World War had proved Douhet wrong on "almost every salient point he made." *Strategy in the Missile Age*, p. 101.

4. Brodie, "Strategic Bombing: What It Can Do," *The Reporter*, August 15, 1950, pp. 27–31. Brodie's brief career with the Air Force is the subject in Barry Steiner, "New Light into the Legacy of Bernard Brodie," Center for International and Strategic Affairs, UCLA, 1981; and Kaplan, *Wizards of Armageddon*, pp. 36–48.

5. Herken, *The Winning Weapon*, pp. 196–9.

6. *The Winning Weapon*, pp. 219–21; Kelley and Ball, "Strategic Nuclear Targeting," pp. 10–16; and Rosenberg, "American Atomic Strategy," pp. 68–71.

7. The importance of the "fractional crit" to the growth of the stockpile is noted in Hans Bethe, "Comments on the History of the H-Bomb," *Los Alamos Science*, Fall 1982, pp. 43–53. Other technological developments in weaponry are discussed in David Rosenberg, "The Origins of Overkill: Nuclear Weapons and American Strategy, 1945–1960," *International Security*, Spring 1983, pp. 19–20.

8. Herken, *The Winning Weapon*, pp. 258–63.

9. Brodie to David Rosenberg, October 22, 1977, Box 9, Bernard Brodie MSS, UCLA.

10. Kelley and Ball, "Strategic Nuclear Targeting," pp. 10–11.

11. Brodie to Rosenberg, Box 9, Bernard Brodie MSS, UCLA.

12. Steiner, "New Light into the Legacy of Bernard Brodie," pp. 4–6. On the targeting of cities in nuclear war plans, see Jeffrey Richelson, "Population Targeting and U.S. Strategic Doctrine," Center for International and Strategic Affairs, UCLA, May 1982, pp. 7–12.

13. MacIssacs, *Strategic Bombing in World War II*, pp. 19–21.

14. Barry Steiner, "Bernard Brodie and the American Study of Nuclear Strategy," unpublished manuscript, pp. 59–63.

15. Herken, *The Winning Weapon*, pp. 295–7; Brodie to Rosenberg, Box 9, Bernard Brodie MSS, UCLA; Kaplan, *Wizards of Armageddon*, pp. 40–4.

16. Brodie to Rosenberg, Bernard Brodie MSS, UCLA.

17. Brodie to Rosenberg, Bernard Brodie MSS, UCLA. The "collapse thesis" found expression in a 1947 war plan's assumption that use of the atomic bomb "would create a condition of chaos and extreme confusion" in Russia. The collapse would come about, the planners thought, as the result of "an increased element of hopelessness and shock resulting from the magnitude of destruction; the fear of the unknown; the actual lingering physical after effects of atomic explosions; the psychological effect arising from the necessity to evacuate large densely populated areas; and the attendant psychological state which these factors will create." The two studies whose conclusions challenged the collapse thesis were the Hull and Harmon reports. See Herken, *The Winning Weapon*, 228–9, 293–8. Excerpts from the Harmon report may be found in Thomas Etzold and John L. Gaddis, eds., *Containment: Documents on American Policy and Strategy, 1945–1950* (Oxford University Press, 1978), pp. 360–3. By 1952 the Air Force itself had begun to develop some doubts about its collapse thesis. Ironically, the advent of the H-bomb that year resolved them. See Walter Poole, *The History of the Joint Chiefs of Staff: The Joint Chiefs of Staff and National Policy*, v. 4, 1950–52 (Michael Glazier, 1981), p. 166.

18. Steiner, "Bernard Brodie and the Study of American Nuclear Strategy," pp. 61–71.

19. Brodie, *Strategy in the Missile Age*, pp. 156–9. NSC-20, which contained the declaration of war aims, concluded: "We must recognize that whatever settlement we finally achieve must be a *political* settlement, *politically* negotiated." Italics are in the original. NSC-20 is discussed in Herken, *The Winning Weapon*, pp. 276–9, and is excerpted in Etzold and Gaddis, eds., *Containment*, pp. 203–10.

20. Brodie, "Schlesinger's Old-New Ideas," Box 33, Bernard Brodie MSS, UCLA. Steiner, "Bernard Brodie and the American Study of Nuclear Strategy," pp. 12, 64–9.

21. The "sample attack" idea is noted in Steiner, "Bernard Brodie," pp. 68–72.

22. Steiner, "Bernard Brodie," pp. 68–72; Brodie, "Schlesinger's Old-New Ideas," Bernard Brodie MSS, UCLA.

23. Brodie to Rosenberg, Box 9, Bernard Brodie MSS, UCLA.

24. Ferrell, *Off the Record,* pp. 55–6.

25. The aide, Gordon Arneson, is quoted in Herken, *The Winning Weapon,* p. 262fn.

26. Herken, *The Winning Weapon,* pp. 271, 283.

27. The lecture was titled "Air Power in an Overall Strategy." See Steiner, "Bernard Brodie," pp. 28, 63.

28. Kaplan, *Wizards of Armageddon,* pp. 46–9.

29. Brodie, ed., *The Absolute Weapon,* p. 51.

30. Poole, *The History of the Joint Chiefs of Staff,* v. 4, p. 145.

31. Brodie, "New Techniques of War and National Policies," in William F. Ogburn, ed., *Technology and International Relations* (University of Chicago Press, 1959), p. 173. See also Brodie, "The Atom Bomb as Policy Maker," *Foreign Affairs,* October 1948, p. 21. Brodie thought it safe "to say with a good deal of assurance that our present superiority in atomic armaments will increase considerably before it begins to wane, and that it may continue to increase even after the Soviet Union is producing bombs, and that it may be a long time in waning thereafter." Concerning the Truman administration's belief that the atomic monopoly would be enduring, see Herken, *The Winning Weapon,* pp. 97–113.

32. Regarding the effect of the Super's development upon Brodie, see Brodie to B. H. Liddell-Hart, April 26, 1957, Box 1, Bernard Brodie MSS, UCLA; and Brodie, *Strategy in the Missile Age,* pp. 152–5.

33. Among them Vannevar Bush, an adviser to Roosevelt on the atomic bomb; and SAC commander Curtis LeMay.

34. See, for example, John Greenwood, "The Air Force Ballistic Missile and Space Program, 1954–74," *Aerospace Historian,* December 1974, pp. 190–200.

35. Brodie, "Nuclear Weapons: Strategic or Tactical?" *Foreign Affairs,* January 1954, pp. 218–19. Steiner, "New Light into the Legacy of Bernard Brodie," pp. 4–9, 75.

36. One military historian has described *Strategy in the Missile Age* as "a gloomy book." Freedman, *The Evolution of Nuclear Strategy,* p. 133. Steiner, "Bernard Brodie and the American Study of Nuclear Strategy," pp. 456–7. The comment by Adam Smith is noted in Brodie, *War and Politics,* p. 417.

37. One other problem with a counterforce strategy, Brodie thought, was that the location of the targets in Russia was simply not known. Steiner, "Bernard Brodie and the American Study of Nuclear Strategy," pp. 106–7, 221–3.

38. Borden to Brodie, October 11, 1954; and Brodie to Borden, October 20, 1954, Box 1, Bernard Brodie MSS, UCLA. My thanks to Barry Steiner for bringing the Brodie-Borden correspondence to my attention.

39. Brodie had earlier written that the atomic bomb was "not so absolute a weapon that we can disregard the limits of its destructive power." By comparison, he thought the destructiveness of the Super virtually without limit. The test of the first American H-bomb in October 1952 had a yield of almost ten and a half megatons, and obliterated a Pacific atoll. Kaplan, *Wizards of Armageddon,* p. 79.

40. Poole, *The History of the Joint Chiefs of Staff,* v. 4, pp. 142–50. Rosenberg, "The Origins of Overkill," pp. 15–18. Rosenberg argues that the aiming points for SAC's 1948 war plan were "selected with the primary objective of the annihilation of population, with industrial targets incidental."

41. Concerning the growth of the target list at this time, see Kelley and Ball, "Strategic Nuclear Targeting," pp. 15–39; Lewis, "Strategic Bombing," p. 37; Jeffrey Richelson, "Population Targeting and U.S. Strategic Doctrine," May 1982, Center for International and Strategic Affairs, UCLA; and General Richard Ellis, "The Joint Strategic Target Planning Staff" (GPO, 1981), pp. 3–9.

42. Rosenberg, "The Origins of Overkill," p. 15.

43. Brodie is quoted in Norman Moss, *Men Who Play God* (Gollancz, London, 1968), p. 117. Regarding the term "overkill," see Steiner, "Bernard Brodie and the American Study of Nuclear Strategy," pp. 97–8. An effort by SAC's commanders in 1952 to deal with the developing problem of "target overlap"—instances where a particular location was targeted more than once by the competing services or even individual commanders—had to be abandoned when the meetings ended in deadlock. Subsequent attempts to avoid "overkilling" a target failed as well, according to the

general in charge of nuclear targeting. See Ellis, "The Joint Strategic Target Planning Staff," pp. 3–9.

44. Brodie, "Nuclear Weapons: Strategic or Tactical?" *Foreign Affairs*, January 1954, pp. 218–19. Brodie, "Strategy Hits a Dead End," *Harper's*, October 1955, pp. 33–7.

45. Brodie, "Strategy Hits a Dead End," p. 36. Brodie, "Unlimited Weapons and Limited War," *Reporter*, November 18, 1954.

46. Brodie to S. Jones, April 6, 1954, Box 1, Bernard Brodie MSS, UCLA. The "nuclear winter" effect is noted in Paul Ehrlich et al., "Long-term Biological Consequences of Nuclear War," *Science*, December 23, 1983, pp. 1293–1300. Details of the war plan are in Poole, *History of the Joint Chiefs of Staff*, v. 4.

CHAPTER FIVE

1. Brodie wrote: "Our problem now is to develop the habit of living with the atomic bomb, and the very incomprehensibility of the potential catastrophe inherent in it may well make that task easier." Brodie, "The Atom Bomb as Policy Maker," *Foreign Affairs*, October 1948, p. 33.

2. The idea was perhaps not as "inflammatory" as Borden imagined, since Truman on one occasion was urged to issue a nuclear ultimatum to the Russians, and on another wrote in his private journal that he considered such an ultimatum at the time of the Korean War. See Herken, *The Winning Weapon*, pp. 334–6; and Ferrell, ed., *Off the Record*, pp. 251–2.

3. The encounter between Groves and McMahon is noted in Richard Hewlett and Oscar Anderson, *The New World: A History of the United States Atomic Energy Commission, 1939/46* (Pennsylvania State University Press, 1962), pp. 450–2.

4. Even years later, Truman expressed skepticism that the Soviets had learned how to build atomic and hydrogen bombs. On the doubts of Truman and Groves concerning the Russian nuclear arsenal, see Herbert York, *The Advisors: Oppenheimer, Teller, and the Superbomb* (Freeman, 1976), p. 34; and Herken, *The Winning Weapon*, pp. 312–13.

5. *The Winning Weapon*, p. 326. The fear that the Russians might have tested a prototype hydrogen bomb in 1949 proved unfounded. See York, *The Advisors*, pp. 31–5.

6. Like Truman and Lilienthal, Hickenlooper was shocked at how few atomic bombs were in the U.S. arsenal several years after Hiroshima. "I now wish you hadn't given me this thing to read," Hickenlooper told Truman after being given the stockpile figures. "I'd rather not have known anything about it." Herken, *The Winning Weapon*, p. 197fn.

7. "The H-bomb Decision," Videotape History, Alfred Sloan Foundation, New York City.

8. The letters written by Borden for McMahon and sent to Truman are in the "Thermonuclear Weapons Program Chronology" prepared by Henry Smyth for "The H-bomb Decision," Sloan Foundation. I am grateful to Arthur Singer of the Sloan Foundation for a copy of the chronology. Portions of Borden's letter are also in Stanley Blumberg and Gwinn Owens, *Energy and Conflict: The Life and Times of Edward Teller* (Putnam, 1976), pp. 317–18.

9. Concerning the H-bomb decision, see McGeorge Bundy, "The H-Bomb: The Missed Chance," *New York Review of Books*, May 13, 1982, pp. 13–21; David Rosenberg, "American Atomic Strategy and the Hydrogen Bomb Decision," *Journal of American History*, May 1979, pp. 83–5; and Herken, *The Winning Weapon*, pp. 316–21.

10. Borden, *There Will Be No Time*, pp. 218–19.

11. *There Will Be No Time*, p. 216.

12. As of January 1984 the chronologies prepared by the committee had yet to be declassified. Borden to the author, January 19, 1984.

13. Borden thus agreed with the contention of the biographers of Edward Teller that the "H-bomb Chronology" incident was one reason why Eisenhower approved the investigation of Oppenheimer, as a way of emphasizing the danger of security breaches. Blumberg and Owens, *Energy and Conflict*, pp. 317–20, 316fn. Interview.

14. Robert Oppenheimer, "Atomic Weapons and American Policy," *Foreign Affairs*, July 1953, pp. 525–35.

15. Borden's letter to Hoover and Eisenhower is in Blumberg and Owens, *Energy and Conflict,* pp. 317–20.

16. William Borden, "Straws in the Wind," Special Collections, Sterling Library, Yale University.

CHAPTER SIX

1. On demobilization's effects upon U.S. strategy, see Herken, *The Winning Weapon,* pp. 214–17; and Michael Sherry, *Preparing for the Next War: American Plans for Postwar Defense* (Yale University Press, 1977).

2. Concerning Kennan and the origins of containment, see John L. Gaddis, *Strategies of Containment: A Critical Appraisal of Postwar American National Security Policy* (Oxford University Press, 1982), pp. 3–53.

3. Daniel Yergin, *Shattered Peace: The Origins of the Cold War and the National Security State* (Houghton Mifflin, 1978).

4. Interview with Paul Nitze.

5. The history of Kennan's memorandum is noted in Herken, *The Winning Weapon,* pp. 314–16. Much of the text of the memo is printed in U.S. Department of State, *Foreign Relations of the United States: 1950* (GPO, 1975), v. I, pp. 22–44.

6. Comment by Gordon Arneson, "The H-bomb Decision," Alfred Sloan Foundation.

7. Arneson in "The H-bomb Decision."

8. Oppenheimer originally opposed the Super in part because he thought the design initially proposed for it would prove unworkable—as indeed it did. The theoretical thermonuclear breakthrough that occurred in 1951 removed his practical objections to the weapon's development, but his ethical qualms remained. See U.S. Atomic Energy Commission, *In the Matter of J. Robert Oppenheimer* (GPO, 1954), pp. 15–20.

9. NSC-68 and its origins are discussed in Gaddis, *Strategies of Containment,* pp. 89–126. Most of the text of NSC-68 is also in Etzold and Gaddis, eds., *Containment,* pp. 385–442. The entire text of the document is in U.S. Department of State, *Foreign Relations of the United States: 1950,* v. I, pp. 234–92.

10. Nathan Leites, *The Operational Code of the Politburo* (McGraw-Hill, 1950). Bernard Brodie thus wrote of Leites, his colleague at Rand, that the latter "developed the thesis that in Bolshevik ideology there is a *special compulsion* to destroy the opponent's capability to destroy oneself. . . ." Brodie, *Strategy in the Missile Age,* p. 185.

11. On Nitze's role in the drafting of NSC-68, see also Samuel Wells, "Sounding the Tocsin: NSC-68 and the Soviet Threat," *International Security,* Fall 1979; John L. Gaddis and Paul Nitze, "NSC-68 and the Soviet Threat Reconsidered," *International Security,* Spring 1980.

12. Herken, *The Winning Weapon,* pp. 328–9.

13. Etzold and Gaddis, eds., *Containment,* p. 442.

14. *Containment,* p. 403.

15. *Containment,* pp. 403–4.

16. Paul Nitze, "Atoms, Strategy and Policy," *Foreign Affairs,* January 1956, pp. 187–98.

17. "Atoms, Strategy and Policy," pp. 188–9.

18. Brodie to William Golden, December 15, 1953, Box 1, Bernard Brodie MSS, UCLA.

19. Nitze's point about the difficulty of destroying railroads from the air is confirmed by another veteran of the bombing survey. See Walt Rostow, *Pre-Invasion Bombing Strategy* (University of Texas Press, 1981).

20. Nitze, "Atoms, Strategy and Policy," pp. 189–90.

21. "Atoms, Strategy and Policy," p. 193.

22. Acheson is quoted in Gaddis, *Strategies of Containment,* p. 108.

23. Yergin, *Shattered Peace,* p. 403.

24. Gaddis, *Strategies of Containment,* p. 113.

25. Symington's proposal, NSC-100, is noted in Herken, *The Winning Weapon,* pp. 334–6.

26. Herken, *The Winning Weapon,* pp. 335–6.

27. David Rosenberg, "The Origins of Overkill," *International Security,* Spring 1983, pp. 11–27.

CHAPTER SEVEN

1. Oppenheimer's career after Los Alamos is detailed in Peter Goodchild, *J. Robert Oppenheimer: Shatterer of Worlds* (Houghton Mifflin, 1981).

2. Former Manhattan Project director Leslie Groves was one of those to point out the difficulty with "denaturing." Herken, *The Winning Weapon*, pp. 156–7.

3. David Lilienthal, *The Journals of David E. Lilienthal: The Atomic Energy Years, 1945–1950* (Harper & Row, 1964), p. 50.

4. Daniel Kevles, *The Physicists* (Knopf, 1978), p. 395.

5. Regarding the GAC meeting, see McGeorge Bundy, "The H-bomb Decision," *New York Review of Books.* Portions of the GAC report are in York, *The Advisors*, pp. 94–109. York makes the argument as well that the Russians might have gained from American thermonuclear testing. The controversy over the GAC report is covered in detail in the "Thermonuclear Weapons Program Chronology," "The H-Bomb Decision," Sloan Foundation, pp. 26–50.

6. The letter by Rabi and Fermi is printed in York, *The Advisors*, pp. 158–9.

7. "The H-bomb Decision," Sloan Foundation.

8. USAEC, *In the Matter of J. Robert Oppenheimer*, pp. 788–9.

9. Teller made this charge against Oppenheimer as recently as 1983, on the fortieth anniversary of the founding of the lab at Los Alamos. See Edward Teller, "Seven Hours of Reminiscences," *Los Alamos Science,* Winter/Spring 1983, pp. 190–3.

10. "The H-bomb Decision," Sloan Foundation.

11. Richard Hewlett and Francis Duncan, *Atomic Shield: A History of the United States Atomic Energy Commission, 1947/52* (Pennsylvania State University Press, 1969), pp. 406–9; Lilienthal, *The Atomic Energy Years,* pp. 632–3.

12. "The H-bomb Decision," Sloan Foundation.

13. "The H-bomb Decision," Sloan Foundation.

14. "The H-bomb Decision," Sloan Foundation.

15. Edward Teller, "The Two Responsibilities of Scientists," in M. Grodzins and E. Rabinowitch, eds., *The Atomic Age* (Simon and Schuster, 1963), pp. 121–4.

16. "The H-bomb Decision," Sloan Foundation. Oppenheimer's comment is in USAEC, *In the Matter of J. Robert Oppenheimer,* p. 69.

17. "The H-bomb Decision," Sloan Foundation.

18. On Project Lexington and its fate, see John Tierney, "Take the A-Plane: The $1 Billion Nuclear Bird That Never Flew," *Science 1982,* December 1982, pp. 46–57.

19. "Project Charles History," Videotape History, Alfred Sloan Foundation, New York City. MIT was chosen for the Charles study in part because the university's president, James Killian, had co-authored an influential article presenting the case for air defense the year before. See J. R. Killian and A. G. Hill, "For a Continental Air Defense," *Atlantic,* April 1948.

20. "Project Charles History," Sloan Foundation.

21. "Project Charles History," Sloan Foundation.

22. "What hit one hard," Zacharias remembered, "was the difference big bombs made with respect to radioactive fallout . . . and what our group knew was that radioactive fallout had a dimension that had not been studied enough." The belated appreciation of radiation effects from ground-burst nuclear weapons is noted in Kevin Lewis, "Strategic Bombing and the Thermonuclear Breakthrough," Rand Corporation, April 1981, p. 18.

23. "Project Charles History," Sloan Foundation.

24. Interview.

25. "Project Charles History," Sloan Foundation.

26. Massachusetts Institute of Technology, "Problems of Air Defense," August 1951. My thanks to Carl Kaysen for a copy of the Charles report.

27. "Project Charles History." Interview.

28. Garwin's early career is detailed in Tom Buckley, "A Voice of Reason Among the Nuclear Warriors," *Quest,* March 1981, pp. 17–23.

29. Interviews.

30. The meetings of Brodie and Oppenheimer concerning the air warfare study are noted in Steiner, "Bernard Brodie and the Study of American Nuclear Strategy," unpublished manuscript, pp. 86–8. Concerning the exclusion of Oppenheimer from analyzing the results of the atomic tests, see Herken, *The Winning Weapon,* p. 224; and USAEC, *In the Matter of J. Robert Oppenheimer,* pp. 682–96.

31. Oppenheimer, "Atomic Weapons and the Crisis in Science," *Saturday Review of Literature,* November 24, 1945, p. 10.

32. Interviews. On the origins, history, and fate of Vista, see USAEC, *In the Matter of J. Robert Oppenheimer,* esp. pp. 753–5; Stern, *The Oppenheimer Case,* pp. 171–4; and Thomas Wilson, *The Great Weapons Heresy* (Houghton Mifflin, 1970), pp. 119–20.

33. Interviews.

34. Interviews. Portions of the final report on Vista have now been declassified. See California Institute of Technology, "Final Report, Project Vista, A Study of Ground and Air Tactical Warfare with Especial Reference to the Defense of Western Europe," Record Group 407, Records of the Adjutant General's Office, Modern Military Section, National Archives, Washington, D.C. The "Interim Report" on Vista is available from the Albert Simpson Historical Research Center, Maxwell Air Force Base, Alabama.

35. Rosenberg, "The Origins of Overkill," p. 30.

36. Interviews.

37. Portions of the disarmament panel's report are in McGeorge Bundy, "Early Thoughts on Controlling the Nuclear Arms Race: A Report to the Secretary of State, January 1953," *International Security,* Fall 1982, pp. 3–27. I am indebted to Mr. Bundy for a complete copy of the report.

38. Bundy, "Early Thoughts," pp. 18–20.

39. Oppenheimer, "Atomic Weapons and American Policy," *Foreign Affairs,* July 1953, pp. 525–35.

40. ZORC is discussed in Wilson, *The Great Weapons Heresy,* pp. 170–3; and Stern, *The Oppenheimer Case,* pp. 193, 201–3. Curiously, the nuclear-powered bomber the Air Force said the Russians were then developing was supposed to be fueled by a mysterious substance known as "LORS." Tierney, "Take the A-Plane," p. 49.

41. Anonymous [Charles Murphy], "The Hidden Struggle for the H-bomb," *Fortune,* May 1953, esp. pp. 110–11.

42. USAEC, *In the Matter of J. Robert Oppenheimer,* pp. 600, 750, 922.

43. Bundy, "The H-bomb: The Missed Chance," *New York Review of Books,* May 13, 1982, pp. 13–21.

44. USAEC, *In the Matter of J. Robert Oppenheimer.*

45. Rabi once said that the test of anticommunism reminded him of the difficulty of proving sanity. The only individual who could be sure of passing for sane, Rabi noted, was one who had been discharged from a mental institution. Interview with Isidor Rabi. Teller's testimony is in USAEC, *In the Matter of J. Robert Oppenheimer,* p. 710.

46. The incident between Teller, Rabi, and Christy is noted, for example, in Goodchild, *J. Robert Oppenheimer: Shatterer of Worlds,* pp. 285–7. Teller's views on the scientists' split are also expressed in "Seven Hours of Reminiscences," *Los Alamos Science,* Winter/Spring 1983, pp. 194–5.

CHAPTER EIGHT

1. The early days at Rand are recounted in Bruce Smith, *The Rand Corporation: Case Study of a Nonprofit Advisory Corporation* (Harvard University Press, 1966), esp. pp. 30–65, 104–5; and Kaplan, *The Wizards of Armageddon,* pp. 51–73. Rand is also the subject in Paul Dickson, *Think Tanks* (Atheneum, 1971), pp. 51–138.

2. Smith, *The Rand Corporation,* p. 105.

3. Interviews.

4. "No one foresaw just how important the economists and social scientists would be at Rand," Charles Hitch reflected. "If they had, they might not have let us in. We had to find a niche for

ourselves and prove to everybody else at Rand that we had some competence to deal with major problems." Interview with Hitch. Hitch was later director of the Social Science division at Rand.

5. Smith, *The Rand Corporation,* pp. 87–90; Kaplan, *Wizards of Armageddon,* pp. 60–3.

6. Bernard Brodie, "Strategy as a Science," *World Politics,* July 1949, pp. 467–88.

7. Interviews.

8. "While the bombing survey showed we killed a lot of people," Kaysen said, "we had relatively little impact upon German ability to produce weapons." Interview. The activities of the Americans at Princes Risborough are also noted in Kaplan, *Wizards of Armageddon,* pp. 35–6. Concerning operations research and its early application, see Reginald Jones, *The Wizard War: British Scientific Intelligence, 1939–1945* (Coward, McCann and Geoghegan, 1978); and P. M. S. Blackett, *Fear, War, and the Bomb: The Military and Political Consequences of Atomic Energy* (Whittlesey House, 1949). On the attempt to shift the emphasis from bombing civilians by the end of the war, see Rostow, *Pre-Invasion Bombing Strategy.*

9. The fate of Operation Thunderclap is noted in Ronald Schaffer, "American Military Ethics in World War II: The Bombing of German Civilians," *Journal of American History,* September 1980, pp. 318–34.

10. Interview with James Digby.

11. Jay Kelley and Desmond Ball, "Strategic Nuclear Targeting," unpublished paper, IISS, August 1981, pp. 7–14.

12. The Rand group and the Air Force meant quite different things by the term "counterforce." Strategist Thomas Schelling once wrote to Bernard Brodie that counterforce was more properly "a nickname than a label"—"it is a name picked up along the way, not deliberately attached, one that gets stuck to it through a social process that involves slang, journalism, technical jargon, much the way some boys end up being called Skinny, Freckles, Fatso, Ace, or Whizzer." "The name," Schelling wrote, "focuses on one aspect of the kid, a salient but not necessarily the dominant aspect of him, there is a little bit of chance in which the name sticks, and he may go on being called Skinny long after he's put on weight. That is really the kind of name that 'counterforce' is." Schelling to Brodie, February 22, 1965, Box 2, Bernard Brodie MSS, UCLA. Early counterforce targeting by the Air Force is discussed in Lewis, "Strategic Bombing and the Thermonuclear Breakthrough," Rand Corporation, pp. 30–1. The development of counterforce thinking is the topic of Alfred Goldberg, "A Brief Survey of the Evolution of Ideas about Counterforce," Rand Corporation, revised March 1981.

13. Curtis LeMay with MacKinlay Kantor, *Mission with LeMay* (Macmillan, 1965), pp. 495–6.

14. Kelley and Ball, "Strategic Nuclear Targeting," pp. 7–14.

15. Rosenberg, "The Origins of Overkill," pp. 35–8.

16. Rosenberg, "A Smoking Radiating Ruin at the End of Two Hours: Documents on American War Plans for Nuclear War with the Soviet Union, 1954–55," *International Security,* Winter 1981/82, pp. 3–38.

17. Brodie, *Strategy in the Missile Age,* pp. 15–18. As early as the 1950s, Brodie rejected an idea that would eventually grow out of counterforce—that of "decapitating" the Soviet leadership at the outset of a nuclear war. Brodie's concern was thus that "a big and successful atomic blitz might very well incapacitate the government of the target state to the degree that it was unable to surrender." Brodie to G. K. Tanham, July 31, 1957, Box 1, Bernard Brodie MSS, UCLA.

18. Steiner, "Bernard Brodie and the American Study of Nuclear Strategy," p. 153.

19. Bernard Brodie, "Nuclear Weapons: Strategic or Tactical?" *Foreign Affairs,* January 1954.

20. Cohen discusses his own background and that of the new weapon in his book *The Truth About the Neutron Bomb* (Morrow, 1983).

21. Brodie to Max Ascoli, September 6, 1957, Box 1, Bernard Brodie MSS, UCLA. Brodie, *War and Politics,* pp. 65–6. "The Air Force came to regard nuclear weapons as essentially interchangeable with conventional weapons": Goldberg, "A Brief Survey," pp. 11–12.

22. The "Monte Carlo" game played at Rand and the "Carte Blanche" war games conducted in Europe are noted, for example, in Lawrence Freedman, *The Evolution of Nuclear Strategy,* pp. 109–10. On war gaming, see also Andrew Wilson, *The Bomb and the Computer* (Barrie and Rockliffe, London, 1968), pp. 51–65, 91–105. Although Brodie defended the exercises at Rand as contributing to the understanding of war through "the spirit of the game," privately he had some

doubts about their relevance. "It's like the difference, in playing poker, between using matches or playing for real money," he wrote to a friend. Brodie to J. M. Goldsen, February 13, 1964, Box 2, Bernard Brodie MSS, UCLA.

23. Brodie, "Unlimited Weapons and Limited War," *Reporter,* November 18, 1954. Brodie, *Strategy in the Missile Age,* pp. vi–vii.

CHAPTER NINE

1. Brodie also wrote: "If the atomic bomb can be used without fear of substantial retaliation in kind, it will clearly encourage aggression." *The Absolute Weapon,* p. 75.

2. A. J. Wohlstetter, F. S. Hoffman, R. J. Lutz, and H. S. Rowen, "Selection and Use of Strategic Air Bases," Rand Corporation, April 1954. I am indebted to Mr. Wohlstetter for a copy of the report. "My God, you guys have thought of *everything*" was Malcolm Hoag's comment to Wohlstetter after he read the report and was asked to write a summary of it. Interview with Hoag. The Air Force only briefly considered the problem of vulnerability in 1948 when choosing forward bases in England. See Herken, *The Winning Weapon,* p. 384fn. An earlier Air Force–sponsored study by Rand of SAC's vulnerability had been stalled when that service denied the researchers access to its war planning. The study was soon supplanted by Wohlstetter's report, in any case. Concerning the intellectual paternity of the idea of strategic vulnerability, see Steven Miller, "The Quest for Invulnerability: Counterforce Surprise Attack and U.S. Strategic Policy, 1945–61," Center for Science and International Affairs, Harvard University, May 1979. The Rand basing studies are also discussed in Kaplan, *The Wizards of Armageddon,* pp. 85–110.

3. B. W. Augenstein, "A Revised Development Program for Ballistic Missiles of Intercontinental Range," Rand Corporation, February 1954. My thanks to Mr. Augenstein for a copy of his report.

4. A. Wohlstetter and F. Hoffman, "Defending a Strategic Force After 1960," Rand Corporation, February 1954.

5. Interviews. Rosenberg, "The Origins of Overkill," p. 49.

6. Smith, *The Rand Corporation,* pp. 208–10; Kaplan, *Wizards of Armageddon,* pp. 105–7.

7. In the late 1950s Brodie wrote with regard to the idea of preemption: "It is more important in military planning than the relatively small amount of discussion concerning it would lead one to expect." Brodie discussed the rationale behind both preventive war and preemptive attack in *Strategy in the Missile Age,* pp. 227–32. Concerning that rationale in the Truman administration, see Herken, *The Winning Weapon,* pp. 318–19.

8. Ferrell, ed., *Off the Record,* pp. 250–1. Rosenberg, "The Origins of Overkill," pp. 31–3.

9. Herken, *The Winning Weapon,* pp. 334–6.

10. Brodie, *Strategy in the Missile Age,* p. 229. Air Force General George Kenney was apparently another advocate of preventive war in that service, but he avoided Anderson's fate by being more discreet. Rand's William Kaufmann remembered "talking late into the night" with both Anderson and Kenney about a surprise attack on Russia. "Kenney," Kaufmann observed, "said many of the things that Anderson did, but was much coyer." Interview.

11. USAEC, *In the Matter of J. Robert Oppenheimer,* pp. 752–3.

12. LeMay and Kantor, *Mission with LeMay,* pp. 480–1.

13. Thomas Power with Albert Arnhym, *Design for Survival* (Coward-McCann, 1964), pp. 79–84. In his unpublished history of strategic studies, James King wrote concerning the place of surprise attack in American military doctrine:

> The case for pre-emption, short for "preemptive strategic attack," appears to have been developed originally, not by the theorists, but by United States Air Force planners when they became fearful that the budgetary ceilings imposed upon the Strategic Air Command by President Eisenhower would not permit it to retain a position of superiority over the Soviet long-range bomber force adequate to ensure that it would prevail in an encounter that began with a Soviet surprise attack. . . . Their response to this dismaying prospect was the proposition that SAC must never be required to endure the full force of a surprise attack before launching its own strike. The surest course to this end was to be prepared

to launch a preventive attack—a course which had appealed to some Air Force generals since the Russians first acquired nuclear weapons. But even the champions of preventive war were compelled to recognize eventually that such action was incompatible with American ethics and national purposes. Hence the softened form of the alternative: SAC could not plan an unprovoked attack, but SAC would attack if it were provoked by a prior attack upon the United States or its major allies. Why not then agree that SAC would also attack if provoked by the knowledge that the United States or its major allies were *about to be attacked?* [King, "The New Strategy," v. 1, Institute for Defense Analysis, February 1972, pp. 159–60]

14. Herken, *The Winning Weapon,* p. 222–3.
15. *The Winning Weapon,* p. 271. Brodie concluded of the logical problem to preventive war:

> It is somewhat bizarre to argue that it would be wise to choose now an infinitely drastic and terrible course mostly because the problem that would allegedly be liquidated in that way is one which we or our heirs would be too stupid to handle properly later. . . . The development of the Russian nuclear capability was decisive in quashing the school urging preventive war precisely because it reinforced the moral argument against preventive war with one founded on fear. [*Strategy in the Missile Age,* pp. 233, 238]

Daniel Ellsberg, who had access to Air Force and Navy war plans during the Kennedy administration, later commented on the "gray area" in military planning between preventive war and preemption: "There is no word like preemptive or preventive for a first strike that takes place in the context of ongoing hostilities, and amounts basically to an escalation. In the absence of warning, there is no word for what American doctrine really is. And in the absence of a word, people concentrate their discussion on preemptive or preventive. It actually slips out of discussion." Interview with Ellsberg.

16. Rosenberg, "The Origins of Overkill," p. 34. British military historian Lawrence Freedman claims that the National Security Council discussed the possibility of a preventive war against Russia in 1954. *Evolution of Nuclear Strategy,* p. 125–6.

17. Concerning Eisenhower's attitude toward preventive war, see Gaddis, *Strategies of Containment,* p. 149. Gaddis notes that Eisenhower told a press conference in 1954: "A preventive war, to my mind, is an impossibility today. . . . I wouldn't even listen to anyone seriously that came in and talked about such a thing."

18. Herken, *The Winning Weapon,* p. 223; Rosenberg, "The Origins of Overkill," p. 17.
19. *The Winning Weapon,* p. 226.
20. Cited in Rosenberg, "The Origins of Overkill," p. 25.
21. Rosenberg, "The Origins of Overkill," pp. 19–20; Kaplan, *Wizards of Armageddon,* pp. 133–4. LeMay evidently thought that National Intelligence Estimates prepared by the CIA would uncover Soviet preparations for war sufficiently early to warn of a coming attack. Tactical warning would come from NORAD's radars and, starting in the 1960s, from the CIA's satellites. "We tried to be ready to go at a moment's notice—and we were ready," LeMay said. "We operated as if we were at war. Every day we were at war." Telephone conversation with Curtis LeMay.

Defense analyst Fred Kaplan quotes SAC's official history for the years 1954–56 on this point: "The ultimate objective was the ability to launch a multiple wing strike over EWP [Emergency War Plan] targets in a minimum amount of time. . . . The only way to protect the nation was to be able to destroy the enemy's offensive power before it could be completely unleashed." *Wizards of Armageddon,* p. 402 fn.

22. Power and Arnhym, *Design for Survival,* pp. 79–84.
23. Rosenberg, "A Smoking, Radiating Ruin," p. 13. Interview.
24. Rosenberg, "The Origins of Overkill," p. 66.
25. Rosenberg, "A Smoking, Radiating Ruin," p. 25.
26. Paul Kecskemeti, *Strategic Surrender: The Politics of Victory and Defeat* (Stanford University Press, 1958). Thomas Schelling wrote to Bernard Brodie some years later about the furor over the book: "I thought the great surrender flap in Congress in 1958 certified that no red-blooded man could believe in restraining general war and nobody on the federal payroll should be permitted." December 18, 1964, Box 1, Bernard Brodie MSS, UCLA.

27. Henry Kissinger, *Nuclear Weapons and Foreign Policy* (Harper & Brothers, 1957). Brodie to Max Ascoli, September 6, 1957, Box 1, Bernard Brodie MSS, UCLA. Others from whom Kissinger reportedly borrowed in writing about tactical nuclear warfare were Army general James Gavin, Harvard professor Robert Osgood, and Rand's William Kaufmann. Ironically, the previous year Kaufmann had written an essay on the subject but had been reluctant to publish it. See William Kaufmann, ed., *Military Policy and National Security* (Princeton University Press, 1966). Interviews.

28. Kaufmann's review appears in *World Politics,* July 1958, pp. 579–603. Another critical review of Kissinger's book is Paul Nitze, "Limited War or Massive Retaliation?" *Reporter,* September 1, 1957, pp. 40–2. Kissinger initially threatened to sue Nitze over the review, which criticized the author for being too sympathetic to totalitarian leaders. Interview with Paul Nitze.

29. Roberta Wohlstetter, *Pearl Harbor: Warning and Decision* (Stanford University Press, 1962).

30. Brodie to K. Archibald, October 5, 1966, Box 1, Bernard Brodie MSS, UCLA.

31. Norman Moss, *Men Who Play God* (Gollancz, London, 1968), p. 239.

CHAPTER TEN

1. On the Solarium study, see Gaddis, *Strategies of Containment,* pp. 145–6.

2. Interviews.

3. Gaddis, *Strategies of Containment* pp. 128–9.

4. *Strategies of Containment,* pp. 149–50.

5. The fate of Operation Candor is detailed in Pringle and Spigelman, *The Nuclear Barons,* pp. 118, 121–2.

6. Portions of the speech are cited in Gaddis, *Strategies of Containment,* pp. 133–4.

7. Pringle and Spigelman, *The Nuclear Barons,* pp. 121–4, 228–9.

8. Eisenhower is cited in Gaddis, *Strategies of Containment,* p. 160.

9. Interviews.

10. On the Teapot Committee and its work, see Edmund Beard, *Developing the ICBM: A Study in Bureaucratic Politics* (Columbia University Press, 1976), esp. pp. 164, 182, 241; James Killian, *Sputnik, Scientists, and Eisenhower* (MIT Press, 1977), esp. pp. 75–6; Herbert York, *Race to Oblivion* (Simon and Schuster, 1970), esp. p. 39; and John Greenwood, "The Air Force Ballistic Missile and Space Program, 1954–74," *Aerospace Historian,* Winter 1974, pp. 190–200. Because of the hydrogen bomb the accuracy requirement of the first ICBMs—which the Air Force had at first wanted to land within 1,500 feet of their targets—was "radically relaxed" to a radius of three to five miles. See Simon Ramo to Trevor Gardner, "Recommendations of the Committee on Strategic Missiles," February 10, 1954, Albert Simpson Historical Research Center, Maxwell Air Force Base, Alabama.

11. Dyson, *Disturbing the Universe,* p. 145.

12. Regarding the Killian report and its recommendations, see Killian, *Sputnik, Scientists, and Eisenhower,* pp. 67–92. Eisenhower's concern with the danger of surprise attack is also noted in Stephen Miller, "The Quest for Invulnerability," Center for Science and International Affairs, Harvard University, May 1979, p. 23.

13. Killian, *Sputnik, Scientists, and Eisenhower,* pp. 81–2.

14. *Sputnik, Scientists, and Eisenhower,* pp. 70–78.

15. For example, Rosenberg writes: "The advent of U-2 overflight reconnaissance of the Soviet Union in 1956 facilitated counterforce planning. By 1959, over 20,000 targets had been screened and analyzed by war planners." "A Smoking, Radiating Ruin," p. 16.

16. The overflight program is discussed in James Bamford, *The Puzzle Palace* (Houghton Mifflin, 1982), pp. 181–3.

17. Walt Rostow, *Open Skies: Eisenhower's Proposal of July 21, 1955* (University of Texas Press, 1983), pp. 192–3.

18. Killian, *Sputnik, Scientists, and Eisenhower,* pp. 67–92.

19. Eisenhower is quoted in Gaddis, *Strategies of Containment,* p. 149.

20. *Strategies of Containment,* p. 187.

21. Rosenberg, "The Origins of Overkill," pp. 45–6.

22. Kelley and Ball, "Strategic Nuclear Targeting," pp. 7–14.

23. Killian, *Sputnik, Scientists, and Eisenhower*, pp. 73–4. A 1950 report to Truman concluded that just sixteen atomic bombs might "most seriously disrupt" the operations of the U.S. government. Rosenberg, "The Origins of Overkill," p. 31.

24. "The Origins of Overkill," p. 40.

25. Rostow, *Open Skies*, esp. pp. 160–1, 194–6.

26. *Open Skies*, pp. 62, 197.

27. *Open Skies*, pp. 6–8.

28. *Open Skies*, p. 48.

29. The idea of exhausting the Soviet Union by means of the arms race had also occurred to others on the Quantico panel. See *Open Skies*, pp. 150, 160–1.

30. On the first flights of the U-2, see Thomas Powers, *The Man Who Kept the Secrets: Richard Helms and the CIA* (Knopf, 1979), pp. 95–7.

CHAPTER ELEVEN

1. Paul Nitze, "Atoms, Strategy and Policy," *Foreign Affairs*, January 1956, pp. 196–7.

2. On Quarles as the author of the notion of "sufficiency" in national defense, see Gaddis, *Strategies of Containment*, p. 188.

3. *Strategies of Containment*, p. 174.

4. Rosenberg, "The Origins of Overkill," *International Security*, Spring 1983, p. 40.

5. "Project Charles History," Videotape History, Alfred Sloan Foundation, New York City.

6. On the Gaither committee and its origins, see Morton Halperin, "The Gaither Committee and the Policy Process," *World Politics*, April 1961, pp. 360–84. The panel and its work are also the subject in Kaplan, *Wizards of Armageddon*, pp. 125–43.

7. U.S. Congress, Joint Committee on Defense Production, "Deterrence and Survival in the Nuclear Age" [Gaither report] (GPO, 1976), pp. 1–45.

8. Lovett is quoted in Albert Wohlstetter, "Rivals, But No Race," *Foreign Policy*, Fall 1974, p. 85. In a foreword to the 1976 reprint of the Gaither report, Senator William Proxmire argued that the report was the inspiration for the idea of nuclear war-fighting—a conclusion vigorously contested by Paul Nitze. "Deterrence and Survival in the Nuclear Age," pp. 1–4, 25. Interview with Nitze.

9. Kaplan, *Wizards of Armageddon*, pp. 150–2.

10. Concerning *Sputnik*'s effect upon American public opinion, see, for example, York, *Race to Oblivion*, pp. 106–24. The national gloom over *Sputnik* darkened further when a hurried attempt to launch the American counterpart, *Explorer I*, resulted in the explosion of the Vanguard rocket carrying the satellite. The sense of near-despair in the country was typified by Edward Teller's reply when asked what he expected to find when the U.S. finally got to the moon. "Russians," Teller answered. Kevles, *The Physicists*, p. 385.

11. "Project Charles History," Sloan Foundation.

12. Rosenberg, "The Origins of Overkill," p. 47.

13. Interviews. The meeting is also noted in Kaplan, *Wizards of Armageddon*, pp. 141–2.

14. "Deterrence and Survival in the Nuclear Age," p. 26.

15. Concerning the creation and history of PSAC, see Killian, *Sputnik, Scientists, and Eisenhower*, pp. 107–217; and George Kistiakowsky, *A Scientist at the White House* (Harvard University Press, 1976).

16. "Deterrence and Survival in the Nuclear Age," p. 28.

17. On the developing public concern with fallout, see, for example, Robert Divine, *Blowing on the Wind: The Nuclear Test Ban Debate, 1954–1960* (Oxford University Press, 1978), esp. pp. 3–35.

18. Donald Brennan, ed., *Arms Control, Disarmament, and National Security* (Braziller, 1961).

19. "Deterrence and Survival in the Nuclear Age," p. 33.

20. Kaplan, *Wizards of Armageddon*, pp. 152–3. The origins of the first Committee on the Present Danger are discussed in Richard Barnet, "The Search for National Security," *The New Yorker*, April 27, 1981; and Jerry Sanders, *Peddlers of Crisis* (South End Press, 1983).

21. On press accounts of the Gaither report, see *New York Times* and *New York Herald Tribune,* November 23, 1957; and *Newsweek,* December 30, 1957.

CHAPTER TWELVE

1. Gaddis, *Strategies of Containment,* p. 153.

2. The work of the Conference of Experts is detailed in Harold Jacobson and Eric Stein, *Diplomats, Scientists, and Politicians: The United States and the Nuclear Test Ban Negotiations* (University of Michigan Press, 1966), pp. 34–85; and Robert Gilpin, *American Scientists and Nuclear Weapons Policy* (Princeton University Press, 1962), pp. 50–2.

3. Gilpin, *American Scientists and Nuclear Weapons Policy,* pp. 229–30.

4. The contrast between the scientists and the diplomats is noted in "Strategy and the Natural Scientists," Robert Gilpin and Christopher Wright, eds., *Scientists and National Policy-Making* (Columbia University Press, 1964), pp. 174–239.

5. Jacobson and Stein, *Diplomats, Scientists, and Politicians,* pp. 79–85.

6. Wohlstetter, "The Delicate Balance of Terror," *Foreign Affairs,* January 1959, pp. 211–34. The phrase "balance of terror" was apparently coined by a British author, Jonathan Griffin, in a 1936 book published in London and entitled *The Alternative to Rearmament.* Griffin wrote: "It would be a balance of terror—for that is what the balance of power, loaded with bombs, should truly be called." Churchill's comment is cited, for example, in Jonathan Schell, *The Fate of the Earth* (Knopf, 1982), p. 197.

7. Wohlstetter drew the distinction between the missile gap and the deterrence gap in a talk he later gave on the essay. "The Delicate Balance of Terror and the Missile Gap," lecture, Harvard University, February 2, 1959. I am indebted to Mr. Wohlstetter for a copy of his lecture. Concerning his criticism of the scientists, see also Wohlstetter, "Scientists, Seers and Strategy," *Foreign Affairs,* April 1953, pp. 466–78. Wohlstetter's views on the relationship between the problems of accidental war and surprise attack are noted in Herzog, *The War-Peace Establishment,* pp. 64–7.

8. Thomas Schelling, *The Strategy of Conflict* (Oxford University Press, 1963), pp. 207–29.

9. Jacobson and Stein, *Diplomats, Scientists, and Politicians,* p. 83.

10. "Memorandum of Conversation with the President," December 31, 1959, MR 76-56 #13, Dwight D. Eisenhower Library, Abilene, Kansas.

11. Rosenberg, "The Origins of Overkill," p. 55.

12. The history of the SIOP is the subject of Peter Pringle and William Arkin, *S.I.O.P.: The Secret U.S. Plan for Nuclear War* (Norton, 1983).

13. Rosenberg, "The Origins of Overkill," pp. 62–6.

14. Gaddis, *Strategies of Containment,* p. 174.

15. *Strategies of Containment,* p. 175.

16. "Memorandum of Conference with the President," January 25, 1960, JCS memo SM-705-76, Eisenhower Library.

17. "Memorandum of Conference with the President," March 24, 1960, MR 76-56 #28, Eisenhower Library.

18. "Telephone Calls," April 7, 1960, Eisenhower Library.

19. Gaddis, *Strategies of Containment,* p. 197.

20. Symington to Eisenhower, August 29, 1958, MR 76-145, Eisenhower Library.

21. Gates' comment is in "Memorandum of Conference with the President," February 2, 1960, MR 76-56 #26, Eisenhower Library. Eisenhower's remark is quoted in Kistiakowsky, *A Scientist at the White House,* p. 293.

22. Concerning Eisenhower's decisions on the missile force, see Desmond Ball, "The Role of Strategic Concepts and Doctrine in U.S. Force Development," IISS, March 1980. Eisenhower's doubts concerning the missile gap are noted in Killian, *Sputnik, Scientists, and Eisenhower,* p. 222. On the history of the "bomber gap," see John Prados, *The Soviet Estimate: U.S. Intelligence Analysis and Russian Military Strength* (Dial Press, 1982), pp. 41–50.

23. On the U-2: Prados, *The Soviet Estimate,* pp. 30–5.

24. Powers, *The Man Who Kept the Secrets,* p. 201.

25. Kistiakowsky, *A Scientist at the White House,* p. 219.

26. Killian, *Sputnik, Scientists, and Eisenhower,* p. 222.

27. "Memorandum of Conference with the President," February 4, 1960, MR 76-56 #26, Eisenhower Library. Evidently Eisenhower was right—the Russians did encounter many of the same problems in their missile program that plagued initial U.S. efforts. See Andrew Cockburn, *The Threat: Inside the Soviet Military Machine* (Random House, 1983), esp. pp. 187–221.

28. The U.S. satellite reconnaissance program is discussed, for example, in Prados, *The Soviet Estimate,* pp. 107–9.

29. "Memorandum of Conversation with the President," February 2, 1960, MR 76-56 #26, Eisenhower Library.

30. "Statement by the Secretary of State," May 9, 1960, Eisenhower Library.

31. Gaddis, *Strategies of Containment,* pp. 196–7. "Memorandum of Conversation with the President," December 22, 1958, MR 78-44 #24, Eisenhower Library.

32. "Statement of Honorable Thomas E. Morgan, Chairman, Committee on Foreign Affairs," May 26, 1960, Eisenhower Library.

33. "Telephone Calls," May 9, 1960, Eisenhower Library.

CHAPTER THIRTEEN

1. This incident and other mishaps involving nuclear weapons are recounted in "U.S. Nuclear Weapons Accidents: Danger in Our Midst," *The Defense Monitor,* v. 10, no. 5, Center for Defense Information, Washington, D.C.

2. This briefing is recounted as well in Kaplan, *Wizards of Armageddon,* pp. 270–2.

3. Interviews. A no-first-use pledge was advocated in 1949 by George Kennan and explicitly rejected by Paul Nitze in NSC-68 some months later. On the history of the idea, see Robert McNamara, McGeorge Bundy, Gerard Smith, and George Kennan, "Nuclear Weapons and the Atlantic Alliance," *Foreign Affairs,* Spring 1982.

4. That year Bernard Brodie complained to a journalist that the government's insertion of a clause in the contract with the think tank which allowed it to review Rand reports before publication was "henceforth to be for policy statements as well as security." Brodie to Richard Rovere, May 2, 1960, Box 2, Bernard Brodie MSS, UCLA.

5. Enthoven to Brodie, October 6, 1960, Box 1, Bernard Brodie MSS, UCLA.

6. See, for example, Daniel Ellsberg, "The Crude Analysis of Strategic Choice," *American Economic Review,* May 1961, pp. 472–78. On Ellsberg's early career, see Peter Schrag, *Test of Loyalty: Daniel Ellsberg and the Rituals of Secret Government* (Simon and Schuster, 1974), pp. 11–35.

7. Concerning Truman's second thoughts about Hiroshima, see Herken, *The Winning Weapon,* pp. 20–21.

8. Bundy is quoted in Kaplan, *Wizards of Armageddon,* p. 297.

CHAPTER FOURTEEN

1. Concerning the history and political significance of the missile gap, see Edgar Bottome, *The Missile Gap* (Fairleigh Dickinson Press, 1971); Prados, *The Soviet Estimate,* pp. 120–5; and Desmond Ball, *Politics and Force Levels: The Strategic Missile Program of the Kennedy Administration* (University of California Press, 1980), esp. pp. 97–9.

2. The Navy spokesman is cited in Richard Fryklund, *100 Million Lives: Maximum Survival in a Nuclear War* (Macmillan, 1962), p. 98.

3. The "Alternative Undertaking" is noted in Rosenberg, "The Origins of Overkill," *International Security,* Spring 1983, pp. 53–4. See also Pringle and Arkin, *S.I.O.P.: The Secret U.S. Plan for Nuclear War,* pp. 101–25.

4. The Navy briefing of McNamara is noted in Kaplan, *Wizards of Armageddon,* pp. 258–60.

5. On the revival of counterforce thinking at Rand and the Air Force reaction, see Goldberg,

"A Brief Survey of the Evolution of Ideas About Counterforce," pp. 11–12, 18–20; Ball, *Politics and Force Levels,* pp. 32–4; James King, "The New Strategy," v. 1, pp. 188–95; and Kaplan, *Wizards of Armageddon,* pp. 201–19.

6. Goldberg, "A Brief Survey," pp. 18–20.

7. Kaufmann credited two other Rand analysts, David McGarvey and Frank Trinkl, and their study, "The Dynamics of Central War," with inspiring much of his thinking about counterforce. A popularization of counterforce strategy that appeared at this time was journalist Richard Fryklund's *100 Million Lives.* Fryklund was an enthusiast of the counterforce approach, though his rationale for the strategy may ultimately have been more disturbing than comforting to many readers: "Postwar effects of fallout will be great, but they will be too diffused to be noticed by the average person. . . . Even with a third of our population gone, we would still be the fourth largest country in the world. Even with our economy cut in half, we would still be the richest country in the world. . . . Our postwar world could be worse—it could be communist." *100 Million Lives,* pp. 138–40.

8. Enthoven argued in a subsequent book that "civilian analysts are needed to pick up good *military* ideas squelched by the Service bureaucracies." Alain Enthoven and Wayne Smith, *How Much Is Enough?: Shaping the Defense Program, 1961–1969* (Harper & Row, 1971), pp. 27–32.

9. Interview with Herbert York. York discusses the missile and bomber figures in his book *Race to Oblivion,* pp. 49–60, 75–105.

10. Pringle and Arkin, *S.I.O.P.,* pp. 101–26. On the reaction of the Air Force and SAC to the new strategy, see Jay Kelley and Desmond Ball, "Strategic Nuclear Targeting," IISS, August 1981, pp. 24–5; and Henry Rowen, "The Evolution of Strategic Nuclear Doctrine," in Martin, ed., *Strategic Thought in the Nuclear Age,* p. 133. Wohlstetter and Hoffman predicted in their report that "the date at which the Russians will have a missile capable of carrying a 25-megaton bomb with a 1500 foot [radius of accuracy] appears sufficiently far removed to make the defense good, let's say, until the end of the sixties." A. Wohlstetter and F. Hoffman, "Defending a Strategic Force after 1960," Rand Corporation, February 1954, p. 19. See also A. Wohlstetter and F. Hoffman, "Protecting U.S. Power to Strike Back in the 1950's and 1960's," Rand Corporation, September 1956. In fact, the Russians acquired the theoretical capability Wohlstetter and Hoffman had predicted around the year 1969 with their SS-9 missile.

11. In the wake of the Bay of Pigs fiasco, Kennedy allegedly vowed to his brother Robert that he would "never trust in experts again." On the planning for the failed invasion, see, for example, Peter Wyden, *The Bay of Pigs: The Untold Story* (Simon and Schuster, 1979).

12. On the Berlin crisis, see Arthur Schlesinger, Jr., *A Thousand Days: John F. Kennedy in the White House* (Houghton Mifflin, 1965), pp. 353–76; and Theodore Sorensen, *Kennedy* (Harper & Row, 1965), pp. 633–5.

13. Bundy is quoted in Kaplan, *Wizards of Armageddon,* p. 298.

14. The crisis-simulation game is noted in *Wizards of Armageddon,* pp. 302–3.

15. The hypothetical war plan of Kaysen and Rowen is also discussed in *Wizards of Armageddon,* pp. 299–301.

16. Interviews.

17. McNamara's memorandum is quoted in Robert Scheer, *With Enough Shovels: Reagan, Bush and Nuclear War* (Random House, 1982), p. 150.

18. Schlesinger, *A Thousand Days,* p. 363; Sorensen, *Kennedy,* p. 577.

19. The president's instructions to Harriman are cited by Glenn Seaborg, whom Kennedy appointed chairman of the U.S. Atomic Energy Commission. Seaborg, *Kennedy, Khrushchev and the Test Ban* (University of California Press, 1981), p. 239. Seaborg writes that "Kennedy might have been thinking in terms of a preemptive strike against Chinese nuclear facilities."

20. Concerning the evidence that the Russians considered an attack upon the Chinese nuclear weapons facility at Lop Nor in 1969, see Robert Haldeman, *The Ends of Power* (Times Books, 1977), p. 69.

21. "The Cuban Missile Crisis," Videotape History, Alfred Sloan Foundation, New York City.

CHAPTER FIFTEEN

1. One concern of the Europeans with the new strategy was that it seemed to put an undue emphasis upon striking first. Ball, *Politics and Force Levels*, pp. 195–8.

2. *Politics and Force Levels*, pp. 197–8.

3. *Politics and Force Levels*, p. 198. Regarding how counterforce strategy became the no-cities doctrine, and no-cities became identified with striking first, see James King, "The New Strategy," v. 1, pp. 188–95.

4. Ball, *Politics and Force Levels*, pp. 197–8.

5. Reconnaissance satellites had given the United States "a fair knowledge" of military targets inside Russia, a Defense Department spokesman told a congressional committee in 1962. On the implementation of counterforce strategy in the war plans, see Pringle and Arkin, *S.I.O.P.*, pp. 101–26; Goldberg, "A Brief Survey," p. 26; and Prados, *The Soviet Estimate*, pp. 106–10.

6. The unexpectedly high cost of counterforce as one of the reasons why McNamara abandoned the no-cities doctrine is noted by Enthoven in his essay "1963 Nuclear Strategy Revisited," in Harold Ford and Francis Winters, eds., *Ethics and National Security* (Orbis Books, 1977), pp. 72–81.

7. An analysis of the Cuban missile crisis which suggests that the disparity in strategic forces between the United States and Russia was its principal cause is Graham Allison, *Essence of Decision: Explaining the Cuban Missile Crisis* (Little, Brown, 1971). An eyewitness account of the crisis that is particularly sympathetic to the president is Robert Kennedy, *Thirteen Days: A Memoir of the Cuban Missile Crisis* (Norton, 1969). In retrospect, both Bundy and McNamara thought that Robert Kennedy's account might have exaggerated his brother's concern that an accidental nuclear war would develop out of the crisis. Interviews. A videotaped reflection on the crisis and its lessons is "The Cuban Missile Crisis," Alfred Sloan Foundation, New York City.

8. Sorensen, *Kennedy*, pp. 748–9. Another account of Kennedy and the crisis is Schlesinger, *A Thousand Days*, pp. 728–61.

9. Kelley and Ball, "Strategic Nuclear Targeting," pp. 7–16, 105–16; Prados, *The Soviet Estimate*, pp. 122, 188.

10. "The Cuban Missile Crisis," Sloan Foundation.

11. This was almost certainly Curtis LeMay. Years later, LeMay lamented that "the military was entirely cut out of the planning process in the Kennedy administration." LeMay also dissented from what he felt was the popular image of Kennedy as a "hero" because of the crisis: "The facts were that we could have gotten the missiles out of Cuba. And the communists out of Cuba." Concerning the possibility of a U.S. ultimatum to the Russians over Cuba and other Cold War issues, LeMay said: "We had the capability to do it then. . . . I knew there would come a time when we would rue the day when we could get the communists out of Cuba and let the opportunity pass." LeMay is convinced that Kennedy made a secret deal with Khrushchev to trade the Russian missiles in Cuba for American missiles in Greece and Turkey. As evidence, he claims that the administration ordered the intermediate-range missiles removed from allied bases only months after the crisis, justifying the move on the grounds that the missiles were then "obsolete" and about to be replaced by intercontinental-range missiles like Minuteman anyway. "But the concrete for some of the launching pads had just been poured," LeMay notes. "We objected to it at the time. But in vain." LeMay's suspicion that there was a deal over the missiles is shared by others. But Kennedy administration officials have steadfastly denied the existence of any such arrangement.

In 1981, former Italian prime minister Fanfani alleged that he was approached by President Kennedy in 1962 to act as an intermediary with Khrushchev for a missile trade. Kennedy apparently did exchange at least eight private letters with Khrushchev after the crisis. But the president did not reveal the nature of his correspondence to even his closest advisers, and neither the exact number of the letters nor their contents have become known. Interviews.

12. "The Cuban Missile Crisis," Sloan Foundation.

13. McNamara's comment is in Scheer, *With Enough Shovels*, p. 49.

14. *With Enough Shovels*, p. 150.

15. Interview.

16. Rowen, "The Evolution of Strategic Nuclear Doctrine," in Martin, ed., *Strategic Thought in the Nuclear Age,* p. 135.

17. Ball, *Politics and Force Levels,* p. 198.

18. Maxwell Taylor, *The Uncertain Trumpet* (Harper & Brothers, 1959). Concerning Taylor and the other men around Kennedy and McNamara, see David Halberstam, *The Best and the Brightest* (Random House, 1969).

19. Kissinger pulled back from his early theories on limited nuclear war in *The Necessity for Choice* (Doubleday, 1960). Concerning Kissinger's change of mind, see James King, "The New Strategy," v. 2, pp. 134–6, 199–200; and Freedman, *The Evolution of Nuclear Strategy,* pp. 106–8. On Brodie's notion of origin of "firebreak" concept, see Bernard Brodie, *War and Politics* (Macmillan, 1973), p. 125.

20. Enthoven and Smith, *How Much Is Enough?* pp. 117–64.

21. Interview.

22. The bureaucratic struggle over the M-16 is recounted in detail by James Fallows, *National Defense* (Random House, 1981), pp. 76–95. Rand's alumni came under attack at this time by military figures like former SAC commander Curtis LeMay, former Air Force chief of staff Thomas White, and Vice-Admiral Hyman Rickover. White, an early enthusiast of counterforce strategy, now declared himself "profoundly apprehensive of the pipe-smoking, tree-full-of-owls type of so-called professional 'defense intellectuals' who have been brought into this nation's capitol." LeMay and Rickover similarly denounced the civilian theorists as "armchair strategists," "crackpot metaphysicians," "sociologists," and "spiritualists . . . playing at God while neglecting the responsibility of being human." On the whiz kids and their critics, see Herzog, *The War-Peace Establishment,* pp. 34–5. The attack ultimately prompted Alain Enthoven to retitle one of the draft chapters of his book: "The Need for Civilian Analysts" became "Why Independent Analysts?" Interview with Enthoven.

23. An account of the MLF that emphasizes its bureaucratic origins is John Steinbruner, *The Cybernetic Theory of Decision* (Princeton University Press, 1974), esp. pp. 202–6. While the completion of the "Acheson report" is generally considered to mark the official end of the policy of massive retaliation, the report's recommendations on the rebuilding of the West's conventional forces were not accepted even as a goal by NATO until 1967. One of those analysts who urged a greater conventional emphasis in defense thought McNamara made a tactical error in choosing Burton Klein to head a secret delegation to NATO assigned with the task of promoting the idea. Klein, then the head of Rand's economics department, was renowned for his absentmindedness. As a tuba player in the Harvard band while an undergraduate, he had almost electrocuted himself when the instrument touched the overhead lines of the Boston subway during the celebration of a football victory over Yale. Interview.

24. McNamara's comment is cited in William Kaufmann, *The McNamara Strategy* (Harper & Row, 1964), p. 312.

25. Regarding the American University speech and public reaction to it, see Schlesinger, *A Thousand Days,* pp. 822–4.

CHAPTER SIXTEEN

1. One observer of the test ban debate writes: "The rancor and bitterness of the conflict among the scientists over the danger of radioactive fallout was unparalleled in the whole history of the scientific conflict over nuclear weapons policy." Gilpin, *American Scientists and Nuclear Weapons Policy,* p. 167. Concerning the Teller-Pauling feud, see Divine, *Blowing on the Wind,* pp. 184–8. On the views of various scientists regarding the test ban, see Herbert York, "The Great Test-Ban Debate," in Herbert York, ed., *Arms Control: Readings from Scientific American* (Freeman, 1973), pp. 294-302.

2. On Teller's arguments against the test ban, see, for example, his article "Alternatives for Security," *Foreign Affairs,* January 1958, pp. 201–8.

3. Dyson, "The Future Development of Nuclear Weapons," *Foreign Affairs,* April 1960; and *Disturbing the Universe,* pp. 129–30, 134–5.

4. On the "big-hole" theory, see Gilpin, *American Scientists and Nuclear Weapons Policy,* pp. 244–5, 269.

5. Interviews.

6. Khrushchev wrote that he and the Russian atomic scientists agreed not to test such a "monster" bomb again. Strobe Talbott, ed. and trans., *Khrushchev Remembers: The Last Testament* (Little, Brown, 1974), p. 289.

7. Interview.

8. On Teller's argument for "cleaner" nuclear weapons and its influence with Eisenhower, see Gilpin, *American Scientists and Nuclear Weapons Policy,* pp. 168–9; Divine, *Blowing on the Wind,* pp. 148–51; and Seaborg, *Kennedy, Khrushchev and the Test Ban,* pp. 8–9.

9. Cohen claimed in an interview that when he was finally allowed to talk to Eisenhower about the neutron bomb—in the summer of 1961—the former president told him "that it was an interesting concept, but that it had no application." "If a war starts," Cohen said Eisenhower told him, "it's going to be all-out thermonuclear war and such weapons will play precious little role." See also Samuel Cohen, "The Neutron Bomb: Political Technological and Military Issues," Institute for Foreign Policy Analysis, Tufts University, 1978, esp. pp. 8–13, 16–20.

10. Cohen, *The Truth About the Neutron Bomb.*

11. Seaborg, *Kennedy, Khrushchev and the Test Ban,* pp. 82–4.

12. On the creation and the early days of ACDA, see, for example, Herzog, *The War-Peace Establishment,* pp. 113–15; and Dyson, *Disturbing the Universe,* pp. 131–9.

13. The scientists' reactions to the missile crisis are noted in Thomas Powers, "Seeing the Light of Armageddon," *Rolling Stone,* April 29, 1982, pp. 13–17.

14. Seaborg, *Kennedy, Khrushchev and the Test Ban,* pp. 210–12, 181.

15. Dyson, *Disturbing the Universe,* p. 138. The dispute over the number of inspections is discussed in Seaborg, *Kennedy, Khrushchev, and the Test Ban,* pp. 186–200. Nor was the exact number of inspections required for a comprehensive test ban agreed upon. Kaysen later thought that ACDA director William Foster's rigid insistence upon five inspections "blew the comprehensive test ban treaty away."

16. Sorensen, *Kennedy,* p. 836.

17. Seaborg, *Kennedy, Khrushchev and the Test Ban,* pp. 242–3, 300.

18. Cohen, *The Truth About the Neutron Bomb,* pp. 162–5.

CHAPTER SEVENTEEN

1. The early history of the ABM is detailed in Ernest Yanarella, *The Missile Defense Controversy: Strategy, Technology, and Politics, 1955–1972* (University of Kentucky Press, 1977), pp. 1–25; and Abram Chayes and Jerome Wiesner, eds., *ABM: An Evaluation of the Decision to Deploy an Anti-ballistic Missile System* (Harper & Row, 1969), pp. 3–62.

2. Yanarella, *The Missile Defense Controversy,* pp. 34–8.

3. The role of the ABM in the Kennedy administration is discussed in Yanarella, *The Missile Defense Controversy,* pp. 43–78; and Prados, *The Soviet Estimate,* pp. 151–64.

4. Enthoven and Smith, *How Much Is Enough?* pp. 184–90.

5. Concerning the pro-ABM viewpoint, see Herman Kahn, ed., *Why ABM?* (Praeger, 1968).

6. Brennan, ed., *Arms Control, Disarmament, and National Security.*

7. Stone's subsequent book typified the attitude of anti-ABM scientists toward arms control. See Jeremy Stone, *Strategic Persuasion: Arms Limitation Through Dialogue* (Columbia University Press, 1967). Journalist William Safire claims that the terms "hawk" and "dove" were added to the Cold War's lexicon during the Cuban missile crisis. See *Safire's Political Dictionary* (Random House, 1978), pp. 773–4.

8. "National Security and the Nuclear Test Ban," *Scientific American,* October 1964. This article also appears with a critical commentary by pro-ABM physicist Eugene Wigner in York, ed., *Arms Control: Readings from Scientific American,* pp. 129–39.

9. McNamara's view of the reasons for the Soviet military buildup is noted in Scheer, *With*

Enough Shovels, pp. 217–19. Johnson is quoted in John Newhouse, *Cold Dawn: The Story of SALT* (Holt, Rinehart and Winston, 1973), pp. 66–102.

10. Newhouse, *Cold Dawn,* pp. 89–90, 101. Newhouse concludes that the ABM "was an option well worth exploring. It was not, however, explored systematically and dispassionately in 1966 and 1967. Washington instead found itself caught up in a wave of ABM hysteria, and the decision, like so many others, was not measured." The Russian military buildup is the subject, for example, of Prados, *The Soviet Estimate,* pp. 157–64.

11. Concerning the ABM debate in the Johnson administration, see Yanarella, *The Missile Defense Controversy,* pp. 79–142; Prados, *The Soviet Estimate,* pp. 158–71; Enthoven and Smith, *How Much Is Enough?;* and Newhouse, *Cold Dawn,* pp. 66–102. McNamara dealt directly with the president on the question of the ABM and did not ask his staff to prepare any of the draft presidential memoranda he had used with Kennedy; this was unlike his dealings with Johnson on other defense issues.

12. McNamara deleted the phrase "mad momentum" from a subsequent book of his speeches while defense secretary. Significantly, he also relegated the actual announcement of the ABM decision and the rationale behind it to an appendix in the book. Robert McNamara, *The Essence of Security: Reflections in Office* (Harper & Row, 1968), pp. 51–67, 163–5. Albert Wohlstetter challenged the "action-reaction" view of the arms race in a later series of articles. See Wohlstetter's "Is There a Strategic Arms Race?"; "Rivals, but No Race"; and "Optimal Ways to Confuse Ourselves," *Foreign Policy,* Summer 1974–Autumn 1975. MIT physicist George Rathjens defended McNamara's thesis in "The Dynamics of the Arms Race," *Scientific American,* April 1969.

13. While McNamara conceded that there were three possible missions for an American ABM —as a defense for U.S. missiles against Soviet attack, as protection against accidents, and as a counter to Chinese ICBMs—he chose to justify his decision by citing the Chinese threat, which supporters of the ABM thought the least persuasive argument. In his 1968 book, McNamara stressed the ABM's importance as a hedge against the vulnerability of American missiles to Soviet attack. *The Essence of Security,* pp. 163–6.

14. Interviews. Some ABM proponents later claimed that McNamara deceived them into believing that he would support a subsequent expansion of the Sentinel program, and hence fooled them into an endorsement of the anti-Chinese ABM.

15. On the origins of MIRV, see Ted Greenwood, *Making the MIRV: A Study of Defense Decision Making* (Ballinger Press, 1975), esp. pp. 1–50; and Newhouse, *Cold Dawn,* pp. 27–31, 73–7. Newhouse writes: "MIRV, it seemed, was the *rara avis* of the arsenal—competent, versatile, cost-effective, and no threat to stability."

16. Rand physicist Albert Latter, an early proponent of MIRV, cited its pending development as a reason for his opposition to the test ban. See Michael Parfit, *The Boys Behind the Bombs* (Little, Brown, 1983), pp. 3–8; and John Edwards, *Super-Weapon: The Making of MX* (Norton, 1982), pp. 51–4.

17. Kaplan, *Wizards of Armageddon,* pp. 111–24.

18. York, *Race to Oblivion,* pp. 156, 184–7.

19. Kaplan, *Wizards of Armageddon,* pp. 360–7.

20. Greenwood, *Making the MIRV,* p. 179.

21. Newhouse, *Cold Dawn,* p. 82.

CHAPTER EIGHTEEN

1. Herman Kahn, *On Thermonuclear War* (Princeton University Press, 1960). Concerning Kahn and his ideas, see also Kaplan, *Wizards of Armageddon,* pp. 220–31; and Norman Moss, *Men Who Play God,* pp. 243–56. Kahn claimed that the first year at Hudson he and his colleagues attempted "to put in writing everything a good secretary of defense ought to know." They intended to spend the second year writing a similar guidebook for the secretary of state. The initial effort, however, eventually ran to nine volumes before it was abandoned, Kahn said. The second book was never attempted. Though Kahn admitted the original idea was overly ambitious and produced "a monstrosity," he defended it "as a minimum-level project to capture the nuances." The distinctions

Kahn made in *On Thermonuclear War* between various strategies and strategists were equally esoteric to many readers. Kahn said the difference between his view of deterrence and Donald Brennan's, for example, was the difference between his own goal of a "not-incredible first-strike capability" and Brennan's of a "not-completely-incredible first-strike capability." Interview with Herman Kahn.

2. Brodie's "wargasm" comment is noted in Moss, *Men Who Play God,* p. 117. Brodie to Kahn, February 16, 1962, Box 3, Bernard Brodie MSS, UCLA.

3. *On Thermonuclear War,* pp. 145–9.

4. Leo Szilard, "How to Live with the Bomb—and Survive" in Grodzins and Rabinowitch, eds., *The Atomic Age,* pp. 217–44. Though Szilard was one of the first scientists to lobby for the international control of atomic energy, Bernard Brodie claimed that the physicist advocated a preventive war against the Soviet Union in October 1945. Brodie to Thomas Schelling, August 1, 1965, Box 2, Bernard Brodie MSS, UCLA.

5. *Scientific American,* March 1961, pp. 197–200.

6. Schelling, *The Strategy of Conflict,* pp. 207–29.

7. *The Strategy of Conflict,* pp. 53–80.

8. Thomas Schelling, *Arms and Influence* (Yale University Press, 1966), p. 191.

9. The idea that appearing irrational could be an advantage in international diplomacy had also been argued by Daniel Ellsberg and Thomas Schelling. One of President Nixon's aides, H. R. Haldeman, claims that a practical demonstration of this ploy was the "madman theory," which Haldeman argues was behind Nixon's decision to order the bombing of the Vietnamese cities of Hanoi and Haiphong on Christmas Eve in 1972. See Haldeman, *The Ends of Power,* pp. 83–5.

10. One noted critic of Schelling and Kahn is Philip Green, *Deadly Logic: The Theory of Nuclear Deterrence* (Ohio State University Press, 1966), esp. pp. 153–4. Interviews.

11. In a second edition of *On Thermonuclear War* published in 1969, Kahn drew a distinction between a "credible," a "not-incredible," and a "splendid" first-strike capability, admitting that in the first edition of the book he should have devoted more space to discussion of the "splendid" capability, which gave the United States the option of disarming Russia in a surprise attack. Ellsberg's point has been made by others. See James King, "The New Strategy," v. 4, pp. 97–8; and Freedman, *The Evolution of Nuclear Strategy,* pp. 216–17. Freedman suggests that one reason for Kahn's leaving Rand was his advocacy of a first-strike capability for the United States.

12. James King notes, for example, that in Brodie's early work escalation is a danger to be avoided by statesmen and strategists. In the subsequent writings of Schelling and Kahn, however, it is treated as a deliberate tool. King, "The New Strategy," v. 4, pp. 216–17. Freedman, *The Evolution of Nuclear Strategy,* pp. 419–20.

13. Herman Kahn, *Thinking About the Unthinkable* (Horizon Press, 1962), pp. 194–5. Kahn, *On Escalation* (Praeger, 1965). Freedman points out that during the Second World War Germany and Britain skipped five rungs of Kahn's hypothetical ladder in a single, unplanned escalation of that conflict. *The Evolution of Nuclear Strategy,* p. 217. A 1969 Rand study of escalation in the strategic bombing of the Second World War that was commissioned by the Air Force concluded that neither side had intended the increase in violence and destruction. Instead, the author wrote, the "ultimate escalation to total war was not planned so much as it happened." Sallagar, *The Road to Total War,* p. 133.

14. See, for example, Bernard Brodie, "Why Were We So (Strategically) Wrong?" *Foreign Policy,* Winter 1971/72, pp. 151–61.

15. Schelling, *Arms and Influence,* pp. 145–6.

16. Kahn, *On Escalation,* p. 261. Kahn deleted the term "exemplary" in a 1968 revision of the book.

17. On Brodie's early support for the Vietnam war, see Brodie to *New York Times,* April 5, 1965, Box 2, Brodie MSS, UCLA. His change of mind on the war is related in Brodie, *War and Politics,* pp. 113–222. In May 1970, following the Nixon administration's decision to invade Cambodia, Schelling led a delegation of MIT and Harvard professors to the White House to inform their former colleague Henry Kissinger that they now opposed the president's conduct of the war.

18. See Schelling, *Strategy of Conflict,* pp. 195–7; Kahn's essay in Frank Armbruster, ed., *Can*

We Win in Vietnam? (Praeger, 1968), p. 178; and Brodie, "Why Were We So (Strategically) Wrong?" pp. 157–60.

19. The Jasons stemmed from a convocation of second-generation atomic scientists in the summer of 1959 at Los Alamos that was sponsored by the Pentagon's Institute for Defense Analysis. The feeling there, according to Goldberger, was that the solution of modern defense problems required supplementing the "aging warriors" who had been prominent in the Manhattan Project and at MIT's Radiation Laboratory with a group of younger scientists. Goldberger said he was surprised to find himself elected president of the nascent organization when he returned from a trip to the bathroom. His wife chose the title for the group, her inspiration being the Greek temple that was the emblem of the Institute for Defense Analysis. The first problem studied by the Jasons was that of defending against a missile attack. Ironically, one result of that project would be to convince many of the Jason scientists that an effective ABM was technologically infeasible. Concerning the history of the Jasons, see Tom Buckley, "A Voice of Reason Among the Nuclear Warriors," *Quest,* March 1981, pp. 17–23.

CHAPTER NINETEEN

1. Concerning the vision of Armageddon in fiction, see, for example, Philip Wylie, *Tomorrow!* (Rinehart, 1954); Nevil Shute, *On the Beach* (Morrow, 1957); Pat Frank, *Alas, Babylon* (Lippincott, 1959); Mordecai Roshwald, *Level 7* (McGraw-Hill, 1959); Walter Miller, *A Canticle for Leibowitz* (Lippincott, 1959); and Eugene Burdick and Harvey Wheeler, *Fail-Safe* (McGraw-Hill, 1962). In *Tomorrow!* the Russians launch a surprise attack on Christmas Day. The only survivors of the nuclear war in *Level 7* are the occupants of the underground bunkers from which the annihilating missiles are launched. Former enemies become friends after the war, though none is able to leave his shelter, and all are eventually killed when the radiation seeps down to their level. *A Canticle for Leibowitz*—perhaps the most sardonic of the novels—sees the survivors of a nuclear war painfully struggle back to create a new modern civilization, only to destroy it once again in another nuclear war. On this literary genre and the popular culture of doomsday, see Michael Mandelbaum, "The Bomb, Dread, and Eternity," *International Security,* Fall 1980, pp. 3–23; and Paul Boyer, "From Activism to Apathy: The American People and Nuclear Weapons, 1963–1980," *Journal of American History,* March 1984, pp. 821–44.

2. Frank, *Alas, Babylon,* p. 254.

3. Peter George, *Red Alert* (Dell Books, 1959). *Red Alert* was originally published in England as *Two Hours to Doom.* The similarities of *Fail-Safe* and *Red Alert* prompted George to sue the rival novel's American authors, who eventually settled out of court. Critics of both *Red Alert* and *Fail-Safe* challenged the assumption of each book that a nuclear war would stop after the destruction of only two cities. See Sidney Hook, *The Fail-Safe Fallacy* (Stein & Day, 1963). The same point was made with a kind of grim humor by novelist Herbert Gold in a short story of the time titled "The Day They Got Boston." See Groff Conklin, ed., *17 × Infinity* (Dell, 1963), pp. 129–38.

4. Kubrick told an interviewer of the reason for changing his mind about the film: "What could be more absurd than the very idea of two megapowers willing to wipe out all human life because of an accident, spiced up by political differences that will seem as meaningless to people a hundred years from now as the theological conflicts of the Middle Ages appear to us today?" Quoted in Norman Kagan, *The Cinema of Stanley Kubrick* (Holt, Rinehart and Winston, 1972), p. 128.

5. Most civilian strategists admitted that the film was at least amusing and well done, though one particularly conservative theorist denounced it as "the most vicious attack to date launched by one of our mass media against the American military profession." Herzog, *The War-Peace Establishment,* p. 17.

6. Henry Kissinger was also mentioned as a possible model for Strangelove. Kubrick insisted that the character was a composite.

7. Green, *Deadly Logic,* pp. 60, iv.

8. Anatol Rapoport, *Strategy and Conscience* (Harper & Row, 1964), pp. 175–98.

9. Leonard Lewin, ed., *The Report from Iron Mountain on the Possibility and Desirability of Peace* (Dial Press, 1967).

10. Bernard Brodie, *War and Politics* (Macmillan, 1973), p. 125fn. A mistaken belief that he had advocated the use of nuclear weapons in Vietnam was one of the reasons for the extremely hostile reaction that Brodie's book on escalation received from critics. "Not only the threat but the use of tactical nuclear weapons is advocated by Bernard Brodie," began one review of the book. Brodie, *Escalation and the Nuclear Option* (Princeton University Press, 1966). *New York Times Book Review,* October 9, 1966.

11. Dyson, *Disturbing the Universe,* pp. 149–50.

12. Interview.

13. Hoffmann would later be a bitter critic of the war, but in 1965 he expressed a sentiment that was then perhaps the most common rationale for remaining in Vietnam: "One is bound by one's commitments; one is committed even by one's mistakes." Stanley Hoffmann, *The State of War* (Praeger, 1965), p. 171. Concerning Ellsberg's conversion on the war, see Schrag, *Test of Loyalty,* esp. p. 32.

14. Herman Kahn and Anthony Wiener, *The Year 2000: A Framework for Speculation on the Next Thirty-three Years* (Macmillan, 1967).

15. Interviews. Critics of *The Year 2000* after 1973 pointed out, therefore, that the book's index contains no entry for "oil" or even for "energy."

16. Interview.

17. Kahn in Armbruster, ed., *Can We Win in Vietnam?*

18. Kahn, "If Negotiations Fail," *Foreign Affairs,* July 1968, pp. 627–41.

19. Kaplan's stand on Vietnam was influenced, he claimed, by his experience as head of Temple University's Peace Fellowship at the beginning of the Second World War. It was not until the day the Germans marched into Paris, Kaplan said, that he finally realized "what a goddamned fool I'd been." He thought the demonstrators against the Vietnam war similarly guilty of "moral primitivism": "I had not waved the Nazi flag, as many of our young people now wave the North Vietnamese flag, but the brutal and unavailing moral fact was that I had willed, even if only indirectly, the victory of a totalitarian force. . . . I wasn't morally bad; I was morally imbecilic." Morton Kaplan, ed., *Strategic Thinking and Its Moral Implications* (University of Chicago Press, 1973), p. 152.

20. Richard Pfeffer, ed., *No More Vietnams? The War and the Future of American Foreign Policy* (Harper & Row, 1968).

21. *No More Vietnams?* pp. 27–9.

22. *No More Vietnams?* pp. 36–8.

23. Draper thought it "not so clear to the 'limited war' theorists that their recipes of 'graduated response' might be self-defeating in a war between a very great power and a very small one," since "a great power may only use a very limited portion of its power, but it will be enough to make a small power feel that it must fight an unlimited war or not fight at all. . . . In fact, the doctrine of 'limited war' as it was worked out in the latter half of the 1950's outside the government and taken over by the government in the 1960's must be held partially responsible for pulling us in." *No More Vietnams?* p. 30.

24. Schrag, *Test of Loyalty,* p. 32.

25. Kaplan, ed., *Strategic Thinking and Its Moral Implications,* p. 42.

26. Concerning Osgood's change of mind about limited war, see his essay "The Post-War Strategy of Limited War: Before, During and After Vietnam," in Martin, ed., *Strategic Thought in the Nuclear Age,* pp. 93–130.

27. Critic Philip Green charged that in Vietnam as in nuclear strategy "secondary technical matters received the kiss of science, but those concerns that were primary in creating our policies were granted only the careless embrace of unanalyzed passions." Kaplan, ed., *Strategic Thinking and Its Moral Implications,* p. 42.

28. Observed Schelling of the effect of Vietnam : "If you taught anything having to do with foreign affairs you got rocks through your windows." Interview.

29. Brodie, "Why Were We So (Strategically) Wrong?" p. 161.

CHAPTER TWENTY

1. A. Wohlstetter and F. Hoffman, "Defending a Strategic Force after 1960," Rand Corporation, February 1, 1954, p. 19.

2. Wohlstetter to McNamara, February 21, 1967. I am indebted to Mr. Wohlstetter for a copy of his letter.

3. Interview.

4. Richard Garwin and Hans Bethe, "Anti-Ballistic-Missile Systems," *Scientific American,* March 1968. The article is reprinted with commentary in York, ed., *Arms Control,* pp. 164–87.

5. Interview with Richard Garwin.

6. York, ed., *Arms Control,* p. 175

7. For a sympathetic view of the rising popular opposition to the ABM, see Chayes and Wiesner, eds., *ABM;* and York, *Race to Oblivion,* pp. 228–40.

8. Bethe is quoted in York, *Race to Oblivion,* p. 199.

9. On the ABM debate among the experts, see also Yanarella, *The Missile Defense Controversy,* p. 101–29; and J. I. Coffey, "The Anti-Ballistic Missile Debate," *Foreign Affairs,* April 1967, pp. 403–13.

10. York, *Race to Oblivion,* pp. 188–212, 198.

11. Interviews.

12. Interviews. For the pro-ABM position, see D. G. Brennan, "The Case for Missile Defense," *Foreign Affairs,* April 1969, pp. 433–48; and William Kintner, ed., *Safeguard: Why the ABM Makes Sense* (Hawthorn Books, 1969), esp. pp. 370–72.

13. Wolfgang Panofsky, "The Mutual Hostage Relationship Between America and Russia," *Foreign Affairs,* October 1973.

14. Interview with Wolfgang Panofsky. On the debate in Senate hearings, see, for example, U.S. Congress, Senate 91/1, Senate Foreign Relations Committee, *Hearings: Strategic and Foreign Policy Implications of ABM Systems* (GPO, 1969).

15. Interviews.

16. Concerning the Soviet missile buildup and the U.S. debate over its implications, see Prados, *The Soviet Estimate,* pp. 183–99; and Lawrence Freedman, *U.S. Intelligence and the Soviet Strategic Threat* (Macmillan, 1977), pp. 145–55.

17. Yanarella, *The Missile Defense Controversy,* pp. 139–42.

18. George Rathjens, "The ABM Debate," December 30, 1981, unpublished paper. My appreciation to Mr. Rathjens for a copy of his paper.

19. Killian, *Sputnik, Scientists, and Eisenhower,* pp. 255–7.

20. The argument for the ABM as a bargaining chip is noted in Newhouse, *Cold Dawn,* pp. 187–8. Jackson's comment was made during his testimony for the ABM. See U.S. Congress, Senate 92/2, *Hearings on the Military Implications of the Treaty on the Limitations of Anti-Ballistic Missile Systems* (GPO, 1972), p. 472.

21. Charges that the government overestimated the threat to U.S. ICBMs and misrepresented the capabilities of Safeguard are noted in Prados, *The Soviet Estimate,* pp. 209–13; and Freedman, *U.S. Intelligence and the Soviet Strategic Threat,* esp. ch. 8.

22. Snow's influential essay was adapted from his Godkin Lectures at Harvard about the role of the scientists in advising on what he termed "the 'cardinal choices' . . . which determine in the crudest sense whether we live or die." C. P. Snow, *Science and Government* (Harvard University Press, 1961). Wohlstetter's critical views on Snow's essays and on the scientists are noted in his article "Strategy and the Natural Scientists" in Robert Gilpin and Christopher Wright, eds., *Scientists and National Policy-Making* (Columbia University Press, 1964), pp. 174–239; and in Wohlstetter, "Scientists, Seers and Strategy," *Foreign Affairs,* April 1963, pp. 466–78.

23. Rathjens drew the parallel with the Oppenheimer-Teller controversy in his essay "The ABM Debate," p. 33.

24. The complete ORSA report appears in *Operations Research,* September 1971. Concerning reaction to the report, see Charles Frankel, ed., *Controversies and Decisions: The Social Sciences and*

Public Policy (Russell Sage Press, 1976); and *FAS Newsletter,* December 1971, Federation of American Scientists. The ORSA dispute and its significance is also dealt with by Kaplan, *Wizards of Armageddon,* pp. 349–52. Rathjens subsequently admitted that his calculations contained mathematical errors.

25. U.S. Congress, *Congressional Record,* October 15, 1971, Senate, pp. 16332–8.

26. Rathjens, "The ABM Debate," p. 36. Interview with George Rathjens.

CHAPTER TWENTY-ONE

1. Newhouse, *Cold Dawn,* pp. 150–1.

2. On the domestic and international bargaining behind the ABM decision, see Gerard Smith, *Doubletalk: The Story of the First Strategic Arms Limitation Talks* (Doubleday, 1980), pp. 201–21; Morton Halperin, "The Decision to Deploy ABM: Bureaucratic and Domestic Politics in the Johnson Administration," *World Politics,* October 1972; and Newhouse, *Cold Dawn,* pp. 77–101.

3. Newhouse, *Cold Dawn,* p. 272.

4. Interviews. On the origins of Option E, see Newhouse, *Cold Dawn,* pp. 185–6; and Smith, *Doubletalk,* pp. 256–63. Newhouse writes that "Option E was strictly a White House affair." Henry Kissinger's account of Option E and the banning of ABM and MIRV in SALT are in Kissinger, *The White House Years* (Little, Brown, 1979), pp. 541–9, 204–10, 210–13.

5. Smith, *Doubletalk,* pp. 261–3, 479–86. Smith claims that after Nixon's letter the idea of a total ban on ABMs was never introduced again into the negotiations.

6. *Doubletalk,* pp. 261–3.

7. Interviews. Concerning the belated recognition of MIRV's implications for SALT, see Smith, *Doubletalk,* pp. 154–78; and Newhouse, *Cold Dawn,* pp. 158–9.

8. Brennan's early attack on MAD is noted in Freedman, *The Evolution of Nuclear Strategy,* p. 382.

9. See Brennan, "Strategic Alternatives," Op-Ed page, *New York Times,* May 24–5, 1971. Curiously, McNamara's original formulation was "assured destruction," but in later years he, too, used the phrase "mutually assured destruction." See McNamara, *The Essence of Security,* pp. 52–3.

10. Interview with Jeremy Stone. Donald Brennan, "Commentary," *International Security,* Winter 1978, pp. 193–8.

11. Concerning the ethical argument against assured destruction, see Fred Iklé, *Every War Must End* (Columbia University Press, 1971); and his "Can Nuclear Deterrence Last Out the Century?" *Foreign Affairs,* January 1973, pp. 267–85. The slogan of MAD's critics is cited in Newhouse, *Cold Dawn,* p. 176. Its corollary, Newhouse wrote, was "Offense is defense, defense is offense." Rowen is quoted from the transcript of a televised debate on the topic "Should we develop highly accurate missiles and emphasize military targets rather than cities?" "The Advocates," February 14, 1974, WGBH Boston. Regarding both sides in the moral debate over deterrence, see, for example, Walzer, *Just and Unjust Wars;* and Paul Ramsey, *War and the Christian Conscience* (Duke University Press, 1961). Walzer writes: "The secret of nuclear deterrence is that it is a kind of bluff. . . . Deterrence and mass murder are thus very far apart. We threaten evil in order not to do it. . . . the threat seems in comparison to be morally defensible." Ramsey, an advocate of counterforce, responds: "Anything it is wrong to do, it is wrong seriously to intend to do. And deterrence means making oneself conditionally willing to wipe out civilians." Interview with Paul Ramsey. On the resurgence of the ethical debate on strategy, see Albert Wohlstetter, "Bishops, Statesmen, and Other Strategists on the Bombing of Innocents," *Commentary,* June 1983, pp. 15–35, and replies in the December 1983 issue.

12. The text of the SALT treaties is in Newhouse, *Cold Dawn,* pp. 273–81. Brennan's comment was made in the course of testimony advising against SALT's ratification. See U.S. Congress, Senate 92/2, *Hearings on Strategic Arms Limitation Agreements Before the Committee on Foreign Relations,* p. 186.

13. Newhouse, *Cold Dawn,* pp. 263–4.

14. Smith, *Doubletalk,* pp. 41–2.

15. *Doubletalk,* pp. 357–9, 537.

16. Interviews. Concerning Nitze's proposal for the internationalization of the Soviet and American arsenals, see also Kaplan, *Wizards of Armageddon,* pp. 300–1.

17. On the views and background of T. K. Jones, see, for example, Scheer, *With Enough Shovels,* pp. 18–26, 60–4.

18. Interview with T. K. Jones. Scheer, *With Enough Shovels,* pp. 18–26.

CHAPTER TWENTY-TWO

1. The developing recognition of the threat that Soviet MIRVs posed to Minuteman is noted in Prados, *The Soviet Estimate,* pp. 200–25; and Kissinger, *The White House Years,* pp. 210–12.

2. Interviews. Newhouse, *Cold Dawn,* p. 161.

3. Nitze said he "was somewhat surprised" when the Soviets developed their own MIRVed weapons in 1974: "But that doesn't mean we didn't think they'd have it a couple of years later than that." Alain Enthoven remarked in 1981: "I didn't see, and I don't think anyone saw, the implications of MIRV for the strategic balance." Interviews.

4. Soviet Deputy Foreign Minister V. V. Kuznetsov told Kennedy adviser John McCloy after the crisis: "Never will we be caught like this again." The incident is recounted in Newhouse, *Cold Dawn,* p. 68.

5. Kissinger's remark was made in the course of a 1974 press briefing. It is quoted in Smith, *Doubletalk,* p. 177.

6. The story of the American proposals on MIRV is recounted in Smith, *Doubletalk,* pp. 154–78.

7. *Doubletalk,* pp. 175–8, 479–80. Smith wrote in 1980, when both the United States and Russia had accurate MIRVed missiles with counterforce capability: "I think now that I should have pressed the case for a MIRV ban even after the Soviet rejection at Vienna. . . . A MIRVless world would have been much safer."

8. *Doubletalk,* p. 170.

9. *Doubletalk,* p. 178.

10. The debate within U.S. intelligence over whether the Soviet SS-9 missile was an MRV, with multiple warheads, or a MIRV, with multiple independently targetable warheads, is recounted in Prados, *The Soviet Estimate,* pp. 204–24. The Soviets did not deploy a true MIRV until January or February 1974.

11. Nitze's case against the SALT II talks is detailed in his essays "Assuring Strategic Stability in an Age of Equivalence," *Foreign Affairs,* January 1976; "The Strategic Balance between Hope and Skepticism," *Foreign Policy,* Winter 1975; and "Deterring Our Deterrent," *Foreign Policy,* Winter 1976–77.

12. Nitze, "Assuring Strategic Stability," pp. 136–8. Concerning Nitze's argument about Minuteman vulnerability and the possibility of a successful Soviet disarming strike against the United States, see Alan Tonelson, "Nitze's World," *Foreign Policy,* Spring 1979, pp. 74–90; and Garry Brewer and Bruce Blair, "War Games and National Security with a Grain of SALT," *Bulletin of the Atomic Scientists,* June 1979, pp. 18–26. The 1969 controversy over the study by the Pentagon's Defense Intelligence Agency is noted by Prados, *The Soviet Estimate,* pp. 216–17.

13. Interview with T. K. Jones.

14. Jones' civil defense studies are described in Scheer, *With Enough Shovels,* pp. 117–19. For a much more skeptical view of Soviet civil defense, see Fred Kaplan, "Dubious Specter," Institute for Policy Studies, Washington, D.C., 1980, pp. 33–8.

15. Paul Nitze, "A Plea for Action," *New York Times Magazine,* May 7, 1978.

16. Schlesinger's career and his role in bringing Rand's analysts back to the Pentagon is noted in Desmond Ball, "Déjà Vu: The Return to Counterforce in the Nixon Administration," California Seminar on Arms Control and Foreign Policy, UCLA, December 1974; and Kaplan, *Wizards of Armageddon,* pp. 372–9. Ball in his essay used the expression "the cohort of Rand alumni."

17. Ball, "Déjà Vu," pp. 1–15.

18. Schlesinger presented the rationale behind the new doctrine in his article "Flexible Strategic

Options and Deterrence," *Survival,* March/April 1974, pp. 86–90. See also Ball, "Déjà Vu," pp. 1–4.

19. The origins and importance of the Foster panel are noted in Kaplan, *Wizards of Armageddon,* pp. 368–70.

20. Concerning the rapid growth of the U.S. strategic arsenal because of MIRV, and the corresponding increase in the number of targets, see Jay Kelley and Desmond Ball, "Strategic Nuclear Targeting," IISS, August 1981, pp. 105–16; and Pringle and Arkin, *S.I.O.P.,* esp. pp. 172–85. The MIRVing of the U.S. missile-firing submarine fleet temporarily confronted targeters with the prospect of having more warheads than targets. See Kaplan, *Wizards of Armageddon,* pp. 360–1; and Thomas Powers, "Choosing a Strategy for World War III," *Atlantic,* November 1982, pp. 82–110.

21. This point is made by the former director of the Air Force's strategic target planning staff. See General Richard Ellis, "The Joint Strategic Target Planning Staff" (GPO, 1981), pp. 1–10.

22. Interview. On the targeting of Soviet command and control, see Desmond Ball, "Counterforce Targeting: How New? How Viable?" *Arms Control Today,* February 1981, pp. 6–8.

23. Ball, "Déjà Vu," pp. 18–20, 47.

24. Schlesinger's testimony was before the Arms Control subcommittee of the Senate Foreign Relations Committee on March 4, 1974. The relevant portion is reprinted in James Fallows, *National Defense* (Random House, 1981), pp. 155–6.

25. The origins and early history of the MX are recounted in Edwards, *Super-Weapon,* pp. 95–111; and Parfit, *The Boys Behind the Bombs,* pp. 250–7.

26. Garwin's testimony against the new weaponry is noted in, for example, U.S. Congress, Senate 94/1, *Hearings,* v. 2, Committee on the Budget (GPO, 1975), pp. 870–98; *Congressional Record,* House, September 4, 1975, pp. 1700–7; and U.S. Congress, House 96/1, *Hearings on Military Posture,* Committee on Armed Services (GPO, 1980). On Garwin's views, see also his article "Reducing Dependence on Nuclear Weapons: A Second Nuclear Regime" in David Gompert et al., eds., *Nuclear Weapons and World Politics* (McGraw-Hill, 1980), pp. 89–145.

27. Kissinger, *Nuclear Weapons and Foreign Policy,* p. 132.

28. Concerning "sufficiency" and its definition in the Nixon administration, see Ball, "Déjà Vu," pp. 8–9.

29. This incident is recounted in Kaplan, *Wizards of Armageddon,* pp. 370–1.

30. Kissinger's statement is in the U.S. State Department *Bulletin,* July 29, 1974, p. 215.

31. On the critics of counterforce, see, for example, Herbert Scoville, Jr., "Flexible MADness?" *Foreign Policy,* Spring 1974, pp. 164–77; and Robert Aldridge, "The Counterforce Syndrome: A Guide to U.S. Nuclear Weapons and Strategic Doctrine," Institute for Policy Studies, Washington, D.C., 1981.

CHAPTER TWENTY-THREE

1. In his 1966 defense posture statement, McNamara justified his decision to accelerate the development of the MIRVed Poseidon missile as a "hedge against the possibility of . . . a greater-than-expected threat." On the origins and history of the "greater-than-expected threat," see Newhouse, *Cold Dawn,* pp. 72–77.

2. Prados, *The Soviet Estimate,* pp. 216–24.

3. On the "footprint" controversy, see *The Soviet Estimate,* pp. 208–9.

4. Laird is quoted in Prados, *The Soviet Estimate,* p. 210.

5. *The Soviet Estimate,* pp. 212–15.

6. On the controversy surrounding the changed NIE, see *The Soviet Estimate,* pp. 217–18; and Powers, "Choosing a Strategy for World War III," *Atlantic,* November 1982, p. 99.

7. Interviews. On the advent of the Soviet MIRV, see *The Soviet Estimate,* p. 235.

8. Wohlstetter, "Is There a Strategic Arms Race?" *Foreign Policy,* Summer 1974; "Rivals, but No Race," *Foreign Policy,* Fall 1974; and "Optimal Ways to Confuse Ourselves," *Foreign Policy,* Fall 1975.

9. For a critique of Wohlstetter's analysis, see Prados, *The Soviet Estimate,* pp. 196–8; Freedman,

U.S. Intelligence and the Soviet Strategic Threat, pp. 107–8, and *The Evolution of Nuclear Strategy,* p. 238; and Michael Nacht, "The Delicate Balance of Error," *Foreign Policy,* Summer 1975, pp. 263–77. Prados claims that Wohlstetter's arguments on the arms race are "highly misleading."

10. Ball, "Déjà Vu," pp. 25, 47–8.

11. The story of the Vladivostok accord is in Talbott, *Endgame,* pp. 32–5, 46–8. The effect of MIRV upon SALT is discussed in Edwards, *Super-Weapon,* pp. 62–7.

12. Interviews. The history of the original committee and the influence of its successor are the subject of Sanders, *Peddlers of Crisis.* On the activities of the two committees, see also Richard Barnet, "The Search for National Security," *The New Yorker,* April 27, 1981, pp. 1–17.

13. Barnet, "The Search for National Security," pp. 12–13.

14. "Where We Stand: Summaries of Policy Statements, 1976–1977," Committee on the Present Danger, Washington, D.C.

15. "What We Have Said and What Has Been Said About Us, 1976–1980," Committee on the Present Danger.

16. The debate over Russian military spending is noted in Prados, *The Soviet Estimate,* pp. 245–7.

17. See, for example, Franklyn Holzman, "Are the Soviets Really Outspending the U.S. on Defense?" *International Security,* Spring 1980, pp. 86–104.

18. PFIAB's history is recounted in Prados, *The Soviet Estimate,* pp. 249–55

19. The Team-B story is told in Scheer, *With Enough Shovels,* pp. 53–65; and Prados, *The Soviet Estimate,* pp. 248–57. See also U.S. Congress, Senate 95/2, *Report: The National Intelligence Estimates A-B Team Episode Concerning Soviet Strategic Capability and Objectives* (GPO, 1978).

20. Scheer, *With Enough Shovels,* pp. 53–65. Concerning the early views of Pipes, see Pringle and Arkin, *S.I.O.P.,* pp. 246–7. On Ellsworth: Ball, "Déjà Vu," p. 37. On Keegan: Prados, *The Soviet Estimate,* pp. 286–7.

21. On the controversy over the B-team report, see Arthur Macy Cox, "The CIA's Tragic Error," *New York Review of Books,* November 6, 1980.

22. "New CIA Estimate Finds Soviet Seeks Superiority in Arms," *New York Times,* December 26, 1976.

23. Interview. The CIA analyst is quoted in Scheer, *With Enough Shovels,* p. 54.

24. "Viewpoint," *Washington Post,* July 31, 1981.

25. Moynihan is cited in Barnet, "The Search for National Security," p. 16.

CHAPTER TWENTY-FOUR

1. Carter's own, largely uncritical view of his presidency is his autobiography, *Keeping Faith: Memoirs of a President* (Bantam, 1982).

2. Carter's proposal and his early idealism concerning the question of abolishing nuclear weapons are noted, for example, by Powers, "Choosing a Strategy for World War III," *Atlantic,* November 1982, pp. 82–109; and Talbott, *Endgame,* pp. 42–3.

3. Carter, *Keeping Faith,* p. 173.

4. Interviews. Concerning the rivalry of Nitze and Warnke, see Talbott, *Endgame,* pp. 56–7; Sanders, *Peddlers of Crisis,* pp. 206–8; and Scheer, *With Enough Shovels,* pp. 199–205.

5. Paul Warnke, "Apes on a Treadmill," *Foreign Policy,* Spring 1975.

6. Interviews.

7. Brown's comment is cited in Talbott, *Endgame,* p. 52. For two very different interpretations of the Carter administration, see Cyrus Vance, *Hard Choices: Critical Years in America's Foreign Policy* (Simon and Schuster, 1983), pp. 17–25; and Zbigniew Brzezinski, *Power and Principle: Memoirs of the National Security Adviser, 1977–1981* (Farrar, Straus and Giroux, 1983), pp. 36–45.

8. Nitze's attack on Warnke is noted in Sanders, *Peddlers of Crisis,* pp. 206–8.

9. The story of the "deep cuts" proposal is recounted in Talbott, *Endgame,* pp. 57–60; and Brzezinski, *Power and Principle,* pp. 156–64.

10. The Soviet missile tests and U.S. concern are noted in Prados, *The Soviet Estimate,* pp. 271–3.

11. Richard Pipes, "Why the Soviet Union Thinks It Could Fight and Win a Nuclear War," *Commentary,* July 1977.

12. William Van Cleave and W. Scott Thompson, eds., "Strategic Options for the Early Eighties: What Can Be Done?" National Strategy Information Center, New York City, 1979, p. 183.

13. Van Cleave and Thompson, eds., "Strategic Options for the Early Eighties," pp. 119–20. Jones said of a Soviet disarming strike that might kill between ten and twelve million Americans: "It is just unreasonable to expect that U.S. leaders would avenge the death of that many Americans by risking another 180 million."

14. "Strategic Options for the Early Eighties," p. 105.

15. "Strategic Options for the Early Eighties," p. 120.

16. "Strategic Options for the Early Eighties," p. 180. On Perle's campaign against SALT II in the Carter administration, see also Talbott, *Endgame,* pp. 52–4.

17. Eugene Rostow, "The Case against SALT II," *Commentary,* January 1979.

18. Van Cleave and Thompson, eds., "Strategic Options for the Early Eighties," p. 193.

19. A critique of Jones' studies is the subject of Scheer, *With Enough Shovels,* pp. 105–19; and Fallows, *National Defense,* pp. 159–62. See also "Critique of T.K. Jones' Computation of Soviet Fatalities" and "An Analysis of Soviet Civil Defense in Nuclear War," May 3, 1979, and December 1978, respectively, Arms Control and Disarmament Agency, Washington, D.C. A revised study of the possible effects of a nuclear war upon both the United States and Russia is U.S. Congress, Office of Technology Assessment, "The Effects of Nuclear War" (GPO, 1979).

20. See, for example, John Steinbruner and Thomas Garwin, "Strategic Stability: The Balance between Prudence and Paranoia," *International Security,* Summer 1976, pp. 138–70; and Brewer and Blair, "War Games and National Security," *Bulletin of the Atomic Scientists,* June 1979, pp. 18–26. Richard Garwin responded to Nitze's claims regarding Soviet missile accuracy and the feasibility of a disarming strike against the United States in a letter. See Garwin to "SALT connoisseurs," June 28, 1979. My thanks to Mr. Garwin for a copy of the letter. Nitze conceded of his scenario of a Soviet first strike that "it would be a high-risk thing to do—as was the Japanese attack on Pearl Harbor. But that means that you just plan it carefully. It doesn't mean that it can't be done." Interview with Paul Nitze.

21. Stephen Rosenfeld, "A Hawkish Argument with Holes," *Washington Post,* July 8, 1977.

22. Garwin testified against Pipes' assumptions on the Russian civil defense program and regarding Soviet hopes for winning a nuclear war in U.S. Congress, House 96/2, Armed Services Committee, *Hearings: U.S. Strategic National Security Programs* (GPO, 1978).

CHAPTER TWENTY-FIVE

1. Prados, *The Soviet Estimate,* pp. 279–80.

2. Talbott, *Endgame,* pp. 223, 277; and Brzezinski, *Power and Principle,* p. 337.

3. Brzezinski writes in his memoirs: "In my judgment, the President's decision to proceed with MX development and deployment, as well as his earlier bold initiative on China, created a proper strategic and geopolitical context for our forthcoming meeting with Brezhnev." *Power and Principle,* p. 338.

4. One of those writing on the MX decision concluded that, beyond the technological developments which made the missile possible, another "compelling reason" behind it "was the strategy developed for fighting nuclear wars": "The MX decision was as much a product of the way politicians thought about nuclear war as it was of technical developments. . . . MX is necessarily a first strike weapon." Edwards, *Super-Weapon,* pp. 23, 201.

5. Edwards writes of the MX: "The doves were attracted by its mobility. The hawks were attracted by its countersilo capability." *Super-Weapon,* p. 111.

6. *Super-Weapon,* pp. 111–12. Concerning the various basing schemes considered for the MX, see also U.S. Congress, Office of Technology Assessment, "MX Missile Basing" and "MX Missile Basing: Summary" (GPO, 1981); and Herbert Scoville, *MX: Prescription for Disaster* (MIT Press, 1981).

7. On the "MX mafia," see Parfit, *The Boys Behind the Bombs,* pp. 215–98. The political

considerations involved in the choice of the shell game are noted by Talbott, *Endgame,* pp. 168–80; and Edwards, *Super-Weapon,* p. 122.

8. Van Cleave and Thompson, eds., "Strategic Options for the Early Eighties," p. 178.

9. "Strategic Options for the Early Eighties," p. 177.

10. "Strategic Options for the Early Eighties," p. 183; Talbott, *Endgame,* p. 169.

11. Brzezinski, *Power and Principle,* pp. 333–9.

12. *Power and Principle,* p. 333.

13. Carter, *Keeping Faith,* p. 241; *Power and Principle,* p. 334.

14. Edwards, *Super-Weapon,* pp. 187–9.

15. Brzezinski, *Power and Principle,* pp. 337–8.

16. Interview with Paul Warnke.

17. Parfit, *The Boys Behind the Bombs,* pp. 275–6. Interviews with Jasper Welch and Harold Brown. Another important MX proponent, William Perry, concluded of the decision for the larger missile: "The geopolitical arguments outweighed the technical arguments." Quoted in Edwards, *Super-Weapon,* p. 199.

18. On the SUM idea and its fate, see Sidney Drell and Richard Garwin, "Basing the MX Missile: A Better Idea," *Technology Review,* May/June 1981, pp. 20–9; and U.S. Congress, Office of Technology Assessment, "MX Missile Basing: Summary," pp. 1–20.

19. Concerning the element of national resolve in the MX-basing decision, see, for example, the letter to the editor in the *New York Times,* March 31, 1981, from Norman Friedman and Colin Gray of the Hudson Institute, and the response on April 16, 1981, from Garwin and Drell. See also Colin Gray, "Critical Issues: Strategy and the MX," Heritage Foundation, Washington, D.C., 1980.

20. Garwin and Drell thought the MX issue was subtly linked with the pending deployment of American cruise and Pershing II missiles in Europe. Interviews. In 1981, a Reagan administration official, Richard Perle, made this link explicit with the observation that "ground-launched missiles will express alliance solidarity." See "Week in Review," *New York Times,* November 22, 1981.

21. Edwards, *Super-Weapon,* pp. 200–12.

22. Brzezinski, *Power and Principle,* p. 337.

23. Interview with Sidney Drell. See also Drell, "Arms Control: Is There Still Hope?" in "U.S. Defense Policy in the 1980s," *Daedalus,* Fall 1980, pp. 177–87.

24. Daniel P. Moynihan, "Reflections: SALT," *New Yorker,* November 19, 1979, pp. 151–4.

25. Moynihan, "Reflections: SALT," pp. 177–8.

26. Drell, "Arms Control: Is There Still Hope?" pp. 180–1.

27. Brzezinski, *Power and Principle,* pp. 51–2, 455–7; Vance, *Hard Choices,* p. 49.

28. PRM-10 is discussed in Jay Kelley and Desmond Ball, "Strategic Nuclear Targeting," IISS, London, August 1981, pp. 46–8; and Thomas Powers, "Choosing a Strategy for World War III," *Atlantic,* November 1982, pp. 85–91.

29. Brzezinski, *Power and Principle,* pp. 455–6.

30. *Power and Principle,* p. 455.

31. Interview. Powers, "Choosing a Strategy for World War III," p. 86. Powers notes of the briefing, after Brzezinski had asked about how many fatalities were expected among *"Russian* Russians": "The briefer was stunned. He felt that he was listening to the voice of 600 years of Polish history."

32. Brzezinski, *Power and Principle,* pp. 455–6.

33. On Welch and his role in the new targeting doctrine, see *Power and Principle,* p. 457; Edwards, *Super-Weapon,* p. 67; and Prados, *The Soviet Estimate,* p. 250.

34. On the views of Brown, see Kaplan, *Wizards of Armageddon,* pp. 385–6; Fallows, *National Defense,* pp. 39–42; and Edwards, *Super-Weapon,* pp. 123–6.

35. Brown is quoted in *Super-Weapon,* pp. 130–1.

36. Brzezinski, *Power and Principle,* p. 458.

37. Edwards, *Super-Weapon,* pp. 187–99.

38. Brzezinski, *Power and Principle,* pp. 774–6. Brzezinski writes: "Throughout this period, the President kept pressing Brown as to whether the United States still needed a triad."

39. *Power and Principle,* p. 457.

40. *Power and Principle,* p. 457.

41. Edwards, *Super-Weapon*, pp. 171–5; Powers, "Choosing a Strategy for World War III," pp. 104–6.

42. Concerning the shift in American nuclear strategy represented by PD-59, see, for example, Desmond Ball, "U.S. Strategic Forces: How Would They Be Used?" *International Security*, Winter 1982/83, pp. 31–60. The interrelationship of the MX and PD-59 is noted by Edwards, *Super-Weapon*, pp. 173, 261. He concludes that the targeting studies which led to PD-59 "had strengthened the case for a quick accurate missile. At the heart of the controversy over MX, over the most accurate, prompt nuclear weapon ever made, is the question of whether a nuclear war can be controlled."

43. Brown stated: "P.D. 59 is not a new strategic doctrine; it is not a radical departure from U.S. strategic policy over the past decade or so. It is, in fact, a refinement, a codification of previous statements of our strategic policy. P.D. 59 takes the same essential strategic doctrine, and restates it more clearly, more cogently, in the light of current conditions and current capabilities." *New York Times*, August 23, 1980.

44. Brown's statement is cited in Kaplan, *Wizards of Armageddon*, p. 382. On "countervailing," see also Walter Slocombe, "The Countervailing Strategy," *International Security*, Spring 1981, pp. 18–27.

CHAPTER TWENTY-SIX

1. McGeorge Bundy, George Kennan, Robert McNamara, and Gerard Smith, "Nuclear Weapons and the Atlantic Alliance," *Foreign Affairs*, Spring 1982, p. 753–68.

2. McGeorge Bundy, "To Cap the Volcano," *Foreign Affairs*, October 1969, pp. 1–20.

3. Concerning the public expression by McNamara of his views, see "No Second Use—Until" and "Inviting War," Op-Ed page, *New York Times*, February 2 and September 15, 1983; and his essay "The Military Role of Nuclear Weapons: Perceptions and Misperceptions," *Foreign Affairs*, Fall 1983, pp. 68–72.

4. On the call for a new nuclear strategy, see Wade Greene, "Rethinking the Unthinkable," *New York Times Magazine*, March 15, 1981; Herman Kahn, "Thinking About Nuclear Morality," *New York Times Magazine*, June 13, 1982; and Laurence Beilenson and Samuel Cohen, "A New Nuclear Strategy," *New York Times Magazine*, January 24, 1982. See also Leon Sigal, "Rethinking the Unthinkable," *Foreign Policy*, Spring 1979, pp. 35–51.

5. Elaine Pagels, *The Gnostic Gospels* (Random House, 1979), pp. xviii, 152.

6. Colin Gray and Keith Payne, "Victory Is Possible," *Foreign Policy*, Summer 1980, pp. 14–27. On the views of Gray and the "second wave," see also Gray, "Nuclear Strategy: The Case for a Theory of Victory," *International Security*, Summer 1979, pp. 54–87; "Targeting Problems for Central War," *Naval War College Review*, January–February 1980, pp. 3–21; and "Rethinking Nuclear Strategy," *Orbis*, Winter 1974.

7. Gray, "Some Selective Options and Deterrence: Some Issues," Hudson Institute, 1981, p. 6; Gray and Payne, "Victory Is Possible," pp. 24–5; Gray, "What Rand Hath Wrought," *International Security*, Fall 1971, pp. 111–29. Concerning Gray's criticism of the "first wave" of strategists, see his *Strategic Studies and Public Policy: The American Experience* (University of Kentucky Press, 1982); "Strategic Studies: A Critical Assessment," Hudson Institute, January 1980; and "Correspondence," *International Security*, Summer 1981, pp. 185–7. Gray's influence upon American nuclear strategy and doctrine is noted in Freedman, *The Evolution of Nuclear Strategy*, esp. pp. 347–8, 364–5; and Bernard Brodie, "The Evolution of Nuclear Strategy," *International Security*, Fall 1978, p. 27.

8. Payne and Gray write: "Striking the U.S.S.R. should entail targeting the relocation bunkers of the top political and bureaucratic leadership, including those of the KGB; key communication centers of the Communist party, the military, and the government; and many of the economic, political, and military records. . . . A combination of counterforce offensive targeting, civil defense, and ballistic missile and air defense should hold U.S. casualties down to a level compatible with national survival and recovery." "Victory Is Possible," pp. 24–5. Concerning Gray's views on initiating nuclear war, see his letter to the editor, *New York Times*, October 19, 1977. On counter-

command strategy and "leadership targeting" in American doctrine, see Ball, "U. S. Strategic Forces," pp. 55–6. Gray makes this point about "decapitation": "Counter (political) control targeting . . . was 'discovered' (if that is the right phrase) by the DIA in 1969, was recommended in NSDM-242 and has been implemented in sundry ways since 1976. Believe it or not, for more than a year I have been trying to tell the government that they cannot just 'kick the door in' and see the whole structure collapse (à la Hitler)." Letter to the author, June 1, 1981. Elsewhere, Gray has acknowledged the impossibility of a "surgical" nuclear war and the difficulty of destroying Soviet political and military command targets without also devastating Russia. See Powers, "Choosing a Strategy for World War III," p. 109.

9. Gray, "What Rand Hath Wrought," p. 125.

10. Gray, *Strategic Studies and Public Policy,* pp. 342–7, 462–74, 560.

11. Gray, "What Rand Hath Wrought," pp. 122–9. Also on his criticism of Brodie, see Gray, "Across the Nuclear Divide—Strategic Studies, Past and Present," Spring 1980, pp. 24–46; and "Correspondence," *International Security,* Summer 1981, pp. 185–7. Concerning Brodie's view of Gray and the "second wave," see his "The Evolution of Nuclear Strategy," pp. 1–30. An especially critical account of the second-wave strategists and their idea of a controlled nuclear war is Michael Howard, "On Fighting a Nuclear War," *International Security,* Spring 1981, pp. 3–17.

12. Gray, "Some Selective Options and Deterrence," p. 6.

13. One of those involved in the targeting study that led to PD-59 told a reporter at the end of 1977: "In the past, nuclear targeting has been done by military planners who have basically emphasized the efficient destruction of targets. But targeting should not be done in a political vacuum. . . . Some targets are of greater psychological importance to Moscow than others, and we should begin thinking of how to use our strategic forces to play on these concerns." "Pentagon Reviewing Nuclear War Plans," *New York Times,* December 16, 1977.

14. Brodie, "Why Were We So (Strategically) Wrong?," *Foreign Policy,* Winter 1971/72, pp. 151–61.

15. Schelling, "The Terrorist Use of Nuclear Weapons," Center for International and Strategic Affairs, UCLA, August 1981. Schelling commonly used as a scenario for nuclear blackmail the specter of the PLO planting an atomic-bomb-laden rowboat in Baltimore harbor. He chose Baltimore as the target of the terrorist attack, Schelling said, because few people in his lecture audiences seemed to know anyone in that city. On the day of our interview, Schelling had to leave his Harvard office early to be sure of catching an evening flight to Washington, D.C. Ironically, the reason was that demonstrators—adopting a very "Schellingesque" tactic—were then protesting cutbacks in Boston's fire and police service by deliberately stalling their cars in tunnels leading out of the city.

16. Spurgeon Keeny and Wolfgang Panofsky, "MAD Versus NUTS," *Foreign Affairs,* Winter 1981/82, pp. 287–304.

17. The British scientist was Solly Zuckerman. Concerning Zuckerman's views on nuclear weapons and war, see his *Nuclear Illusion and Reality* (Random House, 1982).

18. "Conference on the Prevention of Nuclear War," Erice, Sicily, Summer 1981, pp. 58–64. I am indebted to Richard Garwin for a transcript of the Erice meeting.

19. "Conference on the Prevention of Nuclear War," pp. 85–8. Concerning Garwin's ideas on the future of warfare, see his "New Weapons/Old Doctrines: Strategic Warfare in the 1980s," *Proceedings of the American Philosophical Society,* August 1980, pp. 261–65.

20. Garwin, "Launch Under Attack to Redress Minuteman Vulnerability?" *International Security,* Winter 1979/80, pp. 117–39. A criticism of the launch-on-warning idea is Albert Carnesale and Charles Glaser, "ICBM Vulnerability: The Cures Are Worse than the Disease," *International Security,* Summer 1982, pp. 70–85.

CHAPTER TWENTY-SEVEN

1. Eugene Rostow, "What Is Our Defense Program For? American Foreign and Defense Policy after Vietnam," in Francis Hoeber and William Schneider, eds., *Arms, Men, and Military Budgets: Issues for Fiscal Year 1978* (Crane and Russak, 1977). Richard Pipes, "Strategic Superiority," Op-Ed

page, *New York Times,* February 6, 1977. Norman Podhoretz, "The Present Danger," *Commentary,* April 1980. Interview. Concerning a more skeptical view of the political utility of nuclear weapons by an important Carter administration official who had a role in drafting PD-59, see Walter Slocombe, "The Political Implications of Strategic Parity," IISS, May 1971.

2. The expert on SALT, a military officer, concluded: "The Defense Department is wholly preoccupied with nuclear-war-fighting scenarios." Quoted in John Newhouse, "Arms and Orthodoxy," *The New Yorker,* June 7, 1982.

3. York said of the new SIOP: "What the plan calls for is, not to exaggerate—the strip-mining of the Soviet Union." Quoted in Scheer, *With Enough Shovels,* pp. 147, 269.

4. At the start of 1984, following the breakdown of most Soviet-American negotiations and the Reagan administration's announcement of progress toward a space-based missile defense, Keeny's foreboding was shared by another observer of arms control: "Despite Administration disclaimers to the contrary, an all-out research and development program on military space technology would surely bring the United States sooner or later into violation of all the nuclear arms-control agreements still formally in force between the two countries, the 1972 SALT I Anti-Ballistic Missile treaty, which prohibited the development, testing and deployment of ABMs in space, as well as the 1963 Limited Test Ban Treaty and the 1967 Outer Space Treaty." Strobe Talbott, "Buildup and Breakdown," *Foreign Affairs, America and the World, 1983,* pp. 587–615.

5. "Pentagon Draws Up First Strategy for Fighting a Long Nuclear War," May 30, 1982, *New York Times.* On the Reagan administration's nuclear strategy, see also "Weinberger Said to Offer Reagan Plan to Regain Atomic Superiority," *New York Times,* August 14, 1981.

6. Concerning the changes made in the war plan by the Reagan administration, and particularly the emphasis there upon "decapitation," see Pringle and Arkin, *S.I.O.P.,* pp. 220–52; and Arkin, "SIOP-6," *Bulletin of the Atomic Scientists,* November 1983. The targeting of Moscow is noted in Wohlstetter et al., "Morality and Deterrence," *Commentary,* December 1983, p. 6. On experts' doubts about the administration's nuclear strategy, see, for example, Desmond Ball, "Can Nuclear War Be Controlled?," IISS, Fall 1981.

7. The relationship between Jones and Paul Nitze was commented on by former NSC aide Roger Molander in an interview with journalist Robert Scheer: "When Paul Nitze needed numbers he went to T. K. Jones for his numbers." Jones told Scheer that his own study of civil defense began with Nitze, when he "went back to draw on his [Nitze's] knowledge because he had been vice-chairman of the Strategic Bombing Survey." Quoted in Scheer, *With Enough Shovels,* p. 174.

8. The use of the expression "full-court press" is noted in Scheer, *With Enough Shovels,* pp. 7–8. While ACDA director, Rostow elaborated on this theme in making the point that nuclear weapons had perhaps finally achieved Alfred Nobel's "dream" of making war obsolete: "Just as you can't draw a straight line or a strong wall between small and large nuclear wars, so you can't draw a line between conventional war and nuclear war. . . . The existence of the nuclear weapon requires you to tackle the whole problem—to enforce the United Nations Charter." Rostow thought the United States "had to be prepared to outspend" the Soviet Union in the arms race, though he thought that approach unpromising: "We have the capability, but we're no good at that." More useful because of the nuclear stalemate, he believed, would be a threat to use conventional forces in "peninsular campaigns" where the United States had local superiority. He mentioned Libya and Cuba as examples. Interview with Eugene Rostow.

9. Rostow identified other members of the Madison group as Sven Kramer, Seymour Weiss, Mark Schneider, William van Cleave, and Charles Kupplemen.

10. Another key figure in the negotiations, Richard Burt, assistant secretary of state for European affairs, referred to the talks as "an exercise not in arms control but in alliance management." Burt is quoted in Talbott, "Buildup and Breakdown," *Foreign Affairs: America and the World, 1983,* p. 592. Concerning the Euromissile talks and their outcome, see John Newhouse, "A Reporter at Large (Arms Control)," *New Yorker,* February 28, 1983; "Behind Closed Doors," *Time,* December 5, 1983; and Strobe Talbott, "Buildup and Breakdown," pp. 587–615.

11. A detailed account of the failure of both the Euromissile or INF negotiations and the START talks to the end of 1983 is Strobe Talbott, *Deadly Gambits* (Knopf, 1984).

12. According to Talbott, both Burt and Perle at this meeting "argued strenuously that the sacrifice of the Pershing II would be unacceptable for the United States, primarily because it was

to be deployed in West Germany, and if West Germany was freed from its obligation to deploy the Pershing II on schedule, the other West European nations would abandon their commitment to accept cruise missiles." "Buildup and Breakdown," p. 595.

13. On the very different Russian and American versions of the talks, see Yuli Kvitsinsky, "Soviet View of Geneva," Op-Ed page, *New York Times,* January 12, 1984; and Paul Nitze, "The U.S. Negotiator's View of Geneva Talks," Op-Ed page, *New York Times,* January 19, 1984. Talbott concludes of the "eleventh-hour" proposal that apparently originated with Kvitsinsky: "The motives on the Soviet side were obscure. The incident may have reflected intramural machinations and disarray associated with Andropov's long illness and apparent incapacity. The consequences, however, were plain enough: the unusual, durable, and at times remarkably promising and useful relationship that Nitze and Kvitsinsky had developed was all but ruptured." "Buildup and Breakdown," pp. 602–3.

14. On the MX controversy in the Reagan administration, see Edwards, *Super-Weapon,* pp. 215–73; and U.S. Congress, Office of Technology Assessment, "MX Missile Basing" (GPO, 1981), pp. 269–75. Concerning the various views of MX critics, see, for example, "The Cactus Submarine," Op-Ed page, *New York Times,* July 21, 1981; and "Missile Strategy Draws Challenges," *New York Times,* August 26, 1981.

15. A 1981 study by the congressional Office of Technology Assessment calculated that U.S. civilian casualties after a Soviet attack on MX alone would total between five and twenty million. Since an attack on MX would almost certainly be accompanied by attacks on other counterforce targets in the United States, however, the OTA study concluded that twenty-five to fifty million U.S. fatalities was a more realistic estimate. See "MX Missile Basing: Summary," p. 22. The plan with the Strangelovian touch was described in an interview.

16. On the Townes committee and its report, see Edwards, *Super-Weapon,* pp. 228–40.

17. "The MX's New Clothes," Op-Ed page, *New York Times,* April 20, 1983.

18. Concerning the "Densepack" idea and its suitability to a missile defense of MX, see "Texts of Reagan and Pentagon Statements on MX Missile Basing Proposal," *New York Times,* November 23, 1982; "MX Missile Basing," pp. 111–46; and Harold Brown, *Thinking About National Security: Defense and Foreign Policy in a Dangerous World* (Westview Press, 1983), pp. 67–71. Brown noted the possible role of a missile defense for MX in a speech of May 26, 1982, before the Arms Control Association. My appreciation to former secretary of the army Stanley Resor for the text of Brown's speech.

19. See, for example, " 'Dense Pack': It's the Planning that's Dense," *Los Angeles Times,* May 21, 1982.

20. On the Scowcroft report, see "Excerpts from Report of the Commission on Strategic Forces," *New York Times,* April 12, 1983; and Talbott, *Deadly Gambits,* pp. 303–6.

21. Concerning skeptics and critics of the Midgetman idea, see "As a Bargaining Chip, MX May Be No Bargain for the Soviets," *New York Times,* April 24, 1983; and "Midgetman Has Problems," *Bulletin of the Atomic Scientists,* January 1984, pp. 4–6.

22. Scowcroft said in an interview of his reason for supporting deployment of the MX that it was needed "to demonstrate U.S. national will." "If we back away from it now, it will underscore our paralysis for both our opponents and our friends." President Reagan also spoke of the missile as a way to "demonstrate our resolve, our national will." "The MX's New Clothes," Op-Ed page, *New York Times,* April 20, 1983.

23. Concerning the theoretical importance of perceptions in nuclear strategy, see Robert Jervis, "Deterrence and Perception," *International Security,* Winter 1982/83, pp. 3–30.

EPILOGUE

1. "President's Speech on Military Spending and a New Defense," *New York Times,* March 24, 1983.

2. Concerning scientists' attitudes toward the "Star Wars" defense concept, see, for example, "Fiery Debate over Laser Battle Stations," *San Francisco Chronicle,* July 20, 1981; George Rathjens and Jack Ruina, "100% Defense? Hardly," Op-Ed page, *New York Times,* March 27, 1983; and

Edward Teller, "Reagan's Courage," and Richard Garwin, "Reagan's Riskiness," *New York Times,* March 30, 1983.

3. Teller, "Seven Hours of Reminiscences," *Los Alamos Science,* Winter/Spring 1983, p. 195.

4. The analyst, Angelo Codevilla, a staff member of the U.S. Senate Select Committee on Intelligence, is quoted in Parfit, *The Boys with the Bombs,* p. 256.

5. Brodie's disenchantment is especially evident in his last essays. See "The Development of Nuclear Strategy," *International Security,* Spring 1978; and "Schlesinger's Old-New Ideas," undated, Box 33, Bernard Brodie MSS, UCLA. Brodie's interest in psychology began at Rand, when he underwent psychiatric analysis for insomnia and writer's block. The writer's block disappeared, but the insomnia persisted. It was also while at Rand that Brodie and a colleague, Nathan Leites, began writing a psychological profile of SAC commander Curtis LeMay. Unfortunately, the profile —never completed—is apparently lost. Interview.

6. "Last Paper Written by Bernard Brodie, October 1978," Box 9, Brodie MSS.

7. Brodie to Borden, October 20, 1954, Box 1, Brodie MSS.

8. Aron, *The Great Debate,* esp. pp. 152-4.

9. The idea of "launch under attack" and the option of launching U.S. missiles upon "assessment of attack" were each considered in the course of the MX basing study. See U.S. Congress, Office of Technology Assessment, "MX Missile Basing" (GPO, 1981), pp. 147-66. Garwin has become perhaps the best-known proponent of launch-upon-assessment. See his "Launch Under Attack to Redress Minuteman Vulnerability?" *International Security,* Winter 1979/80, pp. 117-39.

10. Osgood is quoted in Gray, *Strategic Studies and Public Policy,* p. 551. I am indebted to Mr. Gray for a draft copy of his manuscript. The advisability of giving the public a role in deciding on American nuclear strategy was considered in the first government document to deal with the question of whether, when, and how the bomb would be used. The document, NSC-30—"Policy on Atomic Warfare"—was completed in the fall of 1948 after a prolonged intergovernmental debate, and explicitly rejected the public's participation in any decision to use nuclear weapons. It reads in part:

> In this matter, public opinion must be recognized as a factor of considerable importance. Deliberation or decision on a subject of this significance, even if clearly affirmative, might have the effect of placing before the American people a moral question of vital security significance at a time when the full security impact of the question had not become apparent. If this decision is to be made by the American people, it should be made in the circumstances of an actual emergency when the principal factors involved are in the forefront of public consideration. . . . Foreign opinion likewise demands consideration. Official discussion respecting the use of atomic weapons would reach the Soviets, who should in fact never be given the slightest reason to believe that the U.S. would even consider not to use atomic weapons against them if necessary. It might take no more than a suggestion of such consideration, perhaps magnified into a doubt, were it planted in the minds of responsible Soviet officials, to provoke exactly that Soviet aggression which it is fundamentally U.S. policy to avert.

NSC-30 concludes:

> Were the United States to decide against, or publicly debate the issue of the use of the atomic bomb on moral grounds, this country might gain the praise of the world's radical fringe and would certainly receive the applause of the Soviet bloc, but the United States would be thoroughly condemned by every sound citizen in Western Europe, whose enfeebled security this country would obviously be threatening.

NSC-30 is in U.S. Department of State, *Foreign Relations of the United States: 1948,* v. 1 (GPO, 1973), pp. 626-7. Concerning criticisms of NSC-30 and the debate surrounding it, see Herken, *The Winning Weapon,* pp. 268-72.

11. Brodie, *War and Politics,* p. 1.

BIBLIOGRAPHY

INTERVIEWS

Luis Alvarez	April 14, 1983	Los Alamos, N.M.
Bruno Augenstein	April 1, 1982	Rand Corporation, Calif.
Robert Bacher	April 15, 1983	Los Alamos, N.M.
Hans Bethe	March 1, 1983	Telephone conversation
Richard Bissell	May 15, 1980	Farmington, Conn.
Barry Blechman	June 1, 1981	Washington, D.C.
William Borden	November 30, 1981	Washington, D.C.
Robert Bowie	June 3, 1981	Washington, D.C.
Harold Brown	December 19, 1983	Washington, D.C.
McGeorge Bundy	June 9, 1981	New York City
	May 11, 1982	New York City
George Carver	December 14, 1982	Washington, D.C.
Robert Christy	April 15, 1983	Los Alamos, N.M.
Samuel Cohen	April 2, 1982	Marina Del Rey, Calif.
James Digby	July 27, 1981	Rand Corporation, Calif.
	April 2, 1982	Telephone conversation
Sidney Drell	August 3, 1981	Stanford, Calif.
Daniel Ellsberg	June 8, 1981	Berkeley, Calif.
	August 9, 1981	Berkeley, Calif.
Alain Enthoven	July 16, 1981	Stanford, Calif.
Bernard Feld	April 30, 1981	MIT
Richard Garwin	July 21, 1981	Stanford, Calif.
	November 2, 1982	New Haven, Conn.
Marvin Goldberger	March 31, 1982	UCLA
Morton Halperin	June 4, 1981	Washington, D.C.
Charles Hitch	July 22, 1981	Berkeley, Calif.
Malcolm Hoag	July 27, 1981	Rand Corporation, Calif.
Fred Hoffman	April 2, 1982	Marina Del Rey, Calif.
Stanley Hoffmann	May 1, 1981	Cambridge, Mass.
T. K. Jones	June 5, 1981	Pentagon
Herman Kahn	May 13, 1981	Hudson Institute, New York
Morton Kaplan	June 9, 1981	New York City
William Kaufmann	April 28, 1981	MIT
Carl Kaysen	February 9, 1982	MIT
Spurgeon Keeny	December 1, 1981	Washington, D.C.
	May 7, 1982	Washington, D.C.
	December 14, 1982	Washington, D.C.
Klaus Knorr	May 21, 1981	Princeton, N.J.
Curtis LeMay	February 8, 1984	Telephone conversation
Leonard Lewin	May 29, 1981	Guilford, Conn.

Robert Lifton	April 21, 1981	New Haven, Conn.
David Lilienthal	February 24, 1979	Princeton, N.J.
Andrew Marshall	June 5, 1981	Pentagon
	December 1, 1981	Pentagon
	December 15, 1982	Pentagon
David McGarvey	July 27, 1981	Rand Corporation, Calif.
Robert McNamara	June 5, 1981	Washington, D.C.
	May 7, 1982	Washington, D.C.
	December 14, 1982	Washington, D.C.
	December 19, 1983	Washington, D.C.
Paul Nitze	October 18, 1979	Rosslyn, Va.
	June 1, 1981	Rosslyn, Va.
	May 11, 1983	Telephone conversation
	December 20, 1983	Washington, D.C.
Robert Osgood	June 3, 1981	Washington, D.C.
Wolfgang Panofsky	August 3, 1981	Stanford, Calif.
Isidor Rabi	September 21, 1981	New Haven, Conn.
	April 17, 1983	New York City
Paul Ramsey	May 21, 1981	Princeton, N.J.
George Rathjens	February 9, 1982	MIT
Eugene Rostow	May 10, 1982	Washington, D.C.
	May 9, 1983	New Haven, Conn.
Henry Rowen	November 30, 1981	Washington, D.C.
Thomas Schelling	April 29, 1981	Cambridge, Mass.
James Schlesinger	December 14, 1982	Washington, D.C.
	December 20, 1983	Washington, D.C.
Herbert Scoville	May 10, 1982	Washington, D.C.
Robert Serber	April 14, 1983	Los Alamos, N.M.
Gerard Smith	May 10, 1982	Washington, D.C.
John Steinbruner	June 2, 1981	Washington, D.C.
Arthur Steiner	July 30, 1981	Telephone conversation
Jeremy Stone	December 1, 1981	Washington, D.C.
Edward Teller	September 28, 1981	Stanford, Calif.
Kostis Tsipis	April 30, 1981	MIT
Paul Warnke	December 14, 1982	Washington, D.C.
Jasper Welch	December 20, 1983	Washington, D.C.
Jerome Wiesner	February 9, 1982	MIT
Robert Wilson	April 14, 1983	Los Alamos, N.M.
Albert Wohlstetter	July 28, 1981	Los Angeles, Calif.
	April 3, 1982	Los Angeles, Calif.
Adam Yarmolinsky	June 2, 1981	Washington, D.C.
Herbert York	June 10, 1981	San Francisco, Calif.
	March 31, 1982	UCLA
	February 2, 1983	Telephone conversation

The following videotaped interviews were conducted by the Alfred Sloan Foundation of New York between 1981 and 1983 and are referred to as "Videotape Histories" in the Notes:

"The H-Bomb Decision": Symposium held at Princeton University in the summer of 1983 with some of the surviving principals in the 1950 decision to develop the American hydrogen bomb. Present were John Manley, Henry Smyth, McGeorge Bundy, Henry Golden, Kenneth Nichols, Gorden Arneson, Stanley Ulam, and Cyril Smith.

"Project Charles History": Symposium held in 1981 on Project Charles, the air defense study conducted at MIT in 1950–51. Present were Paul Samuelson, James Hubbard, James Killian, Jerome

Wiesner, Francis Bator, Carl Kaysen, Jerrold Zacharias, J. M. Forrester, Daniel Dustin, and Elting Morison.

"The Cuban Missile Crisis": Symposia held in 1982–83 with some of the members of the Executive Committee of the National Security Council who advised President Kennedy during the 1962 missile crisis. Present were Dean Rusk, McGeorge Bundy, Robert McNamara, Richard Neustadt, and Edwin Martin.

BOOKS

Allison, Graham. *Essence of Decision: Explaining the Cuban Missile Crisis.* Little, Brown, 1971.

Armbruster, Frank, ed. *Can We Win in Vietnam?* Praeger, 1968.

Aron, Raymond. *The Great Debate: Theories of Nuclear Strategy.* Doubleday, 1965.

Ball, Desmond. *Politics and Force Levels: The Strategic Missile Program of the Kennedy Administration.* University of California Press, 1980.

Bamford, James. *The Puzzle Palace.* Houghton Mifflin, 1982.

Beard, Edmund. *Developing the ICBM: A Study in Bureaucratic Politics.* Columbia University Press, 1976.

Blackett, P. M. S. *Fear, War, and the Bomb: The Military and Political Consequences of Atomic Energy.* Whittlesey House, 1949.

Blumberg, Stanley, and Gwinn Owens. *Energy and Conflict: The Life and Times of Edward Teller.* Putnam, 1976.

Borden, William. *There Will Be No Time: The Revolution in Strategy.* Macmillan, 1946.

Bottome, Edgar. *The Missile Gap.* Fairleigh Dickinson Press, 1971.

Brennan, Donald, ed. *Arms Control, Disarmament, and National Security.* Braziller, 1961.

Brodie, Bernard. *Escalation and the Nuclear Option.* Princeton University Press, 1966.

———. *A Layman's Guide to Naval Strategy.* Princeton University Press, 1942.

———. *Seapower in the Machine Age.* Princeton University Press, 1941.

———. *Strategy in the Missile Age.* Princeton University Press, 1959.

———. *War and Politics.* Macmillan, 1973.

———, ed. *The Absolute Weapon: Atomic Power and World Order.* Harcourt, Brace, 1946.

Brown, Anthony C., ed. *Dropshot: The American Plan for World War III with Russia in 1957.* Dial Press, 1978.

Brown, Harold. *Thinking About National Security: Defense and Foreign Policy in a Dangerous World.* Westview Press, 1983.

Brzezinski, Zbigniew. *Power and Principle: Memoirs of the National Security Adviser, 1977–1981.* Farrar, Straus and Giroux, 1983.

Carter, Jimmy. *Keeping Faith: Memoirs of a President.* Bantam, 1982.

Chayes, Abram, and Jerome Wiesner, eds. *ABM: An Evaluation of the Decision to Deploy an Anti-ballistic Missile System.* Harper & Row, 1969.

Cockburn, Andrew. *The Threat: Inside the Soviet Military Machine.* Random House, 1983.

Cohen, Samuel. *The Truth About the Neutron Bomb.* Morrow, 1983.

Dickson, Paul. *Think Tanks.* Atheneum, 1971.

Divine, Robert. *Blowing on the Wind: The Nuclear Test Ban Debate, 1954–1960.* Oxford University Press, 1978.

Dyson, Freeman. *Disturbing the Universe.* Harper & Row, 1979.

Edwards, John. *Super-Weapon: The Making of MX.* Norton, 1982.

Ellis, John. *The Social History of the Machine Gun.* Pantheon, 1975.

Enthoven, Alain, and Wayne Smith. *How Much Is Enough?: Shaping the Defense Program, 1961–1969.* Harper & Row, 1971.

Etzold, Thomas, and John L. Gaddis, eds. *Containment: Documents on American Policy and Strategy, 1945–1950.* Oxford University Press, 1978.

Fallows, James. *National Defense.* Random House, 1981.

Ferrell, Robert, ed. *Off the Record: The Private Journals of Harry S. Truman.* Norton, 1980.

Ford, Harold, and Francis Winters, eds. *Ethics and National Security.* Orbis Books, 1977.

Frankel, Charles, ed. *Controversies and Decisions: The Social Sciences and Public Policy.* Russell Sage Press, 1976.

Freedman, Lawrence. *The Evolution of Nuclear Strategy.* Macmillan, 1982.

———. *U.S. Intelligence and the Soviet Strategic Threat.* Macmillan, 1977.

Fryklund, Richard. *100 Million Lives: Maximum Survival in a Nuclear War.* Macmillan, 1962.

Gaddis, John L. *Strategies of Containment: A Critical Appraisal of Postwar American National Security Policy.* Oxford University Press, 1982.

George, Alexander, and Richard Smoke. *Deterrence in American Foreign Policy: Theory and Practice.* Columbia University Press, 1974.

Gilpin, Robert. *American Scientists and Nuclear Weapons Policy.* Princeton University Press, 1962.

———, and Christopher Wright, eds. *Scientists and National Policy-Making* Columbia University Press, 1964.

Goldhamer, Herbert. *The Adviser.* Elsevier, 1978.

Gompert, David, et al., eds. *Nuclear Weapons and World Politics.* McGraw-Hill, 1980.

Goodchild, Peter. *J. Robert Oppenheimer: Shatterer of Worlds.* Houghton Mifflin, 1981.

Gray, Colin. *Strategic Studies and Public Policy: The American Experience.* University of Kentucky Press, 1982.

Green, Philip. *Deadly Logic: The Theory of Nuclear Deterrence.* Ohio State University Press, 1966.

Greenwood, Ted. *Making the MIRV: A Study of Defense Decision Making.* Ballinger Press, 1975.

Grodzins, M., and E. Rabinowitch, eds. *The Atomic Age.* Simon and Schuster, 1963.

Hackett, Sir John. *The Third World War: A Future History.* Macmillan, 1978.

———. *The Third World War: The Untold Story.* Macmillan, 1983.

Halberstam, David. *The Best and the Brightest.* Random House, 1969.

Haldeman, Robert. *The Ends of Power.* Times Books, 1977.

Hastings, Max. *Bomber Command.* Dial Press, 1979.

Herken, Gregg. *The Winning Weapon: The Atomic Bomb in the Cold War, 1945–50.* Knopf, 1980.

Hersey, John. *Hiroshima.* Knopf, 1946.

Herzog, Arthur. *The War-Peace Establishment.* Harper & Row, 1965.

Hewlett, Richard, and Oscar Anderson. *The New World: A History of the United States Atomic Energy Commission, 1939/46.* Pennsylvania State University Press, 1962.

Hewlett, Richard, and Francis Duncan. *Atomic Shield: A History of the United States Atomic Energy Commission, 1947/52.* Pennsylvania State University Press, 1969.

Hoffmann, Stanley. *The State of War.* Praeger, 1965.

Howard, Michael. *Studies in War and Peace.* Viking Press, 1971.

Iklé, Fred. *Every War Must End.* Columbia University Press, 1971.

Jacobson, Harold, and Eric Stein. *Diplomats, Scientists, and Politicians: The United States and the Nuclear Test Ban Negotiations.* University of Michigan Press, 1966.

Jones, Reginald. *The Wizard War: British Scientific Intelligence, 1939–1945.* Coward, McCann and Geoghegan, 1978.

Kahn, Herman. *On Escalation.* Praeger, 1965.

———. *On Thermonuclear War.* Princeton University Press, 1960.

———. *Thinking about the Unthinkable.* Horizon Press, 1962.

———, ed. *Why ABM?.* Praeger, 1968.

———, and Anthony Wiener. *The Year 2000: A Framework for Speculation on the Next Thirty-three Years.* Macmillan, 1967.

Kaplan, Fred. *The Wizards of Armageddon.* Simon and Schuster, 1983.

Kaplan, Morton, ed. *Strategic Thinking and Its Moral Implications.* University of Chicago Press, 1973.

Kaufmann, William. *The McNamara Strategy.* Harper & Row, 1964.

———, ed. *Military Policy and National Security.* Princeton University Press, 1966.

Kecskemeti, Paul. *Strategic Surrender: The Politics of Victory and Defeat.* Stanford University Press, 1958.

Kennedy, Robert. *Thirteen Days: A Memoir of the Cuban Missile Crisis.* Norton, 1969.

Kevles, Daniel. *The Physicists.* Knopf, 1978.

Killian, James. *Sputnik, Scientists, and Eisenhower.* MIT Press, 1977.

Kintner, William, ed. *Safeguard: Why the ABM Makes Sense.* Hawthorn Books, 1969.

Kissinger, Henry. *The Necessity for Choice.* Doubleday, 1960.

———. *Nuclear Weapons and Foreign Policy.* Harper & Row, 1957.

———. *The White House Years.* Little, Brown, 1979.

Kistiakowsky, George. *A Scientist at the White House.* Harvard University Press, 1976.

Koestler, Arthur. *The Call Girls.* Hutchinson, London, 1972.

Leites, Nathan. *The Operational Code of the Politburo.* McGraw-Hill, 1950.

LeMay, Curtis, with MacKinlay Kantor. *Mission with LeMay.* Macmillan, 1965.

Levine, Robert. *The Arms Debate.* Harvard University Press, 1963.

Lewin, Leonard, ed. *The Report from Iron Mountain on the Possibility and Desirability of Peace.* Dial Press, 1967.

Lilienthal, David. *The Journals of David E. Lilienthal: The Atomic Energy Years, 1945–1950.* Harper & Row, 1964.

Lowe, George. *The Age of Deterrence.* Little, Brown, 1964.

MacIsaacs, David. *Strategic Bombing in World War II: The Story of the United States Strategic Bombing Survey* (Garland, 1976).

Mandelbaum, Michael. *The Nuclear Question: The United States and Nuclear Weapons, 1946–1976.* Cambridge University Press, 1979.

Martin, Lawrence, ed. *Strategic Thought in the Nuclear Age.* Heinemann, London, 1979.

McNamara, Robert. *The Essence of Security: Reflections in Office.* Harper & Row, 1968.

Moss, Norman. *Men Who Play God.* Gollancz, London, 1968.

Newhouse, John. *Cold Dawn: The Story of SALT.* Holt, Rinehart and Winston, 1973.

Ogburn, William, ed. *Technology and International Relations.* University of Chicago Press, 1959.

Parfit, Michal. *The Boys Behind the Bombs.* Little, Brown, 1983.

Pfeffer, Richard, ed. *No More Vietnams? The War and the Future of American Foreign Policy.* Harper & Row, 1968.

Poole, Walter. *The History of the Joint Chiefs of Staff: The Joint Chiefs of Staff and National Policy, 1950–52,* v. 4. Michael Glazier, 1981.

Power, Thomas, with Albert Arnhym. *Design for Survival.* Coward-McCann, 1964.

Powers, Thomas. *The Man Who Kept the Secrets: Richard Helms and the CIA.* Knopf, 1979.

Prados, John. *The Soviet Estimate: U.S. Intelligence Analysis and Russian Military Strength.* Dial Press, 1982.

Pringle, Peter, and William Arkin. *S.I.O.P.: The Secret U.S. Plan for Nuclear War.* Norton, 1983.

Pringle, Peter, and James Spigelman. *The Nuclear Barons.* Holt, Rinehart and Winston, 1981.

Quester, George. *Deterrence Before Hiroshima: The Airpower Background of Modern Strategy.* Wiley, 1966.

Ramsey, Paul. *War and the Christian Conscience.* Duke University Press, 1961.

Rapoport, Anatol. *Strategy and Conscience.* Harper & Row, 1964.

Rostow, Walt. *Open Skies: Eisenhower's Proposal of July 21, 1955.* University of Texas Press, 1983.

———. *Pre-invasion Bombing Strategy.* University of Texas Press, 1981.

Sallagar, Frederick. *The Road to Total War.* Van Nostrand Reinhold, 1969.

Sanders, Jerry. *Peddlers of Crisis.* South End Press, 1983.

Scheer, Robert. *With Enough Shovels: Reagan, Bush and Nuclear War.* Random House, 1982.

Schell, Jonathan. *The Fate of the Earth.* Knopf, 1982.

———. *The Time of Illusion.* Knopf, 1975.

Schelling, Thomas. *Arms and Influence.* Yale University Press, 1966.

———. *The Strategy of Conflict.* Oxford University Press, 1963.

Schlesinger, Arthur, Jr. *A Thousand Days: John F. Kennedy in the White House.* Houghton Mifflin, 1965.

Schrag, Peter. *Test of Loyalty: Daniel Ellsberg and the Rituals of Secret Government.* Simon and Schuster, 1974.

Scoville, Herbert. *MX: Prescription for Disaster.* MIT Press, 1981.

Seaborg, Glenn. *Kennedy, Khrushchev and the Test Ban.* University of California Press, 1981.

Sherry, Michael. *Preparing for the Next War: American Plans for Postwar Defense.* Yale University Press, 1977.

Sherwin, Martin. *A World Destroyed: The Atomic Bomb and the Grand Alliance.* Knopf, 1975.

Smith, Bruce. *The Rand Corporation: Case Study of a Nonprofit Advisory Corporation.* Harvard University Press, 1966.

Smith, Gerard. *Doubletalk: The Story of the First Strategic Arms Limitation Talks.* Doubleday, 1980.

Snow, Charles P. *Science and Government.* Harvard University Press, 1961.

Sorensen, Theodore. *Kennedy.* Harper & Row, 1965.

Steinbruner, John. *The Cybernetic Theory of Decision.* Princeton University Press, 1974.

Stern, Philip. *The Oppenheimer Case: Security on Trial.* Harper & Row, 1969.

Stone, Jeremy. *Strategic Persuasion: Arms Limitation Through Dialogue.* Columbia University Press, 1967.

Talbott, Strobe. *Deadly Gambits.* Knopf, 1984.

———. *Endgame: The Inside Story of SALT II.* Harper & Row, 1979.

———, ed. and trans. *Khrushchev Remembers: The Last Testament.* Little, Brown, 1974.

Taylor, Maxwell. *The Uncertain Trumpet.* Harper & Brothers, 1959.

Teller, Edward, and Allen Brown. *The Legacy of Hiroshima.* Doubleday, 1962.

U.S. Atomic Energy Commission [USAEC]. *In the Matter of J. Robert Oppenheimer.* GPO, 1954.

U.S. Department of State. *Foreign Relations of the United States: 1948,* v. 1. GPO, 1973.

U.S. Department of State. *Foreign Relations of the United States: 1950,* v. 1. GPO, 1975.

U.S. Strategic Bombing Survey [USSBS]. *The Effects of Atomic Bombs on Hiroshima and Nagasaki.* GPO, 1946.

———. *Japan's Struggle to End the War.* GPO, 1946.

———. *Over-all Report, European War* GPO, 1945.

Vance, Cyrus. *Hard Choices: Critical Years in America's Foreign Policy.* Simon and Schuster, 1983.

Verrier, Anthony. *The Bomber Offensive.* Batsford, London, 1968.

Walzer, Michael. *Just and Unjust Wars: A Moral Argument with Historical Illustrations.* Basic Books, 1977.

Webster, Sir Charles, and Noble Frankland. *The Strategic Air Offensive against Germany, 1939–1945.* 4 vols. HMSO, London, 1961–5.

Wilensky, Harold. *Organizational Intelligence: Knowledge and Policy in Government and Industry.* Basic Books, 1967.

Wilson, Andrew. *The Bomb and the Computer.* Barrie and Rockliffe, London, 1968.

Wilson, Thomas. *The Great Weapons Heresy.* Houghton Mifflin, 1970.

Wohlstetter, Roberta. *Pearl Harbor: Warning and Decision.* Stanford University Press, 1962.

Wyden, Peter. *The Bay of Pigs: The Untold Story.* Simon and Schuster, 1979.

Yanarella, Ernest. *The Missile Defense Controversy: Strategy, Technology, and Politics, 1955–1972.* University of Kentucky Press, 1977.

Yergin, Daniel. *Shattered Peace: The Origins of the Cold War and the National Security State.* Houghton Mifflin, 1978.

York, Herbert. *The Advisors: Oppenheimer, Teller, and the Superbomb.* Freeman, 1976.

———. *Race to Oblivion: A Participant's View of the Arms Race.* Simon and Schuster, 1970.

———. ed. *Arms Control: Readings from Scientific American.* Freeman, 1973.

Zuckerman, Solly. *Nuclear Illusion and Reality.* Random House, 1982.

ARTICLES, ESSAYS, AND MANUSCRIPTS

Aldridge, Robert. "The Counterforce Syndrome: A Guide to U.S. Nuclear Weapons and Strategic Doctrine," Institute for Policy Studies, Washington, D.C., 1981.

Arkin, William. "SIOP-6," *Bulletin of the Atomic Scientists,* November 1983.

Arms Control and Disarmament Agency. "An Analysis of Soviet Civil Defense in Nuclear War," GPO, Washington, D.C., December 1978.

———. "Critique of T. K. Jones' Computation of Soviet Fatalities," GPO, Washington, D.C., May 3, 1979.

Augenstein, B. W. "A Revised Development Program for Ballistic Missiles of Intercontinental Range," Rand Corporation, February 1954.

Ball, Desmond. "Can Nuclear War Be Controlled?," IISS, Fall 1981.

———. "Counterforce Targeting: How New? How Viable?," *Arms Control Today,* February 1981.

———. "Déjà Vu: The Return to Counterforce in the Nixon Administration," California Seminar on Arms Control and Foreign Policy, UCLA, December 1974.

———. "The Role of Strategic Concepts and Doctrines in U.S. Force Development," IISS, March 1980.

———. "U.S. Strategic Forces: How Would They Be Used?," *International Security,* Winter 1982/83.

Barnet, Richard. "The Search for National Security," *The New Yorker,* April 17, 1981.

Beilenson, Laurence, and Samuel Cohen. "A New Nuclear Strategy," *New York Times Magazine,* January 24, 1982.

Bethe, Hans. "Comments on the History of the H-Bomb," *Los Alamos Science,* Fall 1982.

Borden, William. "Straws in the Wind," Special Collections, Sterling Memorial Library, Yale University.

Boyer, Paul. "From Activism to Apathy: The American People and Nuclear Weapons, 1963–1980," *Journal of American History,* March 1984.

Brennan, Donald. "The Case for Missile Defense," *Foreign Affairs,* April 1969.

Brewer, Garry, and Bruce Blair. "War Games and National Security with a Grain of SALT," *Bulletin of the Atomic Scientists,* June 1979.

Brodie, Bernard. "The Atom Bomb as Policy Maker," *Foreign Affairs,* October 1948.

———. "The Atomic Bomb and American Security," Yale Institute of International Studies, November 1, 1945.

———. "The Development of Nuclear Strategy," *International Security,* Spring 1978.

———. "Nuclear Weapons: Strategic or Tactical?," *Foreign Affairs,* January 1954.

———. "Strategic Bombing: What It Can Do," *The Reporter,* August 15, 1950.

———. "Strategy as a Science," *World Politics,* July 1949.

———. "Strategy Hits a Dead End," *Harper's,* October 1955.

———. "Unlimited Weapons and Limited War," *The Reporter,* November 18, 1954.

———. "Why Were We So (Strategically) Wrong?," *Foreign Policy,* Winter 1971/72.

Buckley, Tom. "A Voice of Reason Among the Nuclear Warriors," *Quest,* March 1981.

Bundy, McGeorge. "Early Thoughts on Controlling the Nuclear Arms Race: A Report to the Secretary of State, January 1953," *International Security,* Fall 1982.

———. "The H-Bomb: The Missed Chance," *New York Review of Books,* May 13, 1982.

———. "To Cap the Volcano," *Foreign Affairs,* October 1969.

Carnesale, Albert and Charles Glaser. "ICBM Vulnerability: The Cures Are Worse than the Disease," *International Security,* Summer 1982.

Coffey, J. I. "The Anti-Ballistic Missile Debate," *Foreign Affairs,* April 1967.

Cohen, Samuel. "The Neutron Bomb: Political, Technological, and Military Issues," Institute for Foreign Policy Analysis, Tuft University, 1978.

Cox, Arthur Macy. "The CIA's Tragic Error," *New York Review of Books,* November 6, 1980.

Drell, Sidney. "Arms Control: Is There Still Hope?" *Daedalus,* Fall 1980.

———, and Richard Garwin. "Basing the MX Missile: A Better Idea," *Technology Review,* May/June 1981.

Dyson, Freeman. "The Future Development of Nuclear Weapons," *Foreign Affairs,* April 1960.

Ehrlich, Paul, et al. "Long-term Biological Consequences of Nuclear War," *Science,* December 23, 1983.

Ellis, Gen. Richard. "The Joint Strategic Target Planning Staff," Department of Defense, GPO, 1981.

Ellsberg, Daniel. "The Crude Analysis of Strategic Choice," *American Economic Review,* May 1961.

Gaddis, John L., and Paul Nitze. "NSC-68 and the Soviet Threat Reconsidered," *International Security,* Spring 1980.

Garwin, Richard. "Launch Under Attack to Redress Minuteman Vulnerability?," *International Security,* Winter 1979/80.

———. "New Weapons/Old Doctrines: Strategic Warfare in the 1980s," *Proceedings of the American Philosophical Society,* August 1980.

———, and Hans Bethe. "Anti-Ballistic Missile Systems," *Scientific American,* March 1968.

Goldberg, Alfred. "A Brief Survey of the Evolution of Ideas About Counterforce," Rand Corporation, revised March 1981.

Gray, Colin. "Across the Nuclear Divide—Strategic Studies, Past and Present," *International Security,* Spring 1980.

———. "Critical Issues: Strategy and the MX," Heritage Foundation, Washington, D.C., 1980.

———. "Nuclear Strategy: The Case for a Theory of Victory," *International Security,* Summer 1979.

———. "Rethinking Nuclear Strategy," *Orbis,* Winter 1974.

———. "Some Selective Options and Deterrence: Some Issues," Hudson Institute, 1981.

———. "Strategic Studies: A Critical Assessment," Hudson Institute, 1980.

———. "Targeting Problems for Central War," *Naval War College Review,* January–February 1980.

———. "What Rand Hath Wrought," *International Security,* Fall 1971.

———, and Keith Payne. "Victory Is Possible," *Foreign Policy,* Summer 1980.

Greene, Wade. "Rethinking the Unthinkable," *New York Times Magazine,* March 15, 1981.

Greenwood, John. "The Air Force Ballistic Missile and Space Program, 1954–74," *Aerospace Historian,* December 1974.

Halperin, Morton. "The Decision to Deploy ABM: Bureaucratic and Domestic Politics in the Johnson Administration," *World Politics,* October 1972.

———. "The Gaither Committee and the Policy Process," *World Politics,* April 1961.

Holzman, Franklyn. "Are the Soviets Really Outspending the U.S. on Defense?," *International Security,* Spring 1980.

Howard, Michael. "On Fighting a Nuclear War," *International Security,* Spring 1981.

Iklé, Fred. "Can Nuclear Deterrence Last Out the Century?," *Foreign Affairs,* January 1973.

Jervis, Robert. "Deterrence and Perception," *International Security,* Winter 1982/83.

Kahn, Herman. "If Negotiations Fail," *Foreign Affairs,* July 1968.

———. "Thinking About Nuclear Morality," *New York Times Magazine,* June 13, 1982.

Kaplan, Fred. "Dubious Specter: A Skeptical Look at the Soviet Nuclear Threat," Institute for Policy Studies, Washington, D.C., 1980.

Keeny, Spurgeon, and Wolfgang Panofsky. "MAD Versus NUTS," *Foreign Affairs,* Winter 1981/82.

Kelley, Jay, and Desmond Ball. "Strategic Nuclear Targeting," IISS, August 1981.

Killian, James, and A. G. Hill, "For a Continental Air Defense," *Atlantic,* April 1948.

King, James. "The New Strategy," 4 vols., Institute for Defense Analyses, February 1972.

Latt, John, and W. M. Wheeler. "Reaction to John Hersey's *Hiroshima,"* *Journal of Social Psychology,* August 1948.

Lewin, Kevin. "Strategic Bombing and the Thermonuclear Breakthrough: An Example of Disconnected Defense Planning," Rand Corporation, April 1981.

Mandelbaum, Michael. "The Bomb, Dread, and Eternity," *International Security,* Fall 1980.

McNamara, Robert. "The Military Role of Nuclear Weapons: Perceptions and Misperceptions," *Foreign Affairs,* Fall 1983.

———, et al. "Nuclear Weapons and the Atlantic Alliance," *Foreign Affairs,* Spring 1982.

Miller, Stephen. "The Quest for Invulnerability: Counterforce Surprise Attack and U.S. Strategic Policy, 1945–61," Center for Science and International Affairs, Harvard University, May 1979.

Moynihan, Daniel P. "Reflections: SALT," *The New Yorker,* November 19, 1979.

Murphy, Charles [Anonymous]. "The Hidden Struggle for the H-bomb," *Fortune,* May 1953.

Newhouse, John. "Arms and Orthodoxy," *The New Yorker,* June 7, 1982.

———. "Behind Closed Doors," *The New Yorker,* December 5, 1983.

———. "A Reporter at Large (Arms Control)," *The New Yorker,* February 28, 1983.

Nitze, Paul. "Assuring Strategic Stability in an Age of Equivalence," *Foreign Affairs,* January 1976.

———. "Atoms, Strategy and Policy," *Foreign Affairs*, January 1956.

———. "Deterring Our Deterrent," *Foreign Policy*, Winter 1976/77.

———. "Limited War or Massive Retaliation?" *The Reporter*, September 1, 1957.

———. "A Plea for Action," *New York Times Magazine*, May 7, 1978.

———. "The Strategic Balance Between Hope and Skepticism," *Foreign Policy*, Winter 1975.

Office of Technology Assessment, U.S. Congress. "The Effects of Nuclear War," GPO, Washington, D.C., 1979.

———. "MX Missile Basing" and "MX Missile Basing: Summary," GPO, Washington, D.C., 1981.

Oppenheimer, J. Robert. "Atomic Weapons and American Policy," *Foreign Affairs*, July 1953.

———. "Atomic Weapons and the Crisis in Science," *Saturday Review of Literature*, November 24, 1945.

———. "On the Military Value of the Atom," *Bulletin of the Atomic Scientists*, February 1951.

Panofsky, Wolfgang. "The Mutual Hostage Relationship Between America and Russia," *Foreign Affairs*, October 1973.

Pipes, Richard. "Why the Soviet Union Thinks It Could Fight and Win a Nuclear War," *Commentary*, July 1977.

Podhoretz, Norman. "The Present Danger," *Commentary*, April 1980.

Powers, Thomas. "Choosing a Strategy for World War III," *Atlantic*, November 1982.

———. "Seeing the Light of Armageddon," *Rolling Stone*, April 29, 1982.

Rathjens, George. "The ABM Debate," unpublished manuscript, December 30, 1981.

———. "The Dynamics of the Arms Race," *Scientific American*, April 1969.

Richelson, Jeffrey. "Population Targeting and U.S. Strategic Doctrine," Center for International and Strategic Affairs, UCLA, May 1982.

Rosenberg, David. "American Atomic Strategy and the Hydrogen Bomb Decision," *Journal of American History*, May 1979.

———. "The Origins of Overkill: Nuclear Weapons and American Strategy, 1945–1960," *International Security*, Spring 1983.

———. "A Smoking, Radiating Ruin at the End of Two Hours: Documents on American War Plans for Nuclear War with the Soviet Union, 1954–55," *International Security*, Winter 1981/82.

Rostow, Eugene. "The Case Against SALT II," *Commentary*, January 1979.

Schaffer, Ronald. "American Military Ethics in World War II: The Bombing of German Civilians," *Journal of American History*, September 1980.

———. "American Military Ethics in World War II: An Exchange," *Journal of American History*, June 1981.

Schelling, Thomas. "Bernard Brodie (1910–1978)," *International Security*, Winter 1978.

———. "The Terrorist Use of Nuclear Weapons," Center for International and Strategic Affairs, UCLA, August 1981.

Schlesinger, James. "Flexible Strategic Options and Deterrence," *Survival*, March/April 1974.

Scoville, Herbert, Jr. "Flexible MADness?," *Foreign Policy*, Spring 1974.

Sigal, Leon. "Rethinking the Unthinkable," *Foreign Policy*, Spring 1979.

Slocombe, Walter. "The Countervailing Strategy," *International Security*, Spring 1981.

———. "The Political Implications of Strategic Parity," IISS, May 1971.

Steinbruner, John, and Thomas Garwin. "Strategic Stability: The Balance Between Prudence and Paranoia," *International Security*, Summer 1976.

Steiner, Barry. "Bernard Brodie and the American Study of Nuclear Strategy," unpublished manuscript, undated.

———. "New Light into the Legacy of Bernard Brodie," Center for International and Strategic Affairs, UCLA, 1981.

———. "Using the Absolute Weapon: Early Ideas of Bernard Brodie on Atomic Strategy," Center for International and Strategic Affairs, UCLA, January 1984.

Talbott, Strobe. "Buildup and Breakdown," *Foreign Affairs, America and the World, 1983*, February 1984.

Teller, Edward. "Alternatives for Security," *Foreign Affairs*, January 1958.

———. "Seven Hours of Reminiscences," *Los Alamos Science*, Winter/Spring 1983.

Tierney, John. "Take the A-Plane: The $1 Billion Nuclear Bird That Never Flew," *Science 1982*, December 1982.

Tonelson, Alan. "Nitze's World," *Foreign Policy*, Spring 1979.

van Cleave, William, and W. Scott Thompson, eds. "Strategic Options for the Early Eighties: What Can Be Done?," National Strategy Information Center, New York City, 1979.

Warnke, Paul. "Apes on a Treadmill," *Foreign Policy*, Spring 1975.

Weisskopf, Victor. "On Avoiding Nuclear Holocaust," *Technology Review*, October 1980.

Wells, Samuel. "Sounding the Tocsin: NSC-68 and the Soviet Threat," *International Security*, Fall 1979.

Wohlstetter, Albert. "Bishops, Statesmen, and Other Strategists on the Bombing on Innocents," *Commentary*, June 1983.

————. "Defending a Strategic Force After 1960," Rand Corporation, February 1954.

————. "The Delicate Balance of Terror," *Foreign Affairs*, January 1959.

————. "Is There a Strategic Arms Race?," *Foreign Policy*, Summer 1974.

————. "Optimal Ways to Confuse Ourselves," *Foreign Policy*, Fall 1975.

————. "Rivals, But No Race," *Foreign Policy*, Fall 1974.

————. "Scientists, Seers and Strategy," *Foreign Affairs*, April 1953.

————, et al. "Morality and Deterrence," *Commentary*, December 1983.

————, et al. "Selection and Use of Strategic Bases," Rand Corporation, April 1954.

————, and Fred Hoffman. "Protecting U.S. Power to Strike Back in the 1950's and 1960's," Rand Corporation, September 1956.

INDEX

A NOTE ABOUT THE TYPE

The text of this book was set by CRT in a film version of a typeface called Times Roman, designed by Stanley Morison (1889–1967) for *The Times* (London) and first introduced by that newspaper in 1932.

Among typographers and designers of the twentieth century, Stanley Morison was a strong forming influence as a typographical advisor to The Monotype Corporation, as a director of two distinguished English publishing houses, and as a writer of sensibility, erudition, and keen practical sense.

Composed by The Haddon Craftsmen, Inc.,
Scranton, Pennsylvania
Printed and bound by Fairfield Graphics,
Fairfield, Pennsylvania
Designed by Mark Argetsinger